Twentieth Century

AMERICA

FOSTER RHEA DULLES
OHIO STATE UNIVERSITY

* *

Published for Reynal and Hitchcock by

HOUGHTON MIFFLIN COMPANY

Boston · New York · Chicago
Dallas · Atlanta · San Francisco
The Riverside Press Cambridge

26089

The Riverside Press

CAMBRIDGE · MASSACHUSETTS

PRINTED IN THE U.S.A.

"THE ONLY LIMIT TO OUR REALIZATION OF TOMORROW WILL BE OUR DOUBTS OF TODAY. LET US MOVE FORWARD WITH STRONG AND ACTIVE FAITH."

Franklin Delano Roosevelt

Preface

THE PURPOSE OF THIS BOOK is to tell the story of the growth of American democracy and of the expanding rôle of the United States in world affairs since the opening of the twentieth century. It is an attempt to weave the threads of the more significant political, economic, and social developments of the nation into an integrated account of national progress. Few if any periods of history have been packed with such momentous happenings and startling incident as the years between 1900 and 1945. Great events were continually in the making. If the following pages do not reflect something of the drama which has marked the triumphs of industrial civilization in the United States, the American people's persistent quest for social justice, the emergence of the United States as a great power, and its participation in two world wars to defend the American way of life, they have failed indeed to tell the story for which they were designed.

Writing upon so recent a period of history, an author naturally reflects his own opinions without the benefit of long perspective or cloistered contemplation. These are times through which he has lived, which he has known at first hand. In using the phrase "national progress," a very definite point of view is already betrayed. For a conviction that the United States during the past half-century has made a great advance not only in raising the standard of living of the American people, but in securing for them a greater measure of both political and economic freedom has been strengthened through the very telling of this story. This is not to say that the basic conflict in modern society between liberty and security has been fully resolved here in the United States. But the path along which the American people are traveling, for all its twists and turns, its occasional back-trackings, has led the nation forward, however distant the ultimate goal of a truly effective democracy may still be.

If democracy has not yet been made wholly safe for the world, neither has the world been made safe for democracy. The record of the twentieth century, however, shows a developing trend, despite tragic setbacks, toward a more sober realization on the part of the American people of their international responsibilities. A time of war holds out the promise of peace. Today more than ever before in our national history, there would appear to be greater promise of a peace which the United States is prepared, as a result of the experiences of the past, to uphold — a rôle which its economic and political power imposes upon it.

These are optimistic concepts in the interpretation of recent American history. Is there any substantiation for them?

Let's look at the record . . .

FOSTER RHEA DULLES

Contents

The Opening of the Century

The Progressive Era

The Stakes of World Power

From Prosperity to Depression

The New Deal

Peace and War

The Opening
of the Century

Ring Out the Old, Ring in the New

AMERICA AND THE TWENTIETH CENTURY

AS THE UNITED STATES OF AMERICA entered the twentieth century, there was a general feeling that the country had reached maturity. Since the Civil War the population had more than doubled to a total of nearly seventy-six millions, and the settlement of the West marked the passing of the traditional frontier. At the same time the exploitation of the nation's great natural resources and the tremendous growth of manufactures had created both a higher standard of living than the American people had ever before known and a national position of impressive economic power. And while the pattern of domestic life was modified by these far-reaching changes, the United States had also entered a new era of international relations. The strident imperialism of the Spanish War had led to the acquisition of overseas possessions that gave us dominance in the Caribbean and a commanding influence in the Pacific. The United States had in 1900 become a world power.

The American people faced the new century with a pervasive optimism. There were a few dissident voices questioning the basis for such high confidence in the national destiny, but it was more generally believed that democratic aims and aspirations were being fulfilled and that the future for America was big with promise. "An air of contentment and enthusiastic cheerfulness characterized the thought and temper of the American people," wrote William Graham Sumner, the distinguished economist and sociologist, while Walter Hines Page, editor and later first World War diplomat, declared that the keynote of national life on the threshold of the new century was "the note of joyful achievement; and its faith is the evangelical faith in a democracy that broadens as fast as social growth invites."

The common man was deeply imbued with this confidence. Despite the hard times of the early eighteen-nineties, the farmers and small businessmen of the Midwest kept alive the hopeful spirit which had first made possible the conquest of the frontier. In spite of depressed conditions of work in factories and mines, industrial workers believed in a greatly improved future. Moreover, the faith of the common man was both individual and collective. The opportunity for the enterprising to rise above their environment in seeking wealth and happiness, and the advancing standard of living for the country as a whole, both seemed to be guarantees of continuing economic and social betterment.

The issues forecast in 1900 as likely to block further "progress" were rarely those which time was actually to emphasize, and among popular publicists at least, there was seldom very keen insight into deeper economic and international problems. In a symposium upon the greatest menace of the new century in the *New York World*, fears were expressed of the increasing influence of wealth, of Oriental competition with American labor, of the degrading effect of drink upon national life, of the artificiality of social activities, of the influence of a sensation-mongering press, and of legislation based upon self-interest. Here were minor prophets of minor dooms. On far safer ground was the Archbishop of Canterbury. Asked what was the chief danger facing the world in the new century, he replied: "I have not the slightest idea."

The American scene did not everywhere justify the complacency with which the national blessings were so often counted. Urban slums were an ugly sore. Hundreds of thousands of workers, their ranks continually swollen by newly arrived immigrants, lived in congested squalor in the big cities. In many rural areas, hard-pressed farmers, struggling with debts and mortgages, often earned only the most scanty livelihood. Progress was flanked by poverty. Nevertheless, in the country as a whole, and especially on the farms and in the towns of the great midwestern Valley of

Democracy, there was prosperity. Less happy scenes were dimmed by what William Dean Howells cheerfully called "the more smiling aspects of life that are the more American."

Visitors to the United States at this time were most impressed — as they have been in both earlier and later days — by the immensity and diversity of the national scene. Nothing was more typical of the United States, as one English traveler observed, than the contrasts to be found on every side.

Contrast between the busy manufacturing cities of the Northeast, where the smoke billowed from countless factory chimneys, and western prairies of waving corn or golden wheat. Contrast between the iron mines, copper mines, silver mines of Minnesota, Nevada, Utah, Colorado, and the white-tufted cotton fields of Mississippi and Alabama. Contrast between the Yankee farmer of New England and the Slavic steel worker of Chicago or Pittsburgh, between the lumberjack of the Oregon forests and the fruit-grower in California, between the drygoods clerk of an eastern city and the cowboy of Wyoming or Arizona, between the Negro lazily hoeing his garden patch in a southern hill town and the Jewish garment worker slaving in a New York sweatshop. Contrast between the forward-looking enterprise of a midwestern town in Illinois or Indiana and the decayed gentility of many southern cities. Contrast between the intellectual snobbishness of Boston's Beacon Hill and the rank illiteracy of Chicago's Packingtown. Contrast between the neat, monotonous suburb and the tumbledown shacks littered about mill or factory. Contrast between the simple, homely life of the small town anywhere and the crowded activities of the metropolis.

Underlying such diversity, however, was the great pulsating force of a nation in many ways closely knit together and confronting the world with a power only gradually unfolding; a nation dedicated to the principles of democracy; a nation rich in resources, rich in people, rich in faith. Over the horizon there were questions perhaps more difficult of solution than the American people had ever known. The challenge to our democracy of monopolistic capitalism at home and of imperialistic aggression abroad were to test the validity of "the American way of life" as sharply as had the issues raised in the Civil War. But coming events cast only a dim and wavering shadow at the opening of the century. While there was already an undercurrent of protest against social abuses that was soon to give rise to the progressive movement, there was nothing to point to the world economic crises and world wars that in a few short decades were to engulf the United States as they engulfed the nations of both Europe and Asia. Prosperity and peace appeared to be newly ensured. A dynamic America stood confidently on the threshold of an epochal period in its own and the world's history.

The Triumph of Capitalism

NATIONAL GROWTH AND EXPANSION

THE SPECTACULAR GROWTH that gave the United States its position of world power in 1900 had resulted in large part from the release of those expansive forces that had been held in check in such large measure by the domestic conflict centering upon slavery. After Appomattox a stream of land-hungry pioneers from the older states converged with a stream of European immigrants to pour out over the western plains. A generous land policy, a growing network of transcontinental railroads, the development of new methods of farming, vastly extended the inhabited area of the United States. The mining frontier and the cattle kingdom were the precursors of a new era in continental expansion that gradually filled in the gaps left by those earlier settlers who had followed the Oregon Trail or flocked to California in forty-nine. The West had grown up in the eighteen-seventies and eighties as the scattered camps of prospectors grew into mining towns and as the homesteader, with his womenfolk, his steel-molded plow, and his barbed wire, encroached more and more upon the free range.

The passing of a great epoch in our national history was, indeed, marked by the clamor for admission into the Union of territories which a few short years earlier had known only the Indian, the buffalo, and the occasional prospector or trapper. The two Dakotas, Washington, and Montana became states in 1889; Idaho and Wyoming in 1890; and six years later belated recognition was accorded the Mormon territory of Utah. Oklahoma, Arizona, and New Mexico were the only territories in 1900.

The vast resources of this great area had been rapidly developed. Its mines had been made to disgorge huge quantities of gold, silver, and copper; the herds of cattle grazing on the plains became the principal source of supply for a gigantic meat-packing industry, and thousands upon thousands of new quarter sections planted to wheat and corn more than doubled the acreage of the nation's farms. The Government had disposed of the riches of the West with a lavish and prodigal hand. It had alienated some 80,000,000 acres to homesteaders by 1900, and turned over to the railroads 131,000,000 acres — an area more than three times that of all New England. It had freely granted mining rights, timber rights, and grazing rights. There appeared to be enough for everyone: no need to curb the extravagance and reck-lessness with which the forests were felled, the prairie grass plowed under, and the hillsides laid bare. None stopped to think of future generations which would pay the penalty for exhausted soil and erosion. None could foresee such a day as that in May, 1934, when a dust storm would carry three hundred million tons of the topsoil of Texas, Oklahoma, Colorado, and Kansas out into the Atlantic Ocean.

With the expansion of wheat and corn production in the prairie states, agriculture maintained its vital position in our national economy. "Destroy our farms," William Jennings Bryan declared dramatically in 1896, "and the grass will grow up in the streets of every city in the country." In the latter half of the nineteenth century the granary of the Middle West largely ac-counted for a gain in wheat production from one hundred to six hundred million bushels, while the slowly reviving South in-creased the cotton crop from two and a half to ten million bales. Declining prices held down the value of farm products, account-ing for sharp agrarian distress in the eighteen-nineties, but there was a fivefold increase in the value of all farm property to an aggregate total of twenty billion dollars.

Far more important than these agricultural gains was the tre-mendous advance in the development of manufactures. Here the census figures revealed a rise in values which wholly eclipsed anything which farming could show. In contrast to their total value of one billion dollars in the middle of the century, the products of industry at its close amounted to more than thirteen billion dollars. The industrial area which had been largely limited to the Northeast — New England, New York, New Jersey, and Pennsylvania — had spread out over the western slopes of the Appalachians, embracing such states as Ohio, Michigan, Indiana, and Illinois. The rise of a great steel industry, drawing upon the immense iron resources of the Mesabi Range and the coal and limestone of Pennsylvania; the growth of oil refineries following upon the discovery of petroleum in Pennsylvania and Ohio; the rapidly increasing manufacture of agricultural and industrial machinery; astounding new advances in the production of electric light and power — these were the most significant economic developments since the Civil War.

Our growing foreign commerce, rising to almost two billion dollars annually by 1900, further reflected the new importance of industry in our national economy. For while agricultural products still led all other exports, their proportion of the total trade was declining while that of manufactures had almost doubled. The United States continued to send abroad vast quantities of wheat, cotton, and meat products. They were still our stable exports. But the really significant aspect of trade statistics was the persistent increase in the annual value of exports of machinery, iron and steel products, copper manufactures and petroleum.

Industrialization was not, of course, peculiar to the United States. The entire western world was undergoing the same sweeping changes caused by the economic revolution. But our immense natural resources and the opportunity for their profitable exploitation offered by an ever-expanding domestic market made industrial development possible in this country on an heroic scale. The railroads spread their lines of steel over an entire continent, knitting together the largest area of free trade in all the world. Freight trains traveled continuously from east to west, from north to south, exchanging the products of factory and farm. The rapidity of this economic growth was in many ways terrifying. For so long had the great majority of men been closely tied to the soil, dependent almost wholly on their own individual labor, that the sudden emergence into an age of mechanical power and mass production inevitably created almost insoluble economic and social problems. Little wonder that the nineteenth century deferred these problems until the twentieth, or that the present generation is still seeking to adjust itself to the vast complexities of the new industrial order.

Trusts and Monopolies

The rise of manufactures was marked by the nationalizing of business, the corporation rather than the small individual enterprise or partnership becoming more and more the accepted form of business organization. In 1900, corporations already accounted for some two-thirds of all manufacture, and there was a natural and steady trend toward larger and larger business units. Railway consolidations and then industrial mergers were promoted to lessen competition and give greater efficiency and economy. Manufacturers spread across state lines in their development of national markets. Properties were merged, rival concerns absorbed or driven out of business, and new consolidations effected in the fields of both production and distribution. Combination and monopoly became the order of the day, with the rise of trusts the most salient feature of the economic scene.

The Census of 1900 reported one hundred and eighty-five of these great industrial corporations, their aggregate capitalization totaling three billion dollars. Seventy-three of them, with individual capitalization in each instance of ten million dollars or more, turned out fourteen per cent of the country's industrial products. The very next year was to see this movement come to what appeared to be a peak with the formation of the United States Steel Corporation, the country's first billion-dollar concern. The trusts dominated all important industries — steel, oil, sugar, meat-packing, tobacco, farm machinery, copper manufactures — and they exercised economic controls that were virtually crushing all competition.

There were two sharply contrasting aspects of the industrial development which monopoly promoted. On the one hand, it was responsible for the rapid and successful exploitation of the country's natural resources, the mass production on a relatively cheap scale of countless goods which had never before been available to the common man, and a tremendous increase in the national wealth and national income. But it also caused a striking concentration of wealth and economic power in the hands of a few corporations, wholly controlled by men responsible to no one but themselves. Monopoly meant order, economy, and stability, but it left entirely to the monopolist how far the benefits of order, economy, and stability were to be passed on to the public.

Improvements were brought about in transportation and communications. New types of agricultural machinery proved a tremendous boon to the farmer. Countless labor-saving devices entered into the home and the office. The machine was harnessed to everyday needs as never before in all history, and held out the promise of a more abundant life for millions of people. Yet there was an increasing inequality in the living standards which these developments made possible. The rich were becoming richer, and the poor poorer. Where mid-nineteenth-century travelers had been struck by the general diffusion of prosperity, those at its close were often shocked by the evidence of great wealth set over against dire destitution. There were those who feared that for all that might be said for our economic advance, we were merely "breeding the two great classes — tramps and millionaires."

Twelve per cent of the population, estimates had revealed in 1896, owned almost nine-tenths of the wealth. One per cent controlled half of it — or as much as the other ninety-nine per cent. There had been perhaps nineteen millionaires in the country in 1850; there were several thousand in 1900. The fears of those who had long foreseen the danger of creating an aristocracy of wealth seemed to be confirmed and there was no apparent way of bringing the process to a halt. When in 1894 the attempt was made to enact a moderate income tax, the Supreme Court promptly declared it unconstitutional. Responding to Joseph H. Choate's protest that the principles underlying such a tax were "communistic, socialistic — what shall I call them? — as populistic as ever have been addressed to any political assembly in the world," the Court agreed that such an assault upon capital was but the beginning of a war of the poor against the rich and that the rights of property had to be sustained.

An even greater consequence of the growth of trusts and monopoly was the increasing political power given to organized industry. Its influence appeared to some to overshadow that of Government itself. Through control over local politicians, state legislatures, sometimes even over the judiciary, the power of industry was dangerously threatening the bases of American democracy. "In the encouragement of the investment of capital," so conservative an observer as William Howard Taft later wrote, "we nearly transferred political power to those who controlled corporate wealth and we were in danger of a plutocracy."

Laissez-Faire and the Gospel of Wealth

Supporting the movement which led to such phenomenal industrial advance and to this new concentration of economic power was the prevailing philosophy of *laissez-faire*. Derived from the social doctrines of Herbert Spencer, given further emphasis by the individualistic spirit born of the frontier, *laissez-faire* called for full freedom for the individual — and for the corporation in its legal status as a person — in every phase of economic activity. There should be no interference on the part of Government in the economic development of the country, and no attempt whatsoever to regulate business or industry. National progress was believed to be largely dependent upon such a hands-off policy, and the rise of trusts and monopolies was considered the natural and beneficent working-out of economic laws.

Even the greatest foes of this system could not wholly deny its benefits. Edward Bellamy wrote in his socialistic novel, *Looking Backward*:

> Oppressive and intolerable as was the régime of the great consolidations of capital, even its victims, while they cursed it, were forced to admit the prodigious increase of efficiency which had been imparted to the national industries, the vast economies effected by concentration of management and unity of organiza-

tion, and to confess that since the new system had taken the place of the old, the wealth of the world had increased at a rate before undreamed of. . . .

Nevertheless, certain of the manifestations of *laissez-faire* appeared to violate its own basic tenets. Monopoly tended to stifle the free competition which was the theoretical basis of nineteenth-century capitalism, and the rising trusts actually profited immensely from direct governmental aid. They secured important economic concessions often denied small business through grants of land, timber rights, and mining concessions from the public domain. They throve upon a currency policy generally devised in the interests of capitalist finance rather than of labor or agriculture. They flourished under the protection of customs duties effectively cutting off all foreign competition. The protective tariff was indeed attacked as "the mother of trusts." *Laissez-faire* was twisted into a program for fostering monopoly rather than promoting competition, its critics declared, and the only freedom it upheld was that of the large corporations to control both production and prices in their own interests.

If there was a certain inevitability in the growth of monopoly under the pressure of mass production and mass distribution, this entire process was also hastened by the driving force of as remarkable a group of men as America ever produced. Farsighted and ruthless, they sensed the opportunities· which developing industrialism presented, and proceeded to take every advantage of them. Robber barons or industrial statesmen, they fashioned the image of modern America and eclipsed all other national leaders in the era in which they lived. John D. Rockefeller shrewdly building up the great monopoly of the Standard Oil Company; Andrew Carnegie skillfully bringing one steel company after another under his control; James J. Hill consolidating the railroads of the Northwest; J. P. Morgan establishing a new empire of finance — these were the men, unswerving and audacious in pursuit of their aims, who stamped upon their times the strong imprint of their domineering characters.

In justification of their attitude, the principles of *laissez-faire* were supplemented by an even simpler philosophy which Andrew

Carnegie popularly designated as the "Gospel of Wealth." He stoutly maintained that it was the opportunities afforded by America for winning a fortune which had made it such a great nation, and that on these grounds alone there should be no restraints upon the freedom of individual or corporation. Any governmental restrictions would be a denial of the American heritage and a brake upon national progress. But the rich man, Carnegie further declared, not only promoted economic advance through the wealth he created and made available for the public welfare. He was destined to serve as a guardian for the poor. He could bring to their service "his superior wisdom, experience, and ability to administer, doing for them better than they would or could do for themselves. Thus is the problem of Rich and Poor solved. The laws of accumulation will be left free; the laws of distribution free. Individualism will continue, but the millionaire will be but a trustee for the poor."

Carnegie lived up to his theories. He had risen from bobbin boy to ironmaster, becoming one of the rich, the good, and the wise through his own character and ability, and at the peak of his career he gave over making money to distributing it for the public good. There were some few others who followed his example. But the idea of trusteeship was more generally ignored than observed. Despite all Carnegie might say, the creators of the new industrial order had for the most part only the slightest concern for the public interest. Any feeling of social responsibility was often submerged in the bitter economic struggle in which the law of the jungle, survival of the fittest, overshadowed more charitable considerations. Whereas democracy's doctrine of individualism had once meant the equal right of every person to life, liberty, and the pursuit of happiness, the buccaneers of industry and finance interpreted it as the right to trample underfoot all those who could not protect their own interests. "What do I care for the law?" that ruthless railroad baron, Commodore Vanderbilt, is reputed to have exclaimed. "I got the power, ain't I?" Industry fully believed in its right to bend the Government and the courts to its own purposes. There could be no higher goal than consolidation and monopoly. Property rights held precedence over human rights, and the greedy exploitation of natural resources was matched by an almost equally wanton exploitation of labor.

For the middle class generally the example of their leaders, the opportunities for making money which the country afforded, and the underlying idea that nothing succeeds like success, placed a new emphasis upon wholly material standards of achievement. Many of the traditional ideals and social concepts of the American people appeared to be transformed under the influence of a pervasive attitude that placed the pursuit of riches above every other goal. With the heroes of the age, those industrialists, capitalists, or speculators whose wealth was accepted as unmistakable proof of their ability, the public cared little about whom they might have pushed aside or trodden underfoot in the mad scramble for financial rewards. Speculation in western lands, fraudulent purchase of government franchises, manipulations in stocks and bonds, the juggling of secret railway rebates, outright fraud and corruption — the end justified the means. "The dollar is the measure of every value," wrote William Dean Howells; "the stamp of every success."

Even the pulpit gave its benediction to the triumph of materialism in American life, the Church falling back upon old Puritan traditions to hold riches in the highest esteem as unquestionable proof of hard work, frugality, and righteousness. Wealth was a sign of heavenly as well as worldly approval. God might still love the poor, for certainly there were many of them in the America of 1900, but it was believed that he admired the rich. "In the long run," declared Bishop Lawrence of Massachusetts, "it is only to the man of morality that wealth comes. . . . Material prosperity is helping to make the national character sweeter, more joyous, more unselfish, more Christlike." The Church did not seek to impose any restraints on the methods by which a fortune was accumulated; it only requested that some part of it should be given away in charity. "Men should make money according to the laws of business," another religious leader stated, "and spend it according to the laws of God." John D. Rockefeller, who was undoubtedly sincere in saying "the good Lord gave me my money," was not disabused of this comforting thought by his church. It had hopes of largess for itself.

There were many other indications of the high repute in which business success and riches were held. Newspapers and magazines underscored the important rôle of the wealthy in our national life by widely publicizing everything they did. The success story, symbolized by Horatio Alger's endless tales of the poor boy making good, came to its flowering. Even more significant, the urge to prove that one was among the elect led to extravagant spending as concrete evidence of the possession of wealth. What Thorstein Veblen called "conspicuous consumption" was widely in evidence in urban society and among those social climbers who sought to breathe its rarefied atmosphere.

The lavish expenditures of the new gold rush of millionaires especially dazzled a public which eagerly read all accounts of their spectacular lives. The homes of these newly rich were gaudy show places crowded with the loot of foraging expeditions to the Old World. Yachts, four-in-hand coaches, and polo ponies typified their recreational life. When they entertained, squadrons of butlers and footmen, in silk stockings and powdered hair, served epicurean feasts on massive gold plate. Incredible sums were spent upon the costumes for their elaborate fancy-dress balls. At one party described by the historian of New York's Four Hundred, a miniature lake was built into the dinner table, surrounded by a network of golden wire, within which four swans swam placidly before the diners. Cages filled with singing birds hung from the ceiling; waterfalls splashed upon banks of flowers around the sides of the room. On another occasion such was the display of jewels and expensive Paris models at the new Metropolitan Opera House that a cynical critic found the air perfumed with the odor of crisp greenbacks while "the tiers of boxes looked like cages in a menagerie of monopolists."

METROPOLIS AND THE URBAN WORKER

With material advance so important a goal in American life, the bright lights of the city exerted a far stronger pull at the opening of the century than the old ambition for a homestead in the West. However unimportant the prospective job in factory, store, or office, it held out the romantic possibility of commercial success. Consequently, both boys and girls flocked to the town in such droves that in some states the rapid growth of urban communities was paralleled by a corresponding decline in the rural population. Prosperous farming areas reverted to land half pasturage and half forest, villages were almost wholly deserted, and farmhouses were abandoned as the younger generation crowded to factory town or metropolis.

At the same time the cities were also attracting hordes of immigrant workers from the Old World. As early as the eighteen-eighties there had been a decided change in the character of the arrivals to the Land of Promise. Ignorant and penniless peasants from southeastern Europe began to replace the earlier immigrants from the British Isles and northwestern Europe who had crossed the Atlantic to take up land in the West, and these newcomers were almost inevitably sucked into the industrial vortex of the East and Middle West. They provided the bulk of the unskilled workers necessary for expanding cotton mills, shoe factories, slaughter-houses, steel mills, iron foundries, and oil refineries; they became the day laborers in the building trades of the rapidly growing cities and manufacturing towns.

Under the impact of such a general movement to the city, the proportion of urban dwellers to country dwellers in the United States as a whole rapidly changed. Whereas in the middle of the nineteeth century only one-eighth of the American people lived in towns and cities, by the close of the century this proportion had risen to one-third. There were 547 nation-wide communities with a population of over eight thousand by 1900, and even more significant, thirty-eight had more than one hundred thousand inhabitants. In many instances the size of a city's population was matched by its polyglot character. New York had become a great commercial and manufacturing center of three and a half million with as many Jews as Warsaw, twice as many Irish as Dublin, as many Germans as Hamburg, and one-half as many Italians as Naples. In the Midwest, Chicago boasted of a population of more

than a million and a half, and the number of foreign-born exceeded
the over-all total a decade or so earlier. Its streets were thronged
with Germans, Swedes, Norwegians, and Irish, and also Italians,
Poles, Lithuanians, Hungarians, and Slovenes. Philadelphia had
a population of more than a million and St. Louis, Boston, and
Baltimore each had more than five hundred thousand.

The cities had grown far too fast. They were densely over-
crowded. Particularly in those areas to which the foreign-born
found their way, the congestion was often appalling. One city
block in New York, awarded the dubious distinction of being
called "the most congested block in the world," was found to
house 6888 persons. Living in dark, dingy, and sometimes un-
ventilated, tenement apartments, they had only the most primi-
tive sanitary conveniences and but two bathrooms. If such a
block was the worst example of overcrowding, the tenement
districts in most large cities rapidly deteriorated into dirty,
unsanitary slum areas. It was estimated in 1900 that some ten
per cent of the entire urban population lived in slums, and the
municipal authorities consequently found themselves facing almost insoluble problems of disease, vice, and crime.

Workers living under such conditions, either in the large cities
or smaller factory towns, hardly profited from the country's general economic advance. The increase in real wages and shorter
working hours enjoyed by labor as a whole did not reach down
to these submerged slum dwellers. Current statistics, in fact, indicated that it was only the skilled workers, the aristocrats of
labor, who were profiting from industrialization. With the
average pay of the twelve million persons employed in non-agri-
cultural occupations estimated in 1900 at $490 a year, it was all
too clear that the great mass of workers received a barely living
wage.

Hours of work also remained long and arduous. While a ten-
hour day was perhaps more general, millions of workers were
still called upon for twelve hours' daily labor. The constant pressure of the speed-up in the country's mines, steel mills, and factories was a further aggravation, in many instances more resented
than the long hours. A movement for an eight-hour day was

under way, but it encountered heavy opposition. "A consummate piece of humbuggery — too silly to merit the attention of a body of lunatics," was the flat assertion of one midwestern newspaper.

All efforts to remedy this situation encountered the two formidable obstacles of industry's highly organized control and the constantly replenished reservoir of cheap labor made up of the newly arrived immigrants from Europe. Management still held firmly to the idea that labor was a commodity, to be bought as cheaply as possible in the current market. Labor had no real bargaining power, and even the strike proved a generally ineffective weapon in the face of such large reserves of potential strike-breakers. It might under certain circumstances prove difficult to replace skilled workers, but there was no end to the availability of the unskilled.

The organized labor movement reflected these conditions. At the end of the eighteen-eighties the Knights of Labor, a national organization which was in effect an industrial union for all workers, skilled or unskilled, claimed a membership of seven hundred thousand and for a time exerted a powerful influence upon industrial relations. But a series of disastrous strikes, the diversity of its aims, incapable leadership, and the fact that the time was not yet ripe for industrial unionization led to its rapid decline. Its place was then taken by the American Federation of Labor, established in 1886 along craft lines. It represented an attempt upon the part of skilled workers to promote a highly practical program, in their own interest and to some degree at the expense of the unskilled, limited to higher wages, shorter hours, and better conditions of employment. While the violent industrial strife of the last quarter of the nineteenth century — marked by such outbreaks as the great Pullman strike of 1894 — had been largely resolved by capitalist victories and the decline of unionization, the American Federation of Labor nevertheless succeeded in establishing itself and it grew gradually stronger. In 1900 its membership, far more compact and homogeneous than the old Knights of Labor, was some three hundred thousand.

The great mass of workers, however, remained unorganized, almost wholly at the mercy of their employers. The unskilled were not welcomed into the American Federation of Labor and they had no means to combat the pressure which industry was free to exercise in regard to both wages and hours of work.

REVOLUTION ON THE FARM

Manufacturing progress affected farming as it did every other phase of economic life. In the latter half of the nineteenth century there was an increasing use of agricultural machinery which pointed toward something like the mass-production methods of industry. The farmer was more and more raising staple crops — wheat, corn, hogs, or cotton — for which he found his market either in the principal centers of industry or in export trade. Other foodstuffs were grown where they could be raised most economically and the large-scale farmer of the Midwest consequently bought for consumption many of the products which he had formerly raised for himself. The rise of the baking industry, the canning of fruits and vegetables, new methods of refrigeration, all contributed to this change in farming which transformed it more and more from a way of life to an organized business.

There were many by-products of such change. Concentration on staple crops compelled the farmer to expand his acreage and to purchase more machinery. It tended to involve him heavily in debt and to increase the financial risks of his occupation. During the eighteen-eighties and early nineties declining prices for farm products made this burden of debt more and more onerous, with widespread distress in many agricultural areas. The farmer found himself at the mercy of the railroads for the transportation of staple crops to market; he was indebted to eastern financial interests for the money he had borrowed on mortgages or to finance purchases of farm machinery, and he was dependent on world markets, about which he knew little or nothing, for the price he obtained for his produce. He was losing his independence in an increasingly industrialized world.

Such considerations affected the southern farmer as well as the midwestern farmer. The break-up of the old plantation system had led to an increase in small farms rather than the extension of existing holdings, but with falling cotton prices financial problems weighed heavily upon the agricultural community. Only a little more than half the farms in southern states were operated by owners in 1900, and the remainder were worked by tenants of whom over fifty per cent were Negroes. Conditions for these tenant farmers were perhaps as oppressive as those for any other group in American life, the Negroes particularly often living in degrading poverty.

The difficult position of the farmer in an industrialized society had become a basic problem of American life. It was not to be easily solved. Nevertheless, at the opening of the twentieth century a reversal of the downward trend in prices which had prevailed since the Civil War was apparently bringing back some of the former prosperity. With both an increasing demand for their produce, and more favorable weather conditions in the Midwest than had been experienced for many years, the farmers generally were able to share in the good times that prevailed throughout the country and there was a greater measure of contentment than had seemed possible even a few years earlier.

Largely dependent on the farms were the small towns of the agricultural states. In many ways they were the real backbone of the country, and far more typically American than the new industrial centers with their varied population of immigrant workers. Our traditional institutions retained their old hold upon social life in the small town; democracy was far more real and meaningful than in the large cities. And for the plain folk in these communities or on near-by farms, life at once lacked the dramatic contrasts of the cities and provided a measure of leisurely and pleasant living that the urban dweller might never know. Neither the ostentatious wealth of the Four Hundred nor the grinding poverty of the "most congested block in the world" was known in the small towns and villages scattered over the length and breadth of the United States, from Maine to California, from Oregon to Florida. There was no acute concern over the issues which in the cities divided class against class, and a certain aloofness from the mad scramble for riches that in so many ways emphasized the material aspects of American civilization. Life continued to have a flavor that was a heritage of simpler days and of a less complex order of society.

THE ATTACK ON LAISSEZ-FAIRE

During the years which had witnessed such unexampled growth in the United States, politics was almost wholly subordinate to economic forces. In post-Civil-War days there was no Clay, Calhoun, or Webster to dominate the scene, as there had been during the first half of the century. The leaders of the United States were its railroad magnates, its industrial barons, its financiers. Both Republicans and Democrats accepted this leadership with little questioning of where it might be taking the country. Their politics was the politics of *laissez-faire*, whatever the party label. Political campaigns became largely shadow-boxing over secondary questions that barely concealed the fact that the struggle was primarily one of the "outs" against the "ins." Although the Republicans were considered more the party of big business, the Democrats in power never departed very far from their rivals' policy of non-interference with industry. "No period so thoroughly ordinary had been known in American politics," Henry Adams commented caustically, "since Christopher Columbus first disturbed the balance of American society."

This easy acceptance of industry's domination of governmental policies, indeed, the whole theory of *laissez-faire*, began to be questioned toward the close of the century, especially by farmers and workers. The railroads fattened upon government land grants, and then turned around to extort the last penny in freight charges from the helpless farmer or small-town shipper. The trusts expanded their monopolistic control with the aid of the protective tariff, and then compelled the even more helpless consuming public to pay exorbitant prices for their manufactures. An anti-monopoly movement, started by the Grangers in the eighteen-seventies to establish some sort of regulation over the railroads, slowly gathered strength.

State laws to control both railroads and industrial monopolies were first sought, but when they proved ineffective, either through lax enforcement or adverse court decisions, the fight was carried to Congress. Public pressure finally compelled it to take action. The Interstate Commerce Act, setting up some measure of federal control over railroad operations and rate-making, was passed in 1887, and three years later the Sherman Anti-Trust Act marked a first move against monopolies by declaring illegal all combinations or conspiracies in restraint of trade among the several states.

These laws were immensely important. They were a frontal assault upon the whole theory of *laissez-faire*, an entering wedge for a broad program of railroad and business regulation based on the constitutional powers of the Federal Government to regulate interstate commerce. Nevertheless, it was evident at the time, and became increasingly so in the next few years, that the Government had little interest in their strict enforcement. Congress had felt it advisable to bow before the popular storm in so far as passage of such regulatory measures was concerned, but until the twentieth century little more was done in the face of the strong opposition of big business to any policy that would actually curb its freedom.

If the Government was reluctant to enforce these laws, the courts were also strongly inclined toward the economic doctrine of *laissez-faire*, and successive decisions in regard both to railroad regulation and to the control of trusts further protected the interests of industry. The right of the state to regulate any business affected with a public interest had been recognized as early as 1876, but the Supreme Court soon began to restrict all such legislation through its interpretation of the due-process clause to be found in the Fourteenth Amendment to the Constitution. This provision, expressly stating that no person could be deprived of property without due process of law, was so construed as to apply to corporations, and to mean that regulation such as that attempting to fix railroad rates was not an unlimited function of the legislature but subject to court approval. "The question of the reasonableness of a rate of charge for transportation by a railroad company," the Supreme Court stated in *Chicago, Milwaukee and St. Paul Railroad Co. v. Minnesota*, in 1889, " . . . is eminently a

question for judicial investigation, requiring due process of law
for its determination." In subsequent decisions, applying this
principle both to the Interstate Commerce Commission as well
as to state railroad commissions, it further declared that the basis
for the reasonableness of rates must be the fair value of the railroad's property, taking into consideration original costs, the
market value of stocks and bonds, present cost of construction,
and probable earning capacity.

Under such restrictions as interpreted by the courts, effective
control over railroad rates became virtually impossible. State
legislatures could do little or nothing, and having lost all but one of
sixteen appeals from its decisions made by the railroads during
the first decade of its existence, the Interstate Commerce Commission issued a despairing annual report in 1898 confessing complete failure. Shippers had even ceased to file complaints against
railroad abuses; they knew their case was hopeless.

At about the same time a similar breakdown took place in regard to enforcement of the anti-trust laws. The Sherman Act was
greatly weakened by the courts, not on the ground of violating
due process of law, but as unduly stretching the constitutional
powers of the Federal Government under the commerce clause.
The Supreme Court rendered a significant decision in the E. C.
Knight Company case in 1895. Although this corporation controlled ninety-five per cent of the production of sugar in the entire
country, its operations were freed of the charge of being in
restraint of interstate trade. They involved manufacture, and
such manufacture "bore no relation to commerce between the
states." In later decisions before the close of the century, the
Supreme Court gave a somewhat more liberal interpretation of
the law, but the Knight decision nevertheless remained a strong
barrier to any effective control of the trusts.

The attitude of the Government toward enforcement was significantly illustrated in the comment upon the Court's decision
in this case by Attorney General Olney, charged with its prosecution. He wrote:

You will observe that the Government has been defeated by

the Supreme Court on the trust question. I always supposed it
would be, and have taken the responsibility of not prosecuting
under a law I believed to be no good.

Indeed, only fifteen suits were instituted under the Sherman
Act during the administrations of Presidents Harrison and Cleveland, and but three during that of McKinley.

One exception to the inaction of the Department of Justice was
highly revealing. The Sherman Act was invoked against labor
unions. Attorney General Olney, so complacent over his inability
to proceed against the Knight Company, obtained an injunction
in the Pullman strike of 1894, which was in part based upon the
provisions of the law outlawing any conspiracy in restraint of
trade. Eugene V. Debs, leader of the American Railway Union,
together with a number of his aides, was clapped into jail under
contempt proceedings — an ironical twist in application of a
measure designed to control the power of the trusts.

The underlying fact, at the opening of the new century, was
that the power and influence of big business still overshadowed
that of both the Government and the courts. The public was
slowly becoming aware of this, but it was not yet sufficiently
aroused to demand that its representatives really assert their authority. Discontent with railroad and trust abuses had compelled Congress to pass the Interstate Commerce Act and the
Sherman Anti-Trust Act, but the movement of revolt against
monopoly was not yet articulate enough to compel their strict enforcement. The theories of *laissez-faire* still had far too strong a
hold upon the country as a whole. "The power of the mighty industrial overlords of the country," Theodore Roosevelt was later
to write in his *Autobiography*, "had increased with giant strides,
while the methods of controlling them, or checking abuses by
them on the part of the people, through the Government, remained archaic and therefore practically impotent."

The Verdict of 1896

The only time these underlying issues were squarely faced on
the political stage was in the election of 1896. In that campaign

the old elements of discontent among western farmers, which had regrouped in the eighteen-eighties to form the People's Party, captured control of the Democratic Party. With the country still seething with unrest as a consequence of an economic depression that had developed three years earlier, William Jennings Bryan was nominated as the champion of a program of radical reform. A demand for the free and unlimited coinage of silver, to combat the scarcity of currency which the Populists held responsible for falling farm prices, was the dominant issue of the campaign. "You shall not crucify mankind upon a cross of gold," Bryan thundered in vehement denunciation of conservative insistence upon maintaining the gold standard. At the same time Populists and Democrats attacked the national banks, trusts and monopolies, the railroads and the protective tariff. They insistently demanded strict governmental control and regulation, "to protect the people from robbery and oppression." Free silver was the popular slogan of the Democratic campaign of 1896, but in reality it was the symbol of a much broader revolt against things as they were. The West and the South had arisen in a desperate attempt to wrest control of the National Government from the industrial East and restore a balance of political power more favorable to agrarian interests.

Against this threat the Republicans rallied all the strength of business and finance. With Mark Hanna, industrialist statesman, pulling the strings behind the scenes, they nominated the dignified, affable, and eminently safe William McKinley to oppose that "blatant wild ass of the prairies," as John Hay described Bryan. Without reproach in either public or private life, the Republican candidate was thoroughly sound in all his political and social views. There had been a time when he leaned toward free silver, but under Hanna's careful coaching he had seen the error of his ways. His name was a symbol of high protection. Neither his loyalty to the party nor to the business interests which it represented could possibly be questioned.

McKinley was elected. The Republicans were swept into office with the first clear majority in a popular presidential vote since the election of Grant. The danger that the conservatives had seen threatening the nation's internal stability in an alliance of farmers and workingmen was dispelled. In some quarters it was felt that the country had narrowly survived a major crisis. On the part of those for whom any change or disturbance in the social system threatened loss of privilege, there was heartfelt relief as with the *New York Tribune* they consigned these western rebels, and especially "the wretched, rattle-pated boy" who posed as their leader, to political oblivion. "God's in His Heaven, all's right with the world," Mark Hanna joyfully telegraphed the successful candidate. But it was not the victory of William McKinley and the Republican Party that gave such a deep significance to the election of 1896. It was the victory of conservative capitalism. It was the victory of the industrial East. It was the victory of *laissez-faire*.

During the next four years the promise of this victory appeared to be fulfilled. The attention of the country was for a time largely diverted from domestic issues to foreign affairs. Revolt in Cuba, American intervention in behalf of the rebels, war with Spain, and the march of empire absorbed our political energies. McKinley's domestic policy, however, was carefully geared to the needs of the business interests largely responsible for his election. Not only was the high tariff maintained, but through passage of the Dingley Act in 1897, existing duties were raised and a number of articles removed from the free list to share the benefits of protection. After trying to appease the advocates of free silver by nominally re-examining the possibilities of bimetalism, passage of a gold standard act in 1900 finally and definitely established what the Republicans were convinced was the only sound basis for the national currency. And in strict compliance with the principles of *laissez-faire*, both the Interstate Commerce Act and the Sherman Anti-Trust Act were allowed to become virtual dead letters. Business was given every encouragement to continue the process of consolidation and merger that had been so characteristic of the last quarter of the nineteenth century.

By 1900 the country had fully recovered from depression and the Republicans naturally assumed full credit for the striking improvement in both economic and social conditions. They maintained it was the consequence of the confidence inspired by their

return to power and the soundness of their policies. Actually
many other things came into play. As we have seen, a series of
good crops at home combined with poor crops abroad to restore
the market for agricultural products, while prices were further
stimulated by an increase in the currency made possible through
additional gold reserves obtained from new mines in the Klondike
and South Africa. Although political defeat had not reconciled the
Populists to the gold standard, the inflationary effect of this increase in the currency was laying the ghost of free silver. As prosperity returned to the agricultural states, the farmers could not
be so easily persuaded "to raise less corn and more Hell."

Even more striking than improvement on the agricultural front
were the gains made by business and industry. Production rose
to new peaks, foreign trade expanded with a favorable balance
of exports over imports, industrial employment increased, and
there were fewer business failures than at any time in the past
eighteen years. Whatever the relative importance of the various
factors responsible for such gains, the triumph of capitalism appeared at the opening of the new century to have ushered in
unexampled good times.

The United States Looks Outward

A WORLD POWER

As THE UNITED STATES embarked upon its program of overseas expansion following the war with Spain in 1898, Mr. Dooley, that alert commentator on the American scene created by the humorist Finley Peter Dunne, regarded our new foreign policy with a certain skepticism. We find him telling his friend Mr. Hennessy:

> I sigh f'r th' good old days befur we became what Hogan calls a wurruld power. In thim days our fav'rite spoort was playin' solytare, winnin' money fr'm each other, an' no wan th' worse off. Ivry body was invious iv us. We didn't care f'r th' big game goin' on in th' corner. Whin it broke up in a row we said: "Gintlemin, gintlemin!" an' maybe wint over an' grabbed somebody's stake. But we cudden't stand it anny longer. We had to give up our simple little game iv patience an' cut into th' other deal. An' now, be Hivens, we have no peace iv mind. . . .

That, in homely terms, was exactly what had happened. The mounting economic and industrial strength of the United States had combined with the expansive ambitions of the American people to broaden immensely our international horizons. There were widespread doubts upon the advisability of the new policies we had adopted. There was serious questioning as to just where we were headed. To sigh for the good old days before we had become a world power, however, was to blind ourselves to responsibilities and obligations that our geographic position and economic strength necessarily imposed upon us. Mr. Dooley was thoroughly right in declaring that now we had no peace of mind. Had he been able to look further into the future his nostalgia for the days when America felt no need to break into the big game would have been even greater. Ahead lay 1917 and 1941.

The imperialistic fervor that led the nation to acquire the Hawaiian Islands, Puerto Rico, the Philippines, Guam, and Samoa as overseas possessions was the expression of forces that had been released rather than brought into being by war. Long before 1898 there had been evident a mounting ground swell of aggressive nationalism in the United States which accorded with that cosmic tendency toward imperialist expansion, as John Hay phrased it, which was everywhere so pronounced at the close of the nineteenth century.

Richard Olney wrote in 1900:

> Though historians will probably assign the abandonment of the isolation policy of the United States to the time when this country and Spain went to war over Cuba, and though the abandonment may have been precipitated by that contest, the change was inevitable, had been long preparing, and could not have been long delayed.

THE BACKGROUND OF IMPERIALISM

The ultimate background for expansion overseas was our historic march across the continent — the steady pushing back of the frontier from the days of Jamestown and Plymouth. There had also been throughout our history a consistent national interest in the Pacific, based upon the importance of this great ocean as the trade route to the commerce of the Far East. Before the outbreak of war with Spain, we had already made three moves reflecting this interest. We had acquired Alaska; in co-operation with England and Germany we had established a joint protectorate over Samoa, and the ground had been prepared for the annexation of the Hawaiian Islands. Now new forces were developing that urged us to discover an outlet for national energies in still further overseas expansion as the natural expression of our "manifest destiny."

"Whether they will or no," Captain Alfred Thayer Mahan, naval strategist and historian, wrote in a significant article in the

Atlantic Monthly as early as 1890, "Americans must now begin to look outward." The United States was bound, because of its geographic position, he declared, to be "one of the frontiers from which, as from a base of operations, the Sea Power of the civilized world will energize." Urging the annexation of Hawaii as a first step toward this goal, he strenuously denied that it would be a "mere sporadic effort, irrational because disconnected from an adequate motive." On the contrary, he envisaged it as "a first-fruit and token that the nation in its evolution has aroused itself to the necessity of carrying its life — that has been the happiness of those under its influence — beyond the borders which heretofore have sufficed for its activities." As we followed this policy of expansion, Senator Albert J. Beveridge attributed it to "the unseen hand of God"; William Allen White declared it to be the working of Fate — "it is so written — it is to be."

The Spanish War, providing the opportunity to seek out these new and ambitious goals, was itself a crusade, eagerly entered upon by the American people, to bring freedom to Cuba. Neither President McKinley nor those business interests which stood behind his administration wanted war. It was a public whipped to patriotic fervor by sensational newspaper exposures of Spanish brutality toward the Cuban rebels, and by the dramatic sinking of the *Maine* in Havana Harbor, that swept along with it an administration which dared not stand out against the popular clamor for war. After adoption of a self-denying pledge not to seek the annexation of Cuba, the country succumbed wholly to the martial spirit. While the *Outlook* soberly reported that the American people "had been moved to battle by the demand of an awakened conscience answering the call of outraged humanity," the troops marched gaily off to war to the stirring strains of "There'll be a Hot Time in the Old Town Tonight."

Fortunately for the United States, in view of its total military unpreparedness, the blunders and mistakes of the War Department, and the general air of improvisation which marked our strategy, Spain was completely unable to offer any real resistance to our superior naval forces. This was not war as the twentieth century was to know war. Apart from a moment of panic over the possibility of the Spanish fleet raiding the Atlantic coast, an excited public thoroughly enjoyed the brief but thrilling spectacle to which it was treated in the summer of 1898. Commodore Dewey valiantly destroyed a Spanish squadron in an engagement at Manila Bay which cost us not a single ship and the death of only one man — an engineer who died of a heat stroke; the army landed in Cuba, and Theodore Roosevelt and his Rough Riders made their memorable charge up San Juan Hill; after a swift attack upon enemy forces trying to steal out of beleaguered Santiago, Admiral Sampson offered the nation as a Fourth-of-July present the whole of the Spanish battle fleet, and, finally, Puerto Rico was occupied after a desultory mopping-up operation which Mr. Dooley characterized as "Gin'ral Miles' Gran' Picnic and Moonlight Excursion." Within a brief three months Spain's power in the New World was shattered and her Government was suing for peace. "It has been a splendid little war," John Hay wrote complacently, "begun with the highest motives, carried on with magnificent intelligence and spirit, favored by that fortune which loves the brave."

Expansion Wins the Day

As for possible spoils of victory, the United States was committed to uphold Cuba's freedom. Puerto Rico was the only territorial cession we were definitely prepared to demand. Were the ambitions born of the spirit of Manifest Destiny to be so easily satisfied? The answer was soon apparent as the thrilling news of victory at Manila Bay opened up new horizons before the American people. An enthusiastic member of Congress proclaimed triumphantly:

> The booming guns of Dewey's battleships sounded a new note on the Pacific shores, a note that has echoed and re-echoed around the world, and that note is that we are on the Pacific, that we are there to stay, and that we are there to protect our rights, promote our interests, and get our share of the trade and commerce of the opulent Orient.

The cry for further annexations was at once taken up with new vigor by those who had dimly but confidently foreseen the national future in pre-war years. Theodore Roosevelt, Senator Henry Cabot Lodge, John Hay, and Senator Beveridge were among the most enthusiastic advocates of what they termed "the large policy." Soon they were able to report that President McKinley, who had stated so emphatically in his inaugural that "we want no wars of conquest; we must avoid the temptation of territorial aggression," was swinging into their camp. "The whole policy of annexation," Lodge wrote optimistically to Roosevelt that stirring summer, "is growing rapidly under the irresistible pressure of events."

The business interests of the country had generally opposed our entry into the war against Spain. The possible acquisition of the Philippines, however, awoke new dreams of extending our commerce with the Orient. With international developments appearing to threaten our trade in the Far East at the very time that we were growing newly dependent upon foreign markets, the Philippines came to be regarded as a potential entrepôt for commerce with China and an equivalent to the privileged positions and actual concessions being won in that country by our commercial rivals. A poll of merchants and manufacturers convinced the *Chicago Inter-Ocean* that business was "very generally waking up to the opportunities which the war has brought us at a moment when the immense increase of our manufacturing capacity has rendered foreign outlets absolutely necessary to us." The blunt and forthright Mark Hanna, who had opposed war, rushed into print with an unequivocal statement upon the importance of obtaining the Philippines as a safeguard for our trade with China. "If it is commercialism to want the possession of strategic points giving the American people an opportunity to maintain a foothold in the markets of that great eastern country," he declared, "for God's sake let us have commercialism."

The expansionists found other allies among church and missionary groups. Our duty to annex the Philippines had suddenly become more important than our duty to free Cuba, and on every hand there was vigorous support for the "imperialism of righteousness." The religious press was generally agreed that the United States could not refuse the responsibilities thrust upon it, and that the times were ripe for it to extend the blessing of free government to those parts of the world where the fortunes of war had extended national influence or control. "Woe to any nation," the *Churchman* stated, "brought to a pass where it is called upon to guide a weaker people's future which hesitates for fear its own interests will be entangled and its own future imperiled by the full discharge of an unmistakable duty."

A first step along this inviting path had been taken before the war with Spain was over. We finally annexed the Hawaiian Islands in July, 1898, by joint resolution of Congress. Not a change, President McKinley declared, but a consummation.

Step by step we now moved toward taking over the Philippines as well as Puerto Rico and Guam. McKinley first favored the acquisition of a naval base in the Philippines, then advanced the view that we could not accept less than the cession of Luzon, and finally instructed the delegates to the peace conference that we would have to have the whole archipelago. Public opinion was clearly demanding it even though Mr. Dooley countered his friend Mr. Hennessy's pleas for such action by shrewdly commenting, "'tis not more thin two months since ye larned whether they were islands or canned goods." Moreover, the international situation appeared to leave us little choice. If the United States did not annex the Philippines, there was reason to fear that Germany would, and none could say to what dangerous complications that might not lead. In any event, President McKinley felt that it was futile to stand out against such strong pressure from so many directions. He wrote his peace envoys in frank acceptance of the dogma of Manifest Destiny:

> The march of events rules and overrules human actions. Avowing unreservedly the purpose which has animated all our effort, and still solicitous to adhere to it, we cannot be unmindful that, without any desire or design on our part, the war has brought us new duties and responsibilities which we must meet and discharge as becomes a great nation on whose growth and career from the

beginning the Ruler of Nations has plainly written the high command and pledge of civilization.

To this eloquent statement, so clearly reflecting the imperialist sentiment that had blossomed in the heady atmosphere of war, he added, almost as if an afterthought: "Incidental to our tenure in the Philippines is the commercial opportunity to which American statesmanship cannot be indifferent. . . . "

The die was cast. Our final demands upon Spain were freedom for Cuba, the cession of Puerto Rico, Guam, and the Philippine Islands. Completely humbled by war, this proud but impotent nation had no alternative but to surrender its territories. The United States became for the first time a colonial power. There were American outposts in the Caribbean and in the Pacific. We had turned our back upon the relative isolation of the nineteenth century to enter the twentieth with territorial commitments overseas that would never again allow us to return safely to the policies followed when we were no more than a continental power.

The Senate debated the treaty with Spain long and vehemently. Imperialism had produced an inevitable reaction. Forces which broke across all party lines, with the inclusion of such Republicans as Senator Hoar and Speaker Reed as well as such Democratic leaders as former President Cleveland and William Jennings Bryan, rose up in strong opposition to any departure from our traditional policies. They were determined to prevent the annexation of colonies. Entirely apart from all arguments based on trade or expediency, the anti-imperialists declared that there was no place within our republican form of government for colonial possessions. We had no possible moral right to impose our government upon peoples compelled by force to submit to American rule. To every statement that the United States could not shirk the responsibilities thrust upon it, they replied that there could be no reconciliation between imperialism and those ideals of self-government and democratic equality which underlay American political institutions. But for all the vigor and vehemence of such opposition — although by the margin of only one vote over the necessary two-thirds majority — the treaty was finally ratified.

CUBA AND PUERTO RICO

By freeing Cuba from Spanish rule and annexing Puerto Rico, the United States wholly replaced Spain as the dominant power in the Caribbean. It was soon to take advantage of this by undertaking the construction of the Panama Canal. Nevertheless, the nation was prepared to honor its pledge in regard to Cuban independence. A temporary military administration was set up, but the policies adopted by General Leonard Wood looked toward the immediate establishment of complete self-government and withdrawal of the American forces. The island was rapidly pacified, separation of Church and State effected, and a broad program of economic and social improvement carried through with highly effective results. Most notable of all American achievements was the dramatic and successful fight, with which the name of Walter Reed is immemorially associated, against the dread scourge of yellow fever. On all fronts such progress had been made that the Cuban people were busily engaged in 1900 in drawing up their own constitution.

There was to be one important reservation, however, in regard to their independence. By the terms of the so-called Platt Amendment, attached to the army appropriation bill for 1901, Cuba was constrained to write into its constitution a provision acknowledging the right of the United States to intervene in the country's internal affairs whenever such action was felt to be necessary to preserve Cuban independence or maintain a stable government. Together with our retention of naval and coaling stations, the Platt Amendment thus in effect established a semi-protectorate over the island, narrowly circumscribing its independence. On four separate occasions in the ensuing years, moreover, we were actually to intervene in Cuban affairs in the interests of law and order, and not until 1934 was the Platt Amendment finally abrogated.

The status of Puerto Rico was of course that of a dependent territory or colony, and passage of the Foraker Act in 1900 established a civilian government to replace the temporary military administration that had followed General Miles's conquest. In pursuit of the policy adopted toward all our new dependencies "not to exploit but to develop, to civilize, to educate, to train in the science of self-government," the Puerto Ricans were allowed an elective assembly and representation on an appointed council. Final authority, however, was maintained by an American governor-general. In later years native powers of self-government were further amplified. Passage of the Jones Act in 1917 granted American citizenship to the Puerto Ricans and made both houses of the legislature elective with powers subject only to presidential veto. Economic issues were both at the opening of the century and in later years to prove more difficult of solution. Despite progress along many lines, reflecting the constructive aspects of American colonial policy, the lot of the great mass of Puerto Rican peasantry did not materially improve. Absentee American landlords diverted production more and more to sugar and tobacco for continental markets at the expense of subsistence crops; overpopulation made the struggle for bare existence unbelievably severe, and there would come a day when Puerto Rico appeared to be treated very much as an unwanted stepchild.

A further question had also arisen immediately upon annexation, involving our other overseas territories as well as Puerto Rico, but applying more particularly to this island. What was its exact constitutional status? A protectionist Congress desired to apply the tariff to Puerto Rican products, but if the island were in every sense a part of the United States, this would obviously be discriminatory. On other counts as well it appeared inadvisable, if not wholly impractical, to extend to Puerto Ricans all the civil rights constitutionally guaranteed in the United States. When cases involving these complicated issues came up for final decision, the Supreme Court found itself confronted with a highly puzzling dilemma.

It resolved the question, in the most important of the so-called Insular Cases in 1901 (*Downes v. Bidwell*), in a manner which gave full satisfaction to protectionist congressmen, but involved as tortuous reasoning as perhaps any decision that the Supreme Court has ever handed down. Indeed, the several judges reached their conclusions by almost as many different paths. The general

purport of their five-to-four ruling was to make a distinction between what were to be called "incorporated" and "unincorporated" territories. " . . . The island of Puerto Rico is a territory
appurtenant and belonging to the United States," Justice Brown
said, "but not a part of the United States within the revenue
clauses of the Constitution. . . . " In other words, Congress could
govern Puerto Rico very much as it saw fit, and apply the tariff
to Puerto Rican imports. In later decisions this obscure classifica-
tion of overseas territories was further sustained and the principle developed that while their inhabitants were entitled to such
"fundamental" rights guaranteed in our Constitution as freedom
of religion or freedom of the press, so-called "formal" rights relating to protection from discriminatory laws did not necessarily
apply to them. There appeared to be little question, at least in
the minds of critics of our new policies, that imperialism had done
strange things to the Constitution.

STATUS OF THE PHILIPPINES

These problems of administration and legal status in the Caribbean, however, were nothing compared to those created by our
colonial expansion in the Pacific. This was not true of our smaller
island possessions. Hawaii was given a territorial status. Guam
was taken over as a naval station. American Samoa, which had
come directly under the American flag by an international agreement with Great Britain and Germany in 1899 that abrogated the
old tripartite control, also fell naturally into the hands of the
Navy Department. The trouble was with the Philippine Islands.
Their population of some eight million had no desire whatever
to find themselves a part of the United States — incorporated or
unincorporated. They had fought for their independence against
Spain and had believed that American intervention would bring
them their freedom. On the very eve of ratification of the treaty
that transferred them to American control, they took up arms
against those whom they now regarded as new conquerors. Having fought Spain to assure the freedom of Cuba, the United States
found itself at war to suppress the liberty of the Philippines.

This campaign, breaking out in February, 1899, was to last three years, involving some 120,000 American troops, costing the nation almost as much as the war with Spain, and taking a far heavier toll of lives. In undertaking "to civilize 'em with a Krag," we were to find ourselves involved in a far more arduous job than we had contemplated. Before the new war had dragged on to its weary end after the capture of the Filipino leader Aguinaldo in 1901, our high-minded attempt to extend the benefits of American rule to these Pacific islands found our military forces employing tactics which grievously shocked public opinion at home. Prisoners were killed, the natives brought in to concentration camps, and the water cure adopted as a means to break the Filipinos' spirit and overcome their highly effective guerrilla warfare. In caustic comment upon our use of the very methods which we had so bitterly condemned Spain for using against the Cubans, William Graham Sumner wrote *The Spanish Conquest of the United States*.

Following such reports, the anti-imperialists vigorously renewed their campaign against taking over the islands. Mark Twain declared that the American flag should have its white stripes painted black and its stars replaced by a skull and cross-bones. Carl Schurz condemned the slaughter of innocent people and wanton sacrifice of the lives of American soldiers as a "horrible blood guiltiness without parallel in the history of politics." William Vaughn Moody called eloquently upon the spirit of those who had died for the preservation of American liberties —

> For save we let the island men go free,
> Those baffled and dislaureled ghosts
> Will curse us from the lamentable coasts
> Where walk the frustrate dead. . . .

The McKinley Administration was not deterred by such criticism of its policies. It went obdurately ahead with its inescapable task of stamping out rebellion, and the appointment of William Howard Taft as the islands' first civil governor in 1901 established American rule on a permanent basis. Even though crushed by force of arms, the Filipinos were neither then nor in later years reconciled to our occupation. Their goal remained self-government and independence. The United States was ready to recognize such ultimate objectives, and the colonial policy followed by Governor Taft and his successors was sincerely directed toward preparing the Filipinos to take over increasingly larger responsibilities. It was not until passage of the Jones Act in 1916, however, that the Filipinos were given manhood suffrage, control of the legislature and the explicit promise of full independence as soon as a "stable government" was established. Almost twenty years were to pass before this final pledge was made good with the passage of the Tydings-McDuffie Act of 1934, establishing a Philippine Commonwealth that was slated to achieve complete independence in 1946.

DECLARING THE OPEN-DOOR POLICY

In the meantime our occupation of the Philippines had led at the opening of the century to the ambitious development of American policy in the Far East marked by the famous Open-Door notes of Secretary of State John Hay. The establishment of American control over the Caribbean was a first direct consequence of the Spanish War, but the intervention of the United States in the political situation in China was of even more far-reaching significance. For while the Open-Door policy was in fact a projection of principles that had governed our relations with China since the establishment of treaty relations more than sixty years earlier, it dramatically underscored our new rôle as a Pacific power.

On the eve of our territorial advance to the shores of the Pacific through occupation of the Philippines, our commercial rivals in the Far East had extorted valuable leaseholds from the crumbling Chinese Empire and divided that country into foreign spheres of influence. Germany, Russia, Great Britain, and France successively demanded concessions which China had no alternative other than to grant. "The various Powers," declared the redoubtable old Empress Dowager Tzu Hsi, the last strong figure of the Manchu dynasty, "cast upon us looks of tiger-like voracity, hustling each other in their endeavors to be the first to seize upon our innermost territories." The United States sought no territory, but it was determined not to be frozen out of this great far-eastern market toward which it had always looked so expectantly. The purpose of the Hay notes, as first dispatched at the close of 1899, was to safeguard our commercial interests by winning international support for complete trade equality within all foreign spheres of influence.

Some such move had actually been suggested by Great Britain. Hay was in a sense acting independently on this proposal somewhat as President Monroe had responded to British overtures in declaring the Monroe Doctrine. But there was also strong support in commercial circles within the United States for more effective measures to protect our trade interests in China, and a widespread feeling that we should make the most of the opportunities provided by possession of the Philippines. The Secretary of State's notes, in any event, went no further than to ask the Powers' adherence to three very limited propositions. He sought assurances that they would not interfere with any treaty port or vested interest within their respective spheres of influence in China; that the Chinese tariff would be applied equally to the nationals of whatever country, and that there should be no discrimination in harbor dues or railroad charges. He accepted the existence of spheres of influence; he had nothing to say of China's sovereignty.

Even to these moderate requests the replies of the Powers were evasive and conditional. They would not commit themselves. Nevertheless, Hay chose to interpret their answers as complete acceptance of the American program in order to marshal behind the Open-Door policy the support of world public opinion. In the United States his diplomacy was hailed as having won a brilliant triumph. The exchange of notes, the *Philadelphia Press* proudly stated, "protects the present, it safeguards the future, and it establishes the United States in an impregnable position." Abroad it was viewed with a good deal more skepticism.

A few months later, in the summer of 1900, the Boxer Rebellion broke out in China. Fanatic bands of Chinese peasants, who had sworn to drive the foreigners into the sea, ravaged the northern provinces, burning, looting, and killing. In Peking the legations of the Powers were besieged with the crafty connivance of the Empress Dowager herself. They were entirely cut off, and not until a hurriedly organized international expedition went to the rescue was a worried world assured that the foreign envoys had not all been massacred. American troops took part in this interallied expedition, but for all Secretary Hay's concern over the immediate safety of his countrymen in Peking, he was also anxious to reaffirm the policy behind his original Open-Door notes. He did not wish to see the Boxer Rebellion made the excuse for further encroachments upon Chinese sovereignty that would endanger American interests. The occasion was therefore seized to announce, in the hope of forcing comparable action on the part of the Powers, that this country sought no special privileges in China. It was the policy of the United States, Hay declared in another circular to foreign capitals, to preserve the territorial and administrative integrity of China, protect the rights of all friendly Powers, and safeguard for the world the principle of equal and impartial trade with all parts of the Empire.

Although no replies were received to these second notes, China's independence was preserved in the ultimate settlement of the issues rising out of the Boxer Rebellion. European rivalry over any possible division of the spoils of dismemberment may well have been as much responsible for this as the stand taken by the United States. Whatever the contributing causes, the Open-Door policy had triumphed. The United States had taken the lead in formulating a program which held out the promise of continued international respect for Chinese sovereignty. Public opinion in this country again applauded. The happy blend of self-interest and idealism which Hay's policy represented appealed immensely to the American people. Whether or not they were prepared to support the Open-Door policy by force of arms should it be threatened by any one of the Powers was quite another question.

THE ELECTION OF 1900

Against this background of war in the Philippines and exciting drama in China, the country was called upon in 1900 to fight out another presidential campaign. The issue of imperialism, of where our new foreign policies were leading us, naturally bulked large in the popular mind. The Republicans were prepared to stand on the record; the Democrats condemned it utterly.

The Republican platform heartily endorsed retention of the Philippines and declared it to be "the high duty of the Government to maintain its authority, to put down the insurrection, and to confer the blessings of liberty and civilization upon all the rescued people." After making this clear, the convention thereupon enthusiastically renominated McKinley for the presidency, with Theodore Roosevelt as his running mate.

While thus prepared to meet the challenge of anti-imperialists, the Republicans nevertheless relied even more heavily upon their achievements in domestic policy to win popular support. They pointed toward the prevailing good times as irrefutable proof that McKinley had made good the promise of being Advance Agent of Prosperity.

The Democrats once again named William Jennings Bryan. And once again they came out in favor of free silver and even more vigorously attacked the trusts. But imperialism, which they assailed as threatening "the very existence of the republic and the destruction of our free institutions," was declared to be the paramount issue. "No other question can approach it in importance," Bryan stated in another barnstorming swing around the country in which he accused the McKinley Administration of embarking upon a program that might well lead to dangerous militarism.

This challenge was gladly accepted by the expansionists within Republican ranks whose most flamboyant spokesman was Senator Beveridge of Indiana. No doubts ever assailed him as to the justice of our course. He found that the highest honor liberty could bestow was "the sacred order of the Stars and Stripes" without unduly concerning himself over the feelings of this honor's recipients. He declared on one memorable occasion:

> The Philippines are ours forever. And just beyond the Philippines are China's illimitable markets. We will not retreat from either. We will not abandon our duty in the Orient. We will not renounce our part in the mission of our race, trustee, under God, of the civilization of the world. . . . The Pacific is our ocean. . . . And the Pacific is the ocean of the commerce of the future. Most future wars will be conflicts for commerce. The Power that rules the Pacific, therefore, is the Power that rules the world. And, with the Philippines, that Power is and will forever be the American Republic.

Confronted with such impassioned oratory, the anti-imperialist Democrats could make little headway. Their arguments were negative; those of the Republicans were positive.

When November finally arrived, McKinley was once again elected — elected by a far larger popular majority than he had obtained in 1896 and an electoral vote of 292 to 155. But while the election might be accepted as a popular mandate for imperialism, and there was little question that a majority of the people favored retention of the Philippines, the prosperity of 1900 was the underlying reason for the Republicans' triumphal return to office. Good times, rather than his foreign policy, elected McKinley. The most telling slogan of his campaign was "The Full Dinner Pail." His administration was credited with successful prosecution of the war with Spain and a vigorous policy of overseas expansion, but even more it was credited with the country's unexampled economic growth. The Democrats never had a real chance in the face of mounting business profits, rising farm prices, and high wages. Attacks upon the trusts and money power, let alone upon imperialism, could make no real dent upon a people so generally content.

Nevertheless, the change in our foreign policy which the people endorsed at least by default in re-electing McKinley in 1900 had a far deeper significance than was generally realized. The basic question before the country was this: How far was the

United States prepared to go in exerting its newfound influence in world affairs?

As the twentieth century advanced, it was to become increasingly clear that the American people did not know the answer to this vital question. The "large policy" of the expansionists had won the day in 1900, but even then it did not command universal support. Many persons who voted for McKinley, as well as those who cast their ballot for Bryan, were deeply concerned over what seemed to them so dangerous and radical a departure from our historic traditions. Their ranks would swell rather than diminish as time proved that the consequences of territorial expansion were new foreign entanglements. Certainly imperialism, as so fervently proclaimed in the hectic aftermath of the war with Spain, had no real roots in the American way of life. In days to come political alignments were to shift back and forth, but the sharp division of public opinion, first marked in the bitter debates of 1900, persisted, albeit in new shapes and forms, as we became more and more involved in the changing balance of international power politics. The United States had lost the certain touchstone of national interest found in the immediate needs of continental self-defense, that had made the determination of foreign policy in the nineteenth century relatively simple.

Could all this have been in any way avoided? Theodore Roosevelt was to write a few years later:

> In foreign affairs we must make up our minds that, whether we wish it or not, we are a great people and must play a great part in the world. It is not open to us to choose whether we will play that great part or not. We have to play it. All we can decide is whether we shall play it well or ill.

American Life: 1900

Housekeeping Becomes Ready-Made

AMERICANS at the opening of the century were greatly concerned over trusts and monopolies, imperialism and the Open-Door policy, but these important issues did not make up the stuff of everyday life. Whatever might happen in the world of politics, men and women went about their daily work, sought to enjoy themselves in their leisure time, and were naturally absorbed in the many cares and pleasures of family activity. It is never possible to give a complete picture of such life: it is too many-sided, too varied, to be caught up in a few pages of description. Yet how the American people lived, what were their sports and amusements, what they wore, how they made use of the new products of an industrial age, what books they read and what songs they sang — all this is a part of the warp and woof of history as well as the great events that draw newspaper headlines. Some attempt must be made to weave these strands of American life into the general pattern of the times.

With two-thirds of the people living on farms or in small villages in 1900, the simplicity of an agrarian civilization was still preserved in many parts of the country. Farmers worked their fields with the benefit of new machinery, but theirs was still a relatively isolated life, little touched by the phenomenal changes being introduced in the larger towns and cities. Living conditions were much as they had always been. The farm wife struggled through her housekeeping as had her mother before her, and recreation centered upon farm festivals and rural sports. The county fair, Chautauqua, and the annual advent of the circus were gradually supplemented by other trips to near-by towns as improved roads made for easier traveling, and rural free delivery was a new link with the outside world. But telephones, automobiles, and the radio were still in the future.

The small town was also for the most part outside of the stream of larger events in the growing cities, and as already noted it kept alive the traditions of democracy far more than the metropolis. White frame houses along quiet, elm-shaded streets, groups of people gossiping during the evening on the front porch, the Saturday night band concert on the village green, political discussions at the general store or post office, buggies drawn up at the hitching post, the ball game on the high-school playing field — these were American scenes, familiar and traditional.

Nevertheless, the rise of industry was modifying the simple pattern of nineteenth-century life, and the surging activity of city, suburb, and larger town was to become more and more typical of the United States. For mass production not only meant the nationalization of business and the growth of trusts; it wrought increasing changes in every phase of daily living for ordinary people throughout the nation.

The end results of many new inventions and new processes of manufacture were found in the American home. In 1879 Thomas Edison had invented the incandescent lamp, and twenty years later the gas fixtures in city and suburban houses were being wired for electricity, with excited housewives screwing the curious new bulbs into old wall brackets and chandeliers. The miracle of modern lighting — cheap, safe, and efficient — was being realized. Electrical appliances — toasters, chafing dishes, and percolators; irons, vacuum cleaners, and washing machines — were just over the horizon. Here was easy reading for all the family, and less drudgery in the laundry and in the kitchen.

The closing years of the old century had also seen the introduction of hot-air furnaces; gas stoves were beginning to drive out coal ranges and kerosene stoves; iceboxes had become a familiar feature of innumerable back stoops. Aluminum kitchenware replaced the heavy iron pots and pans of an earlier day, and window screens were a helpful innovation. The most revolutionary household development perhaps was sanitary plumbing. The modern bathroom, in all its glistening, porcelain glory, was just emerging in 1900 as one of the enduring triumphs of American civilization. Few homes yet boasted of a telephone; there were only seven hundred thousand in the entire country. "The day is coming," the *Providence Journal* nevertheless stated confidently, "when practically every household will have a telephone, just as it has other conveniences."

Baker's bread, refined sugar, canned goods, and packaged cereals were freeing women from much of their labor in the kitchen.

THE VOGUE OF SPORTS

As life became somewhat easier with these new conveniences in the home, and hours of work gradually grew shorter for city workers, leisure became a phenomenon that many persons had never before known. There was a consequent demand for new forms of recreation to meet new needs. This was particularly true of communities where people were largely shut off from the simple, informal pleasures of the countryside, and organized sports and commercial entertainment became of ever-increasing importance.

An epic of the day, recited countless times on vaudeville stages throughout the country, concluded with the sad lament:

> But there is no joy in Mudville,
> Mighty Casey has struck out.

Its popularity was symptomatic of the pervasive interest that had grown up in organized sports, and of baseball's rôle as the great national game. Baseball had become professionalized in the eighteen-seventies, and to compensate for their own lack of opportunity to play, urban workers crowded the city ball parks to watch league games. The National League had been formed in 1876, the American League, growing out of the old American Association, in 1899. Within three years the annual World Series was to be inaugurated. Such players as "Pop" Anson, "Iron Man" Joe McGinnity, and "Slide, Kelly, Slide" were heroes to a nation of sports fans. "Let me say," said Cardinal Gibbons, "that I favor baseball as an amusement for the greatest pleasure-loving people in the world."

The crisp days of autumn also brought out large spectator crowds for the increasingly popular sport of intercollegiate football, which had gradually evolved from the English Rugby introduced to this country in 1870. The games of the Big Three — Harvard, Yale, and Princeton — set the pace with crowds of thirty and forty thousand in 1900. "They came by the railroads, horsecars, drags, coaches, and afoot," the *New York Tribune* reported on one occasion. "The air was tinged with the blue and the orange and the black as the great throngs poured through the city over the bridges, invaded Brooklyn, and swept like a rising tide into Eastern Park." The press gave front-page headlines to the championship games (one paper featuring the story, "The Journal's Woman Reporter Trains with the Little Boys in Blue"), and already we find President Eliot of Harvard soberly stating that "the pecuniary aspects of the sport are not agreeable."

The emphasis upon the new spectator sports did not mean that there was no active participation in games. Golf was beginning to outgrow its first class of devotees, the elderly men to be seen going about the links in red coats and visored hats, and it was perhaps the leading pastime of vacationists in New England. Although still considered a fashionable game "essentially for ladies and gentlemen," tennis was also making rapid headway. Basketball, first introduced at the Springfield (Massachusetts) Y.M.C.A. in 1891, was winning a following.

The most popular of all active forms of recreation was still bicycling. "There were eighty-one starters in the century run," reads a typical Monday morning report of the day, repeated in countless newspapers. " . . . Medals of neat design went to the survivors." Annual manufacture of wheels exceeded a million. But bicycles had a greater significance than their contribution to sport. The Census of 1900 stated that few articles ever used by man had created so great a revolution in social conditions. Bicycling opened up the country for city dwellers, it was an important influence in the emancipation of women and in dress reform, it provided an early impetus for the good-roads movement. Bicycling was a world of its own — the League of American Wheelmen, madcap scorchers, Daisy Bell —

> But you'll look sweet
> Upon the seat
> Of a bicycle built for two!

MELODRAMA AND HOTDOGS

Commercial entertainment other than professional sports events also played an expanding rôle in providing year-round recreation for the urban masses. The popular theater was in its heyday at the opening of the new century. For drygoods clerks and stenographers, streetcar conductors and servant girls, newsboys, house painters, hotel waiters, bricklayers, teamsters, and charwomen, going to a show in 1900 did not mean the movies, it meant melodrama, high comedy, burlesque, vaudeville, or the penny arcade.

Tremendous playhouses (admission ten, twenty, or thirty cents) catered to this growing demand for cheap entertainment, with galleries crowded, as another redskin bit the dust or some lovely working girl sacrificed her life to maintain her unsullied honor. *The White Slave, Nellie the Beautiful Cloak Model,* and *On the Bowery* were favorites; and also the girl shows luridly featuring "50 — Pairs of Rounded Limbs, Ruby Lips, Tantalizing Torsos — 50." The new refined vaudeville for family entertainment brought to the two-a-day circuit Weber and Fields, Lillian Russell, Montgomery and Stone, Master George Cohan. There was another world of the theater in which such famous stars as Sarah Bernhardt and Richard Mansfield, Ellen Terry and Henry Irving, drew the carriage trade. The common people were content with *Under the Gas Light, The First Scalp for Custer,* or *Lily Clay's Colossal Gaiety Company.*

Traveling stock companies brought every kind of theatrical fare to the opera houses of Main Street ("first class attractions only"), putting on with equal zest minstrel shows, *East Lynne* and *The Old Homestead,* vaudeville skits, musical comedies, and Shakespeare. "Doubtless there are worse theatrical companies than those which visit Kansas," William Allen White wrote caustically, "but no one has ever described them." In any event, some five hundred companies were on the road in 1900, and generally doing very well.

There were few more popular ways of spending a Saturday afternoon or Sunday than at the amusement park found at the end of almost every suburban trolley line. Coney Island, a popular resort as early as the eighteen-fifties, set the standard with its roller coasters, shoot-the-chutes, merry-go-rounds, Ferris wheels, and fun houses. It also boasted of an innovation at its refreshment stands described by one visitor as "a weird-looking sausage muffled up in two halves of a roll." And so popular was that delectable concoction now known as a "hotdog" that it quickly spread from coast to coast. All in all the trolley park provided not only recreation, but one of the few means of escape from crowded cities. Here democracy could be found at play — fortified with its muffled sausage.

This growth of organized sports and popular entertainment was a significant expression of American life, not only showing new ways in which the urban democracy was spending its leisure time, but also reflecting a shift in emphasis in regard to older traditions of simplicity, thrift, and industry in national life. In the cities, at least, puritanical concepts of work as the only means to avoid the temptation of evil were undergoing a radical change. A problem had been posed for the churches no less far-reaching than had been the impact of scientific thought on traditional religious beliefs. And just as the Church had gradually swung over to more liberal doctrines in the conflict between science and faith, so did it gradually broaden its point of view toward leisure-time activities in the cities. It accepted amusements, including the theater, as wholly justified, and met the challenge of the times in many instances by itself providing recreational opportunities. Institutionalized churches in the large cities organized clubs, set up study and discussion groups, and sponsored all manner of new activities from sports to amateur theatricals. "If amusing young people aids to save them," the *Northwestern Christian Advocate* stated, "then the work is fully and gloriously worthy of the Church."

POPULAR READING AND POPULAR MUSIC

People were reading more as well as playing more. In an era of sensational yellow journalism, newspaper circulation grew by leaps and bounds, with both Pulitzer's *New York World* and Hearst's *New York Journal* passing the million mark. The Sunday paper, with its sports section and colored comics, became an institution. Popular-priced magazines so multiplied that the number of buyers rose to nearly three million. And books poured from the presses in an increasing stream even though they could not compete with either magazines or newspapers among the general public.

The serious authors of the day were deeply concerned with the changing pattern of national life, and an undercurrent of realism was reflected in the writings of William Dean Howells and Frank Norris, Hamlin Garland and Stephen Crane. Theirs were not the books, however, which reached the best-seller lists, let alone the magazine and newspaper reading public. Contemporary critics held the woman reader — "the Iron Madonna who strangles in her fond embrace the American novelist" — responsible for the trend in popular fiction, but wherever the responsibility lay, the public wanted not realism but romance. Mary Johnston's *To Have and To Hold* was the best-seller of 1900, and the sales of other current favorites that year showed totals of 650,000 copies for *Ben-Hur*, 390,000 for *David Harum*, 245,000 for *Richard Carvel*, and 125,000 for *When Knighthood Was in Flower.*

Music played a greater part in everyday American life at this time than it ever had before. Thomas Edison had invented the phonograph in the eighteen-seventies, but it was still in its awkward age, and broadcasting was, of course, undreamed of. Music was home-made. "There is no country where there are so many pianos and players on them," a French visitor commented, and informal sings (as well as even more informal barber-shop quartets) were a favorite evening entertainment. Popular songs — and never was their composition more prolific — faithfully mirrored the spirit of the times, revealing, as did the vogue for melodrama in the theater and romance in the popular novels, an unconscious escapism. Such southern melodies introduced by the minstrels as *Old Black Joe* and *The Old Folks at Home*; Scotch and Irish ballads, as *John Anderson, My Jo, Annie Laurie*, and *Coming Through the Rye*; and *Juanita, Oh, My Darling Clementine*, and *In the Gloaming* were old favorites. *The Rosary* had a tremendous vogue. Among contemporary hits were *The Bowery* and *The Sidewalks of New York*, but more typically sentimental were *On the Banks of the Wabash, Just Tell Them That You Saw Me*, and *After the Ball* —

> Many a heart is aching
> If you could read them all;
> Many the hopes that have vanished
> After the ball.

FADS AND FANCIES

Other aspects of the daily life of the American people are intimately revealed by contemporary records in magazines and newspapers, and by their advertisements. It was the era of the Gibson Girl. Formal dances featured the Lancers and the Virginia Reel, and progressive euchre was a favorite card game. The well-dressed man was advised that "much latitude is allowed in waistcoats . . . derbies have little brim . . . four-in-hands tied with a small knot are worn with the high banded collar." Sarsaparilla, patent cuff-holders, chewing gum, and Milwaukee beer were highly popular.

Fashion plates revealed that skirts still swept the ground and wide-brimmed hats fluttered in every breeze. But there were also indications that the growth of a business civilization was affecting the way women dressed. For salesgirls in the department stores, operators in the new telephone exchanges, secretaries and stenographers, something new in costume was essential. "The shirtwaist has come to stay," commented one fashion writer, and the *Ladies' Home Journal* advised that if one were tempted "to give a gown for office wear, let it be one of black, brown, or gray cravenetted serge."

For the young lady of 1900 going in for sports, other new and daring costumes were suggested. There was "a skirt short enough not to become entangled in the skates"; the bicyclist was advised to wear bloomers, engagingly described as "bifurcated garments extending from the waist to the knee," and *Vogue* suggested for bathers "a turkey-red costume with full drawers, to be worn with a sash around the waist; black stockings, and a straw hat."

"Boy wanted to work in saloon and learn bartending," read one classified ad; another called for "lady cashier for store; salary $8 a week"; a third was "Situation wanted: Coachman — first-class family; strictly sober; careful, stylish driver; can drive tandem or four." There were display advertisements of brass bedsteads, golden-oak parlor sets, and rolltop desks.

The automobile had been invented in the eighteen-nineties and some eight thousand cars were on the road in 1900. But it still appeared to be an expensive, unreliable plaything, and few people believed that it could ever compete with such important new means of transportation as the street railways and suburban trolley lines that were so rapidly multiplying. "The ordinary 'horseless carriage' is at present a luxury for the wealthy," one newspaper stated, "and although its price will probably fall in the future, it will never, of course, come into common use . . . "

Life parodied the social fad of motoring:

> Half a block, half a block,
> Half a block onward,
> All in their automobiles,
> Rode the Four Hundred.

In many ways the year 1900 carried over the flavor of life in the Golden Nineties; in others it foreshadowed the changes to be introduced with the new century. And in addition to all the innovations in the home and new fashions in dress, current vogues in sports and amusements, popular literature and popular songs, were the far-reaching developments taking place in various other phases of social life. There was a steady broadening of popular education and important advances in science and medicine; the status of women was undergoing a highly significant change; a revolution in transportation was in the making, and the expanding cities were being transformed by new developments in urban planning and architecture. To such topics we shall return with the unfolding history of the twentieth century. As revealed in matters that have been touched upon, however, it is already evident that the everyday life of the American people in 1900 was in countless ways directly affected by the impact of the new industrialism. A machine-made civilization was developing which was not only raising the standard of living, but introducing new customs, ways of thought, and popular attitudes in the business of daily life.

The Progressive Era

5

The Background of Reform

ALTHOUGH the election of 1900 was a triumph for conservatism, discontent with the influence of big business had not wholly subsided at the opening of the century. Under the surface of apparent acquiescence with the principles of *laissez-faire*, the spirit of reform was everywhere quickening. It was reaching out to all manner of people who saw a growing danger to democracy in what they had come to regard as a corrupt alliance between political bosses and corporate interests, and who by no means despaired of recovering greater power over government and broader recognition of popular rights. The liberal ranks were to swell as the century advanced, gaining new recruits and developing new tactics to redress the political and economic balance in the interests of the people as a whole. There was a general stirring of reform activity that was destined to usher in one of the most forward-looking and hopeful epochs in our national life.

The Progressive Movement, as it came to be called, may be said to have begun when Theodore Roosevelt assumed the presidency upon the death of McKinley in 1901 and to have lasted until the eve of America's entry into the first World War in 1917. Cutting across party lines, it was neither Republican nor Democratic. After the political battles of 1912, the Wilson Administration carried forward the principles of progressivism even more aggressively than had the preceding Republican administrations. Moreover, the movement was advanced in states and municipalities by governors, mayors, and other leaders irrespective of party affiliations. Progressivism, in other words, reflected a strong, popular demand on the part of the people as a whole for political reform in every branch of government. While Theodore

Roosevelt, Robert M. La Follette, William Jennings Bryan, and Woodrow Wilson were the outstanding leaders on the national stage, there were scores of less well-known progressives who did yeoman work in other fields and who sometimes achieved more effective results.

The movement was fundamentally one of those periodic swings toward democratic progress that have been characteristic of American history since revolutionary days. It owed its strength to the support it commanded among so many different elements in the national life. The direct frontal assault on privilege launched by the Populists had failed because it alarmed the middle class, but progressivism was a liberal rather than a radical uprising. Senator Beveridge was one among many political leaders of that day to realize clearly what was happening. He wrote in 1905:

> I have been carefully studying the present unrest and interviewing numbers of people about it. I am coming to the conclusion that it is not a passing whim, but a great and natural movement as occurs, in this country, as our early history shows, once about every forty years. It is not like the Granger episode or the Debs episode. The former . . . affected only the farmers; the latter, only the workingmen. The present unrest, however, is quite as vigorous among the intellectuals, college men, university people, etc., as it is among the common people.

The scope of progressivism was as broad as the American scene. Roosevelt battled the trusts and fought for conservation of the country's natural resources. La Follette led an intensified drive for regulation of railroad rates. Woodrow Wilson sponsored legislation to reduce the tariff, strengthen the anti-trust laws, and curb the money power. At the same time, a long line of state governors backed the passage of laws to remedy the conditions under which industrial labor was forced to work; to provide workmen's compensation; and especially to protect both child labor and women workers. Reform mayors in cities scattered throughout the country sought to clean up conditions in municipal government and to break the power of corrupt political machines. Gathering support from many sources were such nation-wide drives as those which led to adoption of the initiative and referendum, the secret ballot, and direct primaries, as well as to the constitutional amendments authorizing the income tax, providing for the direct election of senators, and establishing woman suffrage. All of this — and much more — was a part of the progressive movement.

The final results of this spirited activity did not wholly fulfill the promise of the progressives' early hopes. In their confident faith in the workings of democracy and progress, they sometimes blinded themselves to the sharper economic issues created by the new economic order. As we look back from the vantage-point of later years, their achievements may appear disappointing. Nevertheless, this nation-wide liberal uprising, whose roots may be found in Populism and which in some ways foreshadowed the New Deal, brought about great changes, both political and economic, in American society. If its major objectives of recovering for the people the political power usurped by big business and of enacting a broad program of social and economic reform were not wholly attained, at least the bases of democracy were greatly strengthened. The common people succeeded in making their influence felt. The leaders of both business and politics discovered that the liberal and humanitarian sentiment of the American people, once it had been aroused to a determined demand for greater social justice, could not safely be ignored.

Reformers and Muckrakers

The underlying forces that accounted for such a drastic swing away from the earlier philosophy of *laissez-faire* had first found expression in the trenchant criticism of the existing order made by a small minority in the latter decades of the nineteenth century. The note of protest was voiced by economists questioning the way in which free competition, the theoretical basis of *laissez-faire*, was giving way to monopoly. It found expression among humanitarians, skeptical of the validity of the Gospel of Wealth, who proposed a new and more responsible Social Gospel. It was further emphasized by the advocates of socialism and direct political action among the Populists. The critics and reformers of the early nineteen-hundreds, so generally held responsible for the new climate of public opinion in the progressive era, were the amplified chorus of nineteenth-century dissent.

Henry George had been one of the earliest of these dissenters, and in writing *Progress and Poverty* he made a notable contribution to economic discussion. It was his conviction that the growing disparity between the rich and the poor in modern society was primarily due to the profits made by landlords from the unearned increment in the value of land. Accepting the theory that the land properly belonged to the people as a whole, George maintained that any increase in its value created by society rather than by the individual tenant belonged to society. To meet this problem, and thereby erase all inequalities in the distribution of wealth, he specifically proposed the confiscation of this unearned increment in land values through taxation. His program awoke nation-wide discussion and won thousands of converts. Even though the single tax was itself never adopted on any broad, comprehensive basis, there was no question of the tremendous influence *Progress and Poverty* exercised upon the thinking of many twentieth-century progressives.

An even wider audience was aroused to question the existing economic system by Edward Bellamy's *Looking Backward*. This book, published in 1888, was a popular Utopian romance which pictured a future United States in which the movement toward consolidation in industry had been carried through to its logical conclusion — the formation of one all-embracing trust that controlled the labor of all workers and distributed the benefits of their labor to all alike. As the directing agency of this monopoly, according to Bellamy's thesis, the State would wholly control all production and distribution and thereby guarantee economic security for every man, woman, and child in the nation. Although Bellamy maintained that his plan would safeguard individual rights, its apparent denial of individualism was too direct a violation of American tradition for it to win lasting support. But in the early eighteen-nineties his radical ideas spread rapidly across the country. Nearly two hundred Nationalist clubs were formed to promote the doctrine so engagingly elaborated in *Looking Backward*.

An even more direct link between nineteenth- and twentieth-century reformers was Henry Demarest Lloyd, who in 1894 published *Wealth Against Commonwealth*. This book proposed no new economic order. It was an impassioned account of just what was happening as a consequence of the growth of trusts and monopoly, the Standard Oil Company serving as the most horrible example of a concentration of wealth which was yielding "incalculable power and pleasure for a few, and partial existence for the many . . . " Lloyd's disclosures provided the ammunition that liberals needed in their demand for more effective curbs upon monopoly, and they established a pattern for much of the reform literature of the progressive period.

There were other attacks on the social and economic order before the close of the century, but it was after 1900 that criticism and protest began to gather impressive volume. In newspapers and magazines, even more than in books, scores of writers turned to the new theme with missionary zeal. The popular newspapers — the so-called Yellow Press — were in the van of this movement. Both Pulitzer and Hearst were aggressive champions of the common man against capitalistic exploitation, and however much they may have sought out the sensational to gain circulation, they played no small part in laying the foundation of reform. The popular magazines also discovered that articles upon political corruption, monopolistic practices, and other social abuses were good copy, and in meeting the public demand for such literature, they both reflected the growing spirit of revolt against the more flagrant injustices of contemporary society, and also served greatly to intensify it. Political writers were encouraged to delve deeper and deeper into the relationship between corporate wealth and government. They relentlessly tore apart the veil which had heretofore shrouded back-room politics. Political chicanery, corporate bribery of judges, business disregard of law, the skulduggery of high finance were all grist to their busy mill.

Theodore Roosevelt was to owe a great deal to these newspaper and magazine writers. They paved the way for his leadership in the fight against plutocracy. Yet it was he who in a moment of sharp irritation was responsible for fastening upon them the opprobrious term of "muckrakers." It was taken from the description in *Pilgrim's Progress* of the man with the muckrake — "the man who could look no way but downward with the muckrake in his hands; who was offered the celestial crown for his muckrake, but would look neither up nor regard the crown he was offered, but continued to rake the filth from the floor." The men and women to whom it applied ignored the presidential attack upon their methods. They accepted the designation of muckrakers as a badge of public service.

Two series of articles that began in *McClure's Magazine* in 1902 are generally accepted as the pioneer contributions in this school of writing. They were Lincoln Steffens's memorable exposure of municipal corruption, later published under the title of *The Shame of the Cities*, and Ida Tarbell's famous *History of the Standard Oil Company* with its precise and unerring narration of the steps whereby this great corporation had risen to almost unchallenged industrial power. While the latter series, in somewhat more popular form, was doing what Henry Demarest Lloyd had already done in *Wealth Against Commonwealth*, Steffens was breaking new ground. He was not attacking individuals in his exposures so much as "the system" that made possible graft and corruption. The tie-up between the political boss and the special interests seeking municipal favors had developed, he declared, out of the failure of the people to hold their elected representatives responsible for good government. Steffens reported how he found Boss Cox of Cincinnati, for example, treating the elective officers as he would any other instrument for carrying out his own program. Asked in the course of Steffens's investigation of his political machine whether there were not a mayor, a council, and judges in Cincinnati, Cox admitted there were — " 'but' — he pointed with his thumb back over his shoulder to his desk — 'I have a telephone, too.' "

These articles were attacks upon the trusts and municipal corruption, but indicative of the all-inclusive attitude of *McClure's* toward reform, was another series that started within two months on quite a different topic. Ray Stannard Baker began to disclose with the same objectivity and care the corrupt conditions existing within certain labor unions. In "The Right to Work" he sought to show that the little fellow was being pushed about and often deprived of his rights quite as much by union bosses as he was by either political or business bosses.

These revelations of the apparent failure of democracy in government, industry, and labor were drawn together in an editorial note in *McClure's* that discovered a connecting link in a general contempt for law:

> Capitalists, workingmen, politicians, citizens — all breaking the law, or letting it be broken. Who is left to uphold it? . . . There is no one left; none but all of us. . . . We forget that we are the people; that while each of us in his group can shove off on the rest the bill of today, the debt is only postponed; the rest are passing it back to us. We have to pay in the end, every one of us. And in the end the sum total of the debt will be our liberty.

Publication of these exposures was an immediate success. The steadily increasing circulation of *McClure's* — it was soon to pass the five-hundred-thousand mark — proved beyond doubt that they touched a chord of deepening popular interest. Other magazines began to follow *McClure's* promising lead — naturally more interested in its rising circulation figures than its reformist editorial notes. The *Cosmopolitan, Everybody's, Collier's, Hampton's,* and *The American Magazine* — all popular publications — opened their pages to muckraking articles and thrived upon the public response to their keen probing into economic and political abuses.

Charles Edward Russell attacked the meat-packers in "The Greatest Trust in the World"; Ray Stannard Baker shifted his ground to go after transportation in "The Railroads on Trial"; Burton J. Kendrick, taking his material from investigations already under way in New York, wrote his revealing "Story of Life Insurance"; and Thomas Lawson, a spectacular plunger in stocks temporarily turned reformer, disclosed in "Frenzied Finance" the hocus-pocus which went into the organization of the Amalgamated Copper Company. Nor was Lincoln Steffens alone in unmasking political corruption. As his series in *McClure's* continued with "Tweed Days in St. Louis," "Pittsburgh, a City Ashamed," and "Philadelphia: Corrupt and Contented," other writers uncovered the trail of party bosses leading into state and even national politics.

It was a sorry tale of graft, bribery, and unsavory scandals. The power of "an invisible government" appeared everywhere to have replaced that of the elected government. David Graham Phillips even dared trace it to Washington. He struck directly at the National Government in an outspoken article (and it was this attack that inspired Roosevelt's outburst against the muckrakers) entitled "The Treason of the Senate." He called to account those members of what was then popularly known as the "Millionaires' Club" whose loyalty to their business masters he believed to be stronger than their concern for the interests of the people. He named names: Depew of New York, Aldrich of Rhode Island, Gorman of Maryland, Spooner of Wisconsin, Lodge of Massachusetts. This was sensationalism, but although there were laws of libel in the land, Phillips was never taken into court.

While these writers trained their batteries upon the whole complicated network of financial interests and political power, others undertook to expose the conditions for which the combination of predatory wealth and corrupt politics was held responsible. They hammered away remorselessly at such denials of social justice as child labor, the inferior status of women in industry, sweatshop employment, discrimination against Negroes, and urban conditions that provided fertile breeding ground for delinquency, prostitution, drunkenness, disease, and crime.

Jacob Riis had pioneered in such fields in the nineties with his telling indictment of slums in *How the Other Half Lives*. His vivid descriptions of crowded tenement districts had first awakened the public conscience to the influence of slums, not only upon the lives of slum dwellers, but upon society as a whole. The muckrakers, believing that municipal corruption was at least in part responsible for blocking legislation which might have remedied such conditions, took up with a new wealth of detail various phases of this same basic problem. Ray Stannard Baker again entered the lists with a startling revelation of what was happening in regard to the northward migration of Negroes in his article, "Following the Color Line." John Spargo exposed the long hours, low wages, and harsh working conditions imposed on child labor in "The Bitter Cry of the Children." George Kibbe Turner turned the full glare of publicity upon the growing evil of the white-slave traffic in "Daughters of the Poor."

The novelists, too, were concerned with social problems. In the nineties William Dean Howells had written of industrial unrest, although without penetrating very deeply beneath the surface, in *A Hazard of New Fortunes*. He had contributed to the decade's prolific Utopian literature with *A Traveller from Altruria*. But with the turn of the century the realistic school he had fathered began to lay bare the inequalities of American life with a biting effectiveness he could not command. Jack London, Frank Norris, Upton Sinclair, Theodore Dreiser — their books were harsh, realistic pictures of conditions that cried aloud for reform. Norris vividly dramatized, in *The Octopus*, the strangle-hold of the Southern Pacific Railroad over California's politics and the helplessness of the farmers in attempting to defend their rights. In *The Titan* and *The Financier*, Dreiser novelized the muck-rakers' exposures of financial buccaneering. Upton Sinclair disclosed in *The Jungle* the shocking conditions among the immigrant workers of the Chicago stockyards. Even the more popular books were touched by the brush of reform — Booth Tarkington's collection of short stories, *In the Arena*, William Allen White's *A Certain Rich Man*, and the political novels of Winston Churchill — *Coniston* and *Mr. Crewe's Career*.

The muckrakers themselves wrote with the hope that their exposures would quicken the movement for progressive reform rather than with despair over either democracy or capitalism. They were not, as had been the case with such men as Henry George and Edward Bellamy, necessarily interested in radical ideas. They were first of all journalists — and also historians, economists, and sociologists — who were engaged in a critical

survey of the bases of American society rather than in an attempt
to blueprint a future Utopia. There were some socialists among
them. Indeed, there never was a time when socialism had more
adherents among both American intellectuals and the general
public. Its strength is indicated by the five-hundred-thousand
circulation of the official organ *The Appeal to Reason*, and the
steady rise in the socialist vote from less than one hundred thousand in 1900 to almost nine hundred thousand in 1912. Under
the dynamic leadership of Eugene V. Debs, socialism had become
a force with which both Republican and Democratic political
leaders had to reckon. Nevertheless, the muckrakers, whatever
the effect of socialist pressure, generally reflected a much more
conservative point of view. They were liberals who felt confident
that the correction of the abuses to which they called attention
was all that was necessary to create the good society.

"Is this socialism?" asked one writer of this school in outlining
his program of moderate reform. "Quite the contrary, it strives
to give the individual a better opportunity to possess property —
the very antithesis of socialism." The progressive movement,
drawing its strength from this literature of protest to a very considerable degree, was liberal, forward-looking, reformist. But it
advanced no program for overturning the capitalist system or
even seriously modifying it. For the most part its leaders were
confident that the prosperity which capitalism continued to promote during these years could be even further developed, and
much more equitably distributed, if the Government would but
undertake to exercise more effective controls over monopolistic
business. They thought along political rather than economic lines.
They believed that more responsible leadership and a broader
social outlook, together with a reinvigorated political democracy,
were the keys to future progress.

This note of confidence was sounded again and again, but perhaps Herbert Croly most clearly revealed the progressive outlook in *The Promise of American Life*. Published in 1909, this
book had a sale of only some seventy-five hundred copies, but it
influenced deeply both Roosevelt's New Nationalism and Wilson's New Freedom. While he thoroughly believed in democracy

and in the future of America, Croly felt that grave abuses in our national life were casting "a deep shadow over the traditional American patriotic vision." It was no longer enough just to proclaim one's faith in "an indubitable and a beneficent national future." If the American dream was to come true, it was essential, Croly declared, that a broad program should be consciously adopted to redefine the bases of national life in the interests of the economic as well as the political freedom of the individual.

His own ideas emphasized the need of social planning (foreshadowing the New Deal rather than the New Nationalism or the New Freedom), and the intelligent application of scientific processes to all governmental activity. He believed that the movement of progressive reform should be lifted beyond the state and municipal governments which had first responded to the muckrakers' exposures. "The problem belongs to the American national democracy," Croly declared, "and its solution must be attempted by means of official national action."

These were the varied forces making for the progressive movement — or at least the expression of forces whose real basis was the industrial revolution and the changes it had effected in American society. The country was aroused. It attacked the problem of municipal corruption, it sought to break the power of invisible state governments, and it demanded the regeneration of democracy on the national stage. The recovery by the people of their right to self-government, and once such power was recovered, a comprehensive program of social and economic reform, were to remain the progressives' chief objectives — until the shadow of war diverted the country's attention from domestic to foreign affairs.

Reasserting Democratic Rights

The opening years of the century found many cities in revolt against the conditions that Lincoln Steffens described so graphically. One of them was Cleveland. Its municipal government had been wholly in the grip of the local Republican machine dominated by Mark Hanna until a popular revolt in 1901 elected the reform administration of Mayor Thomas L. Johnson. While this wealthy manufacturer, whose ideas had been revolutionized by reading Henry George, failed in an attempt to establish municipal ownership of public utilities, he gave Cleveland for eight years an honest and effective government free of all entanglements with "the system." Steffens declared he was the "best mayor of the best governed city in the United States."

Another Ohio city had much the same experience. In Toledo the reform mayor, "Golden Rule" Jones, sought to apply an entirely new set of principles to municipal government. In the interests of the people, he not only fought corruption, but improved the city parks, established free kindergartens, and inaugurated free outdoor concerts. It was his attempt to act upon Christian ideals in dealing with the outcasts of society, symbolized by depriving the police of their clubs, that earned him the nickname of "Golden Rule" Jones. His popularity was so great that despite the opposition of Toledo businessmen, he was re-elected three times on an independent ticket. Other political rings were also broken up — although in many cases only temporarily — in San Francisco, Jersey City, St. Louis, Denver, and Minneapolis. Even New York for a time shook off the toils of the Tammany Tiger and elected as its mayor Seth Low, president of Columbia University.

Home rule and commission government were more permanent reforms sought by some cities to strengthen the forces of good government. It was recognized that corruption was only partially responsible for municipal troubles since existing administrative machinery often could not cope with the new demands being made upon it. The provision of adequate housing for rapidly increasing populations, control of public utilities, necessary measures to enlarge services of sanitation, improve police and fire protection, and handle traffic congestion presented new and serious problems. They could only be solved by experts with full authority. When ultimate responsibility was vested in absentee state legislatures, inefficiency as well as corruption could hardly be avoided. The cities at first found it difficult to secure the necessary authority to frame their own charters and wholly administer their own affairs; but by 1915 the constitutions of eleven states had been amended to provide for urban home rule. Commission government also made considerable headway. Galveston, Texas, driven to some such reform in order to meet the emergency caused by the disastrous flood of 1900, paved the way, and within little more than a decade some two hundred cities had installed municipal commissions. In 1913 Dayton, Ohio, took still another step along these advanced lines by introducing a city manager, an executive officer responsible to the commission.

Among the states, Wisconsin and Oregon most gallantly carried the progressive banner. In the former, Robert M. La Follette served as governor for the first six years of the century before moving on to the Senate. A man of steadfast devotion to democratic principles, absolutely honest and aggressively courageous, he successfully fought the conservative interests in Wisconsin, smashed an alliance between the Republican machine and the railroads, and persuaded the legislature to enact a broad program of reform. William S. U'Ren led the crusade for better government in Oregon. A convert, as were many other progressives, to the ideas elaborated in *Progress and Poverty*, he held public office only once. But as the secretary of various voters' organizations, he was more responsible than any other individual for his state's renovation of its political system.

Although legislation to regulate railroad rates and improve industrial conditions had its place among the reforms promoted in Wisconsin and Oregon, the two states' more important contributions to the progressive movement were in the passage of such political measures as those providing for the secret ballot, the direct primary, the initiative and referendum, and the recall. Both the "Wisconsin Ideal" and the "Oregon System," as their experiments in popular government became known, attracted nation-wide attention. Woodrow Wilson declared that the effect of the laws adopted in Oregon had been "to bring government back to the people and to protect it from the control of the representatives of selfish and special interests." Theodore Roosevelt wrote that "thanks to the movement for genuinely democratic popular government which Senator La Follette led to overwhelming victory in Wisconsin, that state has become literally a laboratory for wise experimental legislation aiming to secure the social and political betterment of the people as a whole."

Under such progressive governors as Joseph W. Folk in Missouri, Albert B. Cummins in Iowa, Hiram Johnson in California, Woodrow Wilson in New Jersey, and Charles E. Hughes in New York, other states followed the pioneering lead of Wisconsin and Oregon. Taking up the challenge of party bosses and entrenched privilege, they drove through their political and social reforms in the confident belief that once "the system" was broken up, the people would really govern themselves. By 1915 some two-thirds of the states had adopted the direct primary, twenty were using some form of the initiative and referendum, and there were eleven (all but one west of the Mississippi) with the recall, Arizona extending it to judges and Colorado to judicial decisions.

At the same time progress was being made toward two further reforms which the progressives linked with these measures as equally important in reasserting democratic rights. These were the direct election of senators and woman suffrage. Constitutional amendments were necessary before either of these objectives could be fully attained, but state action by no means waited upon Washington.

The prevailing system of selection of senators by state legislators was at this time held largely responsible for the Senate's extreme conservatism and unresponsiveness to public opinion. Only direct election by the people, the progressives maintained, could break the control the large corporations were able to exert over this branch of government. To this end constitutional provisions were circumvented by the states through a requirement that the legislatures name candidates for the Senate who had first been chosen by popular vote. Twenty-nine commonwealths were following this procedure by 1912, and the final capitulation of Congress to the popular demand for reform meant practical recognition of a system already in effect in a majority of the states. The Seventeenth Amendment, officially providing for the direct election of senators, was consequently ratified in 1913 with little opposition.

Woman suffrage had a longer history and was more obstinately opposed. As a result of continued agitation throughout the greater part of the nineteenth century, women had by 1900 been granted the vote in various local elections throughout the country and four western states had extended to them full rights of suffrage. But while this movement continued to make some headway during the first decade of the new century, it was not until after 1910 that it began to get real results. Washington's adoption that year of full suffrage started what was gradually to become almost a stampede: California followed in 1911; Arizona, Kansas, and Oregon in 1912; Illinois fell in line in so far as presidential and municipal suffrage was concerned in 1913, and Nevada and Montana granted full suffrage in 1914.

The suffrage movement won these gains under the direction of such prominent leaders as Carrie Chapman Catt and Anna Howard Shaw, but impatient with what still appeared to be slow progress, younger members of the National American Woman Suffrage Association began about 1913 to campaign more militantly for an immediate constitutional amendment. Their demands were nevertheless repeatedly rejected by Congress, and they were told by President Wilson to go out and get more states before worrying over an amendment. Organized as the Congressional Union, the militant wing thereupon resorted to mass demonstrations and picketing of the White House to publicize their rights. American entry into the first World War and women's increasing participation in the economic and social life of the nation, however, marked the decisive turning point in the movement. In January, 1918, President Wilson finally endorsed the proposal that was to become the Nineteenth Amendment, Congress approved it the next year, and before the 1920 national election it was duly ratified by the states.

It is impossible to evaluate with any great satisfaction the results of these changes in the political machinery of municipality, state, and nation. The power of the boss, of the machine, and of organized wealth was not, as the progressives had so hopefully predicted, wholly eliminated. No one of the devices on which the reformers had set such store was to prove entirely successful in providing the democracy with representatives who had no other thought than the public good. The direct primary, the initiative and referendum, and the recall were to prove disappointing as politicians discovered various ways to get around their clear intent. The responsiveness of the Senate to public opinion as a result of the direct election of its members was hardly revolutionary in its effects. It is extremely difficult to point to any marked changes in political life that may be directly attributed to giving women the right to vote in national and state elections. Special interests still found ways to make their influence felt in government circles through highly organized pressure groups and political lobbies that all too often succeeded in obscuring what was really best for the public welfare.

Nevertheless, the reforms of progressivism introduced a new spirit of social responsibility into government. Philip Loring Allen wrote as early as 1906:

> That there has been an awakening of the American people during the opening years of the twentieth century is now an accepted fact. It has manifested itself in two main forms, the warfare against political bosses and the warfare against specially privileged corporations. . . . Above and beyond these concrete achievements there has been a bracing of the moral sense of the country that is none the less real because it cannot be accurately measured.

It would never again be quite so easy for railway magnates or industrial barons to boast, as in the eighteen-nineties, of being above the law and able to bribe legislatures and judges to do their bidding.

Social Legislation in the States

Running parallel with these political changes was the economic and social legislation enacted by the states during the progressive era. The United States lagged far behind European countries in laws safeguarding the health and safety of industrial workers. Until the twentieth century, there were few statutes on the books of state governments, to say nothing of those of the Federal

Government, dealing with such problems. The basic reason for this humanitarian lag was again a general acceptance of the principles of *laissez-faire*. When state legislatures did try to act, they were met by judicial limitations upon their constitutional powers which left them almost impotent in this field of legislation. Any interference in the relations between capital and labor, the courts widely held, was not only a violation of the property rights of the employer, but also an infringement upon the liberty of the employee. As in the case of early attempts to regulate the railroads and the trusts, any effort on the part of the states to improve factory working conditions appeared to be blocked by such constitutional barriers as the due-process clause of the Fourteenth Amendment. Only gradually were these barriers broken down — at least in part — as the judiciary itself responded to "the felt necessities of the time" and slowly began to accept the new social concepts of progressivism.

A first successful step toward reform was the enactment of the state legislation providing for workmen's accident compensation. Although many states had long had employers' liability laws, the difficulties placed in the way of employees' actually collecting damages made them of little value for industrial workers. It was only necessary for the employer to demonstrate that the accident had occurred through the contributory negligence of either the injured employee or that of "a fellow servant" for the court to set aside all claims. The workmen's compensation laws, however, placed responsibility directly upon the employer, requiring him to pay benefits for all injuries occurring in factory or mine, regardless of the question of immediate responsibility. The first of these laws, passed by Maryland as early as 1902, was declared unconstitutional, but a comparable federal statute, applying to interstate railways, was upheld by the Supreme Court in 1908 and thereby opened the way for further action. The states swung quickly into line, and between 1910 and 1920 all but six passed new laws providing accident compensation on relatively liberal terms. The movement was an important one. It improved conditions for industrial workers, not only through the guarantee of accident insurance, but through the pressure it exerted upon employers to provide adequate safeguards against the hazards of power-driven machinery.

Child-labor laws also met the challenge of constitutionality and by 1912 thirty-eight states enacted legislation prescribing age limits, hours of work, and types of employment. However, attempts in 1916 and 1919 to extend the scope of this reform by federal action were declared by the Supreme Court to be unconstitutional. The first of the congressional child-labor enactments, forbidding the shipment in interstate commerce of the products of any factory or mine employing children under fourteen, was said to exceed the regulatory powers of Congress over commerce, constituting in effect an unwarranted interference in matters reserved to the states; and the second, imposing a tax on interstate shipments, was judged to be an unlawful exercise of the taxing power. While state child-labor laws greatly improved conditions as they had existed at the opening of the century, no further progress toward nation-wide controls was to be made until the nineteen-thirties.

Limitations upon the hours of work for men and women factory workers were also urged by the progressives and the period is marked by the gradual acceptance of this principle despite early opposition on the part of the courts. A first important test grew out of the passage of a New York law seeking to limit the working day in bakeries to ten hours. A case involving the constitutionality of this statute, *Lochner v. New York*, reached the Supreme Court in 1905 and the issue was clearly drawn between the police power of the state to safeguard public health and the protection of individual rights. On the ground that any limitation of hours both deprived the employer of the full use of his property and the employee of his liberty of contract, the Supreme Court refused to uphold the New York measure. "We think the limit of the police power has been reached and passed in this case," the Court declared. "There is, in our judgment, no reasonable foundation for holding this to be necessary or appropriate as a health law to safeguard the public health, or the health of the individuals who are following the trade of baker."

Despite this setback, the progressive states persevered in their efforts to protect industrial workers against conditions of employment considered prejudicial both to their health and that of the public. Oregon, leader in political reform, was again a pioneer. In 1908 it finally won court approval for a law which established a ten-hour day for women employees in laundries, and nine years later a measure setting up a ten-hour day for all employees in manufacturing establishments was sustained. The two cases in which the Supreme Court upheld these laws — *Muller v. Oregon* and *Bunting v. Oregon* — did not actually reverse *Lochner v. New York*, but they revealed a much broader interpretation of the state's police powers. Under the strong pressure of progressive public opinion, a more liberal Supreme Court was questioning the basic assumptions of *laissez-faire* in protecting property interests at the expense of individual rights.

Justice Oliver Wendell Holmes played a highly influential rôle in this judicial swing toward a more liberal interpretation of the Fourteenth Amendment. In a vigorous dissent in *Lochner v. New York*, he had declared that the Constitution was not intended to embody any particular economic view, whether of paternalism or of *laissez-faire*, and that the states were free to regulate life in many ways which as legislators the Court might find injudicious or even tyrannical. " . . . The accident of our finding certain opinions natural and familiar, or novel, and even shocking," he warned his brethren, "ought not to conclude our judgment upon the question whether statutes embodying them conflict with the Constitution of the United States." In approving Oregon's maximum-hour bills, the Court was following Justice Holmes's advice.

These victories for the states opened up the field for further labor legislation as had the Supreme Court's favorable decision on workmen's compensation laws. Limitations on hours of work for both men and women employees became a generally accepted principle before the end of the progressive period, federal legislation extending it to employees of interstate railways when they were given an eight-hour day through passage of the Adamson Act in 1916. Moreover, many states, Massachusetts leading the way in 1912, sought to supplement such measures by minimum-wage laws. They did not receive judicial approval during the progressive period, however, and when the issue again came before the Supreme Court in 1923, any limit on wages was declared to be a definite impairment of freedom of contract.

The progress made in workmen's compensation laws, child-labor laws, and maximum-hours laws, to which might also be added the adoption of more liberal factory codes and the beginnings of old-age pension legislation, was one of the most significant developments of the entire progressive period. It marked a victory for the basic theory that in a modern industrialized society, old ideas of the employer-employee relationship had to give way before the necessity of governmental action to promote the public welfare. In flat contradiction to the tenets of *laissez-faire*, the courts had begun to recognize that under certain circumstances the state could intervene, was perhaps compelled to intervene, in the interests of safety, health, or morals. New precedents were being established in the field of economic legislation which were to be even further extended in the federal controls adopted by the New Deal.

THE CHALLENGE OF LABOR

While industrial workers profited greatly from this remedial legislation, the organized labor movement itself was making further progress. The American Federation of Labor, avoiding the temptation of entering directly into politics and pursuing a generally conservative course based upon the traditional principles of trade unionism, had seen its membership grow to over two million by 1914 in comparison with its three hundred thousand total at the opening of the century. With the inclusion of members of such unaffiliated unions as the Railway Brotherhoods, these figures revealed that over seven per cent of all wage-earners were now organized, double the proportion in 1900. Even though the great mass of unskilled workers were still outside union ranks, labor had won new recognition of its rights. Under the leadership of Samuel Gompers, the A.F. of L. had become a powerful force.

For a time at the opening of the century there had appeared to be an unexpectedly friendly *rapprochement* between capital and labor. The National Civic Federation, with Mark Hanna as its president and Samuel Gompers as its vice-president, was a hopeful attempt to work out industrial relations on the basis of union recognition and mutually acceptable trade agreements. Its early promise was not fulfilled. Although co-operation was maintained in some instances, the inevitable differences developed, and as labor pressed its campaign for higher wages and shorter hours, industry threw its strength behind a powerful anti-union movement. Other organizations of quite a different character from that of the National Civic Federation, such as the National Association of Manufacturers, ceaselessly campaigned against unions, and by both legal and extra-legal means sought to break their rising power.

The response of the unions was to resort both to strikes and to boycotts directed against unfriendly management. Perhaps the most significant of such outbreaks of industrial warfare early in the new century were the strikes in the anthracite coal fields called by the United Mine Workers, then on the threshold of their tempestuous career. The miners had long been struggling against admittedly shameful conditions. Average wages in Pennsylvania were variously estimated at the turn of the century at anywhere from two hundred and fifty to five hundred dollars a year, but an even greater grievance than this meager pay was the almost feudal controls exercised by the operators, who compelled their employees to live in squalid, filthy company houses and to make all their purchases at company stores. The miners had consequently welcomed the chance to organize in defense of their interests when the United Mine Workers of America, under the able direction of John Mitchell, invaded the Pennsylvania area. A first strike had been called in 1900, but a truce was patched up in that election year with a ten per cent increase in wages. When two years later the still restive miners again demanded higher wages, a shorter working day, and recognition of their union, the operators were determined to fight it out. They refused even to consider the union demands and one hundred and fifty thousand men at once laid down their tools.

It was a strike that had unusually widespread repercussions because it steadily drove up the price of coal. The public was alarmed, and the obdurate refusal of the operators to make any concessions whatsoever in the interests of industrial peace caused sympathy to turn more and more toward the miners. Nor was it lessened when George F. Baer, spokesman of the operators, arrogantly stated the case for his associates. "I beg of you not to be discouraged," he answered a correspondent who had written him that it was his duty to end the strike. "The rights and interests of the laboring man will be protected and cared for — not by the labor agitators, but by the Christian men to whom God in His infinite wisdom has given the control of the property interests of this country. . . . " Even the most reactionary blanched at this naïve assertion of the divine right of the coal barons. The *New York Times* said with marked restraint that the letter appeared to "verge very close upon unconscious blasphemy." The religious press had no doubts of it. "This is the sort of thing," one shocked Baptist paper declared, "that makes anarchists."

Appeals began to pour in upon Washington for governmental intervention, and President Roosevelt, ignoring the fact that he had no direct constitutional authority to intervene, decided that the ugly implications of the strike demanded action. With widespread popular support from many quarters, he not only appointed a committee of investigation, but held out over the heads of the operators the thinly veiled threat that if they did not accept arbitration, he would call in the army, dispossess the owners, and run the mines as a receiver. The country had to have coal. Before any such radical move was made, however, Secretary of War Root had persuaded J. P. Morgan of the gravity of the situation and the latter had in turn impressed upon the coal operators the dangers of the course they were following. Under such pressure they had no recourse but to give way, and they at last petitioned the President to appoint an arbitration commission whose award they agreed to accept. It granted the miners a ten per cent wage increase, established a nine-hour day, and set up a board of conciliation for future disputes. The real significance of the settlements, however, is not found in the terms of the award, but in the fact that Government had intervened in an industrial dispute — not in the interests of capital, nor yet of labor, but for the sake of industrial peace.

The example of the miners in striking for better working conditions was followed in other industries, but, without comparable government intervention, such disputes more generally resulted in victory for the employers. An important exception was the dramatic struggle of the workers in New York's garment industry. Under the leadership of the International Ladies' Garments' Workers they went out on strike first in 1909, and again the next year, and ultimately succeeded in winning higher wages, better working conditions, and abolition of the subcontracting system. Although the employers refused to grant a further demand for recognition of the closed shop, the machinery was set up for the settlement of future disputes and the embittered relations formerly prevailing in the industry were measurably improved.

In its attempted use of the boycott as a further means of enforcing its rights, labor found itself confronted with the injunction. Employers were able to obtain court orders, whose violation led to contempt proceedings, enjoining the unions from boycotting their products on the ground that such measures constituted conspiracy in restraint of trade under the terms of the Sherman Act. When the Hatters' Union in 1902 declared a nation-wide boycott of the products of D. E. Loewe and Company, of Danbury, Connecticut, its members were so charged, and the Supreme Court sustained the findings of a lower court that had held for the company against the union. The American Federation of Labor itself ran into comparable trouble when in support of a metal polishers' strike against the Buck Stove and Range Company of St. Louis, it placed that firm's name on its unfair to labor list and urged its members not to buy the company's stoves. An injunction was granted the company restraining the Federation from its boycott, and when it was ignored, the officers of the labor organization were found guilty of contempt of court. Eventually settled without the jail sentences actually being enforced, this case, together with the Danbury Hatters' case, convinced labor that the courts were abetting the employers in mak-

ing the injunction an anti-labor weapon against which the workers had no redress.

Even when driven to strikes and boycotts, the American Federation of Labor tried to refrain from violence. It was in no sense
a radical organization. Its philosophy was based on the principle
of "a fair day's wage for a fair day's work." It had no quarrel with
the capitalist system and sought adjustment of industrial strife
through union recognition and collective bargaining. A minority
would have committed the organization to socialism. But even
the growing influence of socialist thought in the country as a
whole, as already noted in the strong political following attracted
by Eugene V. Debs, failed to make any serious inroads in the
ranks of organized labor.

A radical movement developed outside the Federation, however, and it led in 1905 to the organization of the Industrial
Workers of the World. While this organization never obtained
a membership of more than sixty thousand, it became, under the
aggressive leadership of William D. ("Big Bill") Haywood, unexpectedly strong, instigating violent strikes in many industries
and exerting an influence out of all proportion to its numbers.
Its goal was the establishment of one big union; it was revolutionary in its aims, and it sought to abolish the wage system rather
than to make it workable. In strikes of the textile workers of
Lawrence, Massachusetts, and silk workers in Paterson, New
Jersey, I.W.W. leaders played a prominent part, and scenes of
shocking brutality were enacted for which both strikers and employers were responsible. Public sympathy led to a victory for
the strikers at Lawrence, but they were defeated in Paterson.

Another violent strike of this period, involving not the I.W.W.
but a branch of the United Mine Workers, broke out among the
Colorado coal miners in 1913. It was a revolt against the intolerable conditions among the employees of the Rockefeller-con-
trolled Colorado Coal and Iron Company, and it led to a bloody
pitched battle at Ludlow in which twelve women and eleven
children were among the victims. Despite public sympathy for
the miners and attempted mediation by the Government, the employers in this case refused either negotiation or arbitration, and

by the use of strike-breakers, protected by armed guards, they successfully broke the back of the strike.

The close of the progressive era thus marked a somewhat para-doxical situation in so far as labor was concerned. The more radical elements within the labor movement were in almost open conflict with the more reactionary groups among employers, and the consequent industrial strife was both more widespread and more violent than in many years. At the same time the American Federation of Labor was pursuing its own conservative course and had succeeded in meliorating the lot of many organized workers among its union members. Also the general status of labor appeared to have improved in so far as wages and hours were concerned, and it had particularly benefited, as already noted, from the progressive economic legislation enacted by the states.

PROHIBITION AND OTHER REFORMS

The ferment of the progressive era was not restricted to poli-tical reform, social legislation, or new movements within the ranks of labor. The revelations of the muckrakers in regard to condi-tions among the poor and oppressed, especially in the big cities, inspired attack upon such conditions from many other angles. It was an age of reformist and humanitarian crusades as well as political activity — crusades against poverty, against disease, against vice, against crime, and against drinking. The latter crusade fostered the prohibition movement, and while it did not win its final triumph until after the progressive era, both in its political and social implications it was a part of the history of these times.

The origins of prohibition can be traced back to the middle of the previous century, but for a time in the early nineteen-hundreds it appeared to be making little progress. Only four states — Kansas, Maine, Nebraska, and North Dakota — were completely dry. There was no cessation, however, to the vigorous temperance campaign being waged by such organizations as the Anti-Saloon League and the Woman's Christian Temperance

Union. The former, under the energetic leadership of Wayne B. Wheeler, was spending some four hundred thousand dollars a year to support the election of "drys" to public office. They gradually gained new converts and more and more attention began to be paid to prohibition. In many quarters it was felt that drinking was more responsible than any other one factor for the degradation of life among the city poor. Protected from really effective regulation by the close tie-up between the liquor interests and machine politics, the saloon was believed to be a major source, not only of poverty and ill health, but of crime and vice. There appeared to be evidence on every hand that an uncontrolled liquor traffic tended to nullify everything that social reform sought to accomplish. To the laments of the reformers were also added those of employers who saw excessive drinking impairing the efficiency of industrial workers and increasing the hazard of factory accidents, while the South generally endorsed prohibition as a means of keeping liquor from the Negroes.

With support from such quarters, and the militant backing of all the forces of evangelical Protestantism, the drive for prohibition began to gather great headway after 1905. State after state was brought into the temperance fold, while an even greater triumph was the passage by Congress, in 1913, of the Webb-Kenyon Act, forbidding the interstate transportation of liquor into states where its sale was illegal. On the eve of American entry into the first World War, twenty-six states had prohibition laws, thirteen of them being absolutely bone-dry. Action was pending in many others with every chance of success and local option barred the sale of alcoholic beverages in almost three-fourths of the country's total area. The "drys," in short, were within sight of the promised land and only one further step remained to be taken. The Eighteenth Amendment, adopted by Congress in the first year of the war and ratified in January, 1919, was to provide the complete and absolute prohibition which had always been their ultimate goal.

Another problem to awaken public attention was the status of the Negro. Despite general economic improvement in the South, the colored population in those states found its position — economic, social, and political — at almost the lowest point since the Civil War. The emigration of Negroes to the North, just getting under way in full force, was also in some instances creating situations in eastern and middle-western industrial cities that were little better. Disfranchisement by southern states through special literacy tests, poll taxes, and grandfather clauses was an old story. So was the segregation of Negroes in all public conveyances and public places. But far more serious than even such denial of democratic rights was the frequency of lynchings — the annual number between 1900 and 1910 averaging sixty — and the outbreak of race riots where the Negroes were trying to find a place for themselves in previously white communities.

The growing tension in race relations resulting from these developments was offset to some degree by the efforts to combat it. Among the Negroes themselves there were two approaches to this question, the one based on gradual adjustment in a white world through education and work, the other on more forthright agitation in behalf of Negro rights. Booker T. Washington was the leader of the former program, W. E. B. DuBois of the latter. Perhaps the most forward step in meeting the problem as a whole was the organization of the National Association for the Advancement of Colored People. Both whites and Negroes were associated in this organization in a common effort to apply the principles of democracy to race relations.

Charity as distinct from reform also sought to cope with the depressed conditions among the urban poor. Newly organized societies set up shelters for the homeless, took over the care of dependent children and wayward girls, and established settlement houses, visiting-nurse services, and free milk depots. Community playgrounds sought to keep children off the streets, four hundred cities having established them by 1915. The whole question of juvenile delinquency was brought into the open by Judge Ben Lindsey's pioneer work in the Denver Juvenile Court. It was during these years that the Boy Scouts, the Camp Fire Girls, and the Girl Scouts were organized — the Boy Scouts obtaining by 1913 some three hundred thousand members.

Prostitution and the white slave traffic awoke reformist and humanitarian instincts. The effect of muckraking disclosures in the former instance was heightened by official vice reports in many cities, one sponsored by Chicago authorities revealing the existence of five thousand houses of ill-fame in that city alone. The close connection shown between commercialized vice, white slavery, and the liquor traffic, together seeking protection through the bribery of corrupt police officials, led to clean-up campaigns throughout the nation. The crusade against prostitution gradually became a part of the general "battle of the slums," and this in turn involved the whole issue of municipal reform and the smashing of the political machines under which the saloon, gambling, vice, and crime so generally flourished.

For all the merits of these charitable and humanitarian activities, social workers and reformers were among the first to realize that they were palliatives rather than cures for the ills of society. Jane Addams, founder of Hull House in Chicago, explicitly stressed the paramount need for a more equitable distribution of income if there were to be social justice. She quoted Saint Augustine: "Thou givest bread to the hungry, but better were it, that none hungered and thou had'st none to give him." Conscientiously carrying on their work in city slums, in prison reform, and juvenile delinquency, in combating prostitution and white slavery, these twentieth-century reformers looked to legislation which would equalize tax burdens, maintain wage standards, enforce shorter working hours, and provide decent housing as the only solution for the problems of industrialization and urban growth.

6

Roosevelt Takes the Helm

THEODORE ROOSEVELT became President under highly dramatic circumstances. When on September 6, 1901, McKinley was shot by a half-crazed anarchist at the Pan-American Exposition at Buffalo, Roosevelt had at once rushed to the stricken man's side by special train. Assured that his chief's life was in no danger, he had then rejoined his family in the Adirondacks. But within a few days news of the relapse which was to end in death was brought to him by special courier. There was a wild night ride by buckboard to the nearest railroad station, another special train thundering through the countryside, but McKinley was dead before Roosevelt arrived. All except two members of the cabinet were in Buffalo and arrangements were at once made to administer the oath of office. Deeply moved, his face almost expressionless, Roosevelt stared straight ahead: "I wish to say that it will be my aim to continue, absolutely unbroken, the policy of President McKinley for the peace, the prosperity, and the honor of our beloved country."

It was a natural statement to make under the stress of such a tragic moment, but whatever else may be said of the policies that Roosevelt was to follow in the ensuing years, they were not those of his predecessor. Far more symbolic of the new administration than this solemn reaffirmation of McKinleyism were the circumstances that ushered it in. The country hardly knew what to expect of this dynamic young man so unexpectedly elevated to the highest post in the land. It was whispered about that J. P. Morgan had collapsed upon learning of McKinley's death, and that Mark Hanna was in a nervous frenzy when he realized that

"that damn cowboy" had become President. The fears of these eminent business leaders were not wholly confirmed, but Roosevelt by no means subscribed to their "stand-pat" political theories. He was aware of the changing trends in popular thinking. He sensed the need for reform and feared that unless it was adequately met, far more radical demands than those of the progressives would eventually command popular support. He believed it to be the rôle of the Republican Party, to which he was completely loyal, to carry forward a constructive program that would at once avert any danger of radicalism and quell the rising popular discontent.

Although the youngest man — only forty-three years old — ever to assume the presidency, Roosevelt had already had a spectacular career. His exploits in Cuba, which he had not hesitated to publicize in a book which Mr. Dooley thought should have been entitled "Alone in Cubia," had first won him popular recognition. There were, however, other claims to fame. While his background was inherited wealth, Groton and Harvard, he had early plunged into politics and shown an independence of spirit and zeal for reform that singled him out among the politicians of his day. After serving in the New York Assembly, he had been appointed by President Harrison to the Civil Service Commission and then had accepted the post of president of New York City's Police Board. His strenuous activities as Assistant Secretary of the Navy in 1897 and enthusiastic leadership of the Rough Riders were next in order, and it was from the governorship of New York that he had stepped into the vice-presidency. As a governor he had shown what was to the party bosses an alarming indifference to their vested rights in the spoils system. He proved himself more concerned with the public interest than the conservatives in his state thought wholly wise. "A little loose in the relations of capital and labor, on trusts and combinations," as Senator Platt significantly phrased it.

The fears of radicalism in the White House were hardly substantiated by anything in this record, however. Roosevelt had revealed himself as impetuous and somewhat erratic, pugnaciously certain of himself, and rather naïve in many of his views.

Still, there was no question of his fundamental belief in the capitalist system or of his basically conservative approach to economic problems. Against his reformist activities could be set his militant support of President McKinley in both 1896 and 1900. No one had more extravagantly assailed the "socialism" of Bryan and the Populists. How careful he was prepared to be in taking over his new responsibilities was indicated in his prompt reply to a cautioning letter from Mark Hanna. "It would not be possible to get wiser advice," he wrote, "and I shall act exactly upon it. I shall go slow."

The new President, nevertheless, did have some very definite ideas of his own. He believed firmly in strengthening the political prestige of the United States as a world power, in establishing the supremacy of the Federal Government over all rivals to its control, and in strongly asserting the authority of the Chief Executive. Roosevelt was a man of dynamic energy — Henry Adams once characterized him as "pure act" — and he was prepared to exercise this energy as leader of the nation. In marked contrast to the easy-going McKinley, he believed that it was not only the right, but the duty of the President to do anything that the needs of the nation demanded, unless such action was expressly forbidden by the Constitution or existing law. As events were to prove, he was prepared on occasion to go further than this: he would act first and then seek out the authorization for what he had done.

In pursuing his policies he did not always show a very profound understanding of the basic problems facing the country. They were too often economic in nature, and he had only a slight interest in economics. His concern was with morality, with righteousness. It was his characteristic approach to the issues raised by the power of monopoly or the growing conflict between capital and labor. Dealing with moral issues he felt himself on sure ground. "How do you know that substantial justice was done?" he was asked on one occasion. "Because I did it," he answered, "because . . . I was doing my best."

It was only natural for him under such circumstances to dismiss the economic implications of monopoly and to base his attitude toward the trusts on a moral judgment as to whether they were "good" trusts or "bad" trusts. It was only natural for him in considering the rights of labor to be principally concerned with his own conception of "the square deal." Roosevelt basically believed in compromise. And he believed in it, not merely because it was politically advisable, but because righteousness could only be established by maintaining a proper balance between the divergent elements in American life.

This attitude characterized his relations to the progressive movement. It was to incur the conservative charges that he had become a reckless radical, and the complaints of the more extreme progressives that he had betrayed their cause. There is no question that he swung back and forth, tending to compensate for every move he made toward liberal reform with a placating gesture toward the forces of conservatism. When the dust stirred up by his prodigious activities settled down, his followers sometimes felt they had made very little real progress. Roosevelt was mighty in battle, yet his much-trumpeted victories were not always as decisive as he liked to believe.

But he held his followers in line. Where another man would have been accused of straddling, he won a reputation for political fearlessness. When he was attacking capital, he let out the full stops; in his assaults upon labor, he pulled no punches. His speeches were studded with fighting words. He struck at big business — "malefactors of great wealth" and "industrial overlords"; then turned on its enemies — "demagogic reformers" and "tyrannical labor unions." Only the plain people escaped his bludgeoning blows.

While it may be true that Roosevelt's acts were not always commensurate with the sound and fury of his presidential dictums, his leadership of the progressive cause nevertheless had immense significance during these years. From one point of view he merely rode the crest of a movement which sprang from the deepest instincts of the American people, but in another sense he *was* the progressive movement. "President Roosevelt has crystallized public sentiment and elevated civic standards," was Senator La Follette's tribute in 1908. " . . . He has touched the conscience of the foremost nation in the world, lifted its people on to heights, and made them ready for the greatest work that any nation ever did."

Other qualities than his aggressive leadership more particularly endeared him to the public. The youthfulness which he never outgrew had a wide appeal. Responsibility could not crush the perennial boy; he was forever charging up San Juan Hill, forever waving aloft his victorious sombrero. His enthusiasms, his vitality, his terrible energy, his combativeness, awoke a universal response. There were some who feared Theodore Roosevelt, some who despised him, and others who laughed at him, but the great majority could not help admiring him. They believed that for all his vagaries he had at heart the best interests of the American democracy. And everyone enjoyed the gorgeous show he put on as he strutted across the national stage, talking, gesticulating, shaking his clenched fist, gnashing his gleaming teeth. "Do you know the two most wonderful things I have seen in your country?" John Morley, the noted English statesman and writer asked. "Niagara Falls and the President of the United States, both great wonders of nature."

FIGHTING THE TRUSTS

Among the important issues before the country in 1901, control of the trusts held a foremost place. The failure of the McKinley Administration to take any effective steps to enforce the Sherman Act and the continued growth of monopoly, marked by such mergers as formation of the huge United States Steel Corporation, had intensified popular distrust of the growing power of big business. It was widely felt, as already noted, that unless something were done to bring these gigantic industrial combinations under effective government regulation, the bases of democracy would be seriously endangered. "When I became President," Roosevelt himself later wrote in his *Autobiography*, "the question as to the methods by which the United States Government was to control the corporations was not yet important. The absolutely vital question was whether the Government had power to control

them at all." Under such circumstances, there was keen anticipation throughout the country as to how the new administration
might deal with this pressing problem. Roosevelt's first message
to Congress was eagerly awaited — somewhat fearfully by those
who could not disabuse themselves of the idea that he was "un-
safe"; and hopefully by the liberals who remembered his days as
a reformer.

Delivered in December, 1901, this message proved to be a
politically shrewd compromise. Roosevelt had the forthrightness
and courage to call attention to evils about which his predecessor
had been inclined to be discreetly silent; he also advised caution
in taking any action that might disturb the delicate adjustment of
the economic machinery responsible for the prevailing prosperity.
There were no fireworks. He did not sidestep the trust issue and
he definitely recommended strict supervision and regulation, but
he carefully avoided any direct attack on big business. "'Th'
trusts,' says he," to quote Mr. Dooley's gentle satire of his message, "'are heejous monsthers built up be th' enlightened inter-
prise iv th' men that have done so much to advance progress in
our beloved country,' he says. 'On wan hand I wud stamp them
undher fut; on th' other hand not so fast.'"

The business interests of the country were greatly relieved.
Placing their reliance upon the "not-so-fast" phase of the message,
they felt they had no reason to fear governmental interference
with the continuing process of consolidation among both railroad
and industrial corporations. And this was particularly reassuring
to the men behind the formation of one of the most important
mergers which had yet been carried through. In co-operation
with Edward H. Harriman and James J. Hill, the country's two
leading railroad operators, J. P. Morgan had but recently completed consolidation of the properties of the Northern Pacific,
the Great Northern, and the Chicago, Burlington and Quincy
into a gigantic holding company known as the Northern Securities
Company. It was proving to be an unusually successful venture,
with immense potentialities for the further development of the
Northwest.

Everything was going well — when within two months of the

presidential message, out of a clear sky and without any prior notice, came a dramatic announcement from the White House. The Government was prepared to seek dissolution of the Northern Securities Company as a combination in restraint of trade under the terms of the Sherman Anti-Trust Law. Roosevelt had discovered a "heejous monsther." He was ready to strike at the very fountain-head of finance capitalism.

The effect was sensational. The Sherman Act had for so long been a dead letter that its sudden resurrection created consternation in financial circles which had previously been lulled to a false security. An impressive delegation, including Morgan, Senator Depew, and Mark Hanna, at once descended upon Washington. The financier suggested that if anything wrong had been done he was sure his lawyers and the Attorney General could "fix it up," but he stated his conviction that there was nothing illegal about the Northern Securities Company. Roosevelt was adamant. He indignantly rejected the idea that things could be "fixed up" — by a sort of agreement between rival operators, as he sarcastically described the Morgan proposals to his Attorney General — and he made it clear that what the Government sought was thoroughgoing dissolution. Morgan hastily retreated to the fastnesses of Wall Street.

Big business had failed to realize that while Roosevelt was uncertain on the economic aspects of monopoly, he was absolutely sure of himself where he felt that any aggregation of capital might become so powerful as to overshadow the Government itself. On this issue he was prepared to fight things through. The further concentration of financial interests which would result from a merger of the railways in the Northwest had stung him into action to assert governmental authority.

The wheels of judicial machinery ground slowly. It was two years before the government suit against the Northern Securities Company finally reached the Supreme Court. The result was a victory for Roosevelt and his administration. By a five-to-four decision, the Court held the merger to be in restraint of trade and sustained a lower court decree ordering dissolution. Although the Supreme Court's stand in other cases had already partially opened the door to prosecution of the trusts, this decision against a holding company revealed a striking liberalization of its earlier attitude. The Sherman Anti-Trust Law had suddenly been vitalized. Roosevelt would later write that this success in securing a reversal of the Court's restrictive opinion in the old E. C. Knight Company case was solely responsible for establishing the Government's power to deal effectively with the trusts. This was an exaggeration. Nevertheless, the Supreme Court decision in 1904 was an important development in the gathering movement to enforce the law against the country's industrial and financial overlords.

The public had interpreted the Government's suit against the Northern Securities Company as conclusive evidence that the new administration sought to protect the national interest against the domineering influence of big business and to uphold the rights of democracy as opposed to those of plutocracy. Roosevelt was encouraged to continue along this path. Proceedings were gradually initiated against other alleged monopolies and after 1904 they were pushed with renewed vigor. The Department of Justice prosecuted the so-called beef and powder trusts, haled the sugar trust into court on charges of defrauding the Government of customs duties, and finally climaxed these activities by bringing suit to dissolve both the American Tobacco Company and the Standard Oil Company. The country applauded these moves. Roosevelt's reputation as a trust-buster was firmly established. In all, forty-four Sherman Act suits were filed during his two terms of office and the Department of Justice obtained twenty-five indictments. In comparison with the record of former administrations, here was substantial achievement.

Nevertheless, closer examination of the results of Roosevelt's anti-trust activities clearly reveals that the popular idea of the President as a valiant and intrepid David successfully overcoming the Goliath of business monopoly was largely a myth. Even though the Government won its decrees of dissolution, the trusts soon reorganized on the basis of community-of-interest agreements and went on merrily doing business at the old stand. "Don't be downhearted!" a cartoonist depicted a group of trusts encouraging a new victim of the government attack. "Dissolution gives you that nice legal feeling." It proved impossible to unscramble the eggs. There was no real halt in the process of industrial concentration; monopoly was fully as widespread when Roosevelt went out of office as when he entered it. Moreover, the Supreme Court, while it eventually upheld the Government's suit for dissolution of the Standard Oil Company and the American Tobacco Company, stated in its decisions on these cases in 1911 that a "rule of reason" should henceforth apply in regard to charges of monopoly. No matter how large or how extensive their holdings, only those corporations whose practices could be construed as "unreasonable" restraint of trade were subject to dissolution. This was a definite reversal of the Court's former attitude, and it reflected a growing conviction that the Sherman Act could not be literally enforced. A wide latitude in interpretation would be exercised by the Supreme Court in all future trust decisions.

Roosevelt had from the first recognized that "trust-busting" was perhaps not the most effective answer to the growing power of monopoly. Throughout his years in office he again and again recommended further legislation for their control and regulation which would in effect safeguard the legitimate interests of the "good" trusts and break the power of the "bad" trusts. He advocated national licensing of all corporations engaged in interstate commerce, full publicity for corporate accounts, and the prohibition of certain specific abuses in business practice. If there was not legal provision for such legislation, he favored a constitutional amendment. His primary interest remained the assertion of the Government's right to bring under closer control these "subjects without a sovereign," and he wanted to do so "without paralyzing the energies of the business community." Congress paid little heed to his demands. Except for authorizing establishment of a Bureau of Corporations, forerunner of the Federal Trade Commission, to investigate the operations of all companies engaged in interstate trade, it completely ignored the President's proposals.

Failure to secure further regulation of the trusts and the ineffectiveness of dissolution decrees do not wholly invalidate

Roosevelt's anti-trust record. In bringing the Sherman Act to life again, he succeeded in asserting the power of Government as opposed to the power of industry. He placed monopoly on the defensive. He forced upon the business and financial leaders of America the realization that they could no longer disregard the public interest. His activities both reflected the protest stirred up by the disclosures of the muckrakers and intensified the popular demand that big business mend its ways. While the trusts escaped further regulation for the time being, and although dissolved soon reassembled their component parts, they were taught a salutary lesson which was not lost upon their directors. Finally, Roosevelt's demand for further regulation was to be reaffirmed by President Taft and was ultimately to bear fruit in the first administration of Woodrow Wilson.

THE ELECTION OF 1904

Soon after his first move against the trusts, Roosevelt found himself involved in the great coal strike of 1902. As we have seen, intervention was none of his own choosing. He was driven to secure adequate production of an essential commodity, and the intransigence of the coal operators then led him further afield than he had originally contemplated. The episode was highly important in the history of organized labor's rôle in our national life. It also served to demonstrate the attitude of Roosevelt upon the whole question of industrial relations.

The President had not acted as either friend or foe to either party in this dispute. His concern was with the public interest. But unlike his predecessors he did not always identify the public interest with capitalism, and he was aroused by the operators' arbitrary defiance of all authority except their own. He was ready if necessary to assert again the superior power of the Government, just as he had done when it was challenged by industrial monopoly on other counts. Apart from this aspect of the question, he believed that labor was entitled to a square deal. "The man is no true democrat," he wrote in explaining his position, " . . . who, in problems calling for the exercise of a moral judgment, fails to take his stand on conduct and not on class." So in the coal strike he favored labor against capital, but this did not imply any special sympathy for unionization. Even within these limitations, however, his attitude was markedly different from that of Cleveland and McKinley. In the interests of the square deal, Roosevelt also proposed that one of the functions of the new Department of Commerce and Labor should be the protection of workingmen's rights, and he strongly opposed the use of the injunction as "an engine of oppression against the wage-worker."

Apart from the unexpected prosecution of the Northern Securities Company and intervention in the coal strike, Roosevelt's first term did not witness any startling developments. In other respects he felt obliged as McKinley's successor to follow a somewhat cautious policy. He was perhaps primarily interested in re-election in 1904, and he did not wish to alienate any of the conservative support that had brought the Republican Party into power. On a political swing about the country in 1903, pleasantly interrupted by a few bear hunts in the West, he made every effort to conciliate all factions within his party, praising the achievements of industry and making it clear that labor would be held just as strictly accountable to law as would capital.

There was never very much question of his nomination to succeed himself, and after the death of Mark Hanna in February, 1904, it became a virtual certainty. When the Republican convention met he was named by acclamation. Conservative party members may have had their fingers crossed in supporting a candidate who had given signs of a far less amenable policy toward big business than previous Republican nominees, but they almost universally gave Roosevelt their backing. "I am convinced that Republican rule is best for the country," Andrew Carnegie declared, and Wall Street generally echoed this authoritative statement of faith. "Theodore! with all thy faults . . . " was the single-line editorial in which the *New York Sun* tersely announced its support of the Roosevelt candidacy.

The Democrats found themselves in a quandary. They had gone down twice to overwhelming defeat under Bryan and they felt that only new blood offered them any chance of success.

Although the nation as a whole was becoming far more liberal in spirit than it had been in either 1896 or 1904, they made the ironical selection of as conservative a candidate as they could find. Alton B. Parker, Chief Justice of the New York State Court of Appeals, was nominated in the hope that he could hold the party together and at the same time attract conservative support among Republicans who might be fearful of Roosevelt's sympathy for progressivism.

They could not have miscalculated more grievously. In effect they gave the election to Roosevelt almost by default. For the Republican candidate held the conservative majority of his party, and he drew heavily upon the liberal vote which had nowhere else to go except to vote the Socialist ticket, which once again named Eugene V. Debs. The Democrats were completely snowed under and Roosevelt was re-elected by the largest majority — in both the popular vote and the electoral college — which up to that time the country had ever accorded a presidential candidate. With a total of 7,629,000 votes to his opponent's 5,084,000, giving him an electoral college majority of 336 to 140, Roosevelt carried every state outside of the Solid South, even breaking into this Democratic stronghold by winning Missouri and one electoral vote in Maryland.

His victory — and it was a personal triumph far more than a Republican one — could hardly have been more decisive. Elected now in his own right, Roosevelt prepared to advance his own policies and carry out his own ideas with greater freedom from party restrictions. He was prepared to exert a leadership in both domestic and foreign affairs that graphically illustrated his conception of the rôle the Chief Executive should assume. Abroad he pursued a spirited foreign policy in Latin America and the Far East, and even dabbled in European affairs. These were the imperial years — of which we shall speak further.

At home he vigorously assailed the representatives of corporate wealth and attempted to impose upon them, in the face of the stubborn opposition of many congressional spokesmen in his own party, the reforms which he felt necessary to protect them from their own folly. Debs had won four hundred thousand Socialist votes in the election, strengthening Roosevelt's conviction that if the Republican Party wished to maintain its hold upon the electorate, it had to meet the growing popular demand for reform or give way to the advocates of much more radical policies. He had no intention of going too far in his liberalism, or of breaking with the conservative wing in his own party, but he now felt more free to set his own pace. And while his course never actually departed very far from the middle of the road, he dramatized his progressivism so successfully that, for millions of his countrymen among the ranks of the plain people, he became a crusading knight arrayed in shining armor for the defense of democracy.

Railroad Regulation

Roosevelt's first drive after his re-election was in support of effective regulation of railroad rates. During his campaign in 1904, stealing the old thunder of Populists and Democrats, he had declared it to be the paramount issue before the country. He was determined to carry through a fight to the finish for broader powers for the Interstate Commerce Commission. Congress had already passed, in 1903, the Elkins Act which provided stiffened penalties for rebates. It was an important and long overdue measure, now welcomed by the railroads themselves, but the larger question of specific rate regulation remained. In his message to Congress in December, 1905, the President consequently demanded such additional legislation "as shall summarily and effectively prevent the imposition of unjust rates."

The need for such a law grew out of the failure of the Interstate Commerce Act, as we have seen, to provide effective means which the courts would uphold for coping with a problem that had become of fully as much public concern as the monopolistic practices of the trusts. Through their domination of virtually all interstate commerce, in a day before the general use of the automobile and the motor truck, the railroads were free to impose whatever freight charges they felt the traffic would bear. The restrictive influence of such competition as did exist, moreover, was being steadily weakened as the progress of railway con-

solidation swept ahead. With adverse court decisions whittling
away its theoretical powers, the Interstate Commerce Commission had long since given up the effort to control these giant
transportation systems and frankly admitted its helplessness.
Shippers felt themselves to be fully as much at the mercy of the
railways as they had been in the eighteen-eighties and nineties.
Discrimination and favoritism in the interests of large corporations was the rule rather than the exception. The elimination of
rebates by no means prevented the railroads from imposing
charges which bore unfairly on the farmer and small manufacturer, and the wide distribution of free passes was an undercover
form of bribery to forestall legislative interference and silence
newspaper criticism. The muckrakers had seized upon railroad
abuses as one of the chief targets in their general attack upon the
arrogant power of industry and finance; the Socialists were hammering away at the old Populist demand for government ownership as the only solution of the problem. In taking up the cudgels
for more effective control over common carriers, Roosevelt was
adopting one of the most popular of progressive causes.

His program commanded the instant support of liberals and
awoke the no less vehement opposition of big business. For rate
regulation constituted a challenge, not only to the railroads themselves, but to all corporate industry. It was attacked as socialism,
and under the pressure of a powerful railroad lobby, conservatives rallied their forces to meet the President's attack. In the
House they were unable to prevent quick passage of a bill which
would have empowered the Interstate Commerce Commission
definitely to reduce rates which it found to be unreasonable. But
they strongly stood their ground in the Senate. Here the President was deserted even by such close friends as Henry Cabot
Lodge and Philander C. Knox, his former Attorney General. He
could count upon a senatorial progressive bloc, including a few
younger Republicans and liberal Democrats. La Follette, newly
arrived in the Senate, fought valiantly in behalf of a cause which
he had already advanced so successfully as governor of Wisconsin.
But under the masterly leadership of Senator Aldrich, Republican
Party whip, the Old Guard employed every possible trick and

stratagem to undermine the President's position. The resultant deadlock threatened passage of any legislation at all and Roosevelt finally felt compelled to compromise. He reached an understanding with the opposition — to the embittered discomfiture of his Democratic allies — whereby the original bill passed by the House was modified to provide for judicial review when the Interstate Commerce Commission undertook to prescribe maximum rates. In this form the Hepburn Act, as it was called, was finally passed in June, 1906. It had various other provisions: the abolition of free passes, establishment of a uniform system of bookkeeping, the prohibition of carriers engaging in the transportation of commodities they themselves produced, and the inclusion within the control to be exercised by the Commission of express and sleeping-car companies, bridges, ferries, and pipe lines. But the heart of the bill was the new authority granted for reduction of unreasonable rates.

Judicial review was a weakening limitation upon the original bill because of the conservatism of the federal courts. That could hardly be gainsaid. There was justification for the disappointment of the progressive bloc. Nevertheless, the Hepburn Act served to revitalize the Interstate Commerce Commission and gave it an entirely new rôle in railroad regulation. It now had powers of control which heretofore it had completely lacked. For all the skepticism of critics of the new law, this soon became clearly apparent. In the nineteen years since the Interstate Commerce Commission had been established, only 878 formal complaints had been brought before it by shippers. Within two years of passage of this strengthening legislation, some fifteen hundred such complaints were filed. And in its standardization of schedules the Commission had by 1911 halved 194,000 of the rates existing in 1906.

The principle of federal control over common carriers engaged in interstate commerce had at last been established upon a definite footing. Shippers had a new confidence in the administrative efficiency of the Interstate Commerce Commission. Moreover, the courts steadily strengthened its regulatory powers over aspects of railroad administration other than rate-making, and with the support of Roosevelt's successors, new legislation carried forward the general movement to which he had given such important momentum. The Hepburn Act was in some sense a halfway measure, but never again would the Interstate Commerce Commission be so completely helpless. The abuses which the Grangers, the Populists, and the progressives had in turn attacked were no longer outside the pale of control.

PROTECTING NATIONAL HEALTH

At the same time that the Hepburn Act was making its difficult way through Congress, a movement was gathering momentum which would result that same year in the passage of a Pure Food and Drug Act and a Meat Inspection Act. The progressive elements in Congress, spurred on by the shocking disclosures of the muckrakers, were primarily responsible for this legislation. Roosevelt championed the two measures without any hesitation, however. The bitter opposition of the food manufacturers, the proprietary drug industry, and the meat-packers, commanding a powerful lobby at Washington that secured the support of all conservatives for the protection of corporate interests, could hardly have been overcome but for the President's vigorous insistence upon action.

The need for pure food and drug legislation had long since been called to public attention. Doctor Harvey W. Wiley, chief chemist of the Department of Agriculture, had conducted a series of investigations, in which a volunteer "poison squad" served as guinea pigs, conclusively proving that the adulterants and chemical preservatives commonly used in the processing of food products and the manufacture of drugs were highly injurious to health. The public was not only being imposed upon by false and misleading advertisements in their sale; it was being subjected to very real dangers to life itself. The use of benzoic acid and coal-tar dyes in foodstuffs was anything but harmless, while an even greater hazard was the vicious cure-all drugs, some of them containing morphine or opium, sold as patent medicines. These disclosures were not sufficient to stir Congress out of its lethargy, but when they were more widely publicized by the muckrakers, an aroused public began to demand effective regulation. A series of patent medicine articles in the *Ladies' Home Journal* and *Collier's Weekly* sounded the call for reform. With the support of the American Medical Association — 135,000 physicians strong — a pure food campaign got under way. Roosevelt had fallen in line with the demand for legislation by 1905, and early the next year a bill was driven through the Senate. The opposition did not surrender, however. This time action was held up in the House where the bill's enemies succeeded in having it smothered in committee.

In the meantime Upton Sinclair published *The Jungle*, a scathing indictment of conditions prevailing in the Chicago slaughterhouses. The public was aroused to a new peril. Sinclair's real objective had been to draw attention to the deplorable status of stockyard workers. His gruesomely descriptive passages of the doctoring of poisoned beef, of the prevalence of tuberculosis among the meat-handlers, and of the general dirt and filth characteristic of the cutting rooms were far more effectual, however, in depicting the dangers to national health.

> There was never the least attention paid to what was cut up for sausage [ran one memorable passage]; there would come all the way back from Europe old sausage that had been rejected, and that was mouldy and white — it would be dosed with borax and glycerine, and dumped into the hoppers, and made over again for home consumption. There would be meat that had tumbled out on the floor, in the dirt and sawdust where the workers had tramped and spit uncounted billions of consumption germs. There would be meat stored in great piles in rooms; and the water from the leaky roofs would drip over it, and thousands of rats would race about on it. It was too dark in these storage places to see well, but a man could run his hand over these piles of meat and sweep off handfuls of the dried dung of rats. These rats were nuisances, and the packers would put poisoned bread out for them; they would die, and then rats, bread, and meat would go into the hoppers together.

Among the readers of *The Jungle* was President Roosevelt.

"Tiddy was toying with a light breakfast," ran Mr. Dooley's picturesque account of the scene at the White House table, "an' idly turnin' over th' pages iv the new book with both hands. Suddenly he rose from th' table, an' cryin': 'I'm pizened,' began throwin' sausages out iv th' window . . . since then th' President, like th' rest iv us, has become a viggytaryan. . . . "

The meat-packers denied the truth of the picture drawn by Sinclair, insisting that their plants were as clean as any kitchen. But when Roosevelt instituted an investigation, with disclosures that in some instances went even beyond the semi-fictional record of *The Jungle*, they changed their tune. The sale of meat products began to fall off — the most telling argument the proponents of regulation could have advanced — and the harassed industry was prepared to accept additional federal inspection as a lesser evil than the loss of markets.

The collapse of resistance to meat inspection was paralleled under these circumstances by retreat on the part of those manufacturers who sought to block the pure food bill. There was still some congressional opposition on constitutional grounds. Many Democrats sincerely felt that the proposed measures were a dangerous invasion by the Federal Government of a sphere which should be reserved for action by separate states. The public demanded protection, however, which could only be made effective through exercise of the National Government's powers over interstate commerce. Congress thereupon quickly passed in June both the Pure Food and Drug Act and a new Meat Inspection Act.

CONSERVATION

The final important movement forwarded by this administration in the field of domestic politics, and perhaps the one most closely associated with the name of Theodore Roosevelt, was conservation. It primarily sought to protect the public from industry's exploitation of natural resources which belonged by right to the country as a whole. Yet it had a broader basis than this. The conservation movement also aimed to safeguard the people from their own shortsightedness, and to preserve for future generations the great heritage of our national wealth in arable land, water power, timber resources, oil reserves, and mineral deposits. The measures actually taken along these lines during Roosevelt's term of office were important; even more memorable was the awakening of the nation to an interest in conservation. Nothing accomplished during these opening years of the twentieth century had a greater significance for the future of America.

There had been a faint beginning to the conservation movement in the eighteen-nineties. The Carey Act had provided for the gift of irrigable land to the western states on condition that they should permit the construction of irrigation works by private companies. Following upon surveys of the national wealth made by the United States Geological Survey, Congress had also taken preliminary steps to provide for the removal of forest land from public sale in order to create nationally owned reserves. During the administrations of Presidents Harrison, Cleveland, and McKinley some forty-seven million acres of timber had been placed under the administration of the General Land Office. However, these reserves were entirely inadequate to the national needs and their administration was separated from the Bureau of Forestry which was alone concerned with scientific control over forests.

Roosevelt wrote in his *Autobiography*:

> The idea that our natural resources were inexhaustible still obtained, and there was as yet no real knowledge of their extent and condition. The relation of conservation of natural resources to the problems of national welfare and national efficiency had not yet dawned on the public mind. The reclamation of arid public lands in the West was still a matter for private enterprise alone; and our magnificent river system, with its superb possibilities for public usefulness, was dealt with by the National Government not as a unit, but as a disconnected series of problems, whose only real interest was in their effect on the re-election or defeat of a congressman here and there. . . .

Roosevelt imparted to the conservation movement something

of the driving force of his own personality. It appealed to him
immensely. His love of the outdoors and of nature, his interest
in the West where he had lived as a rancher, and his ardent
patriotism all worked together to the same end. The conservation and proper use of our natural resources, he stated in his
annual message to Congress in 1907, was the fundamental problem underlying every other problem in our national life. He saw
it as a whole — not merely preserving trees or damming rivers, but
recovering for the American people their own land, safeguarding
its resources, whether on the surface or below the ground, for the
general welfare. He believed thoroughly — as a later Roosevelt
was to believe with the same intensity — that the National Government should promote planned and orderly development in the
control of our great rivers through a combined program of flood
prevention, water-power development, and improvement of navigation. There should be no further despoiling of the land, no
robbing of the future for a selfish and thoughtless present.

The first step taken to implement the general conservation
program was passage of the Newlands Act in 1902. This measure
authorized the use of money obtained from the sale of public
land in sixteen western states and territories for reclamation and
irrigation. Within four years, twenty-eight different projects,
looking toward the irrigation of three million acres, had been
successfully launched. The most ambitious of these undertakings
was the impounding of the waters of the Colorado River at the
Roosevelt Dam in Arizona. Other projects were the Shoshone
Dam in Wyoming, the Elephant Butte Dam in New Mexico, the
Gunnison Tunnel in Colorado, and the Arrowrock Dam in Idaho.
The cost of the irrigation works on which the Federal Government now found itself engaged was assessed against the settlers
taking out tracts on the improved land, and it was then returned
to a revolving fund for further projects.

While these important plans were taking shape, Roosevelt also
breathed new life into the program for creating forest reserves.
Here he was aided by James R. Garfield, who became his Secretary of the Interior, and Gifford Pinchot, head of the Bureau of
Forestry. One of his first moves was to transfer the forest reserves

from the General Land Office to a newly created United States Forest Service, where they could be administered with the benefit of Pinchot's skilled training. It was the President's further intention to go the limit of his authority in enlarging these reserves. In 1906 a total of 64,000,000 acres of forest land was set aside — more than all the land withdrawn by his three predecessors. By the end of his second administration this figure had swelled to 148,000,000 acres. In addition, 85,000,000 acres — largely coal land and water sites in the Northwest and Alaska — were withheld from public sale pending further study of their natural resources by the Geological Survey.

There was opposition to these moves. "What's posterity ever done for us?" asked those who favored cutting up the national pie at once. Congress refused passage of a law which would have provided permanent retention of all land bearing coal, oil, or natural gas.

Roosevelt could not be stopped so easily. He recognized that conservation was a state problem as well as a national one, and that effective action by either governmental agency demanded both further study of the whole problem and popular education as to its importance. For these purposes the Inland Waterways Commission was created in 1907 to investigate the interrelation among forests, water power, soil erosion, and river transportation; and upon publication of its findings a national conservation conference was summoned to meet the next year in Washington. With the attendance of the governors of twenty-four states, members of the cabinet, the Supreme Court, members of Congress, federal officials concerned with every phase of the conservation movement, and a notable array of public-spirited citizens, this White House gathering proved to be perhaps the most influential move made by the President in forwarding his program. At its conclusion an important declaration of principles was adopted. It demanded the conservation of all forest lands, the regulation of private timber-cutting, the improvement of navigable streams and conservation of their watersheds, and the retention by the Federal Government of all land containing coal, phosphate rock, oil, natural gas, and water-power sites.

Shortly afterward a National Conservation Commission was created and forty-one states soon fell in line with establishment of state conservation commissions. The President had succeeded in focusing public attention on his favorite issue and had given tremendous impetus to a movement long overdue. The magnificient system of national parks and forest reserves which has become such a striking feature of national development in the West, as well as the vast power and irrigation projects that have been constructed in river valleys throughout the country, largely grew out of these forward-looking measures which were Roosevelt's greatest achievement during his seven years in the presidency.

ROOSEVELT GIVES WAY TO TAFT

As the Roosevelt administration drew to a close, its deeds bulked large in the popular mind. The President was at the peak of his popularity. If he had often been swept along by the progressive movement rather than leading it (as he liked to assume), greater progress had nevertheless been made in strengthening the powers of the National Government to protect the public interest than in any previous administration since the Civil War. There was also the promise of further advance to which the President pointed the way. His final years in office found him demanding new controls over big business, additional powers for the Interstate Commerce Commission, regulation of the stock market, modification of the prevalent use of the injunction in labor disputes, income and inheritance taxes.

There had been only one threat to the general good fortune and public support which his administration enjoyed. A sudden financial panic had developed in the fall of 1907 and for a time the economic skies appeared lowering. Business held the President responsible. "Hail Caesar!" the *New York Sun* ironically declared. "We who are about to bust salute thee!" Roosevelt struck back at business. He charged that "ruthless and determined men" had sought to bring about financial stress solely to discredit the Government. He declared their objective was to force it to reverse its policy so that they could "enjoy the fruits of their evildoing." Nevertheless, he was sufficiently frightened to make an unexpected concession. When the House of Morgan declared that the stability of the New York stock market could be upheld only through the United States Steel Corporation's acquisition of the Tennessee Coal and Iron Company, which would otherwise fail and drag down all business in its collapse, Roosevelt hurriedly promised immunity from the anti-trust laws.

The storm soon blew over. With the opening of the election year of 1908, the skies were again serene. Roosevelt had been able to maintain the public good will that accompanies prosperity. Despite the alienation of many conservatives, who could not stomach his attacks upon wealth and privilege, and despite some doubts in the progressive camp as to his real orthodoxy on reform, the plain people for whom he had made himself spokesman enthusiastically approved what they considered his constructive efforts to maintain a just balance between the warring elements in American life. They believed in his square deal for both capital and labor alike. And they continued to enjoy the exciting aspects of his exuberant personality —

> T. R. is spanking a Senator,
> T. R. is chasing a bear,
> T. R. is busting an awful Trust
> And dragging it from its lair.
> They're calling T. R. a lot of things —
> The men in the private car —
> But the day-coach likes exciting folks
> And the day-coach likes T. R.

Roosevelt might well have succeeded himself, but in the excitement over his election in 1904, he had put aside a possible third term and declared he would not accept renomination in 1908. He could, however, choose his successor. For a time he hesitated between the rival claims and political availability of Charles Evans Hughes, Elihu Root, and William Howard Taft. The mantle fell upon Taft, his Secretary of War and one of his closest personal friends. There were forebodings in some quarters as to the wisdom of this choice, but no real possibility of successful opposition. The Republican convention, after adopting a platform which was a strong endorsement of Roosevelt's policy, dutifully named Taft its presidential candidate on the first roll call.

After their futile venture into the conservative camp in 1904, the Democrats returned to the liberal fold and nominated their traditional standard-bearer — William Jennings Bryan. The progressive advance of the past few years had embodied so many of his own ideas that his rôle as a critic of the Roosevelt Administration was not an entirely happy one. Nevertheless, the Democratic platform stated that the overwhelming issue before the country was, "Shall the people rule?" The political pressure and control of delegates which had enabled Roosevelt to choose his successor were attacked as violating the principles of democracy. Taft himself was assailed as an undercover representative of corporate wealth, and the continued influence of "the interests" in party councils was declared proof positive that for all their much-trumpeted reforms, the Republicans could not carry out the popular will.

It was on the whole a rather apathetic campaign. "Hit them hard, old man!" was Roosevelt's constant advice, but Taft had little of his chief's force. Nor did Bryan supply a great deal in the way of political fireworks with so much of his ammunition stolen. The result was never in doubt. Taft was elected with a popular vote of 7,679,000 to his opponent's 6,409,000, and obtained 321 electoral votes as against Bryan's 162. It was not the popular landslide that Roosevelt had won in 1904, but it put Taft safely in the White House and left the Republicans in control of Congress. It was a famous victory — not for Taft, not for the Republicans, but for Roosevelt.

Would the new President continue his predecessor's policies? Would he maintain the battle against "the abuse of wealth and the tyranny of power"? Or would he revert to the more conservative program formerly associated with the Republican Party and still stubbornly upheld by the Old Guard? As Roosevelt sailed for Africa on a big-game hunting expedition in order to leave Taft a clear field, these were the questions to which an interested public awaited an answer.

7

Taft and the Election of 1912

A MAN OF PEACE

THE TAFT ADMINISTRATION played an unexpected part in the developing history of the progressive era. The new President was believed to be wholly committed to the policies introduced by Roosevelt and in many respects he successfully carried them forward — even more successfully for a time than had his predecessor. Nevertheless, when his term of office was only half over, Taft had allowed himself to become so closely identified with the more reactionary elements within his own party that an insurgent revolt broke out among the progressive Republicans. This deepening cleavage soon led to an embittered split with Roosevelt, and as the Old Guard candidate for re-election in 1912, Taft found himself opposed by a new Progressive Party made up of Roosevelt adherents who had followed their leader out of the Republican Party in fervent support of what he termed the New Nationalism.

There were many reasons for Taft's political failure, and we may today deal more leniently with his administration than did his contemporaries. The growing discord between the two wings of the Republican Party created almost insuperable obstacles to any sort of legislative co-operation. Alarmed over what they considered Roosevelt's precipitate course, the conservatives were doggedly determined to block any further assaults upon *laissez-faire*, while the progressives, who eventually closed their ranks to form an insurgent bloc, were determined to throw off the Old Guard's repressive control. Between these two conflicting forces, Taft at first wavered helplessly. "I am not so constituted," he wrote on one occasion in rueful comment on his inability to maintain party harmony, "that I can run with the hare and hunt with the hounds." As conservatives and insurgents grew more and more antagonistic, he consequently gave up the struggle and almost against his better judgment aligned himself with the former. For all his early sympathy with progressivism, his basic conservatism was reasserted when he found himself, as he thought, misunderstood and unfairly condemned by his former political friends.

Even apart from the unusual difficulties which his administration faced, Taft would probably have had a hard time. He was not cut out for the presidency. His real interest was the law and his ambition the Supreme Court. Although he had already in 1908 had a notable career in public office — Solicitor General under President Harrison, federal judge, Governor General of the Philippines, and Secretary of War — these were appointive rather than elective positions. A "big, generous, high-minded fellow," as Roosevelt affectionately described him, his temperament hardly fitted him for the usual hurly-burly of politics, let alone the embittered partisan strife that lay ahead of him. He recognized his own limitations and had accepted his nomination with reluctance. He never felt quite at home or comfortable in the White House. Shortly after the inauguration he plaintively confessed that every time he heard someone say "Mr. President," he looked around for Roosevelt. The responsibilities of his office, the great burden of work placed on him, the demands of politics, were not at all to his liking, and they proved even more distressing than he had anticipated.

The times demanded aggressive leadership, and Taft almost completely lacked assertive qualities. The times demanded skill in the handling of men and issues, and Taft was the most politically inept of presidents. While he enjoyed considerable personal popularity, for his lovable traits were undeniable, he had no real gift for winning the crowd and maintaining the popular support upon which a president's effectiveness so largely depends. His judicial, objective attitude of mind was also a liability rather than an asset under the circumstances that marked his administration. He could not act with Roosevelt's easy and sometimes careless disregard of precedent and constitutional restraints. Slow and deliberate, Taft had to be certain of his ground. He could not rush ahead and later seek justification for what he had done. No president ever had greater reverence for the Constitution and respect for law — admirable characteristics but not popularly exciting after Rooseveltian fireworks.

From the very first his conservative interpretation of presidential powers led to the resumption by Congress of much of the initiative in legislation. Taft's presidential messages were often strong, forthright documents, but he made little effort to force acceptance of his views. It was his instinct to avoid political strife and to try to hold himself aloof from congressional battles. He was not to find this altogether possible, but he remained at heart a man of peace and good will — again admirable characteristics, but somewhat uninspiring to a public that had grown to enjoy the noisy excitement of party conflict.

For all his achievements — and as already suggested they were more important than his contemporaries were prepared to admit — Taft could not overcome the immense handicap of succeeding the meteorlike brilliance of Roosevelt. His own steadier star was dimmed. Elihu Root once remarked that the shift from the Roosevelt to the Taft Administration was "a good deal like that from an automobile to a cab." The new President would have been among the first to accept such an analogy. "It is a very humdrum, uninteresting administration," he said himself toward the close of his term of office, "and it does not attract the attention or enthusiasm of anybody."

The Battle Over the Tariff

Upon assuming office in 1909, the first issue which Taft felt compelled to take up was the tariff. It had again and again proved to be political dynamite. Roosevelt had shrewdly avoided it. There had been agitation for tariff revision during his administration, but in the face of Old Guard opposition he had neatly ducked out from under all responsibility. "Whence comes this so-called demand for tariff tinkering?" "Uncle Joe"

Cannon, dictatorial Speaker of the House, had demanded. "Aren't all our fellows happy?" And Roosevelt took his advice. "For the last two years," he wrote Cannon in 1907, "I have accepted your view as to just what we should say on the tariff — or rather as to what we should not say — and I am satisfied that it was wiser than the course I intended to follow." The popular demand for revision of existing duties had nevertheless continued to make itself felt. Taft had to face it. During the election campaign the Republicans had pledged themselves to revision and Taft had made it clear that he interpreted the party platform as meaning downward revision.

The demand for lowering the tariff reflected the growing belief that its high rates were primarily responsible for the rising cost of living through the protection afforded domestic monopolies. The country was prosperous, but prices for manufactured goods were out of line with those for other commodities. Even the farmers had at last come to realize that the high duties which had been adopted in the Dingley Act, passed in 1897, benefited them not at all. On the contrary, they tended to increase the cost of the articles they had to purchase, notably farm machinery, and at the same time limited the export market for their own produce. Maintenance of existing schedules was consequently seized upon as but another example of the subserviency of government to big business. Only by combating "the mother of trusts" as well as the trusts themselves, it was maintained, could the new administration prove its devotion to progressive principles and the rights of the common people.

This was all good Democratic doctrine, as preached in election years if not always practiced when the Democrats were in office; but it had now also been adopted by the insurgent Republicans. In response to the growing agrarian discontent with monopoly-protected industrial prices, the progressive senators from midwestern states were on the warpath. Whatever the attitude of the Old Guard in seeking to maintain the Republicans' traditional high-tariff policies, they were determined not to let downward tariff revision again go by default.

Under such pressure, Taft summoned a special session of Congress to deal with the issue and a comprehensive bill for tariff reform was promptly introduced into the House. Its purpose was not complete abandonment of protection — even the western insurgents had no such radical idea — but a reasonable reduction in rates. Existing duties were to be maintained in so far as they were necessary to equalize the cost of production at home and abroad, and extension of the free list was restricted to non-competing imports. The House promptly passed the bill embodying these principles and it was sent to the Senate — only to be so amended by the Finance Committee that the result completely nullified any promise of effective tariff reduction. Some six hundred increases over the House rates were proposed, and under the domineering leadership of Senator Aldrich, whose friendship for the industrial interests had been so strongly demonstrated in his opposition to both railroad regulation and the Pure Food Bill, the Senate protectionists demanded their adoption.

The Republican insurgents, rather than the low-tariff Democrats, provided the excitement in the ensuing debate. With such senators as La Follette of Wisconsin, Beveridge of Indiana, Bristow of Kansas, Dolliver and Cummins of Iowa, each taking up some particular schedule in turn, they tore the amended bill to shreds. They ruthlessly exposed the relationship between the tariff and the trusts. They dragged before the bar of public opinion those senators whom they accused of acting as spokesmen for corporate wealth. They declared that in their fight against protection, they were defending the interests of the people against "privilege, plutocracy, and betrayal of party faith."

Taft was more alarmed by the bitter dissension within Republican ranks than by the fate of tariff revision. He sought a compromise. Finally the protectionist bloc agreed to putting hides on the free list, adopted a corporation tax as partial compensation for the benefits big business might be expected to derive from the continuance of generally high schedules, and approved establishment of a bipartisan tariff board to prepare future schedules on a scientific basis. Taft accepted these concessions and felt that they brought the proposed bill reasonably in line with his campaign promises. The insurgents were not at all mollified. They fought on vigorously in favor of lower rates all along the line. But theirs was a hopeless cause. The conservatives controlled the Senate and as finally enacted in August, 1909, the Payne-Aldrich Tariff was another victory for protection.

Instead of the promised downward revision, the new law actually raised the average rate on dutiable goods. The wool schedule, over which had been fought one of the fiercest battles of the whole struggle, was maintained and the much-criticized duties on sugar were also left at approximately their former level. A few reductions were made, in such goods as coal, lumber, iron, and steel, but the insurgents maintained that on such products there was not any real danger of foreign competition. The free list appeared to be largely a fraud. We find Mr. Dooley explaining to Mr. Hennessy:

> Th' Republican Party has been thru to its promises. Look at th' free list if ye don't believe it. Practically ivrything nicessary to existence comes in free. Here it is. Curling stones, teeth, sea moss, newspapers, nux vomica, Pulu, canary bird seed, divvy-divvy, spunk, hog bristles, marshmallows, silkworm eggs, stilts, skeletons, an' leeches. Th' new tariff puts these familyar commodyties within th' reach iv all.

There was immediate and widespread indignation over such a travesty of tariff revision. The importance of the corporation tax and of congressional support for a proposed income-tax amendment, which came up at the same time, was overlooked by the insurgents in their general disappointment. Taft attempted to defend the law as best he could, describing it as under existing circumstances "a sincere effort . . . to make a downward revision." While such statements by no means satisfied the insurgents, who felt he should have vetoed the bill, popular resentment might not have turned so strongly against the President had he not felt called upon about a month later to go much further in self-defense. In a speech at Winona, Minnesota, he made the grave political mistake of saying, almost inadvertently, that the new law was "the best tariff bill that the Republican Party ever passed."

His earlier statements showed that Taft did not really feel this to be so, but his opponents immediately seized the opportunity for a concerted attack upon his handling of the whole controversy. The newspapers, particularly incensed at the new tariff because of its duty on newsprint, tore the ill-advised phrase from its context and played it up in front-page headlines. The congressional insurgents, and progressives generally, now became convinced that Taft had betrayed them utterly. It was the first instance which appeared to show that for all his nominal support of progressive principles he was really in close alliance with the political representatives of corporate wealth. His reputation never fully recovered from its effects.

Two years later a further attempt to deal with the tariff issue was made through negotiation of a trade reciprocity treaty with Canada. Its proposed reductions on imports of Canadian agricultural commodities, however, met the opposition of the western farm bloc whose interest in downward tariff revision was confined to the duties on manufactured goods. Nevertheless, with the aid of Democratic votes, Taft pushed his proposals through successfully, only to have the whole project collapse when Canada rejected it as a result of certain extravagant statements made in the course of debate in Congress. Taft himself declared that reciprocity would "make Canada only an adjunct of the United States," and the Speaker of the House looked forward to "the day when the American flag will float over every square foot of the British North American possessions clear to the North Pole." An alarmed Canadian public would have nothing to do with reciprocity under these circumstances.

TAFT LOSES MORE GROUND

While passage of the Payne-Aldrich Tariff had greatly disappointed all progressives, other phases of President Taft's general program should have softened their rancor. He was prepared to carry on the prosecution of trusts inaugurated by Roosevelt. "Every trust of any size that violates the statute," he publicly stated in explaining his attitude toward enforcement of the

Sherman Act, "will, before the end of this administration in 1913, be brought into court. . . . " And he generally upheld this pledge. Ninety anti-trust suits were filed in his four-year term of office in comparison with forty-four during Roosevelt's seven and one-half years. The Supreme Court's decision asserting the new rule of reason in the American Tobacco and Standard Oil cases of 1911 underscored popular doubts of the effectiveness of such actions, but Taft chose to assume that the Sherman Act had actually been given a "vivifying potentiality" and instructed the Department of Justice to continue its work.

He also recognized that other measures than anti-trust prosecutions were necessary to meet the problem of monopoly. He asked Congress for legislation definitely outlawing the specific abuses whereby the trusts infringed upon fair trade practices, and he strongly insisted upon the need for federal incorporation of all companies engaged in interstate commerce. "No other method can be suggested," Taft declared, "which offers federal protection on the one hand and close federal supervision on the other of these great organizations that are in fact federal because they are as wide as the country and are entirely unlimited in their business by state lines." It was Congress, not the President, which was responsible for failure to make any further progress along these lines until the Wilson Administration.

In addition to action against the trusts, another development carrying forward progressive principles was a further tightening of railroad rate regulation by the Interstate Commerce Commission. Passage of the Mann-Elkins Act in 1910 enabled it to suspend new railroad tariffs while they were under investigation, set up a new Commerce Court to handle litigation, and extended the Commission's powers to embrace telegraph and telephone companies. Three years later a Physical Valuation Act sought to provide practical procedure for determining railroad property values which would enable the Commission to fix rates on the basis of a reasonable return on investment. These two laws were pushed through Congress under the leadership of the insurgents rather than as a result of insistence by Taft. Nevertheless, they bore his signature and they were a part of the record of his administration.

For all such activity — and at least one political commentator wrote in 1910 that Taft had "somehow managed to produce more results than anybody else who has sat in his chair since the Civil War" — the new administration was losing public confidence. Its failure to bring about downward revision of the tariff outweighed what could be said in its favor on other counts, and in a period that continued to be dominated by the spirit of progressivism, Taft's caution and in some instances apparent timidity alienated a great deal of popular support.

There was, for example, the question of his attitude toward conservation. Actually he was thoroughly in sympathy with it. During his administration the Bureau of Mines was established, the public land laws strengthened, and extensive coal, mineral, and oil lands, as well as additional timber land and water sites, were withdrawn from public sale. However, Taft became involved in 1910 in a bitter quarrel among the officials in charge of carrying out the conservation policy which eventually led Chief Forester Pinchot to charge Secretary of the Interior Ballinger with protecting private interests at the expense of public rights. The President investigated, became convinced that on legal grounds Ballinger was justified, and subsequently dismissed Pinchot. In his opinion the issue did not involve conservation so much as simple justice between two men. "If I were to turn Ballinger out, in view of his innocence and in view of the conspiracy against him," the President wrote, "I should be a white-livered skunk. I don't care how it affects my administration. . . . "

Affect his administration it did. Pinchot had been a Roosevelt appointee and a prominent leader in the whole conservation movement. His devotion to this popular cause was in striking contrast to Ballinger's careful legalism, and the public inevitably sided with him throughout the controversy. Could the Taft Administration be covertly betraying conservation and trying to undo Roosevelt's work? Progressives feared that this was the real explanation of the President's attitude.

Another episode causing a decline in Taft's popular stock grew out of a violent struggle in the House of Representatives this same year to deprive the Speaker of his arbitrary control over legislative procedure. In the hands of "Uncle Joe" Cannon this control was being exercised to block all reform, and the revolt against "Cannonism" developed into an important phase of the general progressive drive to revitalize American democracy. The liberal Republicans naturally looked to the White House for support. It was not forthcoming. Even though his private papers clearly reveal his disapproval of Cannonism, Taft maintained a hands-off attitude throughout the congressional fight on the grounds that it was none of his business. Eventually the battle was won. The Speaker was stripped of much of his power through a modification of House rules that was an important victory for the democratic forces in Congress. But the insurgent bloc, interpreting Taft's silence as tacit support for the Speaker's reactionary adherents, again found him betraying progressivism.

The mid-term elections of 1910 shortly demonstrated both the waning public confidence in the Taft Administration and the growing rift within the Republican Party itself. The Democrats won a decisive victory, securing control of the House, and the insurgent Republicans further strengthened their intra-party position at the expense of the Old Guard. It was all too clear that whatever might be said in explanation or extenuation, Taft had lost control of the political situation. His very real services to progressivism were forgotten or ignored. The insurgents were prepared to deny his leadership and seek control of the Republican Party in order that it might be rededicated to the principles which Roosevelt had preached so eloquently and which they felt Taft was betraying.

What of progressivism's former leader? What of Roosevelt? His attitude under these new political circumstances became of the utmost importance. And about that dramatic figure were to rage the political quarrels that in another two years would result in victory for neither the conservative nor progressive Republicans, but for the Democrats.

THE SPLIT WITH ROOSEVELT

Roosevelt had returned on the eve of the elections of 1910 from a grand hunting trip in Africa and a spectacular tour of European capitals. His bag included nine lions, five elephants, thirteen rhinoceroses, and seven hippopotamuses. He was still a popular hero, perhaps more than ever a popular hero since Taft's failure to provide the dramatic showmanship to which the country had become accustomed, and an eager public waited expectantly to see whether he would re-enter politics and which side he would take in the growing split within Republican ranks.

It was not left very long in doubt. For a time Roosevelt attempted to remain strictly on the sidelines, staying quietly at Oyster Bay, Long Island, but both circumstances and his own inability to hide his light under a bushel brought him prominently into the congressional campaign. Undoubtedly he hoped to heal the growing rift in the party, to maintain a fair balance between his successor and the insurgents, but he was even more concerned over the continuation of his own policies. He talked with many of his old followers, and while there was as yet no open break with Taft, he clearly showed his disappointment over what he considered the President's failure to provide more aggressive leadership for reform. Taft had not proved to be the greatest chief executive since Lincoln, as his sponsor had once confidently forecast; his course was "absolutely inexplicable." Roosevelt felt himself obliged to make thoroughly plain just what Republican progressivism actually meant. He did so in a notable speech at Osawatomie, Kansas on August 31, 1910, in which he outlined the principles of what he called the New Nationalism. He proclaimed with convincing intensity:

> I stand for the square deal. But . . . I mean not merely that I stand for fair play under the present rules of the game, but that I stand for having those rules changed so as to work for a more substantial equality of opportunity and reward. . . . The betterment which we seek must be accomplished, I believe, mainly through the National Government. The American people are right in demanding that New Nationalism without which we cannot hope to deal with new problems.

Upon conclusion of the 1910 campaign, Roosevelt necessarily retired again to the political sidelines and the center of the stage was shortly taken over by the congressional insurgents. In January, 1911, they made their first overt move to overthrow the Republican Old Guard's domination of the party. They established the National Progressive Republican League and adopted a broad program for transferring power from the bosses to the electorate. The guiding spirit of the new organization was La Follette. The progressive Wisconsin senator and his co-workers, moreover, not only had political reform in mind; they sought also to control the Republican presidential nomination of 1912. If the party was to repudiate Taft's growing conservatism and adopt a liberal stand, La Follette felt that he had earned the right to be considered its standard-bearer. No one had more earnestly or more consistently championed progressive principles, in season and out, and the insurgent group announced itself solidly in his favor.

Many progressives throughout the country, however, were looking hopefully toward the vigorous advocate of the New Nationalism rather than to La Follette, and the former President did nothing to make them feel their hopes were altogether in vain. Roosevelt had said he would not again consider the presidency. He had given certain assurances to the Winconsin senator which the latter had interpreted as a promise of support for his own candidacy. But as popular attention swung more and more in the direction of Oyster Bay, the great warrior for righteousness sagely held his peace until his very silence began slowly to undermine the La Follette boom. Finally in February, 1912, responding to a carefully engineered but apparently spontaneous demand from seven progressive governors, he made a startling and dramatic announcement — "My hat is in the ring."

Roosevelt had been unable to resist the call of duty. It had not been difficult for him to convince himself that he alone could carry the banner of progressivism to victory. La Follette had done the pioneer work and would now be pushed aside, disappointed and embittered, but Roosevelt felt that the field had to be cleared for the re-establishment of Republican leadership

where it had originally belonged. As for Taft, the growing cool-
ness between the two former friends had become more and more
pronounced. Roosevelt was persuaded, in part because of that
supreme egotism which made it impossible for him to believe
that anyone else could faithfully represent the people's interests
either as party leader or president, that Taft had completely surrendered to the party machine and the control of the bosses.
Worse than that, he was "disloyal to our past friendship . . . disloyal to every canon of ordinary decency." In September, 1910,
Roosevelt had still thought Taft "thoroughly well-meaning and
upright"; now less than two years later he was "not merely a fool,
but . . . a good deal of a blackguard."

There was still no thought of a third party. The contest was
one for Republican leadership and the presidential candidacy.
The country braced itself for an "elegant row." It looked forward,
in some cases with mixed emotions, to the possibility of another
Roosevelt administration. "The cold chills race up and down our
spine," the magazine *Life* declared. "The Roosevelt Presidency
was one of the most interesting national moving-picture films that
was ever unrolled before us. We haven't a single regret for the
time and money spent upon it. But to have to sit through it
again!"

For Taft the blow was a bitter one. For long he refused to believe that Roosevelt had in reality turned against him. He would
not be goaded into any counter-attack and he told a mutual friend
that he could not be induced to say anything against Roosevelt
personally. While his onetime mentor, having made up his mind,
rushed joyously into the fray, Taft remained heavy of heart. It
was only what he considered the increasingly radical implications
of the New Nationalism, now defiantly shouted from the house-
tops, that at last goaded him into action. He went into the contest for renomination not so much to defend himself as to safeguard the country from what he considered reckless demagogy.
"I am a man of peace," Taft stated. "I don't want to fight. But
when I do fight, I want to hit hard. . . . "

The issue which most aroused him was Roosevelt's advocacy
of the recall of judicial decisions. This had also alienated other

conservative and moderately liberal support, but because of his devotion to the law and unshakable faith in the judiciary, Taft was especially outraged. "When a judge decides a constitutional question, when he decides what the people as a whole can or cannot do," Roosevelt had stated in the address which sounded the opening note of his pre-convention campaign, "the people should have the right to recall that decision if they think it wrong. We should hold the judiciary in all respect; but it is both absurd and degrading to make a fetich of a judge or of anyone else. . . ." This was anathema to the constitutionalist. At such statements, even though Roosevelt limited the recall of judicial decisions to those made by state judges, Taft struck back with unexpected vehemence. "Such extremists are not progressives," he declared; "they are political emotionalists or neurotics." Roosevelt's attitude reinforced the President's basic conservatism. While he might well have withdrawn from the contest for renomination had any other man been the contender, Taft steeled himself for a fight to the death because of his conviction that Roosevelt, in this new radical incarnation, had become a menace to national stability.

"Which Corpse Gets the Most Flowers"

The Republican convention was a bitter contest between a man who was almost surely the popular choice of the rank and file of the party, as proved by the primaries in which his name was entered, and a man who by virtue of his position commanded the support of the party machine. Roosevelt arrived on the scene girded for battle. He felt "like a Bull Moose" — a phrase that would be enthusiastically adopted by his adherents — and he was determined to win this new war for righteousness. "Our cause is the cause of justice for all in the interests of all," he told his enthusiastic followers gathered to hear one of his most memorable fighting speeches in the Chicago Auditorium. " . . . We stand at Armageddon, and we battle for the Lord." Over against this enthusiasm and eloquence, the promoters of President Taft's candidacy had the votes of a majority of the delegates in their pockets. There was a wrangle about credentials, but steam-roller tactics — the same procedure Roosevelt had himself employed in securing the nomination of Taft four years earlier — prevailed. With 561 votes to his opponent's 107, President Taft was renominated on the first ballot.

There were 344 delegates, however, who had not voted, and the implication of their abstention was clear. The insurgents would not accept defeat on the floor of the convention. They were prepared to split the party, carry the fight to the country. The very night of the vote nominating Taft, amid charges of theft, brigandage, and treason, Roosevelt's loyal supporters met separately and pledged him their support on an independent ticket. "If you wish me to make the fight, I will make it," he answered, "even if only one state should support me."

The die was cast. Shrewd observers already foresaw the Democrats driving triumphantly through that disastrous breach in the Grand Old Party. Had either Taft or Roosevelt any chance for election? "The only question now," one Republican leader sardonically commented, "is which corpse gets the most flowers."

The convention of Roosevelt adherents, prepared to organize themselves into a new and independent Progressive Party, was held in August. There was no question of its candidate, and a platform embodying virtually every general progressive principle was quickly adopted. It called for direct primaries and the popular election of senators, woman's suffrage, currency reform, conservation, anti-injunction laws, minimum wages for women, the eight-hour day, social insurance, recall of judicial decisions. There was something for everyone; it was a fervid promise of Utopia. Nevertheless, there was at least one significant omission. No definite promise of downward revision of the tariff was included. Roosevelt was not prepared to throw away all possible conservative support. The fine hand of his financial backers — such men as George W. Perkins and Frank A. Munsey, the one a wealthy director of the United States Steel Corporation and the other a powerful publisher — could be clearly discerned in certain of the party proposals.

Actually there was not so great a difference between the Progressive Party platform and that of the Republicans as might have been expected. The former, however, was backed by the dynamic personality of Roosevelt and the enthusiasm of liberals who saw over the political horizon the dawn of a new era. The campaign was to be a crusade — a crusade for social justice. The heterogeneous assortment of western insurgents, reformers, social workers, wealthy disciples of the Rooseveltian cult, and crackpot visionaries who gathered for its launching transformed a political convention into a stirring revival meeting. "Onward, Christian Soldiers," was its theme song. Whatever their chosen leader might do, the army of the righteous would march at his command —

> Follow! Follow!
> We will follow Roosevelt,
> Anywhere! Everywhere,
> We will follow on.

In the meantime the Democrats had not withdrawn from the presidential race out of respect for the quarreling Republicans. With greater hope and confidence than they had been able to muster since 1896, they were prepared to take every advantage of the glorious opportunity afforded them by the split in the enemy ranks. Their platform, too, conformed to the spirit of progressivism. It definitely called for additional trust control, anti-injunction laws, banking and currency reform, railroad regulation, conservation, and a lower tariff. The Democratic candidate, nominated after a prolonged convention battle, also stood out as a strong adherent of these liberal principles. He was Woodrow Wilson, governor of New Jersey, and the Democrats threw him their united support in the hope of avenging the defeats they had suffered in the last four elections.

For all the excitement occasioned by these maneuvers, and the able addresses of the three candidates, the presidential campaign of 1912 did not greatly stir the electorate. Taft soon realized that he was virtually ruled out of the race as nominee of the conservative party in a liberal year. The contest between Roosevelt and Wilson involved no important differences in principle. The chances of election were heavily in the Democrats' favor and public apathy increased as the campaign wore on. When the vote was counted, Wilson was found to have been elected, according to general expectations. He had a heavy majority — 435 votes — in the electoral college, but only a slight plurality in the popular vote, Roosevelt running second and Taft making a poor third. As evidence of the extent to which people stayed away from the polls, the combined vote for Taft and Roosevelt was actually less than the former's vote had been in 1908, and Wilson's total was smaller than that of Bryan in any of his campaigns as Democratic candidate. The final count was 6,286,000 votes for Wilson, 4,-126,000 for Roosevelt, and 3,484,000 for Taft.

The outcome of the presidential campaign of 1912 graphically illustrated the difficulties which any third party movement faces in American politics, and it underscored the irremediable blunder the Progressives had made in attempting to launch one. Roosevelt recognized the completeness of his defeat. "There is only one thing to do," he told a friend, "and that is go back to the Republican Party." Even more noteworthy, the election was a clear-cut and impressive triumph for progressive principles. And this result, as demonstrated in the overwhelming majority for the two liberal candidates as opposed to the vote for the more conservative Taft, was further highlighted by a striking increase in the Socialist poll. As candidate for that party, Eugene V. Debs had a popular vote of 897,000 — or more than twice his total four years earlier. The country was demanding further reform. It had unmistakably endorsed that broader program of progressive action of which Roosevelt, La Follette, and Wilson alike were the popular champions.

8

The New Freedom

SCHOLAR IN THE WHITE HOUSE

THERE HAVE BEEN MANY ROADS to the White House, but that followed by Woodrow Wilson was perhaps the most unusual of them all. In 1910 he had been elected governor of New Jersey, and this was the only political office he had ever held. His career had been professorial — a long period of teaching and writing in the fields of history and political science. He knew much of government, but it was book knowledge. Except for his two brief years at the New Jersey State House, he was without any practical experience in the knock-down, drag-out battles of American politics. The actual record of his life before that significant day in March, 1913, when he was inaugurated President of the United States is a brief and simple one: student at Princeton and Johns Hopkins, recipient of various academic appointments culminating in a chair of political science at Princeton in 1890, promotion to the presidency of Princeton twelve years later, and finally, election as governor of New Jersey.

Far more important were certain aspects of his background that served to mold the mind and temperament of this brilliant scholar in politics. He came of Scotch and Irish ancestry; on both sides of his family there was a long line of Presbyterian ministers. High thinking and plain living were the inheritance from his forebears. Roosevelt enthusiastically battled for justice and righteousness; Taft's probity and integrity were never challenged; but with Wilson, moral earnestness rose above everything else. He judged men and events from a lofty plateau where he walked alone with God. His vocation was teaching, but his real forte was preaching — to his students, to politicians, to the

American people, to the entire world. Coldly intellectual, little given to warmth or affection except in a few close personal relationships, scornful of the ways of the demagogue, he nevertheless exercised tremendous power. In his years as a reformer on the national stage, he demonstrated an unexpectedly shrewd mastery of practical politics, but his real strength lay in his absolute certainty that he knew what was right, and in the inspired eloquence with which he could express his convictions. Opposition only served to increase the inflexibility of his purpose, and on occasion, as later events were tragically to demonstrate, it transformed determination into stubborn obstinacy.

The public never quite knew how to evaluate this single-minded reformer in the White House. Seldom has a president inspired both such devoted disciples and such implacable enemies. He singularly lacked the common touch. An idealist and visionary, he remained aloof from the everyday concerns of men. Roosevelt had entered into every phase of American life; Taft's interests were not all-inclusive but they ranged broadly. Woodrow Wilson never swerved from his self-appointed task of regenerating the spirit of the American people, and later that of the world. He completely lacked the zest for life itself, the exuberance and hearty enthusiasms, which had characterized both his predecessors. The popular support which he commanded was for his ideas and sincerity of purpose rather than for the man himself.

Wilson was a thoroughgoing liberal, completely in sympathy with the underlying tenets of the progressive movement and passionately devoted to the principles of democracy. His zeal for reform had first been demonstrated as president of Princeton where he had fought valiantly and tenaciously, although without complete success, for academic freedom and a more democratic organization of college social life. As governor of New Jersey he had revitalized the state by asserting its freedom from boss control and pushing through a constructive and forward-looking legislative program. His candidacy for the presidential nomination had been promoted by the liberal wing of the Democratic Party and the platform on which he stood was a platform of reform.

In so far as the powers of the presidency were concerned, Wilson emphatically believed in the need for a strong executive. This had been made clear in his authoritative books on political science. The President was the unifying force in the complex system of government that had grown up in the United States, he wrote some time before his own entry into politics, and he should stand forth as "the leader both of his party and of the nation." In carrying out his policies he should look for support to the American people, and not to the party bosses or even elected representatives. While Wilson sought to uphold the traditional Democratic doctrine of state rights against the usurping power of the National Government, his assertion of presidential leadership actually accentuated the trend toward further centralization which had already become so pronounced in the political evolution of the twentieth century. In some measure he went even further than Roosevelt. He was prepared to play the rôle of a powerful prime minister.

Although the program which he sought to implement had been persuasively set forth during the electoral campaign in the political creed to which he gave the name of the New Freedom, his idealistic purposes were perhaps even more eloquently proclaimed in his inaugural. He interpreted his election, together with the Democratic triumph in securing control of Congress, as a challenge to redress the evils which had crept in with the good in our national development.

It means much more than the mere success of a party. The success of a party means little except when the nation is using that party for a large and definite purpose. No one can mistake the purpose for which the nation now seeks to use the Democratic Party. It seeks to use it to interpret a change in its own point of view. . . . Our duty is to cleanse, to reconsider, to restore, to correct the evil without impairing the good, to purify and humanize every process of our common life without weakening or sentimentalizing it. . . . The nation has been deeply stirred, stirred by a solemn passion, stirred by the knowledge of wrong, of ideals lost, of government too often debauched and made an instrument of evil. The feelings with which we face this new age of right and opportunity sweep across our heartstrings like some air out of God's own presence, where justice and mercy are reconciled and the judge and the brother are one. ... This is not a day of triumph; it is a day of dedication. Here muster not the forces of party, but the forces of humanity. Men's hearts wait upon us; men's lives hang in the balance; men's hopes call upon us to say what we shall do. Who shall live up to the great trust? Who dares fail to try? I summon all honest men, all patriotic, all forward-looking men, to my side. God helping me, I will not fail them, if they will but counsel and sustain me!

The address was an appeal to idealism with a very definite bill of particulars. The President called for immediate tariff revision, for establishment of a new banking and currency system, and for further control over the trusts. He emphasized the paramount need for conservation. He asked for sanitation laws, pure food laws, and labor laws that would safeguard the rights of the people in their struggle for existence when they could not be protected by individual effort. These reforms were among those to which the Populists had first called attention at the close of the nineteenth century and which all progressives had consistently championed. They were the basic ingredients of the New Nationalism quite as much as of the New Freedom. Wilson merely made them his own.

His speech had an enthusiastic reception. The *New York Mail* declared it expressed a spirit "to which the whole country can respond," and even the conservative and Republican *New York Tribune* said that "the nation is hungry for leadership like that." Somewhat more colloquial was the comment of the *Louisville Courier-Journal*: "Assuredly the new president has the right pig by the ear."

Until the shadow of the World War fell across the country and domestic policy was subordinated to the larger interest of foreign policy, Wilson pursued his program with striking success. It met opposition. Conservative interests continued to combat tooth and nail the reassertion of the rights of the democracy over against those of plutocracy. *Laissez-faire* refused to surrender without a struggle to this further extension of governmental regulation.

The masters of capital and industry fought vigorously, but not so vigorously as the tight-lipped, moralistic reformer in the White House. He did not hesitate to use every device of political strategy in translating his principles into action, quietly cracking the whip of party patronage to keep his congressional majority under control. His main reliance, nevertheless, was upon popular support — the backing of liberals, regardless of party — and his accomplishments were largely made possible by the consummate skill with which he rallied to his support all the forces of progressivism.

The Tariff Once Again

The first problem which the Wilson Administration took up, as in the case of the Taft Administration, was tariff revision. Democratic policy on this issue was clear-cut: duties providing for "effective competition" between American and foreign manufacturers would be substituted for the protection afforded by the Payne-Aldrich Tariff. The President called Congress into special session in April, 1913, and in a dramatic personal appearance, which shattered a precedent maintained since the administration of John Adams, he set forth without equivocation what he thought should be done.

> We must abolish everything that bears even the semblance of privilege or of any kind of artificial advantage, and put our businessmen and producers under the stimulation of a constant necessity to be efficient, economical, and enterprising. . . . The object of the tariff duties henceforth laid must be effective competition, the whetting of American wits by contest with the wits of the rest of the world.

To this end an administration bill was introduced by Representative Underwood which called for reductions all along the line and broad extension of the free list.

It quickly passed the House, and then ran into the same obstacles which every attempt to lower the tariff had always faced in the Senate. Representatives of special interests of every kind descended upon Washington *en masse* and called upon the protectionist senators to take matters in hand, as they had in the case of the Payne-Aldrich Bill, four years earlier. The hotels swarmed with lobbyists. Pressure politics had gained tremendous scope and spokesmen for the Chamber of Commerce of the United States, the National Association of Manufacturers, and scores of other specialized business organizations concentrated their powerful influence against tariff revision. They bore down so heavily upon individual senators that there appeared to be every prospect that the proposed bill would be amended out of all semblance to its original form.

President Wilson's answer was immediate action. He made no attempt to wring minor concessions from the adherents of protection as had Taft. He took the issue to the country. In a scathing public statement he denounced the activities of the tariff lobby as unbearable and insidious interference on the part of "great bodies of astute men to create an artificial opinion and to overcome the interests of the public for their private profit." At the same time, he held the Senate sharply to account. By keeping in close touch with committee consideration of individual items, he prevented the log-rolling and trading of special privileges which had always in the past gone into tariff making. The result was passage of the bill almost exactly as first approved by the House. In this campaign the President had the advantage of a closely knit Democratic majority, and also the support of two Republican insurgents, La Follette and Poindexter, but it was his own direct intervention and appeal to public opinion that induced the Senate to resist the pressure of the protectionist lobby.

The Underwood Tariff Act marked the first departure since the Civil War from the principles of protection as upheld by the Republican Party. It was a triumph for the consuming public. This is not to say that the tariff wholly abandoned protection or could be termed one for revenue only. But it reduced the average rate on dutiable goods from approximately thirty-seven per cent to a little more than twenty-six per cent, including the tariffs on fabricated steel products and on cotton and woolen manufactures.

More important, it added to the free list a large number of articles which were necessities of everyday use for everyone, and particularly for the farmer. Wool and sugar, long the backbone of protection, were to be admitted free, and also such products as scrap iron and steel rails, coal, cement, wood and wood pulp, leather, boots and shoes, agricultural implements, barbed wire, and many foodstuffs. These were important changes, making the Underwood Act a milestone in tariff history.

Another feature of the new law, added to make up for the expected deficit in revenue, was a graduated income tax introduced by Representative Cordell Hull of Tennessee. Its adoption had finally become possible through ratification of the Sixteenth Amendment. It affected relatively few persons — only 357,500 paid taxes the first year — and the rate was very low: one per cent for the normal tax and a surtax which rose only to six per cent on incomes over five hundred thousand dollars. Even then it was assailed by reactionary newspapers as "taxing the life out of thrift and industry," "inquisitorial interference with the citizen," and "wrong in principle and un-American in spirit." The country as a whole, however, accepted it as a valid method of taxation based upon democratic principles in regard to ability to pay. Its importance was soon to be demonstrated with the wartime need for revenues which could be secured in no other way.

The Underwood Act generally was highly approved by the Democrats and condemned by the protectionist Republicans. The latter held out the most dire prospects of immediate ruin for industry. While these gloomy forebodings were not realized, the full consequences of tariff reduction could hardly be gauged. The outbreak of the first World War within a year introduced so many complicated factors into the economic setup that the effects of the change in import duties could not possibly be isolated.

THE FEDERAL RESERVE SYSTEM

While Congress was still wrestling with the tariff, the President had again appeared in person and called for action on the second of his promised reforms — establishment of a new banking and currency system.

> We must have a currency [he stated], not rigid as now, but readily, elastically, responsive to sound credit. . . . Our banking laws must be mobilized reserves; must not permit the concentration anywhere in a few hands of the monetary resources of the country or their use for speculative purposes in such volume as to hinder . . . more legitimate uses. And the control of this system of banking and of issue which our new laws are to set up must be public, not private, must be vested in the Government itself, so that the banks may be the instruments, not the masters of business and of individual enterprise and initiative.

The need for such reform had long been recognized, but it was brought home to the entire country with great force during the so-called bankers' panic of 1907. As an aftermath of that incident, a Republican Congress had passed the Aldrich-Vreeland Act. This was a stop-gap measure providing somewhat greater elasticity for the currency by allowing the banks, under careful restrictions, to use certain other securities than government bonds as a basis for their note issues. At the same time, Congress also created a National Monetary Commission to study the entire problem. The report of this commission, not issued until 1912, recommended establishment of a strong central bank. In the meantime, however, the Democrats had won control of the House and instituted an investigation which sensationally exposed the tremendous concentration of control over banking and credit already lodged in the hands of few men. The muckrakers had been viciously attacking the Money Power. Here was the substantiation of their charges. It appeared to be glaring proof that there was need for reform measures much beyond the highly conservative proposals of the National Monetary Commission.

The Pujo Committee, as the investigating committee of the House was called, summoned to its hearings representatives of banks, investment houses, and brokerage companies, subjecting them to a grueling examination at the hands of Samuel Untermeyer as special counsel. Although J. P. Morgan stubbornly testified that "all the money in Christendom and all the banks in

Christendom could not control money; there could be no Money Trust," there were other prominent financiers, among them George F. Baker, head of the First National Bank of New York, who frankly admitted that the control of credit was dangerously concentrated. The facts appeared to bear out the latter opinion — certainly they did so in the minds of a large part of the public.

It was revealed that the three great financial institutions centered in New York — J. P. Morgan and Company, the First National Bank, and the National City Bank — had combined resources aggregating $632,000,000. If the funds of the Morgan-dominated Equitable Life Assurance Society and of other affiliated banks and trust companies controlled by the three leading banks were included, the total was estimated at over $2,000,000,000. Firm members or directors of these dominating financial institutions, moreover, held 341 separate directorates, thereby exercising a large measure of control in no less than 112 different banking, transportation, and industrial corporations whose aggregate resources totaled more than $22,000,000,000. Through joint stock ownership, mergers and consolidations, interlocking directorates, and other legal devices, the committee's final report stated, there was in the United States a "great and rapidly growing concentration of the control of money and credit in the hands of these few men."

In the light of these revelations, made on the eve of his inauguration, President Wilson was voicing an almost universal demand when he asked Congress for a reform in the banking and currency system that would prevent such concentration of monetary resources and place the control of credit in public, not private hands. Two years earlier he had said that "the great monopoly in this country is the money monopoly." He now amplified this statement by bluntly declaring that "the banking system of this country does not need to be indicted. It is convicted. . . . "

A comprehensive bill carrying out the President's recommendations, largely the work of Carter Glass, chairman of the House Banking and Currency Committee, was promptly introduced, and its passage by Congress in December, 1913, created the Federal Reserve System. It established full government control over banking, made possible the rapid mobilization of bank reserves, and provided that elasticity of currency which experience had shown so necessary for the avoidance of money stringency. The governing body of the new system was to be the Federal Reserve Board, comprising the Secretary of the Treasury and the Comptroller of the Currency as *ex-officio* members, and five additional members appointed by the President, subject to confirmation by the Senate. Its powers were broad and far-reaching.

There was to be no central bank. The country was divided into not fewer than eight nor more than twelve regional districts (later fixed at twelve), and in each of them there was to be a federal reserve bank, whose stock would be owned by member banks required to subscribe six per cent of their capital and surplus. All national banks were obliged to join the Federal Reserve System; state banks and trust companies were permitted to do so. The federal reserve banks were to hold the reserves of the member banks, the latter maintaining deposit credits as a basis for their own transactions, and they were to act solely as bankers' banks in their members' interest.

They were empowered to make loans upon the government securities deposited with them as collateral, and to rediscount the commercial and agricultural paper of all member banks. Perhaps most important, this rediscounted paper was to provide the basis for a new currency. The federal reserve banks were authorized to issue federal reserve notes, subject to the limitation of a forty per cent gold reserve, up to the full total of their holdings. Through this provision it would be possible to maintain a volume of currency that depended, not upon rigidly fixed reserves, but upon the needs of business, both from year to year and also from season to season. The federal reserve banks also acted as depositories for government funds and could buy and sell gold, and foreign and domestic bills of exchange. It was a thoroughgoing and highly complicated reform, completely transforming the entire banking and currency system of the country.

Passage of the bill through Congress had been attended by prolonged debate and controversy. Reactionary members of the banking fraternity declared the measure to be a socialistic expedient that would plunge the national finances into complete chaos. More responsible bankers accepted the need for reform in principle, but opposed such complete government control. The American Bankers' Association strongly advocated direct bankers' representation on the Federal Reserve Board. In time the bankers became more reconciled to the obvious advantages of the scheme and when the bill was finally passed, they were prepared to give it a fair trial.

It proved an immediate success. The provisions for an elastic currency, the mobilization of reserves, and general decentralization of banking went far toward meeting the real needs of the country. Through its control over the rediscount rate and power to sell both government bonds and commercial paper in the open market, the Federal Reserve Board was in a position to exercise some measure of authority over credit inflation. By 1915, almost a third of the nation's twenty-five thousand banks, holding about half the entire banking resources of the nation, had become members of the Federal Reserve System. Every year thereafter saw a steady increase both in membership and in the proportion of national banking resources held by member banks. The Federal Reserve System proved of immense value in enabling the country to withstand the stresses and strains imposed upon its finances by the first World War.

While there were to be no further general readjustments in banking or currency until the depression of the nineteen-thirties, one other measure designed to ease the credit situation as it applied directly to farmers was the Federal Farm Loan Act, adopted in May, 1916. Agricultural borrowers invariably found it difficult to obtain the loans necessary for financing their operations and they always labored under a heavy mortgage debt. The Federal Reserve Act had sought to aid them through its provisions for rediscounting agricultural paper and authorizing short-term loans on farm mortgages. But this did not entirely meet the needs of the situation. The Federal Farm Loan Act consequently established twelve federal land banks, closely patterned on the federal reserve banks, "to provide capital for agricultural development, to create standard forms of investment based upon farm mortgages, and to equalize rates of interest upon farm loans." Through the formation of co-operative loan associations, to which each member subscribed five dollars in stock for every one hundred dollars he wished to borrow, the farmers could then jointly apply to the federal land banks for loans up to fifty per cent of the value of their land, and an additional twenty per cent on permanent improvements, which would be granted at an interest rate of five to six per cent. In order that the government banks should not entirely monopolize this field, provision was also made for establishing private joint-stock banks empowered to make direct loans on farm mortgage security.

New Attacks on Monopoly

With both the tariff issue and banking and currency reform successfully disposed of within less than a year of his inauguration, Wilson turned at the opening of 1914 to the third major problem facing his administration. He asked for further legislation to control the trusts. He sought both creation of a Federal Trade Commission and amendments to the Sherman Act which would specifically outlaw unfair trade practices. The purpose behind his proposals, he stated, was "to make men in a small way of business as free to succeed as men in a big way, and to kill monopoly in the seed."

The popular demand for stricter regulation of the trusts had increased with every year. We have noted both President Roosevelt and President Taft's reiterated recommendation for federal incorporation of all companies engaged in interstate trade and strict governmental supervision of their activities. The Democratic Party was even more fully committed to regulatory measures with a platform stating that "private monopoly is indefensible and intolerable." Many of its members desired far more drastic action than the President. "If I had my way," Champ Clark, Speaker of the House, said, "I would fill the penitentiaries and jails of the United States so full of trust magnates that their arms and legs would stick out of the windows."

There were months of discussion in committee and debate on

the floor of both House and Senate, but in September, 1914, Congress passed and the President approved the Federal Trade Commission Act. It set up a commission of five members, bipartisan in character and appointed by the President, with full authority to investigate the activities of all companies engaged in interstate trade and to regulate such unfair methods of competition as it found being practiced. The procedure to be followed, after investigation had shown violation of the anti-trust laws, was the issuance of "cease and desist" orders. Appeal from such orders could be made to the courts, but the findings of the Federal Trade Commission were to be accepted as fact. No criminal or civil penalties were provided for failure to obey the cease and desist orders, but this weakness was remedied by a companion bill which was more strictly regulatory in character.

This was the Clayton Act, an amendment to the Sherman Anti-Trust Law, and it was adopted within a month of creation of the Federal Trade Commission. Its primary purpose was definitely to proscribe those corporate practices which tended to lessen competition or create a monopoly. They were carefully listed. Among them were unwarranted price discriminations, exclusive selling or leasing contracts, establishment of interlocking directorates in formerly competitive industrial corporations, and acquisition by one corporation of another corporation's stock when the effect would be substantially to lessen competition. To enforce these provisions of the law it was stipulated that individuals could bring suit against offenders for triple damages, and that the directors, officers, and agents of the corporations concerned were responsible for all violation of the law.

These were the measures, preventive rather than punitive in their approach to monopoly, whereby Wilson hoped to "check and destroy the noxious growth in its infancy." Their value in strengthening the Sherman Act was generally accepted, but their efficacy was seriously doubted in many quarters. Senator Cummins bluntly stated that some of the clauses in the Clayton Act did not have enough teeth to masticate milk toast. The President was far more hopeful. He believed the Government's attitude toward trusts was now so clarified and specific that the problem was solved. "Our program of legislation with respect to business is now virtually complete," he stated upon signature of the Clayton Act. " . . . The road at last lies clear and firm before business."

Apart from its regulatory features in regard to business monopoly, the new law also contained equally if not more important provisions relating to the status of labor unions. In response to their growing demand for protection, arising from the court decisions upholding injunctions against both strikes and boycotts as conspiracies in restraint of trade, the Clayton Act sought to exempt unions from any prosecution under the anti-trust laws. The need for some such measure had long since been recognized by all progressives as labor found itself more and more restricted in the use of the only weapons whereby it could hope to promote collective bargaining and sustain its demands for higher wages, shorter hours, or union recognition. The decision in the Danbury Hatters' case, already noted, had especially aroused labor sympathizers, and each of the three political parties in 1912 had promised relief from "government by injunction." The Democrats had been particularly explicit in their promise of reform, and in this respect the Clayton Act was therefore carrying out a campaign pledge that had been instrumental in winning labor support for Wilson as a presidential candidate.

Section six of the new law laid down the general principle that the labor of a human being was not a commodity or article of commerce, and expressly stated that nothing in the anti-trust laws should be construed to forbid the existence and operation of labor unions or apply to their members. Going still further, section twenty provided that no restraining order or injunction should be granted by the courts in the case of a labor dispute unless it was necessary to prevent irreparable injury to property for which there was no adequate remedy at law. Labor was to be upheld in its right to strike, to picket, and to boycott.

These new guarantees were at once hailed by labor as the greatest triumph it had won in its long struggle for union recognition. President Gompers of the American Federation of Labor optimistically called the Clayton Act "Labor's Charter of Free-

dom." Time and circumstance were considerably to dampen this
early enthusiasm. The courts still found authority to impose injunctions under cover of the qualifying phrase in regard to irreparable injury to property. The charter of freedom was found
to be deceptive, and almost two decades were to pass before a
more drastic curb on injunctions was finally enacted. Nevertheless, these provisions of the Clayton Act appeared at the time to
constitute a strong reinforcement of the rights of labor as well as
a strict limitation upon those of industry. Regardless of later developments, they at least demonstrated a dramatic reversal of the
earlier attitude of Government toward industrial disputes.

The record of the Wilson Administration in respect to the rôle
of business and industry is not confined to passage of the Trade
Commission Act and the Clayton Act. The President also sought
actual enforcement of these laws with impartial vigor. The new
commission actively undertook the investigation of prevailing
trade practices and drew up a long list of those which it considered unfair. During Wilson's Administrations, 788 formal
complaints were served against corporations charged with such
practices and 379 cease and desist orders were issued.

Prosecutions against monopoly under the terms of the Sherman
Act were also continued. They were not relatively as numerous
as during either the Roosevelt or the Taft Administration. The
greater number of outstanding trusts had already been called into
court, and application of the rule of reason further restricted
proceedings which might otherwise have been instituted. Nevertheless, forty-one bills in equity were filed and fifty-one indictments obtained in criminal cases during this eight-year period.

THE PROGRESSIVE BALANCE SHEET

Shortly before passage of the Clayton Act events abroad had
diverted public attention from Wilson's domestic policy to foreign
affairs. War had broken out in Europe. While there was not at
first much thought of our possible participation in that seemingly
remote struggle, the maintenance of neutrality was soon to become an engrossing problem. Nevertheless, there was no imme-

diate cessation of reform. A number of other measures served to round out the program which President Wilson had stipulated as necessary to carry out the purposes for which the Democratic Party had been brought into office. His policies still commanded widespread popular support. The reforms already enacted had served to strengthen public confidence in his administration.

The sympathy for the interests of labor reflected in the anti-injunction provisions of the Clayton Act found further expression in several other measures which carried forward the progressive drive to remedy industrial working conditions. Congress passed in 1915 the La Follette Seamen's Bill, a measure providing for improved conditions in the forecastle and also restricting the tyrannical control traditionally exercised by shipmasters. A year later, the Adamson Act established an eight-hour day for all employees on interstate railways. These pro-labor measures were in keeping with the liberal spirit of the times, but they aroused as much conservative opposition as any of the other legislation Wilson sponsored. This was particularly true of the Adamson Act. The President was attacked for surrendering to labor's demands upon threat of a railway strike, and for setting up a precedent for governmental intervention in labor disputes that would have dangerous consequences.

Finally it should be recalled that it was while Wilson was President, although not forming part of his own program, that the three amendments to the Constitution to which reference has already been made were formally ratified: the Seventeenth Amendment providing for the direct election of senators; the Eighteenth, establishing prohibition, and the Nineteenth, granting woman's suffrage.

Whether or not the progressive movement had spent its force with the achievements credited to the first Wilson Administration remains an interesting question. Liberal leaders fully realized that there was still much to be done, and that such social legislation as had been enacted could hardly be said to have completely realized its ultimate objectives. On the other hand, the public already appeared to be growing somewhat weary of reform by 1916. There were signs that it wanted a period of adjustment after what had already been accomplished, rather than further activity. In any event, war intervened, and it was not until the advent of another Roosevelt in 1933 that the challenge to society to provide greater economic security and social justice for the masses of people was again to be taken up aggressively. The New Deal was then to attempt, however different the circumstances and actual program, to carry on where the New Nationalism and the New Freedom had left off.

In surveying the progressive era, throughout the entire period from 1901 until 1917, the background of the country's material development must not be disregarded. It was on the whole an epoch of widespread prosperity, although toward its close there were signs of a slackening in business activity. The value of manufactures more than doubled during these years; exports rose even before the outbreak of European war by some seventy-five per cent; and there had been by 1914 an increase of six per cent in real wages. For all the inequalities in the distribution of wealth against which the reformers hurled their blasts, both the farmers and labor were getting a greater share of the national income at the close of the period than at its opening. These were substantial gains, and they provided a basis for the hope and confidence which enabled the progressives to believe that once their reforms were adopted, national well-being would be assured on a broader scale than ever before.

The spirit of the times, however, interpreted the promise of American life not so much in material as in spiritual terms. The basic objective of the progressive movement was to recover the freedom and opportunity which had been so greatly curtailed by the rise of industrialism. Its adherents sought to overthrow that interpretation of *laissez-faire* which in the name of individual liberty had served to increase the power of the strong at the expense of the weak, and was undermining democracy in the interests of an arrogant plutocracy. Along these lines we have seen that there was real advance, and for all the stagnation of the post-war years, the gains of the progressive era were not lost. Although industry was to maintain a substantial hold upon power and there was actually to be an even further concentration of wealth, Government did not abdicate its newly asserted authority. The progressive era, for all the superficiality of some of its reforms, and its halfway measures in dealing with certain fundamental economic problems, had strengthened the bases of American democracy. It was a period not only of high endeavor, but of real achievement.

The Fruits of Imperialism

AN EXPANDING FOREIGN POLICY

AMERICAN FOREIGN POLICY during the progressive era reflected both the strong nationalism that was so pronounced in internal affairs and something of the period's reformist zeal. The United States had become a world power, and it had a new international mission. If our efforts to strengthen the bases of democracy at home and our occasionally cavalier attitude toward other nations' rights of self-government sometimes appeared to be contradictory, this was rationalized on the ground that America had responsibilities that could no longer be reconciled with a complete hands-off policy. The nation was prepared to strengthen the hold it had already won in the general area of the Caribbean through the establishment of a semi-protectorate over Cuba and possession of Puerto Rico. It appeared to be ready to pursue the policy of intervention in the Far East already marked by acquisition of the Philippines and John Hay's declaration of the Open-Door policy. In both these new fields of activity, however, the development of national power was closely associated with an idea of international stewardship which served to justify what might otherwise appear — and did so appear to some of the countries concerned — the pursuit of wholly selfish political and economic aims.

To uphold these new policies, the United States also moved far from that limited program of continental self-defense that had characterized the nineteenth century. We had taken on new commitments as a result of the Spanish War; we sought the means to protect them. A navy that had become by the opening of the century secondary only to those of Great Britain and Germany was built up still further; its bases both in the Caribbean and

Pacific were developed in line with entirely new concepts of naval strategy, and the Panama Canal was constructed to link our two ocean fronts.

Theodore Roosevelt was wholly sympathetic with these expansive ideas. Primarily concerned with the enhancement of national power, he brandished "the big stick" with magnificent assurance in compelling respect for American rights. He intervened aggressively in the Caribbean, notably in regard to the Panama Canal and the so-called Roosevelt corollary to the Monroe Doctrine, and he sent the fleet around the world with the specific aim of impressing Japan with our newfound power. He even dabbled in European politics, making the proud boast on one occasion that he had stood the German Kaiser on his head.

Taft sought to advance American interest no less strenuously. He was primarily interested in commercial expansion, however, rather than in the demonstration of political power, and his program won the derogatory name of "dollar diplomacy." In spite of criticism, Taft vigorously defended this substitution of dollars for bullets on the broader grounds of "appealing alike to idealistic humanitarian sentiments, to the dictates of sound policy and strategy, and to legalistic commercial aims." His more pedestrian approach naturally suffered — once again — in comparison with Roosevelt's dash and exuberance. Taft would never have taken San Juan Hill at the head of a troop of Rough Riders, but he might have captured the position by enabling American bankers to foreclose a mortgage.

Wilson both opposed the obstreperous Rooseveltian technique and roundly condemned dollar diplomacy. Nevertheless, he, too, intervened forcefully in the affairs of other countries, and long before the first World War crusade for democracy, he revealed in action his conception of the international rôle that he felt the United States was called upon to play. He was even more convinced than his predecessors of a mission to spread abroad American ideals and promote "the development of constitutional liberty in the world." These objectives, indeed, led him to follow much the same path in foreign affairs as that traveled by both Roosevelt and Taft, for all their greater emphasis on national power and expansion.

The American people were not always sure where this was leading them or how much they approved of foreign adventure in Latin America and the Far East. As we have seen, the country had been swept from its moorings by the events of 1898, and the conflict between imperialists and anti-imperialists continued in new forms. Did expanding foreign interests reach even farther than Latin America and the Far East? It was already dimly realized that our international commitments could hardly fail to involve us in the growing rivalries of European imperialism.

Roosevelt had no mind to avoid this new aspect of our world rôle. When controversy over German and French rights in Morocco led to a serious crisis, he used his influence to persuade the powers to meet at an international conference in Algeciras in 1906. Moreover, the United States officially participated in the conference and signed the convention settling the Moroccan dispute. Upon ratifying it, the Senate expressly stated that our concern was only with American interests in Morocco, and that adherence to the Algeciras Convention did not mark any departure from the doctrine of non-entanglement in European affairs. The United States had revealed its sympathies, however, in supporting the Anglo-French cause against Germany and it almost unconsciously appeared to be swinging toward an alignment in defense of what Henry Adams called "the Atlantic System." Here was at least one observer who felt that he saw the handwriting on the wall. " . . . If Germany breaks down England or France," he wrote in 1906, "she becomes the center of a military world and we are lost."

On far safer ground than such intervention in Europe, the new American concern over world affairs found expression in fervent backing of the peace movement. The United States had taken part in a first international peace conference at The Hague in 1899; it attended the sessions of a second in 1907. Neither meeting was successful. The first completely failed to bring about a proposed limitation of armaments; the second could reach no agreement on a suggested world court. A new tribunal for arbitration and a convention codifying the rules of warfare were their only practical results. Undeterred by these disappointments, the State Department turned to arbitration treaties with individual countries. Twenty were concluded during Roosevelt's Administration; Taft then sought to extend their scope, but with little success, and finally Williams Jennings Bryan, Secretary of State under Wilson, negotiated thirty new accords providing for "cooling-off" periods of a year in the event of any dispute threatening war. At the close of 1914, only Germany, Austria-Hungary, Turkey, Japan, and Mexico — a highly significant list — were not included among the important nations to have signed such agreements.

For all this activity, the peace movement appeared vague and tenuous in the face of gathering tensions in Europe and the growing armaments race among the powers. Algeciras was more significant than The Hague. And despite the strength of traditional isolationism in the United States, our part in the former international conference appeared a logical projection of our active interest in both the Caribbean and the Far East. Our new foreign policies were carrying us far afield. What price world power?

"I Took the Canal Zone"

While the first important move in foreign affairs at the opening of the century had been the declaration of the Open-Door policy in China, which has already been discussed, steps were simultaneously being taken to acquire the rights to construct what was to become the Panama Canal. It, too, was a part of the general program for expanding American interests abroad that grew out of the imperialism of the Spanish War days. Building up the navy, acquiring overseas naval bases, and a trans-isthmian canal were closely linked.

A necessary preliminary to construction of a canal was abrogation of the fifty-year-old Clayton-Bulwer Treaty, wherein the United States and Great Britain had agreed that neither nation would ever seek exclusive control over such a canal or attempt to fortify it. This was accomplished when Great Britain agreed to withdraw in favor of the United States through her signature of the Hay-Pauncefote Treaty in November, 1901. We were given a free hand to build, control, and fortify an isthmian canal, subject only to a pledge of non-discrimination in regard to the tolls to be charged.

On the eve of signature of this treaty, Roosevelt had become President. If certain hesitations marked the development of other aspects of his foreign and domestic policies, he was ready to deal with this issue at once. As Assistant Secretary of the Navy, he had received a letter from Captain Mahan urging action in regard both to the annexation of Hawaii and the building of a canal. "Do nothing unrighteous," the eminent naval strategist had written, "but as regards the problem, take the islands and the canal site first and solve the problem afterwards." It was advice very much to Roosevelt's heart. "I take your views absolutely," he promptly answered. Now as President he was prepared to carry them out.

Even for the impetuous Mr. Roosevelt, however, it was necessary to decide just where the canal should be built before he could "make the dirt fly." There were two possible routes — Nicaragua and Panama, the latter at this time a province of Colombia. While Panama had many advantages, an old French concession which Ferdinand de Lesseps, the famous engineer of the Suez Canal, had unsuccessfully sought to develop was held by an organization calling itself the New Panama Canal Company. It was asking no less than $109,000,000 for its rights, and largely in view of this tremendous expense the Walker Commission, appointed by President McKinley to investigate the whole question, had just brought in a report recommending the Nicaragua route. Roosevelt was prepared to accept this recommendation, but the New Panama Canal Company at once reduced the price for its concession to $40,000,000 and its representatives began a high-pressure campaign to persuade Congress to buy out its rights.

The active members of this group — Philippe Bunau-Varilla, chief engineer of the original French company, and William N. Cromwell, a New York lawyer — were both ingenious and enterprising. They left no stone unturned in their lobbying activities and the providential eruption of a volcano in Nicaragua gave them a wonderful opportunity. It so happened that this very volcano was engraved on Nicaragua's postage stamps. Bunau-Varilla at once obtained ninety of them and presented one to each member of the Senate with the inscription: "An official witness of the volcanic activity of Nicaragua."

However decisive this piece of propaganda may have been, the Senate was won over to support of the Panama route. A measure favoring Nicaragua that had already passed the House was amended, and as finally passed in June, 1902, the Spooner Act authorized the President to purchase the concession of the New Panama Canal Company for $40,000,000 and to enter into negotiations with Colombia for a right of way across the Isthmus of Panama. It was further stipulated, however, that if this right of way could not be obtained within a reasonable time and upon reasonable terms, negotiations should then be taken up with Nicaragua.

The Administration now went to work. An accord was signed with the Colombian chargé d'affaires in Washington — the Hay-Herran Treaty — whereby in return for a cash payment of $10,000,000 and an annuity of $250,000, Colombia agreed to grant the United States a canal zone six miles wide. It was promptly approved by the Senate on March 17, 1903. All was going well, almost too well, when the program struck an unexpected snag. Colombia refused to ratify the Hay-Herran Treaty. Its Congress declared that it infringed upon Colombia's sovereignty and had been signed without proper authorization. There was also the little matter of the sum agreed upon in payment for the canal site. Why should the New Panama Canal Company get $40,000,000 for a mere concession, the legislators asked, and Colombia itself only $10,000,000? Should not the entire sum be more properly paid Colombia? There was a measure of justice in this point of view, but it found little support in Washington. It was felt that Colombia was simply trying to hold up the United States for what she could get out of the transaction, and that the members of her Congress were not entirely disinterested in the disposal of these larger sums.

Roosevelt, indeed, was shocked. Rejection of the treaty was a breach of good faith. It was an attempt at highway robbery. In his official capacity he brought all possible pressure to bear upon Colombia and explored every means of obtaining the canal zone with or without her consent — except that of forcing the New Panama Canal Company to share its $40,000,000. His private strictures upon the members of the Colombia Congress almost exhausted even his ample vocabulary of abusive epithets. They were contemptible little creatures, they were jack rabbits, they were foolish and homicidal corruptionists, they were members of a corrupt, pithecoid community. Finally, after declaring in exasperation that you could no more make an agreement with Colombia than nail currant jelly to the wall, he prepared to adopt other measures. "I feel we are certainly justified in morals, and therefore justified in law," Roosevelt wrote Mark Hanna in October, 1903, "in interfering summarily and saying that the canal is to be built and that they must not stop it."

His impatience for quick action was fully shared by the New Panama Company. After all, it had $40,000,000 at stake. Its directors feared that the United States, under the terms of the Spooner Act, would revert to the Nicaragua route. Somewhere the idea was consequently born that the province of Panama, which had once been independent of Colombia and was chronically discontented with Colombian rule, might again revolt and sign in its own behalf the treaty Colombia had rejected. There was no conspiracy along these lines, no evidence of direct collusion, but most certainly a tacit understanding prevailed among all concerned that in the event of such a revolt the United States would not allow it to be crushed. Bunau-Varilla conferred with both President Roosevelt and Secretary Hay — that is known, however much we may be in the dark as to just what was said — and American naval vessels were dispatched to Columbian waters to watch developments.

Suddenly things began to happen. On November 2, 1903, an American cruiser, the U. S. S. *Nashville*, reached Colon, the port on the Atlantic side of the Isthmus of Panama; on November 3, a patriot army including 287 members of the local fire brigade and 300 section hands of the Panama Railroad, rose in revolt, while the American naval forces, on the basis of an old treaty giving the

United States the right to keep communications open across the isthmus, refused to allow transit for Colombian troops seeking to suppress the uprising; on November 4, the independence of the Republic of Panama was declared; on November 13, the Panamanian envoy, who surprisingly enough turned out to be Bunau-Varilla, was received at Washington, and on November 18, a treaty was signed in which the Republic of Panama ceded to the United States a ten-mile canal zone on the same general terms as those Colombia had rejected.

Roosevelt heatedly denied the charge that his conferences with Bunau-Varilla had plotted the revolution. Such intrigue was perhaps hardly necessary. "He is a very able fellow," the President wrote some time afterward of this enterprising Frenchman, "and it was his business to find out what he thought our Government would do. I have no doubt that he was able to make a very accurate guess, and to advise his people accordingly. In fact, he would have been a very dull man had he been unable to make such a guess." The trick had, indeed, been turned very neatly: the United States had its canal zone, the New Panama Canal Company had its $40,000,000, and the citizens of Panama had their independence, plus the $10,000,000. Only the Colombian Government had lost out. Moreover, the rebels against its authority knew very well whence all blessings flowed. "The world is astounded at our heroism," the prospective President of the new Republic of Panama declared in an eloquent oration to the fire brigade and section hands. "Yesterday we were but the slaves of Colombia; today we are free. . . . President Roosevelt has made good. . . . Free sons of Panama, I salute you! Long live the Republic of Panama! Long live President Roosevelt! Long live the American Government!"

For a time Roosevelt refused to admit that he had followed Captain Mahan's old advice to take the canal site first and solve the problem afterward. In the face of the protests from Colombia and the criticism of anti-imperialists at home, he not only declared that his actions were "justified by the interests of collective civilization," but that every move had been made "with the highest, finest, and nicest standards of public and governmental ethics." Nevertheless, he appeared somewhat on the defensive. There is a story told of one occasion when he sought to explain himself at a cabinet meeting. "When he had finished," the account runs, "he glared around the table, finally fixing his eye on Secretary Root. 'Well,' he demanded belligerently, 'have I answered the charges?' 'You certainly have, Mr. President,' Root suavely replied. 'You have shown that you were accused of seduction and you have conclusively proved that you were guilty of rape.'" *

As time went on and the dirt began to fly on actual construction, the righteousness of what he had done no longer appeared to demand explanation. His final word on Panama was in a speech in 1911: "I took the Canal Zone and let Congress debate; and while the debate goes on the Canal does also."

The building of the canal was a great feat of engineering carried out under the authority of Colonel George W. Goethals, but it would not have been possible except for the work first done in removing the danger of tropical diseases in one of the world's most unhealthy localities. For this stupendous task the credit goes to Doctor William C. Gorgas who supervised the necessary sanitary and preventive measures. The canal was opened to traffic in 1914, although the work was not fully complete until six years later. Total cost was $275,000,000 for the canal itself, and $113,000,000 for its fortifications.

In the very year the canal was opened, an incident occurred showing that however debonair Roosevelt may have become about the diplomacy of 1903, the conscience of the United States was not altogether easy. A treaty was concluded with Colombia expressing regret for what had taken place and offering that country compensation totaling $25,000,000. It was rejected by the Senate, where Senator Lodge came vigorously to Roosevelt's defense, but seven years later the matter was again brought up. A new convention was ratified in 1921, with deletion of the expression of regret but the same financial balm for Colombia's wounded feelings. But was this entirely due to belated generosity? Oil had been discovered in Colombia. Her friendship somehow appeared more important than it had in earlier days.

* Philip C. Jessup, *Elihu Root*, I, 404-405.

INTERVENTION IN THE CARIBBEAN

The canal project from the very first gave a new emphasis to the problem of the strategic security of the Caribbean. As Roosevelt viewed the situation, the United States had both the right and the responsibility of maintaining order among the little Latin-American republics in this general area to ensure them against intervention on the part of any European nation. In 1902, Great Britain and Germany (with Italy's later participation) had blockaded Venezuela to enforce payment of certain outstanding financial claims. Two years later, the foreign creditors of the Dominican Republic began under somewhat similar circumstances to press for payment of a very considerable debt largely owned by European nationals. In the first controversy, the powers concerned had consulted the United States, and the issue was eventually settled by arbitration. Nevertheless, Roosevelt saw dangerous possibilities in foreign intervention in Latin America even under such restricted circumstances, and with the development of the crisis in Dominican affairs, he consequently sought to forestall any move whatsoever on the part of European nations by having the United States get there first.

The groundwork for his new corollary to the Monroe Doctrine was laid in his annual message to Congress in December, 1904, without reference to the prevalent difficulties in Santo Domingo, but clearly pointed in the direction of the Caribbean. Roosevelt stated:

> If a nation shows that it knows how to act with reasonable efficiency and decency in social and political matters, it need fear no interference from the United States. Chronic wrongdoing, or an impotence which results in a general loosening of the ties of civilized society may in America, as elsewhere, ultimately require intervention by some civilized nation, and in the Western Hemisphere the adherence of the United States to the Monroe Doctrine may force the United States, however reluctantly, in flagrant cases of such wrongdoing or impotence, to the exercise of an international police power.

Two months later, he demonstrated just how this policy might be applied. To meet the just claims of foreign creditors in Santo Domingo and yet prevent their Governments from obtaining any influence over Dominican affairs harmful to the United States, Roosevelt compelled the island Government to conclude an agreement virtually surrendering all financial controls to the United States. He made it clear that the United States did not seek any new territory — it had no more desire to expand than "a gorged boa constrictor to swallow a porcupine wrong-end-to," as he happily phrased it in private correspondence — but the collection of all customs duties was to be taken over under an arrangement allocating fifty-five per cent for foreign debt payments, and the remaining forty-five per cent to internal finances.

This was an entirely new departure in policy. However American exercise of an international police power might be justified or condoned as the only means to prevent foreign intervention in the Caribbean, nothing of the sort was contemplated in the original Monroe Doctrine. The Senate consequently looked upon the Dominican agreement, concluded in February, 1905, with a somewhat suspicious eye and finally refused to ratify it. Undaunted by this rebuff, Roosevelt proceeded to ignore constitutional restrictions on the treaty-making power and applied his policy by means of an executive agreement that lasted until 1907. By then conditions in the Dominican Republic had so greatly improved that foreign debt payments were being met in full, and the remaining portion of customs collections actually exceeded total collections prior to assumption of control by the United States.

Roosevelt's procedure, although subject to criticism for its offhand disregard of the sovereign rights of smaller nations, provided a precedent that both Taft and Wilson were to follow. His Republican and his Democratic successor alike intervened in the affairs of the nations of the Caribbean to maintain order and financial stability, thereby forestalling interference from abroad. During the Taft Administration such moves sometimes appeared to be more in the interest of private United States bankers than in the national interest, but this was often a too simple explanation of what was actually happening. The State Department on occasion had to hector and bully Wall Street interests into making investments whose real purpose was to protect our political stake in the Caribbean. One example was the pressure exercised to induce American bankers to take over certain English bonds in Honduras; another was the introduction of American capital into the National Bank of Haiti. Naturally the bankers then expected protection. Whether such investments had been made on their own initiative or through State Department pressure, however, the end result of this dollar diplomacy was the same. American capital exercised a dominant influence over the affairs of the countries concerned and behind American capital stood the United States Government.

Nicaragua, a country in which our interest was particularly great because of the possibility that there might some day be a second isthmian canal, provides the outstanding example of the development of an American fiscal protectorate. It was governed, according to Latin American fashion, by a dictator who not only recklessly plunged his country into debt, but defied his foreign creditors. "I ridicule the United States, laugh at Germany, spit on England," declared the estimable José Zelaya. Foreign intervention under such provoking circumstances was a constant threat, and on the occasion of a revolt against Zelaya in 1909, Secretary of State Knox consequently hurried to forestall any such action. He threw American support behind the insurgents, and as the price for our recognition of the new régime insisted upon the introduction of American capital to refund all foreign debts. When further disturbances broke out in 1911, the United States again took a hand in Nicaraguan affairs, landing naval forces and marines. The little republic was compelled to accept an American collector of customs and also to sign a treaty granting the United States, in return for payment of three million dollars, the right of way for an interoceanic canal, a naval base on the Gulf of Fonseca, and long-term leases of Great Corn and Little Corn Islands.

In conjunction with other moves in the Caribbean to protect American investments, this intervention in Nicaraguan affairs provoked sharp criticism. Despite the political implications of the treaty, the landing of marines was construed as having had no other purpose than to protect the loans of American bankers. The Senate refused to ratify the Nicaraguan treaty — as it had Roosevelt's treaty with the Dominican Republic — and the Taft Administration came to a close without further action being taken.

Confronted with this situation upon coming into office in 1913, Wilson, for all his opposition to dollar diplomacy, could not overlook the political and strategic implications of Secretary Knox's proposed treaty. The agreement with Nicaragua was in fact strengthened by Secretary Bryan through a new clause that would have given the United States control of the Republic's foreign policy as well as its finances — an equivalent of the Platt Amendment governing our relations with Cuba. Observers found the Democrats not merely continuing but expanding the program they had formerly denounced. The *New York Times* sarcastically observed that the dollar diplomacy of the new administration was making that of Taft and Knox "more nearly resemble ten-cent diplomacy." Again the Senate balked, and it was only after the Platt Amendment feature had been eliminated that the Bryan-Chamorro Treaty was finally ratified in 1916.

Nor was this the sum of Wilsonian intervention in the Caribbean. In 1915, a revolt broke out in Haiti in the course of which an angry mob tore President Sam limb from limb because of his massacre of some one hundred and sixty of his political enemies. American naval forces were rushed to the scene, their commander acting under specific orders to place Haiti's political reorganization under American control. "No opportunity for argument should be given to any person or faction," were the President's instructions. "It is desired that you present the plan and see that it is complied with." After the restoration of order by these arbitrary measures, a treaty was concluded establishing another fiscal protectorate.

A year later, further troubles in the Dominican Republic led to even more drastic action than Roosevelt had taken in 1905. The navy took over complete control in the interests of internal stability and debt collection — the latter doubly important as a result of loans made by the National City Bank. Both here and in Haiti, United States marines remained in occupation to uphold law and order and safeguard American interests.

Through such successive moves on the part of Roosevelt, Taft, and Wilson, the United States added to the protectorate originally established over Cuba and our ownership of Puerto Rico, three fiscal protectorates that further consolidated our control over the entire Caribbean. With them should also be included the Republic of Panama, a virtual dependency; the Canal Zone itself, and also the Virgin Islands, purchased from Denmark in 1916 for twenty-five million dollars. Our policy was directed solely toward safeguarding our own national security from the possible encroachment of any European power. The Caribbean had been transformed into an American lake with the defense of the all-important canal route between the Atlantic and the Pacific placed upon what appeared to be an impregnable basis.

Successful as this policy may have been strategically, and also in the economic and social reforms gradually introduced in the nations over which we had established protectorates, the United States nevertheless paid a heavy price for its Caribbean policy. Intervention in Colombia and Nicaragua, Haiti and the Dominican Republic, could hardly have had a more adverse effect upon our general relations with Latin America as a whole. The offer of our services as mediator in various local quarrels and our part in the formation of the Central American Court of Justice were slightly mitigating features of our policy, but protestations of friendship and sympathy made little headway against what Latin America regarded as an aggressive imperialism that paid scant respect to the rights of small nations.

DEFENDING THE OPEN DOOR

Turning from Latin America to the Far East, the policy initiated by Secretary Hay was undergoing during these same years certain shifts and changes under the impact of startling new developments. There was no abandonment of the Open Door, or of the corollary doctrine of support for China's independence, but events revealed that the American people were hardly prepared to uphold our new position by force. Roosevelt, Taft, and Wilson were each in turn forced to modify or reinterpret their original conception of the Open-Door policy as a new far-eastern power rose to challenge American political and commercial interests.

Japan had been prepared to support the Open-Door policy when it was first announced. It was to her interest that China should not be dismembered, and what she feared above everything else in the Far East was the Russian advance in Manchuria. When the United States refused to meet this challenge of Russia's encroachments in North China, indeed, Japan felt compelled to take it up. Her national security was menaced. She fought the Russo-Japanese War in 1904-05 because of an immediate threat to her interests and also to open the path for her own expansion on the Asiatic mainland.

Upon the outbreak of this struggle, American sympathies were largely with Japan. It was believed that in combating Russian aggression in Manchuria and Korea, she was actually upholding the Open Door and China's independence. She was defending, President Roosevelt declared, what "all civilized powers in the East" were seeking. The American press favored the Japanese cause; American bankers lent the Japanese Government money. As Japan went on to win that series of spectacular victories on both land and sea that so dramatically revealed her rising military and naval power, however, a remarkable change occurred in public sentiment. The American people began to see a potential rival in the upstart island kingdom rather than the grateful ward that Japan had heretofore seemed to be. Roosevelt, too, began to revise some of his earlier ideas. It became the aim of his policy to prevent Japan from winning such a complete victory over Russia as to upset entirely the old balance of power in the Pacific. His good offices were made available for bringing about a compromise peace, not only for peace itself, but as the best means of safeguarding the far-eastern interests of the United States.

In this policy he was only partially successful. The two powers finally agreed to discuss peace terms and met in conference at

Portsmouth, New Hampshire in the summer of 1905. Japan had won the war and it was largely through Roosevelt's mediation that her peace terms were not more onerous than they were. The Tokyo Government, for example, agreed to forego any money indemnity. Otherwise, however, the final settlement reflected a decisive Japanese victory. Russia undertook to withdraw entirely from Korea, which thereby fell wholly under Japanese influence and was soon to be annexed; she surrendered all her special rights and privileges in southern Manchuria, and also ceded to Japan the southern half of the island of Sakhalin. The balance of power in eastern Asia had been completely upset. Japan fell heir to the position Russia had formerly held and boasted a firm foothold on the Asiatic mainland.

It was all too soon revealed that Japan had not driven Russia out of southern Manchuria to re-establish the Open Door for American trade. She had taken the first step in an imperialistic advance that had supremacy over all eastern Asia as its ultimate goal. Our Pacific policy was challenged by a far more dangerous rival than any of the European powers whose interests in the Orient remained secondary to other aspects of their foreign relations. For events were to prove that Japan was not afraid to run the risks of war in seeking to dominate China and promote her own territorial expansion.

As these political shifts took place, a further cause for controversy between the United States and Japan arose over the problem of Japanese immigration in the United States. On the West Coast, and particularly in California, there had long been a growing resentment against the influx of Japanese laborers whose willingness to work for exceedingly low wages appeared to threaten the American standard of living. In 1906, it suddenly flared up dangerously and found expression among other anti-Japanese measures in an order of the San Francisco School Board segregating all Oriental children in a special school. The Tokyo Government at once protested vehemently against this act of discrimination which an incensed Japanese people interpreted as an insult to their national honor. Feeling ran high in both countries; and on either side of the Pacific there was jingoistic talk of possible war.

Roosevelt believed the crisis to be a serious one. If the basic issue in Japanese-American relations was the new political rivalry in the Far East, the immigration quarrel might nevertheless have more immediately dangerous consequences. He undertook to meet it, in his famous phrase, by "speaking softly and carrying a big stick." As the first step in such a policy, he persuaded the San Francisco authorities to rescind their order segregating Japanese children and concluded with the Japanese Government the so-called Gentlemen's Agreement of 1907 whereby Japan herself undertook to withhold passports from coolie labor seeking to enter the United States. This done, he sent the American fleet into the Pacific, on the first stage of a projected round-the-world cruise, in order to impress upon the Japanese the full might of American naval power. These moves had a salutary effect. All talk of war quickly subsided. "Every particle of trouble with the Japanese Government and the Japanese press," Roosevelt later wrote, "stopped like magic as soon as they found that our fleet had actually sailed, and was obviously in good trim."

The President's attitude toward Japanese expansion on the Asiatic mainland also showed a strong desire to maintain friendly relations. He had in 1905 agreed in principle to Japan's annexation of Korea, and he now made a further concession which appeared to involve an additional modification of the underlying principles of our far-eastern policy. For while the Root-Takahira Agreement, concluded in 1908, expressly reaffirmed the Open Door in China, it also recognized "the *status quo* in the Pacific area," thereby going far toward accepting Japan's right to the special economic and political concessions she had obtained in Manchuria. The new accord was a realistic acceptance of two facts: first, that Japan had interests in Manchuria which she was prepared to uphold by force, and, second, that those of the United States did not appear sufficiently important to justify active intervention in their support.

"The Open-Door policy in China was an excellent thing," Roosevelt wrote Taft in explanation of his policy two years later, "and I hope it will be a good thing for the future, so far as it can be maintained by diplomatic agreement, but . . . the Open-Door policy, as a matter of fact, completely disappears as soon as a powerful nation determines to disregard it, and is willing to run the risk of war rather than forego its intention."

Taft did not entirely accept Roosevelt's appraisal of the far-eastern situation. When he came into office in 1909, the concern of his administration in promoting foreign trade made maintenance of the Open Door seem too important to be neglected. Dollar diplomacy was practiced in China as well as in Latin America. Secretary of State Knox undertook to safeguard our rights in Manchuria, where the Open Door was slowly swinging shut, by proposing the internationalization of its railroad system. However, this valiant attempt "to strike the pick into the very heart of the far-eastern question," awoke little support outside the United States. Both Japan and Russia, having agreed upon a division of Manchuria into southern and northern spheres of influence, would not brook such interference in their plans. They bluntly rejected the scheme and nothing more came of it. Efforts were also made to protect American financial interests from being frozen out in China itself by insisting upon our right to take part in various loans which the foreign Powers were negotiating with the Chinese Government. By dint of a personal appeal from the President to the Prince Regent of China, American capital was admitted to a proposed four-power banking group for making such loans, but the outbreak of the Chinese Revolution in 1911 interrupted these transactions.

The Taft Administration, whether in Manchuria or in China proper, had little to show in the way of concrete results when its term of office came to an end. Its policy had not aroused much enthusiasm even among American bankers, and the country as a whole was far from impressed. International repercussions, however, were important. Secretary Knox's efforts to revivify the Open-Door policy to support both our financial and commercial interests had newly aroused Japanese resentment. Tokyo was convinced that the United States more than any other nation blocked the fulfillment of its expansionist ambitions. The basic conflict between Japanese imperialism and the Open-Door policy had been strongly emphasized.

Upon his inauguration in 1913, President Wilson immediately abandoned dollar diplomacy. This did not mean either retreat before a Japanese advance or surrender of the principles of our far-eastern policy. On the contrary, Wilson believed that the loans which the State Department had been supporting infringed upon China's sovereignty, and he bluntly informed the bankers that they could no longer count on government protection. In time he was to be compelled to reverse this stand, promoting the organization of a new international banking group, but in 1913 he was determined to keep his hands clean of any financial intervention in China's affairs.

When Japan took advantage of the outbreak of the first World War to renew her imperialistic advance and force new economic and political concessions from China, the Wilson Administration further demonstrated its friendship by seeking to call Japan to account. The United States protested vigorously against Japanese seizure of the former German concession of Kiauchow in the Chinese province of Shantung. It took immediate exception to the Twenty-One Demands whereby Japan tried in 1915 to establish a virtual protectorate over China. The United States would not recognize, Tokyo was bluntly informed, any changes or agreements in the Far East impairing American treaty rights, China's sovereignty, or the Open-Door policy.

Two years later our diplomatic defense of China's integrity, which at least served to soften somewhat Japan's demands on Peking, appeared to be modified by the Lansing-Ishii Agreement. This pact once more reaffirmed both American and Japanese adherence to the principles of the Open Door, but in very ambiguous terms it also stated that the United States recognized Japan's "special interests" in China. Just what this meant was interpreted differently by Secretary Lansing and Viscount Ishii, and the agreement clearly represented an attempt, under the stress of a war which now found the United States and Japan allies against Germany, to reconcile, at least temporarily, differing views that might otherwise prejudice wartime unity. At the Paris Peace Conference, however, President Wilson stood forth without equivocation as a valiant if not entirely successful champion of Chinese interests.

THE MEXICAN CONTROVERSY

Although both our Caribbean and far-eastern policies were highly important in their long-range effect, popular attention during the final years of the progressive era was much more concentrated on quite a different phase of foreign affairs. After a long period of peace and tranquillity, relations with Mexico had become severely strained. On several occasions between 1913 and 1917 the United States appeared on the very verge of actual war. It was avoided because of the conciliatory attitude adopted by Wilson, significant in itself and as revealing future trends in his world policy.

For over a quarter of a century our southern neighbor had been under the iron rule of Porfirio Diaz. He had successfully maintained peace and order; he had welcomed the introduction of foreign capital for the development of Mexico's immense natural resources. American funds had flowed south of the Rio Grande, together with capital from Great Britain, France, and Germany, for the construction of railroads, the opening of oil wells, the development of silver, lead, and copper mines, and the formation of great stock-raising ranches. Total American investments in these various enterprises were estimated in 1910 at $1,000,000,000. More than fifty thousand Americans lived in Mexico and annual trade between the two countries had passed the $100,000,000 mark.

This was only one side of the picture, however. The resources of Mexico were not being developed in the interest of the Mexican people; they were being ruthlessly exploited for the benefit of foreigners. Officialdom was greedily selling out the national wealth for a mess of pottage, while the great majority of Mexicans were landless serfs. Ground under the heel of a tyrannical dictatorship, these peons had no voice whatsoever in either the political or the economic control of their country. Discontent inevitably spread beneath this deceptive façade of peace and prosperity, and widespread forces of revolt were impatiently waiting the day when they could effectively strike down the Diaz Government.

This movement reached a climax toward the close of Taft's

Administration — to the great distress of that peace-loving executive. Under the leadership of Francisco Madero, the revolutionary party marched on Mexico City in 1911, and President Diaz, realizing that the game was up, hastily resigned and fled the country. Madero took over power and in line with his democratic ideals sought to establish a new liberal régime. But Madero was a visionary who proved to be wholly incapable of meeting the practical problems of government. The revolution had let loose forces that he could not control. Within a few months Mexico was seething with new political plots, peasant uprisings, widespread violence, attacks on foreigners and their property.

Out of this welter of confusion, there gradually grew a strong counter-revolutionary movement, supported by the foreign capitalists who feared Madero's projected reforms. Its leader was Victoriano Huerta, and early in 1913 the forces under his command overthrew Madero and installed themselves in power. A few days later, Madero was shot down in cold blood, under circumstances giving every indication of official assassination, and Huerta set himself up as Provisional President. Promising the restoration of law and order, together with protection of foreign concessions, he at once asked recognition of his new régime.

The United States had watched these developments with alarm. Our financial stake in Mexico was important — almost four times the total of all investments in the Caribbean. The Madero Administration had been sharply warned that it would be held strictly accountable for American lives and property, and troops had been massed on the Mexican border. In the face of an active demand for immediate intervention, President Taft had nevertheless held firm. Although he admitted in his private correspondence that if the new Government could not establish control it would have to be shown that "there is a God in Israel and He is on duty," Taft was reluctant to undertake this avenging rôle. The need to do so appeared to be at least temporarily averted when Huerta came into power, and Taft happily passed on the problem of Mexican relations to the incoming Democratic Administration.

President Wilson's attitude was most clearly stated in an important address at Mobile, Alabama, in October, 1913. In this speech he held out the hand of friendship to all Latin American peoples, caustically criticizing intervention in their affairs and definitely pledging that the United States would never again seek one additional foot of territory by conquest. "We must show ourselves friends," the President stated, "by comprehending their interest whether it squares with our interest or not. It is a very perilous thing to determine the foreign policy of a nation in the terms of material interest. It is not only unfair to those with whom you are dealing, but it is degrading as regards your own actions." The President was thinking of more than Mexico in his address, but he was to apply his principles far more determinedly in our relations with Mexico than in those with the little republics of the Caribbean where he so soon found himself following the lead of Roosevelt and Taft.

His policy, directed specifically toward Mexico, was based upon a refusal either to countenance active intervention in that country or to recognize a government that had come into power through violence. Departing from the traditional American doctrine, originally laid down by Thomas Jefferson, that recognition automatically followed establishment of political power, he would not accept the Huerta Government simply because it was in *de facto* control. The United States was the custodian "of the principles which have made men free and governments just," Wilson declared. " . . . We dare not turn from the principle that morality and not expediency is the thing that must guide us and that we will never condone iniquity because it is most convenient to do so. . . . "

At the same time, American citizens were advised to withdraw from Mexico to lessen the risk to lives and property, and an embargo on the shipment of arms originally adopted by Congress was expressly reaffirmed. Whatever the provocation, the United States would preserve an attitude of watchful waiting. "We can afford," the President said, "to exercise the self-restraint of a really great nation which realizes its own strength and scorns to use it."

An immediate storm broke out in the United States as the implications of Wilson's policy became clear. Financial interests with large capital investments in Mexico, especially the oil industry, loudly demanded a course of action that would protect their property. There should be either recognition and effective support for Huerta, it was asserted, or intervention enabling the United States itself to restore order. As the rule of violence in Mexico inspired new revolutionary outbreaks and further attacks on Americans, public opinion generally swung more and more in line behind such demands for action. The Hearst press, not un-influenced by its proprietor's extensive oil interests in Mexico, was beating the tom-tom of war as it had in 1898. Screaming head-lines told of brutal assaults upon Americans and the wanton de-struction of lives and property. The President was fiercely at-tacked for his weak-kneed caution, for his deadly drifting, for his lack of virility. One of his critics called him "a damn vegetarian." "He kissed the blood-stained hand that slapped his face," shouted the excited Theodore Roosevelt. But Wilson refused to be budged. "I have to pause and remind myself that I am President of the United States," he told his secretary, "and not of a small group of Americans with vested interests in Mexico."

The only change in his policy was the gradual adoption of more active measures to support a new political faction, the Con-stitutionalists, who were seeking Huerta's overthrow under the leadership of Venustiano Carranza. The resignation of Huerta was formally demanded, and in February, 1914, the arms em-bargo was lifted to enable his opponents to obtain supplies. Still the "desperate brute" clung to power and still Mexico was a scene of widespread disorder. Attacks on foreigners continued (more than seventy Americans were to lose their lives between 1913 and 1915) and the clamor for intervention grew every day more insistent.

Finally, in April, 1914, an incident occurred that even Wilson felt he could not ignore. A boatload of sailors from an American naval vessel at Tampico were arrested by the Mexican authorities for alleged violation of certain provisions of martial law. While they were immediately released, their commanding officer, Admiral Mayo, demanded official apologies and a twenty-one-gun salute to the American flag. Huerta was prepared to apologize, but he refused the salute. Public opinion at home interpreted this as an insult to the national honor and clamored for revenge. "I'd make them salute the flag," shouted Senator Chilton of West Virginia, "if we had to blow up the whole place." Reluctantly accepting the situation created by Admiral Mayo's ultimatum, Wilson went before Congress and asked for authority to take retaliatory measures.

The decision to intervene on the basis of such a minor incident, while refusing to do so to protect American lives and property, placed the President in a strange position. He apparently believed that if national honor were not vigorously upheld the moral authority of the United States — to which he gave such transcendent importance — would be seriously weakened. He made it clear that the Tampico incident was but the culmination of a long series of outrages, and he also declared — as he was later to do in the case of Germany — that our quarrel was not with the Mexican people but with their government. Perhaps even Wilson's forbearance was becoming quite humanly strained and he felt that a little chastisement was in order on general principles. "I am going to teach the South American republics," he had once exclaimed in a moment of exasperation, "to elect good men."

In any event, Mexico was blockaded by American naval vessels, and when an attempt was made to smuggle arms into Vera Cruz from a German ship, the order went forth to bombard and capture the city. It was occupied in April, 1914, at the cost of the lives of eighteen United States marines. Was this war? Diplomatic relations with Mexico were at once severed and an hysterical wave of excitement engulfed both nations. Wilson's position could hardly have been more difficult. He was still determined to stand by his original policy. He resolutely opposed active war. Yet he could not completely back down, having gone as far as he had. At this point, Argentina, Brazil, and Chile offered their joint services for mediation and the President eagerly grasped at this possible means of escape from his dilemma. He accepted the offer of the ABC Powers at once. While the resulting conference was not in itself entirely successful, the increasing pressure upon Huerta at last forced him to resign, and in August he was succeeded by Carranza.

While the *New York Times* stated that these developments constituted "such a triumph for President Wilson's much-misunderstood policy as to astonish even the staunchest supporters of the President," the restoration of orderly conditions within Mexico actually appeared almost as distant as ever. New contestants sprang up to challenge Carranza's right to the presidency. While United States' recognition in October, 1915 (accorded in co-operation with the principal Latin American countries), strengthened his position, he was unable to quell these disturbances. A former supporter, Francisco Villa, headed a formidable revolt and in angry defiance of the aid accorded Carranza by the United States, he began a series of systematic attacks upon American citizens. In January, 1916, he took eighteen Americans from a train near Santa Ysabel and summarily executed them; two months later he crossed the American border to raid the town of Columbus, New Mexico, leaving seventeen dead in his wake.

Once again there arose an outraged demand for intervention to restore order in Mexico. Villa's escapades immeasurably strengthened the hand of those who declared that Wilson's entire policy had been a failure, and that the United States could no longer avoid the responsibility of going in and cleaning up Mexico once and for all. The entire country should be occupied, it was stated, even if it called for raising an army of half a million men. Under such pressure, Wilson sought and obtained in March the grudging permission of Carranza to dispatch a punitive expedition into Mexican territory. Under the command of General John J. Pershing, ordered to take Villa dead or alive, it crossed the border in pursuit of the elusive rebel.

Despite the permission originally granted, the attitude of the Carranzistas became increasingly hostile as General Pershing penetrated deep within Mexico. Friction inevitably developed between the United States and Mexican Governments and there was every possibility of such a tense situation leading to war. The militia was called out and stationed on the Mexican border. Whatever the consequences of this move might have been, however, they were averted by the rise of a much more serious danger to the United States. Germany was preparing to embark on her program of unrestricted submarine warfare, and with this crisis at hand, President Wilson felt compelled to recall General Pershing and seek friendship with Mexico in order to strengthen the national front for possible European hostilities. Diplomatic relations with Mexico were once again renewed in January, 1917, and for the time being at least border troubles subsided.

Wilson's policy had not permanently settled anything. The problem of Mexican relations was to arise again in 1919 and 1920, and remain to plague successive post-war administrations. But he had preserved peace. His refusal to be stampeded into intervention in behalf of American financial interests had in considerable measure counteracted Latin American fears aroused by our actions in the Caribbean. He had stood by the pledges made in his Mobile speech. He succeeded in guiding the policy of the United States along lines that served to encourage the growth of constitutional liberty in Mexico, instead of looking solely to the promotion of our own material interests.

10

American Life: On the Eve of War

Two Million Automobiles

ON THE EVE of the first World War, one of the most characteristic features of American life appeared to be its rapid tempo. There was nothing new about this: observers had for a century boasted or complained about it. Nevertheless, the pace was growing faster and faster. Streetcars and subways made "step lively" the *leit motif* of city life; suburban commuters were always on the run to make their morning or evening trains. The telephone, now almost universal through six million nation-wide installations, was responsible for a quickening in communications comparable to that in transportation. Although radio broadcasting was still in the future, the wireless linked ships and land. The drive for greater efficiency in manufacturing processes was introducing the speed-up, the stretch-out, and the assembly line, directly affecting the daily life of millions of industrial workers.

There were innumerable new time-saving gadgets in the office and in the home: adding machines and dictaphones, vacuum cleaners and safety razors. The quick lunch had long since become an institution. "This is a get-things-done-quick age," the magazine *Life* declared. "It is a ready-to-put-on-and-wear age, a just-add-hot-water-and-serve age, a new-speed-record-every-day age, a take-it-or-leave-it-I'm-very-busy age."

The automobile, however, was more responsible than any other one thing for this growing emphasis upon speed. It was no longer a plaything of the rich, and it could not be said, as had Woodrow Wilson in 1907, that "nothing had spread socialistic feeling in this country more than the use of the automobile." For small cars were being manufactured at a price — $490 for the famous Model T Fords — that made them widely available to the general public. Even though a still greater expansion in transportation by automobile, truck and bus was to develop in the nineteen-twenties, there were almost two million cars in 1914, and annual production had risen to over three hundred and fifty thousand. Automobiles were being increasingly used by businessmen and traveling salesmen, by suburban commuters and country dwellers. Farmers were beginning to discover their usefulness in taking produce to town; factory workers were beginning to adopt them to go to and from their work. The automobile was gradually breaking down the isolation of rural areas, linking the farm and the city, and further stimulating the good-roads movement that was changing the face of the countryside. The habits and ways of life of the entire nation were in the process of being revolutionized.

The ubiquitous Fords — universally known as flivvers or tin lizzies — inspired a host of jokes. Turned out at ever-increasing speed — the five hundred thousandth Model T came off the assembly line in 1914 — it was said that the enterprising manufacturer planned to paint them yellow so that he could sell them in bunches like bananas. Then there was the Illinois farmer who stripped the tin roof off his barn and sent it to Detroit, receiving the prompt reply: "While your car was an exceptionally bad wreck, we shall be able to complete repairs and return it by the first of the week." Mr. Ford did not object to these jokes: he had them published in pamphlet form. His sales boomed.

At the annual automobile show in 1914, eighty-four different manufacturers exhibited their models. There were Studebakers, Cadillacs, Buicks, Pierce Arrows, Hudsons, Oaklands, Locomobiles, Wintons . . . The price range was anywhere from several thousand dollars for the new "streamlined limousines" to $395 for the little open Saxon. While the inexpensive closed car of today had not yet been developed, there were innumerable improvements over the original automobile. Self-starters had been introduced, making it possible for women to drive as easily as men. One-man tops, klaxon horns, and even electric gear shifts were advertised.

Touring was still limited for all this progress. The Automobile Club of America recommended trips of one hundred and thirty miles as constituting a good weekend's motoring. The open road and the open car, the likelihood of breakdowns, and the inevitable tire trouble involved all sorts of discomforts, notwithstanding the cheery promises of manufacturers. It was still the day of linen dusters (natural and oyster shades), veils, goggles, wind cuffs, laprobes . . .

THE MOVIES COME OF AGE

Just as the automobile was driving out the horse-and-buggy, so the new invention of moving pictures was slowly pushing melodrama and old-fashioned vaudeville into the background, sounding the death-knell of the traveling road companies of the turn of the century. The urban theater still maintained its more cultured following. Mrs. Fiske, John Drew, Otis Skinner, Sothern and Marlowe were on the legitimate stage; there was a vogue for Gilbert and Sullivan, and both the Provincetown Players and the Washington Square Players were founded in 1915. But the movies were coming into their own as a cheap and popular entertainment with which stage plays, either in the city theaters or in Main Street opera houses, could not compete successfully.

The beginnings of the movies may be traced back to the days of the first horseless carriages. In the early eighteen-nineties Thomas Edison was experimenting with a contraption that gradually evolved into the "vitascope" and was capable of throwing what were then called "living pictures" on a large screen. The novelty of these dim and flickering shots of sneezing babies and dancing girls, of prize fights and street scenes, soon wore off. The first movies were relegated to the darkened back rooms of penny arcades for the amusement of poorer workers in the big cities who could not afford the melodrama and musical comedy of the popular theaters.

With improved techniques and the production of picture stories, initiated with *The Great Train Robbery* in 1903, the movies eventually graduated to a new class of small five-cent theaters called "nickelodeons." They had an astonishing growth, and with increasingly better films, the public began flocking to their performances. When about this same time the movies discovered love themes — *Cupid's Barometer, The Gaieties of Divorce* — things began to look up even more.

On the eve of the first World War, the nickelodeons ("two-reel features, two comedies, and an illustrated song — all for a nickel") were in turn giving way to elaborate and higher-priced movie theaters ("a concert orchestra will play incidental music harmonizing with the various themes of the pictures"). The star system was introduced. Mary Pickford led all the rest as "Little Mary — America's Sweetheart," but there were a host of other glamorous figures on the silver screen. Broncho Billy and William S. Hart thundered across the western plains; Theda Bara aroused new and disturbing emotions in at least the male element of the movie audiences, and the appearance in *Tillie's Punctured Romance* of a pathetically appealing little man, with cane, derby, clumsy shoes, and baggy trousers, launched the triumphant career of Charlie Chaplin. The production of far better pictures was also marked in 1914 by the filming of *The Birth of a Nation,* a sensationally successful movie whose earnings were eventually to total eighteen million dollars. While it established new standards of entertainment, the most popular films of the day were still the weekly adventure serials — *Dolly of the Dailies, Lucile Love, The Perils of Pauline* —

> Poor Pauline, I pity poor Pauline.
> First they tied her to a tree,
> Then they sent her out to sea.
> I wonder what the end will be —
> Poor Pauline . . .

THE EMANCIPATION OF WOMEN

While speeding automobiles and flickering movies were a sign and symbol of the advance of the mechanical age, other new developments were causing just as significant changes in very different phases of social life. The continuing progress of science and invention had at once served to relieve women of even more of their traditional chores than had been the case in 1900, and also to open up for them increasing opportunities in the world of business. There was no longer anything new or strange about women in offices, stores, business or even the professions. They were making their way in the world on terms of increasing equality with men. But their new independence in these days was in many quarters believed to be highly ominous for the future of America. "Modern womanhood," cried the alarmists, "shirks its duty."

The divorce rate was rising. It had almost doubled since the opening of the century and was higher than in any other country except Japan. Margaret Sanger had started her campaign for birth control, and while the first issue of *The Woman Rebel* was barred from the mails, observers believed that they saw the dangerous consequences of this agitation in a declining birth rate. A magazine writer sadly lamented that "having a family is not an American ideal." Theodore Roosevelt denounced race suicide.

Whatever the effect of the emancipation of women on family life, divorce, and the birth rate, relief from much household drudgery afforded those who did not work increasing leisure.

There was a tremendous expansion in women's clubs; membership in those associated with the General Federation of Women's Clubs rose to over a million. The temper of the times was also reflected in the feeling that reform and politics, rather than cultural pursuits, should be the principal interest of these organizations. Not Dante's *Inferno* but the social order, one club leader stated, should be the twentieth-century woman's field of study. "Suffragettes March on Capitol" was a rival headline to the murder of an Austrian Archduke on June 29, 1914.

These years also saw women asserting their independence by going in for more active sports, flouting the convention that they had always to be escorted by men in public places, and taking up cigarette smoking.

EDUCATION AND SCIENCE

Educational advance, scientific activities, intellectual and artistic ferment were further evidence of the period's expansive spirit. Between 1898 and 1914, the number of children in public schools rose from fifteen to twenty million and the high-school population doubled. The "little red schoolhouse" was giving way to larger consolidated schools, in part due to the introduction of school buses in outlying districts. The enforcement of compulsory education laws was being tightened up throughout the country. Yet at the same time that one in every twenty-five persons between nineteen and twenty-three was attending college, the average period of schooling for the population as a whole was only six and a half years.

The airplane was still in a highly experimental stage in 1914. Eleven years earlier, Orville and Wilbur Wright had made the first successful flight in a heavier-than-air machine at Kitty Hawk, North Carolina, but further progress in American aviation had been relatively slow. Europe showed much more interest in flying than the United States. Glenn H. Curtiss, however, designed a hydroplane whose flight from Albany to New York won the inventor a ten-thousand-dollar prize, and only the difficulty of keeping the motor cool by some other means than having the assistant pilot lower a can to draw up sea water, kept him from attempting a trans-Atlantic crossing. The outbreak of the European war impelled airplane designers to embark upon new designs. "The potential results of swooping aircraft armed to the teeth with death-dealing bullets are staggering," one observer declared. "Where will this lead?"

The achievements of science were not only reflected in the practical application of new means of power, but in discoveries and fresh developments (winning Nobel prizes for three Americans) in chemistry, physics, biology, and bacteriology. In medicine particularly there were important forward steps. The death rate in typhoid, tuberculosis, diptheria, and scarlet fever was greatly reduced. X-ray and radium experiments held out hopes of finding a cure for cancer. And among other engagements in the constant warfare of science against disease, Doctor Charles Stiles won one of the most publicized victories of that day. Having discovered what contemporary newspapers happily called "the germ of laziness," he initiated a campaign against hookworm that was to have epochal consequences for the South.

Research and study also led to a broadening of ideas in the social sciences. In history and sociology, political science and economics, there were new co-operative undertakings, important studies were published, and scholarly work was encouraged in all the universities. Psychology first began to feel the impact of the new ideas that were introduced with psychoanalysis. Sigmund Freud visited the United States in 1909, and intellectuals were discussing inhibitions and complexes.

ART AND LITERATURE

Possibly this had a relationship to the strange stirrings that began to affect literary and artistic circles. Young poets encouraged a vogue for *vers libre* and young artists experimented with post-impressionism, cubism, and futurism. The new art forms were first introduced from the Continent at the New York Armory Show in 1913. They were interpreted by painters as an expression of the dynamics of modern industrialism, but to the uninitiated they remained completely unintelligible abstractions:

> Power that breaks like a great wave in spray —
> And what it means we'll let Tomorrow say!

Something has already been said about the literature, both fiction and magazine articles, inspired by the spirit of progressive reform. Otherwise the period was not a very significant one in this respect, even though the publication of books increased and Andrew Carnegie made possible through his benefactions the building of a thousand libraries. Poetry, however, had something of a renaissance on the eve of war.

Edgar Lee Masters wrote his *Spoon River Anthology,* Carl Sandburg published *Chicago,* Robert Frost depicted the New England scene in *North of Boston,* and Vachel Lindsay wrote *The Congo* and *General William Booth Enters Heaven.* The popular novels of the day were still largely romances, although with a contemporary rather than historical background, and those which reached the best-seller lists seldom concerned themselves with social problems. Harold Bell Wright, whose *The Winning of Barbara Worth* sold two million copies, led the field among popular authors, but he was closely matched by Zane Grey, Rex Beach, and Gene Stratton Porter. *Pollyanna* was published in 1913, but the best seller both in that year and in 1914, as reported by the *Bookman,* was Winston Churchill's *The Inside of the Cup.*

While the proportion of fiction to all books published declined, between 1901 and 1914, from twenty-seven to less than nine per cent, the explanation was to be found, not in a more serious-minded public, but in the continued growth of low-priced magazines publishing fictional stories. They had become legion in number and their circulation tripled and quadrupled that of a few years earlier. The *Saturday Evening Post* was on its way with over a million readers, and even this total was doubled by the *Ladies' Home Journal.* There was a beginning of new adventure magazines — westerns and detective stories.

Newspapers were also reporting larger circulations — the

nation-wide total was double that of 1900 — and while sensationalism was somewhat toned down, both Sunday and daily editions
were running more features, adding rotogravure sections, bed-
time stories, and women's pages (with Beatrice Fairfax's "Advice
to the Lovelorn" or Laura Jean Libbey's "First Aid to Wounded
Hearts"). Countless readers first turned to the Sunday comics,
where they followed the engrossing adventures of Buster Brown,
Happy Hooligan, Foxy Granpa, Bringing Up Father, and the
Katzenjammer Kids.

SPORTS, RAGTIME, FASHIONS . . .

Apart from such forms of recreation as the movies, motoring
and reading, sports were booming. The Giants and the White
Sox made a triumphal world tour; American athletes swept the
field in track events at the Olympic Games; intercollegiate football became even more popular after a death roll of forty-four
players in a single season forced revision of the rules, and Jack
Johnson won the prize-fight championship. "He said he'd bring
home the bacon," exclaimed his rapturous mother, "and the honey
boy has gone and done it."

A dancing craze engulfed the country in pre-war years. One
of the most popular tunes was "Everybody's Doin' It" — and this
was almost literally true. Mr. and Mrs. Vernon Castle were the
bright particular stars of the day, introducing the hesitation waltz,
the tango and the maxixe. Ragtime and the animal dances, however, became the popular rage — the fox trot and the bunny hug,
the lame duck, the turkey trot, and the grizzly bear. "Are we
going to the dogs by the ragtime route?" asked the *New York
Sun.* "A substitute for the Turkish bath and the masseuse," said
another critic; "threatening to force grace, decorum, and decency
out of the ballrooms of America." But there was no withstanding
"The Devil's Ball," or "The Dixy Rag."

> Come on and hear, come on and hear
> Alexander's ragtime band;
> Come on and hear, come on and hear,
> It's the best band in the land.

As for women's fashions, long tunic dresses, often trimmed with fur and "slashed in a modest way to give freedom to the feet," had succeeded in driving out the "short, outlandish, tight-gripping hobble skirts" before war broke out in Europe. There had been what some fashion writers considered an advance in hats. It was apparently upward — to new and astounding heights where Ostrich Feather Fantasies awed all beholders. The more epochal changes in women's clothes were along interior lines. The press reported "hot debate over corset"; the new silk stockings were decried as "the foundation of needless extravagance"; and the President of the New York Cotton Exchange stated that "the scantiness of female underclothing has reduced consumption of cotton fabrics by twelve yards per adult female."

Contemporary newspapers published situation wanted notices for "Chauffeur — American, sober and reliable; makes repairs any car. Pierce Arrow preferred"; "Stenographer — experienced, neat, accurate; not afraid of hard work — $10"; and "Tutor — desires position as guide for tourists in Europe." Advertisers sang the praises of Arrow Collars, B.V.D.'s, and the elegant, ready-made suits of Hart, Schaffner & Marx. Others inquired, "Good Morning — Have You Used Pear's Soap?," advised the use of Listerine, and called graphic attention to wrist watches, Parker Fountain pens, and Lucky Strike roll cut tobacco.

Pingpong and pianolas were all the rage. Whist grew into auction bridge. A mild sensation was caused by the exhibition of "September Morn," a painting whose only notable feature was that the subject, however demure, was "clothed as she was born." Popular songs of the day were, "My Wife's Gone to the Country," "O, You Great Big Beautiful Doll," "The Trail of the Lonesome Pine," and "Give My Regards to Broadway."

The basic factor in our national development during these years just before the first World War was further industrial advance, and the underlying spirit was one of progressive reform. This inventiveness, vitality, and spirit of change were largely responsible for the revolution in transportation and entertainment typified by the automobile and moving picture; the feminine quest for social equality; advance in education and insurgency in art; the growth of newspapers and magazines; and the pulsating rhythm of rag-time. Whatever else may be said of America in these days, there was a remarkable zest and drive in national life which found expression in changing social customs as well as in business advance and political reform. "To stay where you are in this country," a contemporary commented, "you must keep moving."

The Stakes
of World Power

11

The Challenge of War

THE ROAD TO INTERVENTION

IN HIS ANNUAL MESSAGE to Congress in December, 1913, President Wilson undertook to review the general international situation. It was his considered opinion that "a growing cordiality and sense of community interest among the nations" foreshadowed "an age of settled peace." Eight months later the first World War broke out. Its tragic implications were only partially realized by an astounded American public, and it was not believed possible that the United States could become directly involved. The President called upon the country for a neutrality that would be "impartial in thought as well as in action."

Why Wilson's sanguine expectations in 1913 were so completely wrong is no part of our story; it is our concern why the United States departed from the neutrality confidently proclaimed in August, 1914. The immediately compelling cause was Germany's adoption of unrestricted submarine warfare early in 1917. In his message to Congress on April 2 of that year, the President solemnly stated that the torpedoing of American ships constituted war against the United States. From Germany's point of view, however, this country had already anticipated war by supplying the Allies with the munitions that threatened her downfall and by refusing to hold England to that strict accountability in the observance of international law which it insisted upon in Germany's case. However the issue of immediate responsibility be resolved, it is clear that the real question is a much deeper one: Why did the United States align itself so definitely with the Allies that Germany should attack our shipping in 1917 and the United States accept such attacks as the challenge of war?

Three closely related and highly complicated factors came into play, factors generally paralleling those that had motivated our foreign policy since 1900. In respect to economic interests, subordinate as they may have been to other considerations, the United States had acquired a huge stake in an Allied victory. The immense export trade in war supplies built up since 1914 and financed in large part by loans to England and France, geared our national economy so closely to the cause of the Allies that it was believed that their defeat would have a catastrophic effect upon American trade, industry, and agriculture. Those who were prepared to fight to promote our economic well-being seized upon Germany's announcement of unrestricted submarine warfare as final justification for their stand.

From the point of view of persons primarily concerned with American political power, apart from matters of trade and commerce, a German victory seemed to hold out a definite threat to our national security. It would have transferred control of the Atlantic from an increasingly friendly power, Great Britain, to one whose ambitious imperialism we already had reason to suspect. Germany would have been in a position to challenge our interests in both Latin America and the Far East. In the light of such considerations, submarine warfare was interpreted as a threatening bid for German naval supremacy.

Finally, there was the idealistic viewpoint. Most Americans had come to identify the cause for which the Allies were fighting with that of democracy and peace. They felt an Allied victory was imperative, not only to safeguard the democratic way of life in the United States, but to make good its future promise for all the world. In their eyes Germany's ruthless naval policy was conclusive proof that justice and decency could not be maintained until this aggressive imperialism was overthrown. "We are," the President stated, "but one of the champions of right."

The American people went to war in 1917 — for it was the American people and not just their Government — because the affront to national honor and threat to national safety in Germany's attacks upon our shipping served to translate into direct action their slowly matured belief, arrived at by these various paths, that the defeat of Germany was more important than the maintenance of their own peace.

SENTIMENT AND PROPAGANDA

On the outbreak of European hostilities in August, 1914, the first reaction of the American people was one of shocked horror, only slightly mitigated by our heartfelt thankfulness for the comforting barrier of the Atlantic Ocean. The nation was determined to remain neutral. The placid impartiality in thought urged by President Wilson proved to be a different matter. It was soon evident that public opinion predominantly favored the Allied cause — not universally but predominantly. There was sympathy for Germany among members of the important German-American bloc in our population, totaling more than eight million, and that country's contributions to civilization had won her a host of devoted non-German friends and admirers. The Central Powers were also favored by many anti-British elements, notably the large numbers of Irish who did not so much love Germany as they hated Great Britain. Nevertheless, our sense of kinship with the English people and a deep sentimental sympathy for France provided the basis for a steady growth in pro-Ally sentiment.

The ties of language and race with England had been supplemented by the trend of world events since the opening of the twentieth century. The end of rivalry in the Caribbean, and a general policy of co-operation in the Far East, emphasized the underlying community of interest existing between the Anglo-Saxon powers. We might still be rivals in trade and commerce, but British imperialism no longer threatened our own spheres of influence, and the British fleet upheld a balance of world power leaving the United States entirely free in the Western Hemisphere. On the other hand, the foreign policy pursued by Germany had on various occasions appeared to run directly counter to American interests. In Samoa, in the Philippines, and in the Far East, even in the Caribbean, minor clashes presaged a day when the Kaiser's imperialistic ambitions might lead to more direct and open conflict. Apart from these considerations, the

United States had become a world power whose widespread interests would necessarily be gravely affected, if not directly endangered, by any change in the *status quo*. British imperialism was static; German imperialism was dynamic. As Henry Adams had long since foreseen, the substitution of German military might for British naval supremacy in the European balance of power would have had the most menacing potentialities.

Once the war had started, actual events in Europe directed public opinion more and more into channels already carved out. Germany's invasion of Belgium in violation of definite commitments to safeguard Belgium's neutrality carried its own lesson as to the attitude of a resurgent militarism. The German Chancellor's blunt reference to the treaty of neutrality as "a scrap of paper" merely underscored his Government's callous disregard of international morality. When a German submarine sank the *Lusitania*, pride of the British marine, with an appalling loss of innocent lives, the American people were still more horrified. "The torpedo that sank the *Lusitania* also sank Germany in the opinion of mankind . . ." the *Nation* declared. "It is at once a crime and a monumental folly. . . . She has affronted the moral sense of the world and sacrificed her standing among nations."

Allied propaganda played insistently upon our underlying sympathy for the people of England and France; it subtly fed our latent hostility toward Germany. Through the great advantage of a common language and also complete control of the cables, the British were able to place their own interpretations of events before the American public so successfully that our picture of the war became wholly one-sided. The United States was told, with such insistent reiteration that it came to be generally believed, that the Central Powers were entirely responsible for starting the war. Every possible emphasis was placed upon those developments — such as the invasion of Belgium — which served to build up the idea of German aggression. Atrocity stories were magnified without compunction to convince the American public that the Germans, individually and collectively, were bloodthirsty Huns. In a report issued in 1915 with the authoritative backing of Viscount Bryce, fantastic tales since largely disproved were told of

Belgian babies with their hands cut off, crucified Canadian soldiers, and German corpse factories.

Against this picture of German aggression and ruthlessness, there was held up the contrasting picture of the Allies fighting humanely for the maintenance of peace and justice. The English propagandists knew the strength of American idealism. They completely suppressed discussion of their own territorial aims and of the treaties which provided for division of the anticipated spoils of war. For American consumption the emphasis was always placed upon preservation of the rights of democracy and the independence of small nations.

Germany was peculiarly inept in this war on the propaganda front. Her agents simply did not understand the American mind. Their attempts to influence public opinion were easily seen through and when they sought to retrieve such failures by sabotaging the munitions industry, they made the irremediable blunder of being caught. Soon after the discovery, in July, 1915, of a briefcase full of damning secret documents, carelessly left in a New York elevated railway car by one of the chief German agents, the trail of propaganda and sabotage was directly traced to both the German and Austrian embassies at Washington. Secretary Lansing demanded the recall of the German military and naval attachés, and intimated to the Austrian Government that Ambassador Dumba was no longer welcome. As a contemporary versifier expressed it:

> O Constantin Theodor Dumba,
> You've roused Uncle Sam from his slumba:
> That letter you wrote
> Got the old fellow's goat —
> Now his path you'll no longer encumba.

The influence of propaganda upon public opinion between 1914 and 1917 nevertheless remains hard to assess. The impact of actual events certainly had greater effect than any interpretation of them. Even had the Allies not made such skillful use of enemy violations of international law, the harsh facts of German policy spoke for themselves. The American people could not reconcile them with their own ideas of justice and decency, unrealistic though such ideas may sometimes have been. And basically more important, the British were building upon a sympathy that already existed while the Germans were combating a prejudice whose roots were deeper than the war.

There remained throughout the period from 1914 to 1917 a strong body of opinion that considered the European quarrel so little our concern that we had no justification for taking sides. Especially in the Midwest there were many men and women, and not only among those who remained consistently pro-German because of their racial inheritance, who felt that the responsibility of the Allies for the war was fully as great as that of Germany. The possibility of Allied defeat and the collapse of British sea power did not represent for them the menace to our national liberties fearfully held out by pro-Ally sympathizers. They were largely indifferent to the pervasive influence of British propaganda.

The gradual swing of the country as a whole into the Allied camp was attested, however, by newspaper editorials, magazine articles, the statements of public men, and all other available criteria for measuring popular opinion. President Wilson could not himself maintain his professed impartiality in thought. "England is fighting our fight," he stated privately in 1915. The entire cabinet was pro-Ally with the possible exception of Secretary of State Bryan, and upon his resignation at the time of the *Lusitania* incident, no more outspoken friend of the Anglo-French cause than his successor could have been found. Secretary Lansing believed firmly that German absolutism was a menace to American liberties and democratic institutions. "In dealing with the British Government," he later wrote, "there was always in my mind the conviction that we would ultimately become an ally of Great Britain. . . ." Among other close advisers of the President, Colonel E. M. House, who was to be sent abroad as a special emissary, was equally convinced that Germany's defeat was necessary for the peace and security of the world, while our envoy in London, Ambassador Page, was so much of an Anglophile that even Wilson once said that he badly needed "a bath in American opinion." On at least one occasion in presenting an official protest against

British infringements of our neutral rights, Page sought to explain it away as of little significance, and then aided the British Foreign Secretary in drawing up a proper answer.

National leaders outside the Administration were no less favorable toward the Allies. No one could have supported their cause more strongly throughout the entire period than Theodore Roosevelt. Leaders in industry and finance, long before economic ties could be held entirely responsible for their views, also emphatically upheld the Entente. J. P. Morgan and Company, it was later stated by Thomas W. Lamont, one of the partners, "had never for one moment been neutral; we didn't know how to be. From the very start we did everything that we could to contribute to the cause of the Allies."

Tightening Economic Bonds

Entirely apart from all political or idealistic considerations, our ties with the Allies were steadily strengthened through the early years of the war by the tightening bonds of economic interest. The circumstances of British control of the seas, whatever might have happened under other conditions, directed our trade and commerce almost entirely into Allied channels. The dictates of material self-interest as well as sympathy made us want to see the Allies win. Soon after the start of war the attempt was made to prevent such considerations from governing or affecting national policy through the adoption of an arms embargo. It failed. We were unwilling to forego the advantages of the munitions trade. "We need it," the editor of the *Annalist* bluntly stated, "for the profits it yields."

While the Wilson Administration did not support an embargo, it at least sought for a time to prevent the extension of financial credits to any belligerent nation. As early as August, 1914, J. P. Morgan and Company asked what the Government's attitude would be toward its giving credit facilities to the Allies. Upon the advice of Secretary Bryan, who feared the implications of such a move upon the neutrality that he was determined to uphold at all cost, Wilson withheld official approval. "Loans by

American bankers to any foreign government which is at war," a presidential memorandum stated, "are inconsistent with the true spirit of neutrality."

Enforcement of this decree would in time have meant curtailment of our foreign trade and the collapse of the burgeoning wartime prosperity, just as surely as adoption of an embargo. Representatives of the international bankers consequently made every effort to persuade the President that it was entirely impracticable. It would force the Allies to look elsewhere for their supplies and curtail our commerce, they stated, "at the time of our greatest need and greatest opportunity." The President thereupon reversed his original stand. In October he indirectly informed the bankers that while the Government would not expressly sanction granting credits, it would not forbid them. J. P. Morgan at once arranged to act as purchasing agent in the United States for the British and French Governments, extending ample credits to enable them to meet their immediate needs.

Short-time credits did not long prove sufficient to finance this rapidly increasing trade. The bankers were soon back in Washington seeking permission to float long-term loans on the Allies' account. They had staunch supporters in official circles. "Our duty is to protect the commerce of the United States," Secretary of the Treasury McAdoo flatly declared. In his opinion it had become imperative that outstanding short-term credits should be refunded and public loans officially authorized to prevent the collapse of American prosperity.

Wilson had invited this situation. He was now faced with a condition, not a theory: the maintenance of national well-being made impossible the strict neutrality he had originally envisaged. With sympathy for the Allies already bolstering national self-interest, he again capitulated to the bankers' demands. J. P. Morgan acted quickly. Following the arrival in September, 1915, of an Anglo-French financial mission, he formed a banking syndicate to underwrite the purchase of a $500,000,000 bond issue jointly guaranteed by the British and French Governments. The day was saved for the munitions trade and for American prosperity. There were uneasy voices prophesying war as a consequence of such open support for the Allied cause, but the die had been cast.

Other loans to the Allies followed in due course as their purchases of war supplies steadily mounted. In the first eighteen months of the European conflict our export trade in munitions amounted to $500,000,000; between January, 1916, and March, 1917, it was $1,680,000,000. Total exports rose to double the pre-war average, and, in the last year of neutrality, those to the Allies grew to $3,215,000,000, or almost four times the total in 1914. The funds advanced for financing these purchases in the American market aggregated $2,300,000,000 upon our entry into the war, and Allied war bonds were held by perhaps five hundred thousand American citizens.

It was not only international bankers and munitions makers who were concerned in the maintenance of this economic and financial stake in Allied victory. We were sending abroad raw materials and foodstuffs as well as munitions and other manufactured products. The effect of the general expansion of exports was a widespread diffusion of prosperity — greater profits for the manufacturer, higher wages for labor, and increased income for the farmer. There was no part of the country which did not feel the quickening effect of wartime demand. The interrelation between our material and ideological ties with the Allies, and the extent to which the latter may have been in any sense a rationalization of the former, went far deeper than the profits of any single group or class in American society.

The Defense of Neutral Rights

In the meantime the official policy of the United States was primarily directed toward support of our position as a neutral. This involved us in prolonged controversy with Great Britain and, far more important, it caused repeated and increasingly dangerous clashes with Germany. Both nations completely disregarded our rights. But there was this important difference. British encroachments upon American neutrality involved property losses; those of Germany led to the loss of American lives. Wilson repeatedly insisted upon this important distinction.

With the outbreak of war Great Britain issued a series of orders in council that declared a general blockade of Germany and set aside the entire North Sea as a military area. The Admiralty proceeded to give its own interpretation to the scope of visit and search; enlarged upon the old doctrine of continuous voyage whereby the ultimate destination, rather than port of entry, made cargo liable to seizure, and assumed full authority for asserting what goods should be considered contraband of war. It carried out its blockade with scant regard for any neutral rights and refused to consider the provisions of the Declaration of London, a partial codification of international law drawn up in 1909, on the ground that it had never been formally ratified. England was fighting for her life. She was determined to prevent supplies of whatever nature from reaching Germany regardless of how it might affect the commerce of other nations. In a measure it was the situation which had prevailed a century earlier during the Napoleonic era.

As the war continued, the Admiralty extended its restrictions. It haled American ships bound for neutral countries into British ports where they were subjected to long and costly delays, even if they escaped outright seizure of cargo, and it strictly limited neutral imports to peacetime needs. It steadily expanded the list of contraband goods to include metals, cotton, and food stuffs. It interfered with American mails and subjected our shipping to petty annoyances that appeared designed to hamper our trade quite as much as to maintain the blockade of Germany. Finally, in 1916 it issued a blacklist of eighty-five American firms and persons charged with aiding Germany and declared they would be cut off from all trade with Great Britain.

The United States protested against these successive infractions of international law and what it regarded as flagrant violation of its neutral rights. It entered into long and protracted discussion on each issue from England's disregard of the Declaration of London through the issuance of the black list. But our protests were either completely ignored or the answers so long delayed

and couched in such evasive terms as to constitute complete repudiation of our position. At any time during these years of
controversy we might well have forced our views upon Great
Britain. "The Allies soon became dependent for an adequate
supply on the United States," the British Foreign Secretary wrote
in his memoirs. "If we quarreled with the United States we
could not get that supply." Sympathy for the Allies and our own
trade interests, however, robbed our protests of the effectiveness
which they might otherwise have had.

In the meantime our policy toward German violation of our
neutral rights had developed along diametrically different lines.
In retaliation for the British blockade, the German Government
established in February, 1915, a war area about the British Isles.
All enemy merchant ships in this zone were declared to be fair
game for German submarines, and Berlin issued a grave warning
that "it cannot always be avoided that neutral vessels suffer from
attacks intended to strike enemy ships." The United States at once
protested. The State Department dispatched a strong note declaring that it could hardly view any action resulting in the loss
of American ships or American lives as other than an "indefensible violation of neutral rights." In sharp contrast to the moderate tone employed in our controversies with Great Britain, it
was further stated that in the event of such losses, the United
States would hold the German Government to a "strict accountability."

The issue involved was far more difficult and complex than
was indicated by our hasty and highly significant decision to
hold Germany so strictly to account. The submarine was a new
weapon of naval warfare. It could not be used effectively unless
the traditional rules of international law governing search and
seizure were waived. A U-boat commander, waiting to make
certain of the identity of the vessel he had intercepted before attacking it, was in imminent danger of having his submarine sunk
should his quarry turn out to be an enemy ship. The British were
arming their merchantmen, sometimes disguising their identity
under a neutral flag, and a single shell from such a vessel could
destroy a submarine. In insisting that neutral commerce should

not be endangered in the war area, the United States would consequently have deprived Germany, at least in large part, of any effective use of the only weapon with which she could successfully counter the British blockade.

Our position was based upon precedent, that of Germany upon ruthless logic. It was the inhumanity of submarine warfare, however, rather than the question of its legality that made it such a burning issue. "The sinking of passenger ships," Wilson declared, "involves principles of humanity which throw into the background any special circumstances of detail. . . . The United States is contending for something much greater than mere rights of property or privileges of commerce. . . . " This was actually only one phase in the change from the limited war of the nineteenth century to the total war of the twentieth century. We were contending, hopelessly, against the forces of history. Nevertheless, the decent opinion of mankind could not easily accept the implications of what was happening. Germany was condemned out of hand for brutally violating traditional codes of conduct.

Submarine Warfare

Although there had been some few earlier losses at sea, it was the sinking of the *Lusitania,* on May 7, 1915, that thoroughly aroused the American public and caused a first crisis in German-American relations. The *Lusitania,* carrying no armaments but with a cargo that included forty-two hundred cases of rifle cartridges, was torpedoed without warning off the Irish coast and sank in eighteen minutes, with the loss of some twelve hundred persons, including one hundred and twenty-eight American citizens.

President Wilson prepared a vigorous protest, demanding Germany's complete disavowal of the act and full reparation for the loss of American lives. Yet he refused to allow his outraged feelings to sway his judgment as to the proper course for the United States to follow. Germany's real crime, in his opinion, was against humanity. The objective of American policy should be to set an example in upholding the ideals of international conduct rather than to insist solely upon protection for our rights as a neutral. "There is such a thing as a man being too proud to fight," he declared in a public address three days after the disaster, clearly echoing the philosophy which had been the basis for his watchful waiting attitude toward Mexico. "There is such a thing as a nation being so right that it does not need to convince others by force that it is right."

Germany, nevertheless, refused to disavow the sinking of the *Lusitania* and maintained that her contraband cargo made the act one of "just self-defense." Wilson thereupon dispatched a second note whose uncompromising insistence upon our rights was the cause for his Secretary of State's resignation. Not that Bryan was pro-German, but he feared that Wilson had closed the door to any amicable agreement on the submarine issue and that the eventual consequence would be war. The President nonetheless persisted in his course and sent still a third note stating that repetition of such incidents as the attack on the *Lusitania* would be regarded as "deliberately unfriendly."

The controversy, heightened by Bryan's resignation, stirred up nation-wide excitement. The most vociferous elements in the population were not those who agreed with the Secretary of State, although he had much support in the Midwest, but those who felt that the President should have gone even further. During the apparently fruitless exchange of notes between the two Governments, criticism of the President's handling of the dispute grew increasingly caustic. "We have not yet begun to write," one newspaper paraphrased the heroics of John Paul Jones. The belligerent Theodore Roosevelt, not unaffected by his chagrin that Wilson should be President instead of himself in such a period of national emergency, had a great deal to say about the "note-writing professor" in the White House, and the "flubdubs," "mollycoddles," and "flapdoodle pacifists" who supported him. Still, there was no widespread popular demand for war. Contemporary comments of the more bellicose adherents of the Allies reflected their disappointment. "Rotten spirit in the *Lusitania* matter. Yellow spirit everywhere in spots," General Leonard Wood noted in his diary.

While Germany refused to abandon her right to sink merchant vessels on sight, the *Lusitania* controversy did cause her to modify her policy. She could not yet risk an open break with the United States. The German Admiralty consequently issued instructions for sparing large liners and every precaution was supposedly taken against further attacks on passenger ships. The expected calm on the high seas proved to be short-lived, however, for on August 19 a German U-boat commander violated these orders, sinking the *Arabic,* with the loss of two more American lives.

Public opinion in the United States again flared up dangerously. The second crisis in German-American affairs appeared to be even more serious than that created by the sinking of the *Lusitania.* Secretary Lansing, who had now replaced Bryan at the State Department, summoned the German ambassador and threatened to break off diplomatic relations. Count von Bernstorff was thoroughly alarmed. Without awaiting instructions from Berlin, he at once issued a conciliatory statement declaring that the attack on the *Arabic* had been a mistake. Going even further, he promised that no passenger liners would be sunk in the future "without warning and without safety of the lives of noncombatants, provided the liners do not try to escape or offer resistance." While the German Government censured him for going so far in an unauthorized pledge, it offered assurances that orders to submarine commanders were being made so stringent "that a recurrence of incidents similar to the *Arabic* case is considered out of the question."

Germany had not surrendered her assumed right to attack all ships entering the war zone, neutral or otherwise. Her concession involved only restrictive orders to the submarine commanders that might be withdrawn at will. Nevertheless, settlement of the *Arabic* case was accepted as a great victory for President Wilson's diplomacy. While his note-writing policy had been sufficiently conciliatory to avoid war, or even any break in diplomatic relations, Germany had been called to account and compelled to leash the submarine. There was a widespread feeling of relief throughout the country. Even Roosevelt declared that settlement of the *Arabic* crisis was "most gratifying."

In the hope of avoiding further difficulties various efforts were now made to lessen the risks of another clash with Germany. One proposal, supported by Secretary Lansing, was to compel England to give up her practice of arming merchantmen by forbidding them the use of neutral harbors, thereby nullifying Germany's claim that the submarine had to attack without warning in self-defense. In January, 1916, identical notes were addressed to both the British and German Governments urging that with such a general prohibition on armaments, both belligerents promise to adhere strictly to the traditional rules governing the stoppage and search of merchantmen. Germany was willing to accept this proposal; Great Britain refused to do so. The United States might still have acted on its own initiative in forbidding armed merchantmen to enter American harbors, but it took no further action. President Wilson was afraid that the ensuing negotiations would somehow provide Germany with an excuse "to throw off all restraints in undersea warfare."

At about the same time a congressional move to forbid travel by any American on a belligerent ship was also sidetracked. While such a step, originally recommended by Secretary Bryan at the time of the *Lusitania* controversy, would not have protected American ships, it would have greatly reduced the danger of possible loss of American lives. Resolutions embodying this proposal, closely paralleling the provisions of the neutrality law to be adopted two decades later, were introduced into the two houses of Congress and might well have passed had it not been for the opposition of the President, who felt that they represented a cowardly surrender of principle. He wrote to the chairman of the Senate Foreign Relations Committee:

> For my part, I cannot consent to any abridgment of the rights of American citizens in any respect. . . . What we are contending for in this matter is of the very essence of the things that have made America a sovereign nation. She cannot yield them without conceding her own impotency as a nation, and making virtual surrender of her independent position among the nations of the world.

The lull in German-American controversy lasted for seven

months despite these setbacks to the movement for minimizing the risks of neutral trade. In March, 1916, however, another crisis developed when a French vessel, the *Sussex,* was torpedoed in the British Channel with the loss of three more American lives. Incensed at Germany's disregard of her pledged word that passenger ships would not again be attacked, Secretary Lansing was convinced that further negotiations were now useless. He was ready to send the German ambassador packing. Wilson still held back. He felt that the country would support him in one further effort to persuade Germany by diplomatic pressure that submarine warfare had to be abandoned. The note dispatched to Berlin on April 18, 1916, was nevertheless a definite ultimatum. "Unless the Imperial Government should now immediately declare and effect an abandonment of its present methods of submarine warfare against passenger and freight-carrying vessels," it emphatically stated, "the Government of the United States can have no choice but to sever diplomatic relations. . . . "

There was no avoiding the implications of the *Sussex* note. Having refused to endorse measures that would have forced the disarmament of British merchantmen and protected American travel in belligerent ships, Wilson was prepared to enforce his original stand of holding Germany to a strict accountability. Still undecided as to her ultimate policy, unwilling to throw down a challenge which the United States would now perforce have to accept, Germany again temporarily retreated. She promised not to attack merchantmen without warning, and to make every effort to provide for the safety of passengers and crew unless these ships attempted to escape or offered resistance. There was a string to this pledge, however. If the United States could not also induce the other belligerents to observe the "laws of humanity" — or in more direct language persuade Great Britain to relax the blockade — the German Government reserved complete liberty of action. President Wilson accepted this reply, without its reservation, as a satisfactory answer to his ultimatum. But the issue had now been clearly drawn. The pledge of the German Government was no stronger than the needs of military policy. Whenever the Admiralty decided that unrestricted submarine warfare held out the promise of real success, there was every reason to believe that it would be adopted. And in that event, the United States was fully committed to breaking off diplomatic relations.

THE ELECTION OF 1916

The situation which thus presented itself in the summer of 1916 was both dangerous and highly confused. While the *Sussex* pledge ushered in the longest period of comparative quiet since 1914, the drift toward war was unmistakable. The continued expansion of our trade with the Allies and the persistent growth of sympathy for their cause stiffened our determination to safeguard our neutral rights. The disclosure of German sabotage activities in this country, on top of the submarine sinkings, revealed that the long arm of Germany might conceivably stretch out across the Atlantic. The American people were becoming more and more conditioned in favor of intervention.

One clear proof of this changing sentiment was the preparedness movement. The need to arm against all eventualities had long been urged by the more belligerent elements in the population, and their demand for strengthening our naval and military forces was steadily winning more popular support. President Wilson had at first held himself strictly aloof from this movement. He believed that a nation prepared for war was all the more likely to be drawn into the conflict. He hoped to maintain a position that would demonstrate our national reluctance to employ either force or the threat of force in international relations. He finally swung over into the preparedness camp, however, and during the summer of 1916 the influence of the Administration was thrown behind a series of measures to promote national defense. With the backing of such organizations as the National Security League and the American Defense Society, gigantic preparedness parades, one of which was led by the President in person, were held throughout the country and Congress was finally goaded into action. A National Defense Act provided for raising army enrollment to 175,000 men, increased the National Guard to 450,000 and set up an officers' reserve corps; a Naval Appropriation Act authorized the expenditure of $1,500,000,000 over a three-year period for the construction of four dreadnoughts, four battle cruisers, and other auxiliary craft; and an Army Appropriation Act not only approved additional funds for military expansion, but created a Council of National Defense to undertake the co-ordination of the necessary measures for economic preparedness. A little later, the United States Shipping Board was established with a $50,000,000 appropriation for the construction of merchant vessels.

While public opinion generally accepted the need for this legislation, the new measures did not by any means command universal support. Pro-Germans and pacifists openly opposed every move toward preparedness. "This nation does not need burglars' tools," was the latter's thesis, "unless it intends to make burglary its business; it should not be a pistol-toting nation unless it is going to adopt a pistol-toter's ideas." And apart from these extremists there were many other elements in the population which feared that preparedness would push us over the brink of war for all the disclaimers of those who stated it was necessary only for national defense.

Nineteen-hundred-sixteen was not only a year of increasing international tension and of strenuous efforts to prepare for possible war. It was also an election year. The public had to decide whether the course President Wilson was following should receive public sanction through the maintenance of the Democrats in power. Other considerations entered into the minds of many voters. There were marked differences of opinion upon domestic issues and upon our policy toward Mexico. But the European war and our attitude toward it bulked largest in the political foreground.

After an attempt by the former Progressives to select Theodore Roosevelt had completely missed fire, the Republicans nominated Charles Evans Hughes, an associate justice of the Supreme Court and former governor of New York. He was a strong candidate, identified with the progressive cause, but a regular Republican in so far as party alignments were concerned. No one was more admirably fitted to heal the breach resulting from the insurgent revolt of 1912. He suffered from the disadvantages, however, which any opposition candidate faces when the principal campaign issue involves foreign policy. Adhering to the general viewpoint of Republican leadership in being strongly pro-Ally and highly critical of what was regarded as Wilson's weak diplomacy, the only clear-cut alternative he could urge to the policy the Administration was pursuing was immediate intervention in the war. For this the country was not yet prepared. Hughes consequently felt compelled to adopt a position which his opponents attacked as a meaningless straddle. His ambiguous slogan, "America first and America efficient," was designed to win the backing of preparedness advocates without alienating the support of more conservative upholders of a cautious neutrality, particularly the German-American voters who were largely Republicans. Despite these compromises, however, Republican strength throughout the country, now that the Progressives had returned to the fold and Roosevelt himself was taking the lead in calling for party harmony, was believed to give Hughes every chance of success.

President Wilson was enthusiastically renominated by the Democrats and they were prepared to go before the country on the success of his record, both in domestic legislation and foreign policy. The salient feature of the campaign was emphasized in the slogan, "He kept us out of war." The obvious inference was that, if re-elected, the President would continue to keep us out of war. Wilson himself never made any such pledge. In January, indeed, he had given a clear intimation of quite a different policy should conditions materially change. If the choice became one between peace and national honor, he had said, "Do not expect of me an impossible and contradictory thing." As the campaign progressed, he was at one and the same time accused of being pro-German and "the best President England ever had," but his appeal was to loyal Americans to uphold a policy which had so far succeeded in maintaining both honor and neutrality.

The campaign was hard-fought and exciting. Early returns appeared to bear out the forecasts that Hughes would be chosen.

Newspapers on the day after the election actually announced a Republican victory. Only the final returns revealed that an extremely close vote in California, where Hughes had failed to win the support of the Progressives, had unexpectedly thrown that state into the Democratic camp and given the election to Wilson. The President's vote in the electoral college was 277 to his rival's 254, and the popular poll 9,129,000 to 8,538,000. However narrow the majority, Wilson interpreted the election as an expression of public confidence in his Administration and as a popular mandate for the maintenance of neutrality in so far as it could be upheld with respect for American rights.

The Collapse of Neutrality

Events had fully convinced the President by 1916 that neutrality was going to be even more difficult in the future than it had been in the past. The only certain way of avoiding war, it was now becoming apparent, was somehow to bring an immediate end to European hostilities. There had been earlier occasions when Wilson had sought to relieve the pressure upon the United States by attempting to induce the warring nations to undertake peace negotiations. In the spring of 1915, and again early in 1916, he had sent Colonel House abroad as his personal envoy to explore the situation. Nothing had come of these efforts. The strongly pro-Ally emissary — for no American was more convinced of the justice of the Allied cause or saw the war more completely through British eyes than Colonel House — had hardly been the best instrument for such negotiations. On his latter trip he reached an understanding with the British Foreign Secretary, Sir Edward Grey, that upon hearing from England that the time was opportune, the President would call an international conference to end the war, and should Germany then prove recalcitrant, the United States would intervene on the side of the Allies. With the insertion of an additional "probably" that in effect nullified its importance, the President had approved this declaration of policy, but Great Britain made no further move to enlist our cooperation in bringing Germany to the conference table. Now in

December, 1916, a further and desperate effort was to be made to bring about peace as a last resort to forestall our being drawn into the struggle.

Other considerations also influenced the President. His attitude toward the war had undergone certain changes in the course of two years. He had originally asked for neutrality in thought as well as action, and he had opposed granting loans to the Allies. Subsequently he had reversed his position on loans and shown a marked sympathy for Great Britain. He had opposed any move, such as banning armed merchantmen from our harbors, which might have weakened the British position in resisting German submarine warfare. On the occasion of Colonel House's second mission, and in talks with Democratic leaders of the House, he had apparently contemplated intervention on the Allied side under certain conditions as early as the spring of 1916. But there was now to be a further shift in his viewpoint. Possibly England's failure to respond to his previous overtures had raised doubts in his own mind as to whether a decisive Allied victory would actually be much more to American interests than a German victory. Would it really assure permanent peace and security? And what would be the rôle of America in a world in which the old European balance of power was so completely destroyed?

Wilson was also vitally interested in furthering those ideals of international morality for which he had made himself spokesman and he had apparently come to the conclusion, despite his earlier statements expressing sympathy for England, that a freely negotiated peace rather than a decisive victory for either side was the best guarantee of their attainment. Spurred to action in order to attain this objective, as well as to halt our drift toward war, he dispatched identical notes to the Powers on December 18, 1916, asking them to state their war aims and suggesting immediate negotiations on the ground that "the objects which the statesmen of the belligerents on both sides have in mind are virtually the same. . . ."

His pro-Ally advisers were shocked. They had always favored a complete Allied victory and in their minds that could be the only possible objective of American intervention. Secretary

Lansing was "worried sick," as he confided to Colonel House, by the startling failure of the President to grasp the "full significance of this war or the principles at stake." In Great Britain the reaction could hardly have been more violent. "Everybody is mad as hell," Lord Northcliffe told Ambassador Page. The King is reputed to have broken down and wept.

The replies to the President's notes got the peace movement nowhere. Generally victorious on the battlefield, Germany would have welcomed the end of hostilities. But the terms upon which she insisted, as privately relayed to Wilson, were a victor's peace. She demanded territorial concessions from France, economic control of Belgium, and indemnities. Nor was Great Britain, despite her relatively weaker military position, any more willing to make the concessions that might have opened the road to negotiations. Her declared goal was the restitution of conquered territories, full reparations, and guarantees for the future. Completely failing in his attempt to discover a basis for negotiations, Wilson still refused to despair. He planned to put the entire issue before the bar of world public opinion. In an address to the Senate on January 22, 1917, he made an eloquent appeal for "peace without victory," outlining the terms on which he believed the war could be stopped and which would receive the full support of the United States.

The proposals he advanced were those which underlay all his thinking upon international affairs and embodied the views for which he would continue to fight — valiantly, stubbornly, and unsuccessfully. He envisaged a new world order based upon government only with the consent of the governed, freedom of the seas in time of war as well as peace, limitation of all armaments, and the avoidance of entangling alliances in favor of "a peace made secure by the organized major force of mankind." A settlement reached in violation of these basic principles, a peace forced upon the vanquished by the victors, Wilson declared, could not possibly endure. "It would be accepted in humiliation, under duress, at an intolerable sacrifice," were his prophetic words, "and would leave a sting, a resentment, a bitter memory upon which terms of peace would rest, not permanently, but only as upon quicksand. Only a peace between equals can last."

At home the speech aroused both tremendous enthusiasm and chilling criticism. Abroad its reception was wholly negative. There was no official reply from the belligerents. They were committed to war to the bitter end and Wilson's great effort collapsed. It was based upon an idealistic vision whose fulfillment demanded a measure of statesmanship of which the world was completely incapable in the opening months of 1917.

The President had also failed, as events quickly proved, to prevent our own engulfment in the whirling vortex of war. Some three months earlier, the German Government had resolved its own internal controversies and decided upon a policy of unrestricted submarine warfare. The announcement of this decision was delayed until the failure of the President's peace efforts was clearly apparent, but on January 31, 1917, Germany declared that henceforth all merchant vessels, armed or unarmed, would be sunk on sight in the war zone. The single exception, doubly insulting to our national sovereignty, was that the United States might send one ship a week to the British port of Falmouth, provided this vessel carried no contraband and was identified by broad red and white stripes painted on her sides.

The German Government adopted this policy in full realization of its possible consequences. Our protest in the *Sussex* case had committed us to severance of diplomatic relations should submarine warfare be renewed. But the unhampered flow of American supplies to Great Britain was dangerously threatening the German war effort. It was felt in Berlin that the United States was affording England as direct and as important assistance as though it was already definitely aligned with the Allies. Moreover, the German Admiralty, with a large submarine fleet now at its command, was confident it could break up the trans-Atlantic trade and starve out England before possible American intervention could become effective.

Announcement of the new policy was a grievous blow for President Wilson. Yet he felt he had no alternative to breaking off diplomatic relations. On February 3, he consequently appeared before Congress to announce that he had taken the action made imperative by Germany's declaration of unrestricted submarine warfare.

Public opinion was shocked, confused, and also aroused to bitter anger by Germany's defiance. While some people clung to the hope that war might somehow be avoided, there was general recognition of the necessity for breaking off relations and a frank realization of what it probably meant. "The hour for temporizing is past"; "If war comes, it will be a holy and righteous one — war on war, a war for peace, a war for a better world"; "If to maintain our rights means war, so let it be," were typical comments in the nation's press. "From the quixotic adventure of imposing upon the Old World a 'peace without victory,'" the *Boston Transcript* declared, "we are brought up with a sharp turn by the imperative necessity of defending American honor, American rights, American lives, and American property — against a war without quarter with which Germany has threatened, not the New World only, but the whole world . . ."

Still stoutly maintaining that "war can come only by the willful acts and aggressions of others," Wilson sought to meet the immediate issue by arming American merchantmen. Congressional authorization for this move was held up by a twelve-man filibuster led by Senator La Follette. "A little group of willful men representing no opinion but their own," the President bitterly declared, "have rendered the great Government of the United States helpless and contemptible." Nevertheless, after the adjournment of Congress, armaments were provided by executive decree. The United States would defend its interests; it would meet attack with counter-attack.

While the country nervously awaited developments, fearful of the overt act which now almost surely meant war, anti-German feeling was still further inflamed and our solidarity with the Allies strongly reinforced by two new developments. On March 3, there was published an intercepted note from the German Foreign Minister to the German minister in Mexico. It proposed in the event of war the formation of a Mexican-German alliance, with the possible adherence of Japan, for the recovery by Mexico of Texas, Arizona, and New Mexico. Some ten days later, word reached the United States that revolution had broken out in Russia with the overthrow of the absolutist monarchy and establishment of a liberal and democratic régime. In world history these two events have a somewhat disproportionate significance. In March, 1917, their effect upon American public opinion was of very comparable importance. The so-called Zimmermann Note was accepted as definite proof that Germany's aggressive designs endangered our national security; the Russian Revolution removed the only obstacle to our idealistic conception of the Allies as fighting the battle of democracy.

In the exciting atmosphere created by these events, banner newspaper headlines also told of those final decisive acts on Germany's part that brought the gathering storm to its seemingly irrevocable climax. The unarmed American merchantman *Algonquin* was sunk by a submarine on March 12. Within a week three other ships were lost. There was at once a popular demand for an immediate declaration of war. The cabinet unanimously agreed that national honor permitted no other course. Feeling deeply the grave responsibility that confronted him, as a consequence in considerable measure of policies he had himself promoted, President Wilson was momentarily torn by doubt and indecision. "What else can I do?" he asked a visitor at the White House. "Is there anything else I can do?" There was no answer, and he reluctantly prepared to go before Congress, called into special session, and advise a declaration of hostilities.

The scene in Congress on April 2, 1917, was a stirring one. His mind finally made up, his momentary hesitations swept away in a new vision of the righteousness of the course upon which the United States was about to embark, the President faced his tensely expectant audience — members of Congress, his cabinet, the justices of the Supreme Court, members of the diplomatic corps:

> With a profound sense of the solemn and even tragical character of the step I am taking and of the grave responsibilities which it involves, but in unhesitating obedience to what I deem my constitutional duty, I advise that the Congress declare the recent course of the Imperial German Government to be in fact nothing less than war against the Government and people of the United States. . . .
>
> It is a fearful thing to lead this great peaceful people into war,

into the most terrible and disastrous of all wars, civilization itself seeming to be in the balance. But the right is more precious than peace, and we shall fight for the things which we have always carried nearest our hearts — for democracy, for the right of those who submit to authority to have a voice in their own Governments, for the rights and liberties of small nations, for a universal dominion of right by such a concert of free peoples as shall bring peace and safety to all nations and make the world itself at last free. To such a task we can dedicate our lives and our fortunes, everything that we are and everything that we have, with the pride of those who know that the day has come when America is privileged to spend her blood and her might for the principles that gave her birth and happiness and the peace which she has treasured. God helping her, she can do no other.

As the President concluded, there was a moment of hushed silence, then a deafening roar of applause. The President stood silent. "My message today was a message of death for our young men," he later said to his secretary. "How strange it seems to applaud that."

Four days later, Congress passed a joint resolution declaring war on Germany.

A Nation Under Arms

RESPONSE TO CRISIS

THE AMERICAN PEOPLE generally welcomed the final break with Germany, but the country was almost totally unprepared for war. Within a few weeks military missions from the Allies descended upon Washington. The British sent Lord Balfour, their Foreign Secretary; the French delegation included former Premier Viviani and Marshal Joffre, legendary hero of the Marne. The needs of the Allies were urgent — supplies and more supplies. Marshal Joffre made an even more dramatic appeal — "Let the American soldier come now." Neither the public nor the Government had actually contemplated an expeditionary force. Our participation in the war had been envisaged as providing economic and naval assistance. Could a democracy meet this great emergency with the unity and effectiveness which alone could assure victory? This was the grave challenge facing the United States in April, 1917.

Costly mistakes, colossal waste, tragic bungling marked our preparations. With so little to guide us in our past experience, valuable time was lost before the economic resources of the country were mobilized and an efficient military machine created out of the raw materials of American manpower. Nevertheless, the national accomplishment was stupendous when viewed against this background — and it achieved its purpose in making possible the final defeat of the Central Powers.

The United States succeeded in expanding the economic aid already being given to the Allies to a point that ensured them a heavy preponderance in armor over the enemy. It raised, trained, and equipped an expeditionary force which greatly bolstered the armies on the actual fighting front. American intervention in the first World War proved decisive. Had it not taken place, there is every reason to believe that the Central Powers would have triumphed. Germany's campaign on the eastern front was making important gains in the spring of 1917; the attempted Allied offensive in the West had collapsed. There was a defeatist spirit abroad in France, and England did not know how long she could hold out against the submarine blockade. No conclusion upon the wisdom of our entry into the war is valid which fails to recognize that it almost surely forestalled a German victory.

With the declaration of hostilities, the mobilization of both our industrial power and our manpower started immediately. The Council of National Defense, with its all-important advisory commissions appointed the previous summer from among the nation's business leaders, was given the responsibility of organizing industry. Congress promptly appropriated four billion dollars to meet immediate military and naval needs, together with three billion dollars in additional credits for the Allies, and then in May, after prolonged and often acrimonious debate, adopted a Selective Service Act subjecting all men between the ages of twenty-one and thirty to military call. A few weeks after passage of these bills, the President officially announced that in response to the requests of the Allies an expeditionary force would be sent abroad. The first contingent, to be made up of army regulars, was to sail "at as early a date as practical" and would be placed under the command of General Pershing, who was already on his way to France.

This was the framework of our war effort: organization of our industrial resources with establishment of a service of supply for both our own troops and those of the Allies, and the creation and transportation overseas of a great national army. It demanded a concentration of political authority and broadening of governmental functions on a scale never before known. The cumbersome machinery set up for the exercise of these powers for a time creaked alarmingly. There was widespread criticism, bitter attacks on the Administration. "The military establishment of America has broken down," the chairman of the Senate Committee on Military Affairs declared ominously in January, 1918. " . . . It has almost ceased functioning." Nine months later three and one-half million men were under arms, and two million of them were serving overseas. Order had been brought out of threatened chaos in large part through passage of the Overman Act, giving the President authority to reorganize in any way he saw fit the executive agencies of the Government, and by the establishment of virtually dictatorial economic control. Everything else was sacrificed to meet a crisis that was accepted as being the most serious the country had faced since the Civil War.

PATRIOTISM AND HYSTERIA

Although the European conflict had been going on for over two and a half years when the United States intervened, an important factor in the situation was the almost total ignorance of the American people as to what war actually meant. They knew nothing of the methods of trench warfare, of fighting with machine guns and tanks and airplanes, except as reported by war correspondents. The United States was a nation devoted to peace. Two decades earlier, a handful of hastily enrolled volunteers and national guardsmen had marched gaily off to free Cuba, and within a few months had been home again with their mission accomplished. Otherwise the country had not known war since 1865 and its memories of that great struggle were dim and hazy. There was no military tradition among the people. Few of them had even seen uniformed troops except for militiamen or Civil War veterans at some flag-waving, band-playing Fourth-of-July celebration. What sacrifices war demanded on the home front as well as on the battle line, what far-reaching interruptions of normal life it involved, were lessons still to be learned.

And for all the general support that President Wilson had won for his policies, there was not that overnight national unity as to our course which was to mark our entry into the second World War in 1941. Six senators and fifty members of the House voted against the declaration of war on April 6, 1917. While there were no dissenting voices to the first appropriation bill, opposition to the draft was strong and vehement. Germany's unrestricted submarine warfare was universally interpreted as an attack upon the United States, but it could hardly have the direct and immediate repercussions that were to result from the assault on Pearl Harbor. The American people had to be convinced of the necessity for war, in 1917, and public leaders adopted every possible means to resolve all lingering doubts there might be about the justice of our cause. The very fact that there were misgivings, perhaps, soon gave rise to a highly emotional — almost hysterical — fervor. It was not long before the public was caught up in a war frenzy that led to the ruthless and intolerant suppression of those small minority elements in the population which continued to remain out of step. The national unity without which victory would have been impossible was forged under the impact both of events and of propaganda. It was not entirely spontaneous.

President Wilson set the tone in creating our war spirit. There was the inevitable appeal to fear and hatred of the enemy — not of the German people, but of the tyrannical force typified by their militaristic government. "This intolerable Thing . . . " he declared, "this menace of combined intrigue and force which we now see so clearly as the German power, a Thing without conscience or honor or capacity for covenanted peace, must be crushed." At the same time he attempted to maintain the conflict upon the high, idealistic level of a great crusade to uphold right and justice. The eloquent phrases of his war message were echoed in many other addresses. The summons to wage a war that would end all war and make the world safe for democracy carried its stirring challenge to every home in the country. "For us there is but one choice," the President stated. "We have made it. Woe be to the man or group of men that seeks to stand in our way in this day of high resolution. . . . Once more we make good with our lives and fortunes the great faith to which we were born, and a new glory shall shine in the face of the people."

The President's speeches and public statements, as well as those of other American leaders, were given nation-wide currency by the Committee on Public Information. Under the dynamic leadership of George Creel, it became one of the most effective agencies of propaganda the country had ever known. It reached out to every town, village, and isolated farmhouse throughout the land. An army of seventy-five thousand "four-minute men" volunteered to speak in support of the draft and to promote the sale of Liberty Bonds. They made their brief appeals at moving-picture theaters, lodge meetings, farmers' granges, labor meetings, church socials, and gatherings of school-children — 7,550,000 speeches, the exuberant Creel later estimated, to audiences totaling 315,454,000. The country's artists were enlisted to placard the country with patriotic posters. Writers, novelists, and college professors were called upon to prepare popular pamphlets. "Loyalty Leaflets" and "Red, White, and Blue Books" poured from the presses — "Why We Are Fighting," "The Meaning of America," "Maintaining Morals and Morale." Six million copies of President Wilson's address on "How War Came to America" were printed, and almost seven million of his Flag Day Address.

These pamphlets were published not only in English, but in order to reach the foreign-born they were printed in Swedish, Polish, Italian, Bohemian, Spanish, and Portuguese. It was impossible for anyone to escape the emotional impact of this patriotic barrage. The omnipresent "four-minute men" were called Creel's Stentorian Guards; a dignified Senator from Ohio, later to become President, complained that their activities were "hysterical and unseemly." But Creel was out to make America war-conscious — and his success was phenomenal.

It was so successful in fact that the Committee on Public Information soon undertook the even more grandiose project of spreading its war messages throughout the world. The peoples of every country were to be told that the war was one to make the world safe for democracy and that victory for the Allied cause was the only alternative to being ground under the iron heel of German military despotism. Pamphlets were distributed in the countries associated with the Allies, the neutral nations, and even in enemy territory. Farmers in the Balkans, the uneasy peasants of Spain, workers in Holland, Norway, and Sweden, Russian muzhiks, and Chinese coolies were taught to dread a German victory and urged to support the Allies. Before the

Armistice brought his astounding labors to a close, Creel had let loose upon the world — in this country and abroad — seventy-five million pieces of war literature.

Apart from this official propaganda there were countless self-appointed spokesmen who undertook to arouse their countrymen. To a far greater degree than in the case of the activities sponsored by Creel, their appeal was to hatred rather than loyalty to American ideals. College teachers and clergymen revealed a new capacity for startling invective. A professor from the University of Nebraska told the country that the Prussian was "a moral imbecile, an arrested development"; a prominent historian warned of "the total pollution of our people by letting loose of the Prussian moral sewers"; the President of another college lyrically wrote:

> The clock has struck! The death-smeared double vulture
> Shall swoop no more adown the insulted skies,
> To spill the venomous bacterial Kultur . . .

Henry van Dyke, clergyman, declared that he would "hang every one who lifts his voice against America's entering the war." The evangelist Billy Sunday excoriated Germany in a prayer in the House of Representatives: "Thou knowest, O Lord, that no nation so infamous, vile, greedy, sensuous, bloodthirsty, ever disgraced the pages of history."

Some of the manifestations of anti-German feeling born of wartime hysteria had an almost pathological aspect. German music was proscribed on the concert platform; German literature and poetry widely banned; the study of German forbidden in schools. Sauerkraut was patriotically renamed "Liberty cabbage," and German measles became "Liberty measles." The residents of Berlin, New Hampshire, were one group that valiantly stood out against such absurdities; they rejected by a vote of 933 to 566 a proposal to change their town's name.

Of more importance were those examples of excessive patriotism that led to intolerant attacks upon anyone who dared to question in any particular the justice of the Allied cause or to criticize any phase of America's war effort. The few dissenting — or even mildly critical — voices in the general chorus of patriotism were rudely suppressed. German-Americans were suspect, whatever they said. While they were almost universally loyal, standing squarely behind the Government in support of the war, the possibility that their loyalties might be divided or that they might still feel some sympathy for the mother country was enough to condemn them in the eyes of super-patriots. In many communities they were virtually ostracized and regarded by hostile neighbors as potential if not actual spies.

An Espionage Act, primarily aimed at overt crimes of obstruction or conspiracy, was passed in June, 1917, and four months later there followed a Trading-with-the-Enemy Act. Treasonable matter was barred from the mails and censorship established over foreign communications, but the general provisions of these two laws were relatively mild. It ultimately appeared necessary, as a reflection of the growing spirit of intolerance, to clamp down more heavily upon individual liberties and freedom of speech. Under the terms of a new Sedition Act, passed in May, 1918, the utterance of disloyal, profane, scurrilous, or abusive language directed against the form of government of the United States, the Constitution, the flag, the army, or navy became a criminal offense, punishable by a fine of ten thousand dollars or imprisonment up to twenty years.

Passage of this law was intended to place the responsibility of ferreting out any treasonable activities on the shoulders of the Department of Justice. Its investigations, however, were outdone by those of self-appointed sleuths. Moreover, the more conservative elements in the country, as represented by such organizations as the American Security League, took advantage of the popular hysteria to broaden the hunt for suspected pro-Germans by seeking out any person or organization whose radical sympathies laid them open to the charge of subversive behavior. Pacifists, socialists, labor sympathizers were hounded from pillar to post. The Home Guards took it upon themselves to break up public meetings, however peaceful, where they thought seditious statements might possibly be made. Treason was discovered everywhere. Men or women who spoke slightingly of the Red Cross or the

Y.M.C.A., critics of the Government's fiscal policies, those who failed in proper respect for our Allies — anyone out of step with majority opinion — ran the danger of denunciation, arrest, and prosecution.

Constitutional guarantees were forgotten in this witch hunt to stamp out not only sedition but radicalism. The Department of Justice made in all 1597 arrests under authority of the Espionage and Sedition Acts, and forty-one persons were given prison terms running from ten to twenty years. Eugene V. Debs, still leader of the Socialists, received a ten-year sentence and was to run for the Presidency in 1920 while still imprisoned at Leavenworth. Victor L. Berger, Socialist member of Congress, was given a twenty-year term. "Big Bill" Haywood, leader of the I.W.W., went to jail with ninety-four other members of this radical organization on conspiracy charges. Among the scores, the hundreds, arrested on suspicion of espionage, sabotage, or aid to the enemy, the courts nevertheless found relatively few against whom there was any evidence other than the nervous imaginings of excitable patriots. There were sensational charges of plots to poison Red Cross bandages and put germs in local water supplies, but none of them was ever substantiated. "I assert as my best judgment," Federal Judge George W. Anderson, before whom many of the espionage cases came, "that more than ninety per cent of the reported pro-German plots never existed."

There was no intelligent program comparable to that adopted after 1941 for dealing with pacifists and conscientious objectors. Public opinion intolerantly considered them slackers or draft-dodgers. While a large majority of the four thousand-odd men who refused military service on religious grounds were assigned to noncombatant activities, some four hundred and fifty were sentenced to federal prisons.

President Wilson had foreseen the danger to our democratic standards in wartime excitement and hysteria. "Once lead this people into war," he told Frank Cobb of the *New York World,* on the eve of our intervention, "and they'll forget there ever was such a thing as tolerance. To fight, you must be brutal and ruthless, and the spirit of ruthless brutality will enter into every fiber of our national life, infecting Congress, the courts, the policeman on the beat, the man in the street." He did not believe that the Constitution, the rights of free speech and assembly, could possibly survive. Events appeared to be proving the President right. Patriotism often became intolerance. Deep as was the wound individual freedom suffered, however, it did not prove fatal. The Constitution was to prove stronger than either wartime or postwar hysteria.

MOBILIZING INDUSTRY

The all-important economic front was a first consideration for the American people. The Allies needed steel, cotton, coal, foodstuffs; they wanted — and so did our new armies — tanks, airplanes, motor trucks, ordnance, rifles, and munitions. And there had to be ships to transport these materials of war overseas. The Council of National Defense soon realized that new agencies would have to be created to deal with the diverse and often overlapping economic functions that had become a primary responsibility of Government. Six key boards finally emerged from the confusion after a long and often disheartening process of trial and error.

The principal one was the War Industries Board. It evolved gradually out of the committees originally set up by the Council of National Defense, and only after passage of the Overman Act, early in 1918, was it finally given the authority which enabled it to cut through the red tape previously hampering its activities. Its chairman, Bernard M. Baruch, was then assigned absolute powers for the over-all regulation of industry, the synchronizing of American and Allied purchases of war supplies, and the establishment of priorities in all raw materials. Control over prices also fell within the War Industries Board's range, but this job was actually administered by a special price-fixing committee directly responsible to the President. Apart from this limitation, Baruch's letter of appointment stated that the ultimate decision upon all questions coming before the War Industries Board rested in his hands.

The controls introduced by the War Industries Board touched almost every phase of the country's economic life. Peacetime manufactures were wholly subordinated to the greater needs of the army and navy. Iron and steel were not released for building operations that could possibly be postponed; other metal supplies were either withheld for war purposes or strictly curtailed; factories were converted from their ordinary manufactures to produce ordnance, tanks, rifles, or munitions. An entirely new industry was set up under War Department control for airplane manufacture, creating the "Liberty engine" and building some twelve thousand planes.

The standardization of innumerable consumer products to conserve raw material supplies through the elimination of waste and duplication was also decreed. The War Industries Board ordered a reduction in the types of automobile tires from some three hundred to nine; it limited the manufacture of shoes to certain specified styles, and among many other things it prescribed definite regulations for the manufacture of baby carriages, buggy wheels, clocks, and furniture. It forbade the use of tin in toy carts, and it placed restrictions on the manufacture of corsets that released eight thousand tons of steel.

In comparison with the all-embracing conversion of industry to wartime production during the even greater national emergency twenty-five years later, these regulations appear hardly surface-scratching. Still, they were something entirely new to the United States in 1917 and 1918. They were immensely important both in forwarding the success of our war effort at that time and in the precedents they provided for the future. They furnished a basis for many of the regulations adopted by the New Deal in its experiments with a planned economy, as well as pointing the way to the complete control of all industry during the second World War.

The second of the great wartime agencies was the United States Shipping Board. Its task was to provide the means for the overseas transportation of war supplies, an undertaking only less important than the work of the War Industries Board. "Ships Will Win the War" was a valid slogan. While naval operations were a first answer to the dangerous threat of the German submarine campaign, the need for more and more shipping was absolutely imperative. U-boats were reported in July, 1917, to be sinking Allied vessels at a rate three times faster than they were being built. Desperate warnings of the imminence of British collapse reached this country. While the Emergency Fleet Corporation, a subsidiary agency, pushed ahead as rapidly as possible with a far-reaching building program, the Shipping Board itself undertook to bring under its immediate control all available tonnage upon which it could get its hand — enemy, neutral, or American. Under the authority of its chairman, Edward N. Hurley, German ships interned in the United States were seized, and other vessels purchased, chartered, or commandeered to build up a great fleet allocated to the war service.

The building program had tremendous ramifications. Existing naval yards had to be expanded and new ones constructed; ports and dockyards made available, and shipyard workers collected and housed. Plans were drawn up for every type of vessel — steel ships, partly prefabricated; wooden ships, composite ships, and even concrete ships. The Emergency Fleet Corporation established four new shipyards, with ninety-five ways, and concluded contracts for twenty-five hundred vessels. At Hog Island, on the Delaware near Philadelphia, a dismal marsh was transformed into the world's largest shipyard with two hundred and fifty buildings, eighty miles of railway tracks, fifty ways capable of launching fifty ships at a time, and an army of thirty-four thousand workers. By midsummer of 1918, after the appointment of Charles M. Schwab to the corporation's chairmanship, its ambitious program was fully under way with results which then appeared to be spectacularly successful.

Nevertheless, few of the ships that the Emergency Fleet Corporation constructed were completed in time to see service in the war. July 4, 1918, witnessed the dramatic launching of one hundred vessels to celebrate the national holiday, but of the nine million tons of shipping eventually brought under the control of the Shipping Board, only five hundred thousand tons were newly built. The great shipyard at Hog Island was laying six keels a week at the time of the Armistice; its first delivery of a completed ship took place a month later. If the navy had been less successful in curbing the submarine menace, the result might have been disastrous. The contribution of the Shipping Board was its management of existing tonnage rather than new construction. As it was, the tremendous fleet over whose preparation it struggled became a peacetime white elephant whose disposal was one of the most vexing of post-war economic issues.

Problems of internal transportation led to creation at the close of 1917 of a third important agency when Secretary of the Treasury McAdoo was appointed Director-General of Railroads. For a time a Railroads War Board had done what it could to meet national needs through the voluntary co-operation of the railroads themselves. But a system based upon competition had broken down under the strain. Without the motor trucking service of post-war years to share its burden, railway transportation became so tied up that traffic was impossibly congested. Freight shipments throughout the country, but particularly on the eastern seaboard, were subject to delays seriously threatening the whole war effort. The new Railroad Administration, given full authority over all lines, thereupon undertook to co-ordinate traffic, eliminate all nonessential and competing passenger services, consolidate railroad terminals and ticket offices, and speed up freight deliveries. While peacetime executives remained in immediate control of operations, they acted under orders from the Director-General as the managers of a unified, national rail network. The new system worked so efficiently under McAdoo's able supervision that the movement of both troops and supplies was greatly facilitated and freight congestion largely relieved.

Industry and transportation were of vital importance, but a fourth key agency — the Food Administration — even more directly affected the lives of the American people. There was a tremendous demand on the part of the Allies for foodstuffs of all kinds. They needed cereals and meat products in immense quantities to feed both their armies and civilian population, and they looked to the United States as their chief source of supply. "Food Will Win the War" was another slogan placarded throughout the country. The national effort was bent to increase production in every possible way, and at the same time to reduce consumption at home to free supplies for shipment abroad. The head of the Food Administration was Herbert Hoover, whose previous work as chairman of the Commission for Belgian Relief had won him well-merited public recognition, and he carried out his new duties with a success that contributed materially to the Allied victory.

The task of increasing agricultural production was undertaken by authority of the Lever Act, passed by Congress in August, 1917. This measure granted the President full control over every phase of the production of foodstuffs, feed, fuel, fertilizer, and farm machinery, together with the power to fix the price of wheat over and above a base of two dollars a bushel. While enactment of this bill had been strongly combated by the congressional farm bloc, it nevertheless gave a tremendous impetus to production. A Grain Corporation set up by the Food Administration agreed to buy the entire 1917 wheat crop at $2.20 a bushel and that of 1918 at $2.25 a bushel. With this guarantee the acreage planted to wheat increased from 45,000,000 acres in 1917 to over 75,000,000 in 1919 and the yield rose from 636,655,000 to 967,979,000 bushels.

In reducing consumption, the Food Administration relied throughout the war upon voluntary action. While certain licensing controls were established over dealers and processors, the public response to Hoover's appeals for co-operation was so satisfactory that no attempt was made to institute rationing. Indeed, no really serious shortages developed. Wheatless and meatless days were observed without any compulsion other than popular opinion; substitute articles of diet were widely introduced to take the place of foods Hoover declared our Allies needed more than we did. In response to nation-wide preaching of the Gospel of the Clean Plate, housewives took care to avoid the waste so generally characteristic of the American home. It was reported that garbage collections were declining so rapidly under the wartime urge "to hooverize" that the collectors feared loss of their jobs! At the same time the countryside broke out in a veritable rash of war gardens as thousands of people tore up their lawns and flower beds to plant vegetables. Boy Scouts undertook to have each troop raise enough to feed a soldier; young women and girls enrolled as farmerettes in a volunteer Land Army.

A Fuel Administration, closely paralleling the Food Administration and also deriving its authority from the Lever Act, was established under the chairmanship of Harry A. Garfield as a fifth wartime agency. Increased coal production and the maintenance of uninterrupted work in the mines were its primary responsibilities. The severe cold of the winter of 1917-18 combined with congestion in railway traffic, however, to produce a coal shortage that confronted the Fuel Administration with a serious crisis. Manufacturing plants in the East were threatened with curtailed production, and, even more important, hundreds of vessels at Atlantic ports were tied up at the docks awaiting bunker coal. Private consumers were urged to be as sparing as possible in their use of coal, and daylight saving was introduced for the first time to lighten the load for power plants, but such limited measures were not enough. In January, 1918, Garfield thereupon ordered plants not engaged in essential industries to close down for a period of five days, and instituted a series of fuelless Mondays that was to last nine weeks. Unable to appreciate the need for such drastic action, the public strongly criticized these regulations. President Wilson, however, stood firmly behind the Fuel Administrator, telling the country in no uncertain terms that "we are on a war footing."

The motoring public was also asked by the Fuel Administration to restrict its consumption of gasoline. For a time "gasless Sundays" were observed in the same spirit as wheatless and meatless days. However, no such problem developed as the country faced during the second World War. Sufficient supplies of gasoline were generally available, and no need developed for strict rationing. The country was not yet as dependent on the automobile as it was to be in later years. It could have adjusted itself far more easily to restrictions than the United States of the nineteen-forties. But it was not called upon to do so.

The sixth of the major wartime agencies was the War Trade

Board, under the chairmanship of Vance C. McCormick. It not only controlled exports and imports in the interests of wartime economy, but it also bought the products of foreign countries to prevent their falling into Germany's hands. An increasing list of commodities was placed under a licensing system applying to neutral as well as American shippers. Under the terms of the Trading-with-the-Enemy Act, the War Trade Board was also empowered to take over all enemy property in the United States. An Alien Property Custodian, A. Mitchell Palmer, was appointed to administer the affairs of some thirty-two thousand foreign corporations whose aggregate capitalization totaled five hundred million dollars. One of the most important phases of this work involved the Americanization of German patents of the utmost value in the chemical industry.

While these six major boards largely controlled the nation's economic life, an important aspect of industrial mobilization beyond their province involved the status of labor. Although Samuel Gompers, president of the American Federation of Labor, early pledged full co-operation in support of the war effort, difficult questions soon arose both in regard to the supply of labor and various aspects of industrial relations. A shortage of skilled workers was an inevitable result of the demand for increased production and the loss of men drawn off by the draft, while the stoppage of immigration depleted the labor reserves upon which industry was accustomed to draw. Although there was no manpower crisis comparable to that which developed during the second World War, and the Government never found it necessary to exercise such all-embracing controls, the problem became acute in some areas. The rush of women into industry, a far more spectacular development in 1918 than in the nineteen-forties, helped out this situation to a great extent. Men were released from other jobs to take up the arduous work of mine, steel mill, or shipyard as women workers not only took over secretarial work and office jobs to a greater extent than ever before, but operated streetcars and elevators, worked on farms, and crowded into the munitions factories.

Strikes were serious for a time. Industrial workers sought to maintain the gains they had made under President Wilson's peacetime administration with the demand that wages be kept in line with the steadily rising cost of living. One violent dispute was a strike instigated by the Industrial Workers of the World in the copper mines of Bisbee, Arizona. The wartime emergency served as a spur rather than deterrent to this organization's program for world revolution. The immediate situation in Arizona was met by intervention on the part of the State Government, which forcibly deported twelve hundred strikers and left them stranded in the desert. President Wilson could hardly countenance such high-handed tactics. His general policy was one of sympathy for labor and he favored the establishment of machinery for conciliation. To provide for an equitable solution of future disputes, he consequently established early in 1918 a War Labor Conference Board, which in turn set up two special agencies: a National War Labor Board, headed by Frank P. Walsh and former President Taft, and a War Labor Policies Board, with Felix Frankfurter as its chairman.

The former board was to serve as a final court of appeal for controversies that could not be settled by other means of conciliation; the latter's function was to determine general policies in the war industries. Something like a bargain was reached between the Government and labor through these agencies. In return for maintenance of the eight-hour day, recognition of the right of workers to join unions, and support for the principle of collective bargaining, labor agreed not to strike for the duration of the war. The situation in 1918 consequently improved very much over that in 1917. The Government found no need to seek either anti-strike or compulsory arbitration laws. With public opinion as well as the conciliatory policy of the Administration exerting strong pressure in support of industrial peace, Secretary Baker declared on one occasion that labor had proved to be "more willing to keep in step than capital."

A final activity on the home economic front was the financing of the war effort. This involved army and navy costs, further loans to our Allies, and the expenses of all wartime agencies. The original appropriations made by Congress early in 1917 were soon exhausted and the cost of war steadily mounted to figures which in all our national history had never before been even remotely approached. Including advances of over ten billion dollars to the Allies, the total bill finally reached thirty-five billion dollars. However much these figures were to be dwarfed by subsequent expenditures either under the New Deal or during the second World War, they seemed in 1918 to constitute a drain upon our national resources that could hardly be met. There was prolonged controversy as to how much of the burden could be passed on to future generations and to what extent a pay-as-you-go policy was practical. The result was a compromise. Taxation was stepped up to meet something like one-third of the war costs, and two-thirds of the necessary funds were raised through public bond issues.

The war revenue acts of 1917 and 1918 increased the new individual income taxes to a basic four per cent, with a surtax that ranged from twelve per cent on all incomes over four thousand dollars to sixty-five per cent on those above five hundred thousand dollars. Corporation levies were also increased, while an excess profits tax took from twenty to sixty per cent of all income earned in excess of the annual average for the period 1911 to 1913. A multitude of special excise taxes were also placed on such articles as automobiles, railroad tickets, bank checks, theater admissions, club dues, chewing gum, and phonograph records. There was an increase in liquor and tobacco taxes, and an advance in postage rates from two to three cents. These taxes bore heavily on the public and they brought the war home to large numbers of people as could nothing else. They failed in large part, however, to take the profit out of war for many manufacturers and contractors. The Government felt compelled to pay terrific premiums for speed in the procurement of army and navy supplies, and in the construction of housing facilities for draftees and shipyard workers. It let many contracts without competitive bids and on a highly expensive cost-plus basis. The excess profits tax hardly touched the large earnings which sometimes resulted from these contracts.

If taxes thus failed to take the profit out of war for contractors and manufacturers, the complete freedom of the bulk of the people, and especially industrial workers, from any income tax whatsoever meant that there were no brakes upon rising salaries and wages. Increased purchasing power thus combined with the curtailment in the production of civilian goods to produce an inflationary spiral that soon got completely out of control and drove up prices all along the line. The cost of living mounted steadily during war days, and then continued upward until the post-war reaction of 1921 finally caused a sudden reversal. At their peak living costs were just twice the pre-war level.

The funds necessary to supplement the revenue raised by taxation were obtained through public loans. Four Liberty Loan drives and a final Victory Loan campaign in 1919 brought the Government a total $21,448,000,000, or almost twice the $11,280,-000,000 raised by taxes. Each of the five loans floated by the Treasury, at an interest rate which rose from 3½ per cent to 4¾ per cent, was heavily oversubscribed. It was estimated that altogether sixty-five million people purchased Liberty Bonds, war-savings certificates, or thrift stamps.

THE MILITARY FRONT

For all the importance of the home front, victory or defeat was to be decided upon the battlefield. As 1917 gave way to 1918, heavy reinforcements for the Allied armies in France appeared to be essential if the democratic cause was to triumph. The military situation was critical; our aid in force was imperative. And it was due to the strenuous activities of the home front that an American Expeditionary Force was now finally available.

While the British and French were holding the line on the Western Front, with the aid of supplies sent overseas under the protection of American naval units commanded by Admiral Sims, the creation of an effective military machine went steadily forward. The National Guard had been called out immediately after the declaration of war and sent to training camps to be whipped into shape as part of the new national army. The first contingents drafted under the terms of the Selective Service Act soon began streaming into hastily constructed cantonments. Their numbers steadily mounted. Some nine and a half million men registered in the first draft in July, 1917; another million a year later, and thirteen million more in September, 1918, when the original twenty-one to thirty age group was expanded to include all men from eighteen to forty-five. Of this total, 2,810,000 men were inducted into the service. With the inclusion of regulars and national guardsmen, our total military forces rose to 3,500,000.

Few major difficulties were encountered in raising this formidable army. Although there were several thousand draft-dodgers in addition to the relative handful of conscientious objectors, general opposition to the draft largely evaporated despite the fears of those who felt that it would create more serious disturbances than had conscription during the Civil War. The real task was housing these huge numbers of men, feeding them, outfitting them, and preparing them for overseas service. The War Department under the administrative direction of Secretary Baker rose admirably to the occasion. The first job — provision of quarters for over two million men — led to great waste and extravagance, but it was carried through with surprising speed. Cantonments sprang up throughout the country and almost as quickly were filled with draftees for whom a hard-pressed Quartermaster Corps then found itself called upon to provide millions of uniforms, overcoats, woolen blankets, pairs of shoes, and innumerable other articles of equipment.

To train the troops so hastily mustered into the service from private life was an even more ambitious undertaking. It was at first largely entrusted to the officers of the regular army, only about half of whom consequently saw service in France, but to an increasing extent men who had gone through the new officers' training camps were called upon. Three months' intensive work was thought to qualify a man to serve as an officer and teach the rudiments of war. For the general rank and file, the program of training was six months in an army cantonment, and then overseas service with two months behind the lines and one month in a quiet sector before going to the active front. The need for troops was so great that further time for training could not be afforded. In many cases men found themselves going into combat with even less experience.

The spirit of this citizen army was one of eagerness to get abroad, to get into the trenches, to get a chance at "the Boche." It grew out of the aggressive character of the soldiers themselves and was further fostered by the nature of their training. "All instruction," an army order of October, 1917, stated, "must contemplate the assumption of a vigorous offensive. This purpose will be emphasized in every phase of training until it becomes a settled habit of thought." Haberdashers and Negro farmhands, brokers' clerks and shoe salesmen, butchers, bakers, and candlestick-makers, took to their new military vocation with an adaptability and zest that won the quick respect of ally and enemy. Camp life was rigorous and the discipline a new and strange experience. There were few diversions, despite the sometimes frantic efforts of the Commission on Training Camp Activities, the Red Cross, and the Y.M.C.A. But there was a deep wellspring of good nature from which the American soldier drew his strength. It was reflected in the songs of army life — "You're in the Army Now"; "Oh! How I hate to get up in the Morning"; "K-K-K-Katy, beautiful Katy"; and "Good Morning, Mr. Zip, Zip, Zip." American troops had marched off to the Spanish War to the tune of "There'll be a Hot Time in the Old Town Tonight." In the first World War they sang "Over There"; "It's a Long Way to Tipperary"; and "The Long, Long Trail." And once abroad it was "Mademoiselle from Armentières," with its refrain of "Hinky Dinky, Parley-Vous?"

General Pershing had sailed for France in May, 1917, with fifty-nine officers and something more than a hundred men. By the end of that year there were fifty thousand troops sailing each month; in another six months they were embarking at the rate of ten thousand a day. There were a million men in France in July, 1918, just fifteen months after our entry into the war. There were over two million in October. So efficiently did the transport system operate, and so successful were naval operations against the submarine, that only two hundred thousand tons of shipping were lost, and only a single troopship with one hundred lives.

Although there were no landings on hostile shores as during the second World War, the advance guard had to make all the preparations for this large army without benefit of any previous experience or training. It had to develop ports for disembarkation, organize a railway service with American locomotives and American cars for moving our troops across France, build roads and cantonments, establish base camps, and provide a service of supply for both the men behind the lines and those at the front. "France was a white sheet of paper, so far as we were concerned," Secretary of War Baker declared, "and on that we had not only to write an army — we had to go back to the planting of corn in France in order that we might make a harvest."

The Allies' idea was that the American troops should be directly associated with their own, serving as replacements to be brigaded with French and British units. From the very first, however, General Pershing was determined to create an entirely independent command. His authority in France was absolute. Secretary Baker later said he gave him only two orders: "one to go to France, and the other to come home." Under such circumstances, he refused to give in to the Allies' demands. He was willing to allow a few token forces to be immediately incorporated with their troops for the moral effect of demonstrating our active participation in the war, but in October, 1917, after establishment of headquarters at Chaumont, American troops began taking over a quiet sector of the front near Toul.

Early in 1918 the situation looked bleak. The Austrians had broken through the Italian front the previous fall, necessitating the transfer of French troops to Italy's assistance. The collapse of Russia's war effort after the Bolshevik Revolution, with complete surrender to Germany in the signing of the Treaty of Brest-Litovsk in March, 1918, had freed additional German forces for action on the Western Front. Under such favorable auspices a great offensive had been launched by the Kaiser's armies that was slowly pushing the Allies back of the lines where they had been so long entrenched. Pershing believed that the retreat was due, not only to the numerical superiority of the German forces, but to war weariness born of years of defensive fighting. He was confident that if a fresh, undefeated American army was thrown into action, it would invigorate the entire Allied war effort.

This could not be done at once. To meet the immediate crisis it was necessary for American troops to reinforce the Allied lines without a moment's delay, and Pershing temporarily waived his own plans. After the German drive had been dramatically checked in the second battle of the Marne in mid-July, however, Marshal Foch, who had in the meantime been appointed to unified command of all Allied forces, was at last prevailed upon to accept the thesis to which Pershing had clung with such tenacity. As preparations developed for a great counter-offensive to the German drive, the First American Army, eighteen divisions strong, came into being.

American troops had already proved their worth in the actions in which they had fought alongside the British and the French — on the Aisne and the Meuse, at Catigny, Château Thierry, and Belleau Wood. Their part in the fighting on the Marne, where six divisions had successfully backed up the French, may well have been decisive. Now these contingents, which had been scattered at various points on the long Allied line, stretching across northern France and Belgium from Switzerland to the sea, were brought together to form a seasoned nucleus for the new American army, a half-million Yanks operating on their own. On the east of the Allies' line they took over an enlarged sector that before the end of the war was to extend westward to comprise almost a quarter of the entire front. Their first important operation, in mid-September, was to reduce a German salient that had been pushed through south of Verdun at Saint-Mihiel. There were two days of fierce fighting. The American troops suffered some seven thousand casualties, but they successfully drove the Germans back, taking sixteen thousand prisoners. A further advance to Metz might have been possible, but Allied high strategy now dictated a shift of the main American forces to a point somewhat farther westward. They were to advance across the Meuse and through the Argonne Forest.

The plans of the Supreme Command contemplated a general offensive along the entire front. It was hoped that the Germans could be thrown back sufficiently so that the initiative would be wholly restored to Allied hands and a final victory drive started the next spring. The whole American war effort, at home and on the front, was geared for an over-all attack in 1919 when our industrial production would be at its peak and far larger forces would be available in France. We know now that the issue had already been virtually decided. Hindenburg had thrown his entire strength into the spring offensive. His failure to break through the Allied lines meant that Germany was already fighting with her back to the wall. The German commander had gambled on victory before American participation could make itself fully felt — and he had lost. The opportunities facing the Allies were far greater than they realized; the end of the war was much nearer at hand.

The final offensive got under way toward the close of September with the total of American troops in the front line swollen to twenty-one divisions and some 1,200,000 men. As the French and British, with the co-operation of a few American divisions, advanced successfully in Belgium and northwestern France, the American forces on the eastern flank of the Allied line fought their way through the Argonne. It was some of the heaviest fighting of the entire war and the casualties were appallingly heavy — 120,000 men. But the German army crumbled. Before the Americans reached their planned objective of Sedan, disorganization had set in along the entire front. Hindenburg was in full retreat. It was a situation, as General Pershing later reported, where "nothing but surrender or an armistice could save his army from complete disaster."

With the Allied troops crashing ahead on the Western Front, there was even greater enemy disintegration in other sectors of the European battlefield. Bulgaria had been knocked out of the war in September, Turkey surrendered a month later, Austria was on the verge of giving way. Informed early in October that its armies in France could no longer hold out, the German Government could see no hope anywhere and it frantically undertook to conclude peace before the disaster facing Germany became complete. There was no popular will to continue a hopeless struggle, and a hastily reorganized cabinet consequently informed President Wilson of Germany's desire to negotiate terms of surrender. The Allies were unwilling to grant an armistice until the absolute supremacy of their military forces was assured, but by the end of the month there was no question of the collapse of the German armies. Mutiny and revolutionary outbreaks at home now rendered further resistance even more impossible, and the forced abdication of the Kaiser early in November was a final sign of the complete disintegration of the empire. The negotiations that had been under way between the Allies and the new German Government were concluded and an armistice was officially signed on November 11.

The news of the end of hostilities was wildly celebrated in the United States. The armistice was hailed as marking a decisive turning point in world history. Immense crowds thronged the streets of every city in the land — cheering, singing, and vociferously expressing their excitement and joy. The war was over. Germany was defeated and the Allies had won a great victory. It remained to be seen whether the "war to end war" could really establish lasting peace, and whether it had in fact made the world safe for democracy.

The Return to Peace

PRESIDENT WILSON'S GOALS

THROUGHOUT 1917 and 1918, President Wilson was greatly concerned over the problems of the future peace. In his own mind the war was above all a crusade for democracy, for the freedom of small nations, for permanent peace. He had aroused the entire country to the high purpose of his own idealism, and he awakened an amazing popular response among the plain people throughout the world. The overthrow of the German Empire meant that the time had now come to realize these ambitions for a new world order based on justice. It represented a tremendous opportunity to carry out what he believed to be America's historic mission for the spread of constitutional liberty.

The outlines of the peace Wilson sought had been nebulously foreshadowed when he called upon the belligerents to lay down their arms early in 1917. His subsequent messages to Congress and to the American people had reaffirmed these general principles. The only change in his point of view was a growing conviction that no lasting accord could be reached with the existing German régime. "The object of this war," he wrote to the Pope in August, 1917, "is to deliver the free peoples of the world from the menace and the actual power of a vast military establishment controlled by an irresponsible government." Finally in January, 1918, he definitely blueprinted his objectives in the famous Fourteen Points. It was with the understanding that peace would be based upon the principles they outlined that Germany had capitulated.

What were the Fourteen Points?

I. Open covenants of peace, openly arrived at. . . .

II. Absolute freedom of navigation upon the seas, outside territorial waters, alike in peace and war. . . .

III. The removal, so far as possible, of all economic barriers. . . .

IV. Adequate guarantees given and taken that national armaments will be reduced to the lowest point consistent with domestic safety.

V. A free, open-minded, and absolutely impartial adjustment of all colonial claims. . . .

VI. The evacuation of all Russian territory. . . .

VII. Belgium . . . must be evacuated and restored. . . .

VIII. All French territory should be freed and the invaded portions restored. . . .

IX. A readjustment of the frontiers of Italy should be effected along clearly recognized lines of nationality. . . .

X. The peoples of Austria-Hungary . . . should be accorded the freest opportunity of autonomous development.

XI. Rumania, Serbia, and Montenegro should be evacuated; occupied territories restored; Serbia accorded free and secure access to the sea. . . .

XII. The Turkish portions of the present Ottoman Empire should be assured a secure sovereignty. . . .

XIII. An independent Polish state should be erected . . . which should be assured a free and secure access to the sea. . . .

XIV. A general association of nations must be formed under specific covenants for the purpose of affording mutual guarantees of political independence and territorial integrity to great and small nations alike.

The Fourteen Points were an expression of Wilson's most sincere convictions, but at the same time they had an immense propaganda value. They could hardly have been more skillfully contrived. They met the basic demands of the peoples of the Allied nations, they raised up the spirits of the small countries seeking freedom, and they reassured the German people that they would be justly treated. "We have no jealousy of German greatness," the President stated, "and there is nothing in this program that impairs it." It is now easy to see that the Fourteen Points created hopes which could not possibly have been fulfilled. They were in certain aspects mutually conflicting. They could not be reconciled with certain of the commitments the Allies had already made in the secret treaties they had concluded for dividing the spoils of war. They ran counter to Allied determination that Germany should pay the costs of war and to the traditional policy of British sea power. The President was compelled to intimate that the United States might make a separate peace before the Allies could finally be persuaded to accept his program, and even then it was modified by reservations in regard both to reparations and freedom of the seas.

Basic to Wilson's whole conception of peace was the proposal to establish an association of nations. This was anything but a new idea. Apart from several precedents for world organization, a widely supported movement in favor of an association of nations had developed in the United States in the early days of the war. There had been formed in January, 1915, a League to Enforce Peace. Its leading adherents, ironically enough in view of subsequent developments, were prominent Republicans. Theodore Roosevelt, who had urged establishment of a world league when he received the Nobel Peace Prize in 1910, strongly supported it. So did former President Taft, Elihu Root, Senator Knox, and Senator Lodge. "I do not believe that when Washington warned us against entangling alliances," Lodge wrote in 1916, "he meant for one moment that we should not join with the other civilized nations of the world if a method could be found to diminish war and encourage peace." It was not until the groundwork had been thoroughly laid by these Republicans that the President declared his sympathy for the general program sponsored by the League to Enforce Peace. After May, 1916, however, he reverted to the idea of world association repeatedly — in his "peace without victory" speech, in his war message, and in later addresses. The proposal in the Fourteenth Point was not merely a crystallization of his own thinking. It was the expression of an idea widely held throughout the country.

Latent opposition both to an association of nations and to the whole concept of a negotiated peace nevertheless developed toward the close of 1918. The intolerance which Wilson foresaw, when he told Frank Cobb on the eve of our intervention that the end would be a dictated peace, was now widely prevalent. Senator Lodge was veering away from his support for a world league and stressing the dangers of a "soft peace." Theodore Roosevelt was expressing his old belligerency. "Let us dictate peace by the hammering of guns," he demanded, "and not chat about peace to the accompaniment of typewriters." Expressing a view that had nation-wide currency, the *Charleston News and Courier* declared there would be no bargaining "with the blood-stained gang of thugs and pirates . . . who deliberately . . . plunged the world into war."

Here were clear indications of a sharp revulsion from the high idealism with which the country had embarked on its crusade. There was also a partisan angle to the growing opposition to the President's program. As the end of the war came in sight, the Republicans felt freed of the patriotic necessity for national union. They began to think of mending their political fences. They felt that something had to be done to prevent the Democratic Party from adding full credit for the conclusion of peace to its wartime laurels. There was also the rising fear of conservative interests throughout the country that if the President came through the peace negotiations with increased prestige, he might be strong enough to take up again the interrupted program of domestic reform implicit in the New Freedom. In so far as his ideas upon peace were open to attack, they felt bound to make the most of every opportunity presented them.

Partisanship and conservative fears were alike heightened by a move made by the President on the eve of the congressional elections in 1918. While Republican sniping had already weakened the uneasy political truce which had been declared in 1917, Wilson completely shattered it by a frankly partisan appeal to the country's voters. "If you have approved of my leadership and wish me to continue to be your unembarrassed spokesman in affairs at home and abroad," he asked, "I earnestly beg that you will express yourselves unmistakably to that effect by returning a Democratic majority to both the Senate and the House of Representatives."

Whatever may have been the effect of this appeal as compared with other aspects of the mounting antagonism to Wilsonian policies, the election was a victory for the Republicans. They won a majority in both houses of Congress. The President nevertheless refused to accept this stinging rebuke as repudiation of his program. He proceeded to carry out his plans for the forthcoming peace negotiations with complete disregard for any possible right of the Republicans to be consulted. Taking the unprecedented step of deciding to head himself the delegation which was to attend the conference to be held in Paris, he failed to appoint to the commission any one of the Republican leaders or any member of the Senate. The delegates, in addition to President Wilson, were Colonel House, Secretary Lansing, General Tasker H. Bliss, and former Ambassador Henry White. The lastnamed, a veteran career diplomat, was nominally a Republican and in intimate contact with the party leaders, but from the political point of view his appointment, rather than that of Taft, Hughes, Root, or Lodge, merely added fuel to the smouldering fire of political discontent.

It broke into raging flame as the President sailed for Europe in December aboard the *George Washington*. He was viciously attacked for leaving the country and for failing to include members of the opposition on the peace commission. He was accused of assuming entirely unwarranted powers in arrogant disregard of the public interest. He was said to be actuated by a messianic complex that made him believe that he alone could bring peace to the world. There appeared more than ever to be strong grounds for the warning which Roosevelt had given "our Allies, our enemies, and Mr. Wilson himself" soon after the congressional elections. "Mr. Wilson has no authority whatever to speak for the American people at this time," the former President had hotly declared on that occasion. "His leadership has just been emphatically repudiated by them. Mr. Wilson and his Fourteen Points and his four supplementary points and all his utterances every which way have ceased to have any shadow of right to be accepted as expressive of the will of the American people."

In marked contrast to the ominous political situation at home, Wilson was welcomed enthusiastically abroad. He was everywhere greeted by cheering crowds and given such a public reception as few statesmen have ever been accorded. "No one has ever had such cheers," wrote one foreign correspondent, "I, who heard them in the streets of Paris, can never forget them in all my life. I saw Foch pass, Clemenceau pass, Lloyd George, generals, returning troops, banners, but Wilson heard from his carriage, something different, inhuman or superhuman." So effectively had he stated the whole world's dream for peace and justice that the President was accepted as a savior of mankind. Hundreds of thousands of persons pinned their hopes of a new international order upon his sincerity and immense influence. It has been said that despite the growing movement against him at home no man ever commanded greater popular support throughout the world than Wilson in the winter of 1918-19. The common people everywhere appeared to have caught a glimpse of his vision that the war which they had gone through was "the culminating and final war for human liberty."

The peace conference in Paris was a momentous affair. There were hundreds of delegates representing the twenty-seven allied and associated nations, and hordes of advisers, experts, minor officials, and secretaries. It was soon found to be impossible to do any business in a full session of the conference, and a more restricted group, the Council of Ten, was charged with the active conduct of the negotiations. It was composed of two representatives from each of the major Powers — the United States, Great Britain, France, Italy, and Japan. There was no representative of the Central Powers, and no delegate from the newly instituted Soviet Government in Russia. Here was a first compromise on Wilson's part when faced with the realities of European politics. The victorious Allies would draw up the terms of peace. Although Germany had predicated her acceptance of an armistice upon a settlement based on the Fourteen Points, she would have no voice in deciding its terms. It still remained to be seen whether they would be mild or severe, but it would be a dictated rather than a negotiated peace.

The Council of Ten soon gave way to a still smaller group. Four men were charged with remaking the world: Woodrow Wilson,

President of the United States; David Lloyd George, Prime Minister of Great Britain; Georges Clemenceau, Premier of France; and Vittorio Orlando, Premier of Italy. In background, in training, in point of view they greatly differed, but among the three European statesmen there was a certain solidarity in their underlying concepts of the future peace which drew them together from the very first and left the spokesman for America solitary and apart. Their primary interest was to build up the political and economic influence of the countries they represented, and so to curtail Germany's power that she could never again threaten her neighbors' national security. They were without many illusions, these three men; they prided themselves upon being tough-minded and realistic. "Mr. Wilson bores me with his Fourteen Points," the cynical old Tiger of France once exclaimed; "why, God Almighty has only ten."

Over against these exponents of European power politics, who were ready to employ every weapon in the armory of diplomacy, stood the schoolmaster president — the idealist, the visionary, the doctrinaire. However shining the armor of his righteousness, however wholehearted his determination to make his dream of a new world order come true, he found himself again and again fighting forces that refused to give way before his onslaughts. He was compelled to compromise his principles and to make concessions that resulted in a treaty departing in many ways from the Fourteen Points. Nevertheless, he succeeded in saving more from the wreckage of his original hopes than is always recognized. The League of Nations, whatever its ultimate destiny, was a striking triumph for an idealism which withstood even the tortuous wiles of European diplomacy. And there were other instances where through skillful yielding on some disputed points, he won more basic concessions to the cause he represented. There is much that is enigmatic about Wilson. How explain his acceptance of the need to compromise in Paris, and his obdurate refusal to do so in Washington? Possibly the human spirit had reached its limits: he could not again compromise to save a compromise.

THE TREATY OF PEACE

The Treaty of Versailles, cornerstone of the series of settlements with the Central Powers which made up the Peace of Paris, dealt with Germany as a defeated nation. On June 28, 1919, she had no alternative other than to sign its harsh terms. She was compelled to restore Alsace-Lorraine to France and to make certain minor territorial concessions to both Belgium and Denmark. She surrendered parts of Silesia and conceded to Poland a corridor to the sea which separated her own territories. She was totally disarmed and stripped of all her colonies. Forced to admit sole responsibility for the war, she was held liable for reparation payments to be determined by an Allied Reparation Commission. And finally the Rhineland was to be occupied for a period of fifteen years and then demilitarized, while the Saar Valley was likewise to be occupied pending a plebiscite to determine its final disposition.

It was a punitive peace, but its terms might have been much more drastic. It was a far more lenient settlement than the Treaty of Brest-Litovsk which Germany had imposed on Russia; it was unquestionably much more moderate than the demands a victorious Germany might have been expected to enforce. It fell far short of the dismemberment of Germany widely called for — and especially in France — by those who felt the Allies should once and forever crush German power. President Wilson, for example, blocked the insistent French demand for either permanent occupation of the Rhineland or for making it an independent buffer state. This issue had led to one of the most serious crises throughout the conference. The President at one time ordered steam up on the S.S. *George Washington* in a dramatic gesture to convince Clemenceau that he would return to America rather than give in. In the final settlement he signed a tripartite treaty with England and France pledging American assistance in the event of an unprovoked German attack, and while this pact was never acted upon by the Senate, it enabled Clemenceau to back down more gracefully from the position that he had been unable to hold against Wilson's inflexible determination.

Greater violation was done the principles of the Fourteen Points, and the basic theory of self-determination, in the supplementary treaties signed at Paris than in the Treaty of Versailles itself. Here the President found himself running headlong against the secret treaties that the Allies had concluded among themselves. He was forced to make concessions which could not possibly be reconciled with his own ideas. After reluctantly admitting Italy's claims to the Dalmatian coast, he succeeded in compelling her to surrender Fiume only after a crisis which caused Premier Orlando temporarily to withdraw from the conference. But even this gesture in support of self-determination proved to be a hollow triumph. Italy later seized the disputed city.

In other respects the establishment of new boundaries in eastern Europe created more problems than it solved. The break-up of the Austro-Hungarian Empire bred international rivalries as dangerous to peace as those which that troubled part of Europe had known before the war. Large blocs of alien peoples were included in the new succession states of Poland, Czechoslovakia, and Jugoslavia. A basis was laid for the claims which Germany would later put forth to union with Austria and for the recovery of the Sudetenland in Czechoslovakia. The desire of France for an eastern bulwark against German aggression governed these territorial settlements far more than the self-determination of peoples.

A further crisis arose when Japan insisted upon retaining the former German islands she had occupied in the North Pacific and also all those rights and special privileges she had seized from Germany in the Chinese province of Shangtung. The former question was settled without great difficulty by awarding the islands to Japan as a mandatory power. No one foresaw the uses to which the Carolines and Marianas were to be put in another two decades, and, ironically enough, it was over the Shantung issue that the great battle raged in Paris. Wilson held out against this outright robbery of the territory of a friendly nation, but fortified by promises made in the secret treaties, Japan threatened to quit the conference if her claims were not maintained. Fearful now of the whole structure of peace, unwilling to face the possible

consequences of Japanese withdrawal, the President agreed upon
a compromise. Japan was allowed to retain Germany's former
economic concessions in Shantung, but she undertook to reach
an accord with China for eventual restoration of the province
itself. Even Wilson could not blind himself to the surrender of
principle this involved; he felt he had no alternative.

There was no denying the patchwork nature of many of the
territorial settlements made in the Peace of Paris. There was no
denying its violation on many counts of the Fourteen Points and
of the principle of self-determination. There was no denying the
ominous character of concessions made in an impossible attempt
to reconcile Wilsonian principles with the Allies' secret treaties.
But in establishing the League of Nations the President scored
one victory which he felt compensated for every sacrifice. Moreover, it was inextricably bound up with the general peace settlement.

He had insisted against all opposition that it be made an
integral part of the treaty and that the covenant should be
adopted before any other questions were decided. It was his
triumph on this major point, to be maintained at all costs, that
induced him to make later concessions. He had given in on
certain of the demands of both Italy and Japan as the price he
felt compelled to pay to retain their support for the League.
Only through these concessions did he believe it possible to
prevent their lining up with Germany in opposition to the new
system of collective security. The irony of this sacrifice need
hardly be pointed out in the light of world political alignments
which brought Germany, Italy, and Japan together in an anti-
democratic alliance just twenty years after the bitter struggle in
Paris. President Wilson was confident in 1919, however, that the
League of Nations would redress the wrongs and injustices of the
peace through its provisions for peaceful adjustment of all future
international disputes. He placed all his bets on the covenant.
"The settlements may be temporary," he declared, "but the
processes must be permanent."

The League of Nations, the inner and supposedly indestructible
core of the entire peace settlement, was an international organiza-

tion to which only the Allied and Associated Powers originally belonged. It was later to be open to membership of all the world. Through its assembly and council, it was charged with administration of a mandate system over Germany's former colonies, the settlement of international disputes before they should lead to war, and collective action against any nation which refused to abide by the League's decisions. The heart of the covenant was Article Ten. This was a collective guarantee of the territorial integrity and political independence of every nation against external aggression.

It had proved impossible to conclude a peace treaty embodying disarmament, the abolition of trade barriers, freedom of the seas, and complete international justice. The League of Nations was intended to achieve these aims. It would give to democratic ideals the validity that otherwise appeared to be so greatly impaired by concession and compromise. Just as the Reparations Commission, established to determine what Germany must pay to make good the damage done by her armies, would work out an equitable solution of this difficult problem, so would the League revise political settlements which proved unsatisfactory. It would develop the mandates system as a substitute for colonial imperialism. It would carry out a program of world disarmament. It was the hope of the future, worth any sacrifice of the present. These were the aspirations of 1919. And from this point of view the tragic failure of the Peace of Paris was not the result of the terms imposed upon the defeated nations, but was due to the way in which they were carried out during the next two decades. The collapse of the League's hopes resulted from its transformation from an agency to promote peace to an agency committed to rigid maintenance of the *status quo*. And this was all the more impossible because the *status quo* was based upon an international settlement which violated many of the League's own principles.

Defeat of the League

American membership in the League was fundamental to the whole idea of a world organization for peace. The President had proceeded on the assumption that whatever difficulties he might encounter in Europe, he could count upon the support of the American people. With a blindness which can never be satisfactorily explained, he ignored the growing indications that the country was gradually turning away from his leadership. He apparently interpreted each instance of opposition to his program as narrow partisanship. He remained superbly confident that the popular support he had been so successful in inspiring during the war was still at his command. The practical necessity of obtaining a two-thirds majority in a Senate controlled by his political opponents he appears to have wholly overlooked in his unalterable belief that where he led, the American people would follow.

A first instance of his naïve assumption that there was no need to placate the Senate occurred during a brief trip he made to this country during the course of the negotiations in Paris — in March, 1919. The League Covenant, just drawn up by a special conference commission, was already subject to attack. Upon the instigation of Senator Lodge a group of thirty-nine senators and senators-elect, six more than the number necessary to defeat any treaty, signed a condemnatory round-robin resolution. It explicitly declared that "the constitution of the league of nations in the form now proposed to the peace conference should not be accepted by the United States. . . . " While Wilson was prepared to incorporate in the covenant certain of the suggestions made by friendly Republican critics, such as adequate safeguards for the Monroe Doctrine, his answer to the senatorial round robin was one of defiance. "When that treaty comes back," he stated on the eve of his return to Paris, "gentlemen on this side will find the covenant not only in it, but so many threads of the treaty tied to the covenant that you cannot dissect the covenant from the treaty without destroying the whole vital structure." The lines were drawn for a struggle in which Republican senators and the President were to clash in embittered, unrelenting opposition.

The Treaty of Versailles, with the League as closely entwined with its other provisions as Wilson had declared it would be, was submitted for senatorial approval in July, 1919. While there is every reason to believe that a great majority of Americans strongly favored it, the general public was already beginning to lose its engrossing wartime interest in foreign affairs and becoming much more concerned with the domestic problems of post-war reconstruction. Senator Lodge, in immediate charge of the treaty as chairman of the Senate Foreign Relations Committee, played for time. His opposition to the League, strangely compounded of sincere fears of the difficulties in which it might involve the United States and of partisan hatred of Wilson, was now so strong that he was prepared to adopt any strategy that he thought might lead either to its emasculation or its defeat. If action could be held up, he believed that the growing apathy of the public would enable the treaty's opponents to write their own ticket.

In the country as a whole the division of opinion on the League crossed all political lines. While it probably commanded much more Democratic than Republican support, such outstanding Republican leaders as Taft, Hughes, and Root thoroughly believed in American membership. It was widely — and strongly — felt that the United States could not now repudiate the promise implied in its intervention in the war to assume its share of responsibility for maintaining world peace. The imperfections of the Treaty of Versailles were fully recognized, the covenant itself was severely criticized. But adherents of the League were convinced that it held out the promise of a better world, and that unless the United States did its share, that promise would be completely nullified. Thirty-two state legislatures endorsed the League; as many governors went on record as favoring it. Senator Lodge himself admitted in May that what he termed the vocal classes of the community — a majority of newspaper editors, teachers, clergymen — "were friendly to the League as it stood and were advocating it."

The opposition was more scattered and more particularized. It included many who were afraid of American entanglement in European affairs and believed in political isolation, and also enemies of Wilson who hardly bothered to disguise a hostility which had nothing whatsoever to do with the principle of a world league. Conservatives still feared a strengthening of the program of domestic reform; liberals felt that Wilson had betrayed their cause by his compromises in Paris. German-Americans were convinced the terms of peace were unfair to the mother country; Irish-Americans saw in the League a new instrument of British imperialism. The Hearst press sounded a terrifying note of alarm about the dangers of creating a superstate and spread the slogan of "one hundred per cent Americanism." But strongest of all the forces operating against the League was disillusionment. The bickering over peace after the idealism of our war aims steadily undermined popular faith in international co-operation.

These cross-currents of popular opinion were responsible for various attempts to find a middle course which would enable the United States to join the League without making commitments that awoke such violent prejudices. There were in the Senate some forty thick-and-thin Democratic supporters of Wilson prepared to accept the treaty without dotting an "i." At the other extreme were thirteen or fourteen Republican irreconcilables, led by Senator Borah, who refused to have anything to do with any League whatsoever. Between them were two shifting groups which favored reservations to the treaty and differed only in so far as to whether the reservations should be "strict" or "mild." If at any time there could have been an agreement among the reservationists and those Democrats willing to accept the treaty exactly as presented, more than the two-thirds majority necessary for ratification would have been easily available. While today many of the arguments over reservations appear picayune, contradictory, or irrelevant, agreement nevertheless proved impossible.

As the debate continued in the Senate, Wilson followed the course he had adopted in so many other political crises. He appealed to the country. In September, 1919, he started on a western tour seeking popular support for the League. In speech after speech he insisted that unless the covenant was ratified, without reservations, the whole movement for international peace would break down. The task he had undertaken was one beyond his physical powers. Worn down by the responsibilities of his position, the President collapsed. He suffered a paralytic stroke that confined him to his bed for several weeks and left the country virtually leaderless for over seven months. The wildest rumors as to his condition were spread about, quieted only when a congressional delegation visited him in his sick-room. He had not altogether lost his keen grasp of affairs. "Well, Mr. President, we have all been praying for you," Senator Fall is reputed to have said. "Which way, Senator?" was the President's quick response.

Under such circumstances Lodge finally carried the Republican majority with him in forcing the adoption of fourteen reservations which would almost surely have reopened the whole League question among the other signatory powers. Several of them were little more than slaps at the President; others were aimed at what was believed to be the preponderant power of the British Commonwealth in the League Assembly. Most important was a reservation which would have released the United States from any commitments in maintaining the territorial integrity of member nations under the provisions of Article Ten. Believing that the real purpose behind the Lodge reservations was so to weaken the League as to render it a meaningless debating society, Wilson flatly refused to consider them. The intransigence of Lodge clashed headlong with the President's stubbornness. Every possibility of compromise was lost in the bitterness, emotional fervor, and heated partisanship which the dispute engendered on both sides. As the reservationists stood firm, Wilson virtually ordered his Democratic supporters to vote against a resolution which he declared "does not provide for ratification, but, rather, for the nullification, of the treaty." When the question at last came to a vote on November 19, the treaty *with* the Lodge reservations was rejected, 39 to 55, through an unhappy alliance of its Democratic supporters and the Republican irreconcilables. Presented *without* reservations, political lines shifted and it went down to a second defeat, by a vote of 38 to 53, through the alliance of irreconcilables and reservationists.

There were shouts of triumph from the anti-League forces. "The greatest victory since Appomattox," Senator Borah declared. The pro-Leaguers refused to accept the decision as final.

Representatives of national organizations whose membership totaled twenty million persons called upon the Senate to reverse its decision. A widespread movement developed to work out reservations which would somehow bridge the gap between the Republican and Democratic positions. While Wilson was by now willing to accept a few mild reservations, he maintained his stubborn and obdurate refusal to make any concessions that proved acceptable to the opposition. He was more than ever convinced that its objective was to kill the treaty. "Either we should enter the League fearlessly," he wrote, "accepting the responsibility and not fearing the rôle of leadership which we now enjoy . . . or we should retire as gracefully as possible from the great concert of powers by which the world was saved."

The President was a sick man. He had broken with his closest friends and advisers. He was out of touch with public opinion. Nothing could be done. When the treaty came up again for vote in March, 1920, twenty Democrats fell away from his leadership to accept a revised set of reservations upon which the Republican majority had agreed. Without a release from the White House, the rest of his followers stood by their guns. The final vote was 49 to 35 — a majority now in favor of ratification but seven votes short of the necessary two-thirds. The decision had at last been made. The United States would not enter the League of Nations. It would not participate in the peace for which it had been so greatly responsible. Sixteen months later, in July, 1921, the war with Germany was declared at an end by the passage of a congressional resolution and in August a separate treaty, incorporating those provisions of the Treaty of Versailles which immediately served our national interest, but omitting the League Covenant, was ingloriously signed.

Back to Normalcy

Eight months after the Senate's final rejection of the League, a presidential election gave the people themselves an opportunity to render a verdict upon Wilson's foreign policy. In the two years since the Armistice, however, much had happened to divert popular attention from the issue in which the country had been so greatly interested when the President first brought his peace treaty back from Paris. It had become more and more obsessed with domestic problems centering on the return to peace, and there was reflected in every political move of 1919 and 1920 an overwhelming desire to get back to the business of ordinary living.

Demobilization of the millions of men who had been called to arms, the resumption by industry of its normal peacetime functions, the liquidation of governmental activities which had been undertaken only because of the wartime emergency — these issues were a compelling challenge to democracy involving almost as much stress and strain as the creation of the machinery of war. The job was done — and in a remarkably short time. The American soldier disappeared from the American scene; factories turned once again to the production of civilian goods rather than tanks, artillery, or airplanes, and beginning with the termination of the activities of the War Industries Board on January 1, 1919, the various wartime agencies were with some few exceptions rapidly liquidated.

The return to peace on the home front, however, was not a carefully planned procedure. Reconversion was carried through, as subsequent events were to reveal, far too swiftly and without adequate provision for a reasonable settlement of post-war problems of economic reconstruction. The compelling interest of the American people was to shake themselves free from wartime restrictions and to re-establish at once the country's traditional freedom of private enterprise. Moreover, there was such a pronounced conservative reaction, not only to wartime restrictions, but to the program of regulation advanced during the progressive era, that the Republican majority in Congress gave short shrift to any ideas for continuing, even temporarily, existing controls over business and industry.

A project for government ownership of the railroads, with operation through a board on which labor, railway management, and the public were to be equally represented, was overwhelmingly defeated and the railways were unreservedly restored to their owners through passage of the Transportation Act of 1920.

Although the powers of the Interstate Commerce Commission were strengthened by enabling it to prescribe rates on the basis of a physical valuation of railroad property, to supervise a highly complicated system of railroad loans, and to bring about further railroad consolidation, these measures were largely in the interests of the railroads themselves. This same year Congress also adopted a Merchant Marine Act handing over to private management the vessels that had been built by the United States Shipping Board. The reluctance of private owners to take over this fleet created a difficult problem, but the terms of the new bill sought to make the process as easy as possible through lowering the prices of the ships, providing loans for prospective purchasers and establishing indirect operational subsidies. If the program even then did not prove successful, and the Government was unable to withdraw entirely from the shipping business, it was not for want of generous encouragement to private enterprise.

In contrast to the aid accorded business interests, labor found itself at the conclusion of hostilities largely deprived of the support it had begun to enjoy from the Government. In an effort to maintain the gains made during the progressive era and secure an increase in wages to meet the continuing rise of prices, there was consequently a widespread resort to strikes. The year 1919 was one of the most turbulent in the annals of labor history. Among many other outbreaks, some three hundred thousand steel workers went on strike under the fiery leadership of William Z. Foster when their employers refused to consider their demand for higher pay, and four hundred and fifty thousand miners in the bituminous coal fields renewed their old struggle for recognition of the United Mine Workers. Equally threatening to the public interest were a five-day general strike in Seattle which aroused the entire Northwest to fear of social revolt, and a strike of the Boston police that for a time deprived that city of its guardians of law and order. In each instance the strikers were defeated. The Government made no move to protect the steel workers when the companies moved in strike-breakers to crush their employees' resistance, and the Department of Justice obtained an injunction against the miners that greatly aided the coal operators in winning an easy victory in the coal fields.

An element in this general situation which accounted in considerable measure for the attitude of the Government was the widespread belief that the strikers were affected by the new communistic theories emanating from Russia, if not acting directly on orders from Moscow. To the circumstances that led to such fears of Bolshevism, we shall return in considering our relations with the Soviet Government. The country, in 1919, in any event, was swept by a Red scare which caused the public to direct against persons suspected of Bolshevik sympathies, or of any radical activities whatsoever, something of the hatred that had been formerly shown to supposed German sympathizers.

In response to such fears and alarms, highly exaggerated even though an American Communist Party had been formed and there was no question that it had some adherents within the ranks of labor, the Department of Justice undertook to expose all suspected Reds. A dramatic raid on New Year's Day, 1920, netted thousands of alleged communists, criminal syndicalists, and other radicals, and while the greater number of those taken into custody were released for lack of evidence, the incident caused nation-wide excitement. Aliens were also hunted down with a zeal reminiscent of the wartime drive against German spies and some two hundred and forty-nine were summarily deported to Russia on the transport *Buford*, popularly know as the "Soviet Ark." "No one who was in the United States, as I chanced to be, in the autumn of 1919," a British journalist later wrote, "will forget the feverish condition of the public mind at that time. It was hag-ridden by the specter of Bolshevism. . . . Property was in an agony of fear, and the horrid name 'Radical' covered the most innocent departure from conventional thought with a suspicion of desperate purpose."

The prompt return to highly conservative policies in supporting the interests of private enterprise, and the hysterical fear that Bolshevism was boring within the labor movement, reflected what was perhaps an only natural reaction from the idealism of the war. The American people had been buoyed up to make real sacrifices in the Allied cause by the hope that the war would in reality make the world safe for democracy and establish lasting accord. Their dreams were cruelly shattered as Europe quarreled over the spoils of war and Wilson himself compromised his high ideals to win a League of Nations which the Senate stubbornly rejected. Any vital interest in reform, in the pursuit of social justice, in strengthening the bases of democracy was at least temporarily dissipated. A crusading spirit had abruptly given way to one of feverish self-seeking as the country turned its back on Europe and the new world order.

Under such circumstances — the first steps toward liquidating the war having been carried through and the country still in the turbulent atmosphere of labor disturbances and Red scares — the American people turned in midsummer of 1920 to the presidential campaign. It was almost certainly a Republican year, and the party's choice of a candidate was all the more difficult on that account. General Leonard Wood and Governor Frank O. Lowden of Illinois were the two leading contenders and their strength was almost equally matched. An influential bloc of Republican senators, however, favored a weaker candidate who would be less likely to assert the influence of the White House over that of Congress. As the convention appeared to be settling into a deadlock, political wires were pulled behind the scenes. A conference of leaders in a "smoke-filled room" decided upon the name of a relatively inconspicuous senator from Ohio whom they thought they could control — Warren Gamaliel Harding. He already had some following, and put forward at the psychological moment as a dark horse candidate who could win the support of both the Wood and Lowden factions, he was given the nomination on the tenth ballot. Calvin Coolidge, Governor of Massachusetts, was later named as his running mate.

The Democratic nominee was Governor James M. Cox of Ohio, a political figure whose stature was not much greater than that of Senator Harding. The illness of President Wilson, apart from all other considerations, made him unavailable for a possible third term and the choice had fallen on Cox after a three-cornered fight with Secretary McAdoo and Attorney General Palmer. The Democratic candidate for Vice-President was Franklin D. Roosevelt, the Assistant Secretary of the Navy in the Wilson Administration.

The nominal issue in the campaign was foreign policy. President Wilson had called for "a solemn referendum" on the treaty issue and persuaded the Democratic candidates to make their appeal for election on the necessity for ratification. And the League still commanded sufficient popular following to compel the Republicans to straddle. In order to keep in line influential pro-Leaguers, including Taft, Hughes, and Root, Harding vaguely declared himself in favor of a new association of nations. Nevertheless, the controversy over the League, for all the speeches made on either side of the question, was a secondary issue. Anti-Wilsonism was the important factor in building up Republican strength. The country as a whole wanted to forget all about foreign affairs in order to concentrate on the problem of economic recovery from the disturbing effects of war. The situation was somewhat analogous to that in 1900 when the issue of imperialism had been dwarfed by the desire to ensure election of an administration which it was believed would successfully promote national prosperity.

Harding had sounded the keynote of his campaign as early as May, 1920. "America's present need," he had declared, "is not heroics but healing; not nostrums but normalcy; not revolution but restoration . . . not surgery but serenity." To a people weary and disillusioned from its overseas adventures, these alliterative phrases struck a responsive chord. A return to the familiar was what they sought above all else. They could not be aroused from this deep desire to get back to ordinary ways of living by any appeal to enlist once again under the banners of either domestic reform or world peace. The immediate post-war period was "the zero hour of our courage and faith," William Allen White declared, and the negative promise of a placid conservatism swept the Republicans into office. The country gave Harding 16,152,000 votes to Cox's 9,147,000, a majority of sixty-four per cent; the count in the electoral college was 404 to 127.

The election was not the great and solemn referendum for which President Wilson had called. Its results were nonetheless interpreted by the victors as a final rejection of the proposal that America should undertake its full responsibilities in maintaining world peace. The theory that Europe's affairs were none of our business, and that we could more securely build our own civilization in political isolation, had apparently won popular endorsement. The trend which foreign policy had followed since the eighteen-nineties toward a larger rôle in international affairs was consequently abruptly reversed when Harding came into office, and it was not to be fully resumed until the dreadful shadow of another war fell over the world. The American people had repudiated a "fruitful leadership for a barren independence," the broken statesman in the White House sadly declared: " . . . They will have to learn now by bitter experience just what they have lost. . . . We had a chance to gain the leadership of the world. We have lost it, and soon we shall be witnessing the tragedy of it all."

From Prosperity
to Depression

Background of the
Nineteen-Twenties

ECONOMIC PROSPERITY

THE ELECTION of President Harding ushered in a period in American history characterized by conservatism and nationalism. Even more striking in its immediate impact, the nineteen-twenties also witnessed unexampled industrial expansion, and, until the dramatic crash of the New York stock market in 1929, what appeared to be limitless prosperity. Caught up in the flood-tide of this economic advance, it was hardly surprising that the public had little time for those ideas of political and social reform considered so important during the progressive era. There was a definite lag in the quest for social justice, further retreat from the liberal spirit of the New Nationalism and the New Freedom. Visiting the country in 1925, André Siegfried found indeed that America had come of age, but with "a materialistic society, organized to produce things rather than people, with output set up as a god."

This was a harsh characterization and far from being wholly true. The nineteen-twenties were materialistic, but they were also dynamic and vigorous, stimulating sweeping advance along the scientific and educational front as well as in the production of goods. Yet output as a god did reflect the prevailing spirit among many elements of the population, and a nation enjoying the highest standard of living it had ever attained was not likely to ponder too deeply over changing social values. Only after time had demonstrated the hollowness of much of the period's prosperity could the American people appreciate the corroding influence of its overemphasis on conservatism and nationalism.

Good times had not followed immediately upon conclusion of the war. A period of readjustment could hardly have been avoided under existing circumstances. Sudden and disastrous deflation was the almost inevitable consequence of wartime price rises that by 1920 had doubled the cost of living. Deflation brought with it industrial stagnation, unemployment, and widespread distress. In 1921 there were over nineteen thousand business failures, involving firms with a total capitalization of almost a billion dollars, and three and one-half million persons were thrown out of work. As the expanded market for agricultural products collapsed, the farmer was even worse off than the businessman or average wage-earner. The precipitate drop in farm prices, preventing the meeting of mortgage payments, meant foreclosure and loss of property. Nevertheless, the turn soon came. Markets gradually revived; pent-up consumer demand halted the downward spiral in prices; the unemployment slack was largely taken up. The wheels of industry began to whir more rapidly and production headed toward new high levels. By 1922 the United States had entered upon its fabulous seven years of plenty.

With an expanding domestic market supplemented by a growing foreign trade, industry now envisioned illimitable opportunities for growth and proceeded to make the most of them. It was true that both the domestic market and foreign markets were buoyed up by somewhat questionable means — installment buying at home and foreign loans abroad. There were other factors in the situation to which a few carping economists pointed — and to which we shall have to return — that threatened to undermine the bases of our newfound prosperity. However, almost every graph of economic activity, whether of production, sales, or employment, showed a persistent upward curve. It became an almost universal belief that the new economic order had averted all danger of the cyclical depressions of the past. "We in America are nearer to the final triumph over poverty than ever before in the history of any land," President Hoover confidently proclaimed in 1928. ". . . We have not yet reached the goal, but given a chance to go forward with the policies of the last eight years, we shall soon, with the help of God, be in sight of the day when poverty will be banished from this nation." The American people saw little reason to question such promises. They were producing more, earning more, spending more, and saving more than at any previous time in their history. They could see no reason why this happy state of affairs should not continue indefinitely.

Industry was able to report between 1921 and 1929 a gain of more than fifty per cent in the value of its products. In the latter year iron and steel, machinery, automobiles, petroleum, textiles, prepared foods, and the thousand and one products of American manufacture reached a total value of $68,000,000,000. At the same time the tremendous task of marketing these products led to a phenomenal expansion in wholesale and retail trade. Selling became quite as important as manufacturing. Advertisements, salesmen, and shopkeepers insistently pressed upon the public this gargantuan supply of goods which had to be absorbed if the factories were to keep up their ceaseless flow of still more products. The measure of their success was total sales of almost $50,000,000,000 through the retail stores dealing directly with the great consuming public. An expanding foreign trade also helped absorb industrial output, total exports rising from $4,485,-000,000 to $5,241,000,000, but even more than in previous years it was the domestic market that enabled industry to expand so spectacularly. While in some instances foreign buyers provided the cream of manufacturing profits, the purchasing power of the American people themselves held the secret of their prosperity.

The national income naturally rose in response to such advances in industry and manufacture. It was estimated at $66,-000,000,000 at the opening of the nineteen-twenties, and at $82,-000,000,000 at their close. This huge total was by no means evenly distributed among American families. Prosperity had wrought no miracle, and we shall, in fact, have occasion to see how the inequitable division of wealth contributed to the later depression. Nevertheless, there were relative gains all along the line. While income taxes and other criteria revealed that the rich were becoming richer, with new additions every year to the swelling roster of millionaires, other classes, including especially professional workers, businessmen, tradespeople, white-collar workers, were also earning more money. The increased purchase of consumer goods demonstrated this, and also the steady rise of both savings deposits and life insurance for the country as a whole. The total of savings in 1930 amounted to almost twice that of 1920, no less than fifty-two million individual accounts being reported with funds aggregating $28,000,000,000.

Labor's share in the national income and its average wages also increased. Although there were many groups out of line, primarily the unskilled workers in the great mass industries, the 8,381,000 wage-earners in manufacturing establishments in 1929, earned total wages of $10,910,000,000 or an annual average of approximately $1300. Adjusted to the cost of living, such figures revealed that between 1922 and 1929 average weekly earnings in industry rose from an index of 92.1 to 104.7. The wave of strikes that had created such widespread industrial disturbances in 1919 gradually subsided under these conditions, and despite sporadic outbreaks the period was generally one of unusual industrial peace.

This situation, from labor's point of view, had a somewhat ironical result. It tended to sap the strength of the organized labor movement. With wages running so high, there was a marked falling off in union membership and particularly in that of the American Federation of Labor. Whereas the total for all union members throughout the country was 5,100,000 in 1921, it had fallen nine years later to 4,300,000. Employers further contributed to this weakening of the labor movement by following a generally conciliatory policy to win their workers' good will and allegiance. Company unions were formed to provide a medium whereby employees could address their complaints directly to management and settle their grievances through arbitration; profit-sharing schemes and elaborate pension plans were established, and comprehensive workers' welfare and recreational programs instituted. The large companies adopting such practices were numbered in the hundreds; millions of industrial workers benefited from them.

Industry's goal in furthering such employer-employee co-operation was not entirely altruistic. It sought to bind the workers so firmly to the chariot wheels of industrial enterprise that they would not dare run the risks of strikes and boycotts. It sought to convince labor that its true interest lay in accepting a generous division of industrial profits as decided by management alone instead of insisting upon union recognition and collective bargaining. And so long as prosperity continued and wages were high, labor widely succumbed to these blandishments. It was persuaded that it had an investment stake in American industry and that its profits would continue to rise. The depression was to be responsible for a rude awakening from these dreams, but that was still over a distant horizon. Even though the great mass of unorganized and unskilled workers were still almost wholly out of this picture, the labor movement as a whole continued on its conservative course, with no great anxiety over its dwindling membership.

Agriculture's relative share in national income did not compare with that of industry, or as the years went on, with that of labor. The farmers had suffered particularly in the sharp postwar depression, and they never fully recovered the prosperity they had briefly known when prices were swollen by wartime demand. The export demand for wheat and cotton fell steadily, with a consequent decline in prices. They still remained well above pre-war levels, and not until the close of the nineteen-twenties was the downward movement to become dangerously accelerated; but the farmers were weighted down by mortgages and other debts contracted in the days when prices were high. Between 1920 and 1930 the ratio of mortgage debts to farm property increased from 29 to 39 per cent, and that of all fixed charges to gross income was in the latter year approximately 12 per cent. One result of such developments was an increase in farm tenancy, with 750,000 share-croppers on the cotton plantations of the South.

This downward trend in agriculture was to give rise to an increasing demand for farm relief. Until the end of the decade, however, little was done for the farmer other than the adoption of several minor measures for extending him credit and seeking to protect him from unfair practices in marketing his produce. There was no question that the emphasis upon industrial development often ignored agrarian interests. Total farm income was in 1929 at the high figure of $10,417,000,000; but in comparison with the gains made in other sectors of the country's economic life, this did not represent anything like the profits enjoyed by the country as a whole.

RISE OF NEW INDUSTRIES

The underlying factors responsible for the general prosperity of the nineteen-twenties, to return to the industrial scene, were the efficient exploitation of natural resources, improved methods of industrial production, and the intensive development of both domestic and foreign markets. Good times were perhaps even more directly due to the spectacularly rapid expansion of a number of key industries. Some of them were entirely new; others were undergoing their period of greatest growth. Together they gave a tremendous impetus to economic development all along the line. Their need for raw materials and for machines stimulated production and employment in the country's mines, steel works, and durable goods industries. Their own operations provided jobs for additional millions of industrial workers, thereby even more directly increasing mass purchasing power from which other manufacturers as well as themselves could profit.

The automobile industry was the most important of them all, and both at home and abroad it became a token of American prosperity during these halcyon days. On the eve of the first World War, some five hundred thousand cars were already being produced annually in the United States, but by the close of the nineteen-twenties this total had been increased tenfold. There were in all twenty-three million passenger cars and three million trucks in operation. No single development, from either the economic or social point of view, was comparable in importance. Automobile manufacture absorbed each year vast quantities of steel, copper, plate glass, rubber, and fabrics, and accounted directly or indirectly for the employment of no less than four million workers. Moreover, the millions of Americans who bought cars also had to buy gasoline for their operation, and another industry was stimulated to vastly increased production. They demanded hard-surfaced and then concrete roads, and the production of road-making machinery and cement greatly expanded. They created a growing need for filling stations, roadside stands, and tourist camps which provided additional employment for thousands of men and women. And finally the states were able to levy automobile and gasoline taxes which soon became an important part of their revenue, expended largely for road construction but sometimes diverted to other purposes as well. Perhaps the full importance of the automobile, and the extent to which the public had become dependent upon it, was not fully realized until the conversion of the industry into wartime production in 1942, together with rationing of tires and gasoline, drove the lesson home with compelling force.

Many other aspects of the industrial expansion of the nineteen-twenties — the further integration of business, the new salesmanship and installment buying, manufacturing profits, and speculation in common stocks — are also graphically illustrated in the story of the automobile industry. There had been scores of independent producers dividing the market before the war; during this decade three major concerns largely controlled it. The Ford Company, General Motors, and Chrysler accounted for ninety per cent of all production. Their popular models were naturally in the low-priced field, but the prosperity of the period was revealed in the improvements for which the general public was willing to pay an increasingly higher price. Ford was driven to complete reorganization by this development. He had long dominated the market for cheap cars by his success in adapting the assembly line to turn out millions of Model T's. When the popular demand for style and appearance as against general utility began to cut into his sales, he shut down his factories, completely retooled, and late in 1927 brought out an entirely different model. So great was the public interest that hundreds of thousands of people flocked to the Ford show rooms to see the first Model A. Its début caused nation-wide newspaper comments; it was one of the events of the year. Ford again was able to compete with the Chevrolets and Plymouths which had threatened his supremacy. His sales spiraled to new high records.

The tremendous profits accruing to the manufacturers were reflected in the steadily rising value of their securities and the creation of a new class of automobile millionaires. General Motors ranked eighth among all American corporations in capital value by the end of the decade. It was earning profits of more than two hundred million dollars a year, and had made a millionaire out of everyone who had invested as much as twenty-five thousand dollars in its stock only eight years earlier. Nevertheless, it was Henry Ford, retaining full control over his tremendous corporation and in one year making profits of one hundred per cent, who remained both here and abroad the outstanding human symbol, not only of the expansion and prosperity of the automobile industry, but of American industrial civilization.

There were other industries showing almost as spectacular growth. The production of electric power, as a consequence of increased demand both in industry and in the home, almost doubled in the nineteen-twenties. A conspicuous feature of this expansion in the public utilities was the rise of gigantic holding companies controlling the actual operating companies which might be scattered in all parts of the country. Through a complicated process of pyramiding, four such corporations, one of them controlling no less than one hundred and fifty local public utility concerns, produced more than half the country's total output of electric power. Paralleling the growth of power companies was the increase in production of electric equipment. The total value of machinery, apparatus, and supplies amounted by 1930 to some two billion dollars. One branch of this industry, the manufacture of electric refrigerators, was itself a striking example of the importance of an entirely new product in industrial production.

Three other highly significant industries were moving pictures, radio, and aviation. Their social implications in the fields of entertainment, communications, and transportation were of greater importance than their contribution to the national economy. To that topic we shall return. But the nineteen-twenties also saw them become big business.

By the middle of the decade there were 20,000 motion-picture theaters in the country with a weekly attendance estimated at the phenomenal figure of 100,000,000. Some $2,000,000,000 was invested in the industry; annual production costs rose to $184,-000,000 (well over twice the figure at the beginning of the decade), and employment was furnished some 20,000 persons. Five hundred feature films were turned out every year in Hollywood, some ninety per cent of them by eight large companies. The control of the greater number of motion-picture theaters also was highly concentrated in four nation-wide chains.

Radio was an entirely new development in so far as commercial broadcasting was concerned. Its economic importance was found not so much in the value of the industry's manufactured products, although, between 1922 and 1929, the total value of the sales of radio sets increased from $5,000,000 to $600,000,000, as in the rôle broadcasting rapidly began to play as an advertising medium. Two great networks, the National Broadcasting Company and the Columbia Broadcasting System, were established in the nineteen-twenties, and through their facilities national advertisers found a new way of carrying their sales talks into the ten million homes which by the end of the decade had radios. The effectiveness of this constant and almost inescapable reiteration of the desirability of purchasing automobiles, washing machines, refrigerators, household appliances, furniture, cosmetics, cigarettes, and toothpaste had no little to do with the increased velocity of business activity in the nineteen-twenties. Radio advertising was just beginning to realize its potentialities — it would become even more important a few years later when virtually every home had a receiving set — but it was already an integral feature of the nation's business structure.

The aviation industry was a laggard in comparison with these other forms of industrial activity, but it underwent a sudden boom in the middle nineteen-twenties as a result of government subsidy through the award of mail contracts to the aviation transportation companies. While important expansion waited until the next decade (the total value of all aircraft produced in 1929 was only $52,000,000), it was foreshadowed by feverish speculation in aviation stocks. Public interest in the whole question of air transport was also stimulated by various spectacular feats awakening a new realization of aviation's tremendous possibilities, feats climaxed by the epochal trans-Atlantic flight of Charles A. Lindbergh in 1927, a non-stop solo crossing from New York to Paris.

The amazing progress in the economic field overshadowed everything else in the history of the nineteen-twenties. The immediate gains in our standard of living obscured basic defects in the economic structure that prosperity actually accentuated. The problems with which the progressives had sought to cope were not solved; they were merely pushed into the background. There still remained a concentration of economic power gravely threatening social democracy. The inequitable distribution of income, however much the total had increased, was an economic as well as a social threat to national well-being. The emphasis had shifted far too much toward industry, at the expense of both labor and agriculture, to provide a truly stable basis for continued development along the lines so confidently projected in the optimistic spirit born of the era of the Big Money. Still, nothing succeeds like success. How could the American people, with so many evidences of prosperity at hand, doubt capitalism's final triumph over poverty?

RUGGED INDIVIDUALISM

The economic philosophy which provided the background for prosperity drew heavily upon the principles of *laissez-faire* in its insistence that there should be no restraining governmental control over business. It could hardly have been in more direct contrast to the popular trend during the progressive era. Government was no longer thinking of regulation, and the attitude of three successive Republican administrations was epitomized in President Harding's statement that there should be "less government in business and more business in government." However, the theory of *laissez-faire* was once again modified, as it had been in the eighteen-nineties, by the Government's pronounced willingness to extend aid to business interests at the expense of other elements in the national life. There often appeared to be something paradoxical about "the American system of rugged individualism" when it maintained a high tariff to protect industry, on the one hand, and on the other, refused to aid the farmer or to safeguard the rights of labor.

Herbert Hoover, the most eloquent spokesman of the new economic order, declared toward the close of the period that the withdrawal of Government from business had been in 1919 and 1920 the most vital issue facing the country. Acceptance of the paternal ideas so prevalent in Europe, he declared, would have undermined the individual initiative and enterprise responsible for our growth to national greatness. The Republican program was to restore to Government its rôle of umpire instead of player in the economic game. In opposition to any move that tended to inject it more directly into business, he called for the preservation of economic freedom as the essential basis of political freedom.

> Even if Government conduct of business could give us more efficiency instead of less efficiency [Hoover said], the fundamental objection to it would remain unaltered and unabated. It would destroy political equality. It would increase rather than decrease abuse and corruption. It would stifle initiative and invention. It would undermine the development of leadership. It would cramp and cripple the mental and spiritual energies of our people. It would extinguish equality and opportunity. It would dry up the spirit of liberty and progress.

As Secretary of Commerce, however, Hoover would appear to have had more practical views on the possible limitations of "rugged individualism" than this glorification of it suggested. "We are passing from a period of extreme individualistic action," he stated on this earlier occasion, "into a period of associated activities." Republican policy often seemed more interested in promoting such associated activities than in insisting upon an interpretation of *laissez-faire* that would have reduced government aid for big business as well as cutting down government regulation.

The Sherman Anti-Trust Act was virtually suspended. As of the close of 1929, over two hundred business mergers, involving twenty-six hundred companies, had taken place. Although the aggregate value of their securities was placed at $21,650,000,000, the Department of Justice showed no alarm. Moreover, the Federal Trade Commission, packed with the friends of big business, was encouraging moves within industry that served even more to strengthen monopolistic controls. The formation of trade associations, numbering over a thousand by 1927, was vigorously promoted. With government protection, they undertook to pool information among member companies, to standardize products and practices, to deal on a co-operative basis with outside agencies, and often to co-ordinate price-fixing policies. At the same time, the new powers granted to the Interstate Commerce Commission in the Transportation Act of 1920 authorized it, as we have seen, to promote railway consolidations and encourage in every way unification of existing railroad lines. The economics of railroad transportation had shown this to be clearly desirable. Nonetheless, it represented a sharp reversal of the attitude which had led to attacks upon railway holding companies two decades earlier.

The transformation of these regulatory commissions into agencies pursuing purposes so much at variance with those for which they were originally established aroused some liberal criticism. Senator Norris of Nebraska, one-time leader of insurgent revolt in the House, charged that this boring from within represented a nullification of federal law which would set the country back twenty-five years in its attempt to establish effective control over business. "If trusts, combinations, and big business are to run the Government," he asked, "why not permit them to do it directly?" But there was little support for such views. William E. Humphrey, a member of the Federal Trade Commission, stated that the Government's alliance with the great corporations was not to benefit them as such, but to benefit the people through them. "It is not that we are less democratic than we were, but more," he wrote in the *Magazine of Wall Street.* "Formerly democracy was confined to politics: now it has permeated business. Formerly the people were the Government; now they are also business."

With Republican control of Congress there was a return to a high-tariff policy. It won general popular support apart from traditional political alignments. The aid it afforded industry was accepted as necessary to safeguard the American standard of living, including the wages of labor quite as much as the profits of manufacturers. Taxation was also channeled in the direction most favorable to business. Andrew Mellon, Secretary of the Treasury throughout the entire period, based his whole program on the premise that high rates in corporation and income taxes tended "to destroy individual initiative and seriously impede the development of productive business."

The attitude of the courts fully sustained the position taken by the Government both in regard to the promotion of "associated activities" and in opposing any further regulation of business and industry. In contrast to the more liberal interpretations of the state's police power that had characterized later Supreme Court decisions in the progressive period, there was now a marked trend in quite the opposite direction. William Howard Taft, appointed Chief Justice of the Supreme Court in 1921, declared that there was no greater issue in domestic politics than maintenance of the court as a bulwark to guarantee that no person should be deprived of property without due process of law.

Perhaps the most striking instance of this new conservatism was the emphatic rejection of a District of Columbia minimum-wage law for women in *Adkins v. Children's Hospital.* In this case, decided in 1923, Justice Sutherland ruled for the Supreme Court that the police powers of the state had been clearly exceeded, and that wage restrictions could in no way be reconciled with the constitutional guarantee of liberty of contract. Even more significant of the attitude of the Court, however, was his cavalier dismissal of all arguments that minimum-wage laws were essential to protect the health of women as "interesting, but only mildly persuasive." "For surely the good of society as a whole," the decision concluded, "cannot be better served than by the preservation of the liberties of its constituent members."

In sharp contrast to their refusal to sustain laws regulating business, the courts upheld those restricting the activities of labor unions. Despite the high hopes for relief held out in the Clayton Act, injunctions were again and again approved. One authorized by a federal court in the case of a strike of railway shopmen not only outlawed any resort to violence, but extended its sweeping provisions to "picketing of all sorts, strike meetings, statements to the public, the use of union funds to carry on the strike, and the use of any means of communication by the leaders to direct it." In *Truax v. Corrigan,* a case coming before it in 1921, the Supreme Court declared unconstitutional an Arizona law that would have prohibited the use of injunctions in labor disputes, and that same year, in *Duplex Printing Press Company v. Deering,* it declared that nothing in the Clayton Act authorized secondary boycotts.

There were dissents to these decisions which patently safeguarded the rights of property against government regulation while limiting the rights of labor unions. Even Chief Justice Taft dissented in the *Adkins v. Children's Hospital* case, while both Justice Holmes and Justice Brandeis again and again stated their belief that the Supreme Court majority was once again trying to write its own social theories into law. Justice Holmes said in his dissent in *Truax v. Corrigan:*

> There is nothing that I more deprecate than the use of the Fourteenth Amendment beyond the absolute compulsion of its words to prevent the making of social experiments that an important part of the community desires, in the insulated chambers afforded by the several states, even though the experiments may seem futile or even noxious to me and to those whose judgment I most respect.

And somewhat later Justice Brandeis, dissenting in *New State Ice Company v. Liebmann,* also warned against this danger of erecting prejudices into legal principles. He declared:

> There must be power in the states and the nation to remould,

through experimentation, our economic practices and institutions to meet changing social and economic needs. . . . To stay experimentation in things social and economic is a grave responsibility.

Despite these voices of the future, asking for an open-minded awareness of changing social needs, the Supreme Court effectively blocked any further progress in the social and economic legislation to which the progressives had pointed the way. It was, however, reflecting the conservative spirit of the time; it was conforming to the general attitude of the American people toward both business and labor.

MATERIALISM, SOCIAL REVOLT AND LAWLESSNESS

In one of his terse statements, President Coolidge declared that "the business of America is business." In the atmosphere of the nineteen-twenties the American people were quite ready to accept this dictum. Upholding the governmental attitude in letting industry have its way and generally approving the Supreme Court's new conservatism, they asked nothing more than to be left free to make money and to spend money. It could perhaps be said of this period, as William Dean Howells had said of the eighteen-nineties, that the dollar was the measure of every value, and the stamp of every success.

There was not an institution which failed to make pious genuflexions before the Great God Business. The university and the Church succumbed to the universal contagion. The doctrine of "the redemptive and regenerative influence of business" was widely preached with the happy discovery that service to society was the real purpose behind manufacturing, merchandising, and selling. Among other organizations the Rotary clubs, welcoming to their membership selected representatives from every walk of life, held weekly luncheons in cities and towns throughout the country at which food, good fellowship, and uplift were neatly blended to promote still greater business activity.

It was left to Bruce Barton, advertising man extraordinary, to express in its most extravagant form the apotheosis of the businessman. In *The Man Nobody Knows,* he taught the surprising lesson that Jesus had won his success through becoming the world's outstanding executive. "He picked up twelve men from the bottom ranks of business and forged them into an organization that conquered the world," wrote Mr. Barton. " . . . Nowhere is there such a startling example of executive success as the way in which that organization was brought together." Jesus might well be called the founder of modern business, he told his readers, because he preached the doctrine of service which business had made its own. In 1925 and 1926 *The Man Nobody Knows* was the country's non-fiction best-seller.

Other manifestations of our business civilization appeared to emphasize profits somewhat more than service. For all the economy of thrift so assiduously preached and practiced by President Coolidge, extravagance and conspicuous display, again as in the eighteen-nineties, were accepted as the hallmark of success. This was particularly true as a booming stock market piled up immense paper profits for the fortunate holders of common stock in United States Steel, General Motors, Montgomery Ward, and many other companies. Entirely apart from its deeper economic implications, speculation — whether in the Coolidge bull market or the Florida real estate boom — immensely fostered the free spending of these expansive days. As stocks soared upward, hesitating at times only to gather renewed strength for their dizzying climb, there seemed no end to the possible profits to be garnered. Not only the capitalist class, but hundreds of thousands of small investors — white-collar workers and wage-earners — lived happily on great expectations.

While those of moderate means went on buying new automobiles, washing machines, electric refrigerators, and radios, the wealthy splurged on expensive luxuries. They built Tudor cottages or Italian villas in the fashionable suburbs and made over colonial houses into elaborate country homes. They vacationed in Florida, Bermuda, and Europe. They joined select country clubs and yacht clubs. They paid fantastic prices for entertainment provided for their pleasure by enterprising showmen and promoters.

The tremendous increase in the amount of money spent by the

American people on recreation, and the corresponding growth of what had become a great amusement industry, may perhaps be taken as almost the most significant illustration of the prevailing prosperity and extravagance. Automobile touring and vacation travel, moving pictures and the theater, sports and other amusements, were estimated as costing the American people anywhere from six to ten billion dollars a year — about a tenth of the entire national income.

This craving for amusement had in the immediate post-war years been accentuated by a restlessness and cynicism growing out of the first World War. Men and women who had been through the trying experiences of 1917 and 1918, only to find that their sacrifices had apparently been futile, readily accepted the idea that the chief objective of life was pleasure. They not only wanted to make money; they were impatient of all restraint on how they might spend it. There was open rebellion against infringement of personal freedom in any sphere of social activity. To a very considerable degree this apparent revolution in manners and morals was the climax of the gradual breakdown of Victorian standards, especially in relation to the rôle of women in society, but it also reflected the underlying spiritual confusion of a secular age in which disillusionment had for so many persons followed swiftly upon wartime idealism.

Among the more exaggerated manifestations of those years, sometimes characterized as the jazz age, were the preoccupation with sex as a conversational topic, the "pleasure-mad" pursuit of every amusement, the popularity of petting parties and drinking. Young people particularly seemed to have lost their moorings. "Here was a new generation," Scott Fitzgerald wrote in *This Side of Paradise*, " . . . grown up to find all Gods dead, all wars fought, all faiths in man shaken." The revolt of youth soon spent its force, and the country survived this period of rebellion which seemed to threaten the very bases of society. But during its height the nineteen-twenties had a hectic, feverish atmosphere that deeply disturbed the social conservatives.

The popular attitude toward prohibition was a not unrelated phenomenon. The long and persistent campaign of the drys for a national amendment had finally achieved success. The way for such action was paved by the wartime prohibition adopted to preserve grain supplies, but while it was often claimed that the Eighteenth Amendment was put over under the stress of war, support for such a move had steadily increased year by year. In any event, the country in 1920 accepted permanently — as it then appeared — a self-denying ordinance that forbade the manufacture, sale, transportation, or importation of intoxicating liquors. To enforce its provisions Congress passed the Volstead Act, defining intoxicating liquors as any beverage containing five-tenths per cent alcohol. For a while the implications of prohibition were generally accepted, but the temper of the times doomed such a drastic reform. It infringed too directly upon the personal liberty and the right to enjoy oneself upon which the post-war generation was so stridently insisting.

Innumerable leaks soon appeared in the dyke that had been confidently erected against the flow of alcoholic beverages. Rum-runners anchored off the Atlantic coast, truckloads of beer smuggled over the Canadian border rumbled southward through the night, alcohol was surreptitiously withdrawn from the Government's medicinal stocks, secret whiskey stills were set up in city cellars and isolated country districts, the manufacture of home-brew became almost a national industry, and many individuals performed alarming experiments with bathtub gin. Bootlegging became big business; the speakeasy flourished throughout the land. Perhaps a majority of the American people continued to uphold the law. There was a wealth of conflicting statistics, and while they apparently indicated a marked reduction in the consumption of liquor from pre-war totals, none could maintain that the country was wholly law-observing or really dry. The most conspicuous drinking was done by a noisy, unashamed minority which made evasion of the law fashionable in urban centers, but the most staid and conservative members of society often followed their example. Country club highballs and suburban cocktail parties became almost a ritual. As expressed in a verse appearing in F. P. A.'s column in the *New York World* —

> Prohibition is an awful flop.
>   We like it.
> It can't stop what it's meant to stop.
>   We like it.
> It's left a trail of graft and slime,
> It's filled our land with vice and crime,
> It can't prohibit worth a dime,
>   Nevertheless, we're for it.

Bootlegging operated through a complicated network of corrupt alliances with the officers of law enforcement. The police were bribed to assure the hijackers' immunity from arrest, and speakeasy proprietors paid recognized tribute for protection. Moreover, an industry based on violation of the law steadily extended the sphere of its criminal activities. Rival gangs sought to establish liquor monopolies in the territories they controlled, and the weapons they employed were intimidation, threats, and murder. The peaceful competition of the business world became open warfare in this industry outside the law, with embittered rivals settling their scores with sawed-off shotguns.

In Chicago, on Saint Valentine's Day, 1929, members of the notorious "Scarface" Al Capone gang, disguised as policemen, lined up seven members of a rival gang and shot them down in cold blood. It was a devastating climax to a period of lawlessness which sent the homicide rate up to over ten thousand murders a year. The bootleggers soon moved on into other rackets. They levied tribute upon legitimate business and operated gambling halls, race tracks, dance halls, and houses of prostitution. Whatever the ethics of law among those who, in insisting upon their right to drink, bought liquor from bootleggers and patronized speakeasies, the system they supported bred a new rule of violence in the underworld of crime.

The Saint Valentine's Day massacre may appear a far cry from the revolt of youth against social restraints, but there were observers of the America of the nineteen-twenties who felt they were but different manifestations of the same underlying spirit. James M. Beck, former United States Solicitor General, found a general lack of respect for authority and universal violation of the law as the most conspicuous phenomena, not only of the post-war decade, but of the entire industrial age. He wrote:

> No one can deny that there is today a revolt against the discipline of law and the wise restraints of human convention such as has not existed within the memory of living man. The reign of lawlessness has crept over the world like the huge shadow of an eclipse, but too few have realized the portentous change that has come over civilization.

THE NEW IMMIGRATION POLICY

The nationalistic spirit of the nineteen-twenties was symbolized by the popular slogan, "One Hundred Per Cent Americanism." It was translated to mean, not only rejection of everything foreign, but insistence upon strict conformity with the prevailing conservative philosophy. There should be no traffic with those who proved, through refusal to accept *in toto* popular ways and popular ideas, that their sympathies were un-American. Although various other important factors also came into play, nationalism provided the final impetus for the exclusion laws that in this period shut off foreign immigration; it fostered the violent attempts to stamp out all subversive activity which could be traced to foreign influence; and it inspired, as a still more ugly manifestation of intolerance, a revived Ku Klux Klan.

The background of the new immigration laws clearly reveals that their enactment was in reality the culmination of a long-time trend marking the gradual abandonment by the United States of its traditional rôle as an asylum for the poor and oppressed of Europe. Much of the expansive strength which had enabled the United States to extend its borders to the shores of the Pacific had been derived from the constant replenishing of native stock with new European blood. The country's rapid industrial development was made possible in large part by the great reservoir of cheap labor built up by immigration. Now that the country was fully settled and free land exhausted, now that our industrial machine no longer needed fresh workers, we were prepared to shut off the flow of immigrants. America was no longer to be the frontier of Europe.

There had been straws in the wind well before the first World War. As the old immigration from northwestern Europe gave way to the new immigration from southeastern Europe, the problem of assimilation had taken on a new importance. Grave doubts were expressed as to whether the American "melting-pot" could indefinitely absorb such huge annual additions to our population. Moreover, the new immigrants, settling in the congested slum areas of the industrial cities of the Northeast, created social and economic problems, as we have seen, which appeared almost insoluble. Various laws had been passed as early as the eighteen-eighties and nineties barring such undesirable aliens as paupers, criminals, convicts, and the insane. A small head tax had been adopted, certain health controls set up, and contract labor had been expressly forbidden entry. Measures had also been taken to exclude Chinese and discourage Japanese immigration. But the really significant change in immigration policy took place at the close of the progressive period when in 1917 Congress finally adopted, over President Wilson's veto, an immigrant literacy test.

Upon the conclusion of the first World War, this underlying opposition to unrestricted immigration became stronger as the heightened spirit of nationalism gave a new emphasis to old fears. Labor felt that the American standard of living would be seriously threatened, industrial management feared the effect of radicalism upon the stability of our institutions and economic system, unless additional barriers were set up to control the influx of ever greater numbers of foreign workers. When these forebodings seemed likely to be confirmed by a rising tide of alien arrivals, totaling eight hundred thousand in 1921, the demand for a complete overhauling of immigration policy became irresistible.

The new program was based upon the principle of quotas. This not only made possible a reduction in the number of immigrants to be admitted annually, but provided the means to control their nationality. A first temporary bill — the Emergency Immigration Act of 1921 — placed these quotas on a basis whereby the entry of nationals from any European country was limited to three per cent of the nationals from that country who were resident in the United States in 1910. The obvious purpose of choosing 1910 rather than the most recent census returns was that it weighted the scales in favor of northwestern Europe, origin of the older and more assimilable immigrant groups.

Three years later a permanent law was enacted. It barred all persons ineligible to American citizenship, thereby definitely excluding Japanese as well as Chinese; reduced existing quotas during a three-year interim period, and, finally, decreed that after July 1, 1927 (later postponed until 1929), total immigration from all European countries was to be restricted on a completely revised basis to one hundred and fifty thousand annually. The new quotas were to be proportionate to the number of persons of a given *national origin* currently residing in the United States. That is, the annual addition to the population by immigration was not only to be limited to a maximum less than one-third the pre-war average, but it was to be divided among the various peoples of Europe according to the existing admixture of racial stocks in the United States. As finally worked out, this meant, for example, that the annual quota from the United Kingdom was 65,721, or almost a third higher than the pre-war average, while that of Italy was 5802, or less than six per cent of the previous average.

During the first decade in which the law was in effect, total immigration fell to seven hundred thousand in comparison with over four million during the previous ten years. As the onset of the depression caused large numbers of the foreign-born to return to Europe, the net result was that alien arrivals and departures were nearly balanced. The trans-Atlantic transit had been shut off. Further increase in the American population was to be left dependent upon natural growth rather than upon new arrivals. The Immigration Act of 1924 marked the end of an epoch in our national history, as significant as the closing of the frontier to which it was so closely related.

RED-BAITING AND THE KU KLUX KLAN

The fear of subversive propaganda, and especially of communism, had been effectively played up in the movement to curtail immigration. And while the original Red scare gradually subsided, the conservative elements in American life remained on guard against all radical influences. They continued to see bogies on every hand. The American Communist Party had been almost immediately driven underground after its emergence in 1919; five Socialists were summarily expelled from the New York Assembly in 1920, and Victor Berger, Socialist member of Congress, was twice denied the right to take his seat. Although left-wing radicalism in general could make slight headway against the prevailing prosperity, such organizations as the National Civic Federation, the National Security League, and the American Legion vigorously kept up their Red-baiting and their super-patriotic crusade for "One Hundred Per Cent Americanism."

All too often they inspired a persecution of supposed radicals leading to suppression of free speech and other constitutional liberties. Although the Supreme Court, in the wartime case of *Schenck v. United States*, declared that restraint on free speech was justified only when the words used were of a nature "to create a clear and present danger," it did not always sustain this principle. Nationalist fears of foreign subversive influences, moreover, found expression in various state criminal syndicalism laws, teachers' loyalty oaths, the denial of citizenship to pacifists, and even the revision and censorship of American history textbooks. It became disloyal, un-American, to criticize the existing institutions of democratic capitalism, let alone favor their overthrow or radical reform.

Justice Holmes, who had been responsible for the Supreme Court's "clear and present danger" phrase, urged a more liberal viewpoint. " . . . The best test of truth," he stated in a memorable dissenting opinion in the conspiracy case of *Abrams v. United States*, "is the power of the thought to get itself accepted in the competition of the market." He gravely called upon his brethren on the bench to be eternally vigilant "against attempts to check the expression of opinions that we loathe and believe to be fraught with death, unless they so imminently threaten immediate interference with the lawful and pressing purposes of the law that an immediate check is required to save the country." Timid or reactionary judges, however, lacked his forthright confidence in freedom of speech.

A *cause célèbre* of the nineteen-twenties was the case of Nicola Sacco and Bartolomeo Vanzetti, two Italian workmen convicted of murder in a Massachusetts court under circumstances that appeared to give every indication that they were being railroaded to their death because of their radical views rather than on clear evidence of guilt for the crime with which they were charged. Liberals everywhere rallied to their support. Sacco and Vanzetti became world-wide symbols for the defense of individual rights and democratic freedom. While the popular outcry caused a thorough review of their case, their conviction was finally upheld. In 1927 they went to their death, hailed as martyrs. "This is our career and our triumph," was their last message to the world.

Even more rabidly nationalistic, even more intolerant than the persecution of alien radicals, was the attitude of the Ku Klux Klan. It was in a sense a horrible travesty upon the booster's drive for conformity and the super-patriotism of those who sought to free the country from radical foreign influence. To make America safe for white, Protestant, native-born Americans, the Klan took the law into its own hands, preached a doctrine of violence, and tried by every means to terrorize all nonconforming elements in the communities in which it operated.

It had started in the South, drawing upon the traditions of the old Civil War Ku Klux Klan, and then spread rapidly through many states of the East and Middlewest. Membership rose to a peak of four million, and the new Klan was able to exert a secret and powerful influence over both state and local politics, an influence invariably representing the most reactionary and intolerant point of view. There was a mysterious ritual binding its members, and a hierarchy of Kleagles and Goblins took their orders from a mysterious Imperial Wizard. Dressed in their white hoods and shrouds, the Klansmen were accustomed to hold great midnight meetings in the fiery glow of burning crosses, symbols of their warped and twisted conception of Americanism. As part of their campaign of terrorism, they beat up, or tarred and feathered, Negroes, Catholics, Jews, and foreigners. There were occasional floggings that resulted in death; there were instances of outright murder. Set against the background of a nation enjoying such freedom and prosperity as perhaps no other country had ever known, these cowardly exhibitions of intolerant brutality had few defenders. Nevertheless, the Ku Klux Klan remained an unlovely feature of the American scene until about 1928, when revelations of political intrigue and corruption, as well as violence, finally led to the submergence of the "invisible Empire."

CRITICISM AND PROTEST

There was in the nineteen-twenties, as in every other period of American history, a minority report directed against the prevailing social concepts of the times. The ideals and hopes of progressive reformers and political liberals were kept alive by writers and critics in many fields. Some few of those who had written during the progressive era continued on during this period, and others joined their ranks. If there was no parallel to the muckraking articles of pre-war days, such magazines as *The New Republic, The Nation, The Freeman,* and *The Survey Graphic* remained acutely aware of social problems, and a number of highly important books, which would include Charles and Mary Beard's *The Rise of American Civilization,* Vernon Louis Parrington's *Main Currents in American Thought,* and Robert K. and Helen M. Lynd's *Middletown,* carefully explored the underlying tenets of American democracy. Intellectuals and liberals, however, were far more generally concerned with individual problems of morals and aesthetics than with the economic and political issues that had absorbed the progressives. The concentration of economic power, social justice for the people as a whole, the distribution of national income, the relations of capital and labor, were not the questions they found most important.

Criticism of America and Americans in contemporary literature could hardly have differed more from that a decade earlier. For not only was it largely concerned with the superficial aspects of American life; it was in the main destructive rather than constructive. It despaired of democracy — not in the sense that democracy would be unable to achieve social justice, but because it was believed incapable of promoting an appreciation of the finer things of life. In the eighteen-nineties critics had seen the possibility of a richer civilization developing in the United States. The period was notable for its Utopian literature. A decade later the muckrakers, while enthusiastically exposing the evils of American society, were nonetheless confident that with political and economic reform the American dream would be realized. But the disillusionment and cynicism of much of the literature of protest in the nineteen-twenties held out slight hope for the future.

The bible of the sophisticates was the *American Mercury*, edited by Henry L. Mencken. Its editorial policy was based upon a belief that civilized life was not possible under a social and political system that fostered prohibition, censorship, One Hundred Per Cent Americanism, and Rotary Clubs. "If you find so much that is unworthy of reverence in the United States, then why do you live here?" Mencken asked himself. The answer was, "Why do men go to zoos?" This scornful attitude toward American democracy was expressed by many other writers. In *I'll Take My Stand*, twelve Southerners inveighed hopelessly against the ugliness of industrialism. Analyzing the current scene in *Civilization in the United States*, a more general group of authors found almost nothing to commend. "The most amusing and pathetic fact in the social life of America today," wrote Harold Stearns, editor of the volume, "is its emotional and aesthetic starvation." James Truslow Adams asked sadly in one magazine article where an American of simple tastes and an interest in things of the mind "is going to be able to live any longer in his native country."

The spiritual confusion that Scott Fitzgerald had first reflected in *This Side of Paradise* also characterized his later books which depicted the hectic efforts of the younger generation to find itself in a world it believed well lost. Ernest Hemingway painted in

The Sun Also Rises the tragic lot of those expatriates who fled to Europe because they found America unlivable. Significant through their very titles of cynicism and despair were T. S. Eliot's *The Waste Land* and Theodore Dreiser's *An American Tragedy*. As far and away the most distinguished dramatist of his day, Eugene O'Neill even more poignantly expressed the conflicting ideas of the age in a long series of notable plays, among which *Strange Interlude* stood out most prominently in these years. Sinclair Lewis, dissecting small-town bourgeois ideals, struck such a responsive chord among the very persons he was satirizing that his books became best-sellers. In *Main Street* and *Babbitt*, he laid bare with devastating irony the cant and hypocrisy underlying many aspects of the nation's business civilization, while Main Street and the Babbitts sent the books into edition after edition.

Again it is necessary to stress that there were writers who probed deeply beneath the surface of life in the nineteen-twenties, and many of them maintained their faith in democracy for all the popularity of "debunking" and Mencken's raucous laughter at "the bilge of idealism." The fires of reform may have been banked during the era of the Big Money; they were not entirely extinguished. Nevertheless, it does remain true, as many of the critics of the period were themselves later to admit, that literary protests often avoided primary issues in their absorption with the idea that American civilization was doomed by its regimentation, hypocrisy, puritanism, and lack of aesthetic appreciation. And this remains highly significant. For in so far as literature may reflect an age, even the criticism of these years indicates how greatly the climate of public opinion had changed since pre-war progressivism and the crusading idealism of 1917.

We are brought back to the underlying prosperity of the period and its spectacular economic progress as the basic factors in its history. They were responsible for a generally conservative and self-satisfied attitude on the part of the American people that drew its strength from the apparent success of existing economic, political, and social institutions. The critics of society were themselves sufficiently impressed by this success, although

they might not have admitted it, to satirize the surface manifestations of the nation's complacent acceptance of things as they
were rather than to seek out the deeper and still unsolved problems of social adjustment in the industrial age. There was to be
no real awakening from these attitudes until the Great Depression shook the post-war world to its very foundations, and democracy found itself confronted by the challenge of an aggressive fascism.

Republican Supremacy

"He Looked Like a President"

THE POLITICAL SCENE during the nineteen-twenties was a pale reflection of economic developments. With Government once again largely subordinate to business, the real leadership of the nation was often found in Wall Street rather than in Washington. The successive Republican administrations of the period were so concerned with promoting industrial expansion that their legislative program seldom extended beyond this immediate horizon. Nor did political opposition to Republican supremacy, except for an unsuccessful progressive uprising under Senator La Follette in 1924, advance any principles of action differing greatly from those which were in force. The Democrats hungered for office, but in so far as economic theories were concerned, their standard-bearers were cut out of very much the same cloth as the Republican presidents. They paid similar obeisance to the desires of big business. Both major parties were expressing the dominant ideas and desires of a great majority of the American people. A Democratic victory at the polls in 1924 or 1928 would not in all probability have substantially changed the course of American life.

Theodore Roosevelt and Woodrow Wilson had tried to mold the development of American industrial capitalism in the interests of the people as a whole. Their goal had been to recover for the American democracy a greater measure of control over its own destiny. They sought assurance that the common man everywhere would be able to enjoy the full benefits of that rising standard of living that economic advance made possible. The Republican presidents of the nineteen-twenties would have professed the same objectives, but they were content to give industry its head as the most practical means toward this end. They believed that the people generally would benefit by the gradual diffusion of business profits even if there was marked inequality in the immediate returns. This was the justification of special privilege and they did not feel that the interests of the common man needed any further protection by the state.

Harding, Coolidge, and Hoover differed from Theodore Roosevelt and Wilson in another respect. They did not attempt to exercise the leadership in public affairs that had brought about such a concentration of authority in the National Government, and in the hands of the President, during their predecessors' administrations. They did not have the necessary qualifications in the first place, and their willingness to follow rather than to lead perhaps reflected inadequacy quite as much as a different political philosophy. Washington became the scene of purposeful and aggressive lobbying on the part of scores of highly organized pressure groups, from the National Association of Manufacturers to the American Federation of Labor, from the American Legion to the Anti-Saloon League. A leaderless and often quarrelsome Congress allowed itself to be pushed about and used for ends that mainly served the interests of strongly entrenched minorities. The result was that with some few exceptions there was very little in the way of constructive legislation during the nineteen-twenties. The gains of the progressive era were not wholly lost; the period was static rather than reactionary. Problems that could not be avoided were as often fumbled as handled efficiently, and much that might have been done was left undone. While industry spread the mantle of prosperity over the country, the Government made little effort to see that it covered rich and poor alike, or that the fabric was so woven that it could withstand the winds of adversity.

The first of the triumvirate of Republican presidents was Warren Gamaliel Harding, elected, as we have seen, as an advocate of "normalcy" after the alarms and excursions of progressivism and war. Perhaps no man elevated to the high office of President of the United States was less suited by temperament or ability to fill that post than this genial, well-meaning, small-town newspaper publisher from Marion, Ohio. He fully recognized this himself. Harding had no delusions of grandeur. He had been reluctantly dragged into the presidential race from a comfortable berth in the Senate by the stronger will of Harry M. Daugherty, a machine politician who ruled his political life. He had a dignified, commanding presence, and was unusually handsome. Daugherty is said to have first recognized the possibilities of his career because "he looked like a president." He attracted people of all kinds, from every walk of life, and he was a natural and unself-conscious mixer. Everyone who came in contact with him felt his "warm and endearing humanity." These were lovable qualities of Harding the man.

In so far as he had political principles, they were conservative, based upon a firm belief in the rights of business and of men of property. His stand upon public questions, however, was actually governed almost entirely by political expediency. As a senator he had proved his loyalty to the Republican Party and he could always be counted upon to support its program. There was nothing in his record which opened him to serious attack; there was nothing there to command much admiration. On the League of Nations issue he had strung along with the mild reservationists and attempted to straddle the question in his presidential campaign. He invariably followed the line of least resistance.

His occasional speeches in the Senate had been undistinguished. Although he was given to flights of patriotic exhortation (in which he was entirely sincere), there were slight substance and little grace of expression in his addresses. William G. McAdoo, a political foe, once described his speeches as leaving "the impression of an army of pompous phrases moving over the landscape in search of an idea." In his presidential campaign he had wisely followed the example of McKinley, staying at home to receive delegations of visitors. As President he enjoyed speaking, and a public, wearied with Wilson's eloquent and moving appeals to its idealism, had no quarrel with his comfortable platitudes.

For all these negative aspects of his character, or perhaps because of them, Harding was exactly the sort of man the American

public wished to see in the White House. Here at last, the plain
people felt, was one of themselves — a man without any special
pretensions or messianic complex. Harding was "just folks." His
small-town background, his conventional middle-class ideas, and
his lack of strong or disturbing convictions, inspired a feeling of
comfortable security. The American people did not want heroics;
they did not want discipline. They liked Harding because he was
Main Street come to Washington. The fact that he enjoyed a good
time — nothing so much as a convivial evening with "the boys" —
was a great relief after the austerity of his predecessor. He was
one of them, but at the same time his formal urbanity and handsome presence appeared to uphold all the dignity with which the
presidential office should be clothed. While his essential lack of
character, his easy-going attitude, his too trusting loyalty in his
friends were to have tragic consequences, this could hardly be
foreseen as he took office in 1921. The promise of his administration was "restoration . . . serenity . . . healing."

Two of his strongest characteristics were at once exhibited in
his selection of a cabinet. In recognition of his own limitations he
called to Washington some of the "best minds" of his party; in
loyalty to his friends and political associates he chose a number
of men who had no other possible claim to high office. In the first
group were Charles Evans Hughes as Secretary of State; Herbert
Hoover as Secretary of Commerce; and Andrew Mellon as Secretary of the Treasury. The latter category included Harry M.
Daugherty, who had been his campaign manager, in the post of
Attorney General; Albert B. Fall, a senatorial associate, as Secretary of the Interior; and Will H. Hays, chairman of the Republican National Committee, as Postmaster-General. All that was
worth while during the Harding Administration was largely the
work of the "best minds," while the personal appointees were to
be responsible for a shocking betrayal of the public trust.

TARIFF, FINANCES AND SCANDAL

As far as domestic policies were concerned, the new administration carried through the program of liquidation of the war ini-

tiated during the last years of the Wilson Administration. It also took up at once, in a special session of Congress summoned by President Harding in May, 1921, enactment of a new tariff law to meet the danger of cheap goods being dumped on the American market from a reviving Europe. An emergency bill for this purpose had been vetoed by President Wilson, but with the Republicans in control of both the Administration and Congress, the Fordney-McCumber Act, finally passed in September, 1922, definitely reversed the downward tariff trend of the Underwood Act and once again wrote into law the protectionist principles for which the Republicans had always stood. The United States took its stand in favor of a highly nationalistic program of safeguarding domestic manufactures rather than attempting to promote world-wide trade through the removal of economic barriers as promised in the third of Wilson's Fourteen Points.

The Fordney-McCumber Tariff, in fact, raised the duties on foreign imports to a level higher than ever before in our history. Moreover, these rates could be based upon either the American or foreign valuation of goods, and they were subject to further adjustment on the principle of equalizing costs of production at home and abroad. The supposedly redeeming feature of the bill was creation of a Tariff Commission empowered to draw up revised schedules which the President, within certain limitations, could then declare in effect. Here was a promise of scientific rate-making which could afford legitimate protection without completely cutting off the American market from European exporters. A commission packed with high-tariff advocates, however, proposed thirty-two upward revisions in existing rates and only five decreases. Moreover, the articles falling in the latter category proved strangely reminiscent of Mr. Dooley's free list in 1909. They were mill feed, bobwhite quail, paint-brush handles, phenol, and cresylic acid.

This abrupt return to economic nationalism completely disregarded changes in our economic and financial status brought about by the war. The United States was no longer a debtor nation owing Europe more than it was owed. It was a creditor nation on all counts. It enjoyed a favorable balance, not only in trade, but in all international transactions. If we were to sell abroad, Europe would have to sell in the American market. Otherwise foreign countries would have no international exchange to purchase our exports. And a high protective tariff made this normal exchange of goods impossible. Wilson had recognized the need to admit imports from abroad if we wished Europe either to settle her debts or to purchase our products. "Clearly, this is no time for the erection here of high trade barriers," he had said in vetoing the first emergency tariff bill. Harding blindly accepted economic nationalism: "The urgency of an instant tariff enactment, emergency in character . . . cannot be too much emphasized," he declared. "I believe in the protection of American industry, and it is our purpose to prosper America first."

Under such circumstances the only way to promote exports was to provide potential customers with the necessary funds to make American purchases through some artificial device. During the ensuing years we did this in two ways — by making extensive foreign loans and setting up American branch factories in other countries. With the funds made available by our favorable trade balance, there were by 1930 private long-term investments abroad totaling sixteen billion dollars. For a time these expedients appeared to work out successfully and during the nineteen-twenties our trade expanded phenomenally, despite our tariff barriers. But a situation was being created in which loan would have to be piled upon loan or our export markets could not be maintained. Not until the advent of the Hoover Administration in 1929 was any attempt made to meet this situation — and the result then was adoption of still higher rates with passage of the Hawley-Smoot Tariff. The policy inaugurated under Harding was consistently maintained so long as the Republicans remained in office.

The general lines of the fiscal policy of the nineteen-twenties were also laid down at the beginning of the Harding Administration in accordance with the basic conviction of Secretary Mellon that high income taxes upon corporations and individuals tended to discourage venture capital and undermine productive enterprise. The need for increased government revenue was all-important. As a result of wartime borrowings, the public debt had risen to $24,298,000,000, some twenty times its pre-war total, and the expansion of governmental functions had increased expenditures (exclusive of any debt retirement) to an annual average of more than three billion dollars, four times higher than in the years before 1914. Nevertheless, Secretary Mellon consistently strove to reduce taxes and after some delay due to congressional opposition his program was adopted. The excess profit and wartime excise taxes were abolished almost at once, and subsequent years saw the steady lowering of the corporation tax, the surtax on incomes, and the normal income tax itself.

General prosperity enabled the Treasury to carry out this policy and both meet revenue needs and provide for some reduction in the national debt. By 1930, indeed, the immediate post-war debt total had been successfully cut by a third and stood at $16,185,000,000. A program of economy in government expenditures, supervised by the Bureau of the Budget, established in June, 1921, helped to make possible this simultaneous lowering of taxes and reduction in debt, but it was primarily a consequence of the rise in industrial profits sustaining revenue collections even with reduced tax rates. In any event the system appeared to work. While critics of Secretary Mellon declared that the burden of debt could have been reduced far more rapidly by keeping taxes on a higher level, the country as a whole was more than satisfied with a policy that could at one and the same time show a persistent reduction in debt and relief for the taxpayer.

While these important developments, establishing both the tariff and fiscal programs of the nineteen-twenties, were getting under way, the dark cloud of official corruption was gradually settling over post-war Washington. In the perspective of history just how the members of the "Ohio gang" and other political henchmen of the easy-going President succeeded in mulcting the Government is not important. The Harding scandals have a real significance, however, as had those of the Grant Administration a half-century earlier, in so far as they reflected the prevailing moral laxity of the nation as a whole. The cynical dishonesty in Washington political circles was but another manifestation of the selfish materialism that in so many other ways revealed the bankruptcy of idealism.

President Harding had allowed himself to become surrounded by a group of self-seeking political parasites whose one idea appears to have been to take advantage of every opportunity that their chief's misguided trust and easy gullibility opened up to them. They were good fellows, and the President liked good-fellowship. Biweekly poker parties in the White House afforded a pleasant escape from the conventional restraints imposed upon the presidency. Gambling, drinking, conviviality, broke down all barriers of official formality. "No rumor could have exceeded the reality," Alice Longworth Roosevelt wrote in description of one of these parties in her autobiographical *Crowded Years*; "the study was filled with cronies, Daugherty, Jess Smith, Alec Moore, and others; the air heavy with tobacco smoke, trays with bottles containing every imaginable brand of whiskey stood about, cards and poker chips ready at hand — a general atmosphere of waistcoat unbuttoned, feet on the desk, and the spittoon alongside." A scene so familiar to the back room of a small-town saloon hardly appeared appropriate in presidential circles, but the real trouble was that these professed friends of the President were callously betraying the trust their genial host placed in them.

Many of their shady transactions centered about the Department of Justice — a corrupt traffic in permits for the withdrawal of medicinal liquor, bribery in cases of criminal prosecution, and the venal sale of paroles and pardons. Little was actually proved in regard to these practices. While Attorney General Daugherty was asked to resign in 1924 and was subsequently brought to court on charges of conspiracy to defraud the Government, he succeeded in winning an acquittal. The heads of two other government agencies, equally at home in the close circle of Harding intimates, were less fortunate. Charles R. Forbes, a casual acquaintance in whose charge Harding placed administration of the Veterans' Bureau, was dismissed early in 1923, brought to trial two years later, and sentenced to Leavenworth for robbing the Government of thousands of dollars in the handling of medical supplies and construction of veterans' hospitals. Thomas W. Miller, Alien Property Custodian, was likewise relieved of his post and convicted of fraud in the sale of properties under his control.

More important than these instances of corruption were the oil scandals resulting from the lease to private interests of certain government-owned reserves at Elk Hills, California, and Teapot Dome, Wyoming. Originally under the jurisdiction of the Navy Department, these reserves were transferred in May, 1921, to the Department of the Interior. On the pretense that operations in adjacent oil fields were tapping the Government's supplies, Secretary Fall thereupon leased Elk Hills to private oil interests represented by Edward L. Doheny, and Teapot Dome to those of Harry F. Sinclair. The leases were made with doubtful legality, in complete secrecy, and on terms highly unfavorable to the public.

Reports of these transactions, which had been completed in 1922, finally got about and upon the prodding of Senator La Follette an investigation was undertaken the next year. There was at first no suggestion of outright fraud, but gossip soon brought attention to a curious coincidence. Secretary Fall, known to be in financial straits, had apparently come into substantial funds. He was reported carrying out improvements on his New Mexico ranch which could hardly be explained on the basis of his twelve-thousand-dollar salary as a cabinet member. The Senator investigators, headed by Senator Thomas J. Walsh, soon found themselves on the trail of something far more malodorous than dereliction of duty. Their hearings provided sensation upon sensation. Fall twisted and turned as he attempted to explain away what he described as purely personal loans extended to him by Doheny and Sinclair. The presence in his bank account of Liberty bonds traced to the Continental Trading Company, a Sinclair corporation, and the mysterious journeyings of a little black satchel containing one hundred thousand dollars in cash which Doheny's son had obligingly delivered at the Secretary of the Interior's home afforded, however, conclusive evidence of bribery.

The Government at once instituted civil suits for the recovery of both the Elk Hills and Teapot Dome reserves, which were finally won in 1927, and it also brought criminal charges of fraud, conspiracy, and corruption against the principals involved. Secretary Fall was convicted of receiving bribes with a sentence of one year in jail and one hundred thousand dollars fine, but both Sinclair and Doheny were eventually acquitted.

Long before this final dénouement, President Harding found himself trapped in the network of corruption that his supposed friends were weaving so tightly about him. There is no evidence whatsoever that he was in any way directly involved, but he could not escape his responsibility as Chief Executive. By the early summer of 1923, after the disclosure of corruption in the Veterans' Bureau and the beginning of the investigation into the transfer of oil reserves, he apparently began to realize what was happening. But somehow even then he lacked the courage to sweep clean the Augean stables himself. Obviously borne down with anxiety, he sought at least temporarily to escape the problems pressing upon him and paid an official visit to Alaska. Upon his return to Seattle, he was suddenly taken ill. For a time he seemed to rally, but he died six days later at San Francisco, on August 2, 1923.

COOLIDGE AND THE ELECTION OF 1924

Upon the President's death, the responsibilities of his office devolved upon the shoulders of the Vice-President — Calvin Coolidge. He was visiting his father in Plymouth, Vermont, and it was in the early hours of the following morning that word reached him of what had happened. With only a half-dozen persons present, including his wife, stenographer, and chauffeur, by the flickering light of a kerosene lamp, he was sworn into office by his father, a notary public. The scene was thoroughly in keeping with the traditions of American democracy, but the contrast between its simplicity and the strident boom times that were to characterize the Coolidge era could hardly have been more striking.

It was not so untypical of the new President himself. Coolidge was a New Englander, the first to be President since Franklin Pierce almost three quarters of a century earlier. More than that, he was a Vermonter. And he embodied many of the qualities of the people of that state which has clung more tenaciously, perhaps, than any other to the traditions of an earlier agrarian civilization. The country knew little about Coolidge — it would not know much more when he left office some six years later. Reticence and self-control were among the salient characteristics of one of the most enigmatic figures that ever lived in the White House.

Coolidge was conservative, cautious, shrewd, and thrifty; he was highly conscientious and completely honest. There was none of Harding's convivial good-fellowship, keen love of life, warmth of personality, about this cool New Englander with his deep strain of puritanism. The myths which were to gain such wide currency as to his taciturnity hardly did him justice, for with his few close intimates he let down the bars and was loquacity itself. Nevertheless, Coolidge held himself apart, awkward and self-conscious, in general society. He commanded respect from the public, but little affection.

He had climbed the political ladder step by step from the lowest to the highest rung. After working his way through Amherst College, he had taken up the practice of law in Northampton, Massachusetts, and almost at once started upon his political career. Assemblyman, mayor of Northampton, state senator, lieutenant-governor, governor, Vice-President, and President — he had not once faltered in his steady progress to political eminence. Luck accompanied him at every stage of his career — it would not desert him when he stepped neatly out from under the impending economic crash at the close of his second term as President — but he had always been fully aware of the main chance.

An ambition bulwarked by calculating caution kept him on the correct path to political preferment. On only one occasion had he sprung into national prominence — and it had much to do with his availability for the vice-presidency in 1920. During the Boston police strike the year before, he had carefully refrained from intervening until the moment when possible advantage far outweighed possible risk. Then, after having authorized the use of state militia and having seen the strike successfully broken, he tersely replied to Samuel Gompers's plea for reinstatement of the police, in a public telegram: "There is no right to strike against the public safety by anybody, anywhere, any time." In the pre-

vailing temper of the country, nothing could have more completely won national confidence.

There was no question of Coolidge's party regularity or of his
support for the dominant interests. He had largely ignored the
progressive movement of pre-war days; he had kept clear of the
political chicanery of the Harding Administration. Yet he had
strong convictions, however limited, to which he adhered without equivocation. Coolidge believed in the moral government of
the universe, the present success and future greatness of America,
the inherent right of conservative wealth to determine national
policies, and the constant need for the American people to practice frugality and simplicity in their living. The fostering and
protection of large aggregations of wealth had his full approval.
He believed them to be the only foundations on which to build
the prosperity of the whole people.

Upon taking office Coolidge promised to continue the Harding
policies. With the guarantee implicit in his personal integrity and
caution that public affairs would now be administered with unim-
peachable honesty, this was altogether satisfactory. The country
wanted no fireworks, no sudden change in pace or direction.
Even full disclosure of the Harding scandals and the new President's contentment with the most casual house-cleaning could not
shake the complacency born of good times. Coolidge was safe —
and that was all that was necessary.

It was late in 1923 that he became President. An electoral campaign was to be under way within a year. Whether or not he
would be the Republican nominee, and what were the chances
of his election, were the political questions of paramount interest
throughout the country. The first was quickly answered. Coolidge skillfully maneuvered his nomination and prepared to go
before the country on the issue of maintaining prosperity. Even
though the long shadow of the oil scandals fell across the party
record, Republican political leaders felt justified in their belief
that rising profits in the business world would blot out all minor
considerations when their candidate was as impeccably honest as
Calvin Coolidge.

His election, however, was not a foregone conclusion. Despite the general acceptance of conservative doctrines there were stirrings of discontent among the old progressives and members of the midwestern farm bloc. A Farmer-Labor Party had entered the field in 1920 and two years later its members joined forces with a new Conference for Progressive Political Action. With the backing of the railway labor unions as well as farm groups, this organization had won considerable congressional strength in the mid-term elections. Under the formidable leadership of Senator La Follette, a revolt comparable to that which had wrought such havoc during Taft's Administration was under way. Here was potential danger for the Republicans, and in 1924 it materialized into the organization of a definite third party.

The new progressives sought to rally farmers and labor, liberal elements of whatever persuasion, behind the independent candidacy of La Follette. Their platform — or rather that of La Follette — adhered closely to the principles advanced by the Progressive Party of 1912. It stated that the great issue before the country was "the control of government and industry by private monopoly." It demanded immediate relief for farmers; effective action to protect our national resources from further plunder; government ownership of water power; tax reduction limited to the lower income brackets; railroad rate regulation based on prudent investment; and abolition of the injunction as a weapon to break the power of labor. In the field of foreign policy it advocated revision of the Versailles Treaty, the outlawry of war, and reduction of armaments. It was a liberal document in the great tradition of progressive reform. La Follette could call upon the support of those elements in the country which had upheld progressivism before the war and his candidacy was specifically endorsed by the executive council of the American Federation of Labor and by the Socialist Party.

Before the Conference for Progressive Political Action had outlined its program, however, the Democrats had obligingly done what they could to help out the Republicans. The prevailing conservatism of the country made a third party a much less dangerous threat than had been the case in 1912, and La Follette could not command the personal devotion that cemented the ranks of Theodore Roosevelt's followers. There was always the chance, however, that he might win sufficient votes from the Republicans to open the way for an aggressive Democratic candidate to drive to victory as Wilson had done in 1912. It was a Heaven-sent opportunity — and the Democrats casually threw it away by choosing this particular year for a disastrous quarrel over their own nominee.

The leading contenders at the Democratic convention in 1924 were William G. McAdoo, former Secretary of the Treasury, and Alfred E. Smith, Governor of New York. The one represented the traditional and more conservative interests within the party, strong in the West and in the South. The other was spokesman for the urban masses, often foreign-born, who made up Democratic strength in the great cities of the Northeast. This sectional alignment, ominous in itself, was further charged with explosive political dynamite. "Al" Smith was not only a product of the sidewalks of New York and of Tammany Hall, he was an outspoken opponent of prohibition and a Roman Catholic. No possible candidate could have more outraged the feelings of southern Democrats. Fanatically dry in theory, largely under the sway of the Ku Klux Klan and imbued with its intolerant doctrine of Protestant, white supremacy, they closed their ranks against the nomination of this representative of everything in American life to which they stood most opposed. The more liberal forces supporting Smith were no less adamant against accepting McAdoo as a nominee of the Klan. A bitter deadlock could not be avoided. Over one hundred ballots were voted, but neither man could secure the necessary two-thirds majority. Finally, after both Smith and McAdoo had withdrawn in despair, John W. Davis, a conservative New York lawyer, was put forward as a compromise candidate and the wearied delegates gave him a nomination that had lost all meaning. The Democratic Party was split asunder. Davis had no chance whatsoever of restoring its unity.

The campaign was itself a dull affair. The weakened Democrats had no will to arouse effective opposition to Republican rule, for all the ammunition afforded by the oil scandals. La Follette had even less chance of awakening a generally satisfied people to the need for progressive reform. The Republicans made the most of two alliterative slogans — "Keep Cool with Coolidge" and "Coolidge or Chaos." Little more was necessary. Their candidate received 15,725,000 votes to Davis's 8,386,500 and La Follette's 4,826,400. The electoral college gave him 382 of its 531 total ballots. The third-party vote was a far stronger protest against both major parties than had been expected, but Coolidge had been safely elected in his own right.

During the next four years no changes were made in Republican policy. On the principle that national prosperity was "predicated on the foundation of a protective tariff," every move toward revising existing customs duties was effectively blocked. The fiscal policies supported by Secretary Mellon were carried forward with a new emphasis placed upon national economy. In some quarters there were rumblings of discontent. The demand which veterans of the first World War had long since voiced for a bonus to supplement their discharge payments came to a head with the passage in 1924 of a bill providing paid-up endowment policies at a total cost of $3,500,000,000. A campaign led by Senator Norris for public ownership of water-power sites resulted in congressional approval of a measure to empower the Government to take over the wartime hydroelectric plant at Muscle Shoals, in the Tennessee River. A farm bloc revolt forced through Congress the McNary-Haugen Bill, a measure seeking to meet the problems of agriculture by setting up a $400,000,000 revolving fund to assist the farmer in marketing the exportable surplus of his crops.

In each instance, Coolidge's answer was an emphatic veto. On the bonus issue he was overridden. Under the insistent pressure of the powerful American Legion lobby, Congress, when it came to war veterans, paid no attention to the President's plea for economy in the disposition of federal funds. He was upheld, however, in his refusal to endorse any step toward government ownership and operation in the sphere of water power, or to countenance such direct aid to the farmer as that contemplated in the McNary-Haugen Bill.

These problems Coolidge left to his successors. For himself, he simply sat tight, as around him swirled the pleasing excitement of boom times, mounting corporation profits, and a soaring stock market. His primary concern was not to interrupt or in any way impede our continued progress toward a new high plateau of material prosperity, and the country fully approved this negative attitude. As the humorist Will Rogers wryly commented, "He didn't do anything, but that's what the people wanted done."

Coolidge might well have received the Republican renomination in 1928, but during the previous summer he startled the nation with an unexpected and characteristically terse announcement, handed in typewritten form to the press: "I do not choose to run for President in 1928." Refusing to amplify this statement in any way despite all the excited conjecture it provoked, he relegated the responsibility of choosing his successor to the party leaders and continued to carry out the formal duties of his office with the passive acceptance of things as they were which had marked his entire political career.

The Engineer in Politics

The Republican choice for a presidential candidate to succeed Coolidge was Herbert Hoover. No one was more closely identified with the policies of the previous eight years. In his rôle of Secretary of Commerce during both the Harding and Coolidge Administrations, he had promoted the interests of big business at every turn. Conservatives had every reason to feel that his election would assure continuance of the Republican policy of leaving industry free to pursue its own ends. The platform on which Hoover was prepared to run praised the party record, and made no further definite commitments.

The Democratic nominee was "Al" Smith. There had been no real healing of the bitter rift of 1924. The southern Democrats were no more enthusiastic over Smith's candidacy than they had been four years earlier. It was recognized, however, that another knock-down, drag-out fight would be suicidal for the party, and Smith's record as Governor of New York could not be ignored by even his most rabid opponents. He had shown in two re-elections a remarkable vote-getting capacity, and his progressive, forward-looking administrations had attracted nation-wide attention. To have refused him the nomination under such circumstances, with no other Democrat of comparable stature available, would have caused complete disintegration of the party.

The Democratic platform, nevertheless, differed little in essentials from that of the Republicans. Even on the tariff question, traditional bone of contention, it favored duties serving to equalize the costs of production at home and abroad in order to maintain legitimate business and a high standard of wages. The country was too obviously content with Republican policies for the Democrats to have the courage to offer very much more than a slightly modified version of the same thing. Smith had certain ideas of his own. He favored farm relief, government control over public utilities, and restrictions upon the use of injunctions in labor disputes. Yet he made every effort to demonstrate his friendly attitude toward big business, even going so far as to choose for his campaign manager an officer of the General Motors Corporation. The only sharp difference in policy between the Republican and Democratic candidates, despite their striking dissimilarities in background and character, was on prohibition. While Hoover upheld what he termed "a great social and economic experiment, noble in motive and far-reaching in purpose," Smith was definitely in favor of repeal.

The campaign became one of personalities — or actually of intolerant attack and warm defense of the unusual attributes and background of the Democratic candidate. Appeals to prejudice soon overshadowed every attempt to keep the election on the level of fair and rational political debate. An undercover campaign of vilification made the election one of the most embittered in our political history. All the latent bigotry in the nation, symbolized by the Ku Klux Klan, came out into the open. An opposition candidate with fewer political liabilities could hardly have hoped to make effective headway against the Republican Party, which had so successfully identified itself in 1928 with prosperity, but as a Catholic and a Wet, "Al" Smith never had a real chance.

Hoover was carried into office by a landslide which made political history. His popular vote was 21,392,000 and that of Smith

15,016,000. The Democratic total closely approximated the vote which Coolidge had obtained four years earlier, but the Republican total was some forty per cent greater. Hoover lost Massachusetts and Rhode Island, but with the support of so-called Hoover Democrats he broke the Solid South. Only six states south of the Mason-Dixon line preserved their traditional allegiance to the Democratic Party. In the electoral college the count was 444 to 87.

While the apparent disintegration of the Democrats was the most startling consequence of the election, even more significant was the almost complete lack of any vote of protest. Four years before, La Follette had won nearly five million votes for progressivism, but there was no equivalent to this vote in 1928. Norman Thomas, the Socialist candidate, received only 267,420 votes, less than a third his party's total in 1920, and William Z. Foster, the Communist, but 48,770. Despite the greatly increased size of the electorate, there had not been such a feeble dissenting voice to the policies of the two major parties since the opening of the century. The conservative program which the Republicans had been carrying out since 1920 could hardly have received a more emphatic and unequivocal endorsement.

As the last of the triumvirate of Republican presidents during the post-war decade, Hoover was destined by a harsh fate to reap the whirlwind where his predecessors had sown the wind. He was in office less than a year when the stock-market crash heralded the long years of the Great Depression of the nineteen-thirties. As a member of the Administrations of Harding and Coolidge, the new President was not without responsibility for the governmental policies which helped to pave the way for complete economic collapse. It was nevertheless ill luck, as pronounced as Coolidge's good luck, that made him the victim of the disaster. And it was a particularly ironic fate for Herbert Hoover in the light of his confident campaign assertions that the country was "nearer to the abolition of poverty, to the abolition of fear of want, than humanity has ever reached before." Seldom has an administration opened with such promise as that of Herbert Hoover. But it was to end with the country economically prostrate, and the Republican Party politically bankrupt.

The gods may have been preparing to make tragic sport of "the great engineer," but upon his inaugural in March, 1929, there was as yet little evidence of it. The public had full confidence in the new President. He lacked Harding's warm-hearted personality and Coolidge's shrewd political sixth sense. But the very fact that he had become Chief Executive without such qualities appeared to be a guarantee that efficiency and the new techniques of science, rather than spoilsmanship and log-rolling, would govern his administrative policy. Moreover, his career was the sort of success story which most appealed to the generation of the nineteen-twenties. Born an Iowa farm boy, Hoover had made his way in the world as a mining engineer and amassed a very considerable fortune. Since the outbreak of the first World War in 1914, however, he had employed his decided administrative gifts in public service rather than for private profit — the Commission for the Relief of Belgium, the Food Administration, and the Department of Commerce. It was the sort of training which a business civilization appeared to demand at a time when Government was considered almost an offshoot of industrial enterprise.

It nevertheless remained true that the presidency needed a politician quite as much as an efficiency expert, and Hoover's limitations on this score soon became apparent. In his previous posts his executive ability had been given full play. He was "the chief," commanding the unquestioning and loyal support of subordinates. As President he had to cope with Congress and professional politicians whose interests could not always be reconciled with effective, businesslike procedure. Hoover's lack of experience in the rough-and-tumble of American politics was a tremendous handicap. He was confronted with strong opposition in both the Senate and House, despite their large Republican majorities, as the farm bloc continued to demand redress of the economic balance which had swung so far in favor of industry. Hoover did not have the training to cope with problems which demanded political quite as much as economic adjustments.

The public also began to find in Hoover too much of the efficiency expert and too little of the popular leader. He was too reserved, too solemn, too stuffy. There was nothing about him to make lively newspaper copy. He did not know how to develop those friendly relations with the Washington correspondents which ensure a good press. He was highly vulnerable to criticism or attack. When troubles began to fall upon him thick and fast, these weaknesses promoted the loss of public confidence. The country not only turned away from him, but it made him the scapegoat for mistakes and errors for which he was at least no more responsible than Coolidge or Harding.

It has already been noted that he believed thoroughly and completely in "the American system of rugged individualism." Nothing that was to happen after 1929 would shake this unalterable faith. But his was not the negative, do-nothing policy of Coolidge. Hoover felt that Washington should encourage and promote our economic expansion — both at home and abroad. "Without intrusion," Hoover stated, "the Government can sometimes give leadership and serve to bring together divergent elements . . . that is reinforcement of our individualism."

He had a broad conception of social planning and was liberal-minded at least in the sense that he had no idea of complete surrender to the powers of big business. He declared on one occasion:

> The very essence of equality of opportunity and of American individualism is that there shall be no domination by any group or combination in this republic, whether it be business or political. On the contrary, it demands economic justice as well as political and social justice. It is no system of *laissez-faire*.

Circumstance compelled the new President to summon a special session of Congress in the summer of 1929. The absence of any real improvement in agricultural conditions was responsible for such a sharp wave of agrarian discontent that the demands of the farm bloc for relief could no longer be ignored. And on an issue closely related with direct aid for the farmers, midwestern spokesmen in Congress were insisting upon downward revision of the tariff in order to reduce the costs of manufactured products and stimulate export markets.

The basic problem of the farmers remained that of maintaining prices in the face of a world-wide overproduction of farm goods, especially wheat and cotton. We have already noted the effect of such conditions, in the midst of general prosperity, upon the status of the farmer in American society. While quite as much opposed to price-fixing or subsidy, to export debenture plans or McNary-Haugen bills, as Coolidge had been, Hoover realized that something had to be done. He knew that the day had passed when agrarian discontent could be stilled by the dispassionate logic of veto messages. Consequently he proposed government aid to the farmer in meeting the problem of surplus crops by a scheme that he hoped would at once stabilize agricultural prices and bring about a better balanced national economy.

In response to his proposals, Congress passed the Agricultural Marketing Act of 1929. It established a Federal Farm Board, with a revolving fund of five hundred million dollars, empowered to advance loans to the farmers, through co-operatives, which would enable them to hold off the market any surplus in basic commodities that threatened the price structure. By temporarily freezing this surplus, price levels were to be allowed gradually to adjust themselves so as to make possible in time the profitable disposal of all warehoused crops. Under ordinary circumstances the plan might possibly have worked and the farmers co-operated by voluntarily limiting their production. Circumstances, however, were not normal in 1929. A world-wide decline in agricultural prices was under way and it could not be so easily halted. Domestic prices were temporarily pegged when tremendous quantities of wheat and cotton were taken off the market, but the cumulative piling-up of these excess stocks injected such an uncertain element into the situation that they could make no real recovery. The Federal Farm Board then had no way to dispose of its withheld supplies without still further depressing prices. As it continued to hold its stocks, mounting storage charges threatened to exceed their total value.

Two stabilization corporations had been established to handle these operations, and by 1931 the Grain Corporation held no less than 330,000,000 bushels of wheat and the Cotton Corporation some 3,250,000 bales of cotton. There were no purchasers for these huge stocks, prices continued to sag ominously, and the funds made available by the Agricultural Marketing Act were soon exhausted. The Federal Farm Board then had no alternative other than to withdraw from the market. Without its support the price of wheat fell to fifty-seven cents a bushel, the lowest since 1896, and cotton plunged to five cents a pound. The Hoover program of farm relief had failed disastrously, and it was left for the New Deal to attempt to meet the critical problem of agrarian distress through far more radical measures.

In the meantime congressional consideration of the allied problem of the tariff found the farm bloc fighting strenuously for adoption of its ideas on downward revision. Party lines were broken as this revolt against protection assumed proportions comparable to that of the insurgents during the Taft Administration. For a time the Senate and the House found themselves in an apparently irreconcilable deadlock and it was not until June, 1930, that a new tariff finally emerged from the confusion — and proved to be another victory for traditional protectionists.

The log-rolling, bartering, and lobbying in behalf of special interests that has always marked American tariff-making had once again produced a measure that raised rather than lowered the general level of existing duties. The Hawley-Smoot Tariff, as this bill was called, greatly accentuated the economic nationalism first expressed in the Fordney-McCumber Tariff, and it was to have far-reaching, world-wide repercussions. A petition signed by over a thousand economists urged the President to veto the bill on the ground that it would raise industrial prices, restrict exports, and interfere with European payment of war debts, but with the lame excuse that the Tariff Commission would enable him to reduce such duties as circumstances showed to be inadvisable, Hoover duly signed it. Other countries immediately took retaliatory measures, as they had threatened to do while the bill was making its hectic way through Congress, and the rise in American tariff rates was met by comparable upward revision in European and Latin American rates. Not only that, many countries felt compelled to establish import quotas, special exchange restrictions, and other barriers to the normal interchange of goods.

Hoover also faced at the beginning of his Administration renewed pressure on the water-power issue and a further demand on the part of veterans of the first World War to be allowed to borrow on their new endowment policies. He followed Coolidge's lead in vetoing legislation upon both water power and the bonus, and like Coolidge, was overridden on the latter issue. The farm relief and tariff acts remained the most important legislation of his first two years in office.

Was he to be left free to develop further the "American system" which he had so hopefully referred to in his campaign speeches as holding the promise of the abolition of poverty and fear? The Agricultural Marketing Act had barely been passed and Congress was still wrangling over the Hawley-Smoot Tariff when deep depression began to settle ominously over the land. Its repercussions were to change the face, not only of twentieth-century America, but of the entire world. Before taking up the economic crisis, we must therefore turn to American foreign policy during the nineteen-twenties and observe the effect of economic nationalism abroad.

World Affairs

Bases of Foreign Policy

During the years of Republican supremacy the American people appeared to subscribe to the statement in Harding's inaugural that the United States sought "no part in directing the destinies of the world." Attention and interest were too largely concentrated upon domestic affairs. Nevertheless, to characterize this period as one of complete political isolation is unwarranted. There were important developments in the three spheres in which American foreign policy operated — Europe, Latin America, and the Far East. As Theodore Roosevelt had long before stated, the United States could not avoid playing a great part in the world, whether it wished to or not.

In the Far East these years opened with an ambitious attempt to strengthen the Open-Door policy and secure naval limitation in the Pacific through the treaties signed at the Washington Conference. They closed with the whole structure of this settlement in tragic collapse and an upsurge of Japanese imperialism ominously foreshadowing a world at war within another few years. Latin-American affairs improved about in proportion to the deterioration in the far-eastern situation. Abandonment of the interventionist program promoted under cover of the Roosevelt corollary to the Monroe Doctrine pointed clearly to the Good Neighbor policy and an era of good will from which we would reap the fortunate fruits in the nineteen-forties. In Europe there was a hesitant trend toward closer co-operation. Our relations with Soviet Russia were a striking exception to this generalization, but the close of the period found the United States participating in almost all of the League of Nations' non-political activities and ready to act in concert with its members in any move toward disarmament.

It nevertheless remains true that economic nationalism, as exemplified in our high-tariff policy and insistence upon payment of the war debts, had more important consequences than our tentative approaches to international co-operation. The attitude of the United States was a contributing factor to the breakdown of world economy that hastened the rise of Nazism in Germany and of militarism in Japan, developments which in turn laid the groundwork for the second World War. The success which attended our policies, in terms of increasing material prosperity, was held to be sufficient justification to refrain from any closer economic collaboration with other nations, just as it excused our failure to carry out further progressive reform in the sphere of domestic policies. While it will never be possible to apportion satisfactorily the ultimate blame for the conditions that in 1939 plunged the world into a conflict so much more devastating than that of 1914, the United States cannot escape its share of the general responsibility.

NAVAL LIMITATION AND THE FAR EAST

When Harding came into office in 1921, conditions in the general area of the Pacific were so chaotic that he called them a grave menace to peace. Japan was firmly entrenched on the Asiatic mainland, not only through her steady encroachments upon China, but by occupation of the Siberian coastline as a carryover from Allied intervention in Russia in 1918. An impending naval race among the United States, Great Britain, and Japan both reflected and intensified a highly dangerous situation. The American people were deeply concerned, and furthermore a postwar demand for government economy left them in no mood to meet the expenses which additional naval construction would involve.

The Washington Conference for the Limitation of Armaments was summoned by the President to meet these issues with both political and naval settlements on its prospective agenda. Great

Britain, having herself suggested our holding just such a conference, accepted the American invitation eagerly. Japan did so
reluctantly. The other participants were France, Italy, Belgium,
Holland, Portugal, and China.

The conference opened at Washington in November, 1921.
With no forewarning of what he was about to say, Secretary of
State Hughes astounded the assembled delegates by dramatically
proposing, in definite and precise terms, that the five powers —
the United States, Great Britain, Japan, France, and Italy — proclaim at once a naval holiday. For ten years, he suggested, there
should be no construction of capital ships. Going still further, he
called for the scrapping of such vessels already built or under
construction as would be necessary to place the relative strength
of the powers' existing vessels in this category upon the basis of
500,000 tons each for Great Britain and the United States, 300,000
tons for Japan, and 175,000 tons each for France and Italy.

The delegates were swept off their feet by the audacity of this
proposal. They had not dreamed of being presented with anything of the sort on the opening day of the conference. But Secretary Hughes had issued a challenge to action which could not
be left unanswered, and after considerable negotiation his plan
was accepted. While it proved impossible to extend the principle of limitation of naval armaments to other vessels, the construction of cruisers, destroyers, and submarines thus being left
unrestricted, the Five-Power Naval Treaty was a substantial
achievement. It was enthusiastically hailed as a milestone in the
history of the disarmament movement.

It contained, however, an important concession to Japan. In
return for her acceptance of naval inferiority under the 5–5–3
ratio, she insisted that the signatory nations agree not to fortify
further their islands in the Pacific. Hawaii was excepted in so far
as the United States was concerned, but we waived our rights to
develop naval bases in the Philippines, Guam, Samoa, or the Aleutian Islands. In so doing we gave up whatever effective naval
power we might have exerted in the western Pacific and we virtually surrendered control of those waters to Japan. The tremendous significance of this concession was not wholly recognized at

the time. In so far as it was, however, it was felt to be justified by two political accords which were believed to provide security for American interests in that part of the world.

The first of these was a Four-Power Treaty in which the United States, Great Britain, France, and Japan agreed to respect one another's insular possessions in the Pacific and to consult jointly should the rights of any one of them be threatened by any other power. The chief importance of this treaty lay in the fact that it abrogated the old Anglo-Japanese Alliance, which was felt to constitute a possible danger to the United States in the event of further controversy with Japan. At the same time it apparently guaranteed our possession of the Philippines and served further to promote the stability of the entire Pacific area.

The second and more important political accord was the Nine-Power Treaty. All the powers represented at Washington definitely and specifically pledged themselves in this pact to respect the political sovereignty and territorial integrity of China, and the principle of equality of trade in all their dealings with her. As between the opposing interests and claims of the United States and Japan, this treaty was a decisive diplomatic victory for the United States. It wrote into international law for the first time our historic far-eastern policy. "The Open Door in China," the American delegation reported, "has at last been made a fact." But while Japan thus appeared to have forsworn her imperialistic policy on the Asiatic mainland, accepting the American viewpoint on the importance of safeguarding China's independence, the Nine-Power Treaty provided no means for its enforcement. The United States placed its whole reliance for the maintenance of far-eastern peace upon Japan's good faith.

When these accords were finally concluded in 1922, there seemed to be every reason for confidence in the results of the Washington Conference. And for almost a decade their high promise of peace and stability in the Pacific was realized. Japan withdrew her troops from Siberia, returned Shantung to China, and annulled the Lansing-Ishii Agreement in which the United States had recognized Japan's special interests in China. In 1930, moreover, the Tokyo Government agreed at another conference in

London to extend the life of the Five-Power Naval Treaty and, in accordance with somewhat more favorable ratios, to limit as well the construction of cruisers, submarines, and other naval vessels. Our intervention and assertion of political leadership in the Far East gave every indication of having established international security throughout the Pacific.

Such difficulties as did develop during the nineteen-twenties actually involved our relations with China rather than those with Japan. For a time the Chinese Nationalists, coming into power under Chiang Kai-shek in 1926, followed such a strongly anti-foreign policy that American interests in China, as well as those of other powers, seemed to be gravely threatened. The danger of any serious conflict was averted, however, and the United States took the lead in recognizing the new Nationalist Government established at Nanking and pledged itself to revision of the so-called unequal treaties, with return of tariff autonomy and the promise to surrender all extra-territorial rights.

The calm so generally prevailing throughout the Pacific at the end of the decade nevertheless proved illusory. Before the close of the Hoover Administration, it was suddenly shattered when Japan cynically violated the pledges made at the Washington Conference, as well as her other treaty obligations not to resort to force as an instrument of national policy. In September, 1931, her troops marched into Manchuria and proceeded to occupy the Chinese provinces lying north of the Great Wall. The American people could hardly credit their senses. For a time it was believed that the Japanese Government would disavow the action of the army in Manchuria, but gradually the sober realization was borne in upon the public that the militarists had once again come into power and that Japan had reverted to her old program of continental expansion.

As it soon became clear, the military leaders had never been reconciled to the self-denying ordinances the Japanese Government had accepted at the Washington Conference, either in regard to naval limitation or policy toward China. They had nursed their resentment and waited for a time to strike. After the London Naval Conference their plans began to mature, and by political pressure and assassination they drove the liberals out of power and took over control of the Government. Their pretext for attack on Manchuria was the threat to Japan's interests resulting from the obstructive policies of the Chinese Nationalists, but their goal reached out far beyond occupation of this territory. They were prepared to brush aside all treaty obligations in vigorous assertion of their political power in eastern Asia. Japan had taken the first step on that march of imperialist aggression that just ten years later led to Pearl Harbor. The hopes of lasting peace in the Far East created by the Washington Conference treaties faded away.

Protests were at once showered upon Japan for resorting to force in contravention of her international obligations. The United States not only sought to call her to account for violation of treaties to which this country was a party; in its concern over the threat to world security in the occupation of Manchuria, it went so far as to allow an official American representative to take part in the League of Nations' discussions on the crisis. There was an outcry from isolationists at this gesture of co-operation. How far we might have carried it can never be known. For beyond repeated protests to Japan and adoption of a condemnatory report submitted by the Lytton Commission, appointed to investigate the situation in 1932, the League itself took no decisive action.

As Japan went about setting up the puppet state of Manchukuo under her complete domination, the United States sought the co-operation of Great Britain in bringing more direct pressure to bear upon Japan than the hard-pressed League was prepared to exert. It was confronted, however, with a policy of let-well-enough-alone on the part of Downing Street, resulting in varied measure from England's absorption in financial crisis, skepticism as to how far the United States was really prepared to go, and a feeling that no important British interests were menaced. Secretary Stimson thereupon decided to take what action he could on his own initiative to give greater weight and force to American protests. In notes dispatched to both the Japanese and Chinese capitals early in January, 1932, he explicitly stated that the United States would refuse to recognize any situation, treaty, or agreement in the Far East which impaired American rights or was brought about by resort to force.

There was a demand from some quarters for more positive action. It was urged that the United States impose economic sanctions or some form of boycott upon Japan. President Hoover believed, however, that any such policy ran the risk of involving the United States in a war for which there was no popular support, and public opinion generally supported his cautious attitude. "The American people," the *Philadelphia Record* asserted, "don't give a hoot in a rain barrel who controls North China." This was far from the mark. The excitement occasioned by Japan's aggressive attack upon China reflected a widespread concern over events in eastern Asia. Nevertheless, it was true that the American people did not consider maintenance of China's integrity and of the Open Door a vital national interest. Under such circumstances Japan paid no more heed to the Stimson Doctrine than she had to either our earlier protests or those of the League of Nations.

The impunity with which Japan was allowed to tear down the whole fabric of collective security in the Far East, ruthlessly violating her treaty commitments in unprovoked attack on China, was the most threatening development in international affairs since the end of the first World War. The inability of the Powers to take joint action to restrain an aggressor nation was a disastrous revelation of the ineffectiveness of the League of Nations. The lesson was not lost upon other potential aggressors. Where Japan had led the way in asserting what she considered her rights by force of arms, Italy and Germany were soon to follow. In many ways 1931 was the turning-point which marked the doom of whatever hopes the world might have had that the international order established by the Treaty of Versailles could endure.

LATIN-AMERICAN RELATIONS

Relations with Latin America followed a rather erratic course before pointing toward the *rapprochement* of the nineteen-thirties. While the Harding Administration maintained a friendly attitude toward the nations south of the Rio Grande, there was a return for a time under President Coolidge to a policy that could hardly be distinguished from the dollar diplomacy of President Taft and Secretary Knox. In its application to the countries of the Caribbean, this policy was upheld, as it had been during the earlier period, on the ground that disturbances in that area were a direct menace to our own peace and safety. Nevertheless, Coolidge also admitted frankly an economic concern in Latin-American developments that in his opinion justified intervention on quite a different basis. He declared:

> The person and property of a citizen are a part of the general domain of the nation, even when abroad. Wherever he goes these duties of our Government must follow him. . . . There is a distinct and binding obligation on the part of self-respecting governments to afford protection to the persons and property of their citizens wherever they may be. . . .

Under cover of a doctrine going much further than had the policies of any of his predecessors in its disregard of the sovereign rights of small nations, Coolidge initiated measures which awakened a storm of protest both among the Latin-American nations and among liberal elements in this country. American bankers were given all possible diplomatic support in safeguarding the security of their loans and strong pressure was applied to promote our foreign trade. Over any government south of the Rio Grande which refused full economic co-operation with American business interests hung the threat of retaliation. In the case of the smaller countries in the Caribbean, even more direct interference was at times practiced through arms embargoes and military force.

Nicaragua was once again a case in point. It will be remembered that a fiscal protectorate had been established during Wilson's Administration. The marines were finally recalled in 1925, but when further political disturbances broke out the next year, they were quickly sent back. Nicaragua was a country whose stability was vitally important for the safety of the Panama

Canal, but this consideration did not appear wholly to govern our policy. We refused to recognize the political faction already accepted as Nicaragua's legitimate government by Mexico and other Latin-American countries, and threw our support behind another party more friendly to American financial interests. A force of five thousand marines was landed to uphold the claims of its candidate for the presidency and all shipments of arms to the *de facto* Government were embargoed. It looked like open hostilities. President Coolidge denied it. "We are not making war on Nicaragua," he stated, "any more than a policeman on the street is making war on passers-by."

Nevertheless, there developed within this country strong opposition to intervention which appeared to be patently in the interests of American bankers. Coolidge was compelled to seek a way out of the imbroglio in which he found himself, and early in 1927 he dispatched Henry L. Stimson as a special envoy to attempt to reconcile Nicaragua's quarreling factions. Stimson succeeded in negotiating an agreement for new presidential elections to be held under American supervision. General order was re-established through these measures, but the refusal of one rebel leader to lay down his arms prevented the complete recall of the marines. They remained in Nicaragua to carry on a private war against the so-called Sandistas, and were not entirely withdrawn until 1933.

A more important controversy developed in our relations with Mexico after the election of President Calles in 1924. The constitution of that country, adopted in 1917 following the disturbances which so nearly brought on war during the Wilson Administration, had vested ownership of all of the country's oil and mineral resources in the Mexican nation. American corporations with investments totaling some three hundred million dollars had at first feared that this provision might be made retroactive. After a period of sometimes angry dispute in which recognition was withheld from the Mexican Government, an understanding had finally been reached which apparently validated existing American property titles. Calles now threatened to upset this accord and introduced a radical agrarian program that renewed the old struggle centering upon foreign rights in the country's natural resources. Various pressure groups in this country, particularly investors in Mexican oil properties, at once demanded intervention to protect American interests.

For a time the Administration appeared to be prepared to enforce American claims. Moreover, Secretary of State Kellogg added fuel to these controversial fires by charging in a note sent to the Senate, in January, 1927, that Mexico had embraced communism and the influence of Soviet Russia lay behind her refusal to heed our protests. As in the closely related controversy with Nicaragua, however, opposition to any interventionist program began to make itself felt. The State Department was accused of "deliberately and consciously driving toward war with Mexico to protect American business interests." In answer to such criticism Coolidge again fell back on a special mission. He dispatched Dwight W. Morrow, a partner of J. P. Morgan and Company, to seek a peaceful solution to the whole controversy.

Summoning to his aid two strangely assorted ambassadors of goodwill, Charles A. Lindbergh, the trans-Atlantic flier, and Will Rogers, newspaper columnist, Morrow undertook to convince Mexico of American good faith and to try to persuade her to adopt a more conciliatory policy. He succeeded in creating so favorable an atmosphere for negotiating that by the beginning of 1928 the controversy was largely settled. Mexico agreed to recognize all oil rights obtained prior to 1917, and to compensate American owners for the expropriation of properties to which title had been acquired since that date. While difficulties were to persist in negotiating these settlements, and further disturbances in Mexico on occasion created friction between the two countries, the Morrow mission marked a turning-point in their relations and successfully averted the recurrence of any further crises threatening war.

It had even greater significance. Our general attitude toward Latin America became much less domineering, and in order to counteract the suspicions of imperialism aroused by actual intervention in Nicaragua and threatened intervention in Mexico, every effort was made to demonstrate our friendship. Coolidge opened in person the Pan-American Conference held in Havana in 1928; that fall President-Elect Hoover made a good-will tour of South America. A larger conception of our national interests, both political and economic, had finally led to the realization that friendship with the nations south of the Rio Grande was far more important than protecting our investments, through force or the threat of force. Co-operation was accepted as the only practical basis on which American solidarity could be built or our ties of trade and commerce successfully expanded.

In his inaugural President Hoover definitely emphasized this new interest in Latin-American friendship, explicitly stating that the United States did not have the remotest desire for territorial expansion or economic domination over other peoples. Moreover, our original policy of recognizing Latin-American Governments solely on the basis of whether or not they exercised *de facto* control was reaffirmed. When arms embargoes were adopted, they were applied only to rebels against constituted authority. And finally, Secretary of State Stimson in effect repudiated the Roosevelt corollary to the Monroe Doctrine by subscribing, in 1930, to a State Department memorandum (drawn up two years earlier by Undersecretary of State Clark) stating that the United States would not again claim the right to intervene in the affairs of any Latin-American country as a self-constituted international policeman. It is true that our tariff policy, particularly after passage of the Hawley-Smoot Act, was responsible for a lingering resentment toward the United States, yet it is not too much to say that before the Republicans went out of office, the foundations of the Good Neighbor policy had been securely laid.

The Peace Movement

Although developments in the Far East and in Latin America dimly foreshadowed the rôle the United States was to play in world affairs in the nineteen-forties, the paradoxical features of our policy toward Europe held no such clue to the future. While the election of 1920 definitely precluded any reconsideration of our decision not to join the League of Nations, and for a time a meticulously correct State Department ignored its very existence, such self-conscious isolation could not be long maintained in a closely integrated world. At first through delegates sitting with League committees in an unofficial capacity, and after 1924, by the action of official representatives, the United States took part in the various international controls set up in regard to health regulations, white slavery, narcotics, and the traffic in arms and ammunition. By the end of the nineteen-twenties we had been represented, all told, in some forty non-political conferences. The closing days of the Hoover Administration then saw us taking part in the World Disarmament Conference and, even more significantly, in the League discussions on the Manchurian crisis.

Nevertheless, there was no bridging the gap between participation in such international activities as directly interested us and assumption of the responsibilities of full League membership. In the fear that such a move might somehow infringe upon our national sovereignty, we even refused to join the World Court. Every President from Harding through Franklin D. Roosevelt believed that we should take this step; there was little question of overwhelming popular support for it, and on one occasion the Senate went so far as to vote qualified approval. Isolationist sentiment, however, remained sufficiently strong to enable a minority to block our adherence on any basis acceptable to World Court members. Even when the question came up in 1935, with new reservations worked out by Elihu Root and definitely approved by all members, the result was still another defeat for this limited gesture of international co-operation.

While refusing to join the World Court, the United States did, however, take the initiative in securing international adherence to another program for maintaining peace. This was the "outlawry of war." The idea of concluding an agreement in which the signatories forswore the use of force as an instrument of national policy had for some time been urged in this country, and one of the leaders in the movement, James T. Shotwell, specifically suggested the plan to Foreign Minister Briand of France in 1927. The latter at once took it up, publicly stating that his country would be willing to conclude such an agreement with the United States. For a time nothing happened, but public opinion eventually galvanized Secretary Kellogg into activity. On the suggestion of Senator Borah and others, he proposed a broadening of the projected French-American accord to enable other powers to subscribe to it. After lengthy conversations this was done, and on August 27, 1928, fifteen powers signed the Pact of Paris, to be more generally known as the Kellogg-Briand Anti-War Treaty. Other nations subsequently adhered to its renunciation of the use of force until the roster included sixty-five states — including Japan, Italy, and Germany.

Optimists hailed conclusion of this treaty as the most magnificent step in the promotion of world peace ever taken. Skeptics wryly noted that it had no provision whatsoever for enforcement, or even consultation, in the event that any one of the signatories should disregard it. It was, in fact, nothing more than a pious expression of hope, as events were all too soon to prove, reflecting that strange misconception of international politics which dominated American thinking during the nineteen-twenties. The theory was widely held that peace could somehow be secured without settlement of the underlying political issues which disturbed it, and without the assumption of any responsibility to act in concert against nations which disregarded the rights of their neighbors. The Kellogg-Briand Treaty, Sumner Welles, one-time Undersecretary of State, was later to write, "lulled to sleep any still lurking feeling of national obligation. It blinded the American people to the danger to their own security in an increasingly unstable world."

In its attitude toward disarmament, the United States also followed a highly unrealistic policy. It again was unwilling to assume the responsibility of taking part in any general political settlements or of making any definite commitments for upholding peace.

During the World Disarmament Conference which opened in Geneva under League auspices in 1932, President Hoover strongly urged the abolition of all offensive weapons of war, and, when this idea awoke no genuine response, he specifically proposed that all nations agree to reduce their existing armaments by one-third. Europe's answer — or more particularly that of France — was to demand some pledge of American willingness to co-operate in supporting collective security. While the United States was willing to make vague promises of consultation should an international crisis arise, it would go no further. Perhaps disarmament was already a lost cause in view of the mounting tensions in world politics, but the equivocal attitude of the United States certainly did not help matters.

NONRECOGNITION OF SOVIET RUSSIA

Another significant phase of our foreign policy during the nineteen-twenties was our continued refusal to recognize Soviet Russia. Antagonism toward this Government stemmed from the earliest days of the Bolshevik régime. The revolution of November, 1917, heralding the rise to power of Lenin and Trotzky and the creation of the Soviet Union, had immediately alarmed public opinion in this country, which saw in the triumph of communism a menace to capitalism the world over. When the Soviets then withdrew from the war against Germany to sign the Treaty of Brest-Litovsk, their abandonment of the democratic cause further confirmed these fears. President Wilson was prevailed upon to lend American support to a program of intervention in Russia with the twofold objective of aiding the anti-Bolshevik forces to overthrow the Soviet régime and re-creating an eastern front against Germany. United States contingents then remained with the Allied forces in both northern Russia and Siberia after conclusion of the war against Germany, and while our theoretical position was one of non-interference in Russia's internal affairs, we actually lent aid and support to the Russian Whites in their continuing civil war against the Reds.

The Bolsheviki gradually suppressed all counter-revolt and Allied forces were finally withdrawn from Russian territory in 1919. In the meantime, however, Moscow was vigorously promoting a program of world revolution, at least partly in the conviction that communism could in no other way protect itself from its capitalistic foes. The Third Communist International had been organized in March, 1919, and for a time Bolshevism threatened to engulf the states of eastern Europe while its revolutionary propaganda reached out across the Atlantic. "It is the declared purpose of the Bolsheviks in Russia," wrote Assistant Secretary of State Colby in November, "to carry revolution throughout the world. They have availed themselves of every opportunity to initiate in the United States a propaganda aimed to bring about the forcible overthrow of our present form of government. . . ."

The impact of the great Red scare upon popular opinion in this country has already been noted. Throughout the nineteen-twenties communism continued to frighten conservatives and the anti-Bolshevik feeling drummed up during the period of intervention in northern Russia and Siberia was heightened by lurid reports of Red atrocities and of the brutal measures adopted by the Bolsheviki to strengthen their hold on power. Under such circumstances our refusal to enter into diplomatic relations with Russia commanded general support. Even the demonstrated stability of the Soviet Government and the recognition accorded it by other nations caused no change in national policy. Russia's repudiation of all foreign debts, her failure to compensate American citizens whose property had been confiscated, and communist propaganda intensified our dislike and fear of the new Moscow régime. The United States could have no relations, Secretary of State Kellogg declared, with "a governmental entity which is the agent of a group which hold it as their mission to bring about the overthrow of the existing political, economic, and social order throughout the world."

Toward the close of the nineteen-twenties a growing minority began to demand the resumption of friendly Russian-American relations. To withhold recognition from a government whose stability could no longer be questioned was felt to be completely unrealistic, and, even more important, American business interests were becoming increasingly anxious to promote Russian trade. As the shadow of depression began to creep over the world, it was felt that despite political antagonism we could not afford to lose the market which Russia offered for our dwindling exports. Regardless of such pressure, President Hoover refused to modify the non-recognition policy, and it was to be left to President Roosevelt to reverse a stand so consistently maintained for sixteen years.

DEBTS AND REPARATIONS

The problem of war debts, a final consideration in reviewing foreign relations of the post-war decade, must be viewed against the background of the tariff legislation that so strongly emphasized our economic nationalism. The limiting of European imports through protective customs rates, culminating in those of the Hawley-Smoot Tariff of 1930, greatly accentuated the difficulties our European debtors encountered in fulfilling their agreements. Nevertheless, the United States refused to consider the war debts as anything other than an entirely separate and distinct problem by themselves. We would not even allow them to be linked with reparation payments from Germany, on which the European powers depended so directly in meeting their obligations, and consequently we would take no official part in any attempt to conclude a general settlement of the whole question of international financial transactions. The American attitude throughout the long controversy was pithily expressed in Coolidge's dry comment, "They hired the money, didn't they?"

The total of the war debts owed the United States was $10,-350,000,000. The greater proportion of them — more than $7,-000,000,000 — represented sums lent to the Allied Powers during the war for the purchase of supplies in this country. The remainder were loans which had been extended after the Armistice, either in the form of cash or supplies, for reconstruction and economic recovery. Great Britain was the largest debtor, with $4,-277,000,000 outstanding; France owed $3,404,000,000, and Italy, $1,648,000,000. Smaller amounts were owed by seventeen other countries, including the new states established in eastern Europe.

The United States had made its foreign loans upon the express agreement of the borrowers that they would be repaid. The money had been raised through the flotation of bonds — the Liberty loans and Victory loan — which the Government was pledged to redeem. If it could not collect from abroad, taxation of the same millions of individuals who had originally bought the bonds was the only way in which our own large public debt could be retired. This seemed obviously unfair to the American public. Furthermore, the United States had won nothing out of the war comparable to the new territories many of the debtor nations had obtained. It had made no claim for reparations.

Europe's reaction was an embittered conviction that this country was insisting upon the pound of flesh which would mean the economic collapse of the debtor nations. The Allies considered the loans a contribution to a common cause. Since England, France, and Italy had made the greater sacrifice of manpower in encompassing the defeat of Germany, they felt it both logical and just that the United States should shoulder the greater financial burden. And ignoring the part these loans had played in making possible European reconstruction, it was further insisted that the immense sums spent in the United States by the Allies were largely responsible for our newfound economic and financial strength.

In an attempt to work out a general solution, Congress established in February, 1922, a World War Foreign Debt Commission and negotiations were at once undertaken with the debtor nations. A first agreement was made with Great Britain, whose desire to maintain her financial credit made her more willing to come to terms than the other debtors. While the full principal of the debt was to be repaid, the United States in effect allowed a reduction of almost one-third by agreeing to lower the interest rate from 5 to 3.3 per cent, and extending the period of repayment over sixty-two years. Negotiations with France and Italy proved more difficult, for in their case debts almost inevitably became enmeshed with the question of German reparation payments.

The total sum for reparations had in 1921 been placed at the impossible total of $33,000,000,000 and the German Republic was soon compelled to default on the payments expected from her. In retaliation France occupied the Ruhr in what was to prove a wholly unsuccessful attempt to collect by force. The *impasse* was so complete that upon the instigation of the United States, but without its official participation, a new reparation agreement was concluded in 1924, known as the Dawes Plan, which reduced the payments required of Germany to a scale more nearly commensurate with her capacity to pay. As money again began to flow from Germany to the Allies, the United States thereupon increased the pressure for settlement of the debt owed us, and the continental nations finally followed England's lead in coming to terms.

Italy concluded an agreement, in November, 1925, in which she was allowed a reduction in interest representing cancellation of more than eighty per cent of the original loan. Five months later an accord with France upon a comparable basis reduced the principal of her debt by over sixty per cent. Additional negotiations resulted by 1930 in agreements with seventeen nations, Russia remaining the only important country with which no understanding was reached. But for all the generosity of these terms, the United States remained "Uncle Shylock" to the European public.

When Germany's difficulties in maintaining even the revised schedule of her payments threatened to cause another breakdown, a further reparation conference was held in 1929, resulting in adoption of the Young Plan. Total reparations were set at $9,-272,000,000 and a Bank for International Settlements was established to handle all payments. Furthermore, the direct relationship between reparations and debt payments to the United States was recognized by provision for scaling down part of the annuities in the event that this country made further reductions in its financial bill. While the economic fact that the former Allies could pay this country only in so far as they were paid by Germany was thus written into the European agreements, the United States refused to accept its implications. President Hoover insisted that "reparations are necessarily wholly a European problem with which we have no relation." He made no move to meet an intensified demand from abroad that the whole problem be reconsidered. He would have nothing to do with debt cancellation.

The hope that we could continue to make full collections proved illusory. Germany soon experienced new troubles under the Young Plan as serious as those that she had encountered under the Dawes Plan. The Allies found it more than ever difficult to acquire the exchange necessary for payments to the United States. Our tariff policy was contributing to the stagnation of international trade; depression was engulfing the entire world. When financial panic spread from Austria into Germany and Great Britain in 1931, the whole shaky structure of international debt was undermined. The United States found itself faced, not only with nonpayment of the governmental war debts, but with possible repudiation of the huge total of private loans whereby it had sought to uphold foreign trade. And the crisis that now developed found this country almost prostrate from the breakdown of its own internal economy.

Under such circumstances Hoover made a desperate effort to save the situation by proposing, in June, 1931, a year's moratorium on all intergovernmental payments, reparations as well as war debts. After some delay it was accepted and the lowering financial skies momentarily brightened. The Allies then sought to take further steps toward settling the entire problem, and at a conference at Lausanne agreed upon virtual cancellation of reparations if a satisfactory solution of war debts could be reached with the United States. At this point Hoover balked. Once again he insisted — and in doing so reflected general American opinion — that reparations and war debts still had to be considered separately. Theories now gave way, however, before the realities of financial and economic collapse. Neither Germany nor the Allies were in a position to maintain further payments. Reparations went completely by the board and when the next installments on the debt owing to the United States fell due in December, 1932, six of the debtor nations, including France, defaulted outright.

For a time Great Britain and a few other countries continued to make small token payments on their account, but one by one they followed France's example. Finland alone kept up her payments. To all practical purposes the debt issue had finally been decided. The United States would not be paid. There was nothing we could do except lock the doors of an empty stable. In April, 1934, the Johnson Act forbade further loans to any country in default on its governmental debt to the United States.

When the final accounts were added up, it was revealed that Germany had in all paid reparations to the Allies amounting to $4,470,000,000. They in turn had passed on something more than half of this sum — $2,606,000,000 — to the United States. During these same years, however, Germany had borrowed from the United States through private loans a sum almost exactly equivalent to what we had been paid on the Allies' account. Since the Third Reich largely repudiated these private loans even before the outbreak of the second World War, our insistence upon repayment of the war debt had profited us little. It served only to intensify Europe's financial troubles. And at the same time the American people, already disillusioned by the political consequences of the Treaty of Versailles, were more than ever convinced that our intervention in European affairs had gained us little more than bad debts. Memories of this prolonged and unfortunate controversy were to have an important influence in determining the neutrality policy of the nineteen-thirties and the lend-lease program of the nineteen-forties.

Economic Collapse

THE STOCK-MARKET CRASH

NOTWITHSTANDING all the difficulties over farm relief and tariff at home, over debts and reparations abroad, post-war prosperity reached a new peak in the summer of 1929. The American people appeared to be happily oblivious of every portent of future trouble in their confident belief that good times had come to stay. Automobiles were rolling off the assembly line at a dizzy rate. Sales of radios, electric refrigerators, washing machines, vacuum cleaners, and oil burners zoomed. Reporting higher profits every quarter, industrial corporations and public utilities were engaged in a frenzy of mergers and consolidations. The total value of manufactures that year rose to $68,178,000,000 — or well over fifty per cent higher than in 1921. Foreign trade was at its all-time high. Indices of industrial production, employment, and payrolls broke all records.

The rise of stocks was even more spectacular. The Coolidge bull market had been under way since March, 1927, and even at this early date there were cautious observers who felt that security prices were too high. But what had happened between March, 1927, and September, 1929? Every decline in the market provided a springboard for still further advance. On an adjusted basis, General Electric skyrocketed from 128 to 396, American Telephone and Telegraph from 179 to 335, Montgomery Ward from 132 to 466, and Radio from 94 to 505. This phenomenal rise appeared to be unquestionable proof that all was well with business and industry — with the promise of growing even better.

Everybody wanted to get into this rising market. Had not John J. Raskob, writing under the inviting title "Everybody Ought to be Rich," advised the readers of the *Ladies' Home Journal* that the road to wealth was investment in good sound common stocks? As paper profits continued to pyramid, orders for the purchase of additional shares poured into the offices of Wall Street brokers. Bank presidents, lawyers, business executives, salesmen, insurance agents, clerks, stenographers, and office boys were avidly playing the tips so freely passed about, scanning the market news in the evening papers on their way home from work to see how much money they were making. Dirt farmers in Iowa, cattlemen in Wyoming, fruit-growers in California, took an occasional flyer as the stories of fortunes to be made spread across the country. Speculation was a disease which spared almost no one, whether college professor or retired plumber, shopgirl or elderly widow, in the exciting summer of 1929. And still stocks continued to soar.

All warnings were brushed aside in the popular mania to get rich. The counsel the public heeded was, "Don't sell America short." As the exchanges began to experience some premonitory qualms in September, 1929, Charles E. Mitchell, chairman of the National City Bank of New York, blandly stated that he knew of nothing wrong "with the stock market or with the underlying business and credit structure." Professor Irving Fisher, a leading economist, expressed the deliberate opinion that stock prices had entered "what looks like a permanently high plateau." Caution and conservatism had few takers in the feverish atmosphere of those exciting days. The banker and the industrialist were making a new America in which the shadow of poverty was to be forever banished. President Hoover, the engineer in politics, and Andrew Mellon, who was being called the greatest Secretary of the Treasury since Alexander Hamilton, stood foursquare behind them.

But something happened to the market on October 24, 1929. A wave of unexpected and unexplained liquidation hit the New York Stock Exchange. Prices plunged precipitately downward as selling orders placed well below market levels were suddenly touched off. Margins were wiped out in a few hours amid hysterical panic and only a hurriedly organized banking pool finally succeeded in checking the disastrous downward spiral. This was but a respite, however; not rescue. Five days later another avalanche of selling orders cracked the market even wider open. Transactions on the Exchange became so jammed that neither buyers nor sellers knew what was happening. The tickers could not possibly keep up with the pace and when the gong which marked the closing of the market finally sounded, there was still no knowing what the actual losses were. Nor did even this tremendous day in which over sixteen million shares changed hands mark the end of liquidation. With only feeble rallies, the market continued its decline until November 13. By that date the *New York Times* average for leading stocks was cut in half. Some thirty billion dollars in capital values had been swept away. A dazed and frightened public was rudely shaken out of its complacency under the terrific impact of developments over which there was no apparent control.

Reassuring statements were quickly forthcoming from both Wall Street and Washington. A phrase was born that would haunt the minds of men for almost a decade: "conditions are fundamentally sound." It was glibly explained that the break in stock-market prices was only a financial panic resulting from over-speculation. It was highly unfortunate, but it had no bearing upon basic economic factors. The flurry in Wall Street would not be allowed to retard the forward march of industrial progress. Hoover summoned a conference of employers in Washington and they agreed that there would be no reduction in wages or dismissal of workers. "I am convinced that through these measures we have re-established confidence," the President stated in December. Ignoring what were now revealed as unmistakable signs of business decline, the Secretary of the Treasury optimistically forecast "a revival of activity in the spring," and the Secretary of Commerce declared "there is nothing in the situation to be disturbed about." Soon Julius H. Barnes, head of the National Business Survey Conference appointed by the President, swelled the hallelujah chorus. "The spring of 1930," he said, "marks the end of a period of concern. . . . American business is steadily coming back to a normal level of prosperity."

A few years earlier the United States had been visited by a cheerful little Frenchman who had gone about the land preaching the doctrine of self-help by suggestion. Thousands had learned to repeat Emile Coué's hypnotic formula: "Day by day in every way I am getting better and better." The country was trying to drive off the specter of economic depression by Couéism. For a time the formula actually appeared to work. Business succeeded in partially recovering its balance; the stock market made substantial gains. The collapse of the previous autumn was prophetic, however, and the day of reckoning could not be so easily averted. Commodity prices were falling off dangerously, industrial activity was slackening all along the line, and thousands of workers were being laid off by harassed employers despite their earlier promises of maintaining the employment front.

When the President again declared that the worst was over — "with continued effort we shall rapidly recover" — the country at last realized that he was whistling in the dark. The harsh fact of serious economic depression could no longer be disguised. Unemployment and lengthening bread lines drove home a lesson which tumbling stock-market prices could never teach. The real dangers of the situation with which the country was confronted could not yet be foreseen, but hard times had become a grim reality. There were those in high places who still insisted that prosperity was just around the corner, but as recovery failed to materialize with the winter of 1930, the only thing the man in the street discovered around the corner was another of the jobless trying to sell apples in the shivering cold.

Throughout the remainder of the Hoover Administration conditions grew steadily worse. The persistent decline in stocks, which in the summer of 1932 touched a point at which the averages were little more than a tenth of their 1929 peak, merely reflected general financial and economic collapse. Deflation undermined all commodity prices, those for farm products falling to some forty per cent of their 1929 levels. Exports dropped to less than a third their former total; industrial production was almost halved; and the balance sheet of all corporate enterprise revealed a net deficit of $5,650,000,000. The pace of economic activity for the country as a whole had been so slowed down that in three years the total national income fell from $82,885,000,000 to $40,074,000,000. The most ominous of all these developments, however, was the steadily increasing unemployment. There had been some six or seven million men out of work by the close of 1930; two years later this huge total was approximately doubled.

Statistics can only hint at the dire effects of the depression. They cannot depict the scrimping and saving forced upon millions of middle-class families, the privations and hardships caused those in lower-income groups, or the cruel suffering of the unemployed and their families. They cannot portray the disappointment of crushed hopes or the dull helplessness of utter defeat. For millions of Americans the sudden descent into hard times after the glowing promise of the Big Money appeared inexplicable. Confusion, uncertainty, despair, took the place of hope and confidence. The one-time rich watched with bewilderment as their thousands of dollars in paper profits mysteriously melted away. The wage-earner knew no answer to his anguished wife's questioning as to why he had been so unexpectedly laid off. The long queues of ragged men waiting in line at food stations and soup kitchens were a sad commentary upon the mirage of the era that was to abolish poverty. And even more tragic was the plight of the armies of young men and boys wandering back and forth across the country, riding the rods, and living in tramp jungles because society had no work to offer them.

CAUSES OF THE DEPRESSION

The causes for the depression were many and varied, closely interrelated, and served only in their cumulative effect to cause such havoc to the economic order. Several of them have been indicated as already at work during even the most prosperous years of the nineteen-twenties. The dwindling market for agricultural products caused widespread agrarian distress with consequent curtailment of the purchasing power of a large segment of the population. The decline in construction contracts, well under way by 1929, reduced demand for steel, concrete, lumber, and other durable goods. Our foreign trade was largely buoyed up by loans, whose ultimate repayment precariously depended on the sale of European goods in the American market. Speculation in the stock market, fostered by a cheap money policy on the part of the Federal Reserve Board, added a new element of hazard to general financial stability.

The basic fault in our economic system, however, appears to have been overexpansion in capital savings. Harold B. Moulton has written in *The Formation of Capital*:

> The rapid growth of savings as compared with consumption in the decade of the 1920's resulted in a supply of investment money quite out of proportion to the volume of securities being floated for purposes of expanding plant and equipment, while at the same time the flow of funds through consumptive channels was inadequate to absorb — at the prices at which goods were offered for sale — the potential output of our existing productive capacity. The excess savings which entered the investment market served to inflate the price of securities and to produce financial instability. A larger relative flow of funds through consumptive channels would have led not only to a larger utilization of existing productive capacity, but also to a more rapid growth of plant equipment.

The distribution of the national income held the key to the situation to a very considerable extent. If less had been paid out in the form of rents, profits, and interest, and a greater share in salaries and wages, the purchasing power of the country would have been more nearly equal to its productive capacity. A closer balance would have been maintained between goods which could be produced and goods which could be sold. The tremendous increase in the national income as a whole, and the extent to which all classes of society were apparently sharing in prosperity, tended to obscure this in the nineteen-twenties. The fact that purchasing power was increasing and the public steadily absorbing an ever greater volume of consumer goods overshadowed the even more significant fact that there was this still greater increase in savings. Only through subsequent studies has the maldistribution of the national income in the nineteen-twenties come to be fully understood.

This situation was primarily a consequence of the persistent and perhaps unavoidable concentration of economic power which had characterized the history of the previous fifty years. According to the Bureau of Internal Revenue, some 618 corporations, or one-fifth of one per cent of the total number reporting, owned over half the corporate assets of the entire country in 1932. Of this small group, 232 earned more than half of total corporation income. The ownership of stock was even more highly concentrated. Three-tenths of one per cent of the population received 78 per cent of all corporation dividends paid to individuals. And largely as a consequence of such conditions, less than a quarter of one per cent of all American families, as reported by the Brookings Institution, received 14.8 per cent of the total national income.

Some thirty-six thousand families in the upper-income brackets, to put it another way, received as much of the national income as eleven million families in the lowest group. Among these low-income families, moreover, there were no less than six million which received less than one thousand dollars a year. Disregarding the personal consequences of such disparity in income, with almost a fifth of all families living in comparative poverty, the effect upon the economic system was to reduce mass purchasing power far below the level at which the industrial machine could continue to operate successfully.

Once the depression was under way, whatever the immediate economic or psychological cause serving to start it off, each breakdown all along the line served to deepen the general distress. Farm purchasing power declined still further as prices broke upon the withdrawal of the Federal Farm Board from its stabilization activities. Unemployment depleted even more severely the consumer market on which all manufacture eventually depended. The rigidities in the industrial price system (the price of agricultural implements, for example, declining only six per cent while that of farm commodities plunged sixty-three) intensified the existing disequilibrium in the economic structure as a whole. With creditors pressing for payment on outstanding loans, the country's immense debt load became an incubus to be removed only through mortgage foreclosures and bankruptcies. Our inability to support foreign trade through further foreign investments sent it spiraling downward, and both agriculture and industry were deprived of their export markets. All the inner stresses and strains under which our economic system had been laboring became so much more acute that the severity of the depression far exceeded anything the country had ever known.

Apart from these immediate factors in the situation, there were others of greater long-run significance. The closing of the frontier and falling-off in immigration meant that the United States no longer enjoyed the rapidly expanding economy of the nineteenth century. New sources of untapped wealth were not being opened up as they once had been. The rate of population growth had appreciably declined. Further opportunities for such economic development as the nation had formerly experienced were largely dependent on new industries, and as the original impetus afforded by the spectacular growth in the manufacture of such products as automobiles, electrical equipment, and household appliances spent itself, there was perhaps an inevitable slowing-down of economic advance. Depression overtook the country before it had been able to make the difficult and far-reaching adjustments which were necessary to stabilize our economy by rendering the products of our industrial plants more generally available to the people as a whole.

Hoover's Policies

After its failure to maintain either employment or prevailing wages by voluntary agreement, the Hoover Administration began to realize that the country was faced with a highly critical situation. The President abandoned the policy of drift that had at first characterized his attitude, and stopped offering reassuring statements to the public. He sought to exert the power and the influence of the Federal Government to meet what had clearly become a great national emergency. Hampered by serious limitations, the program was to fail to meet national needs. Yet it must be realized that Hoover was blazing a new trail in the course of action that he did adopt. Traditional American doctrine held that the possible economic distress of the country was no concern of the Federal Government. Earlier presidents had not considered intervention of any sort during periods of depression. They had left business and industry, agriculture and labor, to work out their own salvation without aid or comfort from Washington. Hoover realized that times had changed. He accepted a responsibility that Government had heretofore avoided. His vision as to how far such new policies should be carried was to prove highly restricted, but he had the political courage to pioneer.

Although many of the measures adopted were delayed past the time when they might have had their greatest usefulness, and then did not go nearly far enough, the Hoover program embraced aid for the farmers, for industry, for finance, for foreign trade, and for labor. The unsuccessful efforts of the Federal Farm Board in attempting to maintain the prices of wheat and cotton have been discussed, and also the President's belated establishment of a moratorium on all intergovernmental debts. The Hoover Administration also sought to stimulate industrial activity and promote employment by expanding the public works program; made credit more easily available to business by liberalizing the discount requirements of the Federal Reserve System; and, finally, afforded even more direct assistance to finance and industry through the Reconstruction Finance Corporation.

In many ways this was a broadly conceived program. The Federal Government for the first time, as Hoover stated, took "an extensive and positive part in mitigating the effects of depression and expediting recovery." The animating idea behind the more important of these measures, however, was that the national welfare could best be promoted by pouring funds into the top of the economic funnel in order to help banks, financial institutions, and the more important business enterprises. There was to be no corresponding action to strengthen the bases of the economic structure by really effective help for small business, agriculture, or labor. It may well be that this program prevented the further spread of bankruptcy among financial institutions, insurance companies, railroads, and public utilities, but it fell far short of solving the problems of millions of persons suffering so severely from the depression that direct government aid was the only way through which they could ever hope to get back on their feet.

As early as January, 1930, Hoover first suggested that the industrial pump should be primed and employment stimulated, through an extensive public works program, and some two years later he specifically recommended, in his message to Congress in December, 1931, that all such activities should be "consolidated into an independent establishment under the President to be known as the Public Works Administration." The construction of public roads, river and harbor improvements, and other large-scale projects was undertaken at an increasing rate. One important undertaking, for example, was the construction of a great dam across the lower reaches of the Colorado River — later to be named the Boulder Dam — to store up water in a combined flood-control, irrigation, and power project. Before Hoover went out of office, expenditures on public works had risen to some six hundred million dollars annually and employment was provided for seven hundred and fifty thousand men.

The President did not intend, however, to let such a program go very far. When an increasingly restive Congress, in which the Democrats controlled the House after the mid-term elections of 1930, took up consideration of a proposed public works appropriation of two billion dollars with unemployment relief as its principal objective, he emphatically intervened. "This is not unemployment relief," Hoover declared caustically. "It is the most gigantic pork-barrel ever proposed to the American Congress."

If expanded public works were a striking instance of the Federal Government's new concern over economic depression, the Reconstruction Finance Corporation broke away from tradition much more radically. It was set up in January, 1932, with authorization to extend government loans to banks, agricultural credit associations, life insurance companies, railroads, and state governments. Despite charges that in some instances it was bolstering up weak and overcapitalized institutions, which might better have been allowed to go into bankruptcy than kept alive

by artificial respiration, advances totaling some two billion dollars
were made before March, 1933. And here again the Hoover
Administration provided the New Deal with a program which it
took over without hesitation. The Reconstruction Finance Corporation was not only continued after Roosevelt came into office;
its activities were greatly expanded.

Despite such governmental activity, the back of the depression
was not broken. As 1931 gave way to 1932, the pall of economic
distress spread ever more widely over the country. Unemployment became not only a basic economic problem but a burning
political issue. The failure of Hoover to tackle it more directly,
either through a much vaster public works program or some form
of direct relief, led to bitter attacks upon his Administration in
and out of Congress. There was a rising demand for immediate
aid for the growing millions of persons out of work.

Hoover, nevertheless, maintained his unequivocal opposition
to any further direct intervention by the Federal Government.
Although he had said in 1930 that "as a nation we must prevent
hunger and cold to those of our people who are in honest difficulties," he strongly felt that this obligation rested solely upon
individuals, communities, or at best the states. An Emergency
Relief Corporation was established to co-operate with local communities and private agencies, the surplus food stocks held by
the Federal Farm Board were made available for the needy in so
far as possible, and eventually the Reconstruction Finance Corporation made loans totaling some three hundred million dollars
for the relief activities of state and municipal governments. But
with a consistency born of absolute conviction, the President
would not go beyond these limits and he blocked every further
move by Congress to provide direct relief. He feared it would
lead to an unwarranted centralization of authority, set up bureaucratic controls that could not be removed when the emergency
had passed, and undermine the bases of American individualism.
He emphatically stated in February, 1931:

> The moment the responsibilities of any community, particu-
> larly in economic and social questions, are shifted from any part
> of the nation to Washington, then that community has subjected

> itself to a remote bureaucracy. . . . It has lost a voice in the control of its own destiny. . . . Where people divest themselves of local government responsibilities they at once lay the foundations for destruction of their liberties. . . . At once when the Government is centralized there arises a limitation upon the liberty of the individual and a restriction of individual opportunity . . . [which] can lead but to the superstate where every man becomes the servant of the State and real liberty is lost.

His position was strongly approved in conservative circles and in later years these same people were to feel that everything against which he warned had come to pass. It was condemned by liberals who saw him stubbornly upholding doctrinaire principles based upon a nineteenth-century conception of *laissez-faire*. And in the meantime millions of people were hungry and in want, if not actually starving. A distraught public, not concerned with political theory, interpreted his adamant stand against direct relief as callous disregard of human suffering.

There were occasions when this interpretation of his actions — or rather lack of action — appeared to be substantiated. During a drought in Arkansas in 1930, the President was willing to appropriate money to provide seed and feed for the farmers, but no funds for their own direct relief. Hoover would not save the starving farmers, it was said, but he was willing to save their starving mules. When congressional Democrats sought to provide more substantial help, he accused them of playing politics at the expense of human misery. Barring every move beyond a small loan, he declared that direct relief for the farmers "would have injured the spiritual responses of the American people."

Again when veterans of the first World War attempted in the summer of 1932 to obtain governmental aid through the immediate payment of a bonus as final liquidation of their adjusted service certificates, his attitude showed a harsh severity which lost him much popular support. He had strongly opposed the bill to increase the borrowing power of these certificates, which, as we have seen, was passed over his veto the previous year; but what most disturbed the country in 1932 was his dispersal of the so-called Bonus Expeditionary Force which marched on Washington, some ten thousand strong, to back up the American Legion's new demands. When the veterans refused to disband, many of them because they had nowhere to go, Hoover gave orders to have them driven out by force. The job fell to a subsequent hero of the second World War, General Douglas A. MacArthur. Four troops of cavalry and four of infantry, a machine-gun squadron and six tanks took part in the action. The veterans' encampment was burned to the ground and the Bonus Expeditionary Army successfully dispersed. Law and order had been maintained in the national capital, but the country was shocked by the forcible methods employed.

It was the failure of Hoover to convince an increasingly restive people of the idea that he had any real understanding of their needs, quite as much as the inadequacy of the measures he adopted, that led to increasing lack of confidence in his Administration. What profit public works and governmental loans to business, when vast numbers of people were in actual want and the Federal Government refused them relief? Hoover had cut a new trail in attempting to meet the urgent problems of business recovery, but his conservatism prevented him from broadening his program so as to make it truly effective.

18

American Life: The Nineteen-Twenties

Era of Wonderful Nonsense

THE nineteen-twenties may stand out in formal history as a period of conservative politics and heightened nationalism, as the years of tariff protection, a new immigration policy, and the industrial boom. They were also "the era of wonderful nonsense," with a nation-wide absorption in "tremendous trifles" which were played up by the newspapers in a spirit of ballyhoo possible only in the United States. The jazz age and the revolt of the younger generation, speculation in stocks and Florida real estate, speakeasies and bathtub gin, high-pressure salesmanship and installment buying, spectator sports, Rotary and Kiwanis ("Don't Knock, Boost"), flappers and lounge lizards, radio and the movies, success stories and true confession magazines . . . the nineteen-twenties were unique.

In 1925 the little town of Dayton, Tennessee, was inundated by the special writers dispatched by newspapers, magazines, and tabloids to report what they gleefully called the Scopes monkey trial, a legal case in which William Jennings Bryan battled valiantly to uphold a Tennessee law forbidding the teaching of evolution. A year later, an even greater army of reporters descended upon Somerville, New Jersey, to cover the notorious Hall-Mills murder case, and in eleven days sent out over the wires five million words of lurid copy. And then in 1927, every known record in all the history of newspaper ballyhoo was smashed when Lindbergh flew the Atlantic. After the flier's public welcome in New York, the quantity of ticker tape, torn-up telephone books, and waste paper swept up weighed over one hundred times that collected after the Armistice celebration in 1918 — an estimated eighteen hundred tons.

A legal battle over fundamentalism, a murder trial, and a trans-Atlantic flight bore little relation to one another. Yet each was built up by a sensational press to provide a Roman holiday for the great American people. This was the spirit of the times. And there were innumerable other colorful events in the post-war decade to be set against the more sober background of national growth and development. Atlantic City's famed bathing-beauty contests introduced the vogue of one-piece swim suits. There were nation-wide dance marathons, and C. C. Pyle staged a cross-continent Bunion Derby. Queen Marie of Rumania made a triumphal tour of the country, Admiral Byrd flew to the South Pole, and Gertrude Ederle was tumultuously acclaimed in New York as the first woman to swim the British Channel. Shipwreck Kelly perched for twenty-three days on a flagpole.

Amid all such sensations and aberrations, the craze for sports perhaps most consistently held the spotlight of newspaper publicity. People as ever — more than ever — were playing games as well as watching them. College football, world championship prize-fights, semi-professional tennis and golf tournaments, however, overshadowed everything else. A contemporary could write with little exaggeration that spectator sports seemed "to be almost the national religion."

Millions of persons packed the stadia that had mushroomed throughout the country to take care of the football crowds during the short autumn season, and millions more hugged their radios every Saturday afternoon to follow play-by-play accounts of the games. The "praying colonels" of Centre College blazed through the sky like a meteor, and as quickly faded out; Princeton's "team of destiny" briefly brightened the dimmed prestige of the one-time Big Three; the Four Horsemen of Notre Dame marched on down scores of fields to win new laurels for Knute Rockne, and Red Grange, the Galloping Ghost of Illinois, flashed past all other heroes in football's hall of fame.

Equally sensational were the triumphs of prize-fighting staged under the brilliant showmanship of Tex Rickard. In 1921 the Battle of the Century at Boyle's Thirty Acres in Jersey City, when Jack Dempsey knocked out the French fighter, Georges Carpentier, marked the beginning of million-dollar gates. Six years later, the climax was reached when Gene Tunney outboxed Dempsey before 145,000 hysterical customers at Chicago's Soldiers Field. Twenty-four special trains had rolled into town for this epochal event; two hundred millionaires had seats in the first ten rows, and five radio listeners were reported to have dropped dead of heart failure during the bout.

While big-league baseball suffered somewhat, as football and prize-fighting rose to rival its traditional popularity, Babe Ruth, the redoubtable Sultan of Swat, nevertheless became the idol of every small boy throughout the land as he knocked out a record sixty home runs. "Big Bill" Tilden dominated tennis, with

Helen Wills a close rival in her own class, and Bobby Jones was the super-champion of golf. Horse-racing too had its hero in Man o' War, whose sensational victories helped to swell race-track attendance to record totals.

MOVIES, RADIO, TOURING

The flamboyant spirit of the nineteen-twenties also found expression in current moving pictures. "Brilliant men, beautiful jazz babies, champagne baths, midnight revels, petting parties in the purple dawn," one producer enthusiastically advertised. For all the protests of Will H. Hays, motion-picture czar, that the industry still held Service as its Supreme Purpose, there was a plague of trashy films under such titles as *Flaming Youth, Sinners in Silk,* and *Women Who Give.* When Rudolph Valentino, the passionate sheik of millions of lovelorn maidens' dreams, died in 1926, crowds of hysterical women, stopping traffic for blocks, milled about the funeral parlor where his body lay in state.

Yet there were also many admirable pictures, showing a tremendous advance over those of pre-war days. *Ben Hur, The Covered Wagon, The Thief of Bagdad, The Gold Rush, The Three Musketeers,* are but a few samples of what the producers, now settled in Hollywood, were able to turn out — and did turn out at production costs that skyrocketed from the one hundred thousand dollars paid for *The Birth of a Nation* to three and four million dollars. A new galaxy of stars became the most expensive entertainers any country had ever known. Mary Pickford (she signed her first million-dollar contract in 1917) was still America's Sweetheart, but more exciting were Gloria Swanson, Constance Talmadge, and Clara Bow. Among the men, Charlie Chaplin had made his own unique place, and then there were, among others, Douglas Fairbanks, John Gilbert, Wallace Reid.

If the movies were making substantial progress in the early nineteen-twenties, an event took place in 1928 that was to give them a greater impetus than anything that had happened since the days of the nickelodeon. Warner Brothers released a new film — Al Jolson in *The Jazz Singer.* Here were the talkies, and within a year their conquest of the silent film was virtually complete. Weekly attendance at the movies was reported to have soared to an estimated 100,000,000.

Another and even more novel form of entertainment forging ahead in the nineteen-twenties was the radio. Something has already been said upon its importance in advertising and salesmanship, but perhaps even more significant was the impact of nation-wide broadcasting on other phases of American life. Its influence in creating a popular demand for the products of its advertisers was supplemented by its rôle in disseminating news, opening up new vistas for those otherwise cut off from the outside world, and especially in providing recreation within the home. Radio's growth was indeed phenomenal. The first broadcasting station, KDKA in East Pittsburgh, went on the air on November 2, 1920, to give a handful of excited listeners the results of the Harding-Cox election. Twelve years later, seventeen million owners of home radio sets were able to tune in to hear the news of the first election of Franklin D. Roosevelt.

Headphones ("ear muffs" as they were called) marked radio's advent, but they were soon followed by loud-speakers. As the listening audience grew, broadcasting studios fumblingly experimented with every possible type of program. As early as 1923, WJZ pioneered with an all-day performance from early morning setting-up exercises to midnight dance concerts. As other stations followed its lead, however, the *New Republic* sternly commented that, apart from jazz, these continuous programs were ninety per cent sheer rubbish. When a few years later, chain broadcasting awoke national advertisers to radio's sales possibilities, sponsored programs over national networks made possible at least relative improvement.

Popular orchestras filled the air with the dulcet strains of "Mister Gallager and Mister Shean," "Barney Google" or "Valencia." "Ol' Man River" was kept endlessly rollin' along. Rudy Vallee stirred millions of feminine hearts crooning "I'm Just a Vagabond Lover," and torch singers soothed masculine breasts with "Moanin' Low" and "Am I Blue?" The night air was strangely troubled as Roxy and his Gang, the Happiness Boys, or the Clicquot Club

Eskimos marshaled their saxophones, trombones, and ukeleles to create "the greatest single sweep of synchronized and syncopated rhythm that human ingenuity has ever conceived."

The frontier was closed in 1890 — but the American people kept restlessly on the move. They toured over the entire country as the automobile gave them a new vacation mobility; they visited the great national parks in the West by the hundred thousand, camping and fishing; and they went to Europe in increasing droves to rediscover the Old World (almost half a million in 1928 alone). "It's the Thing to Do — To Go to Europe," the steamship companies advertised; "See America First," urged the proponents of tourist travel at home. Thousands of miles of hard-surfaced roads became lined with filling stations, tourist camps, and roadside stands catering to the great traveling public. "Tell the family to hurry the packing and get aboard," full-page spreads in the popular magazines invitingly proposed, "and be off with smiles down the nearest road — free, loose and happy — bound for green wonderlands."

SCIENCE — PURE AND APPLIED

Automobiles and airplanes, moving pictures and the radio, together with the electric refrigerators, washing machines, and vacuum cleaners to be found in the home, demonstrated emphatically the ever-mounting importance of the machine in the nineteen-twenties. And again science was making other contributions to American life no less significant if not always so apparent. It was constantly pushing back the horizons of human knowledge, setting up new ways to harness power and raise the standard of living.

More than ever before research had become a co-operative undertaking and was supported not only by universities and research foundations, but by industry itself. Physicists, chemists, astronomers, biologists, and bacteriologists vied in making new discoveries and developing new techniques. Determining the weight of the electron, measuring cosmic rays, testing the theory of relativity, discovering new galaxies of stars and new chemical elements, researches in the never-ending fight against disease, were but a few of the pursuits of contemporary scientists. The work of chemists, biologists, and bacteriologists, in concert with preventive medicine, modern sanitation, and better hospitalization, improved public health and lengthened the average span of life. The incidence as well as the death rate in typhoid, tuberculosis, diphtheria, and scarlet fever was still further reduced; yellow fever and small pox were virtually wiped out, and deaths from pneumonia greatly declined. More healthful dietary habits, and the knowledge of vitamins, strengthened resistance to other diseases. During the first third of the century, average life expectancy increased from forty-nine to fifty-nine years — and over the horizon were adrenalin, sulfanilamide, and finally, penicillin.

Advances in all branches of engineering were another sign of the times. The George Washington Bridge over the Hudson River, and the Holland Tunnel under it, were two impressive achievements. The rapidly growing cities also introduced new developments in highway approaches, improvements in public utility services, and general urban planning.

The most conspicuous contribution of American architecture has been the skyscraper. The Woolworth Building, sixty stories in height, was erected in 1913, but during the nineteen-twenties the Manhattan skyline became a more amazing, breath-taking spectacle than ever. The Chrysler Building and Al Smith's Empire State Building (with a mooring mast for dirigibles) were to soar to spectacular new heights as the depression settled over the country. Other cities followed this lead to a limited extent and there were many architectural developments of lasting significance in post-war years. Adopting the dictum that "form follows function," experiments were made in constructing public buildings, offices, and factories that introduced startling and sometimes impressive changes from the imported styles of the nineteenth century. Frank Lloyd Wright had long been the outstanding pioneer in architectural experimentation, his "prairie houses" marking a distinctive approach in adaptation to environment.

New Trends in Education

At the same time, there was also further progress along the general educational front. The increase in students in elementary schools, high schools, colleges, and universities, already noted for pre-war years, still continued, with especially spectacular gains in college enrollment. It had reached a total of three hundred thousand in 1914, yet by the end of the nineteen-twenties this figure was approximately a million. Summer schools, extension courses, and correspondence courses flourished; junior colleges and state teachers' colleges multiplied; and at the top of the educational ladder, graduate schools attracted more and more students.

The traditional calm of academic halls was disturbed by discussion and debate over the purposes and methods of education in a democracy. In large part through the influence of John Dewey, educator and philosopher, there was widespread experiment in progressive schools, and for all the criticism evoked in conservative circles, the new principle of "education for life" made many converts among educators. In the realm of higher learning, there were attacks upon the traditional curricula, while proponents of a return to the classics repudiated the elective system. Underlying all such controversy — the science of education, the one hundred best books, progressive schools, humanism, freedom of the individual, and pedagogical discipline — there nevertheless appeared to be a trend away from the liberal arts with increasing emphasis upon scientific, professional, and even vocational training.

In so far as such advances in education might have been expected to affect the reading habits of the people as a whole, there was little evidence of any real change in popular standards. Rather than rushing to read the new school of realism in modern fiction, to which reference has already been made, the great American public was still primarily interested in newspapers and tabloids, in the *Saturday Evening Post, Collier's, Liberty,* and the *American Magazine,* and in the new rash of detective-story magazines, motion-picture magazines, and confession magazines. Culture of a sort was zealously pursued outside academic halls, however, through five-foot shelves of books, popular encyclopedias, outlines, and books of knowledge. "They laughed when the waiter spoke to me in French," read the advertisements of language study in a few easy lessons; "they laughed when I sat down at the piano," countered the appeals for correspondence courses in music. The Book of Etiquette was a best-seller, and Simon and Schuster sold almost two million crossword-puzzle books.

The Contemporary Scene

The flavor of life in the nineteen-twenties, as in previous periods, is revealed in other advertisements than those showing how to become educated through easy and painless doses of manufactured culture. Gigantic billboards disclosed that countless smokers were walking a mile for a Camel, lighting Murads to remain nonchalant, finding satisfaction in Chesterfields, and "slenderizing in a sensible way" by reaching for a Lucky instead of a Sweet. It was widely proclaimed that yeast was restoring the nation's health and Simmons beds enabling it to catch up on its sleep. Major P. F. O'Keefe won a gold medal for coining the phrase, "Say It With Flowers." Copy-writers also found new ways to create self-consciousness among a gullible public through the discovery of pyorrhea, halitosis, and B.O. — "Often a Bridesmaid but Never a Bride."

Mahjong was introduced from China in the post-war decade; Elinor Glyn discovered "It"; Abie's Irish Rose ran for five years and five months on Broadway; and automatic traffic lights were installed throughout the country. Behaviorism had its brief day, and one of the most popular songs of the decade was, "Yes, We Have No Bananas." Soft hats were driving out the derby and soft shirts the stiff, detachable collar. There was a suntan vogue, golfers affected baggy plus-fours, eskimo pies flourished, and Judge Ben Lindsey advocated companionate marriage.

During the nineteen-twenties women wore progressively less and less, and the little they did wear was designed to accentuate the slender, boyish figure. The skirt rose alarmingly (in conservative eyes) from the ankle to the knee, or, as the statistician carefully figured it all out, from a level above the ground the equivalent of ten per cent of a woman's height to an equivalent of more than twenty-five per cent. Consequently, silk stockings became all-important.

Bobbed hair had come in with the war, and women invaded the hallowed sanctity of the barber shop until the beautician came into his own and the permanent wave rolled over the land. Make-up lost its earlier intimations of immorality as the use of rouge and lipstick brightened the faces of all womankind. Fingernails were still untinted.

The question continually on the lips of the older people was, "Is the younger generation in peril?" The flapper, however, nonchalantly went her own way, petting in the parked sedan, sharing her escort's hip flask, checking her corset in the ladies' room at the college prom, and dancing cheek-to-cheek to "The Japanese Sandman," "Tea for Two," or "It Ain't Gonna Rain No More." Churchmen and college presidents sadly deplored this state of affairs. "The low-cut gowns, the rolled hose, and short skirts are born of the devil," the President of Florida University cried out; "the music is sensuous, the embracing of partners, the female only half-dressed, is absolutely indecent," lamented the *Catholic Telegraph*. But there was no stopping the younger generation:

> We all went to the party, a real high-toned affair,
> And then along came Lulu, as wild as any Zulu.
> She started in to "Charleston,"
> And how the boys did stare! . . .

It was in many ways a crazy decade, those feverish, frenetic nineteen-twenties, with a booming prosperity the backdrop both for its obsession with tremendous trifles and its solid progress in scientific and material developments. There were those who declared that automobile touring, the movies, the radio, spectator sports, the swollen mass circulation of newspapers and magazines, and national advertising were imposing upon the American people a dull uniformity. They were doing the same things, seeing the same things, reading the same things, buying the same things. Yet such an interpretation of the significance of these by-products of a mechanized age overlooked the far greater uniformity of life in the days when the great bulk of the people were held closely to farms and villages with almost no outlook upon the urban world. Regimentation was more apparent than real. The automobile took the bank clerk on a solitary fishing trip as well as to a crowded football game; the radio brought symphony orchestras into the home as well as endorsements for hair tonics, and news reels followed the Hollywood dramas in the moving-picture theaters. Even though the nineteen-twenties were indeed a materialistic age, and their gaudy prosperity was destined for bankruptcy, the infinite variety of contemporary life left room for social gain as well as failure.

The New Deal

19

New Doctrines for Old

THE ELECTION OF 1932

As POLITICAL LINES were drawn for another presidential campaign in the disturbed summer of 1932, the virtual certainty that the electorate would demand a change in the Administration made the position of the Republicans almost hopeless. They had no alternative other than to renominate Hoover. To have cast him aside would have been to condemn the entire party record, not only during the two and a half years of depression, but throughout the preceding decade. Their only hope was that conditions would somehow improve sufficiently by election time to persuade the public that Hoover's tactics were proving successful and that another Republican Administration would bring back the piping days of prosperity.

For a time there were faint signs of an upward turn. The President consequently took the position that domestic recovery was now being held back only by foreign complications which blocked the essential re-establishment of lost export markets. A World Economic Conference had been called for the next year. Hoover agreed to American participation and held out the promise of international agreements which would once again open up the channels of world trade. Any departure from the tried principles of Republican rule at this stage, he gravely warned, would risk the collapse of these hopes. To turn the country over to the Democrats would bring inevitable disaster — "the grass will grow in the streets of a hundred cities, a thousand towns."

In happy anticipation of the victory that had for so long eluded them, the Democrats prepared to take the offensive. Their platform not only held the Republicans responsible for the de-

357

pression and condemned them for their failure to cope with it; it also promised direct and immediate action in dealing with every phase of the national emergency. It stated:

> In this time of unprecedented economic and social distress, the Democratic Party declares its conviction that the chief causes of this condition were the disastrous policies pursued by our Government since the World War, of economic isolation, fostering the merger of competitive businesses into monopolies and encouraging the indefensible expansion and contraction of credit for private profit at the expense of the public. . . . The only hope for improving present conditions, restoring employment, affording permanent relief to the people, and bringing the nation back to the proud position of domestic happiness and of financial, industrial, agricultural, and commercial leadership in the world lies in a drastic change in economic governmental policies.

The major proposals of the Democrats nevertheless appeared to be basically conservative. A reduction in governmental expenses and strict balancing of the budget, together with maintenance of a sound currency at all hazards, were explicitly promised. The Government was to be taken out of all fields of private enterprise except where necessary to develop public works and natural resources in the public interest. Other planks then went on to express support for a competitive tariff and reciprocal trade agreements, the extension of federal credit to the states for unemployment relief, the planning of public works, unemployment and old-age insurance under state laws, the restoration of agriculture and effective control of crop surpluses, strengthening of the anti-trust laws, regulation of public utility holding companies and security exchanges, repeal of the Prohibition Amendment.

The selection of a presidential candidate was far more important. Yet it did not take very long. The pre-convention campaign of Franklin D. Roosevelt, then governor of New York, placed him well ahead of all other aspirants for the nomination. After conclusion of a political deal inducing his principal rival, John N. Garner, Speaker of the House of Representatives, to accept the vice-presidential nomination, Roosevelt was enthusiastically named on the fourth ballot. Spectacularly flouting tradition, he at once flew to Chicago to accept the nomination in person and in a short, dramatic speech confidently sounded the keynote of his campaign: "I pledge you, I pledge myself, to a New Deal for the American people."

Roosevelt's family background was one of inherited wealth, and he had been educated at Groton and Harvard. There was little here to foreshadow the career which lay before him, but his family had a tradition of public service which did not make it so unusual for him to escape the conservative influences of school and college and plunge into New York's state politics as a liberal and independent Democrat. Elected to the state senate in 1910 from Dutchess County, he soon distinguished himself as a vigorous opponent of Boss Murphy of New York, and three years later he was rewarded for his support of Wilson's presidential candidacy in 1912 by appointment as Assistant Secretary of the Navy. His practical experience in this post, and general participation in a wartime government, greatly broadened the range of his interests and demonstrated both administrative and political abilities of a high order. He was nominated by the Democrats as their vice-presidential candidate in 1920, taking his stand in forthright support of the liberal, international outlook bequeathed to his party by President Wilson.

So far his record closely paralleled that of his distant cousin, Theodore Roosevelt, but his campaign in 1920 was unsuccessful and soon afterward his political future appeared to have been brought to a final close by an attack of infantile paralysis. It was only through courage and tenacity that he conquered the illness, refusing to allow it to thwart his plans and ambitions. It was a brave victory of the human spirit. Its effect upon the character of the man, and consequently upon the history of his country and the history of the world, could hardly be foreseen.

During the years he was waging this dramatic personal battle, moreover, Franklin D. Roosevelt had taken the opportunity to build up his political contacts through wide correspondence among party leaders. It was he who put the name of Alfred E. Smith before the Democratic convention in 1924, dragging himself to the rostrum on crutches. And four years later, Smith had persuaded him to run for governor of New York in order to strengthen the Democratic ticket in that state.

To the surprise of even his admirers, Roosevelt had run ahead of his party in that disastrous Democratic year and had been elected to office. His record as governor, which won him re-election in 1930, increased his political stature. He had proved himself to be an able administrator, a man of strong progressive, liberal principles, and highly popular with the people of his state. Still, his reputation did not extend very far beyond the borders of New York and his earlier career in national politics was largely forgotten. Even among those who knew his record, nothing in it seemed to give unusual evidence of capacity to deal with so great an emergency as that which the country faced in 1932. "An amiable man," wrote Walter Lippmann, "with many philanthropic impulses . . . who, without any important qualifications for the office, would very much like to be President."

As the campaign opened, however, Roosevelt gave immediate proof that there were stronger strains in his character than amiability. The cards were stacked in his favor. The country was prepared to vote the Republicans out of office almost regardless of what the Democrats might do. He was reasonably sure of election so long as he did not make too many mistakes. Instead of sitting on the sidelines and waiting for the anti-Hoover votes to carry him into office, however, he undertook an aggressive nation-wide campaign, traveling some twenty-five thousand miles.

The impression he made upon the country was highly favorable. His positive personality, confidence, and forceful public speaking were something fresh and new in the political life of the times. There was a magnetism about Roosevelt that only Al Smith had possessed among the presidential candidates of the nineteen-twenties, and he did not arouse the prejudices and antipathies that the Happy Warrior had inspired. He could also project the warm, human aspects of his personality over the air, and since the radio had become a most important way of reaching the public, to be able to do this proved to be an incalculably valuable political asset. He was to demonstrate this even more convincingly after his election, when he instituted his familiar, intimate "fireside chats" with the American people; but during the campaign of 1932 his persuasive radio voice unquestionably won him votes.

His speeches were also forceful and dynamic. The Hoover Administration, he charged with great vigor, had encouraged speculation through its false economic policies, attempted to minimize the stock-market crash and mislead the people, erroneously attributed the cause of the depression to conditions in other nations, and refused to recognize and correct the evils at home which had brought hard times forth. But Roosevelt was not content with destructive attack. As the campaign progressed, he developed and effectively elaborated a positive theory of government, going much further than the Democratic platform, which gave form and substance to his promise of a New Deal.

In working this out he had the able assistance of a group of advisers to which the newspapers soon gave the name of the "brain trust." Included in it were Raymond Moley, Rexford G. Tugwell, Hugh S. Johnson, and Adolf A. Berle. Roosevelt owed a great deal to these men for information, for ideas, and for the expression of those ideas. Yet they were not the New Deal. While they gave valuable aid in formulating a practical program for the prospective Democratic Administration when it should come into office — as they were all confident it would — there was no time when Roosevelt did not very well know what he was doing. He was prepared to take up the thread of progressive reform where it had been broken off by war and post-war reaction, evolving from past experience those measures which would not only meet the immediate problems of economic recovery, but would lay the basis for renewed progress toward effective social democracy.

There is more than an echo of Theodore Roosevelt in such a speech as that which Franklin Roosevelt made before the Commonwealth Club in San Francisco during his western campaign tour. America owed much to the financial and business leaders who had built up our industrial system, the presidential candidate of 1932 declared. Realization of the dream of an economic machine capable of raising our standard of living had been made possible only through the force of their tremendous will and tremendous ambition. Nevertheless, there was a shadow over that dream in the creation of great uncontrolled and irresponsible units of power within the state.

> Clearly, all this calls for a reappraisal of values [the later Roosevelt said]. A mere builder of more industrial plants, a creator of more railroad systems, an organizer of more corporations, is as likely to be a danger as a help. The day of the great promoter or financial Titan, to whom we granted anything if only he would build, is over. . . . The day of enlightened administration has come.

Against the background of this philosophy — the philosophy of Bryan, Theodore Roosevelt, and Wilson — he specified in general terms what he meant by enlightened administration. He endorsed the Democratic platform. He urged governmental economy and lower tariffs, unemployment relief and social security, support of the interests of the "forgotten man." With greater precision he came to grips with the farm problem, announcing himself definitely in favor of crop control. There would be no more temporizing as in the case of the Hoover Administration — "it delayed relief, it forgot reform." The new program, Roosevelt declared with buoyant, infectious optimism, would create a new America.

It may be doubted whether the people pondered very deeply the significance of what Roosevelt proposed. They did not give much thought to how his ideas might be translated into action. Hoover soon realized, however, that the election was bringing out a real clash of political philosophies. In a speech at Madison Square Garden at the close of the campaign, he declared that the "changes and so-called new deals" that the Democrats proposed meant nothing more nor less than destruction of the American system.

Developing his concept of this system as the ordered liberty, individual freedom, and equal opportunity through which alone initiative and enterprise could be summoned to spur the march of progress, Hoover declared that the program of his opponents meant, on the contrary, government intervention in business at the expense of free enterprise, the creation of a huge bureaucracy, the regimentation of the American people, and the stifling of liberty. Under the policies adopted by his Administration, he proudly claimed, the American system had weathered the storm of depression without succumbing to any of these evils or any other infringement of its basic principles.

> I therefore contend [President Hoover stated] that the problem of today is to continue these measures and policies, to restore this American system to its normal functioning, to repair the wounds it has received, to correct the weaknesses and evils which would defeat that system. To enter upon a series of deep changes, to embark upon this inchoate new deal which has been propounded in this campaign, would be to undermine and destroy our American system . . . you cannot extend the mastery of government over the daily life of a people without somewhere making it master of people's souls and thoughts. . . . My countrymen, the proposals of our opponents represent a profound change in American life. . . . Dominantly in their spirit they represent a radical departure from the foundations of one hundred and fifty years which have made this the greatest nation in the world. This election is not a mere shift from the ins to the outs. It means deciding the direction our nation will take over a century to come.

Here was a keen realization of the implications of the New Deal in terms of Hoover's conservative doctrines. It called upon the American people to look beyond politics, and assess the real values of the American way of life. But whatever the merit of his summons, the public was thinking in terms of immediate relief from an almost unendurable situation. There was little worry over people's souls when the compelling need was jobs and enough to eat.

It was perhaps remarkable that an election in a year of such deep depression did not result in more violent expressions of popular discontent. There were demagogues who sought to sow the seed of hatred against the bankers, capitalists, and industrialists whom they held responsible for the depression. Senator Huey P. Long of Louisiana, preached a Utopian doctrine of "Share Our Wealth" and "Every Man a King." Father Coughlin, a radio priest of the Shrine of the Little Flower near Detroit, called for immediate currency inflation. Doctor F. E. Townsend advanced an impossible program of old-age pensions of two hundred dollars a month. But while these men attracted huge followings, their support, in 1932, went to the Democrats. Only the Socialists and Communists, in both of which parties the ranks were divided, definitely campaigned against the capitalist system.

When the country finally went to the polls, it did not vote for Roosevelt and reform so much as it voted against Hoover and stagnation. It was bent on throwing the Republicans out of office much as it had been determined twelve years earlier to throw out the Democrats. The result was an overwhelming victory for Roosevelt. He obtained 22,822,000 votes to 15,762,000 for Hoover, while less than one million ballots were cast for all minority candidates. The Democrats carried all but six states — Maine, New Hampshire, Vermont, Connecticut, Delaware, and Pennsylvania — with an electoral vote of 472 to 59. Their majority in both houses of Congress was overwhelming. Whether or not the election represented a definite mandate for a New Deal, it was a striking demonstration that the country wanted something other than a continuation of Republican policies.

Roosevelt's Inaugural

Four months passed between the election and Roosevelt's inauguration. The economic situation steadily deteriorated. When the triumphant Democrats gathered in Washington on March 4, 1933, some two hundred and fifty thousand strong, to celebrate the start of the new Administration, the depression had tightened its paralyzing grip upon every phase of the country's life. It was a national crisis comparable only to the great emergencies of war.

In industry after industry production had been cut down to a minimum, and workers laid off by the thousands. Factories were in many cases lying idle, mines were shut down, business offices were going through little more than the motions of routine work. Ships were tied up and rotting at the wharves; empty freight trains cluttered the railway yards. Perhaps as many as fifteen million men were unemployed. Desperate farmers were taking the law into their own hands to prevent mortgage foreclosures and hunger marchers in the big cities were sullenly demanding relief. Those who still had money were nervously hoarding gold and currency. On the eve of the inauguration, the banks had been officially closed in almost every state in a final, desperate effort to stave off complete chaos. The President-elect had narrowly escaped assassination. A frightened people gave uneasy credence to all sorts of impossible rumors of impending violence. Never had a presidential inauguration — except that of President Lincoln — been awaited with more nervous anticipation than that of Franklin D. Roosevelt.

On that raw March fourth the new President spoke to a tremendous crowd, but his message was addressed directly to the whole American people and its tone was pre-eminently one of calm confidence. He struck this note at once. The condition of the country was grave, but the nation would endure. It would revive and prosper. "The only thing we have to fear," Roosevelt declared, "is fear itself — nameless, unreasoning, unjustified terror which paralyzes needed efforts to convert retreat into advance." The responsibility for the crisis, and he outlined it candidly, lay in no failure of substance. Plenty was at our doorstep. The generous use of it languished primarily "because the rulers of the exchange of mankind's goods have failed through their own stubbornness and their own incompetence, have admitted their failure and abdicated." The President called first of all for new ethical principles: a recognition of the falsity of material wealth as the standard of success and repudiation of the leadership of those who knew only the rules of a generation of self-seekers. "They have no vision, and when there is no vision, the people perish."

Changes in ethics, however, were not enough. The nation was calling for action. "Our greatest primary task," Roosevelt declared, "is to put people to work." Direct recruiting by the Government could accomplish this in part. It could be furthered by other measures. The new President advocated raising agricultural prices, preventing mortgage foreclosures, unifying relief activities, national planning for and supervision of all forms of transportation, communications, and other public utilities. Also it was essential to have strict banking supervision over all credits and investments, and to maintain an adequate but sound currency.

> I am prepared under my constitutional duty to recommend the measures that a stricken nation in the midst of a stricken world may require. These measures, or such other measures as the Congress may build out of its experience and wisdom, I shall seek, within my constitutional authority, to bring to speedy adoption. But in the event that the Congress shall fail to take one of these two courses, and in the event that the national emergency is still critical, I shall not evade the clear course of duty that will then confront me. I shall ask the Congress for the one remaining instrument to meet the crisis — broad executive power to wage a war against the emergency as great as the power that would be given me if we were in fact invaded by a foreign foe.

It was a speech that electrified the nation with its vigorous assertion of national leadership, awakening a public response that crossed all party lines. "Strikes the dominant note of courageous confidence" — *Chicago Tribune*; "new steel in the nation's spirit" — *Norfolk Pilot*; "like a true leader, who realizes the difficulties before him, and faces them unafraid" — *New York Herald Tribune*; "the determination to act, and to act heroically, strikes the popular chord" — *Washington Post*; "well calculated to inspire confidence" — *Los Angeles Times.* There was recognition of the fact, as expressed by *Business Week*, that "never had a man entered the White House with whose policies and theories, associations and record, Business, particularly Big Business, was so completely in disagreement." Business, however, had abdicated its leadership. It was prepared to accept that of Roosevelt. He promised the action which only a national administration, with popular support, could bring to bear upon the crisis. A joint statement signed by the heads of the American Federation of Labor, the National Grange, the Union Pacific Railroad and the Baltimore and Ohio Railroad; by Alfred E. Smith, Nicholas Murray Butler, Cardinal Mundelein, and Walter Lippmann, spoke glowingly of the "spontaneous and spiritual uprising of confidence and hope in our chosen leader."

THE HUNDRED DAYS

The outgoing Administration had blamed continuance of the depression, first on foreign complications, and then on fears and uncertainties as to what the Democrats might do. Hoover had felt his hands to be tied in taking any effective measures to cope with the emergency during his last months in office. His policies had been definitely repudiated; he had no further mandate from the American people. Under these circumstances he had sought the President-elect's co-operation in developing a national program for the forthcoming World Economic Conference and in meeting the banking emergency. Roosevelt had refused to commit himself. The issue was a critical one. Hoover was convinced that Roosevelt's temporizing was in large measure responsible for the collapse of the banking system. He believed that if the President-elect had given definite assurances that he intended to follow a sound policy on the currency and the national budget, the day would have been saved. Roosevelt felt that announcement of his program would serve no good purpose until he was in a position to carry it out. He would not accept responsibility without authority.

Once in office, however, the promise of action made in his inaugural was quickly fulfilled. The immediate declaration of a national banking holiday closed every bank in the country and Congress was at once summoned into special session. It met on March 9. Before the day was over, an emergency bill had been passed by both houses and received the presidential signature. It authorized the Secretary of the Treasury to call in all gold and gold certificates, provide for the opening of such banks as federal inspectors judged to be sound, and appoint "conservators" for all others. Public confidence was at once restored. With the provision of emergency currency to meet possible runs on the banks, the deposits that had been withdrawn during the crisis began to flow back. Normal financial activity was resumed with amazing rapidity. Three quarters of the member banks of the Federal Reserve System reopened within three days. There was an immediate upswing of prices. Markets which had been completely in the doldrums sprang into new life.

This was only the first of the many measures — already looking toward the broader program of relief, recovery, and reform — which the President was prepared to place before Congress and drive through to enactment while the iron was hot. On the day after passage of the Emergency Banking Act, an economy bill was introduced providing a fifteen per cent reduction in all federal salaries and cutting prevailing payments to war veterans by $460,000,000. Another three days, and the President sent a message to Congress urging repeal of the Volstead Act as a preliminary step looking toward the end of prohibition which would at once provide new revenue through federal taxes on beer. And close on the heels of this move, he proposed establishment of a Civilian Conservation Corps as a first direct attack upon unemployment. Before the close of this fateful month of March, 1933, he had also introduced a far-reaching program for aiding the farmer, urged establishment of a special relief administration, called for expansion of public works, and recommended a securities bill for the protection of investors.

April saw no letup in these feverish activities. Having asserted title to all gold in the country, the Government established a complete embargo on shipments of the metal and introduced a program for specific dollar devaluation. Measures began making their way through Congress to provide mortgage relief for both home-owners and farmers. A bill proposing establishment of the Tennessee Valley Authority was presented, and the President intimated he would soon ask authority for negotiating reciprocal trade agreements. Then in May, after introduction of a railroad transportation bill, the capstone of the New Deal program was set in place when Roosevelt called for establishment of a National Recovery Administration to meet the needs of business and labor, with appropriation of $3,300,000,000 for a vast program of public works.

Never before in the history of the country had such a mass of far-reaching, if not revolutionary, legislation been introduced with such breath-taking rapidity. And before Congress adjourned in June, within a hundred days of Roosevelt's inaugural, every one of the Administration's principal measures had been enacted into

law. The Economy Act had gone into effect before the end of
March and the Civilian Conservation Corps was set up early in
April. The Agricultural Adjustment Administration was being
organized in May. The National Industrial Recovery Act, characterized by the President as probably "the most important and far-
reaching legislation ever enacted by the American Congress," was
signed by the middle of June. Both the Federal Emergency Relief Administration and the Public Works Administration had
come into being. "The nation asks for action, and action now,"
Roosevelt had stated in his inaugural. Whatever the value or
advisability of certain of these measures, whatever the faults
naturally resulting from such terrific haste, Roosevelt had made
good his pledge to meet this demand.

There had been, indeed, no withstanding the dynamic force of
his leadership. His program had been pushed through Congress
with amazing success, and business interests no less than labor
and agriculture applauded such forthright action. "Never in the
history of the nation," Henry I. Harriman, president of the Chamber of Commerce of the United States, stated on the occasion of
a meeting addressed by Roosevelt in the middle of May, "has an
Administration more courageously and fairly attempted to deal
with so many and such far-reaching problems."

Such praise from business could not last indefinitely, and there
were signs of a different attitude even before the end of the
hundred days, with the more conservative elements in the
country striking out at what appeared to be the radical implications of some of the new measures. The Economy Act was
termed an abdication of congressional power and assertion of
presidential dictatorship. Senator Couzens hoped that he would
be struck dead before voting for it. The Civilian Conservation
Corps was said to involve the regimentation of labor; the Agricultural Adjustment Administration was attacked as destroying
the independence of the farmer; the abrogation of the gold-pay-
ment clause in government bonds was caustically declared to be
both "immoral and dishonest," and the National Recovery Administration was condemned as "the most sweeping and perilous
experiment in economic revolution since the Soviet régime was

set up in Russia." Moreover, these attacks multiplied when recovery really got under way and bankers and business executives emerged from the cyclone cellars to which they had retreated, to save what they could of special privilege. As the long decline in prices was checked, employment and payrolls turned upward, and other business indices began to show real improvement, there was a swelling chorus of conservative criticism aimed at the New Deal's social implications.

Nevertheless, when Congress finally adjourned in June, approval for what Roosevelt had accomplished far overshadowed all such complaints. The American people took up enthusiastically the three "R's" — not of Reading, 'Riting, and 'Rithmetic, but of Relief, Recovery, and Reform. It learned a new alphabet — the AAA, the NRA, the TVA, the CCC, the FERA, the HOLC. It was widely believed that through his energy, determination, and aggressive leadership, the President had reversed the downward course of economic activity. With its confidence restored, the country could carry on to full recovery. "We have shown the world," Roosevelt declared, "that democracy has within it the elements necessary to its own salvation."

New Deal Philosophy

The hundred days laid the groundwork for the New Deal's entire program. Its underlying philosophy, as already indicated in the President's campaign speeches and in his inaugural, was diametrically opposed to the principles and ideas forming the basis for the Republican policy of the nineteen-twenties. The New Deal was based upon a far broader conception of the responsibilities and obligations of the Federal Government. It necessarily involved a tremendous stride toward centralization of authority in Washington at the expense of states' rights. It had as a primary objective the safeguarding and promotion of the interests of the great masses of people rather than those of the more privileged classes. Roosevelt was later to justify this expansion of governmental functions by falling back upon the authority of Lincoln. "The legitimate object of government," he quoted Lincoln as saying, "is to do for a community of people whatever they need to have done, but cannot do at all, or cannot do so well, for themselves, in their separate and individual capacities."

By some of both its adherents and its critics the New Deal was called revolution. This could hardly be historically justified. Although precedents were shattered and drastic changes introduced, the main lines of reform projected by Roosevelt marked no real break with the past. What gave such a revolutionary aspect to the New Deal was the great speed with which its general program was developed. As it went on to elaborate its policies for promoting social security, protecting the interests of labor and agriculture, supervising the security exchanges and regulating the production of power, it made up in a few brief years for the time lag in social legislation resulting from the highly conservative philosophy of the nineteen-twenties. Almost overnight, the United States caught up with developments which in the more advanced European countries had already compelled drastic social change and adjustment to the new conditions of industrial civilization.

More important, the actual roots of the New Deal were deeply embedded in American experience. Just as Progressivism had developed out of Populism, so did the New Deal develop logically out of Progressivism. It sought above everything else — in theory if not always in practice — to reassert the powers of American democracy over against those of economic autocracy. Its fundamental aim was to bulwark political liberty by an economic liberty interpreted as the right of every man to social security. "If the tendency in the dozen years following the World War had been permitted to continue," Roosevelt later stated, " . . . the inevitable consequence would have been the destruction of the base of our form of government. For its splendid structure there would have been substituted, as a natural result, an autocratic form of government."

Yet he also recognized that there was some danger that the New Deal would create the very thing he professed to fear because of the new instruments of public power built up in Washington. The issue was one of control. "In the hands of a people's government," he declared, "this power is wholesome and proper. But in the hands of political puppets of an economic autocracy such power would provide shackles for the liberties of the people."

Opponents who looked beyond immediate legislation to the principles underlying it believed that such shackles were already being forged. They felt that centralization of authority and establishment of a parasitical bureaucracy were destroying individual freedom. The controls established over agriculture, over wages and hours for labor, over the operations of business, were denounced as definite steps toward establishment of an authoritarian government completely regimenting the American people. Asserting vehemently his opposition to anything savoring of either Fascism or Communism, Roosevelt met such charges by declaring that the primary purpose of the measures he advocated was to prevent the growth in this country of any analogous system of government. His foes, nevertheless, felt that unless he was restrained on the course on which he had set out, the result would be the overthrow of American democracy rather than its salvation.

It was also asserted that the New Deal was undermining the bases of capitalism by socialistic reform. On this issue, however, there was ample evidence that Roosevelt believed completely in the basic concepts of free enterprise. Many New Deal measures which at the time appeared most radical may be fairly interpreted as representing an effort to preserve capitalism from the grave dangers confronting it during the dire days of the depression. Like Theodore Roosevelt before him, Franklin Roosevelt attacked, not capitalism, but those in high places who he believed were betraying it. The "malefactors of great wealth" became "unscrupulous money-changers" and "economic royalists." He sought to root out abuses and evils in order that free enterprise might be able to function more effectively. He would, however, have broadened the conception of property rights which is at the basis of capitalism. He believed every man was entitled "to make a comfortable living" and "to be assured to the fullest extent attainable, in the safety of his savings. . . . " In other words, the right of property was not limited to those who controlled great aggregations of capital. It applied more immediately to the savings of the individual. "In all thought of property, this right is paramount," Roosevelt declared; "all other property rights must yield to it."

In *The People, Yes,** Carl Sandburg wrote:

> Stocks are property, yes,
> Bonds are property, yes,
> Machines, land, buildings are property, yes,
> A job is property,
> No, nix, nah, nah.

Should not the New Deal also attempt to assure the workingman of job protection? To this, too, it would turn as it developed its program of social security.

During the early stages of the Roosevelt Administration there was heavy thunder on the Left as well as onslaughts from the Right. The President was continually under pressure from more radical elements in the country whose proposals, sometimes strongly supported in Congress, might well have led to the destruction of free enterprise. In steering his course, he was buffeted from all sides. He was continually being urged to take over the banks or to take over the railroads. The popular clamor for currency inflation, at whatever cost, became almost irresistible. Huey Long and Father Coughlin and Doctor Townsend could not be entirely ignored. Their crack-brained schemes for sharing the wealth and redistributing the national income gained more adherents, vociferous and demanding, every day. Roosevelt's success in standing out against all such radical pressure was his answer to his conservative critics' charge of socialism. "It was this Administration," he declared in 1936, "which saved the system of private property and free enterprise."

To preserve capitalistic democracy, the threefold program of relief, recovery, and reform had to be closely correlated and skillfully worked out. The President relied, to an extent which his

* Sandburg, Carl, *The People, Yes.* Harcourt, Brace and Company, New York; 1936.

opponents believed increasingly dangerous, upon the suggestions and proposals of the members of his "brain trust." They were inclined to be long on theory and short on political experience. They were perhaps responsible for the contradictions in certain phases of the general program. Much of the New Deal, indeed, was frankly experimental. The President compared the situation to that which the quarterback of a football team faces in trying out various plays to break through the opponents' defense. And apart from experimentation, there was also no question but that the speed with which legislation was hurried through Congress, subject to only the briefest debate during the hundred days, made for serious mistakes. It led to extravagance and bureaucratic inefficiency. In spite of all this, there was an underlying consistency to the New Deal as a whole, and a general correlation of its various parts. Roosevelt repeatedly emphasized this in the radio "fireside chats" that enabled him, as no other President before him, to speak directly to a nation-wide audience of millions of American families.

"Higher wages for workers, more income for farmers, mean more goods produced, more and better food eaten, fewer unemployed and lower taxes," he declared in 1936. "That is my economic and social philosophy, and, incidentally, that is my political philosophy as well." Another time he stated that the first objective of the New Deal was to establish "the security of the men, women, and children of the nation." It was a program which envisaged provision for decent living conditions, provision for the greatest possible use of all our national resources, and provision against misfortune — that is, "the security of the home, the security of livelihood, and the security of social insurance." These were the minimum requirements of democracy, the President said. They constituted "a right which belongs to every individual and every family willing to work. They are the essential fulfillment of measures already taken toward relief, recovery, and reconstruction."

The attempt to go beyond a recovery which would mean no more than re-establishment of conditions as they had existed in the nineteen-twenties conformed to the general sentiment of the nation. The inequalities as well as the precarious basis of the prosperity of the nineteen-twenties had finally been recognized. Measures looking toward relief for agriculture, recognition of the rights of labor, minimum wages and maximum hours, unemployment, and old-age insurance were in the spirit of the times. The pendulum had swung back to reform. These measures reflected the climate of public opinion during the nineteen-thirties just as the campaign for railroad regulation, anti-trust activity, and pure food laws had mirrored popular sentiment in the progressive era. The New Deal was not operating in a vacuum. It was expressing the national will. And in taking up the broken thread of reform, it was renewing that search for social justice and a more abundant life for the people as a whole which is the integrating factor in all American history.

20

The Recovery Program

"THE GOLD NOBODY KNOWS"

THE UNDERLYING PURPOSE which bound together the New Deal program of relief, recovery, and reform was the restoration of those basic values in the American way of life that the prolonged depression had so seriously threatened. It was immediately necessary to provide relief for the unemployed both for their own sakes and to prevent further demoralization in the country as a whole. Yet recovery was even more essential to enable the unemployed to obtain the jobs in private industry which would re-establish their status in society, while its broader aspects also involved the economic security and well-being of every group within the country — industry, agriculture, and labor. Nor was reform altogether an end and aim in itself. While its primary goal was to promote a greater measure of social justice for the underprivileged, many of the reform measures adopted were designed as well to reinforce recovery by sustaining the economic system against the shocks of further depression.

This close interrelation among the various phases of New Deal activity should be more clearly revealed as we consider them in some detail. In taking up recovery first, it is recognized that relief had priority in President Roosevelt's policies. "Our greatest primary task," he had said in his inaugural, "is to put people to work." Nevertheless, recovery directly affected this phase of his program, and it was to demand the continued attention of the Government for the very reason that it was to prove so difficult to attain. The elusive search for some way to bring into proper adjustment the various elements in our national life in order that the American people might again enjoy prosperity underlay the entire history of the years between 1933 and 1940. "What we seek," again to quote Roosevelt, "is balance in our economic system — balance between agriculture and industry and balance between the wage-earner, the employer, and the consumer. We seek also balance that our internal market be kept rich and large, and that our trade with other nations be increased on both sides of the ledger."

The most important legislation directed toward this goal was the devaluation of the currency, the program for agricultural relief, the attempt to aid both industry and labor through the National Recovery Administration, and reciprocal trade agreements.

As we have seen, the country was taken off the gold standard in April, 1933, the public being called upon to surrender all gold coin or gold certificates in its possession while an embargo was placed on shipments abroad. A month later, specific authority for a policy of devaluation was granted by the Thomas amendment to the Agricultural Adjustment Act. It provided for a reduction in the gold content of the dollar up to fifty per cent and authorized $3,000,000,000 in new currency. The abandonment of the gold standard was then further affirmed in the Gold Repeal Joint Resolution, passed in June, 1933, which abrogated the gold clause in all public and private contracts and made debts payable in legal tender.

For a time there were considerable doubt and confusion as to just what these steps foreshadowed. They were first of all an answer to the rising popular clamor for currency inflation. It was only the President's promise to meet the need for an expanded currency in other ways that enabled him to keep congressional inflationists under control and to block the demand for immediate issuance of greenbacks. While these measures were being taken, however, Roosevelt also dispatched an American delegation to the World Economic Conference, held that June in London, pointedly emphasizing the importance of establishing financial order in place of the prevailing chaos "by a stabilization of currencies, by freeing the flow of world trade, and by international action to raise price levels."

The phrase "international action" was significant. Did it mean that the authority to devalue the dollar would be exercised only in so far as was necessary for the international stabilization of exchange rates? But the other nations had already drastically devalued their currency. The objectives of our program in raising domestic commodity prices could hardly be achieved with stabilization at existing levels. International negotiations were already under way in London when the President apparently became convinced that they were premature from the point of view of American domestic interests. After issuing a frank warning that his policy was to create a managed currency which would establish "the kind of dollar which, a generation hence, will have the same purchasing and debt-paying power as the dollar value we hope to attain in the near future," he suddenly withdrew American support from the World Economic Conference. It was left to flounder hopelessly as the United States embarked on its own nationalistic approach to the entire currency question.

This program involved the purchase of gold at increasing prices arbitrarily determined by the Treasury. Designed by Professor G. F. Warren of Cornell to meet the demand for a managed currency, it sought to stimulate a rise in commodity prices proportionate to the dollar's declining gold value and to this extent, therefore, was a form of moderate, controlled inflation. The plan was successful in raising the dollar's exchange value, but it did not lift the domestic price level. While the Reconstruction Finance Corporation bought gold during the remainder of 1933 at prices ranging from $29.80 to $34.45 an ounce, the wholesale price index (on the basis of a 1926 average of 100) rose only from 71 to 72. Since further manipulation consequently appeared inadvisable, the President recommended stabilizing the devalued dollar at approximately the level it had already attained. The Gold Reserve Act, adopted in January, 1934, reasserted the Government's title to all gold, fixed the gold content of the dollar at approximately sixty per cent of its former value, and set up a $2,000,000,000 stabilization fund.

It was still "the gold nobody knows." At a press conference in January, the President was asked whether he looked for any immediate effect on prices from the new legislation. "I don't know," he answered; "I have no idea."

In its major objective of trying to lower the value of the dollar, thereby serving the interests of all debtors, this policy conformed to the traditional doctrines of the nineteenth-century Populists. There was consequently little reason to be surprised in the demand that soon arose for the Government to purchase silver as well as gold. With the strong support of representatives of the silver-producing states, Congress thereupon passed, in June, 1934, a Silver Purchase Act, directing the Treasury to nationalize all domestic stocks of the metal and to continue its purchases until the price should either equal $1.29 per ounce or there should be a three-to-one ratio between gold and silver in the country's monetary holdings. Silver prices immediately spurted upward, but our continuing acquisition of gold made it impossible, despite this artificial value for silver, to attain the required ratio between the stocks of the two metals.

It is impossible to appraise satisfactorily the results of this monetary policy. It led to the accumulation in this country of huge and unnecessary reserves of both gold and silver. By the end of 1937, the Treasury had in its possession over $17,000,000,-000 of gold coin and bullion and $2,000,000,000 of silver. American control of such a great proportion of world monetary stocks, however, greatly contributed to the further dislocation of international exchange, and unnecessarily large reserves were of no intrinsic value to our own economy. They were out of all proportion to the total money in circulation which amounted to only $7,600,000,000, or less than half our metallic stocks. While this sum represented a very substantial increase over available currency at the time the dollar was first devalued, money in actual circulation remained dependent, not upon gold or silver stocks, but upon the credit controls of the Federal Reserve System. Had devaluation then raised domestic prices in the long run any more effectively than in the first nine months? A general price recovery had of course taken place, the wholesale average rising, between 1933 and 1939, from 66 to 77. This did not, however, correspond with the cut in the value of the dollar. It could not be directly attributed to it. Too many other factors came into play. Currency manipulation had had no definitely appreciable effect upon the national economy, and after 1934, in fact, the Government gave up its attempt to lift us back to recovery by such means.

Conservatives consistently criticized and opposed the entire program. Although J. P. Morgan admitted when the country was first taken off the gold standard that it was "the best possible course under the circumstances," bankers generally felt that the later New Deal measures along this line were steps toward outright currency inflation and constituted a dangerous threat to economic stability. The abrogation of the gold clause in public and private contracts was also bitterly attacked as going beyond the constitutional powers of Congress and as a callous betrayal of public faith. The constitutionality of dollar devaluation was subsequently passed upon by the Supreme Court in a series of highly technical decisions. While the Government was upheld in its general policy, the right to abrogate the gold clause in government bonds was denied. This adverse decision, however, was in effect nullified on the ground that since possession of gold had been made illegal, a person deprived of payment in gold could not show damages. Here was perhaps a moral rebuke for the New Deal, but the devaluation policy was not practically affected.

Roosevelt's monetary program did not live up to the hopes of its friends in raising prices, but on the other hand it did not lead to the disasters predicted by its critics. Its real significance lay in its success in staving off the popular demand for direct, all-out currency inflation. The possibility that such a course might have been forced upon the Administration by a panicky Congress was very real in 1933. The authorization for issuing $3,000,000,000 in bank notes included in the Agricultural Adjustment Act stands as clear proof of dangers narrowly averted. That authority was never used because gold devaluation silenced the inflationary clamor.

In other phases of its fiscal program, the New Deal followed a line which also alarmed conservatives and continued throughout the nineteen-thirties to arouse the greatest opposition to the

Roosevelt Administration. The tremendous increase in federal expenditures resulting from expanded governmental functions in every direction could only be met by deficit financing. Three sets of figures graphically tell this story. Between 1933 and 1940 the annual total for all federal expenses rose from $3,864,000,000 to $8,995,000,000 — or more than doubled. At the same time receipts from all sources increased from $2,006,000,000 to $5,669,000,000 — an even greater relative gain. But in every year there was, nevertheless, a heavy deficit and it could be met only by public borrowing. The consequence was a rise in the federal debt from $22,539,000,000 to $44,458,000,000.

Low interest rates saved the Government from a comparable increase in the carrying charges for this tremendous debt, but there was no closing the gap between outgoing and incoming funds. The New Deal raised the rates on gift and inheritance taxes, on income taxes in the higher brackets, and on corporation taxes. It experimented with a special levy on undistributed corporation profits — which was so strongly opposed by business that it was subsequently repealed — and in every way tried to increase revenue. With maintenance of relief and public works on the colossal scale considered necessary, it nevertheless proved impossible to balance the budget.

Critics repeatedly emphasized that this phase of the Roosevelt program held out the gravest danger to the financial stability of the country. The process of borrowing and piling-up debt could not be continued indefinitely without disaster. Business could never regain real confidence, it was stated, until the threat of an unbalanced budget was put to rest. New Deal supporters, on the other hand, declared that the expenditures were necessary and that governmental debt should be measured, not in terms of governmental income, but of national income. So long as the latter increased, according to this thesis, there was no cause for alarm. Eventually it would prove possible to balance the budget, and in the meantime a swollen public debt was itself no criterion of the country's financial condition. The experience of the British Government in supporting a much higher per capita debt than that of the United States appeared to afford ground for these contentions, and the progressively lower yield on government bonds demonstrated continued confidence in the credit of the National Government.

AGRICULTURAL RELIEF

The Agricultural Adjustment Act, initiating the currency policy through the devaluation provisions of the Thomas amendment, was in its main aspects a direct attack upon the problem of overproduction on the nation's farms. President Hoover's program to support purchasing power had completely failed. As we have seen, the Agricultural Marketing Act had been unable to stem the persistent decline in farm prices and when the Federal Farm Board was compelled to withdraw from its stabilization operations, agriculture was in a worse situation than ever. The New Deal consequently accepted the impossibility of depending upon foreign markets for absorbing surplus farm crops, and undertook to limit production to a closer approximation of the needs — or rather effective demand — of the domestic market.

This meant an economy of scarcity instead of an economy of abundance. It led to the distressing spectacle of cotton plowed under, wheat crops destroyed, and little pigs wastefully slaughtered while millions of people still remained in want of adequate food and clothing. The harsh fact remained, however, that it was not possible to utilize a high rate of production to relieve these widespread needs. There was no way in which surplus crops could be converted into food and clothing, and then economically distributed, without even further national dislocations. Overproduction meant falling prices for the farmer. It made it impossible for him to meet his fixed charges, let alone keep up his end in the purchase of industrial products. Impoverishing the most important single element in our population, it benefited neither industry nor labor.

Apart from the immediate goal of raising agricultural prices, there were two further objectives behind the AAA program. Roosevelt was intensely interested in soil conservation. To take marginal lands out of production, preserve soil fertility by crop rotation, reinvigorate exhausted lands by planting with legumes and other soil-building crops, appeared fully as important to him for the sake of the future as any immediate increase in farm purchasing power. "We must avoid any national agricultural policy," he stated, "that will result in shipping our soil fertility to foreign nations."

As basic to the program as long-term conservation, moreover, was the desire to sustain and uphold agriculture as a way of life deeply embedded in the American tradition. The mounting indebtedness of the farmer, the deadly process of mortgage foreclosures, the increase in farm tenancy, had to be combated because of their effect in breaking down the farmer's independence. "The American farmer, living on his own land," was Roosevelt's expression of this feeling, "remains our ideal of self-reliance and of spiritual balance — the source from which the reservoirs of the nation's strength are constantly renewed."

The Agricultural Adjustment Act specifically provided for the conclusion of contracts with individual producers whereby, in return for benefit payments to be made by the Government, they would voluntarily reduce the acreage planted to basic crops. Cotton, wheat, corn, hogs, rice, tobacco, and milk were included in the program as originally drawn up, and this list was later extended still further. The funds for the benefit payments were to be obtained from a tax levied on the processing of these commodities, and the whole system was consequently to be made self-supporting. While it was placed on a voluntary basis, the cooperation of farmers was held to be assured. They would profit, not only from the benefit payments made for taking land out of production — land which would then be planted to soil-building crops — but also from the rise in farm prices expected to result from an economy of scarcity. While operation of the program was in the hands of the newly established Agricultural Adjustment Administration, its enforcement was largely left to the farmers themselves as a further means of guaranteeing their support.

More than ten million acres of land were taken out of production in 1933 — most spectacularly through plowing under cotton crops already planted — and farm prices responded with gains all along the line. The program even so proved inadequate. More intensive cultivation of the acres actually planted and the generous use of fertilizer kept production in some commodities at a much higher level than had been contemplated. In 1934, Congress consequently supplemented the original program through additional legislation imposing definite production quotas upon cotton and tobacco with farmers who exceeded their quotas subject to penalty taxes. In order to meet problems of marketing which even effective control of production did not solve satisfactorily, additional aid was also extended the farmer through commodity loans, special marketing agreements, and the purchase of surplus foodstuffs for distribution among the needy.

In 1934 and 1935 more than thirty million acres of land were taken out of production each year, marketing supplies were greatly reduced (a severe drought adding to the effectiveness of the curtailment program), and farm prices continued to rise. It was estimated in the latter year that the agricultural cash income had increased almost fifty per cent, with even more marked gains in such crops as wheat, cotton, tobacco, corn, and hogs. In the ratio of prices received and prices paid, moreover, the farmer was some thirty-five per cent better off than he had been three years earlier. From the point of view of agriculture, the program was a success. A referendum showed 3,700,000 out of the 4,300,000 farmers taking part in it voting for its continuance.

On other counts, however, the AAA came under increasingly heavy attack. It was benefiting the large growers of staples more than the smaller farmers who were actually in greater need. The rise in agricultural prices had been too rapid; it was throwing the economic system out of balance in a new direction. The regimentation of the farmer's life involved in the AAA's operations was undermining his independence. And an economy of scarcity, with a third of the population, as Roosevelt himself admitted, undernourished, was widely denounced as a travesty. Accepting the New Deal claim that this phase of the program was only a temporary expedient to meet an immediate emergency, it was still hard to reconcile it with the needs of the country as a whole.

In January, 1936 — under circumstances to which we shall return — the Supreme Court declared the Agricultural Adjustment Act unconstitutional. The whole problem of farm relief was again thrown into the lap of Congress. Its answer was to adopt another program, with the same objectives, but designed to overcome constitutional barriers by basing crop control directly on the need for conserving land. The Soil Conservation and Domestic Allotment Act, passed the next month, established a system of direct federal subsidies for producers who would substitute soil-conserving crops for commercial staples. It was a temporary expedient. When changes in the attitude of the Supreme Court opened the way to further legislation, a more permanent program was adopted with enactment of a second Agricultural Adjustment Act in February, 1938.

According to the terms of this highly complicated measure, the AAA was to administer a still more elaborate form of crop management, placing the emphasis upon controlled production rather than controlled acreage. The conservation phases of the earlier program were continued, with direct benefit payments made to the farmers for their withdrawal of land from commercial crops and its use in raising soil-building crops, while additional subsidies were also to be granted to all growers of wheat, corn, tobacco, cotton, and rice who accepted specified acreage allotments judged necessary to meet both domestic and foreign requirements, together with an adequate carry-over. The purpose of the latter subsidies was to provide the farmers with an income equivalent in purchasing power to that of their income in the five-year period from 1909 to 1914. These so-called parity payments, as well as the conservation payments, were to be drawn from the Government's general funds. Should overproduction develop despite these precautions, specific marketing controls could then be established with a penalty tax on all sales over specified allotments, subject to approval by two-thirds of the growers of the affected commodities. In addition to these provisions, the AAA was empowered to extend commodity loans to uphold the price on the reserve supplies, stored in government warehouses in order to provide "an ever normal granary," and to set up a system of federal crop insurance to protect the farmer against a bad harvest.

The AAA did not by any means represent the full measure of aid extended to the farmer by the New Deal. Various measures were passed to make credit more easily available for agricultural borrowers, to prevent mortgage foreclosures, and to provide for mortgage refinancing. Under the direction of the Farm Credit Administration, something like half the farm mortgage debt was taken over by governmental agencies. Lower interest rates were charged and the principal of outstanding indebtedness was reduced by almost a fourth. Farm bankruptcies at the close of the nineteen-thirties had declined by seventy-one per cent.

Attempts were also made to do something for destitute farmers on submarginal lands and to meet the problem of farm tenancy. First through a Division of Subsistence Homesteads, and then through the Resettlement Administration, loans and other assistance were extended to needy families for establishing co-operative communities in which part-time farming could be combined with part-time work in industry. Sanguine hopes for the creation of a new type of social organization were held out by the promoters of these schemes and over a hundred co-operative communities established. They did not prove practical. In the meantime, the problem was being approached from another angle by the Farm Security Administration. It provided loans on easy terms for the purchase of new land and also aided tenant farmers through so-called rehabilitation loans. For a time this agency also experimented with a co-operative village-community type of rural organization, but again this did not prove altogether feasible. The interrelated problems of submarginal production, farm tenancy, and share-cropping proved to be the most difficult of the various phases of agricultural relief.

The New Deal policy as a whole unquestionably served to better the condition of American agriculture. With almost six million farmers whose holdings represented three-fourths of all crop lands, taking part in the AAA program, agricultural cash income had risen in 1939 to $8,540,000,000 — or almost twice that of 1932. Nevertheless, it was not a wholly satisfactory solution of the basic problem of agriculture's status in the national economy. Overproduction in wheat and cotton continued; little progress was made in recovering export markets. Reductions in acreage and the increasing use of farm machinery proved to be a depressing influence for share-croppers in the South and agricultural laborers everywhere. Together with some of the small farmers, these classes suffered rather than benefited from the AAA. Subsidies averaging over a half-billion dollars yearly were a terrific drain on the national treasury. With American participation in the second World War, this entire picture underwent a complete change. Farmers were urged to increase production in every possible way to meet new demands both at home and abroad, and only government controls held down runaway price inflation. Nevertheless, there was a clear foreshadowing of the day when action might again have to be taken to limit production and sustain prices against a disastrous post-war collapse. There was no certainty that the farmer's security and well-being in our social and economic system had been permanently established.

THE NATIONAL RECOVERY ADMINISTRATION

The National Industrial Recovery Act sought to provide for recovery in industry much as the goal of the Agricultural Adjustment Act was recovery in farming. Its immediate purposes were threefold. Production in heavy industries would be stimulated by the demand resulting from a sweeping program of public works. Business enterprise in general was to be assisted by shelving the anti-trust laws and permitting the adoption of codes of fair competition to prevent disastrous price-cutting. The establishment of maximum hours and minimum wages for labor, together with a guarantee of its right to collective bargaining, would serve to increase employment and enhance labor's purchasing power. Perhaps no bill ever passed by Congress had a broader scope or such far-reaching implications. And few have ever been so generally supported upon their enactment, and yet proved such a complete failure.

The public works program provided by the National Industrial Recovery Act contemplated the expenditure of $3,300,000,-000 — a figure approximately the annual total of all ordinary expenditures of the Federal Government during the nineteen-twenties. It was to be used for the construction of public highways and public buildings, conservation of natural resources, development of water power and transmission of electrical energy, river and harbor improvements, low-cost housing and slum clearance. A Public Works Administrator, to which post Secretary of the Interior Ickes was at once appointed, was empowered to allocate these funds either directly to federal projects or to non-federal projects through grants-in-aid to local governmental units.

The need to draw up individual plans and specifications, and the difficulties experienced in making the necessary arrangements with local governments which often found themselves unable to raise the funds entitling them to grants-in-aid, caused considerable delay in getting the program started. Within a year, however, allotments had been made for 13,266 federal and 2407 non-federal projects. With construction at its peak in July, 1934, employment was furnished by the Public Works Administration to some 650,000 workers.

It was impossible to gauge the full effect of these undertakings upon recovery, but the Administration soon decided that large-scale public works did not provide enough employment to justify their tremendous expense in materials. Consequently, appropriations for a time were withheld and greater reliance placed upon more direct relief agencies, such as the Works Progress Administration. Taking into consideration later allotments, however, the over-all total of the loans and grants made by the PWA before its wartime liquidation in 1943 amounted to $4,253,000,000, accounting for the construction of more than 34,000 separate projects at an aggregate cost of $6,000,000,000. Public buildings, roads, dams, sewage systems, bridges, and housing were the most important projects undertaken, but allocations had also been made for waterworks, power stations, airfields, and aids to navigation. The long-term value of these projects to the nation, whatever their rôle in the recovery program, could hardly be disputed.

While public works construction was thus launched upon a grandiose scale in the opening months of the New Deal, it was actually only a by-product of the real purposes of the National Industrial Recovery Act. The more important assistance it hoped to render business — and the really striking departure in public policy it represented — was the establishment of industrial codes of fair competition. These agreements were to be drawn up by the industries themselves, subject to presidential approval, and in the event that any industry failed to carry out this program, the President was empowered to act for it. The provisions of the codes, having the force of law, were to be administered by Code Authorities. In return for the privileges specifically allowed in regard to price-fixing, of which the great majority of codes took quick advantage, industry was to make important concessions to the needs of labor in order to increase employment and raise wages. Section 7A of the new law obligated all employers to accept maximum hours of work and minimum rates of pay, approved or prescribed by the President, and to bar the employment of children. Also, employees were guaranteed "the right to organize and bargain collectively through representatives of their own choosing."

During the summer of 1933 the National Recovery Administration was launched with a burst of feverish activity. Under the dynamic direction of Hugh S. Johnson, appointed national administrator, industry hurriedly adopted over five hundred codes while labor drove ahead quite as rapidly with the organization of workers. Here was the final answer to industrial co-operation. Government and Business were working hand in glove; Capital and Labor had buried the hatchet. Amid general enthusiasm great parades were held throughout the country to introduce the new era and Blue Eagles were formally awarded to all firms participating in the national program. The country was at last pulling together and recovery seemed surely to be under way.

This happy phase of the NRA, however, was short-lived. The elaborate machinery set up to administer its program somehow did not function as smoothly as had been hoped. Opposition developed on a broad front as the fair promise of immediate recovery failed to materialize. Industry made the most of its opportunities for price-fixing, and a helpless public began to feel the severe pinch of the rising costs of living. The small businessman found operation of the codes to be so much to the advantage of big business that he was being squeezed out. Labor found that the safeguards in maximum hours and minimum wages failed to improve its position as prices began to rise. And the large industrialists suddenly became aware of certain unforeseen consequences of the government regulation which they had so blithely accepted. Section 7A especially aroused their ire. The rights guaranteed to labor, especially that of collective bargaining through unions of the employees' own choosing, were a concession they were unprepared to accept as the full implications of the new law became clear. Some employers, most notably Henry Ford, had obdurately refused to have anything to do with the NRA, and soon many others began to challenge the whole system.

Attacked on all sides, by capital, labor, and the consuming public, the NRA was placed on the defensive. In May, 1934, a National Recovery Review Board, appointed under the chairmanship of Clarence S. Darrow, made public a report which stirred up still further discontent. Its conclusion was that the new economic setup was fostering monopoly. Small manufacturers and distributors were being oppressed; consumer prices were dictated by the large industrialists. Hugh S. Johnson resigned as administrator, code provisions began to be widely violated, strikes belied the promise of industrial peace. The NRA could no longer be effectively administered. As it drew to the verge of complete collapse, the Supreme Court finally stepped in to deal the final blow. In a decision handed down in May, 1935, the National Industrial Recovery Act was unanimously declared unconstitutional.

It was difficult to see what had been achieved. Statistics showed a reduction in the average working day for labor and some gains in average wage rates. Nevertheless, there was still paralyzing unemployment. Economic activity had been stimulated for a time, but the impetus of this upward movement had quickly died. The index for industrial production in 1934 was only six points higher than in 1933. There seemed little reason to regret NRA's passing and the public wasted few tears.

The Administration could not be so easily persuaded, however, to abandon the entire program. While it made no further attempt to regulate industry through the adoption of codes, it instead revived the anti-trust laws, seeking to keep monopoly in check by more traditional methods, and threw its support even further to the side of labor. The National Labor Relations Act, passed in July, 1935, again guaranteed workers the right to collective bargaining; the Walsh-Healey Contracts Act the next year applied to corporations accepting government contracts the wage and hour rules which NRA had sought to impose on all industry, and, finally, the Fair Labor Standards Act, which Congress adopted in 1938 after one of the longest, most hard-fought legislative battles of the entire period, fully regained the ground lost in this phase of the New Deal program. Maximum hours and minimum wages were fixed, and child labor expressly barred, in all industries engaged in interstate commerce. The wage scale was to start with a minimum of twenty-five cents an hour and rise to forty cents within seven years. Hours of work were to be at once restricted to forty-four a week and reduced to forty during the next two years, with time-and-one-half pay for overtime. To the implications of these new developments, both from the point of view of the rising power of labor and changes in the Supreme Court's approach to the constitutional issues involved, we shall return. What had started out as a program for immediate recovery under the NRA was translated into an attempt to bring about permanent reform through government regulation of labor-capital relationship.

RAILROADS AND SHIPPING

In the meantime the problems of the railroads and of shipping called for special attention. The railroads' position in our national economy was particularly important. Their function as the foremost transportation agency, despite the growing use of the automobile and motor truck, was still supreme. In addition, railroads represented, under normal conditions, large purchasers of the products of the heavy-goods industries. To aid them was both to keep the transportation system operating effectively, and also to build up a market for manufactures. The Interstate Commerce Commission consequently permitted the railroads to raise their rates and the Reconstruction Finance Corporation, carried over from the Hoover Administration, continued to grant them extensive loans. Through passage of the Emergency Railroad Transportation Act of 1933, further encouragement was also given to the consolidation of existing services. This law provided for the appointment of a Co-ordinator of Transportation to advise and aid the railroads in a common program looking toward economy and savings for the transportation network as a whole.

The real problem of the railroads, however, remained the huge debt resulting from their overcapitalization. Some sixty-two per cent of their securities were bonds, held largely by insurance companies and philanthropic organizations, and these heavy fixed charges made improvement or even maintenance of right of way and rolling stock increasingly difficult. The loans granted by the RFC, which reached a total of over $350,000,000, served to protect the holders of railroad bonds. On the other hand, they prevented the drastic refinancing, with the squeezing-out of watered stock, which was perhaps the only way in which the railroads could have effectively solved their problems and renewed equipment buying on a large scale. To many observers government ownership appeared the only way out. Joseph B. Eastman, the Federal Co-ordinator, indicated such a solution in a report to Congress, but he did not specifically recommend it because of the prohibitive cost. Conditions gradually improved for the railroads despite these unfavorable circumstances, but progress was disappointingly slow.

The shipping problem was a carry-over from the nineteen-twenties. The aid then extended in an effort to build up an adequate American merchant marine had proved insufficient. With the depression our shipping was even less able to hold its own among the world's merchant fleets. Indeed, so few ships had been built under the subsidies granted by the laws of 1920 and 1928, that it was estimated that some eighty-three per cent of the gross tonnage in existing vessels would be obsolete in 1942. To meet this emergency, pointed up by the growing possibility of war even more than by normal commercial needs, Congress passed the Merchant Marine Act of 1936. In place of mail contracts it applied a new form of subsidy. Construction and operating differentials were granted to equalize costs at home and abroad, and should private industry still fail to provide the shipping necessary, provision was made for a government financed program. A Maritime Commission was established with broad authority over both trade routes and construction.

Private industry continued to lag in meeting the requirements for an adequate merchant fleet, estimated at some seven million gross tons, and the Government consequently undertook in 1938 a long-range program for the construction of five hundred new vessels. Three years later, two hundred and eighty-three were either ordered or being built. The needs of national defense necessitated further construction by that year, however, and appropriations were made for additional emergency shipping. On the eve of American intervention in the second World War, the building program provided in all for 1383 ships.

RECIPROCAL TRADE AGREEMENTS

A final and interrelated phase of the general economic policy of the New Deal was the adoption of tariff reciprocity in June, 1934, through the Trade Agreements Act. In the discussion of any other administration, a change in the tariff law would necessarily bulk large. This was the case under Taft, under Wilson, and under Hoover. And it was important under Roosevelt, introducing an entirely new departure in meeting this perennially difficult and controversial problem. But perhaps nothing more tellingly demonstrates the tremendous range of economic legislation during the nineteen-thirties than the fact that tariff revision falls into place as only one of a long series of measures which drastically changed the entire economic pattern of the previous decade.

The Democratic platform had originally advocated lower duties, but international economic co-operation had apparently been sidetracked for economic nationalism when President Roosevelt torpedoed the World Economic Conference in 1933. Primarily through the persistent efforts of Secretary of State Hull, the New Deal nevertheless got back on the low-tariff track the next year. It was Hull's conviction, held to unswervingly, that "full, stable, and durable business recovery can only be effected by the restoration of international trade and finance. . . ."

The Trade Agreements Act, breaking all past precedent in American tariff-making, delegated to the President authority to conclude reciprocity treaties in which tariff reductions up to fifty per cent of the prevailing duties could be granted in exchange for comparable concessions on the part of the signatory nations. The tariff, that is, was taken out of congressional politics. It was freed from the log-rolling and bartering of special privilege in which it had traditionally been enmeshed. Special committees, to which representatives of business were invited to make their suggestions or complaints, were to work out the new schedules, with the actual negotiations with other countries conducted by the State Department.

Before the outbreak of the second World War, reciprocal trade agreements had been concluded with twenty nations. The greater number of them were in Latin America, but there were also treaties with Canada, Great Britain, France, Belgium, and the Netherlands. Altogether these nations accounted for over half of our shipments abroad and under the stimulation of the new agreements our exports to them soon showed an increase relatively greater than our trade with the rest of the world. The program could not be fully carried out, however. Its long-range possibilities of promoting a general reduction in trade barriers were not realized because of the outbreak of war.

Secretary Hull's policy was opposed by industrialists who still upheld protection as the best means of safeguarding the domestic market for American manufacturers, and by farmers who felt that reductions were being granted on agricultural imports without any equivalent expansion of the farm export market. It won the strong support of all elements in the country's economic life primarily interested in foreign trade, and also of those who felt that beyond immediate questions of exports and imports, a solution of the world's economic and political problems depended upon closer international co-operation. On balance, the trade reciprocity program stood forth conspicuously as one of the few constructive efforts made during these years by any country to combat the growing trend toward economic nationalism throughout the world. Secretary Hull was widely credited with a high measure of statesmanship in pursuing the goal of economic collaboration with such unflagging zeal.

ECONOMIC BALANCE SHEET

Whatever the relative effect or contribution of currency legislation, the AAA program, the short-lived experiment of the NRA, and the Trade Agreements Act, we have seen that the United States had achieved a substantial measure of recovery before Roosevelt's first term drew to a close. The total values of both domestic manufactures and foreign exports were in 1936 approximately double what they had been in 1933, and the national income as a whole had risen $30,000,000,000 above the depression lows to a total of $71,000,000,000. Other factors, however, somewhat marred this otherwise encouraging picture. Production in the heavy-goods industry lagged far behind that of consumer goods. Building construction was still in the doldrums. And most important, unemployment persisted alarmingly with some ten million workers still out of jobs.

Nor was it possible to ignore the tremendous increase in the expenditures of the Federal Government as a consequence of its unparalleled relief program. Deficit financing had raised the federal debt to what then appeared to be the colossal total of almost $36,000,000,000. Here was a highly important item on the debit side of the national ledger. What price was being paid for economic gains which still left the country well below the level of prosperity attained in the nineteen-twenties?

Controversy raged throughout the country as to how secure the foundations of recovery actually were, and where a balance could be struck between success and failure in regard to the New Deal program. President Roosevelt's supporters emphasized the gains that had been made, and attributed them to his policies. His political foes were more skeptical of what had been accomplished, maintaining that improvement, such as it was, resulted from natural forces and that the New Deal was the principal barrier to still further progress. The popular verdict, as expressed at the polls 'in November, 1936, was overwhelmingly in favor of the New Deal. Roosevelt was re-elected and he received an overwhelming mandate to continue his policies.

The recovery was not destined, however, to continue uninterruptedly the gains of the previous four years. No sooner had Roosevelt embarked upon his second term than business and industry suffered a sharp relapse. It was called a "recession" rather than a "depression," but by the end of 1937 the country was once again in serious straits. Although the low levels of 1932 were not reached, every phase of economic activity went into a disturbing decline. There was a drop in farm prices and consequent falling-off in farm income; the volume of manufactured products and foreign trade underwent a drastic reduction, and unemployment again soared upward. As a single illustration of what was taking place, government relief rolls, which had been cut down from seven million in Roosevelt's first year in office to well under four million in the summer of 1937, rapidly rose to their former levels. Hard times had returned with a vengeance.

What had happened? Why had the promise of recovery faded out so suddenly? Explanations differed all along the line. Overproduction in consumer goods, at generally high prices, was set against the failure of the capital-goods industry to experience any real revival. The continued maldistribution of the national income was said to have prevented the creation of sufficient mass purchasing power for the broad market on which industry depended. The leveling-off of governmental appropriations for public works was held to have been a vital mistake in that it shut off industrial pump-priming just as it was beginning to become effective. Whatever the cause, the bitter and incontrovertible fact was that the economic machine had again stalled.

More than during the earlier period of depression, Big Business held Government responsible for what was happening, and Government blamed Big Business. Charges and countercharges flew back and forth. Critics of the New Deal attacked it for what they said were its constant shifts and changes in policy, its interference with industry, its wild extravagance, its inability to bring any semblance of order into government finances. The Roosevelt Administration was accused of destroying all business confidence and of discouraging the investments which could alone sustain and forward industrial expansion. The New Dealers countered such attacks by ascribing the nation's ills to what they termed industry's obstructive attitude toward necessary reforms, its refusal to co-operate with the Government, and its blind antagonism to the interests of labor and the consuming public. It was a strike of capital, they declared, that blocked industrial expansion and held back increased production.

To meet the new emergency, in any event, the New Deal felt compelled to increase appropriations for work relief and again sought to prime the pump of industry with an expanded public works program. The reserve requirements of the federal reserve banks were lowered to make credit more easily available, and the Reconstruction Finance Corporation was authorized to make direct loans to industry. In a startling reversal of its attitude in 1933 in upholding prices through the monopoly controls permitted under the NRA, every effort was now made to bring manufacturers' prices down. The Department of Justice started a new campaign under the anti-trust laws, directed not only against corporate price-fixing, but also against the monopolistic practices whereby certain labor unions artificially kept up production costs. On a broader front, Congress undertook a study of the whole problem of monopoly, patent laws, trade associations, and other aspects of the economic system through the establishment of a Temporary National Economic Committee.

By the summer of 1938, whether through these governmental measures or as a consequence of the natural recuperative powers of the nation, conditions were again improving. The lost ground was rapidly regained. By 1939 the Federal Reserve index for production had recovered from its twenty-five point slump and was back again to the high levels registered in 1937. Farm income increased; there were gains in foreign trade; and the national income closely approximated its former recovery record. But the way had not been cleared for permanent recovery with any real certainty. There was still no solution of the unemployment problem, and a balanced federal budget appeared as distant as ever. For all the impressive gains recorded by the available indices of trade and industry, the economic future in 1939 was still clouded.

It had to be recognized that certain of the basic faults which had developed in the economic structure of the nation had not been entirely eliminated. Balance between industry and agriculture, between the employer, wage-earner, and consumer, still eluded the most persistent search. Would subsidies to the farmer have to be continued indefinitely to enable him to maintain his traditional status in American life? Was permanent work relief the only answer to technological unemployment? How could the advantages of monopoly be retained and its tendency toward price-fixing effectively combated? Could a more equitable distribution of the national income provide the purchasing power necessary to sustain full operation of the industrial plant? What of deficit financing and the still rising public debt?

These questions could not be answered easily. They involved the long-term functioning of our economic system. If the New Deal were to be judged on the efficacy of its recovery program as of the close of the nineteen-thirties, the only verdict could be "not proven." There was to be no opportunity, however, to test the permanent value of the changes effected in our national economy under normal conditions of growth and development. The course of domestic progress was rudely interrupted by the outbreak of war in Europe. The nation was soon to be engaged in an all-out program of national defense to meet the challenge of foreign aggression. Its resources were to be mobilized for the single purpose of meeting as grave an emergency as the country perhaps ever faced, and an entirely new direction was given to events as the New Deal was compelled to turn from a peacetime to a wartime economy.

21

Relief and Reform

"Work Must Be Found . . . "

As THE RECOVERY PROGRAM was getting under way in the spring of 1933, the New Deal also took up directly the problem of relief for the unemployed. Roosevelt's ideas were at the opposite pole from those of Hoover. "While it isn't written in the Constitution," he said on one occasion, "nevertheless it is the inherent duty of the Federal Government to keep its citizens from starvation." And no matter what the cost, no matter what the effect upon the budget, the New Deal was prepared to provide the funds to fulfill this duty. Pledges of economy went completely by the board as continued unemployment involved the Government in heavier and heavier relief expenditures. Moreover, while there were many shifts and changes in the approach to this most difficult of issues, the emphasis was placed increasingly upon work relief rather than an outright dole. The obligation to prevent people from starving was translated into an obligation to provide them with work.

The President declared in his annual message to Congress in 1935:

> We have a human problem as well as an economic problem. When human considerations are concerned, Americans give them precedence. The lessons of history, confirmed by the evidence before me, show conclusively that continued dependence upon relief induces a spiritual and moral disintegration fundamentally destructive to the national fiber. To dole out relief is to administer a narcotic, a subtle destroyer of the human spirit. It is inimical to the dictates of sound policy. It is in violation of the traditions of America. Work must be found for able-bodied but destitute workers.

The establishment of the Civilian Conservation Corps was the first measure in the relief program. It provided for the enrollment for six-months periods of young men, unmarried and between the ages of eighteen and twenty-five (later changed to between seventeen and twenty-three), for reforestation work, erosion and flood control, road-building, and other land improvements. A quarter of a million were quickly accepted, largely drawn from the army of jobless youth who had neither homes nor occupation, and they were put to work for a dollar a day and their keep. The experiment proved to be one of the most successful made by the New Deal, both in the aid afforded this group of the unemployed and in the social value of CCC projects. At one time enrollment reached five hundred thousand, but the average remained between two hundred and fifty thousand and three hundred thousand. Before appropriations were cut off in 1942, over two million men and boys had served in CCC camps scattered from Maine to California, from Oregon to Florida. They had planted more than two billion trees, constructed one hundred and twenty-six thousand miles of minor roads and trails, and generally improved four million acres of forest stands.

Only a small fraction of the unemployed were aided in this way, however. A more comprehensive undertaking was the establishment of the Federal Emergency Relief Administration. It operated through the agency of states and local governments, but unlike the procedure followed by the Hoover Administration in extending limited loans, the FERA was authorized to make direct federal grants from an original appropriation of five hundred million dollars. The local governments were expected to match such contributions in so far as they could, and either through work relief or direct home relief expend these funds to prevent actual want and suffering. Under the administration of Harry L. Hopkins, the FERA sought to co-ordinate the activities of the various local governments under this program, and to allocate the available money on the most economic basis.

When the states found themselves increasingly unable to do their part in matching federal funds, local committees gave up the more expensive but socially valuable work relief and resorted almost entirely to the dole. As an admittedly temporary measure, until a more satisfactory solution for the problem could be worked out, Congress consequently established in October, 1933, a Civil Works Administration. Functioning under the direct control of the FERA, and with funds made available through additional federal appropriations, this new agency was to provide work relief to take the place of a dole.

The CWA soon had over three million persons on its rolls. Men were put to work at any job which local authorities could invent or improvise. The latter were under the handicap of being unable to furnish adequate materials or equipment, and consequently landscaping roads and highways, general repair work, and minor improvements on public buildings were about all that could be done. Thousands of men were given tasks which had little practical value, for which they were ill-suited, and which seldom inspired them to any real effort. This was the leaf-raking era of the relief program, the disheartening days of what came to be called "boondoggling." Some nine hundred million dollars was spent in the sorry six months before the CWA was abandoned. Under the circumstances it had proved fully as demoralizing to those employed as an outright dole, and it awakened a storm of public criticism which saw little in the experiment but a careless waste of public funds.

In the meantime, the FERA had undergone a thorough reorganization. It was prepared to substitute for the CWA a revised system of grants-in-aid to the states. Local governments were to be encouraged to provide made-work opportunities more socially valuable than leaf-raking and landscape gardening. Administrative procedure was tightened up, eligibility for employment given more careful consideration, and both working conditions and relief wages subjected to closer supervision. Where there appeared to be no alternative, the FERA continued direct relief, and it also undertook to distribute food and supplies to the needy, and to set up transient camps throughout the country to provide shelter for some three hundred thousand homeless men.

The continuance of the depression through 1934 and into 1935 did not make the task any easier. The failure of recovery meas-

ures to bring about any substantial reduction in unemployment
and the exhaustion of the private funds of those who had been
long out of work progressively increased the burden the Federal
Government had assumed. As hard times hung on, provision for
the unemployed began to take on the aspects of a permanent
problem. Again it became necessary to reorganize the system and
seek a solution which could somehow meet the essential needs of
the unemployed, maintain morale, and keep costs as low as possible. Two classes of relief recipients were now recognized. Direct relief was to be continued for the unemployables, those who
could not work because of age, physical disability, or some other
definite cause. They were to be taken care of by the states, with
financial assistance from the Federal Government, ultimately giving way to nation-wide social insurance. For those whose unemployment resulted from the temporary inability of industry to
give them jobs, work relief was to be provided directly by the
Federal Government on a broad, comprehensive scale.

The agency established to carry out this new program in the
spring of 1935 was the Works Progress Administration. With
huge additional appropriations, amounting in 1935 and 1936 to
some $4,800,000,000, it developed a program of public works,
distinct from that of the Public Works Administration itself, to
give immediate jobs and promote projects that were of real social
value. Moreover, these new government activities were not to
compete with private enterprise, and whenever practical they
were to be developed with the idea of eventual recovery of the
funds expended on them. Every effort was also to be made to
initiate projects which would supply employment not only for
industrial workers, but for technicians, professional men and
women, white-collar workers, and unemployed youth.

The WPA now embarked upon an ambitious course which
touched every phase of the national life. Under its auspices over
one hundred thousand different projects were undertaken during
the next five years. Their scope was almost limitless. The WPA
built the great Triborough Bridge in New York, and it published
a series of guidebooks for every state in the Union. It constructed
thousands of miles of concrete highway and sponsored the paint-

ing of almost as many miles of murals in post offices and other public buildings throughout the country. It built sewage and drainage systems for urban communities from the Atlantic to the Pacific; it established a Federal Theater which produced its plays before nation-wide audiences of twenty-two million. It constructed bridges, schoolhouses, airports, public utility plants, parks, playgrounds, golf courses, tennis courts and swimming pools. It promoted adult education, vocational training, and public health. All in all, it took over some eighty per cent of those formerly on relief, and before its final liquidation in June, 1944, it had provided employment for 8,500,000 persons and expended nearly $13,000,000,000.

Construction activities were the most important phase of the WPA program. It built over 650,000 miles of surfaced roads and 78,000 new bridges; it constructed more than 35,000 public buildings and renovated another 90,000. Airplane landing fields, to a total of 373, became an increasingly important item on the program as time went on, and on the other hand some 10,000 tennis courts and 1600 swimming or wading pools were built in public parks. The entire country was marked with the handiwork of the WPA. The new highways, bridges, sewage systems, schoolhouses, and recreation centers were permanent and valuable contributions to community life throughout the country. They represented, entirely apart from their rôle in providing employment, a material increase in the nation's social resources directly benefiting all classes in society.

From one point of view, the innovations sponsored by the WPA through its writers', art, music, and theater projects were of greatest interest. Unemployed authors, painters, sculptors, musicians, and actors found a new scope for their energies as well as financial support for themselves and their families. The results were not always commensurate with the assistance given by the Government, but work of enduring value was done in many instances. The historical guides were a real contribution to popular knowledge of the country, while the extensive cataloguing of public records was a great boon to scholarly research. The Federal Theater proved to be a notable artistic success, some of its productions winning highly enthusiastic critical acclaim. The intangible results in the field of art and music, both in encouraging artists and in stimulating popular appreciation of things of the spirit, can hardly be measured. A National Youth Administration, whose activities fell within the general WPA program, also performed a highly useful purpose in aiding students and providing them with the work opportunities which enabled them to carry on their studies through college and postgraduate work.

The obverse side of this comprehensive program was its tremendous cost. It was criticized on other counts. Not all its projects were valuable, and all too often the work supplied was far too reminiscent of the CWA. The morale of these job-holders was consequently sometimes low — the WPA could not wholly escape the stigma of relief — and when this was the case, the result was inefficiency and loafing. The program also became on occasion a football of partisan politics. While no national scandal developed, local Democratic politicians sometimes used WPA employment as a means of controlling the vote. Nevertheless, it was the great expense of not only providing wages for these millions of government employees, but of supplying the necessary material and equipment for construction projects, that became the most important point of attack on the WPA. For while every effort was made to enlist the financial support of local governmental units, with a complicated system of loans as well as direct grants, the Federal Treasury could not escape bearing the major part of the burden.

The conservative opposition to the New Deal condemned such expenditures out of hand as monumental waste. Business interests favored a direct dole as cheaper than work relief wherever aid could not be avoided, and they doubted the value of the WPA in maintaining national morale. The shifts and changes in the relief program as a whole from the FERA to the CWA, back to the FERA, and then on to the WPA, were singled out as proving the inept floundering of the Roosevelt Administration. "As each of the alphabetical organizations flares up in folly and waste," former President Hoover said, "its victims and accounts have been buried by juggling of the alphabet. When they are all

buried their spirit will live on as IOU." And again in scorn of
what he considered the pauperization of the nation, he declared
that we were "becoming a nation of prayer wheels directed to
Washington."

The peak for all public assistance and of total numbers employed on the federal work program was reached in March, 1934.
In that month over seven million families, involving twenty-six
million persons, were receiving direct aid in one form or another.
One-fifth of the entire population of the United States, that is,
was at least in part dependent on the Federal Government. There
was some decline in relief demands during the next few years,
but these figures were again approximated, as a result of the recession, in the autumn of 1938. Almost one-half of those being
aided on this latter date were on WPA. The load carried by this
agency came to more than three million persons, and while it was
progressively lightened in 1939 and 1940, there were still over a
million WPA workers when the United States entered the war in
December, 1941.

The swollen rolls of relief organizations and of the WPA were
a demonstration of the New Deal's success in fulfilling its pledge
to keep American citizens from starvation and to provide them
as far as possible with work. They were at the same time the
measure of its failure to stimulate such a degree of economic
recovery as might have enabled private industry to solve the unemployment problem at its source. Even the most severe critics
of New Deal policy, fulminating over the expenditure of so many
billion dollars in relief, could not, however, deny the responsibility of the Federal Government to meet the problem.

BANKING AND SECURITIES

The reform program of the New Deal, in somewhat arbitrary
distinction to the interrelated measures looking primarily toward
recovery and relief, had a broad and comprehensive sweep. Protection of the rights of labor and the provision of maximum hours
and minimum wages were made a function of the Federal Government. The regulation of the stock market and control of se-

curity issues were promoted through establishment of the Securities and Exchange Commission. Various efforts were made to provide low-cost housing and cheap electric power for the masses of the people. A highly significant experiment in water-power control and social planning was launched by setting up the Tennessee Valley Authority, and through this latter agency, as well as the AAA and many of the projects of the CCC and the WPA, the old movement for conservation of the nation's natural resources was revitalized. And finally, the New Deal adopted a comprehensive system of social security involving nation-wide unemployment insurance and old-age pensions.

In substance, these various measures were an attempt to meet, through the powers of the Federal Government, wherever state and local governments were unable to act effectively, the challenge of "a third of a nation ill-clad, ill-housed, ill-nourished." The New Deal committed itself to "nation-wide thinking, nation-wide planning, nation-wide action," when confronted with the old problem of progress and poverty in our industrial civilization. "Democracy assures that the gains of civilization are essentially mass gains . . . " stated a report of the National Resources Board. "Nation-wide planning should be directed toward this end. . . . We do not stand at the end of a worn-out road, but look forward down a broad way to another era of American opportunity."

To the whole question of labor under the New Deal, we shall return in another chapter. Among other reforms, almost the first to which the Roosevelt Administration turned its attention was control over financial operations. No drastic change was sought in the country's banking system. Although there was a demand in some quarters for the assertion of a greater degree of government regulation, the Banking Act of 1933 was a moderate and conservative bill. It ordered the member banks of the Federal Reserve System to divest themselves of their security affiliates, and compelled private bankers to choose between doing a deposit or an investment business. The Federal Reserve Board was given power to restrict credit for speculative uses, and a Federal Deposit Insurance Corporation was established to guarantee all bank deposits up to a maximum of five thousand dollars. Through these provisions a curb was placed upon speculative operations on the part of the banks and individual depositors were assured of the safety of their funds.

Equally important was the passage of the Securities Act in May, 1933, and of the Securities Exchange Act in June, 1934. These two bills, based upon the new principle of "let the seller beware," sought to protect the public from ever again being drawn into such a speculative orgy as that which had led to the market crash of 1929. The disclosures of a Senate investigating committee in 1932 had clearly revealed the need for government controls. The way in which banks and investment houses had unloaded worthless stocks and bonds on a gullible public, manipulated security prices in order to encourage further speculation, and subordinated sound investment practice to win quick profits from a rising market made sensational reading. "The only thing some of our great financial institutions overlooked during the days of boom," the columnist Heywood Broun wrote, "was the installation of roulette wheels for the convenience of depositors." Even Wall Street was prepared to admit that the exchanges should be licensed and the issuance of new securities more closely regulated in the public interest.

The two new measures specifically outlawed certain forms of stock manipulation popular during the nineteen-twenties, established new rules for the purchase of stocks on margin, and granted the Federal Reserve Board control over brokers' loans. They also set up very definite regulations in regard to the information which should accompany every flotation of new securities, with heavy penalties for any fraudulent or untrue statements. Enforcement of these regulations and control over security markets were delegated to the Securities and Exchange Commission.

In pursuit of another important New Deal objective, the authority of the SEC was extended in 1935 to include the regulation of public utility holding corporations. This new development was the result of passage of the Public Utility Act in August of that year, one of the most hotly contested of all New Deal laws. The President had long warred against the practice of pyramiding in the power industry whereby control over a vast network of widely scattered operating units was concentrated in a single holding company. The owners of $600,000,000 in stock, in one instance, had full direction of corporations whose securities totaled $13,-000,000,000. It was "a ninety-six-inch dog being wagged by a four-inch tail," Roosevelt declared.

While in some instances holding companies could effect important economies, they more generally milked the operating subsidiaries for the benefit of their own stockholders. The principal purpose of the Public Utility Act was consequently to compel the holding companies to limit their control of subsidiaries to "a single integrated public utility system." It also sought to provide for strict regulation of the interstate transmission of electric power. On this latter issue there was already provision for some control under the terms of the Water Power Act of 1920, authorizing the Federal Power Commission to license and regulate power plants on navigable streams. The new law was designed to strengthen a measure, which had proved in practice to be largely ineffective, by broadening the Federal Power Commission's authority.

Representatives of the electric light and power industry, which had campaigned vigorously, and successfully, throughout the nineteen-twenties against any further regulation by the Federal Government, descended upon Washington in outraged wrath when the holding company bill was first introduced. Terming its chief provisions a "death sentence," which in destroying holding companies would destroy the industry, they deluged the country with propaganda and waged one of the fiercest pressure group campaigns the country had ever witnessed. While they succeeded in securing minor modifications of the bill, it was finally passed with its regulatory provisions intact, and the SEC was empowered to supervise the vast financial reorganizations prescribed for breaking up the holding companies. Enforcement of the law was for a time bitterly contested, but after a long-drawn-out court battle the Supreme Court finally upheld it, and practical measures were eventually agreed upon by the SEC and leading public utilities to carry out its provisions. An important reform in the interests of lower light and power bills for the consuming public was gradually effected during the following years.

The Tennessee Valley Authority

The Tennessee Valley Authority, established in 1933, had a far broader scope than any of this legislation. It was in the first instance an agency empowered to produce, distribute, and sell electric power to be derived from the impounded waters of the Tennessee River. Its activities also embraced, however, flood control, irrigation of submarginal lands, reforestation, and the prevention of erosion. It promoted conservation on an all-inclusive scale. Moreover, there were even more far-reaching implications to the TVA. "What we are doing there," President Roosevelt stated, "is taking a watershed with about three and a half million people in it, almost all of them rural, and we are trying to make a different type of citizen out of them from what they would be under their present conditions. . . . So TVA is primarily intended to change and improve the standards of living of the people of that valley."

The New Deal had followed President Hoover's lead at Boulder Dam by undertaking in other parts of the country the construction of several gigantic hydroelectric power plants, notably those at the Grand Coulee and Bonneville Dams on the Columbia River, and the Fort Peck Dam on the Missouri River. The TVA was an experiment in social planning in which the construction of dams, reservoirs, and power plants on the Tennessee River was only a starting point. Where Senator Norris had pointed the way with his original proposal for government ownership and operation of power and nitrate plants at Muscle Shoals, the New Deal did not merely follow, but pushed on far ahead.

Few aspects of New Deal policy, indeed, illustrate more vividly the change in viewpoint between the Hoover Administration and the Roosevelt Administration. It will be recalled that Hoover, following an example already set by Coolidge, had in 1931 vetoed the Muscle Shoals Bill introduced by Senator Norris. In the strongest possible terms he condemned the entry of Government into the field of ownership and operation of public utilities as breaking down the initiative and enterprise of the American people, destroying equality of opportunity, and denying the ideals upon which American civilization was based. "I hesitate to contemplate the future of our institutions, of our country," Hoover had declared in his veto message, "if the preoccupation of its officials is to be no longer the promotion of justice and equal opportunity, but is to be devoted to barter in the markets. That is not liberalism, it is degeneration." Yet here was the Federal Government, upon congressional authority and with the subsequent approval of the courts, embarking upon a program that contemplated not only ownership and operation of a power plant, but embraced far more ambitious plans for economic reconstruction and for the conservation of land.

The program entrusted to the TVA — actually a board of three members — contemplated, then, the economic and social rehabilitation, on a long-range scale, of an area of some forty thousand square miles impinging upon seven states: Tennessee, Kentucky, Alabama, Mississippi, Virginia, North Carolina, and Georgia. This was a territory rich in natural resources, but unusually backward in its development. Its inhabitants were poor and unenterprising. The TVA undertook to sell them inexpensive electric power through a program of rural electrification, to aid them in improving their land, and to provide them with cheap fertilizer. In addition, it planned to promote public health and education, build low-cost housing for its own employees, and develop an extensive recreational program. The facilities of the controlled Tennessee River were to be used "to release the energies of the people."

The TVA was soon successfully launched on this great experiment. It proceeded, with the aid of funds from the Public Works Administration, to build a series of dams on the Tennessee and its tributaries, of which perhaps the Norris Dam was the most notable, with the multiple purpose of improving navigation, providing flood control, and generating electric power. The market for such power steadily broadened as this program progressed, and the TVA, in addition to sales to private industry, extended its power lines throughout the Tennessee Valley.

Through such lines and the distributing facilities of municipalities and co-operatives, 450,000 customers were by 1940 being served with electric current for farm and household uses. In comparison with a national consumption average of 850 kilowatt hours a year at a cost of about $36, consumers in the Tennessee Valley used an average 1179 kilowatt hours at an annual cost of little more than $25. While electrification was the most conspicuous feature in the rise in the standard of living throughout the area, the conservation and social rehabilitation program as a whole held out even greater promise for the future.

The apparent practicality of such social planning led President Roosevelt in 1937 to recommend the creation of seven other public agencies in different parts of the country with comparable functions. Congress refused to grant him the necessary authority. The opposition of conservative business interests, stirred to revolt by the electric light and power industry, had made itself felt too strongly. They aggressively combated any further extension of governmental activity in the public utilities industry, or further experiments in what they called socialistic planning.

The public utilities also had another grievance. In its own sale of power, the TVA had established a "yardstick" that could be used for regulating the rates of private companies. The latter charged that these rates were entirely unfair, inasmuch as the TVA obtained its capital from the Government and was exempted from taxes. A developing quarrel over this issue in the Tennessee Valley itself was settled when the TVA bought out the private companies in the area it served. The larger question, nevertheless, remained of whether the competition of Government in the production of power, with its exacting yardsticks for rate regulation, would not discourage private capital from entering the public utility industry as a whole.

Every attempt to revive the idea of new regional power projects was consequently attacked as a threat to general economic recovery. Wendell L. Willkie, then head of Commonwealth and Southern, the company whose properties had been sold to the TVA, made himself spokesman for the power interests and campaigned against further government entry into business. It was a first step, he declared, toward socialism. While the TVA went vigorously ahead with its own program, further experiments along these lines were effectively blocked.

Low-Cost Housing

The need for adequate housing for the American people — still another important objective of the New Deal — was repeatedly emphasized by President Roosevelt, and various attempts were made to meet it. They had not made very much headway before attention was diverted from the long-term problem to the more immediate task of providing dwellings for munitions workers in the mushrooming wartime industries which grew up after 1940. Very little more can be said of achievement in this field than that the New Deal pioneered in what was for the Federal Government an entirely new undertaking.

To protect existing home-owners, and also to meet the more general problem of mortgage debt, several measures were taken comparable to those adopted to assist farm-owners. The most important was the creation of the Home Owners Loan Corporation in 1933. In three years it granted loans totaling three billion dollars to more than a million home-owners whose mortgages might otherwise have been foreclosed. To encourage further building, a Federal Housing Administration was also set up in 1934. It undertook to underwrite new mortgage loans through providing insurance on approved properties up to eighty per cent (later ninety per cent) of the value of land and buildings.

These agencies did not, of course, touch the real problem — housing for the low-income groups. There was no question whatsoever of the appalling shortage of decent, safe, and sanitary dwellings for the wage-earners of urban communities. To provide them, however, involved, first of all, slum clearance. Private industry could not undertake such wholesale operations; municipalities often lacked the necessary financial resources. It was felt to be a responsibility which only the Federal Government was in a position to undertake. The original public works program included slum clearance and low-cost housing, but little progress was made in this direction by the PWA itself. Finally, in 1937, Congress passed a National Housing Act to provide federal loans, under the supervision of a United States Housing Authority, for the construction of model tenements. Monthly rentals in these new housing developments, it was expressly stipulated, should be kept sufficiently low to allow occupation of the new homes by the dispossessed dwellers of the slums torn down to make way for them. By June, 1941, the USHA had approved loans totaling seven hundred million dollars in some two hundred and fifty communities in thirty-four states and some seventy thousand homes in low-cost apartment projects were in actual occupation. Upon the outbreak of war, provisions of the original law, and also available funds, were expanded to meet wartime housing needs. Until this emergency forced further action, little more than a start had been made toward meeting a problem which remained one of the most distressing consequences of too rapid urbanization. The economic difficulties of slum clearance and low-cost housing appeared almost insoluble. Public opinion needed to be awakened by some new Jacob Riis who could successfully dramatize the battle of the slums.

Social Security

A final reform — and perhaps in some ways the most important achievement of these years — was the passage in 1935 of the Social Security Act. It had three major provisions. A system of old-age and survivors' insurance was established, provision was made for unemployment compensation, and public assistance grants to the states were authorized for an eight-point program of social welfare. The lastnamed included aid for the needy aged and blind, for dependent children, and for the crippled and disabled. There was also assistance for maternal and child health services, for child welfare, for rehabilitation of the disabled, and for public health. Viewed as a whole, the law's various features were an attempt to provide social security for wage-earners and the underprivileged throughout the nation. Other countries had long since adopted such measures. The United States was merely catching up with the trend of the times. While the methods adopted for carrying out the program, and especially those for financing it, were sometimes subject to sharp criticism, public opinion generally applauded. The provision of social security was accepted as an essential function of Government in an industrialized society.

The old-age pensions set up by the new law were to be administered solely by the Federal Government, while unemployment compensation was to be undertaken by the states with federal supervision. In the case of the former, the permanent plan provided for building up an insurance trust fund in the Federal Treasury to which both employers and employees were to make annual contributions. They were to be on an equal basis, starting at one per cent of the employee's wages in each case and rising gradually to three per cent after 1948. Annuities were to be paid to the insured after the age of sixty-five.

The unemployment compensation scheme was more complicated. The Federal Government placed a tax upon all payrolls, rising to three per cent, but ninety per cent of the revenue went to the states if they adopted insurance programs which met federal specifications. Although only Wisconsin had unemployment compensation at the time, every state soon complied with these provisions of the law and the program went into immediate nation-wide effect. The details of the various state plans varied somewhat, but benefit payments to laid-off workers were generally based upon the length of time they had been employed and the amount of their wages. The whole program was to be administered by a newly constituted Social Security Board.

In 1943, old-age assistance payments were being made to some two million persons; and in the old-age insurance program, $155,-000,000 was paid out to 750,000 beneficiaries. Forty million workers had wage credits under state unemployment compensation plans; total unemployment benefits paid out since they first went into operation amounting to more than two billion dollars. Comprehensive as this program appeared to be, agricultural workers, domestic servants, and various categories of salaried employees were not included. Congress failed to respond during the pre-war years to presidential suggestions that it should be enlarged. Nor was any action then taken to provide any scheme for health insurance.

The New Deal reform program was building for the future. The importance of this legislation adopted during the nineteen-thirties lay not so much in its immediate effect upon the social and economic system as in its possible long-term consequences. Each step along the path had been strongly opposed by conservatives. The Securities and Exchange Commission, the Tennessee Valley Authority, the United States Housing Authority, and the Social Security Board had each in turn run the gantlet of violent attack. There was occasional ground for the criticism leveled at both the laws setting up these agencies and at their administration. As pointed out in another connection, the legislation of the New Deal was enacted hurriedly. It sometimes attempted to do too much in too short a time. The newly created agencies were also handicapped by a lack of experience in their work and by the want of trained personnel. With the terrific expansion of governmental functions, some bureaucratic inefficiency was inevitable.

It was significant, however, that as time went on, the attacks directed against New Deal reforms were concentrated more and more on administration rather than on objectives. Even conservatives, by the close of the nineteen-thirties, had generally accepted new departures in governmental activity which had been anathema to them at the beginning of the decade. However critical the opposition might be of the Roosevelt Administration itself, there was no real demand for abandoning crop controls, security exchange regulation, unemployment work relief, or social security. These immensely important New Deal innovations gave every indication of having been accepted as a permanent part of the American system.

The Rise of Labor

New Deal Policy

AMONG the various social developments to which the New Deal gave a fresh impetus, none was more important than the growth of the labor movement. When Roosevelt came into office union membership was estimated at somewhat less than three million; eight years later, on the eve of entry into the second World War, it was well over ten million. Approximately one quarter of the country's industrial workers were organized.

These figures tell only a part of the story. The labor movement had lost its driving force during the nineteen-twenties. The contentment born of prosperity on the one hand, and the effective anti-unionization campaign of industry on the other, left the movement in an almost helpless position when the depression suddenly struck such a devastating blow at the earnings and employment of industrial workers. A generally conservative leadership did not know which way to turn. In 1941, organized labor was a powerful, aggressive, dynamic force. Although its ranks were split by the rivalry between the A.F. of L. and the C.I.O., it exercised a tremendous influence in the life of the nation. Its power in certain respects appeared to rival the power once wielded by industry. No single question in the sphere of domestic policy had a greater significance, nor awoke more impassioned controversy on the part of the public, than where labor was headed and what its rôle in our national life was going to be.

The principal factor in this remarkable change was the friendly attitude consistently shown toward labor by the New Deal. The Roosevelt Administration was the first one in our political history to accept the underlying thesis of the labor movement. It acted upon the principle that only organized workers could deal on equal terms with organized industry in bringing about a proper balance between these two rival forces in a capitalistic society. Consequently, it not only passed legislation directed toward the maintenance of higher wages and shorter hours, together with provision for social security, but, more important, it recognized and upheld labor's right to organize and bargain collectively as vital to the national economy.

Theodore Roosevelt had pioneered thirty-odd years earlier in insisting that capital should give labor a square deal. Franklin D. Roosevelt would have enabled labor to obtain a square deal in its own right. His critics felt that he went much farther than this. They believed he had weighted the scales in labor's favor even more drastically than previous administrations had weighted them in behalf of industry. The occasional turbulence in industrial relationships was held to be a consequence of his policies. The President's answer was that labor was experiencing its growing pains. Only in exercising power could it learn the necessity of social responsibility.

Joseph W. Madden, chairman of the National Labor Relations Board, stated:

> Let the employer make known by word and conduct to his workers that they have the right to organize and meet without interference, that any employee may act like a man and take a man's part in the determination of his affairs, and sound leadership will inevitably emerge. If this be not a sound prediction, the whole basis of American democracy is false.

Despite this attitude on the part of the New Deal, however, there was a growing trend on the eve of our entry into the second World War to curb the powers and privileges accorded labor. The principle of collective bargaining — although it was by no means universally accepted by all employers — had been too firmly established to be overthrown. There was also general recognition of the right to strike as the only effective means whereby workers could uphold their end in coming to terms with management. But it was strongly felt in many quarters that unions should be subjected to strict regulation in order that they should not attain such dominance in the political and economic life of the country as to be able to defy the democratic will. In redressing the balance which in the years of *laissez-faire* had so greatly favored capital, many persons warned, the country should not allow the unions to become the irresponsible and uncontrolled units within the state which the trusts had been before the Federal Government took up the cudgels against industrial monopoly.

Unions of Their Own Choosing

Although President Hoover had summoned labor leaders to Washington in that first series of conferences in 1929 in which he hoped to exorcise the depression, we have seen that agreements upon the necessity of maintaining employment and wages had quickly broken down. Men were soon being laid off in every industry; pay checks steadily dwindled. The elaborate profit-sharing schemes and welfare programs that had grown up during the nineteen-twenties collapsed almost overnight. Hard-pressed employers resorted to the stretch-out, sweatshop practices, and child labor in frantic efforts to reduce their own costs. Their persistent campaign for the open shop and adoption of "yellow-dog contracts," whereby workers were pledged not to join trade unions, made impressive headway as the army of unemployed gradually swelled to immense proportions. Labor was so completely on the defensive that it could not protect its own interests. The membership of the American Federation of Labor, already down to 2,770,000 in 1929, dropped by almost half a million in the next four years.

The only gain which could be recorded in the workers' favor — and virtually the only one since the first World War — was passage of the Norris-La Guardia Anti-Injunction Act in 1932. The continued failure of labor to obtain the protection against the use of injunctions in industrial disputes promised by the Clayton Act had progressively intensified the demand for new legislation. The new bill finally set up safeguards closely restricting the use of injunctions, providing jury trial in cases arising from contempt of court, and outlawing yellow-dog contracts. It also laid down certain general principles in respect to labor relations which were of the utmost significance. The second section of this measure (passed the year before Roosevelt came into office) read:

> Whereas, under prevailing economic conditions . . . the individual unorganized worker is commonly helpless to exercise actual liberty of contract and to protect his freedom of labor, and thereby to obtain acceptable terms and conditions of employment, wherefore, though he should be free to decline to associate with his fellows, it is necessary that he should have full freedom of association, self-organization, and designation of representatives of his own choosing, to negotiate the terms and conditions of his employment, and that he shall be free from the interference, restraint, or coercion of employers of labor, or their agents, in the activities for the purpose of collective bargaining or other mutual aid or protection. . . .

Although President Hoover accepted this statement, it was left to the New Deal to build upon its assumptions. Under Section 7A, the National Industrial Recovery Act for the first time definitely obligated employers to acknowledge their employees' right to bargain collectively through representatives of their own choosing. Hailed as "a new Magna Carta" by President William Green, of the A.F. of L., this provision of the new law gave a great impetus to unionization. Organizers went on the warpath. Making the most of the idea that the President wanted all workers to join a union, they rapidly began to regain the ground lost during the nineteen-twenties. Before the end of 1933, charters were granted to some seven hundred federal unions, many of them in industries where there had previously been no locals. Total membership in the A.F. of L. rose to over four million.

It was not all clear sailing, however. Employers soon began to show their hostility to the movement. Aside from other weapons to combat further unionization, they sought to forestall the A.F. of L. organizers by forming their own company-controlled unions. Labor's answer was to go out on strike in industry after industry to force recognition of genuine collective bargaining. There

were strikes in textiles, work stoppages in the automobile industry, and a general strike in San Francisco. Industry fought back,
and these strikes, poorly organized, were quickly crushed. It was
a turbulent period — strikes involved more workers than in any
previous year since 1919. With the National Labor Board set up
under the NRA lacking any power for effective enforcement of
the guarantees of Section 7A, labor began to lose confidence in
the new program. When a nation-wide strike among steel workers
was threatened, Congress finally felt compelled to provide more
effective machinery for overcoming mounting industrial strife.

In June, 1934, it authorized, through passage of the Labor
Dispute Joint Resolution, the creation of labor boards empowered
to investigate disputes between capital and labor and conduct
elections to determine the representation for bargaining agencies.
A National Longshoreman's Board was set up to deal with a
strike among waterfront workers on the West Coast; a National
Steel Labor Relations Board was established in the hope of preventing conflict in that industry. Finally, the old National Labor
Board was replaced by a National Labor Relations Board. By
this time, however, the NRA was beginning to break down all
along the line. Within a few months it was to be declared unconstitutional. The New Deal's first attempt to handle industrial
relations came to an end with labor fully aroused and aggressively determined upon more effective means for enforcement
of its rights.

The next step was the passage by Congress in July, 1935, of the
National Labor Relations Act, sponsored by Senator Wagner of
New York. This measure reaffirmed the labor objectives previously sought in the National Industrial Recovery Act; workers
were again guaranteed the right to organize and bargain collectively. Far more significant, employers were specifically forbidden to interfere with labor's exercise of these rights, to dis-
criminate against union members in any way, to support company
unions, or to refuse to bargain collectively. The stated purpose
of the bill was to allay industrial strife by restoring equality of
bargaining power between employers and employees. Its privileges were admittedly in the interest of labor; its restrictions imposed solely upon capital.

To enforce the law a new National Labor Relations Board of three members, perhaps the most important of the New Deal's quasi-judicial administrative agencies, was granted authority to prevent any person "from engaging in any unfair labor practice affecting commerce." The specific duties of the NLRB were to supervise the elections whereby workers designated the unit appropriate for collective bargaining, whether an employer, craft, or plant unit; to enforce the provisions against any employer interference in such elections, and to hear and act upon any complaints that the workers might bring against their employers. It was authorized to issue cease-and-desist orders enforceable in the courts. The NLRB was not concerned with the adjustment of industrial disputes which might develop over conditions of employment. That was left to agencies of arbitration or conciliation. Its primary function was to establish collective bargaining on a permanent basis.

Passage of this act was stubbornly fought by industry; its constitutionality was widely questioned. Many employers refused to accept it until it was finally upheld by the Supreme Court in a decision definitely affirming its principles. Collective bargaining, Chief Justice Hughes now stated emphatically, was "a fundamental right." Freed from the injunction suits which had paralyzed its activities, the NLRB thereupon vigorously proceeded to business. It supervised union elections in thousands of plants, intervened in innumerable disputes where unfair labor practices were charged, declared the use of labor spies and formation of vigilante groups illegal, and sought generally to enforce industry's compliance with the provisions of the Wagner Act.

The Board was attacked during the next five years for partiality, a pro-labor bias, and for exceeding its authority. The fact remained, however, that the majority of the twenty-seven thousand cases involving unfair practices brought before it between 1935 and 1940 were settled without prejudice to the interests of industry. Almost half of them were disposed of through mutual agreement between the disputants, over a quarter of them were withdrawn by the unions, and seventeen per cent were dismissed. Only eight per cent reached the stage of an official hearing.

While the workers were upheld in some two-thirds of the last-named cases, this meant that the NLRB took action against employers on only five per cent of the total number of complaints brought before it.

Moreover, in those cases which were appealed to the courts, the NLRB was largely successful in having its powers confirmed. In the first sixteen cases reaching the Supreme Court, it was overruled on only four occasions. Legal sanction was obtained for the disestablishment of a company union, for forbidding interference with peaceful picketing, and for the legality of the closed shop. The conservative press continued to emphasize the NLRB's occasional failures and to underscore those instances where the courts declared it had exceeded its authority, but the new body of administrative law governing labor relations which it built up was an outstanding achievement.

While the Wagner Act and the activities of the NLRB were the most important expression of New Deal friendliness toward labor, they do not tell the whole story. The Walsh-Healey Public Contracts Act and the Fair Labor Standards Act, to which reference has already been made, were more in labor's interests than any laws heretofore passed by either a state government or the Federal Government. The Social Security Act was also labor legislation. In its relief policies, the New Deal showed a consideration for industrial workers which was something new in our national history, and it consistently sought to maintain prevailing wage standards in the work provided through the WPA. Labor stood to profit by these various measures. Its status was greatly improved. While it remained true that unemployment was a threat to the security of the industrial worker which was hardly compensated by anything the Government did to uphold his position, impressive gains were made during the nineteen-thirties in higher wages, shorter hours of work, and better working conditions. At the end of the decade, the index of average weekly earnings in all manufacturing industries stood at 93.8 in comparison with 68.3 in 1933. Work hours per week had fallen to an average of 37.6.

THE CHALLENGE OF THE C.I.O.

The increase in union membership during the period in which Section 7A of the National Industrial Recovery Act was in force was primarily the fruit of organizing activity on the part of individual unions. It had been most noted in certain of the mass-production industries. So-called industrial unions increased their membership by some 130 per cent in comparison with a gain of only 13 per cent in craft unions. The United Mine Workers, under the aggressive leadership of John L. Lewis, made spectacular gains. In 1935 it could count five hundred thousand members as compared with perhaps a fifth of this number three years earlier. There were also large increases in the International Ladies' Garment Workers, under David Dubinsky, and in the Amalgamated Clothing Workers, whose guiding spirit was Sidney Hillman. As a result of this advance on the part of a few industrial unions in comparison with the lack of organization in so many mass-production industries, a restive, insurgent bloc developed within the ranks of the A.F. of L. which charged that its leadership was not taking full advantage of the pro-union sentiment fostered by the Roosevelt Administration.

The A.F. of L. was conservative, slow-moving, and accustomed through its experience of the nineteen-twenties to working in close collaboration with employers. Furthermore, its whole policy, as a consequence of the conditions which had originally given rise to its formation, was predicated on the importance of craft unions as distinct from industrial unions in the continued growth of the labor movement. Whatever validity its theories might once have had, the insurgents felt that they were outworn. John L. Lewis and those who followed his lead insistently stressed the tremendous importance of the masses of workers in the new manufacturing industries who were not yet organized and who could be organized effectively only on industrial rather than craft lines. The A.F. of L. was passing up its greatest opportunity, it was charged, by failing to gather in the full harvest which awaited aggressive leadership in these fields.

At the Federation convention in 1934 a group of leaders representing industrial unions — which constituted almost a third of the total membership — demanded a change in policy. John L. Lewis was the leader of this group. His success in building up the United Mine Workers, largely through the force of his own dynamic personality, enabled him to speak with authority. A violent dispute was precipitated by his demands, but it was finally agreed that the A.F. of L. would grant new charters for industrial unions at the discretion of the executive committee, and "at the earliest possible date inaugurate, manage, promote, and conduct a campaign of organization in the steel industry."

But nothing happened during the following year. The A.F. of L. executive committee was largely dominated by leaders of the building-trade unions. Their interest was in organization along craft lines. They did not think in terms of industrial unions on a nation-wide basis — or rather, many of them considered labor's growth along such lines a threat to the influence of their own unions and their own vested interests. When the A.F. of L. met in 1935, they forced adoption of a report declaring it to be the duty of the executive committee to protect the jurisdictional rights of craft unions by promoting the accession of new members rather than by encouraging the formation of additional industrial unions.

Such a policy was at once vehemently attacked by the insurgents as blindly stubborn if not wholly obstructive. Without wishing to cut into the membership of any union, they insisted upon unrestricted charters which would override traditional craft barriers and "guarantee the right to accept into membership all workers employed in the industry." When their demands were rejected after a bitter debate, enlivened when the belligerent Lewis sought to emphasize his arguments with his fists, nine of the insurgent leaders in November, 1935, organized the Committee for Industrial Organization. With funds amounting to five hundred thousand dollars provided out of the exchequer of the United Mine Workers, the C.I.O. at once set up a Steel Workers' Organizing Committee, under the chairmanship of Philip Murray, and prepared to launch its own unionization campaign.

This was open revolt within labor's ranks. Early in 1936 the

A.F. of L. executive committee consequently summoned the ten unions which had in the meantime become affiliated with the C.I.O. and ordered them to show cause why their charters should not be suspended. Defiantly standing their ground under the leadership of Lewis, they refused to answer this summons, and when duly suspended took no part in the A.F. of L.'s next annual convention. This body upheld the suspension of the C.I.O. unions by a vote of 21,679 to 2043 and declared it should remain in force until "the breach be healed and adjusted under such terms and conditions as the executive committee may deem best." The A.F. of L. and the C.I.O. declared open war. The former took the necessary steps definitely to expel the dissident unions and the latter was reorganized on a wholly independent basis as the Congress of Industrial Organization. At the very time when the opportunity for a united labor movement was greater than ever before, its councils were divided and its energies dissipated in fighting among its own divergent elements.

While the nominal cause for the split was the issue of industrial unionism versus craft unionism, this was in many ways a sham battle. The formation of the C.I.O. represented a revolt on the part of a more aggressive, more radical group of labor leaders against the conservatism of firmly entrenched old-line trades-union politicians. The insurgents sought to invigorate the labor movement and compel it to take more forward-looking action. Both William Green of the A.F. of L. and John L. Lewis of the C.I.O., moreover, craved the power that triumph for their particular cause would mean, and found it impossible to divide the glory. Both men were labor politicians who had made their way up from the ranks through the United Mine Workers. Green was conservative, tenacious, middle-class-minded, and given to preaching and moral exhortation. Lewis was brilliant, ambitious, and self-assertive, reveling in the spotlight. There was a clash of personalities quite as much as a clash of principles.

The C.I.O., in any event, was prepared to seize every opportunity to build up its own strength. The bulk of its original membership of about a million was in the United Mine Workers, the International Ladies' Garment Workers, and the Amalgamated

Clothing Workers. It pushed militantly ahead into other mass industries — particularly steel, automobiles, textiles, radio, lumber, transportation, and rubber. A campaign was also started to organize various groups of white-collar and professional workers, attaining its greatest success with the accession of the American Newspaper Guild. By the end of 1937, that is, within two years of its formation, thirty-two national and international unions, claiming a total membership of almost four million, were affiliated with the C.I.O. and it was still expanding. Moreover, it played an active part in politics, and Lewis was instrumental in organizing Labor's Non-Partisan League to marshal support for Roosevelt and the New Deal.

While the A.F. of L. continued to maintain a more local point of view in union activities and adhered strictly to the policy of not entering directly into politics, it accepted the challenge of the C.I.O. Traditional organizing activities were revitalized by competition. The strength of existing unions was built up, and the efforts of the C.I.O. to monopolize unionization in the mass industries was hotly contested. The gains of the A.F. of L. were by 1937 at least sufficient to compensate for loss of the expelled unions, with total membership well over three million.

The most sensational developments in the feverish labor activity of 1936 and 1937, however, were the victories won by the C.I.O. in the automobile and steel industries. Under the leadership of Homer Martin, the United Automobile Workers of America established a membership of four hundred thousand and secured collective bargaining agreements with all but one of the important automobile manufacturers. The Steel Workers' Organizing Committee, still under the direction of Philip Murray, obtained more than five hundred thousand members. While it failed to win over those companies comprising "Little Steel," an epochal agreement was reached with the United States Steel Corporation. These victories were not won without virulent opposition and they afforded dramatic evidence of labor's newfound strength.

The campaign of the automobile workers led to a series of unusual strikes which first broke out in December, 1936, in the

General Motors Corporation's plants at Detroit. The workers did not walk out and attempt to establish picket lines in the traditional fashion. They adopted a new weapon which had been introduced by strikers in the rubber industry. They sat down by their machines and refused to leave the plant. The employers at once obtained court injunctions against the sit-down strike, but the workers resisted every attempt of local authorities to have them thrown out. With employees virtually besieged, employers clamoring for state troops to storm the plants, and frequent clashes between strike sympathizers and the police, the situation in Detroit became increasingly tense. Governor Frank Murphy of Michigan — later Justice Murphy of the Supreme Court — nevertheless refused to allow the use of state troops and he was upheld by President Roosevelt in his efforts to avert violence and bloodshed. Few strikes have ever attracted greater public attention. Conservatives everywhere denounced what they termed the surrender of the forces of law and order before the threats of a handful of striking workmen, but Governor Murphy stood his ground.

The result was a triumph for the strikers after a forty-day shutdown. General Motors recognized the United Automobile Workers as the bargaining agency for all employees in its plants, and concluded a contract governing wages and hours. Soon afterward another sit-down strike on the part of Chrysler employees again attracted nation-wide attention and fears of violent strife. But that company too was soon forced to surrender. The Ford Motor Company alone among the Big Three in the automobile industry stood out. The United Automobile Workers failed to take this redoubtable fort and not until 1941 did it finally capitulate. Henry Ford then suddenly gave in, granting the union even greater concessions than it had demanded. He not only recognized it as the bargaining agent for all Ford workers, but he signed a closed-shop contract.

The major victory of the Steel Workers' Organizing Committee was an entirely peaceful one. In March, 1937, the entire country was astounded by the announcement that the United States Steel Corporation, which since its formation had been one of the most implacable foes of labor organization, had agreed to recognize the union and granted a forty-hour week and ten per cent wage increase. The importance of allaying a growing discontent among its employees was the apparent cause for a complete shift of policy, and within a short time some two hunded and fifty smaller companies, bringing the number of workers affected up to more than three hundred and fifty thousand, also fell into line.

The "Little Steel" group, composed of the Bethlehem, Republic, Inland, and Youngstown Sheet and Tube Companies, nevertheless obdurately refused to recognize the Steel Workers' Organizing Committee, or to negotiate with it on any terms. As chief spokesman for these intransigent corporations, President Girdler of Republic, one of the arch opponents of the New Deal and of what he regarded as its dangerously radical pro-labor policies, defied the steel workers to do their worst. His attitude paralleled that which George F. Baer had maintained in the coal strike which had called forth another Roosevelt's intervention thirty years earlier. A complete reactionary in his views, he was no more prepared to accept labor's right to collective bargaining than the industrial barons of 1900. The result was a strike in May, 1937, involving some ninety thousand workers in an atmosphere so embittered that violence was inevitable.

Strike-breakers were called in by the steel companies, vigilante groups organized to break up picket lines, and every possible weapon employed to intimidate the workers. As protection was generally given the companies by the local authorities, the strikers found themselves almost helpless. On Memorial Day pickets at a plant of the Republic Steel Company in South Chicago clashed with the police. Shots were fired, and when the sudden battle ended, ten of the strikers were dead and many more injured. Only three of the police were minor casualties. The strike dragged on for almost two months after this massacre, in which the brutality of the police was later condemned by a Senate investigating committee, but in July the steel workers were forced to accept defeat. It was a Pyrrhic victory for Little Steel, however. After its powers to enforce labor's right to collective bargaining had been upheld by the Supreme Court, the National

Labor Relations Board ordered the companies involved to reinstate the strikers whom they had dismissed and to enter into collective bargaining negotiations.

COMMUNISM AND STRIKES

The militant tactics pursued by the C.I.O. unions, dramatized by the strikes in steel and automobile factories, placed the whole labor question very much in the forefront of public interest during 1937. The sympathy shown the unions by the New Deal, and the active support they in turn gave President Roosevelt, created among conservatives a growing fear of labor dominance over national politics. Under such circumstances, industry undertook to fight further unionization harder than ever, and, as later disclosures of the Senate Committee on Civil Liberties revealed, many employers did not wait for the outbreak of strikes to attempt to crush labor's growing power. They employed spies, at a reported cost of hundreds of thousands of dollars, to ferret out every instance of union activity before it could assume formidable proportions. They formed strong-arm squads to discourage labor organizers by physical intimidation, the Pinkerton detective agency alone furnishing over three hundred operatives who joined the unions they were hired to break up, in some cases being elected to posts of official responsibility. In short, the provisions of the Wagner Act were openly defied. "It is those shortsighted ones, not labor," Roosevelt declared in a vigorous attack upon employers who refused to accept collective bargaining, "who threaten this country with the class dissension which in other countries has led to dictatorship."

In their propaganda to enlist public support for their antiunion campaign, one powerful weapon used by employers was to charge that the labor movement, or more particularly the C.I.O., was communistic. There was little ground for this accusation. The Communist Party in this country, supposedly acting upon orders from Moscow, was attempting to bore from within in the C.I.O. and in some instances it made sensational inroads upon union membership. It had introduced its agents into positions of authority in half a dozen of the more important unions in 1937, including the United Automobile Workers, the Transport Workers, the Maritime Union, and the State, County, and Municipal Workers. There was strong Communist influence in the American Newspaper Guild. However, the rank and file of the C.I.O., no less than the membership of the A.F. of L., were basically conservative in their views upon democratic capitalism. A militant left-wing minority was able to exercise an influence out of all proportion to its numerical strength. This group was firmly welded, disciplined, experienced, and energetic. It was prepared to follow the Communist Party line, however erratic it might prove to be. The interest of Moscow in this period was the creation of a united front against fascism. Communists — or more accurately Stalinists — could consequently work their way into posts of importance by shelving at least for a time their revolutionary aims.

There was no more sympathy for communism among the responsible leaders of the C.I.O. — Lewis, Hillman, and Murray — than among the rank and file. Their objective was a powerful labor movement which would be able to protect the interests of the workers through both union activity and political influence. They had no sympathy with any move to undermine either the economic or political basis of American society, and at the close of the nineteen-thirties a vigorous housecleaning was started to free the C.I.O. of all taint of communism. Popular fears of radical infiltration within labor's ranks nevertheless strongly reinforced a nation-wide drive on the part of business leaders to curb labor's growing power and combat the closed shop.

The interests of unions affiliated with the A.F. of L. were endangered by these new attacks quite as much as the interests of C.I.O. unions, but the two national organizations still failed to unite in any common defense of labor's rights. Jurisdictional quarrels of rival unions increased rather than subsided, and strikes grew out of such internal controversies quite as much as from labor-capital disputes involving union recognition or collective bargaining. A natural result of this bickering and disunity, with the cleavage between the A.F. of L. and the C.I.O. steadily widening, was the weakening of control in some union locals. This in turn led to further wildcat strikes, and in some instances to union racketeering which discredited the whole labor movement.

In recognition of the importance of labor unity to industrial relations, efforts were consequently made, with the support of President Roosevelt, to bring the A.F. of L. and the C.I.O. together. Their strength had become relatively equal, each organization claiming some five million members, and the original cause for their dispute had largely lost even the semblance of reality. The A.F. of L. was freely granting charters to industrial unions, and the C.I.O. afforded a hospitable welcome to craft unions. With no substantial differences in principle to prevent a reunion, the only thing which appeared to stand in the way was the ambitious rivalry of their respective leaders. Yet every move toward reconciliation failed. The stubbornness of William Green and the pugnacity of John L. Lewis, neither man at any time showing any desire to bury the hatchet except in his rival's head, continued to block all hope of labor peace.

That Lewis at least was driven by political ambition rather than concern over the best interests of labor soon appeared to be confirmed by an angry break with President Roosevelt. Incensed over what he considered the President's failure to live up to promises made in return for C.I.O. support in the presidential election of 1936, the stormy petrel of the labor movement transferred his political allegiance to the Republicans, and as a threat to hold his followers in line, he declared that he would resign the chairmanship of the C.I.O. should the President be re-elected.

When the Democrats were returned to power in 1940, he fulfilled this pledge, and Philip Murray, head of the Steel Workers' Organizing Committee and his closest collaborator, succeeded him. For a time it was thought that Lewis's stepping down would have a calming effect upon the labor world. Yet it was perhaps inevitable that he was soon quarreling with Murray, and in embittered resentment took the United Mine Workers, for so long the mainstay of the C.I.O., out of this organization he had himself originally formed.

Labor politics had indeed reached a new high of confusion by 1941. The combined strength of the movement had never been more formidable, but it appeared to be hopelessly split among rival factions. The majority of individual unions were pursuing constructive policies which had enabled them to reach collective bargaining agreements to the mutual interest of both employers and employees. Nevertheless, this substantial progress toward allaying industrial strife and improving the status of workers everywhere was overshadowed by the angry recriminations of labor leaders, violent jurisdictional strikes, and occasional highly publicized exposures of union racketeering and graft.

The campaign of industry to restrict labor's power took every advantage of public apprehension over these developments. Further concessions on union recognition were condemned. The closed shop was bitterly attacked as undemocratic and un-American. As the national defense program which had been adopted after the fall of France in 1940 led to increased production and rising employment, the stage consequently was set for a battle royal in which labor sought to promote still further the gains already made, and industry undertook to hold the line or whittle away such gains.

The result was a wave of strikes. The most dangerous of them grew out of the refusal of the National Defense Mediation Board, set up to handle disputes in defense industries, to grant a union shop in the coal mines of the great steel companies. It was eventually settled through arbitration granting the miners' demands, but not until the controversy had caused the collapse of the National Defense Mediation Board. A nation-wide railway strike was also threatened and averted only at the last moment; building-trade workers went out in many parts of the country, and a strike by a handful of electricians in Kansas City completely blacked out that city for a few hours. In all, there were over three thousand strikes, involving two million workers, in the first nine months of 1941.

Actually these work stoppages were far more spectacular than serious, and the number of man-hours of work lost was relatively small. Employees as a whole remained on the job. But the public grew alarmed and the clamor for anti-strike legislation assumed formidable proportions. Labor was losing public support and the New Deal was itself being attacked more fiercely than ever for such admittedly one-sided legislation as the National Labor Relations Act. Anti-labor laws had been passed in twenty-two states and more than thirty comparable bills had been introduced in Congress, ranging from measures for the incorporation of unions to the outlawry of all strikes on defense projects, when the United States suddenly found itself at war.

Politics and the Supreme Court

THE ELECTION OF 1936

IN THE MIDSUMMER of 1936 — a presidential campaign year — the New Deal stood on trial for the first time before the bar of public opinion. There had been sufficient time for the American people to have gained a good idea of how President Roosevelt was playing his cards. What had the New Deal achieved in its zealous pursuit of relief, recovery, and reform? What did the country want as it stood at this periodic crossroads in its political history?

The program for relief was in full swing following the reorganization marked by establishment of the Works Progress Administration, and there were almost two and a half million men at work on government projects throughout the country. The New Deal had made good its pledge of seeing to it that in one way or another people got jobs — even if it had to be made-work. The cost, however, had already proved staggering. Expenditures for the fiscal year 1936 on the entire recovery and relief program amounted to $3,441,000,000, and of this total almost forty per cent was allocated to the WPA. The public debt had already risen to over $33,005,000,000 — approximately fifty per cent higher than when Roosevelt first came into office. Economy and a balanced budget had been ruthlessly sacrificed to fulfill the obligation of direct care for the unemployed.

In so far as recovery was concerned, the summer found indices of production moving steadily upward. Fortunately for the Democrats, there was as yet no sign of the "recession" which in another year was to wipe out so many of these gains. It was true, as previously noted, that the capital-goods industry, and especially construction, were lagging in this upward march. The failure of new investment issues to materialize was a discouraging sign whose significance Wall Street recognized more than other parts of the country. Still, business was making profits, farm income had notably risen, and wages for industrial labor enjoyed a considerable gain. Although full confidence in the permanence of this improvement was still lacking, the country as a whole was clearly far better off than it had been in 1933.

The situation in regard to the reform program was more confused. The basic measures proposed by the New Deal had been passed. There had been placed on the statute books of the nation not only the laws establishing the AAA, the NRA, the TVA, and the WPA, but also the Securities and Exchange Act, the National Labor Relations Act, the Public Utility Act, and the Social Security Act. The Supreme Court, however, had shown little sympathy for the expansion of governmental functions which these measures represented. It placed a chill restraint upon the whole program of reform.

The first Agricultural Adjustment Act and the National Industrial Recovery Act had been declared unconstitutional. Approval had also been refused for a farm mortgage act, a measure providing pensions for railway employees, an act designed to stabilize conditions in the coal industry, and a municipal bankruptcy act. The gold devaluation program had in the main been sustained, the TVA had been at least partially upheld, and a railroad bankruptcy act approved, but this still meant that in the ten most important cases involving New Deal legislation, the Supreme Court had rendered seven verdicts of unconstitutionality. The fate of other basic laws, including the National Labor Relations Act and the Social Security Act, had not yet been decided and hung dangerously in the balance. To this whole issue we shall return. It suffices to say at this point that in its major aspects the New Deal reform program, whatever the public's reaction to it, appeared to be blocked by the courts.

This was the general record as the time approached for the Democrats to ask a renewal of their popular mandate. While it was inconclusive in many respects, the party was confident of popular endorsement. The mid-term congressional elections of

1934 had resulted in Democratic gains in both the Senate and the House. With economic conditions even more improved, a still greater majority for the New Deal might be reasonably expected. Moreover, apart from any general approval for the enterprise and initiative the Democrats had shown, other factors of great political import affected the situation. The Roosevelt Administration could reasonably count upon the support of those elements in the population which its policies had definitely and unmistakably aided. It had proved more friendly to labor than any previous administration in the country's history. It had really attempted to come to grips with the problem of agrarian distress and had generously subsidized the farmer. It had provided relief for the unemployed out of the resources of the Federal Treasury. Labor, the farmers, and recipients of relief had a direct stake in the continuance in office of a régime so favorable to their special interests.

At the same time, the opposition to the New Deal from other quarters was so strong, and so articulate, that the preponderance of strength commanded by the Democrats was not fully realized. Business and industry had so often exerted a decisive influence in political campaigns that their almost universal antagonism to Roosevelt was given great weight. Moreover, newspapers generally throughout the country upheld the conservative point of view and perhaps two-thirds of the press was definitely Republican. Insistent and embittered attacks were made by editorial writers upon what was considered the inept bungling of the threefold policy of relief, recovery, and reform. The New Deal was condemned for reckless waste and extravagance, for the growth of a bureaucracy that was attempting to regiment the life of the people, and for such unwarranted interference with business and industry that all confidence was destroyed and full recovery seriously hampered. And finally, the general trend of developments in Washington was interpreted as revealing a growing disregard of constitutional restraints that could only end in the establishment of a political dictatorship.

Party lines were often crossed in the fury of conservative attack. The anti-New Dealers drew their support from old-line Democrats as well as traditional Republicans. The Liberty League, spearhead of the drive to overthrow the New Deal, included such one-time Democratic leaders as Al Smith and John W. Davis — former presidential candidates. And they were flanked by an impressive array of business executives, Wall Street lawyers, and William Randolph Hearst.

Former President Hoover had also returned to the political scene to make some of the most scathing attacks ever directed against the New Deal. Everything that he had feared would happen once the Democrats were in power, Hoover told his audiences, had actually taken place. They had failed to meet the problems confronting the country, and yet, in their futile attempts to do so, they had sacrificed the liberty of the American people. The former President stated solemnly:

> In the last campaign we charged these men with the intention to introduce these foreign creeds of Regimentation, Socialism, and Fascism into America. They denied it. No proof is needed after three years of these attempts at so-called Planned Economy; this government in business; this breaking down of constitutional safeguards; this reduction of Congress to a rubber stamp; this substitution of personal government of men for government of laws; and these attacks upon the Constitution.

The Republicans were nevertheless confronted by a difficult problem as the time came to open the presidential campaign. It was one thing to condemn the New Deal, but it was quite another to offer a constructive alternative to its policies. After declaring "America is in peril," the platform adopted at the party convention offered little to avert such peril. It favored state administration of relief, enforcement of the anti-trust laws, a return to high-tariff protection, and compacts among the states for the social legislation that the Supreme Court had declared to be beyond the province of the National Government. These proposals were pallid and unexciting, but even more disturbing to Republican followers was the lack of effective leadership in the high command.

The nomination finally fell to Governor Alfred M. Landon of Kansas, with Colonel Frank Knox, at that time publisher of the

Chicago Daily News and subsequently wartime Secretary of the
Navy, as his running mate. Landon was known as a liberal, but
he lacked any effective driving force. During the campaign he
allowed himself to become the mouthpiece of many of the more
reactionary elements in his party, and his own somewhat vague
and colorless personality made very little impression upon the
public.

The Democrats had no doubts or hesitation when their nominating convention met. Having approved a platform that was a
paean of praise for New Deal achievements, they enthusiastically
renominated Roosevelt without a dissenting voice. "The issue in
this election is plain," it was confidently proclaimed. "The American people are called upon to choose between a Republican administration that has and would again regiment them in the service of privileged groups and a Democratic administration dedicated to the establishment of equal opportunity for all our
people." On the vexed issue of the Supreme Court's rejection of
New Deal legislation, the Democratic platform rather cautiously
called for a clarifying amendment that would open up the road
to further social advance.

As the campaign progressed, Republican charges of dictatorship, demagogy, and communism leveled against the New Deal
crackled with anger. So sharp a division of opinion developed
along class lines that attack and counter-attack took on a virulence
going back to the disturbing days of 1896 when conservatives had
feared social revolution. The well-to-do, especially in the cities
and suburbs of the East, became more and more incensed at what
they considered Roosevelt's betrayal of the interests of his own
class. An aristocrat and beneficiary of inherited wealth, he had,
in their opinion, abandoned everything in American society for
which he should have stood, to curry favor with the mob. In
private, if not in public, few epithets were spared in denunciation
of "that man in the White House."

Roosevelt was prepared to strike back at his critics with a
vehemence corresponding to that of their attacks upon him. "The
economic royalists complain that we seek to overthrow the institutions of America," he had declared in accepting renomination.

"What they really complain of is that we seek to take away their power. Our allegiance to American institutions requires the overthrow of this kind of power." As the personal attacks upon him multiplied, he carried the war even more directly into the enemy camp. In a memorable speech delivered at New York's Madison Square Garden at the close of the campaign, he lashed out at his political foes with unexampled scorn and defiance:

> We had to struggle with the old enemies of peace — business and financial monopoly, speculation, reckless banking, class antagonism, sectionalism, war profiteering. They had begun to consider the Government of the United States as a mere appendage of their own affairs. We know now that Government by organized money is just as dangerous as Government by organized mob. Never before in all our history have these forces been so united against one candidate as they stand today. They are unanimous in their hate for me — and I welcome their hatred.

With an election in which the lines were so heatedly drawn between the privileged and the underprivileged, the record of the New Deal gave the Democrats a tremendous advantage and the probable result was foreshadowed with increasing clarity as the campaign went on. Nevertheless, few other than James A. Farley, the Democratic campaign manager, who predicted the outcome with uncanny accuracy, foresaw the full extent of the victory that Roosevelt was to win. For the Democratic landslide in 1936 exceeded anything in our history for at least a century. Only two states — Maine and Vermont — remained in the Republican column. Roosevelt's popular vote was 27,477,000 to Landon's 16,-680,000, and the Democratic majority in both houses of Congress was so great as to be unwieldy. Although a new radical third party was in the field, made up of the followers of Father Coughlin and Doctor Townsend, it polled less than 900,000 votes for its candidate, Representative William Lemke of North Dakota. Norman Thomas, Socialist, received only 188,000 votes, and Earl Browder, Communist, 80,000. The left-wing dissent to the New Deal, that is, was almost negligible. Possibly the country as a whole was still more skeptical of the Republicans and fearful of a return to the policies of the nineteen-twenties, than it was enthusiastic over all phases of the Democratic program. But Roosevelt had won overwhelming popular endorsement.

The Constitutional Issue

In his second inaugural, the President reaffirmed a promise already made in his speech accepting renomination. The struggle against want and destitution and economic demoralization, the fight to preserve the American form of government, he declared, must go on until final victory was fully assured. And he was enlisted for the duration. While little stress was laid upon what was to become the outstanding political issue of the next few months, the Supreme Court was obliquely warned on its attitude in invalidating New Deal legislation. "The progress of our democracy," the President said, "must not be imperiled by the denial of the essential powers of free government."

The judicial issue was not a new one in American politics. Virtually every strong executive had sooner or later found himself in conflict with the courts. No one had taken a more radical stand against what he considered the encroachments of the judiciary upon the powers of the other two branches of government than Theodore Roosevelt in his advocacy of the recall of judicial decisions. The situation in 1937, however, was perhaps more critical than in any previous period of our history — except that following the Dred Scott decision. For there appeared to be little question that a conservative majority of the Supreme Court was determined to block New Deal reform, not so much on constitutional grounds as because of a convinced opposition to the economic and social theories these reforms embodied. In almost every one of the more important cases in which the Court had ruled against the New Deal, the decision had been reached by a closely divided vote. Justices Van Devanter, McReynolds, Sutherland, and Butler were found invariably in opposition to the new legislation; Justices Brandeis, Stone, and Cardozo were prepared to accept the greater part of it. Chief Justice Hughes and Justice Roberts occupied a middle-of-the-road position. How the last two decided had become the determining factor in a succession of five-to-four and six-to-three decisions.

Roosevelt had hit out angrily when the Supreme Court, in this instance in a unanimous decision, invalidated the National Industrial Recovery Act in May, 1935. It had been declared unconstitutional in *Schechter Poultry Corporation v. United States*, on the double grounds of an improper delegation of legislative power to the Executive and, more significantly, as going beyond the powers of the Federal Government over interstate commerce. "Does this decision mean that the United States Government has no control over any national economic problems?" the President asked in one of his press conferences. " . . . We have been relegated to the horse-and-buggy definition of interstate commerce."

As the Court then went on to tear down other laws, he became more and more convinced that it stood as a barrier to the expressed will of the people. "A dead hand was being laid upon this whole program of progress — to stay it all," he later wrote. "It was the hand of the Supreme Court of the United States."

The laws providing pensions for railway employees and regulating the coal industry were both declared unconstitutional as exceeding the powers of Congress under the commerce clause. The former was said to involve merely the social welfare of the worker and was "therefore remote from any regulation of commerce as such"; the latter set up controls over what the Court declared to be in effect a local industry. Striking even more directly at the New Deal program, the six-to-three decision, invalidating the AAA in *United States v. Butler et al.*, stated that the regulation of agriculture was the sole concern of the states, and that the processing tax was unwarranted as being "a mere incident" to the Administration's farm program rather than a *bona fide* revenue measure.

Finally, the Supreme Court handed down, in June, 1936, a decision which seemed to reveal even more directly the conservative viewpoint of the court majority. Once again dividing five to four, it declared a New York minimum-wage law unconstitutional in *Morehead v. New York ex rel. Tipaldo*, on the old grounds of violation of liberty of contract. This decision appeared to establish what Roosevelt called a no-man's land where apparently no government could operate, *laissez-faire* receiving a new and unexpected lease on life.

The idea that the Supreme Court was expressing in these decisions political or economic views, rather than juridically interpreting the Constitution, gained nation-wide currency, not only from the almost invariable conservative-liberal line-up on the bench, but from the vigorous dissenting opinions. In his dissent in the case rejecting the Agricultural Adjustment Act, Justice Stone referred to the majority's "tortured construction of the Constitution." In the New York minimum-wage case, he even more pointedly expressed his doubt as to any basis for the decision "other than our own personal economic predilections." When the railroad pension decision was handed down, Chief Justice Hughes himself not only dissented but bluntly characterized the majority opinion as "a departure from sound principles" and "an unwarranted limitation upon the commerce clause."

Under such circumstances, the need for some action to free social legislation from the restrictions under which it was laboring became almost universally recognized. The Democratic platform in 1936, as already noted, called for a clarifying amendment to the Constitution which would redefine the powers of the National Government over interstate commerce. Other proposals were also put forward with the idea of somehow curbing or limiting judicial review, to the end that it might be made more responsive to popular opinion. It was suggested that more than a Supreme Court majority be required to invalidate congressional legislation, and that Congress should be given the right by a two-thirds vote to re-enact any statute that the Court had disapproved. Strong objections were raised against all such plans, and only one thing seemed clear: something had to be done if the New Deal program, endorsed by the indisputable mandate of the presidential election, was not to be further held up or perhaps permanently sidetracked.

President Roosevelt had given no hint of what he might have in mind along these lines, when, early in February, 1937, he startled the country by unexpectedly sending a message to Congress in which he recommended a drastic reorganization of the entire federal judiciary. His proposal, which was to become known during the following months of feverish debate as the "court-packing plan," provided that whenever a federal judge over the age of seventy did not voluntarily retire, an additional judge should be appointed to aid him in the performance of his duties. The total number of such new judges was not to exceed fifty, with appointees to the Supreme Court limited to six. Instead of candidly admitting that the purpose of the proposed reform was to authorize the appointment of additional justices of the Supreme Court, for six of its members were already over seventy, Roosevelt maintained that the objectives were to invigorate the federal judiciary and enable it to act more efficiently in clearing up an overloaded docket. The recommendation was patently evasive in meeting the issue which had called it forth, as the President himself was later to admit. "I made one major mistake when I first presented the plan," he wrote in 1941. "I did not place enough emphasis upon the real mischief — the kind of decisions which, as a studied and continued policy, had been coming down from the Supreme Court."

A terrific political storm broke out immediately. No earlier proposal by the President, or by any of his predecessors for many years, had created such widespread consternation. The ranks of the New Dealers themselves were shattered. In attacking the Supreme Court, Roosevelt alienated many of his most staunch supporters. Liberal opinion accepted the need for action of some sort, but "packing the court" appeared far too drastic a measure. A constitutional amendment was more widely favored — or even modified recall of judicial decisions. With many of his own friends so vigorously criticizing his program, the attacks by foes of the New Deal rose to a piercing scream of rage. They violently condemned the plan as an attempt to secure executive control of the judiciary. It was an entering wedge to destroy the constitutional liberties of the American people. It was a step toward personal dictatorship.

In one of his most persuasive Fireside Chats, the President sought to defend his plan. He declared that the Supreme Court had been acting, not as a judicial body, but as a policy-making body. Citing Chief Justice Hughes's dictum that "the Constitution is what the judges say it is," he assailed the obstructive rôle of a few men who were reading into that great document what he declared were words and implications that were not there. "We must find a way," he said, "to take an appeal from the Supreme Court to the Constitution itself." He demanded the right — for he had not yet made a single appointment to the Supreme Court — to infuse new blood into its deliberations through the addition of judges with a present-day sense of the country's needs. "This plan," he said, "will save our national Constitution from hardening of the judicial arteries."

As the controversy raged through the country, the Senate Judiciary Committee took up consideration of the proposed bill. But while the President commanded some support from constitutional authorities, as well as among the rank and file of New Deal adherents, it appeared increasingly doubtful if even a preponderantly Democratic Congress would this time follow his lead.

A Battle Lost; A War Won

At this point the Supreme Court itself unexpectedly took a hand in the situation. In a decision announced in March, 1937, upon the constitutionality of a minimum-wage law in the state of Washington, it in effect dramatically reversed the stand it had taken on the New York minimum-wage law. The new legislation was upheld in *West Coast Hotel v. Parrish*. In frank rejection of the earlier principle that such legislation conflicted with liberty of contract, the Court held that "regulation which is reasonable in relation to its subject and is adopted in the interests of the community" did not violate the due-process clause of the Fourteenth Amendment. It was again a five-to-four decision, but the old minority had become the majority through the shift of Justice Roberts into the liberal camp.

This case had far-reaching implications. Far from being an isolated instance of ephemeral liberalism, it marked the beginning of a strategic retreat on the part of the Supreme Court which completely changed the conditions which had called forth the President's proposal. In April, it upheld through a five-to-four decision the constitutionality of the National Labor Relations Act, accepting in *N.L.R.B. v. Jones & Laughlin Steel Corporation* a far broader interpretation of the commerce clause than it had allowed in invalidating the NRA. In May, again dividing five to four, it sanctioned the Social Security Act in *Steward Machine Company v. Davis,* placing a new construction upon the national taxing power as compared with that made in rejecting the AAA. With additional decisions sustaining every other New Deal measure whose constitutionality was under challenge, these startling reversals of opinion swept the ground from beneath the feet of those demanding the Supreme Court's reform. Before a single change had been made in its membership, it had brought itself into harmony with prevailing concepts in regard to social legislation.

"To stay experimentation in things social and economic," Justice Brandeis had long since stated, "is a grave responsibility . . . In the exercise of this high power, we must be ever on guard, lest we erect our prejudices into legal principles." The Supreme Court had apparently remembered this advice, and was finally acting on it.

The immediate change in the position of the Court was primarily due to nothing more nor less than the shift in the views of Justice Roberts, but obviously its new attitude had a more basic significance. The popular endorsement of the New Deal program in the 1936 election may well have exercised a compelling influence in causing it to change its views, and there was also the pressure of the court plan itself. Moreover, the condition in which the country found itself in 1937, with nation-wide strikes threatening even greater social disturbance and a recession looming over the horizon, was convincing evidence that constitutional law might possibly be best preserved by taking public opinion into greater consideration.

It was after these epochal decisions had been handed down that on June 14, 1937, the Senate Judiciary Committee finally made its report on the President's plan. It was an outspoken denunciation. The proposed bill would not accomplish the purposes for which it was framed, the committee stated, and it represented "an invasion of judicial power such as has never before been attempted in this country." In applying force to the judiciary, it would undermine the independence of the courts, make the Government of the country one of men rather than laws, and vitiate every sacred tradition of American democracy. "It is a measure which should be so emphatically rejected," the committee concluded, "that its parallel will never again be presented to the free representatives of the free people of America."

Whatever the force of this indictment — and it appealed strongly to the country's belief in the inviolability of constitutional law — the reversal of the Supreme Court's attitude had already taken the heart out of the drive for its reorganization. The President stubbornly insisted upon the passage of the bill, but Congress was for once prepared to desert him on a major issue. His plan was stripped of all its essential features. The Judiciary Reform Act as finally passed in August said nothing about the appointment of additional judges and it went no further than to incorporate a number of minor reforms in the lower courts.

If Roosevelt had lost a battle, he had nevertheless won a war. The purpose behind his attack on the courts had been achieved and he considered this victory one of the most important of his domestic achievements, a turning point in modern American history. "I feel convinced," he wrote four years after the event, " . . . that the change would never have come, unless the frontal attack had been made upon the philosophy of the majority of the Court." But might it not have been effected in any event? The President's critics insisted that it was only a matter of time. With a little more patience the crisis could have been wholly avoided. They were convinced that a dangerous threat to our whole constitutional system had been narrowly averted, congressional rejection of the court-packing plan saving the country from a major disaster.

As events soon proved, ironically enough, Roosevelt was also going to have the opportunity to appoint new members to the Supreme Court and thereby definitely secure the victory for liberalism. During the midst of the struggle, Judge Van Devanter, one of the most persistent foes of the New Deal, announced that he was prepared to resign. This would of itself have changed the character of the Court. Whatever else might have happened, the President could have counted upon at last one appointment to reinforce the ranks of those who agreed with his general views on social progress. During the next year, moreover, two further vacancies occurred with the death of Justice Cardozo and the resignation of Justice Sutherland. In 1939, Justice Brandeis retired and Justice Butler died. And two years later, Chief Justice Hughes in turn left the bench while death claimed Justice McReynolds. In the brief span of four years, the President thus had the opportunity to appoint seven new members to the Supreme Court. Justices Stone and Roberts were the sole survivors of "the nine old men" about whose heads had swirled such a raging storm.

Roosevelt filled these vacancies, as his predecessors had before him, with men whose ideas he thought conformed to those of the country as indicated in his own election. They were New Dealers. His first appointee was Senator Hugh Black of Alabama, an outstanding liberal. A brief storm of protest arose when it was dramatically revealed that the new justice had once been a member of the Ku Klux Klan, but on the bench he soon proved himself to be no less a friend of civil liberty than a proponent of social reform. Other appointments were Stanley F. Reed, who had been solicitor general; Felix Frankfurter, of the Harvard Law School; William O. Douglas, who had been head of the Security and Exchange Commission; Frank Murphy, former governor of Michigan; Senator James F. Byrnes, and Robert H. Jackson, the Attorney-General. Upon the retirement of Chief Justice Hughes, the President raised Justice Stone to his high post, while the later resignation of Justice Byrnes brought still another new member to the Court in the person of Justice Rutledge.

The new Supreme Court adhered to the judicial philosophy which had already been demonstrated in the majority shift during the hectic days of the spring of 1937. The viewpoint so long urged by Justices Holmes and Brandeis in the earlier days of the century had now apparently become the basic doctrine in judicial review.

In successive cases, the Court modified the traditional interpretation of due process to sustain the Federal Government's right to regulate hours and wages, accepted so broad a concept of its powers under the commerce clause that virtually all manufacture could be controlled by congressional legislation, gave a new and almost unlimited breadth to its taxing and spending powers, and allowed far greater latitude than ever before to the delegation of congressional authority. Between January 7, 1935, and May 25, 1936, the Supreme Court had handed down in all twelve decisions in which congressional statutes were held unconstitutional. After March, 1937, not a single act of this character was invalidated up to the close of 1944.

There was no breakdown in the principles of constitutional law, however. On the contrary, it was maintained by most authorities that the Constitution had been greatly strengthened. The Supreme Court's new decisions afforded striking proof that it was a body of law fully adaptable to the conditions of modern life. Nor was the authority and prestige of the Supreme Court itself impaired. The skeptics of 1937 spoke of "the switch in time that saved nine." There were to be critics who declared that "what the members of the Supreme Court will do with matters that are laid before them is as predictable, these days, as what a cage of chimps would do with a bunch of bananas." Nevertheless, the new justices soon proved that in bringing the doctrines of the Court "in more substantial accord with the main currents of national life," they had not in any sense diminished the judicial character of the Court's functions.

"Our Constitution is so simple and practical," Roosevelt had himself declared in his first inaugural, "that it is possible always to meet extraordinary needs by changes in emphasis and arrangement without loss of essential form. That is why our constitutional system has proved itself the most superbly enduring political mechanism the modern world has produced. It has met every stress of vast expansions of territory, of foreign wars, of bitter internal strife, of world relations." When the shouting and tumult over judiciary reform finally died down, the opinion he had himself earlier expressed upon the elastic qualities of the Constitution appeared to be fully substantiated.

Even more significant, the struggle emphasized the deep respect in which the great majority of American people held fundamental law. The public reaction to the court-packing plan was an impressive demonstration of the popular determination to uphold and defend our democratic form of government. Authorities agreed that there was nothing illegal in the President's plan. The number of justices on the Supreme Court, as Roosevelt was able to point out, had been changed on previous occasions — under John Adams, Thomas Jefferson, Andrew Jackson, Abraham Lincoln, and Ulysses S. Grant. Nevertheless, the mere suggestion — or suspicion — that the President was attempting to alter the traditional balance in our constitutional system aroused the entire country. The huge majority by which he had been re-elected made no difference. The Government of the United States, the people in effect said through Congress, must be a government of laws and not of men.

POLITICAL SETBACKS

In so far as immediate political developments were concerned, the judiciary struggle had distracted Congress from its normal legislative activity and greatly impaired the President's leadership over the Democratic majorities in both the Senate and the House. There could be no denying his political defeat in the blunt rejection of the packing plan. After summoning a special session of Congress in the spring of 1938, he sought to drive ahead once again with his domestic program, but he could no longer count upon the full support of Congress. Three major laws were passed: the second Agricultural Adjustment Act, the Fair Labor Standards Act, and a new Food, Drug, and Cosmetic Act. On two other important measures, however, the President met defeat.

His proposal for extending the TVA program to other parts of the country, through the development of seven additional regional authorities for water-power development and social rehabilitation, was rejected. A plan for the reorganization of the executive branch of the Government, admittedly long overdue since the creation of so many new administrative agencies, was also effectively sidetracked. A year later a somewhat modified version of the latter bill was accepted. The President was empowered to consolidate a number of overlapping agencies into three major governmental bodies, the Federal Security Agency, the Federal Works Agency, and the Federal Loan Agency. But the memories of the court fight were still too fresh for Congress to sanction any move which could possibly be interpreted as another attempt to give dictatorial powers to the executive branch of the Government.

Roosevelt's political difficulties were aggravated in 1938 by the development of the recession which, as we have seen, cancelled a great part of the economic gains of his first administration. With business opposition to the New Deal further strengthened, the mid-term congressional elections consequently assumed unusual importance. The Republicans felt that their opportunity was now at hand. Their chance to retrieve ground lost since 1932 appeared brighter than at any time during the intervening six years. They hoped to take full advantage of the mounting criticism of the President within his own party, and to enlist the support of anti-New Deal Democrats in building up a congressional majority which would curb Roosevelt's power and call a halt to further social reform. The popular reaction to the court plan appeared to hold out every chance of success for such tactics.

There was also a movement among the more liberal elements in the country, never fully satisfied with New Deal reforms, for the organization of a third party which would bring into common alliance all left-wing forces. Its nucleus was the progressive parties in the Midwest which had been organized by Senator Robert La Follette and Governor Philip La Follette, successors to their father's political power in Wisconsin, and by Governor Benson of Minnesota. To these groups were to be added Labor's Non-Partisan League and the American Labor Party. The former organization had been set up under the direction of John L. Lewis and supported Roosevelt's candidacy in 1936. The latter was an independent party in New York State which had also backed his re-election. Leaders in this movement for a nation-wide farmer-labor party looked to the congressional elections of 1938 to promote their cause, just as the anti-New Deal forces hoped to ensure a firm alignment of conservative Republicans and Democrats.

Roosevelt's answer to this challenge to the political dominance of the Democratic Party was an attempt to transform it into a union of all progressive forces regardless of party label. He sought to drive anti-New Deal Democrats, those whom he described as the "yes, but . . . fellows," into the political wilderness. In a vigorous campaign statement, he called for the election of only those congressional candidates who were pledged to support his policies.

The election took place amid far more popular interest than usually attended a mid-term vote. The issues were clearly drawn. And it resulted in a marked defeat for Roosevelt and the New Deal. The Republicans made striking gains in both the House and the Senate. They elected eighteen governors including those of seven key states — Pennsylvania, Ohio, Massachusetts, Michigan, Minnesota, Wisconsin, and Oregon — where the previous incumbents had been either Democrats or Progressives. And even more significant of the President's loss of prestige, was the re-election of conservative Democrats, including the three Senators whom Roosevelt had openly attacked and whose defeat he had made a test of party loyalty. His attempted purge had succeeded in retiring only a single representative.

The independent progressive cause was also hard hit by the virtual collapse of the movement to form a farmer-labor party. Both Governor La Follette and Governor Benson were defeated in the Midwest, while labor groups in the East failed to maintain the hold upon the electorate which they had demonstrated in 1936. The American Labor Party remained an important factor in New York politics, but even its strength had waned.

The President could no longer count upon a Congress prepared always to follow his leadership. The revolt evident in the defeat of the court plan, of the proposal for further water-power developments, and of the reorganization bill had assumed formidable proportions. As a result, the New Deal was compelled to mark time on additional legislation, finding itself very much on the defensive to maintain gains already made. The disposition of

Congress was to curtail the relief and public works program, limit application of social security, and stringently amend the National Labor Relations Act. Roosevelt only partially succeeded in blocking such moves. He was unable to make any further advance. He felt that Congress tied his hands.

The more conservative attitude of congressional members appeared to reflect a general shift in public opinion as well as political revolt. The sands of social reform were beginning to run low. As at the close of the progressive era, what the country seemed to demand was time to consolidate the gains that had been made. Rather than further experimentation, it wanted greater efficiency and economy in the administration of policies already adopted. As business conditions again improved, it was also fearful of additional legislation which might place a brake upon economic progress.

The implications of these developments upon the coming presidential election became for a time the all-important political topic. With the close of 1939, however, domestic issues were completely overshadowed by foreign policy. The outbreak of European war in September of that year, and the fall of France before the armed might of Hitler's Germany nine months later, subordinated every other aspect of national policy to the needs of national defense. The challenge of war, not relief, recovery, and reform, became the conditioning factor in the election of 1940.

24

American Life: The Nineteen-Thirties

The Spirit of the Times

PLUNGED SUDDENLY AND UNEXPECTEDLY into deep depression, recovering slowly and uncertainly, the American people were sore
beset during the nineteen-thirties. The contrast with the nineteen-twenties could hardly have been more pointed. "In its frus-

tration of passionate world-wide hopes," a magazine contributor wrote on the last day of 1939, "this fourth decade has been one of the gloomiest in modern history." The pinched circumstance of millions of families (one-third of a nation ill-housed, ill-clad, ill-nourished), the army of discouraged WPA workers, and unemployment as a harsh, inescapable fact, indelibly stamped the American scene. How can I get a job? was the somber and sometimes hopeless question asked by each succeeding generation of high-school or college graduates. The goal of the nineteen-thirties was not prosperity and riches, but economic security; not a chicken in every pot, but anything at all in the pot.

A popular song of the nineteen-twenties had been, *My God, How the Money Rolls In*; with the depression it was *Brother, Can You Spare a Dime?* but soon American hope reasserted itself — *Who's Afraid of the Big Bad Wolf?* There were idle machines and idle men, but the spirit of the country rose above misfortune. It had become more serious, it was far more socially conscious; the ballyhoo of the nineteen-twenties was greatly subdued. Nevertheless, during these years the American people found enjoyment and pleasure that gradually lifted the depression blues. They spent an eighth of their entire national income on recreation, proportionately more than ever before in their history. They clung to their automobiles (twenty-seven million passenger cars), continued to go to the movies (nineteen thousand theaters), kept their radios (fifty-two million sets), whatever else the debt collector might cart away. They discovered their back yards for games and gardens, and used what was often an enforced leisure to enjoy more sports.

The nineteen-thirties were the era of plowing cotton under and massacring little pigs, of unemployment and home relief, of embittered labor battles, of lowering foreign skies; they were also the era of miniature golf, streamlining, glamour girls, candid cameras, Mickey Mouse, and swing music. "Dear, tough, hungry, dramatic, aspiring Thirties!" exclaimed a *New York Times* editorial writer, and at their close, as Hitler plunged Europe into war, twenty-six million people crowded the World's Fair in New York to gaze dreamily upon The World of Tomorrow.

URBAN LIFE AND PROGRESS

The growth of population, characteristic of every period in American history, had slowed down somewhat during this decade. The basic factors for this, rather than the depression itself, were the declining birth rate and the drastic curtailment of immigration. While total population in 1940 was 131,000,000, the gain during the nineteen-thirties was just half of that during the twenties. More than ever — despite some movement back to the country — people were concentrated in the cities, one-third of them living in centers of over one hundred thousand. The cities were growing larger and larger, with vast metropolitan areas spreading ever farther into the suburbs. But there was no longer the great concern of the progressive era over the assimilation of the foreign-born. With alien departures approximating alien arrivals, a quite different situation prevailed, and a program of Americanization had led to the naturalization of three out of every five of the foreign-born.

The cities faced a new problem, however, as a consequence of the continued influx of southern Negroes, which had first reached sizeable proportions during the first World War. By 1940, New York had as large a colored population as Arkansas; Chicago more Negroes than Kentucky or Missouri. The problem of race relations had not been solved in the South, and it was becoming acute in some parts of the North. While in the southern section of the country there were still Jim Crow laws, poll taxes, and other instances of discrimination, segregation was also a general rule in northern cities, and occasional race riots challenged the validity of professed democratic principles. As already noted, Negro labor was encouraged to join C.I.O. unions, but the Railway Brotherhoods and many A.F. of L. unions shut it out. On the other side of the ledger, the Negroes themselves were gradually improving their lot, taking advantage of educational opportunities and slowly climbing the economic ladder. Their capabilities were demonstrated in the careers of many of their leaders. Perhaps most notable had been the achievements of Doctor George W. Carver, born in slavery yet becoming one of the nation's foremost agricultural chemists.

General conditions of life in the cities and other smaller communities revealed in scores of ways the material progress that even hard times could not halt. Improvements in public services, at least a beginning in better housing, larger parks, and new boulevards as a result of city planning, and, very often, WPA funds, were to be found throughout the country. And everywhere — in rural areas as well as in towns and cities — the transformation of the American home, first observed at the opening of the century, was proceeding apace.

While the depression slowed down industrial production, it appeared to have speeded up invention. New mechanical aids to housekeeping (prefabricated houses were to have an electrical unit as their core) multiplied on every hand as manufacturers vied to meet the wants of a servantless age. Kitchens were modernized, the old-fashioned cellar was metamorphosed into something new and strange with a playroom and oil burner replacing the coal bin, and the bathroom became more than ever a thing of beauty, the plumbers adding a note of color (and also advertising bathtubs for two) to its porcelain gleam. Air-conditioning, widely used in public buildings, offices, department stores, theaters, was a promise (not entirely fulfilled) for private homes as well.

New materials were introduced in building, in household utensils, and in clothing. Celotex was widely used, stainless steel became commonplace, anything and everything was made of plastics, aluminum tableware was advertised, lastex was developed, packages were wrapped in cellophane, and the zipper conquered all.

Science and invention were also still driving ahead in transportation. The country's thousands of miles of concrete and macadam highways (1,200,000 by 1940) were not only crowded with automobiles, but with trucks and busses. By the middle of the decade, trailers had already appeared upon the scene (some 160,000 by 1937), and it was being predicted that they were the homes of the future. The railroads had awakened to the new need of modern improvements, with streamlining, air-conditioning, reclining seats, and chromium-plated fittings providing new luxuries for passengers in the one-time lowly day coach which rivaled the Pullman cars. The country was still in the depression doldrums, but travel had become *de luxe*.

AVIATION COMES INTO ITS OWN

Of much greater importance were the tremendous strides being made by aviation. It had been steadily going forward in the nineteen-twenties, as demonstrated by record-breaking transcontinental and trans-Atlantic flights. With the aid of government subsidies, air mail had become an important factor in communications and new passenger services were being gradually instituted throughout the country. It was not until the nineteen-thirties, however, that air transportation really came into its own, and flying was accepted as safe and practical by the American public.

Remarkable developments in aeronautical engineering produced giant air transports, carrying from a dozen to twenty passengers, with a cruising speed of two hundred miles per hour. Coast-to-coast travel in overnight sleepers was established, and in the persistent extension of its overseas service, Pan-American Airways reached out from its original sphere of Latin America, first to the Far East and then to Europe. The *China Clipper* successfully completed the first round trip to the Philippines in 1936, and three years later, just on the eve of war, the first trans-Atlantic clippers opened a regular service. By the close of the decade, the record flying time across the continent had been cut to seven hours, twenty-eight minutes, and the globe had been circled in only a few more hours than the days consumed by Jules Verne's hero — around the world by plane, that is, in three days and nineteen hours.

After a flurry over the withdrawal of mail contracts in 1934 had been settled by passage of a new air-mail contract act the next year, services on the country's seventeen scheduled air lines expanded more rapidly than ever. In 1939, they were carrying almost two million passengers over eighty-two million air miles, and a total of over fourteen million pounds of freight and express.

In addition to all scheduled air-carrier operations, sixteen thousand private planes were also reported to be flying over two hundred thousand miles annually. The nation had become air-minded; over the horizon were the bombing raids of the second World War.

INTELLECTUAL TRENDS

Whether advances in science were paralleled by intellectual growth poses an unanswerable question. Gallup poll investigators estimated that of the forty-five million persons who voted in the 1936 election, some forty million read a daily paper. How many went beyond the front-page headlines and the comics, the investigators did not say. Editorials apparently did not carry much weight, but at least somewhat more influential were the comments of the columnists — led by Walter Lippmann, Dorothy Thompson, Westbrook Pegler, and Eleanor Roosevelt.

Old-line magazines of the so-called quality group were giving ground before the immense popularity of such relative newcomers as *Time, Newsweek,* and the *Reader's Digest* (all established in the nineteen-twenties), while an entirely new group of picture magazines was led by *Life* and *Look.* Newsstands also remained crowded with westerns, movie magazines, adventure magazines, confession and true-story magazines, and even crime magazines.

There was no end to the making of books — almost ten thousand new ones being printed each year at the close of the decade. Cheap reprints and popular-priced editions were being sold over drugstore counters as never before, while circulating libraries did a rousing business. The Book of the Month Club and other comparable sales organizations emphasized the vogue for best-sellers.

The significance of what one critic called the "hard, bright, creative spirit" in literature was endlessly disputed in intellectual circles. Were the writers of the nineteen-thirties ignoring primary literature? Were they defeatist in so often stressing the drab and ugly in the American scene? Had they turned their backs on real values and betrayed their responsibility to democracy? What of Ernest Hemingway, John Dos Passos, William Faulkner,

Thomas Wolfe, John Steinbeck . . . ? These were among the giants of the literature of the nineteen-thirties, but, except for *The Grapes of Wrath*, their public remained a relatively limited one. Whether the literary leaders were creating or reflecting a mood of cynicism sometimes seemed a minor point when *Anthony Adverse* soared to the top of best-seller lists and a million persons rushed to buy *Gone with the Wind* within the first six months of publication. Another popular novel, of a great deal more significance and point, was Pearl Buck's *The Good Earth*, largely responsible for its author winning the Nobel prize. Among non-fiction leaders — and their titles reveal their significance — were *How to Win Friends and Influence People*, Dale Carnegie's tract for the times; *Life Begins at Forty*, *The Importance of Living*, and *Wake Up and Live*.

American art had attained real eminence by the nineteen-thirties, and it was characterized by an attempt to depict the American scene and catch the American spirit. Where young artists had formerly either followed traditional academic conventions, or palely reflected the course of French painting from impressionism through cubism and surrealism, the new modern school found both dignity and beauty in regional scenes of the United States and painted faithfully what they saw. Thomas Hart Benton, Grant Wood, and John Steuart Curry are but three names among these distinguished artists, but in interpreting the familiar and the commonplace as they found them in the Mississippi Valley, on the midwestern plains and in the South — the people as well as their background — they gave a new validity to native art.

THE USES OF LEISURE

The rôle of both the moving pictures and the radio in American life became increasingly significant during the years of the depression. Their entertainment value was enhanced in the economic circumstances of the time, and they inevitably had an important influence upon cultural patterns. Extravagant girl-and-music shows, blood-and-thunder melodramas, sophisticated comedies, and slapstick farces alternated on the screen; and popular dance music, soapbox operas, quiz programs, and melodramatic skits over the air. Clark Gable, Bette Davis, James Cagney, and Greta Garbo were among the film stars. Buck Rogers, Uncle Don, Blondie, and the Lone Ranger were popular radio features.

Yet, there were also signs that these amusements were perhaps coming of age. Moving-picture photography had become more artistic, actors and actresses more polished, worth-while stage plays and books were being successfully adapted to the screen. In some few instances, timid experiments were made with films that had some idea of social content, while news reels told vividly and well the story of current happenings. To an even greater degree, the broadcasting of symphonies and opera demonstrated radio's cultural progress, and toward the close of the nineteen-thirties, news commentators began to play an important rôle. Such interpreters of the swift-moving panorama of events as H. V. Kaltenborn and Raymond Gram Swing did much to make the American people aware of the outside world.

If spectator sports were featured in the nineteen-twenties, participant sports enjoyed something of a revival with the depression. At the close of 1937, it was estimated that twelve hundred cities had a total of seventeen thousand acres of parks reserved for athletics. Bathing beaches and swimming pools, baseball diamonds, tennis courts, and golf courses (many of them built by the WPA) had an annual attendance ranging from eight million golfers to an estimated two hundred million bathers. Softball had grown into one of the most popular of all games, women factory workers as well as men taking it up enthusiastically. Bicycling and roller skating were revived. The newest sport was skiing. Only a handful of enthusiasts were skiing in 1930; their number by the end of the decade was perhaps two million.

In other respects the depression had unexpected effects on the uses to which people put their leisure time. An almost universal urge to try to get something for nothing appeared to sweep over the country. The game of bingo flourished (one church making the startling announcement of "Bingo Every Night in the Holy Spirit Room"); slot machines and pin-ball games were estimated to draw annually five hundred million dollars in nickels from an ever-hopeful public; the movies added bank nights to the extra attraction of double features; the radio introduced scores of prize contests, and the numbers racket fleeced hundreds of thousands of small-scale gamblers.

In quite the opposite direction, hard times promoted a back-to-the-country movement and emphasized the delights of the simple life. Many people tried to get away from it all. Abandoned farmhouses ("charming colonial ten-room house, gravity water system, two open fires") were sold on a rising market to discouraged bankers, brokers, and business executives.

The habits of at least a part of the nation had been changed by the Twenty-First Amendment — repealing prohibition. The bootleggers, rum-runners, and speakeasies of the nineteen-twenties disappeared as control over the sale of liquor was returned to the states (eighteen of them establishing government monopolies), and drinking became respectable. There was no return to the saloon, and little evidence of any increase in drunkenness. Perhaps the most remarkable change since pre-prohibition days was that the new bars and cocktail lounges welcomed women as freely as men. Drinking as a pastime broke down the barriers of sex, at least in urban circles, as had so many other recreational activities. That the country as a whole was satisfied with repeal appeared to be shown by a favorable vote of two to one in a 1940 Gallup poll.

Ragtime — jazz — swing! Young America, and sometimes middle-aged America, was still caught up in the dance craze. The new generation went in for jam sessions, and by way of truckin', the Big Apple, and the shag, finally arrived at jitterbugging. In 1938, some twenty-three thousand enthusiasts were on hand for a Carnival of Swing at Randall's Island in New York; players in the twenty-five bands assembled for the occasion had to have police protection. Benny Goodman was the King of Swing, but there were also Tommy Dorsey, Artie Shaw, and Duke Ellington. "Hot" bands in hotels and night clubs, radio dance orchestras and juke boxes throughout the land paved the way for the triumphs of boogie-woogie.

The fashions of the nineteen-thirties, after a period in which skirts again fell demurely to just above the ankle, found freedom and glamour marching hand in hand. "Back to curves and hips and bustles," the experts called. "Back to the frankly feminine figure." Advertisements depicting "the uplift bust" and the new foundation garments left little to the imagination. Less intimately, they also portrayed light tropical prints, billowing evening gowns ("ethereal clouds of lustrous Rayon Net"), tailored slacks, "girlish ginghams." There were new styles in shoes, introducing the sandal, while more feminine hairdos revived woman's crowning glory. Hats were indescribable. Far more significant than the fashions themselves, inexpensive reproductions clothed suburban matrons, stenographers, and factory girls very much alike. It was not only *Vogue* that advertised the new styles, but Sears-Roebuck.

TREMENDOUS TRIFLES

As the decade wore on, growing ideological conflict and threatening war heightened the tension under which the American people lived in a depression-born struggle for jobs and livelihood. They sought in many ways to discover new bases for faith in what was essentially a secular age. There was a growing awareness of approaching crisis in world affairs. Yet the nineteen-thirties also had their tremendous trifles, revealing once again the strange diversities and contrasts of the American scene.

In 1933 a midget sat on the lap of John Pierpont Morgan upon the solemn occasion of a senatorial investigation; technocracy was hailed as the hope of ages; contract bridge was being ballyhooed by Ely Culbertson; and Sally Rand's fan dance stole the show at Chicago's "Century of Progress." . . . The Dionne quintuplets were born in 1934; Hugh Johnson, as NRA administrator, was "cracking down on the chiselers"; and J. Edgar Hoover's F.B.I. agents shot John Dillinger, Public Enemy No. 1. . . . During 1935, Sears-Roebuck first advised purchasers of men's bathing suits that they could "take off the shirt for swimming"; and at the close of the year *Tobacco Road* opened in New York for what was to prove an almost endless run. . . . *The Music Goes*

'*Round and 'Round* weighed down the ether in 1936; the New York Yankees won the first of four straight world championships (Lou Gehrig was to retire in 1939 with a record of having played in 2130 consecutive games); King Edward VIII renounced his throne to marry Mrs. Wallis Warfield Simpson. . . . Joe Louis became the world's heavyweight champion in 1937; ever more promising experiments were being made with television; men were wearing play suits.

In 1938, broadcasting had an epochal year with Edgar Bergen and Charlie McCarthy springing into sudden fame, Toscanini conducting the NBC symphony orchestra, and Orson Welles (a month after the Munich Conference) terrifying half his nation-wide audience by recounting a Martian attack upon the United States; the movies celebrated as well with production of what Westbrook Pegler characterized "as the happiest thing that has happened since the Armistice" — *Snow White and the Seven Dwarfs.* . . . In the final year of the decade, college boys took up goldfish swallowing; Shakespeare was declared to be the leading playwright on Broadway; the date of Thanksgiving was shifted; Mrs. Roosevelt served hotdogs to the King and Queen of England . . . and a horrified public read of the march of Hitler's troops into Poland.

* * * * * * * * *

Peace and War

25

The Collapse of Collective Security

THE GOOD NEIGHBOR POLICY

THE INTERNATIONAL SITUATION confronting Roosevelt upon his inauguration in 1933 was confused and threatening. The full significance of foreign developments could hardly be foreseen, but the shadow of the future lay heavily over a disturbed and restless world. Virtual chaos ruled in international finances. Great Britain had gone off the gold standard some eighteen months earlier, the former Allies were on the point of repudiating their war debts, and high-tariff walls everywhere imposed an effective barrier to the normal flow of world trade. Soviet Russia had brought to a successful conclusion its first five-year plan and prostrate capitalism was again fearful of the subversive influence of communism. Just a month before the inaugural, the upstart Hitler had come into power in Germany and the aged President von Hindenburg made his final surrender to the rising power of National Socialism.

In the Far East, militarism tightened its hold upon the Government of Japan. After arrogantly defying the peacemakers at Geneva and ignoring all American protests, the Japanese warlords were stealthily encroaching upon North China from their newly established base in the puppet state of Manchukuo. The League of Nations had been struck a mortal blow. There was still to be talk for another five or six years of collective security as a means of averting the growing peril of war, but it already had a hollow ring as democracy found itself in retreat before dictatorship and aggression.

Roosevelt did not refer directly to these circumstances in his inaugural. The measures that "a stricken nation in the midst of a stricken world" required in March, 1933, had to do with our own immediate recovery from economic collapse. In so far as foreign affairs were concerned, the President made a single, unadorned statement: "In the field of world policy I would dedicate this nation to the policy of the good neighbor. . . . "

The attempt was made to implement this program by closer co-operation with other nations in Europe, in the Far East, and in Latin America. There was no break with the policies promoted by President Hoover; the Democrats picked up where the Republicans had left off. The United States continued its participation in the disarmament conference at Geneva and, as we have seen, sent a delegation to the World Economic Conference in London. While our refusal to consider currency stabilization played an important part in the latter's failure, the collapse of disarmament came about despite announcement by our delegate that the United States was willing to consult with other states in case of a threat to world peace, and, if agreement were reached, "would refrain from any action tending to defeat this collective effort for a restoration of peace." This gesture toward collaboration was still far from a direct pledge to employ sanctions against an aggressor nation and Congress was not prepared to support an arms embargo. Nevertheless, it marked a distinctly forward step in comparison with our attitude a decade earlier.

Another significant development in foreign policy was the recognition at long last accorded Soviet Russia. Where Hoover had refused to respond to the growing feeling in favor of such action, Roosevelt acted promptly. In response to his official invitation, the Soviet Government sent Foreign Commissar Litvinov as a special envoy to Washington in November, 1933, and after a brief eight days of negotiations an agreement was reached reestablishing diplomatic relations between Moscow and Washington. The demand for closer economic collaboration with Russia was primarily responsible for this sharp reversal of the attitude so consistently maintained during the nineteen-twenties, but the rising power of Japan further underlined the advantage of being on as friendly terms as possible with this other great power so influential in the Far East.

Three general questions were settled in the Roosevelt-Litvinov accord. Visiting nationals of the two countries were guaranteed certain fundamental rights on a reciprocal basis; the whole issue of debts and of the counterclaims arising from American intervention in 1918 was made subject to future negotiations, and the Soviet Government expressly undertook to refrain from revolutionary propaganda in the United States. There was nation-wide approval for these common-sense moves. While warnings were expressed in many newspapers stressing the difficult obstacles that still remained in the way of complete Russian-American understanding, it was generally felt that recognition strengthened the cause of world peace.

Apparent progress was also made during the first years of the Roosevelt Administration in easing tension in the Far East through the adoption of a more conciliatory policy toward Japan. Although the President had no intention of repudiating the Stimson Doctrine and recognizing Manchukuo, American protests against Japan's further advances in Jehol and North China were significantly toned down, and every effort was made to discover a basis for common agreement in Japanese-American relations. "I believe that there are in fact no questions between our two countries," we find Secretary Hull writing the Japanese Foreign Minister in March, 1934, "which, if they be viewed in proper perspective in both countries, can with any warrant be regarded as not susceptible to adjustment by pacific processes." Even when a spokesman of the Japanese Foreign Office publicly declared a month later an Asiatic Monroe Doctrine, in effect warning other powers to keep their hands off China, the *caveat* registered by the State Department was couched in such mild terms that Tokyo appeared fully justified in calmly ignoring it.

At the same time the movement to grant freedom to the Philippine Islands, slowly gaining ground over two decades, now came to final fruition. The first concrete step in this direction had been taken in the closing days of the Hoover Administration when Congress, over the President's emphatic veto, adopted an independence bill. The Filipinos themselves, however, rejected this particular measure, and in 1934 it was re-enacted in a somewhat

modified form with passage of the Tydings-McDuffie Act. The
impetus behind the drive for freeing the islands actually came
from various economic pressure groups within the United States,
notably the sugar interests, which wished to bar competing Filipino products from the domestic markets. But while the international situation in the Far East was conspicuously ignored in
much of the congressional discussion of the issue, the repercussions of Philippine independence were highly important.

According to the terms of the Tydings-McDuffie Act, the Philippine Islands were to acquire the equivalent of dominion status
as soon as the Filipinos had drawn up and adopted an acceptable
constitution, and ten years after such action they were to be
granted full independence. Provision was made through a complicated system of quotas and special export taxes for a general
tapering-off of the tariff protection afforded Filipino products in
the American market during the transitional period; American
military establishments in the islands were to be surrendered upon
the attainment of independence, and the disposition of naval
bases was left subject to future negotiations. Having accepted
these terms, the Filipinos drew up a constitution for their commonwealth and elected Manuel Quezon as their first president.
The new status of the islands was thereupon formally proclaimed
in 1936, and the date for full independence definitely set for 1946.

Did our more conciliatory policy toward Japan and independence for the Philippines actually mark full retreat from the Far
East? Appearances were belied by a renewed interest in the
maintenance of naval power. While the American Navy had for
a time been allowed to fall even below the strength permitted in
the Washington and London treaties, Congress undertook in
1934, through passage of the Vinson Bill, to bring it up to allow-
able limits, and a strong stand was taken against any further
concessions to Japan on this important issue. The real basis for
any limitation of armaments, indeed, had been destroyed with
Japan's violation of the Nine-Power Treaty in seizing control of
Manchuria. An attempt was to be made to save something from
the wreckage of the hopes of 1922 by holding another conference
in London late in 1935. Japan denounced the Washington Naval

Treaty, however, and then withdrew her delegation from the futile negotiations in the British capital.

There was one concrete result from this meeting. Spokesmen for the United States and Great Britain agreed that there would be "no competitive building as between ourselves and that the principle of parity as between the fleets of the members of the British Commonwealth and the United States shall continue unchanged." There was no question of the growing Anglo-American community of interest in the Pacific, and the naval construction of both nations in the ensuing years revealed that they were not prepared to surrender full control of the Pacific to Japan. The future was still veiled, however. While the United States had by no means abandoned its position in the Far East, it still moved slowly in building up its naval strength and it took no effective action whatsoever to stem the rising tide of Japanese imperialism.

The most direct, and generally successful, application of Roosevelt's concept of the good neighbor was in Latin America. His administration was able to build securely upon foundations already laid, and the growth of hemispheric solidarity in the New World afforded a striking contrast to the mounting tensions of both Europe and Asia. At the Pan-American Conference held at Montevideo in December, 1933, Secretary Hull emphatically stated that United States policy was firmly based upon the principle that no state, whatever the circumstances, had the right to intervene in either the external or internal affairs of any other state.

Our adherence to such a policy was demonstrated in the attitude maintained toward a revolt that had already broken out in Cuba. Despite strong pressure from financial interests, the Roosevelt Administration stood by its principles and refused to intervene by force of arms. While the Government unquestionably exerted its influence in behalf of order and stability, there was no landing of military forces. Moreover, in May, 1934, the United States gave up all right to intervention by signing a new treaty with Cuba abrogating the Platt Amendment. In that same year, the last of the marines still lingering in Haiti were withdrawn; in 1936, a new treaty with Panama liberalized the terms of the original agreement governing cession of the Canal Zone, and in 1938, the State Department refused to try to coerce the Mexican Government when it once again sought to expropriate the holdings of American oil companies. On this last occasion the companies' claims for compensation received diplomatic support, but the United States acknowledged Mexico's right to take over foreign properties by legal processes, using official influence only to promote a fair adjustment of the controversy.

In the meantime the reciprocal trade agreements had also strengthened Latin-American ties, and President Roosevelt attended in person the Inter-American Conference for Peace held in Buenos Aires in 1936. He failed to attain his major goal of transforming the Monroe Doctrine into a multilateral undertaking for the defense of the Western Hemisphere. The time was not yet ripe. Nevertheless, the principle of non-intervention was definitely reaffirmed by general agreement, and a consultative pact adopted for co-ordinating the peace machinery already in effect. The President felt justified in reporting to Congress:

> Among the nations of the Western Hemisphere the policy of the good neighbor has happily prevailed. At no time in the four and a half centuries of modern civilization in the Americas has there existed — in any year, in any decade, in any generation, in all that time — a greater spirit of mutual understanding, of common helpfulness, and of devotion to the ideals of self-government than exists today in the twenty-one American Republics and their neighbor, the Dominion of Canada. The policy of the good neighbor among the Americans is no longer a hope, no longer an objective remaining to be accomplished. It is a fact, active, present, pertinent, and effective.

Neutrality Legislation

While the United States vainly sought to reconcile Japanese imperialism and the Open-Door policy in eastern Asia, and more successfully followed the path of the good neighbor in Latin America, events in Europe were sharply demonstrating the inadequacy of the structure of international peace centering upon

Geneva. As the continent moved year by year closer to the tragic abyss of war, the American people were driven to decide whether they would try to stave off the impending conflict by throwing their full support behind collective security, or allow Europe to go its own way and withdraw once again into complete isolation.

The unstable nature of the peace proclaimed at Versailles had long since been recognized, but after 1933 the growing power of Nazi Germany gave a new immediacy to the fears that the war broken off in November, 1918, might be renewed. Hitler withdrew Germany from the World Disarmament Conference and the League of Nations; started upon a program of ac ive rearmament; and in 1936, having shrilly demanded the complete revision of the Treaty of Versailles, he boldly marched his troops into the demilitarized Rhineland. As Italy revealed that she, too, had learned the lesson of aggression by making war upon Ethiopia, a next logical step of the German leader was to join forces with Mussolini in establishing a Rome-Berlin Axis. The lines of future conflict were being drawn, as Hitler prepared to challenge England and France in the establishment of a New Order in Europe under German hegemony.

Where did the United States stand as the rift between the democratic and fascist nations widened so inexorably? The answer was soon apparent. The American people were to try to remain aloof from what they insistently told themselves was solely a European quarrel, and the trend toward international co-operation that appeared so promising at the opening of the decade was abruptly reversed. Retreating into a narrow nationalism, the United States sought only insulation from the growing menace of war. The ghosts of Washington and Jefferson walked the land. Collective security was cried down as a modern substitute for entangling alliances. Adopting a policy of strict neutrality, the United States sought to transform the Atlantic and the Pacific Oceans into Chinese walls behind which it could safely go its own way.

The general lines of this policy never commanded the universal support of the American people. There was a pronounced division in public opinion upon its wisdom — just as there had been in

1900 on the issue of imperialism, and in 1920 in regard to membership in the League of Nations. Although there was a popular majority in favor of the neutrality legislation, opposition not only continued, but remained highly vocal. The adherents of isolation carried the day, but those who believed in collective security never wholly gave up the struggle.

Political lines, all other divisions into which the American people normally fall by reason of their liberal or conservative views, were crossed in this bewildering battle. Advocates of closer international collaboration argued that the United States could not escape its responsibilities in a highly interdependent world, and that there was no way for a single nation, however broad the Atlantic or the Pacific, to immunize itself from the plague of war. International health was the only guarantee of national health. If the fabric of peace was shattered in Europe, it was said, no policy of neutrality could permanently keep the United States from becoming involved.

The proponents of an isolationist policy, on the other hand, declared that there was no contribution that the United States could make to peace that could successfully counter the rivalries and jealousies of Europe; that the idea of collective security had already collapsed with the failure of the League of Nations to meet the crisis in Manchuria; and that closer co-operation would have no tangible effect other than to drag the United States into quarrels which were none of its concern. In the event of war in Europe, they further stated, the United States could protect itself. If our neutrality were realistically safeguarded, there need be no fear of war encroaching upon the New World, whatever cataclysm might overwhelm the Old World.

The decisive factor weighting the scales in the isolationists' favor in the nineteen-thirties was the disillusionment resulting from our intervention in the first World War. Why again run the risks of 1917, the American people asked themselves, when it profited the United States so little? The possible consequences of the German victory which American intervention forestalled were quite forgotten in the feeling of frustration growing out of our failure to realize the idealistic purposes for which the nation had

believed it was taking up arms. The general public remer...
only that America had fought to end all wars — and again the
war clouds were gathering; that victory was to make the world
safe for democracy — and democracy was dangerously threatened
by fascism. To many people the only enduring fruits of the first
World War appeared to be the repudiation of international debts,
economic rivalries, and a new armaments race.

With this disillusionment there also came a feeling that the
United States had been tricked into intervention in 1917. The
idealistic phrases of President Wilson were now said to have
hidden the self-interest of international bankers and munitions
makers. British propaganda had falsified the issues for which the
Allies were actually fighting, taking in a gullible public by an appeal to its emotions. The story of the profits made by the bankers
and munitions makers was in 1934 spread upon the records of a
congressional investigating committee, while popular writers sensationally exposed what they declared was the iniquitous influence of the "merchants of death" over government policy here
and abroad. The war which had once been considered a great
crusade was translated into a sordid struggle for commercial
profits. The interplay of factors actually responsible for American
intervention — political, economic, and idealistic — was widely
ignored in favor of an oversimplification of the historical question
that bore little relation to reality.

True, economic factors played a sufficiently important part in
carrying us into the first World War to lend some support to this
interpretation of events, but the popular view basically reflected
an intense desire to maintain peace this time no matter what
might happen in Europe. If the international bankers and munitions makers could be made wholly responsible for American intervention in 1917, then the United States should on another
occasion be easily able to stay out. It would be necessary only
to prevent economic self-interest from again overriding the national interest. Peace could thus be guaranteed by providing in
advance a policy of neutrality that was proof against our acquiring an economic stake in victory for either side and against the
accident of loss of either American ships or American lives in
trade with the belligerents.

The impending outbreak of hostilities between Italy and Ethiopia brought this movement for insulating the United States against war to a head in the summer of 1935. In the growing tension of international politics, here was perhaps the spark to ignite the powder barrel and plunge the entire European continent into war. The Administration favored a program that would have enabled the United States, as a neutral, to exercise its influence in behalf of the victim of aggression, but a Congress fearful that this might lead to involvement refused to make any such distinction between belligerents. It passed a first temporary neutrality measure that prohibited the sale of munitions to all belligerents, barred their submarines from American waters, and gave the President discretionary authority to forbid American citizens from traveling on belligerent vessels except at their own risk. Upon expiration of this bill's temporary features, a second neutrality act was immediately adopted that extended the arms embargo and added a ban on all loans to belligerents. This measure was then in turn replaced in May, 1937, with a so-called permanent neutrality act. The mandatory bans on the shipment of munitions and on belligerent loans were retained; the rule in regard to American travel on belligerent ships was strengthened by expressly prohibiting it under all circumstances; and an entirely new "cash-and-carry" provision stipulated that non-embargoed goods purchased in this country by belligerent nations had to be fully paid for before leaving this country and could not be transported in American ships. A Congress which had stubbornly refused to give the President any discretionary power over the munitions ban authorized him to apply this phase of the law whenever he deemed such action necessary "to promote the security or preserve the peace of the United States." Inasmuch as England and France controlled the seas and could purchase on a "cash-and-carry" basis while the Axis Powers were cut off from the American market, it was clearly enough trying to find a way to aid those nations with which we were in sympathy, should they become involved in war, without exposing the United States to the risks that selling munitions to them was believed to incur. So highly controversial was this compromise between the two opposing views on foreign policy, however, that the "cash-and-carry" provision was to expire in two years.

In terms of our traditional policy in support of freedom of the seas, these successive neutrality measures marked a complete reversal of a doctrine that the United States had consistently upheld ever since the Napoleonic Wars. We would no longer demand the right to trade with belligerents in non-contraband goods, we would no longer seek to compel respect for neutral shipping, we would no longer uphold freedom of travel for neutral citizens. The United States undertook to keep both American ships and American citizens out of harm's way in order to avoid such attacks upon them as had been instrumental in taking us into the first World War. In wholly abandoning the doctrine of freedom of the seas for which President Wilson had so stoutly contended from 1914 to 1917, we were prepared to sacrifice what we had then considered basic rights in the hope that by so doing we could really secure peace.

FURTHER RETREAT

The first application of the neutrality law, as already suggested, was in the Italo-Ethiopian War which broke out in October, 1935. President Roosevelt at once declared the munitions embargo to be in effect and all shipments of arms to the belligerent nations automatically ceased. When the League of Nations made a half-hearted attempt to apply sanctions against Italy as the aggressor in this unprovoked conflict, the State Department sought to impose a moral embargo on the shipment of other supplies in order to bring the United States into line with the League's action. It proved ineffective, especially in regard to oil. The Government had no way to enforce it and in any event the European countries continued their own oil shipments throughout the conflict.

No sooner had the war in Ethiopia drawn to a close in the spring of 1936, with the final crushing of all enemy resistance by the Italian army, than the outbreak of bitter civil strife in Spain between the Loyalist defenders of the existing republican régime and the rebel forces of General Franco created a new problem for American foreign policy.

Our neutrality measures did not apply to civil war; they had been framed to meet international emergencies. In the belief that the alignment of democratic and fascist forces within Spain might precipitate a general conflict, Roosevelt nevertheless induced Congress in January, 1937, to broaden the scope of existing legislation to include civil war, and this provision was then retained in the permanent neutrality law enacted a few months later. A strict ban was imposed upon all shipments of munitions to Spain, whether destined for the Spanish Government or for the rebels.

This policy was both at the time and in ensuing years vigorously criticized by all adherents of collective security as a betrayal of the very principles which Roosevelt had been upholding. The Spanish Loyalists were not only the Government officially recognized by the United States; they were fighting to uphold democracy. The rebel forces under General Franco were trying to impose upon Spain — and eventually succeeded in doing so through their defeat of the Loyalists — a fascist régime to which both Mussolini and Hitler were already extending direct support. Application of our neutrality laws under such circumstances meant that we made it impossible for a friendly government to obtain in the United States the supplies necessary to defend itself, even though it was clearly a victim of aggression.

While Roosevelt, in April, 1938, attempted to justify his stand on the ground that lifting the arms embargo would not help the Loyalists, what he was actually doing was following the lead of Great Britain and France. A non-intervention agreement had been reached among the European powers. Germany and Italy openly flouted its terms in the direct assistance afforded the rebels; Soviet Russia was in some measure aiding the Loyalists. Suspicious of the united front against fascist aggression being urged by communist Russia, and unwilling to accept the Axis Powers' challenge to democracy because of fears of a war for which they were not prepared, England and France continued to adhere to the non-intervention policy. The American position thus conformed to the Anglo-French determination to prevent at all costs the enlargement of the Spanish civil war into a general

European conflict. Our own distrust of the Spanish Government's supposed affiliations with communism and the sympathy of many American Catholics for General Franco may have played some part in determining the Administration's attitude, but the decisive factor was fear of somehow becoming involved in the struggle.

In contrast to application of the neutrality legislation in Spain's civil war, the Administration refused to extend its provisions to the Far East when Japan renewed her imperialistic advance on the Asiatic continent, with direct attack upon the Chinese in the summer of 1937. Here was a further challenge to our whole position in the Pacific, but once again the avoidance of foreign entanglements was the nation's chief concern. Continued normal relations with both Japan and China rather than the adoption of an arms embargo appeared in this instance to be the more practical program. Such a course was made possible, despite the mandatory provisions of the neutrality law, because neither Japan nor China actually declared war and the President was therefore not legally required to recognize a state of hostilities. What Japan consistently referred to as "the China incident" was indeed war in everything but name. Japan was gradually to extend her control over more and more Chinese territory, eventually driving the Nationalist Government out of its capital and setting up its own puppet state in Nanking. Nevertheless, the fiction that it was not war was observed until 1941.

Once again Roosevelt was criticized, but in the Far East he was better able to defend his policy as in fact aiding the victim of aggression rather than the aggressor. Application of the neutrality laws, it was plausibly maintained, would have benefited Japan more than China. Through her control of the seas Japan could have continued trade on a cash-and-carry basis in everything but munitions, while China would have been altogether cut off from American supplies. To allow Japan to obtain some arms from the United States was felt to be less of an advantage to her than the overwhelming disadvantage to China of our recognizing a state of war that would almost surely have driven Japan to blockade the China coast.

The contradictory effects of our neutrality policy — in Ethiopia,

Spain, and China — did not augur well for its effectiveness should it be put to a really vital test. With the European war clouds growing ever more lowering, Roosevelt consequently sought some means to win public support for a program that would throw the full weight of American influence behind international security. In a speech at Chicago on October 5, 1937 — after passage of the permanent neutrality law and while wars were raging in both Spain and China — he dramatically called for a "quarantine" of those aggressor nations which he found spreading abroad an "epidemic of world lawlessness." The President declared:

> The peace, the freedom, and the security of ninety per cent of the population of the world is being jeopardized by the remaining ten per cent, who are threatening a breakdown of all international order and law. Surely the ninety per cent who want to live in peace under law and in accordance with moral standards that have received almost universal acceptance through the centuries, can and must find some way to make their will prevail. . . .

This attempt to win support for a more active American policy, whatever may have been specifically in Roosevelt's mind, awoke little popular response. Those who militantly favored the principle of collective security warmly applauded the quarantine speech; the isolationists condemned it as a move to involve the United States in foreign wars. The country as a whole, however, remained apathetic both to the President's warnings of the dangers confronting the world and to his suggestion that the United States undertake a more active rôle in the search for peace. The majority of Americans were aroused neither by fascist aggression in Spain nor Japanese aggression in China. "Let no one imagine that America will escape, that America may expect mercy, that this Western Hemisphere will not be attacked," Roosevelt had declared, but his words were dismissed as warmongering.

Polls of the Institute of Public Opinion revealed that forty per cent of the persons questioned about the Spanish civil war had no opinion upon the issues at stake, while of those asked their views upon the war in the Far East, fifty-five per cent declared that they sympathized with neither China nor Japan. A further *Fortune* poll, in October, 1937, upon popular feeling toward Germany, Italy, Russia, and Japan, found over sixty per cent of the persons interviewed stating in each case that their attitude toward these nations was entirely neutral. The country apparently still had full faith in the neutrality legislation adopted by Congress, was uninterested in any project for quarantining aggressor nations, and believed that the United States could maintain its own national safety without concerning itself with collective security.

THE ROAD TO WAR

The international situation nevertheless became even more threatening as 1937 gave way to 1938. Having made good her conquest of Ethiopia, Italy withdrew from the League of Nations. With the Versailles Treaty torn to shreds, Hitler was about to occupy Austria in further defiance of the western democracies. All Europe was feverishly arming. The Axis Powers, more firmly united than ever because of their successful collaboration in aiding the cause of fascism in Spain, forged far ahead of the democracies in these preparations for war. England and France hesitated and temporized. With their conservative governments still divided as to whether fascism or communism represented the greater threat to Europe, they held themselves stubbornly aloof from the united front for which Soviet Russia repeatedly called as the only effective barrier to further fascist conquests. Early and late, Foreign Commissar Litvinov declared that his country's policy "was, is, and will be a policy for peace," but his appeals for greater collaboration went unheeded.

Nor was there any improvement in the Far East as Japan continued her relentless warfare against China. An international conference held at Brussels in November, 1937, to attempt to deal with the threat to world peace ended in complete failure. It was all too evident that Japan could be stopped only by force, and the only powers in a position to exercise effective restraint were unwilling to adopt economic sanctions, let alone military or naval pressure. While Tokyo's quick apologies prevented the Japanese bombing of an American gunboat, the *Panay*, from developing into a serious crisis, the incident nevertheless underlined the dangers inherent in the situation to American interests in Asia.

Only in Latin America could the international observer find anything but wars and the rumors of war. Before the close of 1938 another conference of the twenty-one republics of the Western Hemisphere was to meet at Lima, Peru, and once again reaffirm their solidarity. Argentina did not wholly subscribe to the new attitude of international good will born of the Good Neighbor policy, but the Declaration of Lima marked a general agreement for co-operative action in the event the peace of the Americas should be threatened. It called for consultation among the foreign ministers of the several countries whenever any one of them considered it advisable.

In the light of this over-all world picture, popular opinion as to what policy the United States should follow remained confused and contradictory. Adherents of collective security grasped at every straw to urge closer American co-operation with other countries in upholding democracy against fascism. Isolationists were more than ever fearful that participation in any common program directed against the aggressor nations would involve us in the threatened conflict. Where the former called upon America to play its rôle in defending democracy wherever it might be threatened, the latter demanded that we put aside every idea of another idealistic crusade and establish democracy at home before worrying about it abroad. The danger to our own way of life should fascism triumph in the rest of the world was shouted as loudly by the one group as it was vociferously denied by the other.

Roosevelt had been silenced by the adverse reaction to his quarantine speech, and Congress, clinging determinedly to the neutrality policy embodied in existing legislation, came within a few votes of adopting a resolution introduced by Representative Ludlow for a constitutional amendment making any declaration of war dependent upon a popular referendum. At the same time a first step was taken toward building up our national defenses through a billion-dollar appropriation for a huge increase in the American Navy. During the spring of 1938, moreover, public opinion polls reported majorities ranging from sixty-five to seventy per cent against American collaboration in any form of collective action; in favor of the withdrawal of American citizens and military forces from the Far East; and in support of the Ludlow resolution.

September of this year brought to a head the first crisis in that calamitous train of events that was to lead Europe to war. France and England had in March acquiesced in Hitler's incorporation of Austria into the Third Reich, but when he went on to insist upon restoration of the German-populated parts of Czechoslovakia, known as the Sudetenland, resistance to Nazi aggression appeared to stiffen. Would the two democratic powers accept Hitler's challenge? Was war at last about to break out? The entire world waited nervously as the telegraph and telephone lines linking Berlin, Prague, Paris, Rome, and London hummed with frantic diplomatic messages.

President Roosevelt attempted to throw American influence on the side of peace. On September 26 he cabled the powers immediately concerned — Czechoslovakia, Germany, Great Britain, and France — strongly urging settlement of the issue without war, and calling upon them to uphold their pledges in the Kellogg-Briand anti-war treaty. The next day he sent a further appeal to Mussolini, asking him to intervene with his Axis partner, and again called upon Hitler to enter into negotiations. Whatever the effect of these trans-Atlantic appeals — and there is little reason to believe that they played any important part in the negotiations — Hitler held his hand. He agreed to a conference on the Sudetenland. Soviet Russia was not invited, but the heads of government of Great Britain, France, Germany, and Italy met at Munich and an agreement was dramatically reached on September 29, in which England and France bowed to Germany's demands and allowed the Nazis to take over the coveted territory. Appeasement had once again won the day. The democracies surrendered in the face of Hitler's demands, vainly hoping that this major concession would satisfy his ambitions and avert the war which otherwise appeared inevitable. Prime Minister Chamberlain returned triumphantly to tell cheering crowds in England that the Munich accords had established "peace in our time."

Public opinion in this country echoed the relief which swept over Europe. There was outraged criticism of the policy of appeasement by those who saw in the democracies' surrender a triumph for fascist aggression which they were convinced could not end with the Sudetenland. The proponents of a united front against Nazism in which the United States would take part felt that their cause had been betrayed. But the country as a whole looked no farther than settlement of the crisis. The American people made their hopes for peace the basis of a general belief that it had at last been securely established.

Roosevelt did not believe this. He still felt that the only chance of maintaining international order was through concerted action against the aggressors. "All about us rage undeclared wars — military and economic," he stated in his message to Congress in January, 1939. "All about us grow more deadly armaments — military and economic. All about us are threats of new aggression — military and economic. . . . There are many methods short of war, but stronger and more effective than mere words, of bringing home to aggressor governments the aggregate sentiments of our own people."

Popular opinion in this country strongly opposed the aggressor nations. Germany found little support or sympathy anywhere. The threat to peace in Hitler's ruthless foreign policy, and the tyranny of his dictatorship in its suppression of democratic liberties, created an almost universal anti-Nazi feeling. When the persecution of Jews, which had already been revealed as an integral part of Hitler's program, was suddenly intensified on the very heels of the Munich accord, the public applauded the President's recall of the American ambassador in a protest only mildly veiled by the explanation that he had been summoned home to report to his Government. Nevertheless, the public still showed little disposition to allow the President to express the national sentiment by any "methods short of war" which were stronger or more effective than verbal protests. Every suggestion of direct aid to the European democracies aroused a storm of protest. The isolationists increased their attacks upon the President as a warmonger seeking to draw us into the European conflict.

And by now another crisis was developing in Europe. Hitler brazenly flouted the pledge he had made at Munich that with acquisition of the Sudetenland he had no further territorial ambitions. Defying the powers of Europe to restrain him, he sent his armies into Czechoslovakia and in March, 1939, forcibly seized control of the remainder of that truncated country. Again words, not action, was the world's answer to this new aggression. On the part of the United States, Acting Secretary of State Welles declared Germany's latest move to have been an act of "wanton lawlessness and arbitrary force." Protests, however, had long since lost all meaning.

A week later, Hitler seized the territory of Memel. Three weeks later, Mussolini took over Albania. The whole structure of European peace was crashing in tragic ruins, and President Roosevelt did not disguise his fears that a general conflict could not be much longer postponed. "I have had a fine holiday here with you all," he said, on leaving Warm Springs, Georgia, on April 9. "I'll be back in the fall if we do not have war."

His policy had now fully crystallized. He favored, despite congressional opposition, all measures short of war against the threat of fascist aggression. He believed thoroughly in national defense, and was prepared to seek further appropriations from Congress for building up our air strength. He advocated a program of hemispheric solidarity which would join Latin America with the United States in a common front against external aggression. And he still hoped that whatever might happen, the United States could stay out of war.

On April 14, another effort was made to stabilize the situation in Europe when Roosevelt dispatched messages to both Hitler and Mussolini proposing that they agree for a period of ten years not to attack any one of thirty nations which the President specifically named. In the event that they would agree to such a non-aggression pact, he suggested an international conference to take up problems both of disarmament and trade. This proposal fell through, as he must have expected it would. Yet it more than ever served to single out Germany and Italy as the aggressors whose intransigent policy made peace impossible. Roosevelt then turned once more to our own neutrality policy, again seeking repeal of the obligatory munitions embargo in order that the democracies might be assured of obtaining military supplies in this country. He was convinced that declaration to the world that the United States would furnish arms and ammunition to any victim of Nazi aggression was the one thing which might conceivably prevent Germany from plunging the world into war.

Congress refused to heed his words. Although Gallup polls now pointed toward a steadily growing popular majority favoring the wartime sale of arms to England and France — sixty-six per cent of those interviewed in April, 1939 — neither Roosevelt's nor Secretary Hull's statements, upon American responsibility in refusing aid to the democracies should they be attacked, succeeded in breaking isolationist ranks. The cash-and-carry provisions of the Neutrality Act of 1937 were allowed to expire, but the ban on shipment of munitions and instruments of war was left intact.

Events in Europe rushed toward their tragic climax. Hitler was putting forward new claims for recovery of the free city of Danzig and for the Polish Corridor. Finally, convinced that appeasement had failed and that there should be no further concessions, England and France supported Poland in refusing to meet the German demands. The democracies tightened their lines, rushed their preparations for war. At long last they even sought to conclude an understanding with Soviet Russia, rebuffed at the time of the Munich Conference, for common resistance to Nazi Germany. Could the united strength of Britain, France, and Russia bring Hitler to terms? Were his demands upon Poland a bluff which the former Allies could successfully call with a determined show of force? The world was hoping against hope when suddenly, on August 22, 1939, it was announced from Berlin that Germany and Russia had concluded a non-aggression pact. Hitler had won the battle of political maneuver. Any chance for a united front among the democracies and communist Russia was lost. The writing on the wall was there for all that had eyes to see.

Roosevelt for a third time — as he had at the Munich crisis and just after the invasion of Czechoslovakia — sought to intervene in the interests of peace. He dispatched urgent cables, on August 24, to Hitler and to the President of Poland urging them to enter into direct negotiations, or otherwise to accept impartial arbitration or conciliation of their dispute. Poland alone made a favorable reply. The President once more addressed Hitler. He reported Poland's acceptance of his proposals, adding that "all the world prays that Germany, too, will accept." But Hitler's answer was to insist upon the terms of the ultimatum he had already dispatched. When Poland refused to accept them, German troops crossed the border. England and France immediately insisted on their recall. Hitler ignored these demands. And on September 3, 1939, the two democracies declared war on Germany.

War had come this time with the issues more clearly defined in the minds of the American people than when it had broken out just a quarter-century earlier. The public was much more aware of what was happening abroad. Having fearfully followed the development of each succeeding crisis, it was almost universally prepared to condemn Germany as the aggressor. The policies of the Nazis both at home and abroad were thoroughly abhorrent to an overwhelming majority of the American people. Although there was something less than unquestioning enthusiasm for the Allies, since many people felt that they had betrayed the peace which Wilson had endeavored to establish in 1919 and were in some measure reaping the reward of their pusillanimous policies during the long armistice, there was also a general conviction that the defeat of Germany would be a victory for democracy over fascism. It alone could ensure the United States from possible attack in its turn should a conquering Hitler seek world domination. Opinions differed widely upon the emphasis given this ideological interpretation of the war and upon the reality of the threat to the United States of a triumphant Germany, but the American people as a whole strongly favored the Allied cause.

President Roosevelt declared in a fireside chat on September 3:

> This nation will remain a neutral nation, but I cannot ask that every American remain neutral in thought as well. . . . I hope the United States will keep out of this war. I believe that it will. And I give you assurance and reassurance that every effort of your Government will be directed toward that end. As long as it remains within my power to prevent it, there will be no black-out of peace in the United States.

26

National Defense

The First Impact of War

WITH THE DECLARATION of American neutrality in September, 1939, a mandatory ban upon all shipments of arms and munitions to the belligerent powers came into immediate effect. The nation faced a decisive test as to whether our much debated neutrality legislation could really prevent us from being drawn into the conflict. It soon became apparent, however, that the test was not to be made in the form in which the promoters of the neutrality legislation had desired. Within two months of the opening of hostilities, the pronounced sympathy of the American people for the Allied cause and their hostility toward Nazi Germany led to the repeal of the arms embargo in order that England and France might be able to take advantage of their control of the seas to purchase materials of war in the American market.

Roosevelt instituted the drive for repeal and the full power of the Administration was thrown behind it. In conformity with promises previously made, a special session of Congress was summoned on September 21. The Neutrality Act, the President declared, was under existing circumstances affording aid to the aggressor and denying it to the victims of attack. He regretted its passage; he regretted his approval of it. He urged repeal as a return to our historic policy of safeguarding neutral rights of trade, as a means of building up our own armaments industry in the interests of national defense, and as a spur to domestic employment. The risks involved in any policy that served to aid the aggressor were, however, most emphatically stressed in his message to Congress, and Roosevelt expressed his firm conviction that an Allied victory was the only certain guarantee that the

United States would not eventually become involved in war. To avoid the situation created in 1917, he coupled with his suggested repeal of the arms embargo, re-enactment of the former cash-and-carry provisions of the neutrality law. "There," the President stated, "lies the road to peace."

Congress and the entire country hotly debated this issue for the next six weeks. The former advocates of collective security generally favored repeal because of the aid it would afford England and France, while the isolationists strongly opposed it as a first step toward intervention. Charges and countercharges were hurled across the floor of the Senate. The President was accused of trying to carry the country into war as an escape from the domestic failures of the New Deal. The final votes on the measure again revealed the sharp cleavage upon foreign policy that had been so apparent when the neutrality legislation was first adopted and that would become steadily intensified during the next two years. The proposed amendments to existing legislation were adopted in the House by 242 to 172 votes, and in the Senate by 55 to 24 votes. Here was a clear-cut majority, but it was also apparent that the President, signing the new bill on November 4, would have to move cautiously in order to maintain popular support for any further moves to aid the democracies in their fight against Nazi aggression.

With our markets thus opened to all belligerent trade, subject only to the cash-and-carry provisions of the law, the Allies were quick to take advantage of their control of the sea lanes. While exports to Germany immediately fell off to only nominal proportions, those to England and France, especially in airplanes and other munitions of war, rapidly increased. During 1940 their total value was almost double what it had been in 1939.

As the United States made this highly significant change in policy and the American people sought in other ways to adjust themselves to a world at war, events in Europe traced an unexpected and disturbing pattern. Hitler's armies quickly overran Poland, and without assistance from her allies that country soon lay wholly at the mercy of the Nazi conquerer. An agreement was then reached between Germany and the Soviet Union dividing

Poland between them, and Russian forces at once occupied the eastern half of that unhappy country. Nor was this all. Moscow began to put pressure upon the neighboring border states of Latvia, Lithuania, and Estonia, eventually leading to their annexation, and turned upon Finland whose resistance to Soviet demands resulted in October, 1939, in open warfare.

Little happened on the western front while these decisive developments were taking place in eastern Europe. The apparent inability of either Germany or the Allies to launch a full-scale offensive, the opposing forces doing little more than hold their lines behind the fortifications built up in preceding years, created a puzzling situation. American opinion began to doubt whether the deadlock would ever be broken. The war in the West became "the phony war" as public attention was diverted to the far more spectacular events marking the fall of Poland and the Russian attack on Finland. When the latter struggle continued through the winter of 1939-40, with the Finns putting up an heroic fight against the Red armies, popular feeling turned even more strongly against Soviet Russia than against Germany. Stalin was condemned for making himself a partner in aggression with the Nazi dictator, and what was considered Russia's original betrayal of the democratic cause in concluding a non-aggression pact with Germany now appeared to be underscored by her invasion of neighboring states. The hope once held that the influence of Russia was on the side of peace and collective security, Roosevelt declared in an address to the American Youth Congress in February, 1940, "is today either shattered or put away in storage against some better day."

The Russo-Finnish War came to an end with final victory for the Red armies in March, 1940, but still all was quiet on the western front. The American people, lulled into a false sense of security, began to feel that their alarm over the possibility of being drawn into the European struggle had been unnecessary. The war had stimulated trade, and therefore industry. Economic conditions were improving. In the early spring, issues of domestic politics began once more to come to the fore when suddenly, unexpectedly, Germany launched that series of dramatic, lightning-like blows that in a brief three months overwhelmed the democracies of western Europe, left Hitler astride half the continent as a conqueror, and placed the German armies on the British Channel, beyond whose narrow waters England stood alone as the only barrier to a final triumph of Nazi arms.

April brought the invasion of Norway and Denmark, the German armies quickly breaking through their weak resistance; a month later, air attack, parachute troops, and fifth-columnists spearheaded an overwhelming onslaught upon Belgium and Holland. The Allies were forced to fall back steadily before the Wehrmacht's fierce, relentless advance. At the end of May, only the "miracle of Dunkirk" saved the British armies from complete defeat, enabling them to withdraw from the continent. A prostrate France was doomed. Having so far remained neutral, Italy entered the war on June 19, but Germany's victory was already assured as a result of the complete collapse of all French powers of resistance. Three days later, an armistice was signed; and while Marshal Pétain set up a new and nominally independent government at Vichy, Germany remained in occupation of some two-thirds of France.

The United States was abruptly jerked out of its complacency by the shattering impact of Germany's whirlwind triumph. The public had followed the dramatic course of these world-shaking events with nervous intensity. It was not so much the ruthless brutality with which Hitler effected his conquests that alarmed the nation as the terrifying efficiency of his war machine, advancing from victory to victory with clocklike precision and an amazing co-ordination of land and air forces. The *blitzkrieg* had demonstrated with devastating results the potency of the air arm and the extent to which modern mechanized warfare had made obsolete both the weapons and much of the tactics of previous wars. Could Hitler carry forward his campaign to the final defeat of England? Could he win control of the British fleet? Where might he then turn?

The threat to American security in Hitler's conquest of western Europe seized the imagination of the country almost overnight. There was still to be embittered controversy over the aid which should be given England, heroically at bay against Nazi fury, but there was a general demand that the United States take every possible measure to strengthen its own means of protection from foreign attack. After the tragic fall of France, national defense became the major objective of American policy.

President Roosevelt, in a series of special messages to Congress, called for additional appropriations to build up our army, navy, and air force. Stressing the danger to the United States should Hitler overcome Great Britain and then look abroad for further fields to conquer, he dramatically called attention to the actual flying time between air bases on the coasts of Europe or Africa and the principal cities of the United States. There was a real "possibility of attack on vital American zones," Roosevelt declared. " . . . I should like to see this nation geared up to turn out at least fifty thousand planes a year."

Congress responded with alacrity to these appeals. In rapid succession, five major appropriation bills were passed, providing funds for mechanized army equipment, an effective two-ocean navy and airplane construction that dwarfed any comparable appropriations, whether during the first World War or the emergency of the depression. The over-all total made available for national defense before the end of the summer was thirteen billion dollars — a peacetime appropriation more than three times that made when we had actually entered war in 1917.

Comprehensive measures were also adopted to mobilize the industrial resources that would enable the country to carry out this far-reaching rearmament program. The old Council of National Defense was revived, and the President set up the Office of Emergency Management with general supervisory powers over the allocation of war materials and determination of priorities. It was a seven-man board headed by William S. Knudsen, president of General Motors Corporation, and Edward R. Stettinius, Jr., chairman of the United States Steel Corporation. In addition, new heads were appointed to both the War and Navy Departments, Roosevelt shattering precedent in calling to these important posts two outstanding Republicans. Henry L. Stimson, who had been Hoover's Secretary of State, went to the War Department, and Frank Knox, Republican vice-presidential candidate in 1936, to the Navy Department.

Far more important than either appropriations for defense or the marshaling of industrial resources, however, was the enactment in September of a Selective Service Act. Never before in all its history had the United States adopted conscription in time of peace. Administration leaders insisted that the immediate necessity of building up the army could not wait upon voluntary enlistments, and while there was strong opposition to a measure which isolationists declared to be a step toward war, Congress fell in line by a narrow margin. The new law followed the general lines of the Selective Service Act of 1917. All men between the ages of twenty-one and thirty-six were required to register, and the army planned to enroll from this pool of some seventeen million an annual contingent of nine hundred thousand, to be given a year's training and then remain subject to call for ten years. Voluntary enlistments were continued and national guardsmen were called into active service, but the main reliance of the country was to be placed upon the draft. An important stipulation governing this citizen army, adopted to placate isolationist protests, was that it could not be used for service overseas.

As this program for national defense got under way, Roosevelt was also taking important diplomatic action to promote American security. All possible aid to the Allies short of war had been his policy even before the fall of France, and with Great Britain now standing alone, he was even more determined to extend her the utmost material support. All assets in this country of the nations conquered by Hitler were frozen to prevent their falling into Germany's hands; government stocks of certain military supplies were released for sale to England, and finally, acting upon his own responsibility and without congressional authorization, Roosevelt concluded on September 2 a deal with Prime Minister Churchill whereby fifty over-age destroyers were exchanged for naval and air bases on the British island possessions off the American coast. Great Britain made an outright grant of such bases in Newfoundland and Bermuda, and leased the necessary territory in the Bahamas, Jamaica, Saint Lucia, Trinidad, Antigua, and British

Guiana. There was criticism of the method pursued, but general approval in principle for what the President called "the most important action in the reinforcement of our national defense that has been taken since the Louisiana Purchase."

Relations with Canada, to whose protection the United States had already pledged itself, were further strengthened by the creation of a Permanent Joint Board on Defense, and every effort was made to develop the new solidarity with Latin America. Soon after the outbreak of war a meeting of the foreign ministers of the twenty-one republics of the New World had been held at Panama. As a first instance of their united front, a common neutrality zone, stretching three hundred miles off the coast of the Americas, was established "as a measure of continental self-protection." Belligerent activities were not to be permitted within this area and the Latin-American countries agreed to co-operate with the United States in patrolling the waters adjacent to their coasts. Two inter-American committees were also set up, one to consider further measures for enforcing neutrality and the other to provide mutual economic aid.

After Germany's occupation of the nations of western Europe, the possibility that Hitler might attempt to take over their possessions in this hemisphere led to another conference at Havana in July, 1940. At this meeting it was agreed that in the event of any threat to the existing status of the colonies of non-American countries, the American republics were empowered, either individually or collectively, to intervene for their protection. These colonies would then be provisionally administered for the duration of the war as "a collective trusteeship," and at its close either be restored to their former status or granted independence. The United States in no way surrendered its right to independent action in support of the Monroe Doctrine, whose inviolability had already been stressed in stern notes to both Germany and Italy, but it successfully obtained in the Act of Havana a collective guarantee against European aggression. At long last the Monroe Doctrine had been transformed from a wholly unilateral policy of the United States into a multilateral understanding on the part of all nations in the Western Hemisphere.

In adopting these various measures, whether relating directly to national defense, material support for Great Britain, or hemispheric solidarity, Roosevelt repeatedly called upon the American people for national unity and concerted action. The answer to Germany's growing military might, he insisted, should not be appeasement but effective aid for every nation that stood out against Hitler, together with the steady strengthening of our own military and naval defenses. Our goal was not war, the President reiterated on countless occasions; it was peace. "I have one supreme determination," he declared, " — to do all that I can to keep war away from these shores for all time."

The public was on the whole ready to uphold his policies and the thrilling news from the British battle-front as the R.A.F. valiantly fought off German bombing raids was reflected in a slowly growing sentiment in favor of all possible aid to England. Nevertheless, two militantly opposed schools of thought arose as to where our foreign policy was taking the country and what its future course should be. While an overwhelming popular majority wished above all else to avoid war, some of the former adherents of collective security had reached a position where they felt the United States should at once and actively intervene. Approving of the President's program so far as it went, they would have extended it much farther. The future of democracy was at stake, the interventionists believed, and the Nazi threat could be met only by immediate and decisive action. The United States could not afford to wait until Hitler was finally victorious in Europe and able to carry the war against the New World when and where he would. Whatever the risk, it was maintained, America should throw her full force into the scales of conflict while the British fleet still controlled the Atlantic and England itself stood as a bastion of democracy off the European coast.

At the opposite pole were the non-interventionists, who feared that the President, for all his disclaimers, was carrying the country into war and that the United States should not run the risks of involvement under any circumstances. Many of them favored aid to England short of war and upheld the defense program, but the extreme isolationists among them denied both American interest in the European conflict or any danger to the United States even should Germany defeat England. They saw no ideological conflict between democracy and fascism, but rather a decisive struggle between German and British imperialism. In any event, this group maintained, the United States could protect itself behind the bulwark of the Atlantic Ocean, whatever happened in Europe. To intervene in support of Great Britain was actually to weaken our defenses, dissipate our strength, and run the needless risk of a war that could be avoided.

Election of 1940

The calendar willed, in the important year of 1940, that the American people elect a president. Although foreign policy now eclipsed all questions of domestic politics, the country was called upon, in the face of the imminent danger of becoming involved in war, to decide whether it wished a continuation of the Democratic Administration of the past eight years or a return of the Republicans to political power. In some ways the situation was analogous to that in 1916. In that year the drift toward war had been unmistakable. President Wilson was still striving to maintain neutrality, but in declaring that the country could not ask an impossible thing of him, he had clearly intimated how great were the dangers of our becoming involved in the European struggle.

In 1940, despite all President Roosevelt's protestations that his sole object was to preserve peace, the likelihood of our once again finding ourselves at war with Germany seemed to many persons to be rapidly becoming almost a certainty. And there was a further resemblance between the two years in domestic politics. A strong undercurrent of conservatism had developed in each instance which strengthened Republican attacks upon the existing Democratic Administration. The antagonism of business interests to Wilson's New Freedom was paralleled by their even more vehement hostility to Roosevelt's New Deal.

An immediate issue was whether the President would seek a third term. Despite the hoary tradition against it, the European war and internal politics created a situation so unusual that the possibility of his defying precedent to seek re-election overhung all political activity. Roosevelt consistently refused to designate any heir apparent, as the earlier Roosevelt had done in the case of Taft, or to commit himself in regard to his own candidacy. Whether or not he had made up his mind as to the course he should follow, he continued to retain control of the situation by not showing his hand.

It was still uncertain what he might do when the Republicans, meeting as usual before the Democrats, gathered in convention to choose their standard-bearer. Their hopes were high. Things seemed to be looking up for the Grand Old Party. The conservative trend which had been so marked in the 1938 elections appeared to be even more general, and the party platform, while actually upholding in principle many Rooseveltian measures, did not hesitate to declare that the New Deal had "for seven long years whirled in a turmoil of shifting, contradictory, and overlapping administrations and policies." Foreign affairs were more difficult. Although party lines were everywhere crossed, isolationist sentiment was stronger among Republicans than among Democrats, and yet it would have been dangerous to carry partisan opposition on this issue too far. The plank finally adopted was consequently something of a straddle, favoring an "orderly and realistic building of our national defense," but condemning all executive acts that might lead to war and castigating the President's "explosive utterances . . . which serve to imperil our peace."

There were several contenders for the nomination, including Thomas Dewey of New York, Senator Vandenberg of Michigan, and Senator Taft of Ohio, but toward the close of the pre-convention campaign a man who was very much of an outsider began to attract increasing attention. Wendell L. Willkie was a corporation executive with no experience in politics and known to the public only as a vigorous critic of the New Deal in his rôle of spokesman for the public utility interests. His candidacy was promoted by a group of amateur strategists within the Republican ranks who were convinced that only new blood promised any chance of defeating Roosevelt should he run again. Put for-

ward as a plain, common-sense businessman who would give
the country an efficient administration, Willkie won a host of
friends through an arresting personality that radiated confidence
very much as did that of the President himself. To the general
amazement of the country he won the Republican nomination on
the sixth ballot amid scenes of popular enthusiasm reminiscent
of the Bull Moose convention of 1912.

The Democrats met a few weeks later with their course still
uncharted. Their platform was obviously enough an enthusiastic
endorsement of the New Deal and they emphatically upheld
Roosevelt's foreign policy. Their three major objectives, the
Democrats declared, were to strengthen democracy by defensive
preparations against aggression, by economic efficiency at home,
and by improvement of the welfare of the people. But what of
the candidate? A majority of the delegates were instructed for
Roosevelt, and while he had disclaimed any desire to run again,
the movement to draft him was strengthened rather than weakened by his somewhat ambiguous attitude. The Democrats thereupon took the plunge and named him on the first ballot. Without
further hesitation, Roosevelt at once accepted and agreed to run
for a third term. "My conscience will not let me turn my back,"
he declared, "upon a call to service."

For a time Roosevelt took no active part in the campaign, and
Willkie's strenuous efforts to convince the electorate that the
Republicans should be returned to office held the center of the
political stage. His own position, it was soon revealed, differed in
detail rather than in principle from that of the President. He
not only subscribed to the general principles underlying the New
Deal, but he went far toward endorsing Roosevelt's foreign policy.
His claim for votes was based upon what he regarded as the
Democrats' failure to carry out their program effectively, and he
vigorously attacked Roosevelt for seeking a third term.

While Willkie attempted to fight out the campaign on such
issues, the rank-and-file Republicans were far more bitter in their
strictures upon Roosevelt and the New Deal. They largely concentrated their fire upon what they termed the President's attempt to establish a dictatorship, but the isolationists among them

accused him of having reached secret agreements with England, dissipated American military and naval strength, and undertaken to send American troops overseas in contemptuous disregard of the right of Congress to declare war.

In October, the President finally felt driven to refute what he termed such "deliberate falsification of fact." In five ringing speeches he carried the attack to the enemy's camp, charging the Republicans with delaying the rearmament program by "playing politics with national security." He reaffirmed his own conviction that aiding the Allies was the only way to keep war from the United States. "Your President and your Secretary of State are following the road to peace," he declared; and again, even more emphatically, "Your President says this country is not going to war." On the domestic front, he charged that election of the Republicans would mean the destruction of the social gains that he was determined at all costs to maintain: "Democracy, to be dynamic, must provide for its citizens opportunity as well as freedom."

The election results were decisive. Nearly fifty million persons went to the polls in November, a greater number than ever before in American history, and some fifty-five per cent of them gave their votes to Roosevelt, a count of 27,243,000 to 22,305,000. Willkie carried ten states where Landon had carried only two in 1936, and the vote in the electoral college was 449 to 82. Roosevelt had won his third great triumph, breaking all precedents in becoming the first President ever to be elected to a third term.

LEND-LEASE AND ATLANTIC CHARTER

His position reinforced, Roosevelt continued his twofold program of increasing the flow of war materials to Great Britain and pushing ahead our own rearmament. The Battle of Britain had now been fought and won. In a fireside chat in December, the President nevertheless stressed once more the danger to the United States should England fall, the ever-present threat of German bombing raids upon the United States, and the impossibility of peace ever being secure until Hitler was decisively defeated. American economic resources, he told the country, must be thrown into the battle against the Nazis' conquering lust — "we must be the Great Arsenal of Democracy."

When Congress met the next month, in January, 1941, the President had both a new slogan to dramatize what he felt were the aims for which all democratic nations were contending in the struggle against fascist aggression, and a new program to render more effective our aid to those who had actually been the victim of such aggression. He called upon the nation to rally behind the Four Freedoms — freedom of speech, freedom of religion, freedom from want, and freedom from fear — and to do so most effectively, he recommended the adoption of a lend-lease program whereby the United States would undertake to give assistance to any nation "whose defense the President deems vital to the defense of the United States."

The need for such legislation was a logical outgrowth of our increasing shipment of war supplies to England and the gradual exhaustion of British credits to pay for these supplies under the cash-and-carry provisions of the Neutrality Act. Prime Minister Churchill's plea to the United States was: "Give us the tools." What the President now advocated was procedure whereby this could be done, for other countries as well as for Great Britain, without our becoming involved in the entangling mesh of inter-governmental debts that had characterized post-war relations in the nineteen-twenties. Congress accepted this proposal, although only after prolonged and often acrimonious debate, and on March 11, 1941, the lend-lease program was written into law. After consultation with the army and navy chiefs of staff, the President was empowered to sell, transfer title, lease, or lend any defense articles needed by such nations as he designated as eligible to receive them. Additional appropriations to the huge total of seven billion dollars — the largest single appropriation in time of peace throughout the history of the country — were approved to implement this program, over two billion dollars being earmarked for airplanes alone. Under the direction of Harry L. Hopkins, who had been administrator of the WPA, this gigantic program at once got under way.

In order to make possible the production of the materials of war allocated to the Allies, as well as those necessary for our own army and navy, various reorganizations were effected in the agencies originally established to integrate the defense program. The Office of Emergency Management gave way to the Office of Production Management, under the joint control of William S. Knudsen and Sidney Hillman, representing management and labor respectively. While it did not have procurement authority for either the army or the navy, its directive was to establish coordinated control over the production of airplanes, tanks, ships, and all other weapons of war.

Other agencies set up in the spring of 1941 were the Office of Price Administration, under the direction of Leon Henderson, to attempt to control inflationary tendencies resulting from the tremendous impetus being given to industrial production; the Office of Civilian Defense, whose first director was Mayor La Guardia of New York, to provide for emergencies in the event of attack upon this country; the National Defense Mediation Board, charged with adjusting labor disputes which might lead to an interruption of the defense program; and the Office of Facts and Figures, headed by Archibald MacLeish, to marshal public support behind the national policy.

Although still at peace with the Axis Powers, the United States was nevertheless engaged in a war effort under the national defense program that threw into the shadow the preparations that were made in 1917 even after hostilities had actually been declared. "All our domestic problems," the President declared, "are now a part of the great emergency . . . we are committed to all-inclusive national defense."

In the meantime the scope of the war in Europe was steadily broadening and every month appeared to increase the danger of American involvement. Rumania had been brought within the orbit of the Axis Powers, Hungary and Bulgaria became new satellites, and in April, Germany launched an offensive in the Balkans that soon resulted in the conquest of Jugoslavia and Greece. Had the time now come for a final, all-out assault upon Great Britain, or would Hitler turn in some other direction in his apparently insatiable lust for power? The answer came to a fearful world, and an astounded American public, when on June 22, 1941, the German armies, some two hundred and twenty divisions strong, marched against Soviet Russia. While it was at first almost universally expected that the Red armies would crumble before the Wehrmacht as had the armies of western Europe, they retreated so stubbornly that Hitler failed to win the easy victory upon which he had counted. The Soviet forces, pressed deep back into the interior of their country, rallied to the defense of Moscow and gave the world new hope that Germany's heretofore invincible armies could yet be broken.

The United States found itself compelled to reverse its policy toward the Soviets as they became an ally in the struggle against Hitlerism. Isolationists cried out that here was a final and conclusive reason for America to avoid any further involvements. "Just let Joe Stalin and the other dictators fight it out," was Senator Wheeler's terse comment. Nevertheless, every effort was made to re-establish friendly relations with Russia, and arrangements were soon concluded to ship her supplies for carrying on the war. Harry Hopkins was dispatched as a special emissary to Moscow and returned to report to the President that he was convinced that Russia would not make a separate peace with Hitler and was entitled to all the aid we could extend to her.

He did not find the President in Washington on making this report. In dramatic demonstration of how closely our fortunes were now believed to be linked with those of Great Britain, Roosevelt was conferring with Prime Minister Churchill at the famous Atlantic Conference. Meeting at sea somewhere off Newfoundland, as the world was later to learn to its amazement, the two statesmen reviewed the whole problem of lend-lease, agreeing that it was their common policy to expedite the shipment to Russia of the materials sought by Stalin, and on August 14, they issued a joint statement of the principles to govern any future settlement of peace after the defeat of Hitler. In the Atlantic Charter, Roosevelt and Churchill accepted eight principles governing the national policies of their respective countries:

First: Their countries seek no aggrandizement, territorial or other;

Second: They desire to see no territorial changes that do not accord with the freely expressed wishes of the people concerned;

Third: They respect the right of all peoples to choose the form of government under which they will live. . . .

Fourth: They will endeavor, with due respect for their existing obligations, to further the enjoyment by all states, great or small, victor or vanquished, of access, on equal terms, to the trade and to the raw materials of the world which are needed for their economic prosperity;

Fifth: They desire to bring about the fullest collaboration between all nations in the economic field. . . .

Sixth: After the final destruction of the Nazi tyranny, they hope to see established a peace which will afford to all nations the means of dwelling in safety within their own boundaries, and which will afford assurance that all the men in all the lands may live out their lives in freedom from fear and want;

Seventh: Such a peace should enable all men to traverse the high seas and oceans without hindrance;

Eighth: They believe that all of the nations of the world, for realistic as well as spiritual reasons, must come to the abandonment of the use of force. . . .

Freedom of the Seas

The Atlantic Charter was to have widespread and continuing repercussions, was to arouse bitter criticism and lead to interminable debate here and abroad. In the meantime, however, tension between the United States and Germany was increasing dangerously. Upon orders of the President, all German and Italian ships in American ports were taken over in June, the credits of both countries were frozen, and their consulates closed. But the critical issue was that which had been the immediate cause of our entry into the war against Germany a quarter of a century earlier. American shipping was being attacked by German submarines and the two nations were becoming involved in an undeclared shooting war in the Atlantic. Once again the United States, repudiating the policy that had been incorporated in the neutrality legislation first adopted in 1935, was to assert the principle of freedom of the seas and to use force for its maintenance.

The adoption of lend-lease had already greatly modified our neutrality, and the question soon arose as to whether we could afford to extend such important aid to Great Britain and not also seek to safeguard its transportation against the increasing attacks by German submarines. A first step extending our control over the sea lanes was the inclusion of Greenland and Iceland within the American neutrality zone in order to prevent their falling into Hitler's hands or being somehow used by him in submarine warfare. In April, 1941, we reached an agreement with the Danish minister whereby air bases were established in Greenland, and three months later American troops occupied Iceland. The means were thus provided, in theoretical compliance with our neutrality law, to assert American rights over a vast area of the Atlantic whose protection we declared essential to our national security. "Our patrols are helping now to ensure delivery of the needed supplies to Great Britain," Roosevelt stated as early as May 27, 1941. "All additional measures necessary to deliver the goods will be taken."

It was hardly surprising that Germany should resent these moves to keep open the sea lanes to Great Britain. The first attack upon an American ship had been in the South Atlantic rather than in the North Atlantic. The *Robin Moor* was sunk on May 21, en route to South Africa. As summer drew to a close, two other American-owned ships, operating under Panamanian registry, were torpedoed en route to Iceland within our neutrality zone. And then, on September 4, the destroyer *Greer*, carrying mail to Iceland, was attacked by a submarine, although not sunk.

The President stated in a world-wide radio broadcast on September 11:

> These Nazi submarines and raiders are the rattlesnakes of the Atlantic. They are a menace to the free pathways of the high seas. They are a challenge to our sovereignty. They hammer at our most precious rights when they attack ships of the American flag — symbols of our independence, our freedom, our very life. It is no act of war on our part when we decide to protect the seas which

are vital to American defense. The aggression is not ours. Ours is solely defense. But let this warning be clear. From now on, if German or Italian vessels of war enter the waters, the protection of which is necessary for American defense, they do so at their peril. The orders which I have given as Commander-in-Chief to the United States Army and Navy are to carry out that policy — at once. The sole responsibility rests upon Germany. There will be no shooting unless Germany continues to seek it.

It might have been the voice of Wilson upholding freedom of the seas against the menace of unrestricted submarine warfare in 1917 — but still with one important distinction. We made no claim as yet to the right to send American vessels into the war zone. Our shipping was still prohibited from carrying supplies directly to any belligerent power. What we were defending in September, 1941, was freedom from attack in the waters adjacent to our own coasts. Germany was being warned that the United States could not be swerved from its policy of all-out aid short of war to the democracies by any Nazi threat, and that it would defend its interests in its own part of the world at whatever risk.

Germany refused to heed this warning. There were further attacks upon American cargo ships, and on October 9, Roosevelt asked Congress to repeal those sections of the neutrality law that prohibited the arming of American vessels and their sailing to belligerent ports. Even as Congress debated a proposal which the isolationists declared meant war, the destroyer *Kearny* was torpedoed and limped back into port badly damaged and with eleven of her seamen killed. Then two weeks later, the destroyer *Reuben James* was sunk with heavy loss of life.

Hitler charged that the American ships had first fired upon the submarines, but the Navy Department declared that it was the Germans who had attacked. The issue was in a sense irrelevant. The naval shooting war was actually a result of Germany's attempts, very much as in 1917, to hamper the aid that the United States was extending to Great Britain, and our insistence upon our right to do as we pleased. In any event, these sinkings resulted in congressional action in November authorizing American ships to arm themselves and to trade with the belligerents — that is, to transport lend-lease aid to Great Britain. There was no declaration of war against Germany, no severing of diplomatic relations. "We Americans have cleared our decks and taken our battle stations," the President had stated even before repeal of the Neutrality Act, " . . . [standing ready] in the defense of our nation and the faith of our fathers to do what God has given us the power to see as our full duty."

The country was not by any means wholly united behind an undeclared shooting war. The lines were drawn even more sharply between interventionists and non-interventionists. Under the leadership of the Committee to Defend America by Aiding the Allies, headed for a time by William Allen White, the interventionists demanded an end to further temporizing and delay in their growing insistence upon direct entry into the war against Germany.

The non-interventionists, whose isolationist wing was organized as the America First Committee, with the active participation of Senator Wheeler, Colonel Lindbergh, and Robert R. McCormick, owner of the *Chicago Tribune*, declared bitterly that the President was in fact taking the country into war; and they fought tooth and nail every administration measure that they felt prejudiced our neutrality.

Gallup polls, in the fall of 1941, revealed a highly confused public opinion, wavering uncertainly between the positive arguments of both groups. The American people wanted to aid the Allies and to avoid the risks of war, and they hardly knew how to reconcile these two conflicting aims. In Congress, a resolution to extend the original Selective Service Act had passed the House in August by a single vote, while repeal of the Neutrality Act had been accepted only upon the urgent plea of both President Roosevelt and Secretary Hull by a vote of 212 to 194 in the House and 50 to 37 in the Senate.

The country was divided, but the sands of peace were running out. By the end of November, there appeared little possibility that the shooting war in the Atlantic could much longer be kept from developing into an open and complete break with Germany. For all the attacks upon the Administration by bitter-end isolationists, who continued to insist that the war was none of our concern, public opinion seemed to be swinging closer and closer to favoring active participation. Entirely apart from what the country desired, however, circumstances had drawn us to the very edge of the abyss. The United States was no longer wholly in control of its own course of action — when, suddenly and for a great majority of the people quite unexpectedly, the dreaded incident that would precipitate actual hostilities grew, not out of the tense situation in the Atlantic, but from a gathering crisis in the Pacific.

On December 7, 1941, Japanese bombers drove in upon Hawaii to attack Pearl Harbor.

Storm over Asia

The American people had not been unaware of the threatening situation in the Pacific. Glaring headlines telling of the growing crisis in our relations with Japan had throughout the summer and autumn rivaled those reporting the Battle of the Atlantic. A public, as confused over the issues at stake in the Far East as over the situation in Europe, was divided upon the question of whether a general war in the Pacific could possibly be forestalled, or had become so highly probable that the United States might better take the initiative and strike first at Japan. Again, non-interventionists favored a policy of peace; interventionists clamored for decisive action. Yet for all this controversy, popular attention was more generally centered upon our relations with Germany. A direct attack by Japan upon American territory was hardly envisioned by the general public. There was shocked and stunned surprise in millions of American homes as the fateful news of Pearl Harbor broke in upon the usual Sunday afternoon radio programs.

To trace the pattern of events that led to war with Japan, it is necessary to turn back to the outbreak of the "China Incident" in 1937. When Japan first embarked upon her attempted conquest of China, the policy of the United States, as we have seen, was to avoid any entanglement in this distant conflict. A growing sympathy for China soon became manifest, however, and there arose in many quarters a demand that the United States should not stand aside while Japan battered her way to a far-eastern over-lordship. An embargo on the trade still left open to her because of failure to apply our neutrality law was strongly urged by advocates of collective security, and in many parts of the country un-official boycotts were declared on all Japanese imports, with thousands of American women trying to curtail such trade through their refusal to wear silk stockings. When the Japanese began indiscriminately bombing Chinese cities, public indignation flared up on an even wider scale and a moral embargo was imposed upon further shipments to Japan of airplanes and high-quality aviation gasoline.

The Administration, nevertheless, resisted all pressure for any more active measures to restrain the Japanese warlords. While the United States repeatedly warned Japan that it would not under any circumstances recognize the New Order that she was attempting to establish in eastern Asia, our policy was one of studiously avoiding any overt act of opposition that might possibly precipitate hostilities. Secretary Hull urged American citizens to withdraw from China to lessen the risks of any incident that might lead to conflict. Far more significant, Japan was allowed to continue her purchases in this country of many of the commodities that served to maintain her armies in China, and we continued to sell her huge quantities of scrap iron and oil. Not until July, 1939, did we make any move even threatening restrictions on trade. It was then announced that the existing Japanese-American commercial treaty would be terminated within six months.

This move was heartily endorsed by a public anxious to see its implied threat carried out. A majority of more than eighty per cent, on the basis of Gallup polls, approved the Government's action in canceling the trade treaty, and favored upon its expiration a complete ban upon all further shipments of war supplies.

Five weeks after this development, the outbreak of war in Europe rendered this touchy situation both more complicated and more critical. All idea of a trade embargo was put aside.

The problem could no longer be considered as involving only a conflict between Japanese imperialism and the traditional American support for China's independence and the Open Door. Through her signature of the anti-Comintern pact, Japan had already taken her stand with the Axis Powers. Would she now enter into active partnership with Germany and Italy? Would the aggressor nations join forces in a concerted world-wide attack upon the democratic nations? For a time there were no further developments presaging such united action, but after the fall of France in the summer of 1940, the possibilities of a general war breaking out in the Pacific were heavily underlined.

Japan seized the opportunity to broaden the sphere of her operations in eastern Asia. On the ground that China, still unconquered for all the fury of Japanese attacks, was receiving supplies through Indo-China, the Tokyo Government demanded of the helpless Vichy régime the right to send troops into northern Indo-China. The economic pressure that had for some time been exerted upon the Dutch East Indies was increased in an attempt to bring these rich islands within the Japanese sphere. Effectively employing the slogan of "Asia for the Asiatics," the Japanese militarists, now fully in control of foreign policy, were reported by Ambassador Grew in Tokyo as being determined to seize upon what they regarded as a "golden opportunity" to achieve their ambition of making Japan supreme throughout the Orient. And finally in September, 1940, the menace to far-eastern peace in Japan's southern advance was still further emphasized by the announcement that Japan had officially joined the Axis, concluding a treaty of alliance with Germany and Italy apparently aimed directly at the United States.

American policy continued to hew to the narrow line already marked out. The threat to our interests when Japan moved into Indo-China was fully recognized, as revealed in the dispatches of Ambassador Grew, but it was felt even more strongly under these new circumstances that any application of economic sanctions might force war, and that hostilities in the Pacific would block our efforts to aid the democratic forces fighting Nazi Germany. Our rearmament program was just getting under way. It was the hope of the Administration that an attitude of firmness without undue provocation might restrain Japan and at least maintain the Pacific *status quo.*

To implement this policy, some new restrictions were imposed upon our trade with Japan. On the basis of requirements for our program for national defense, export licenses were withheld for aviation gasoline, various types of machine tools, and, finally, scrap iron and steel. There was still no ban upon oil shipments. At the same time, additional loans were granted to the Chinese, total advances by the close of 1940 amounting to $170,000,000; and after passage of the Lend-Lease Act in March, 1941, China was designated as a nation whose defense was vital to that of the United States. The following months also witnessed the dispatch of various missions to Chungking, including economic and financial experts, transportation engineers, and finally a military mission, while as a sign of its friendship, the United States pledged itself to relinquish its extraterritorial rights in China — a pledge that was to be fulfilled when a treaty for their abrogation was signed in January, 1943.

No one of these moves served to halt the Japanese march southward. Having dispatched troops into southern as well as northern Indo-China, occupied the island of Hainan, and swung Thailand within her sphere of influence, Japan steadily expanded her area of control in southeastern Asia. It was a secret, creeping advance, each new move first denied by Tokyo, but the growing threat to British possessions in southeastern Asia, to the Dutch East Indies, and to the Philippines became more serious with each passing month and week. Our policy of "firmness" appeared to have no effect whatsoever, and in open defiance of the interests of all other powers, Japan gave every indication that she was prepared to call the bluff of any nation that sought to restrain her.

The American public grew increasingly restive and increasingly alarmed during the spring and summer of 1941. The demand for action that would call Japan to account gathered added weight, and the Administration found itself under heavy attack for what its critics called a policy of cowardly caution and timidity. But while popular polls revealed a majority opinion in favor of trying to keep Japan from seizing the Dutch East Indies or Singapore, it did not approve running the risks of war to keep these territories out of Japanese hands. There were exactly the same contradictions in popular thinking as in the case of aid to the Allies.

President Roosevelt was, nevertheless, moved in July, 1941, to take that decisive step toward economic sanctions that had long been urged upon him, but from which he had carefully refrained for fear of the consequences. An executive order was issued freezing all Japanese assets in the United States. This was in effect a total embargo on trade, necessarily including oil shipments, and Japan's leaders consequently found themselves facing the alternative of submitting to American pressure and abandoning their program of expansion or trying to break through the American economic blockade.

On the eve of this announcement of the freezing of Japanese credits, the President explained the policy that the Administration had been following, but which it was now prepared to abandon. His sole purpose had been, Roosevelt stated, to prevent "a war from starting in the South Pacific by all possible means, even including the shipment of some supplies to Japan." He expressed his conviction that if the United States had cut off oil any earlier, Japan would have long since attempted to seize the Dutch East Indies in order to assure herself of such an essential commodity, and there would inevitably have been hostilities. "Therefore, there was, you might call it," Roosevelt said, "a method in letting this oil go to Japan, with the hope — and it has worked for two years — of keeping war out of the South Pacific for our own good, for the good of the defense of Great Britain, and the freedom of the seas."

PEARL HARBOR

Although the public hardly realized the full significance of the step that had now been taken and continued to hope that Japan would press no farther southward, events in southeastern Asia revealed a steadily growing tension. Japan's penetration of Indo-

China was not halted; her advance continued relentlessly. The United States hastened the reinforcement of Hawaii, Guam, and the Philippines, placing Major-General Douglas MacArthur in charge of all American troops in the latter islands; withdrew such American forces and gunboats as were still stationed in China, and concluded a close accord for mutual defense with the British and Dutch East Indies Governments.

At the same time, negotiations looking toward a peaceful settlement of Pacific problems, carried on through frequent conversations between Secretary Hull and Ambassador Nomura, were not broken off. Yet, as they continued through the summer, every single exchange, it was later to be revealed, served only to emphasize the widening gap between the American and Japanese positions. Knowing only that negotiations were being held, the public, however, had little realization of how sharp the conflict between the two nations had actually become. Japan proposed a settlement that in effect would have meant American abandonment of China to Japan's tender mercies, and the United States countered with the proposal that it would suggest that China enter peace negotiations with Japan only if the latter nation first communicated its terms to the United States. Many other issues were taken up in these Hull-Nomura conversations, but the crux of the problem remained the status of China, with Japanese imperialism and the Open-Door policy in immediate and direct conflict.

Under such circumstances no headway could be made unless one or the other nation gave way. Neither was willing to do so. The Japanese militarists could not admit the failure of their whole program of national aggrandizement; the United States was unwilling either to sacrifice its interests in eastern Asia or to betray China. Whatever opportunities might once have existed for reconciling such divergent policies, the published correspondence of the two Governments during the crucial summer and autumn of 1941 reveals that the time for reconciliation had long since passed.

Secretary Hull had by autumn given up virtually all hope of a peaceful settlement, and early in November reported at a cabinet meeting a warning from Ambassador Grew that attack by Japan was an "imminent possibility." Nevertheless, he was unwilling to let slip any opportunity, however slight, to reach an understanding. If he could not assure peace, he might at least postpone war a little longer. A second Japanese envoy, Saburo Kurusu, dispatched by the Tokyo Government to join Ambassador Nomura, was consequently welcomed at Washington on November 15, but while the public took new heart at what it interpreted as a mark of Japan's desire to reach an accord, Hull saw no sign that Japan was prepared to make any real concessions.

Eleven days later, in what he recognized was diplomacy's last despairing gesture ("the matter will now go to the officials of the army and navy," he told the British ambassador soon afterwards), the Secretary of State outlined to the two Japanese envoys his final terms for the re-establishment of friendly relations and restoration of normal trade. These proposals contemplated a broad program of mutual commitments governing every phase of Pacific relations. In effect, however, Japan was called upon to acknowledge the territorial sovereignty of China, withdraw from the tripartite pact with Germany and Italy, conclude a general treaty of non-aggression, and recall her troops from both China and Indo-China. In return, the United States would also subscribe to the general terms of this accord, remove the freezing restrictions on Japanese funds, and conclude a most-favored-nation commercial treaty.

Secretary Hull was reaffirming, in perhaps more definite and precise terms than he had ever used before, the attitude he had maintained since the negotiations first started. He was restating our traditional policy. There was to be no more appeasement in the Far East, and the United States was at last prepared to take the consequences of making its position unequivocally clear.

The reply which the Japanese envoys delivered to Secretary Hull, completely ignoring a further appeal for peace directed personally to the Emperor by President Roosevelt, was a blunt rejection of the American plan. "It ignores Japan's sacrifices in the four years of the China affair," the note stated, "menaces the empire's existence itself and disparages its honor and prestige." The impassable gulf between the American and Japanese viewpoints was even more manifest in the Tokyo Government's embittered tirade against American attempts to destroy "Japan's position as the stabilizing factor of East Asia." So extreme was the language of the reply that Secretary Hull indignantly declared that the document was "crowded with infamous falsehoods and distortions — infamous falsehoods and distortions on a scale so huge that I never imagined until today that any Government on this planet was capable of uttering them."

This interview between Secretary Hull and the Japanese envoys took place at 2:20 P.M. on December 7, 1941. Just an hour earlier the final blow to all peace negotiations had been struck by the Japanese air force. Whatever the policy of the United States might have been, had rejection of our proposals been followed merely by a further Japanese advance in southeastern Asia, Pearl Harbor decided the issue of peace or war irrevocably.

On the day after Japan's attack, President Roosevelt went before Congress and asked recognition of the state of war that had been so suddenly thrust upon the country. Both houses acted at once with only a single dissenting vote, and the President was duly authorized to employ all the resources of the Government to bring hostilities to a speedy and victorious end. Three days later, Germany and Italy declared war on the United States, and once again Congress was called upon to take appropriate action, this time not a single voice being raised in opposition.

27

Total War

The First Round Overseas

When President Roosevelt asked Congress to declare war, he did not find it necessary to make any such eloquent appeal for action as had President Wilson in 1917. Events spoke for themselves. Whatever mistakes may have marred the conduct of our foreign policy since the failure to realize the fruits of victory after the first World War — and there was no denying there had been grievous mistakes — war was now a brutal and inescapable fact that the American people had to accept. The divisions in public opinion which had persisted up to the attack on Pearl Harbor were reconciled overnight. The United States, more united than ever before in its history, was at war; and it had entered upon a conflict declared by Roosevelt to be one not only for our survival as a nation, but for the preservation of all those spiritual values which America had always cherished. The country rallied at once to support the measures which had to be taken for national defense and for ultimate attack upon the enemy overseas.

In the first weeks of war, American forces in the Pacific suffered a series of catastrophic reverses that awoke the country to a feeling of actual peril that it had not known since the Civil War. The losses at Pearl Harbor were even more devastating and more dangerous than was at the time realized. Nevertheless, even partial reports drove home the harsh truth that our Pacific fleet had been dealt a well-nigh fatal blow. And in the meantime Japan struck at Wake Island, at Guam, and at the Philippines. A dazed public suddenly awoke to the realization that the United States had already lost the first round in the Pacific, and was engaged in a desperate defense of the Philippines that offered no

real chance of more than temporarily slowing up Japan's relentless advance.

There was no comparable attack on American possessions by
the European partners of the Axis. The fighting on the continent
in the winter of 1941-42 was marked by the first great Russian
counter-offensive, launched after the heroic stand of the Red
Army had saved Moscow, and by the seesaw battle for control of
North Africa which eventually found the British forces grimly
holding a line well within Egypt at El Alamein. More immediately important for the United States was the Battle of the Atlantic. While all available naval forces were thrown into this
critical struggle to keep open the sea lanes to Great Britain and
Soviet Russia, German submarines pressed home their attack on
Allied shipping with such vigor that an alarmingly high rate of
losses recalled the similar situation confronting the United States
when it had been drawn into war a quarter of a century earlier.

The American public had for a time fears other than those of
further defeats overseas. Might not the Japanese Navy, taking advantage of our losses at Pearl Harbor, directly attack the western
seaboard? Might not Germany attempt to bomb cities along our
eastern coast? While all precautions were at once taken by the
army and navy, home defense became an urgent responsibility
for the people themselves. Airplane spotters watched the skies
for enemy bombers; volunteer air-raid wardens prepared for every
emergency, and practice black-outs were held in cities and towns
throughout a large part of the country. Although no direct attacks on either the east or west coast actually materialized, the
possibility, however remote, of their taking place served to
heighten the tension that characterized the first weeks and months
of war. The United States was entering upon a conflict that was
to be fought overseas, on a fluctuating front that girdled the
globe, but for a time there was no certainty that hostilities might
not somehow be brought directly to the Western Hemisphere.

A first dramatic demonstration that the United States did not
stand alone was the arrival in Washington of Prime Minister
Churchill and the formation, through a declaration of policy
issued on January 1, 1942, of the United Nations. The way for

close collaboration between the United States and Great Britain had already been prepared through the Atlantic Conference, and this alliance was now broadened to include Soviet Russia, China, and all other nations at war with the Axis. Twenty-six governments in all — the number would eventually be increased to forty-six — agreed to employ their full forces against those members of the Axis Pact with which they were engaged in hostilities, to co-operate with one another throughout the war, and to refuse to grant any separate peace or armistice to the enemy. Furthermore, the signatories of the Declaration of the United Nations accepted as their common program the statement of principles and purposes that Roosevelt and Churchill had written into the Atlantic Charter as their collective war aims.

While diplomacy was thus setting up a united political front against the Axis, the reverses in the southwest Pacific continued to grip public attention. Abandoning Manila on January 2, 1942, American and Filipino troops, fighting under the command of General MacArthur, retreated to the Bataan Peninsula, where they doggedly resisted far superior Japanese forces until April 8. Even then the fortress of Corregidor held out valiantly for another month, and all of British Malaya, the Dutch East Indies, and southern Burma were in enemy hands before the American flag was finally lowered in the Philippines on May 6. Japan had then successfully completed what she hoped was only the first stage of her conquests. She dominated all eastern Asia and in the broad reaches of the Pacific had extended her control over an area embraced by a vast arc that swung from her own northernmost possessions in the Kuriles, through the Marshall and Gilbert Islands, to the Solomons and New Guinea. Where might she strike next? — at Australia? at India? at Russia? or at the United States?

American interception of a strong Japanese fleet, heading apparently for either Australia or the New Hebrides, was a first answer to such questions, and in the great naval and air battle of the Coral Sea, fought just after the fall of Corregidor, planes from the carriers *Lexington* and *Yorktown* inflicted such heavy damage on the enemy forces that they were turned back. Less than a month later an even more decisive air-naval battle off Midway Island resulted in the dispersal of another Japanese fleet advancing dangerously in the central Pacific. Although still fighting on the defensive and suffering heavy losses, the United States had won its first naval victories, called at least a temporary halt to Japanese conquest, and demonstrated to all the world that while it had been rocked back on its heels by the enemy's first surprise attacks, it had not been driven entirely out of the Pacific. In August the landing of American marines upon Guadalcanal, in the Solomon Islands, marked the first hesitant, costly beginning of offensive operations. Bitter and protracted fighting, both on land and at sea, was stemming the Japanese tide. The first phase of the Pacific war had come to an end.

While these operations in the Southwest Pacific, under the command of General MacArthur, rescued from the Philippines, and Admiral William F. Halsey, were slowly getting under way, a first move was also made to bring more effective support to our allies in the European war zone. On the morning of November 7, 1942 — eleven months after our entry into the war — American and British forces commanded by General Dwight D. Eisenhower landed in North Africa to occupy French Algeria and Morocco. It was part of a grandiose plan, agreed upon in consultations between President Roosevelt and Prime Minister Churchill, to trap the German Afrika Korps under Marshal Rommel in a gigantic pincers movement: the new Allied advance to be co-ordinated with a drive already launched from El Alamein by the British Eighth Army under General Montgomery. There was brief French resistance to our landings, at Casablanca and Oran, but on November 11, as a result of negotiations with Admiral Darlan, who assumed authority in North Africa in the name of the Vichy Government, all fighting ceased. As the Anglo-American forces drove toward Tunisia, and General Montgomery rolled back the Germans in Libya, the most extravagant hopes were aroused of quick and decisive success in clearing the Mediterranean of Axis control and attacking what Churchill described as Europe's "soft underbelly." Their fulfillment was to be agonizingly delayed. Nevertheless, on this front as in the Pacific, the tide of enemy conquests began to recede.

Although the United States had been largely on the defensive since Pearl Harbor, it was finally beginning, as 1942 drew to a close, to gain the initiative. It now could determine how and where it would fight. Moreover, a bombing raid on Japan on April 18 by a squadron of planes led by General Doolittle, and four months later an Allied commando attack on the French coast at Dieppe, had been spectacular if premature harbingers of things to come. Both in the Pacific and in Europe, a start had been made toward bringing the tremendous weight of American arms to bear upon the Axis Powers.

Mobilizing Industry

During the first year of hostilities, the United States was swiftly mobilizing the industrial resources and manpower that were to make possible final victory. The far-flung operations of our naval and military forces, expanding gradually throughout the entire Pacific, eastern Asia, North Africa, the Middle East, and finally western Europe, were naturally the most spectacular and ultimately decisive American contributions to the war. After 1941 as after 1917, however, the production of arms and ammunition, of ships and planes and tanks and guns, of the myriad supplies demanded by modern warfare, was the basic factor in the national war effort.

The conversion of the country from a peacetime to a wartime basis had been a remarkable achievement during the first World War. It was an even more stupendous accomplishment in this far greater national crisis. The United States evolved a war economy that not only continued to send abroad under lend-lease the immense quantities of supplies required by our allies, but by the close of 1944 was sustaining an American army and navy totaling almost twelve million men, of whom over half were serving overseas in the four quarters of the globe.

Although everything was on a much vaster scale, this transformation to a wartime economy followed in many ways the general pattern of 1917. It was once again to prove necessary to advance by trial and error, sometimes repeating old mistakes, before smoothly functioning machinery could be established for making our national resources fully available. There was finally created, however, a hierarchy of special agencies which in the spring of 1943 were made subject to the general control of an Office of War Mobilization. The task of this policy-making board, headed until 1945 by former Supreme Court Justice James F. Byrnes, was to unify the work of all subordinate agencies and to settle questions of overlapping and sometimes conflicting authority.

In the immediate field of industrial mobilization, the job previously handled by the Office of Production Management was taken over by the War Production Board. Until the summer of 1944, when he was replaced by Julius A. Krug, the WPB was directed by Donald M. Nelson, a former executive of Sears, Roebuck and Company. Related problems of manpower soon proved to need special direction, and for this task there was established a War Manpower Commission, headed by Paul V. McNutt, which for a time included among its divisions the Selective Service Bureau, charged with the actual induction of drafted men into the armed services. Only less important agencies in this general category were the War Shipping Administration, whose building program was handled by the Maritime Commission; the War Food Administration, responsible for adequate agricultural production, and the Foreign Economic Administration, which consolidated control of foreign trade, economic warfare, and lend-lease.

To adjust the national economy as a whole to the enforced concentration upon production of war materials, it also proved necessary to expand the controls which before Pearl Harbor had been administered by the Office of Price Administration. An Office of Economic Stabilization was established for this purpose, first under the direction of James F. Byrnes, and then of Fred M. Vinson. It was subject to the supervision of the Office of War Mobilization, but had the immediate task of combating the danger of inflation. The OPA was left in charge of both prices and rents, while a new National War Labor Board, succeeding the National Defense Mediation Board, was made responsible for wage controls.

It was in January, 1942, that the War Production Board took over its functions with full authority to promote "the most effective prosecution of war procurement and war production" — the allocation of raw materials, determination of priorities, conversion of factories to essential war industries, and all related responsibilities. "Debating societies are out," Chairman Nelson declared. "We are going to have action." The WPB brought automobile assembly lines to a full stop to enable that industry to convert its manufacturing facilities to the production of airplanes, tanks, and motorized army equipment; it promoted the construction for war purposes of new industrial plants at a cost of billions of dollars; it seized stocks of essential raw materials throughout the country; and in scores of other ways proceeded to direct the course of American industry.

It banned the making of radios for civilians, limited canning operations, restricted the manufacture, among many other products, of plumbing fixtures, luggage, electrical equipment, cosmetics, and furniture. It halted or drastically curbed production of lawnmowers, typewriters, safety razors, hardware, garden tools, and zippers. It allocated newsprint and prohibited the use of rubber in scores of articles from girdles to golf balls. It simplified styles in women's clothing, doing away with unnecessary frills, and fixing maximum skirt lengths, and it decreed that trouser cuffs and patch pockets should be eliminated in men's clothing. So sweeping, indeed, were the controls exercised that no industry and no factory escaped the WPB directives from Washington. The national emergency compelled the concentration of economic activity throughout the country on the single purpose of military and naval armament.

A first imperative need was expansion of the aviation industry. Not only the automobile makers, but scores of other manufacturers were called upon to convert their plants to the production of airplanes and airplane parts. President Roosevelt had in 1940 declared that he would like to see the United States turning out fifty thousand planes a year. It appeared at that time to be an almost fantastic figure. Nevertheless, the goal was almost reached in 1942, and nearly doubled a year later when annual production reached 85,946. With the output then rising still higher in 1944, it was estimated on the eve of the invasion of France that American industry had already manufactured 170,000 planes since Pearl Harbor (of which 33,000 had been sent to our allies) — a swelling stream of bombers and fighters that gave the United Nations, both in Europe and in the Pacific, air superiority that the Axis Powers were unable to challenge.

At the same time, and equally important, a tremendous impetus was given to the production of both naval vessels and cargo ships. The United States had suffered heavily at Pearl Harbor and there were continued losses in its naval operations in the Pacific and in the Atlantic. Yet the strength of the navy was more than doubled by 1943, and within another year it was tripled. Between July, 1940, and December, 1943, the over-all tonnage of naval vessels rose from 1,875,000 to approximately 5,000,000 tons, and in October, 1944, the number of combat ships was reported at 1100 in comparison with 380 four years earlier. Vessels of all types, including the special landing craft required for amphibious warfare, had in this period been increased from some 2000 to 50,000. With a complement of over 20,000 airplanes, the American Navy had become, as Secretary Knox was able to announce before his death in 1944, "the greatest sea-air power on earth."

The record in constructing cargo vessels was equally impressive. The general demands of global warfare decreed an expansion in our merchant marine far beyond the needs of the "Atlantic bridge," and for a time losses by submarine attack heavily underscored the desperate urgency of more rapid shipbuilding. The program already launched by the Maritime Commission was at once stepped up after Pearl Harbor with plans to construct 24,000,000 tons of new ships in 1942 and 1943. Eighty-one shipyards with 300 ways, representing an investment of $552,-000,000, were built, and it was estimated in 1944 that twice as many vessels could be constructed annually as there had been in the total pre-Pearl Harbor merchant fleet. The fiscal year of 1944 actually saw 1881 vessels, aggregating 19,000,000 tons, sliding down the ways. The introduction of new methods of shipbuilding, such as welding in place of riveting, had so speeded up production that the time for building a Liberty ship had been reduced since the start of the war from 242 to 41 days. In no other way could the tonnage have been made available to transport overseas the men and supplies necessary for our operations against Germany and Japan.

Settling priorities in steel and other materials for such equally imperative needs as those of airplane construction, naval replacements, and the building of cargo ships constituted one of the most complex problems facing the War Production Board. But it also had to meet the demands of scores of other industries providing the sinews of modern war — tanks, automotive equipment, heavy artillery, mortars, machine guns, rifles, shells, bombs, and small-arms ammunition. There was equally urgent need to build up a synthetic rubber industry to replace supplies cut off by Japanese occupation of the sources of raw rubber; to expand essential aluminum stocks; and to provide every possible facility for increasing the production of fuel oil and gasoline. And apart from all such war material, our rapidly expanding army and navy had to be furnished general supplies and equipment on a scale that taxed our national resources as never before in history.

The new rubber industry was by 1944 producing more than the equivalent of all supplies imported from southeast Asia before Pearl Harbor; aluminum production was actually in excess of current needs, and that of aviation gasoline had been increased from 40,000 gallons to 150,000 gallons a day. Almost comparable figures could be given for scores of other products. Three-fifths of the nation's industrial plant was converted to production for war, with the total output for 1944 estimated at approximately $80,-000,000,000, or almost half the value of all goods produced and services rendered in the nation's total economy.

Lend-lease absorbed a huge quantity of these war products, the value of all exports to our allies, between March, 1941, and March, 1945, totaling $32,377,000,000. Munitions accounted for over half the total, and the United Kingdom was far and away the most important recipient of such aid. It was followed by Soviet Russia, with smaller quantities of supplies being shipped to North Africa and the Mediterranean, the China-India-Australia area, Latin America, and Canada. However, the great bulk of all materials — whether ships or uniforms, tanks or food rations, machine guns or medical supplies — went to our own army and navy. On Labor Day, 1944, General Eisenhower expressed in behalf of the army under his command his "grateful thanks to the workers of America for having made this the best-equipped force in history."

The nation's farmers as well as its industrial workers were called upon to increase their output to meet wartime needs, and despite drought and shortages of labor, they responded as did industry with new production records. Under the direction of the War Food Administration, the national crop acreage was expanded to 380,000,000 acres, a larger cultivated area than ever before in our national history. Wheat production soared to a new peak of 982,000,000 bushels in 1942, a banner year for all crops, and then two years later topped even this high figure. Taking agricultural production as a whole, both crops and livestock, each successive year until 1945 saw the establishment of new records.

MANPOWER AND FINANCES

Such stupendous activity all along the home front inevitably posed a highly critical problem in regard to the availability of adequate manpower. Industry and agriculture lost millions of workers to the army and navy, as will be further noted in discussing the draft, but under the pressure of wartime needs the total labor force actually increased, despite such abnormal drains. The number of employed workers was estimated in 1943 at 53,-900,000 — a two-year gain of some six per cent — although there were already nearly ten million men in the armed services. The former unemployed, who had constituted such a vital problem during the nineteen-thirties, were rapidly absorbed in the expanding war industries, and other additions to the labor force came largely from among persons who had not formerly been included in it.

Women took over innumerable jobs that had been the usual prerogative of men. They went into munitions plants, airplane factories, and shipyards, taking their place on the assembly line, sometimes becoming welders and riveters. Between 1940 and 1944, the number of women employed as industrial workers (entirely apart from those who went into the fields to help out in agricultural production) rose from some 10,600,000 to almost 15,000,000.

The task of maintaining employment at the levels necessary for full production nevertheless remained an insistent challenge throughout the war period. The failure to enact legislation authorizing a complete draft of manpower, for industry as well as the armed services, handicapped the War Manpower Commission in attempting to adjust the conflicting demands of the armed forces, industrial management, and agriculture. However, longer hours of work with overtime pay were encouraged, controls were set up over the shift of workers both from industry to industry and from one part of the country to another, and employment ceilings were established in nonessential industries wherever labor shortages developed. Repeated changes of policy on such aspects of manpower control, in part the consequence of unavoidable changes in the requirements of both the armed services and industry, at times caused widespread concern and fears that the whole system was proving inadequate to meet the national need. The high production rate maintained by both industry and agriculture nevertheless demonstrated the over-all success of the country in meeting this problem as so many others.

The financing of the war effort involved unbelievably gigantic sums. Total expenditures on all war activities rose to $72,109,000,-000 in the fiscal year 1943 and for the next twelve months were reported at $87,038,000,000. Between July 1, 1940, when the national defense program first got under way, and July 1, 1944, the American people spent some $200,000,000,000 on the war — or already almost six times the full cost of our participation in the first World War. With the invasion of France and all-out attack on the citadel of Europe, the nation was pouring out its funds at the rate of almost $250,000,000 a day.

Taxes and borrowing were the only ways to meet such tremendous governmental expenditures, and as congressional appropriations steadily mounted, every effort was made to provide for wartime costs so far as possible on a current basis. It was essential not only to hold down a growing public debt, but to absorb the excess purchasing power, represented by the difference between national income and the volume of goods available for civilian buyers. Taxation was a weapon to fight inflation as well as to provide governmental funds. An excess profits tax, levied upon all corporation income that might be left over after the payment of normal taxes, sought to hold business profits down to pre-war levels. The surtaxes superimposed upon normal individual income taxes ranged from nineteen to eighty-eight per cent, while the base for individual taxes was broadened to include all those with an income of five hundred dollars a year, and collections were placed on a pay-as-you-go basis. Special excise taxes were both increased in number and sharply stepped up in rates.

Through such drastic measures, totally eclipsing what had appeared to be the heavy taxation of 1917 and 1918, internal revenue rose to $22,281,000,000 in the fiscal year 1943, and in 1944 had almost doubled even this high figure. While the United States was thus meeting almost half the costs of war through taxation — a far better record than a quarter of a century earlier — the tremendous gap that still remained between income and expenditures inevitably led to a phenomenal rise in the gross public debt. At the close of the fiscal year 1941 — that is, some five months before Pearl Harbor — it totaled $49,000,000,000. Three years later, it was more than four times this figure, and on March 31, 1945, it stood at the astronomical figure of $233,-950,000,000.

Popular loans supplemented the normal borrowings of the Treasury in meeting its obligations, and also served to curtail civilian purchasing power. Until the close of 1942, no special drives were conducted, but thereafter periodic war loan campaigns were held to win wider public participation, involving far larger amounts than those of 1917 and 1918. In each instance they were oversubscribed and when the books of the sixth loan were closed in January, 1945, the aggregate total collected was reported by the Treasury to be $109,300,000,000. While the subscriptions of banks and corporations accounted for the greater part of this total, the public too had responded with generosity.

Holding the Line Against Inflation

What did all this tremendous activity on the home front actually mean to the American people? What was the effect on everyday life of such far-reaching economic adjustments? How was the imperative challenge of total war met by the general public?

As already suggested, a first consequence of the wartime mobilizing of our resources was a great increase in the national income, resulting from expanded manufactures, and a decline in goods and services available for the civilian population due to the concentration of industry upon war production. It was estimated in 1943 that whereas income payments to individuals had soared to $152,000,000,000, the value of goods and services available for civilians was only $82,000,000,000. This excess purchasing power was greatly reduced by tax payments and loan subscriptions, but there was still left an inflationary gap, sometimes estimated to be as large as $20,000,000,000, that could easily stimulate a runaway rise in the cost of living. The prevention of any such breakdown in our economy was the task of the Office of Economic Stabilization, with the OPA empowered to maintain price ceilings, the Treasury controlling salaries, and the National War Labor Board undertaking to enforce a limit upon wage increases.

Although the OPA had been first set up in pre-Pearl Harbor days, it was the Emergency Price Control Act, passed by Congress in January, 1942, that provided the statutory basis for what was gradually to grow into a comprehensive program of controlled consumption that affected every phase of civilian life. At first restricted to the establishment of price ceilings and rationing for a limited group of commodities, this program was extended in October, 1942, after the creation of the Office of Economic Stabilization, to cover ninety per cent of all foods and to provide in addition for the stabilizing of wages and control of rents. The over-all objective, as President Roosevelt stated in a subsequent "hold-the-line" order, was to keep excess purchasing power in check and to make possible the distribution of such civilian supplies as were available upon an equitable and fair basis. In the face of threats that inflation might still break through such controls as had been set up, he urged, in addition to stabilizing prices, rents, and wages, a policy of still higher taxes, increased war bond purchases, and less public spending.

Before this program was fully developed, a first blow had been struck at normal civilian activity by the sudden curtailment of all rubber supplies as a result of Japanese occupation of Malaya and the Dutch East Indies. A public that had grown increasingly dependent upon automobile transportation suddenly found itself, under regulations promptly issued by the OPA, unable to buy new tires. The needs of the civilian home front had to be subordinated to those of the armed forces, and while the successful development of the new synthetic rubber industry was to provide essential supplies for the war effort, there were to be no tires, tubes, or other rubber products available for the public except under the most strict rationing for absolutely essential needs.

Inability to purchase new tires, however, was only the first shock suffered by motorists. The conversion of the automobile industry to the production of airplanes, tanks, trucks, jeeps, and other forms of motorized army equipment meant that no new passenger cars were to be produced for civilians. And then even more onerous, rigid restrictions were clamped down on gasoline sales, as the incalculable wartime demands for fuel steadily mounted. Rationing spread from east to west, was made nationwide, and finally the weekly allowance for passenger cars was cut down in some parts of the country to as little as a gallon and a half a week. There was no pleasure driving under such circumstances; workers dependent upon automobile transportation were required to establish car pools to get any supplementary rations.

These regulations affecting automobiles, gasoline, and tires were supplemented by restrictions upon the sale of countless other commodities. Typewriters and bicycles fell under the same ban as had automobiles; sales of fuel oil and kerosene were curbed, and the rationing of sugar and coffee marked the first curtailment of foodstuffs. Then on March 1, 1943, a point rationing system was set up for processed foods, and soon thereafter was extended to meats and fats. Ration coupon books were issued for every family in the country and community price ceilings established for something like a thousand grocery-store items. Housewives were thus protected from unwarranted price advances and assured an equitable distribution of dwindling supplies, but the business of daily shopping was immensely complicated. The armed services' demand for leather also brought shoes under the point system, and many other products were subject to almost equally rigid restrictions or purchasable only on a priority basis. Shortages that affected clothing, electrical equipment, household supplies, liquor, cigarettes, ice cream, chocolate — the list could be extended almost indefinitely — still further limited, and in some instances wholly prevented, normal civilian purchases.

The control of food prices was in many ways the crux of the problem facing the OPA in its efforts to check the rise in the cost of living, and it was particularly complicated in that it reached back to farm prices and therefore to agricultural production. Farmers generally looked askance at all controls and there was constant danger that, without the incentive of rising prices, they would curtail production. To meet this issue and hold prices all along the line, a system was consequently adopted in June, 1943, whereby the farmers were encouraged to increase essential supplies through special subsidies. These benefit payments were estimated to cost the Government $800,000,000 a year, but they saved the public many times this sum by enabling the OPA to maintain or even to lower prices to the consumer.

Closely interrelated to all such efforts to combat inflation was the control of wages. To prevent the spiraling effect upon the cost of living that wage or salary increases would inevitably have produced, the policy was adopted — after it had been shown to be impractical to freeze wages completely — of allowing no greater increase than the equivalent of the fifteen per cent rise in living costs which was estimated, in the summer of 1942, to have already taken place since January, 1941. The so-called Little Steel formula, as worked out in the National War Labor Board's settlement of a demand on the part of steel workers for higher wages, was thereafter maintained as an integral feature of the general stabilization program.

The danger of prices and wages getting out of hand, and of the country experiencing an inflationary rise in living costs comparable to that of the first World War, repeatedly strained the resources of both the Office of Price Administration and the National War Labor Board. The two agencies were again and again brought under attack in Congress and widely criticized by the public for what appeared at times to be their failure to resist the demands of competing pressure groups. Shifts and changes in procedure, conflict between the Administration and Congress upon basic policies, and replacements in administrative personnel all contributed to the difficulties in maintaining general economic stability. The country was often bewildered by the endless flood of orders, directives, questionnaires, licenses, and special regulations that were issued from Washington. The OPA grew into a huge, unwieldy organization with a staff of fifty thousand employees and more than two hundred thousand volunteer workers, including the nation-wide War Price and Rationing Boards, whose activities interfered directly, and in countless ways, with normal civilian life.

Nevertheless, the controls which it exercised served to hold the line against inflation far more effectively than had originally been thought possible. The cost of living rose gradually after Pearl Harbor, in comparison with pre-war averages, and in May, 1943, was up some twenty-five per cent. A roll-back in prices then checked this trend at least temporarily, and succeeding months revealed so slight an increase that it could be fairly maintained that stabilization had been achieved. At the close of 1944 the index was still less than thirty per cent above the pre-war figure on a newly adjusted basis.

LABOR AND THE PUBLIC

The conversion of industry to wartime production, and resultant problems of assuring adequate manpower for army and navy needs; the stabilizing of prices and wages; and the rationing of so many commodities, together with widespread shortages even in those which escaped rationing, directly affected the members of every class in American life — business, agriculture, and labor. The attitude of labor, both because of its vital rôle in the war effort and the huge size of the labor force, was perhaps of greatest importance in assuring general support for this comprehensive program. There was never any question of its basically loyal acceptance of necessary wartime controls and restrictions. Without such co-operation the amazing records of production all along the line could not have been made. Despite labor support, however, and the no-strike pledges that were made immediately after Pearl Harbor by the leaders of both the A.F. of L. and the C.I.O., there were instances of industrial strife that threatened to impair the war effort. Occasionally serious impairment did occur, though usually of short duration. Industrial workers were as patriotic as any other group in American life and as opposed as any other to war profiteering of any sort, but the threats of anti-strike legislation in 1941 had put them on guard against any infringement of their rights under the stress of wartime conditions. Labor was determined to protect the gains it had made during the nineteen-thirties.

A first serious dispute was precipitated by the insistence of the coal miners, renewing the struggle in which they were engaged just before Pearl Harbor, upon wage increases denied by the National War Labor Board on the ground that they exceeded the Little Steel formula. After the breakdown of negotiations in April, 1943, John L. Lewis ordered a strike in defiance of an ultimatum of President Roosevelt threatening to seize the mines if the workers quit their jobs. As the Government thereupon proceeded to take over control, some 450,000 soft-coal miners and 85,000 anthracite miners laid down their tools. They temporarily went back to work after assurances from Solid Fuels Administrator Ickes that their demands would be met, but when the National War Labor Board again refused to grant their wage increases, they went out on strike for a second time. Only after a serious interruption to coal production was a compromise agreement worked out in which the miners were allowed portal-to-portal pay as a means of raising their wages without technical violation of the Little Steel formula.

That same year a threatened strike of railway workers, growing out of the refusal of the Office of Economic Stabilization to approve wage increases, again forced the Government to take drastic action in behalf of the public interest. For a brief period it nominally took over the railways, but when a new and acceptable wage agreement was concluded, they were promptly returned to private management. Unlike the situation prevailing during the first World War when the railroads were operated by the Government — and this was the only instance in which controls exercised in 1918 were not greatly expanded in the nineteen-forties — it did not prove necessary to assert any more direct authority over railway operation than the general supervision maintained by the Office of Defense Transportation. The immense burden upon the railways was somewhat lightened by the availability of trucks and buses, so that they could transport millions of troops and tons of war munitions without any breakdown in their normal services.

As a result of the labor disturbances and strikes in the first half of 1943, affecting some two million workers, or more than twice the number involved throughout the whole previous year, Congress finally took a hand in the matter. In June, 1943, it passed, despite a presidential veto, the War Labor Disputes Act. This measure, more generally known as the Smith-Connally Act, gave statutory basis to the National War Labor Board, specifically authorized the President to take over control of any industry or individual plant where a serious work stoppage was threatened, and made subject to criminal prosecution anyone who then instigated or promoted a strike. It did not actually deny the right to strike, however, and its ambiguities left it open to attack by both the friends and foes of labor. While the President had occasion to act under its provisions on a number of occasions, the new law did not prove wholly satisfactory. Periodic strikes broke out in 1944 in both industry and transportation. They were generally settled promptly after the Government had once intervened, but such procedure did not prevent temporary interruptions to the war effort. While the newspapers invariably played up these strikes, the man-hours of work lost during the first two and a half years of war were actually the equivalent of only one day for each of twenty million war workers. In 1944 only two-thirds the time lost in 1943 was reported. Absenteeism for wholly personal reasons was a much greater deterrent to full production.

Some measure of industrial strife could not be avoided, and it paralleled other instances of restlessness and lack of co-operation involving every class in American life. There was a natural reaction to the stress and strain of wartime controls. The unity and spirit of sacrifice brought about by the attack on Pearl Harbor could not be completely sustained. As our land and naval victories removed virtually all danger of foreign attack upon continental United States, the public appeared on occasion to be becoming complacent. Profiteering and black-market operations in rationed goods flared up intermittently as a grave menace to the country's continued economic stability.

Nevertheless, the American people generally adjusted themselves to the necessary controls over their daily life and maintained a high level of war production despite all minor setbacks. They accepted price ceilings and rationing; they endured with little complaint the discomfort of crowded traveling, standing in queues at restaurants and stores, walking where they had once ridden in automobiles; they put up with what at times was an almost complete breakdown in the normal services of household economy, and they got along cheerfully without many of the things formerly considered almost essential to existence. In the factory, in the office, on the farm, and in the home, men and women stayed faithfully on the job. There was no real break on the home front or relaxation of the national determination to carry the war through to a final and complete victory.

Volunteers manned the posts to which they were called by the Office of Civilian Defense, serving as airplane spotters, air-raid wardens, and home guards. Women enrolled in the special services maintained by the Red Cross. Thousands of persons worked without compensation on ration boards and draft boards. The country as a whole responded wholeheartedly to the drives instituted for the sale of war bonds and for the collection of scrap iron, tin cans, rubber, paper, fats, and other raw materials needed for the production of military supplies. Millions of pints of blood were contributed to blood banks set up throughout the country. Food shortages were relieved through the cultivation of an estimated twenty million Victory gardens.

Public participation in the war effort exceeded by far that of 1917 and the essential unity of the nation was perhaps even more clearly demonstrated in the different psychological atmosphere that prevailed throughout the country. There was relatively little of the overzealous war propaganda, rabid intolerance, and suppression of individual freedom that had been so characteristic of first World War days. Under the direction of the Office of War Information, headed by Elmer Davis, the radio was widely used in whipping up enthusiasm for war bond and salvage drives, and newspapers and moving pictures played their full part in sustaining national morale. The spirit of the nation, however, was one of steady determination to see a necessary job carried through successfully rather than one of flamboyant patriotism or crusading fervor.

An exception to this more tolerant attitude was the treatment accorded Japanese-American citizens on the West Coast, who were herded into relocation camps because of fears of the aid they might possibly give to the enemy. But more generally the public refused to be thrown off balance by any war hysteria. There was no orgy of spy-hunting, only some seventeen hundred Germans and two hundred and fifty Italians were interned, few if any unwarranted arrests were made for alleged treason, and radicals were not persecuted for so-called un-American activities. The problem of dealing with conscientious objectors was handled by assigning this tiny minority to special work camps rather than imposing prison sentences upon them for their refusal to bear arms. Democratic rights and civil liberties were preserved to a remarkable extent, both in comparison with previous wartime experience and to pre-Pearl Harbor fears that the democratic way of life could not withstand the impact of total war.

THE ARMED FORCES

These manifold activities on the home front were a necessary means to an end: that end was raising, equipping, training, and sending overseas the armed forces that could encompass the final defeat of the Axis. The global character of the war in which we were engaged made this at once a far larger and infinitely more complex task than the nation had ever before faced. Yet under the final responsibility of General George C. Marshall, army chief of staff, and Admiral Ernest J. King, navy commander-in-chief, it was carried through with a success that amazed the nation no less than it did both our allies and our enemies. Our strength in 1945, with an army of 8,000,000 and almost 4,000,000 in the navy, marines, and coast guard, had grown out of a total armed force of some 800,000 but four years earlier. Moreover, the overseas deployment of more than half of our army involved the stationing of American troops in forty-six countries and separate islands, linked to the United States by 56,000 miles of supply lines.

Immediately after Pearl Harbor, our outlying bases in Alaska, the Aleutian Islands, the Panama Canal Zone, and Hawaii were strengthened, as well as those in Iceland and in the Caribbean, and soon army contingents began to make their way to far more distant parts of the world. They were dispatched to Australia, New Zealand, New Caledonia, and other islands in the southwest Pacific; to India as the nucleus of an Allied force for operations in Burma; to Liberia, Egypt, Irak, and Iran to establish lines of communication that would enable the United States to provide supplies for the British forces in the Near East and convey lend-lease aid to Soviet Russia; and, finally, to England and North Ireland which were to become gigantic bases for action in North Africa, and then on the European continent itself.

The strategy behind this world-wide distribution of American forces, as determined upon by the Combined Chiefs of Staff of the United States and Great Britain, was to hold the line wherever Axis attack threatened, wear down the enemy's outer defenses, and ultimately launch offensive operations. "All of these operations," President Roosevelt was to state in 1944, "had to be planned for in advance. . . . It has meant planning in terms of precisely how many men will be needed, and how many ships — warships, cargo ships, landing craft — how many bombers and how many fighter planes — and how much equipment and what types of equipment down to the last cartridge. And it has meant getting all of them to the right place at the right moment."

Raising this huge army and manning the ships of a navy that doubled and tripled in size demanded the induction of every available man who could be spared from the home front. The draft boards, first set up throughout the country in 1940, were under continual pressure to meet the quotas assigned to them. According to new provisions adopted after Pearl Harbor, all men between the ages of eighteen and sixty-five were required to register in December, 1941, with those between twenty and forty-five held liable for military service. Relatively few over thirty-eight were actually called, as the army came to place increasing emphasis upon youth; workers in essential war industries and in agriculture were exempted, and men with dependents were deferred for as long as possible. As the pool of those available under such regulations neared exhaustion, however, the age limit was lowered to eighteen, and more stringent deferment regulations led to the induction of married men and even pre-Pearl Harbor fathers. The list of so-called essential occupations was also progressively cut down. By January, 1945, over 10,000,000 men had been called into service from a total registration (of those between eighteen and thirty-eight) of 22,000,000. As the war went on, there were few families anywhere in the country which did not have husband, father, or son in the armed services, or were not otherwise directly affected by the impact of this sweeping mobilization of manpower.

The allocation of these hundreds of thousands of men to the several branches of the armed services (for after December, 1942, all enlistments by men of draft age were stopped, and the navy and marine corps, as well as the army, relied wholly upon the draft), and their assignment to the specialized units and technical schools necessary to train men for modern warfare, posed many highly complicated problems. Provision of adequate air personnel, both for airplane crews and ground forces, was a primary consideration in building up the new army, and the very flower of the nation's youth was drawn off for concentrated instruction at nation-wide air bases and flying fields. Pilots, navigators, and bombardiers, and also mechanics and maintenance personnel, had to be given thorough schooling. Hardly less important was the need for intensified training for the artillery, the tank corps, chemical warfare units, the engineers, and paratroop units.

The infantry, still the backbone of the army, had also to receive much more extended training than had ever before been considered necessary. Basic training for thirteen weeks was usually but a preliminary to a further period devoted to maneuvers that sought in every way to simulate the conditions of actual combat. This in turn was generally followed by still more preparation at overseas bases and assault training centers before the troops were assigned to actual combat duty. Prior to the invasion of France, the men assembled in England and northern Ireland went through every phase of the amphibious warfare in which they were to be called upon to engage, and thousands of them both in this theater and in the Pacific had the most rigorous instruction in commando tactics and hand-to-hand fighting, as well as in the handling of all kinds of mechanized equipment.

Officers were often drawn directly from civilian life for administrative posts, but again far more training was required to command men in combat duty than had been the case in 1917. The regular army, the national guard, and reserve officers provided the bulk of officer material in the early days of the war, but officer candidate schools and the air cadets thereafter met the needs of the expanding armed forces. Some 140,000 young men were also for a time assigned to college campuses under the Army Specialized Training Program, but the urgent need for manpower led to the abandonment of this program in 1944 except for men engaged in such specialized work as engineering or medicine.

The navy and the marines faced similar problems in training the personnel which they needed to man a constantly growing fleet and naval air force. Enlisted men and subsequently inductees were given "boot" training, and then assigned to active service either ashore or afloat, while officer candidates went through further instruction at training centers set up throughout the country. The navy also instituted a comprehensive program whereby potential officer material was sent to the colleges for general academic work, special instruction and drill, and training at naval flight preparatory schools.

In many ways as vital to the successful conduct of the war as recruitment of army and navy forces was the provision of an adequate force to man the rapidly expanding merchant marine service. The need for seamen on the cargo ships that were responsible for maintaining a steady flow of supplies for the troops overseas was imperative, and this service involved just as much risk and danger, in many cases, as front-line action in either the army or the navy. It was met throughout the war on a voluntary basis with the War Shipping Administration providing both a recruitment and training service which accounted for more than fifty thousand merchant marine officers and men. No greater contribution to the war was made than by the sailors who successfully maintained the overseas transport system, despite the heavy toll that was taken during the early days of conflict by German submarines.

Still another phase of the mobilizing of army and navy personnel was the enlistment of well over two hundred thousand women (entirely apart from army and navy nurses) in all branches of the services to free men for combat duty. WACS, WAVES, Women Marines, SPARS and WASPS — as these army, navy, marine, coast guard, and air service pilots were called — performed highly useful functions as clerks, technicians, telephone and radio operators, supply officers, machinists, parachute riggers, and Link Trainer instructors. Paralleling the important activities of women on the home front, their rôle in the armed forces was but another manifestation of the national response to the country's needs. Faced with the test of whether democracy could wage total war, the United States had given an unequivocally affirmative answer.

The Road to Victory

TURNING OF THE TIDE IN EUROPE

THE FIRST YEAR of American participation in the war was primarily one of preparation at home and, after our first retreats, dogged holding operations abroad. At the close of 1942, however, American forces in the southwest Pacific were consolidating their hold upon Guadalcanal, and, in conjunction with the Australians, were beginning to drive back the Japanese on New Guinea; while on the opposite side of the world, they were ready to take their part in a final Allied push in North Africa directed against the German forces in Tunisia. Together with even more important action on the eastern front, where the Russians had miraculously checked the Germans along the Volga after what had appeared to be the disastrous retreat of the summer of 1942, these developments in the Pacific and Mediterranean war zones had given a new aspect to the over-all picture of the war. Although the United Nations had not yet won any great offensive victories, the New Year was to open with prospects in dramatic contrast to those of January, 1942, in the aftermath of Pearl Harbor.

The great Russian victory at Stalingrad sent a new wave of confidence through Allied ranks, but public attention in this country remained more generally centered on the fighting in North Africa. The battle for Tunisia was the first trial by fire for the American forces in the European theater, and the raw, green troops which had occupied Morocco and Algeria against little resistance were to suffer serious reverses, notably at Kasserine Pass, before they found themselves.

As the British Eighth Army drove the German Afrika Korps into the Tunisian pocket from the east, however, the Americans and British closed in from the west. For a time the Axis forces stubbornly defended the so-called Mareth line, but with the juncture of Allied armies, including Free French troops, General Montgomery at last smashed through this position and the Americans and British surged forward in the north. Tunis and Bizerte fell on May 7, 1943, just six months after the first North African landings, and with all possible means of escape cut off, some two hundred and fifty thousand German and Italian forces finally laid down their arms and surrendered to the triumphant Allies. All danger of enemy activity in North Africa had come to an end, and the way was at last open for further operations to clear the Mediterranean and carry the attack directly to Italy.

Careful preparations were made by General Eisenhower for the next stage in the campaign. Air power had played a tremendous part in breaking the back of Axis resistance in Tunisia, and incessant bombing now paved the way for the advance upon Italy. In early June the island of Pantelleria, a first stepping-stone across the Mediterranean, capitulated after a terrific pounding from the air, and a month later our invasion forces descended upon Sicily. The first landings were highly successful, and despite stubborn resistance the greater part of the island and its capital city were in Allied hands before the end of July.

A sudden and dramatic turn in events occurred before the final conquest of Sicily. On July 25, there burst upon the world like a bombshell the exciting news that Mussolini had been ousted from power and the Fascist régime overthrown. Throughout the fighting in both North Africa and Sicily, German troops had proved to be the tough unbreakable core of the Axis forces. There had been mounting evidence that the Italians had lost what little heart they had ever had in the war. Did Mussolini's downfall mean that Italy would break all ties with Germany? And if she did, indeed, want to get out of the war, would she be able to do so?

As rumor and conjecture spread over the next possible development in the Italian drama, Allied troops in Sicily crushed the last remnants of Axis resistance and after intensive preliminary bombing invaded the Italian mainland. Five days later, on September 8, it was announced that the new Government headed by Marshal Badoglio in succession to the Fascist régime had secretly accepted Allied terms of unconditional surrender. But whatever hope the American public had that the collapse of Italy would also mean the withdrawal or surrender of the German forces fighting in Italy, was quickly dashed. When our troops followed up the original invasion of the Italian mainland with new landings on the beaches of Salerno, they found the Germans in full control and fiercely determined to block any advance on Naples. With the British meeting comparable opposition in their operations, it was October 1 before Naples was finally captured. In the meantime the greater part of the Italian fleet had escaped to the Allies, Sardinia had been turned over to their control, and on October 13, Italy declared war on her former Axis partner and was accepted by the United Nations as a co-belligerent.

As the American and British forces pushed their northward advance, it was confidently believed that they would be in Rome by Thanksgiving — by Christmas — then at least by Easter. But German resistance stiffened, and fighting under impossible conditions of terrain and weather, the Allies finally found themselves stubbornly held in what resolved into a long, bitter stalemate. Even the establishment in January of a new beachhead at Anzio, on the Italian coast between Rome and the Allied line, had failed to break the deadlock. The German command refused to fall into the expected trap, succeeded in closely confining the troops at Anzio, and prevented any union of the Allied forces. It was not until May, 1944, more than six long months after the capture of Naples, that the German line anchored on Cassino was finally cracked and the advance on Rome renewed.

The Mediterranean campaign fell far short of the expected conquest of all Italy, and a public whose hopes had been raised too high was sadly disappointed. Nevertheless, the fighting of 1942-43 brought the Mediterranean entirely under Allied control, greatly shortening the long supply route to Soviet Russia through the Persian Gulf; it exacted a heavy toll upon German forces and tied down thousands of troops in the further defense of Italy, and it enabled the Allies to move up their air base within flying range of southern Germany and the greater part of central and southeastern Europe. Although Italy did not represent a second front in the sense of all-out invasion of western Europe, it was nevertheless a new point of direct attack. The United Nations were on the offensive; Hitler was in retreat.

Simultaneously with these developments, Russia's armies were steadily pressing forward the advance initiated late in 1942, an advance that the Germans could not permanently halt; ever larger bombing raids from British bases were night and day pouring down death and destruction upon German cities, and less spectacularly but with equally great long-range importance, the campaign against German submarines was slowly but surely winning the Battle of the Atlantic. The United States played no part in the Russian advance other than to add to the effectiveness of the Red armies through the swelling volume of lend-lease supplies exported overseas, but an American air force contributed heavily to the success of the bombing of Germany, and the American Navy played a vital rôle in freeing the Atlantic from the menace of the submarine.

Throughout the greater part of 1942, the United States had been engaged in building up its air strength in England, but it was not until January, 1943, that the first all-American bombing assault upon Hitler's European fortress took place. Even then it was to be a long time before our part in this phase of the war could be fully sustained. The general strategy involved American daylight raids, relying upon the precision bombing made possible through our highly developed bombsights, to supplement the night raids of the R.A.F. At first our operations were limited to cities in France, Belgium, and Holland, but the area of attack soon broadened. Flying Fortresses and Liberators, protected by deadly shields of fighter planes, roared out over enemy country in ever-increasing numbers to inflict widespread damage upon German submarine pens, transportation facilities, military installations, industrial plants, and factories.

With the winter of 1943 and during the following spring, this combined Anglo-American air attack gained tremendous power. United States planes based on England bombed the Saar and the Ruhr, Hamburg and Bremen, Berlin itself; they flew from Italian fields in a widening arc to attack Bucharest, Belgrade, and other Balkan cities as well as the Rumanian oil fields at Ploesti. Moreover, the big bombers now went out by the hundreds, and even in occasional thousand-plane raids, pressing forward an almost uninterrupted campaign aimed at driving the Luftwaffe from the skies, disrupting German industry, and generally softening up continental Europe for the final land attack. On the eve of the invasion of France, General Henry H. Arnold, commander of the United States Army Air Force, announced that since the beginning of the war, American planes had flown 746,000 sorties, loosed 463,091 tons of bombs, and while suffering losses of 6154 bombers and fighters, had destroyed or damaged 32,149 enemy planes. Figures could not tell the full story of the effectiveness of these operations; it was revealed only by German weakness in the air when Hitler's armies were put to their final test.

Shipping losses through submarine attacks had given a dangerous immediacy to the Battle of the Atlantic during the first half of 1942. German undersea craft were sinking American oil tankers off the Florida coast, the Virginia Capes, and New Jersey; dimmed-out cities along the eastern shore were a grim reminder to the American people of how much was at stake. With more intensive counter-measures, however, sinkings were cut almost in half during the latter part of the year. Although persistent bombing of submarine pens contributed to this improvement, naval and air patrols throughout the North Atlantic ("Sighted sub, sank same," was the laconic report of one young flier) were the principal weapons of defense. Electronic devices worked their miracles in detecting the submarines, and depth bombs began to take an increasing toll that during one period reached an average of almost one craft sunk every day. For a time early in 1943 a shift in German strategy, the submarines hunting in packs rather than singly, appeared to offer a further threat to the Allied convoys transporting the men and munitions that were to make the invasion of Europe possible. But this new danger too was met.

As the year progressed, the joint communiqués issued by President Roosevelt and Prime Minister Churchill reported a steady decline in all shipping losses, while unofficial compilations for the entire twelve-month period put the total at only one hundred vessels in comparison with almost six hundred during the previous year. The spring of 1944 actually revealed naval and air attacks inflicting more destruction on submarines than they were able to inflict on Allied transports. Eventually no shipping losses whatsoever were reported over month-long periods. The Battle of the Atlantic had been won. Our communications with Europe were so successfully guarded that the supply and reinforcement of our expeditionary forces were fully assured.

ADVANCE IN THE PACIFIC

Simultaneously with these developments on the European front, a tremendous offensive was building up for the war in Asia. The strategy of global warfare had made Germany the Number One enemy. Berlin had to be taken on the road to Tokyo. Nevertheless, the United States was by no means neglecting the Pacific theater. The gradual pushing back of the Japanese forces in actions that ranged from the Aleutian Islands to the Solomons and New Guinea, together with submarine attacks on Japanese shipping that had by June, 1944, accounted for the sinking of some six hundred enemy craft, complemented the general repulse of the German forces on Europe's eastern front and in the Mediterranean.

An offensive aimed at driving the Japanese off the Aleutian Islands, where they had landed in midsummer, 1942, to occupy Attu and Kiska, opened early in 1943 with a heavy bombing attack. Yet not until May could American forces land on the first of these islands. A tough, bloody campaign had to be fought under the worst possible conditions before its Japanese defenders, refusing to surrender, had been virtually annihilated. Then on August 15, again after protracted bombings, landings were made upon Kiska — only to find that the Japanese had fled. Any further threat of attack in the North Pacific was now eliminated, and forces engaged in this area were at least partially freed for operations elsewhere.

In the meantime slow but effective progress was also being made in ejecting the enemy from the Solomon Islands at the other end of the vast arc of Japan's outermost conquests. The last pockets of resistance in Guadalcanal having been wiped out in February, 1943, after a naval victory the previous November had smashed enemy efforts at reinforcement, American fliers opened concerted bombing attacks, steadily mounting in intensity, upon other Japanese strongholds in the Southwest Pacific. The almost total destruction of still another large enemy convoy in the battle of Bismarck Sea on March 2-3, thereupon opened the way for further land attacks. Advancing along the eastern coast of New Guinea, to which the Japanese had been driven back the previous year, Allied forces captured Lae and Salamaua in September, landed at Empress Augusta Bay on Bougainville Island a month later, and secured a position that not only fully safeguarded Australia from any further danger, but made possible the gradual isolation of the important Japanese stronghold at Rabaul, on New Britain. No campaign of the war appeared to meet harder going than that of the Solomon Islands, and it was not to be brought to a final successful end until more than a year after the first landing on Guadalcanal. It was, however, to pay large dividends.

A first indication that this advance was eventually to link up with one in the Central Pacific, developing a powerful pincers movement directed in the first instance against the important Japanese bastion at Truk, was an air attack, followed by naval bombardment, on the Gilbert Islands. The powerful Pacific fleet that was being built up under the command of Admiral Chester W. Nimitz was swinging into action, and toward the close of November, 1943, under cover of its operations, our amphibious forces landed on Makin and Tarawa islands. Some of the bloodiest fighting that had yet occurred in the Pacific took place before Tarawa was conquered. Tokyo recognized the significance of what was happening far more than did the American public; for with the capture of the Gilberts, our Pacific fleet was really on its way.

This hard-won success was followed on the last day of January, 1944, by an invasion of the near-by Marshall Islands, our troops landing on Kwajalein, and then two weeks later occupying Eniwetok. Again there was fierce fighting, but without waiting to bring the Marshalls wholly under our control, the campaign was broadened, first by bombing from the air and then through shelling by naval task forces, to bring Truk under direct attack. In conjunction with the progress in the Southwest Pacific campaign, now marked by new landings in the Admiralty Islands, this advance in the Central Pacific was breaking through the Japanese defenses. Outflanked, by-passed enemy forces were being left "to wither on the limb." Even though the distance to Tokyo was still immense — it lay more than twenty-five hundred miles beyond the most forward American outposts either in New Guinea or the Marshall Islands — the demonstrated might of American arms, on land, on the sea, and in the air, clearly foreshadowed, in the spring of 1944, still further gains and even greater conquests.

CEMENTING THE UNITED NATIONS

Coalition war on a global front was no less demanding in the field of political strategy than in that of military strategy. Our relations with our allies in the struggle against the Axis Powers, our policy toward the exiled Governments or other representatives of the conquered countries, the attitude to be maintained toward the neutrals, considerations involving the future treatment of enemy nations, and the post-war organization of peace, made up a complex of tangled diplomatic issues that tested statesmanship to the utmost.

The public rarely questioned the conduct of military operations, although there was for a time a natural impatience at the delay in the opening of a second front in Europe and some criticism of the failure to exploit more successfully our first victories in Italy, but the handling of foreign affairs became on occasion a source of heated controversy.

The formation of the United Nations at the beginning of 1942 had not provided any certain guarantee of the collaboration so essential for effective war and yet so difficult to attain in any coalition. Subsequent meetings of President Roosevelt and Prime Minister Churchill — including those at Casablanca in January, 1943, and seven months later at Quebec — both assured and publicly demonstrated a close accord between the United States and Great Britain. Not only was their war strategy a common one, but it was directed by the Combined Chiefs of Staff of the two nations, and both in Europe and in the Far East their armed forces served under a unified command. Moreover, at the Quebec Conference, Roosevelt and Churchill gave a new precision to the immediate war aims of the two nations by declaring that the only peace terms the Axis Powers could expect were those of unconditional surrender. The very strength of Anglo-American solidarity, however, raised the question as to whether this accord also embraced Soviet Russia or risked the alienation of so important an ally.

There was no secret made of the fact that the Russians were becoming increasingly anxious for immediate opening of a second front in western Europe to relieve the tremendous pressure upon the Red armies. Apart from the Anglo-American landings in North Africa, however, no such move was made in 1942 and the Mediterranean war fell short of popular Russian expectations. While the delay in launching an invasion of western Europe thus appeared to endanger the Soviet Union's confidence in its allies, public opinion here and in England also seemed to have some cause for misgivings in regard to Stalin's policy as the advance of the Red armies continued without any announced assurances upon Russian war aims. The issue of strategic boundaries, involving the future of the Baltic countries and eastern Poland, complemented that of the second front, and the American people nervously wondered whether the United Nations were drifting apart even before Hitler had been defeated. German propaganda, in any event, made the most of such apparent differences in policy in trying to drive a wedge between Russia and the western democracies.

A dramatic move to allay mutual suspicions and bring about greater unity among the United States, Great Britain, and Soviet Russia was made in the autumn of 1943. Secretary Hull flew to

Moscow to take part in a tripartite conference with the British and Russian foreign ministers at which an accord was reached, with the added adherence of the Chinese Government, reaffirming the solidarity of the Allies in unmistakable terms. The foreign ministers not only pledged their Governments' continued collaboration in war; even more significantly, they stated in a joint declaration of policy, issued at Moscow on October 30, that they were agreed upon the necessity of establishing "a general international organization, based on the principle of sovereign equality of all peace-loving States, open to membership by all such States, large and small."

This accord was at once enthusiastically hailed in the United States both as cementing the wartime alliance of the four powers and holding out the promise of their continued co-operation after the war. Congress had been discussing post-war policy. The House had already adopted a resolution advocating American participation in a world peace organization, and the Senate promptly incorporated the Moscow proposal, by an overwhelming vote of 85 to 5, in a very similar measure. The lowering clouds of international distrust were swept away in a new wave of optimism over the possibilities of preserving future peace once the enemy had been defeated.

Within a month, an even more momentous conference was held at Teheran, where both President Roosevelt and Prime Minister Churchill met Premier Stalin. Only the most meager announcement was made of its results, but the greatest significance was seen in the statement issued by the three national leaders, on December 6, that their respective countries were prepared to "work together in the war and in the peace that will follow." The very fact that the heads of state had met was the best proof of Allied solidarity, and it was generally understood that agreement had been reached upon concerted military plans. "We came here with hope and determination," Roosevelt, Churchill, and Stalin declared. "We leave here friends in fact, in spirit, and in purpose."

Nor were the conferences at Moscow and Teheran the only proofs of unity within the ranks of the United Nations. On the eve of the latter meeting, Roosevelt and Churchill had conferred at Cairo with Generalissimo Chiang Kai-shek upon policy in the war against Japan. Publication of the results of this meeting, on December 1, revealed an agreement to insist upon the unconditional surrender of Japan. Moreover, she was to be stripped, not only of all the islands that she had seized or occupied in the Pacific, but of all the territories "stolen" from China since the first Chinese-Japanese War a half-century earlier. Manchuria, Formosa, and the Pescadores were to be returned to China, and Korea was "in due course" to become free and independent.

Policy toward countries not associated with the United Nations raised problems of quite a different order but almost as important. In order to protect our troops in North Africa, it was felt necessary to maintain friendly relations with Spain even though her Government was both fascist in character and openly sympathetic with the Axis Powers. The cry of appeasement was raised in criticism of the State Department's attitude on this issue, but not until the safety of our troops in North Africa was fully assured did we attempt to exercise any pressure upon Spain to induce her to afford less aid and comfort to the enemy. American policy toward Finland was bedeviled by the fact that while the United States was not at war with her, Russian-Finnish hostilities had been renewed when Germany attacked the Soviet Union in 1941. When Finland hesitated to accept Russia's proffered peace terms in the spring of 1944, we finally broke off diplomatic relations.

This phase of wartime diplomacy was not limited to the European theater. While the greater number of Latin-American countries, following a Pan-American conference at Rio de Janeiro in January, 1942, had fallen in line with our policy toward the Axis, either declaring war against its member nations or breaking off all relations, Argentina obdurately refused to align herself with the other nations of the Western Hemisphere. The problem was gravely complicated by internal political developments. At one time there appeared to be a promise of greater co-operation, and Argentina actually severed diplomatic relations with the Axis in January, 1944, but another shift brought into power a government of such marked fascist leanings that the United States refused to recognize it. Although Brazilian troops fought with the

Allies in the Italian campaign in 1944, Argentina still went her
own way despite all appeals and protests from Washington.

With this situation very much in the foreground, a conference
of all the other Pan-American nations met at Mexico City late in
February, 1945. The principles of solidarity agreed upon two years
earlier were strongly reaffirmed, and in the Act of Chapultepec,
the conferees set up regional machinery for united action, during
the duration of the war, against aggression from any quarter whatsoever. Although conspicuously absent from this meeting, the
way was left open for Argentina to return to the fold. Under such
concerted pressure, she at long last — late in March — declared
war on the Axis Powers and accepted the provisions of the Act of
Chapultepec. Her government was then officially recognized by
her sister republics, including the United States. Complete hemispheric unity, on paper at least, had become an all-inclusive
reality.

Our attitude toward enemy nations was first removed from the
sphere of military action to that of diplomacy upon the capitulation of Italy in the summer of 1943, and it has already been noted
that the Badoglio Government was accepted as a co-belligerent
in the war against Germany. Prolonged controversy grew out of
what was regarded in many quarters as a willingness to compromise with a régime that had not demonstrated that it was wholly
free of fascist influence. Confusions and uncertainties characterized the situation for the better part of a year, the American
public remaining largely ignorant of what had been done or what
had been promised. Premier Badoglio, however, finally undertook to make way for a more democratic régime. After the final
delivery of Rome from the Germans in June, 1944, King Victor
Emmanuel gave way to his son, Prince Umberto, and a new Government representative of all Italian political parties was set up
and duly recognized by the Allies.

More important than relations with any of the other countries
of Europe, except Great Britain and Soviet Russia, were those
with France. Upon that nation's defeat by Germany in 1940, we
had continued to deal with the Vichy Government maintained
by Marshal Pétain. Its façade of independence had, however,

completely collapsed when Hitler occupied all France following the Allied landings in North Africa. The question was consequently posed whether we should consider the colonial authorities in North Africa as the successors to the Pétain régime, or recognize the Free French, who under the leadership of General Charles de Gaulle had maintained a government-in-exile in London, refusing to accept either France's defeat or her surrender. In landing in Algeria and Morocco, it will be remembered, the United States had come to terms with Admiral Darlan, the representative of Vichy France and designated successor of Marshal Pétain, solely on the ground of his influence in North Africa. On December 24, 1942, however, Admiral Darlan was assassinated and General Giraud, with whom the American authorities had also established close relations, took his place. Our co-operation with this North African régime was vehemently resented by the Free French, who charged that it was still permeated by the collaborationist spirit of Vichy, and it also evoked widespread criticism in this country where General de Gaulle's heroic continuation of the war against Germany had won widespread sympathy.

Every effort was made to reconcile the Giraud and de Gaulle factions and in June, 1943, their forces were finally joined to establish a Committee of National Liberation. After a long period of political maneuvering among its members, Giraud was compelled to give way to de Gaulle and on November 9 the latter assumed full control in North Africa. The United States, nevertheless, remained reluctant to extend any further measure of recognition to the reorganized Committee of National Liberation. While its authority in North Africa had to be accepted, President Roosevelt expressly stated that he would not accede to its demands to be recognized as the French Provisional Government until the French people, freed from German control, could make known their own views. However sound such a theory might be, it did not silence criticism of our lukewarm attitude toward the only French leader with whom the Allies could presently co-operate.

It was after the actual invasion of western Europe that final steps were taken to settle this issue. A meeting was arranged between General de Gaulle and President Roosevelt, and following conferences in Washington in July, 1944, it was announced that the United States was prepared to extend *de facto* recognition to the Committee of National Liberation with authority to take over the civilian administration of such parts of France as were freed by the Allied armies, subject only to the military command of General Eisenhower. Some three months later, upon de Gaulle's return to Paris, full diplomatic recognition was granted to his Government, and step by step France began to regain her place as a full-fledged member of the United Nations and one of the great powers.

None of these agreements or understandings, whether between the Anglo-American Powers and Soviet Russia, with the French Committee of National Liberation, or with other European countries, could be construed as permanent accords fully settling the many political problems that the war had created. Their net result, however, was to strengthen the solidarity of the United Nations as they prepared to strike the final decisive blows against Hitler's Germany. The machinations of the German propaganda ministry in its efforts to undermine the Allied front had completely failed. The vast coalition arrayed against the Axis, for all the stresses and strains to which it had been subjected, and for all the diplomatic mistakes that may at times have been made, had stood firm.

Whether it would continue to do so after the European phase of the war had been brought to a close, and whether the embryonic organization called the United Nations would provide the basis for a future world organization to maintain peace, were further questions deeply concerning the American people. As the continuing years of war drove home the realization that the future security of the United States largely depended upon postwar agreements, public opinion began to look beyond the battlefields to the possible shape and form of the coming peace. It was by no means unanimous as to what course this nation should follow. Many isolationists remained unconvinced that American membership in a world peace organization was as certain a guarantee of national security as a more independent nationalist policy. Yet there was striking evidence of an increasing swing in favor of international collaboration, as revealed in public opinion polls in July, 1944, reporting that seven out of every ten persons believed that the United States should participate in a world organization. Moreover, such diverse groups as the Chamber of Commerce of the United States, the A.F. of L. and the C.I.O., the National Farmers' Union, the National League of Women Voters, the National Association of Manufacturers, and the American Legion all adopted resolutions, by overwhelming majority votes, in support of such a policy.

There was no question of where the Administration stood. Its attitude was implicit in our participation in such activities as the Interim Food Commission, the United Nations Relief and Rehabilitation Administration, and the World Monetary Conference. Support for an international organization had been publicly declared in the Moscow accords. President Roosevelt was apparently determined, however, to avoid at all cost the mistakes that President Wilson had made after the first World War. In the development of post-war policies he sought both to draw upon the counsel of all interested groups and associations throughout the country and to co-operate fully with Congress. His first explicit statement of the direction in which he was moving, on June 15, 1944, categorically rejected any idea of a world superstate, and generally outlined a program closely conforming to the principles enunciated at Moscow. There should be created after the war, the President said, an international organization of all peace-loving nations "to maintain peace and security and to assist the creation, through international co-operation, of conditions of stability and well-being necessary for peaceful and friendly relations among nations." He advocated a council of the four major powers, together with a suitable number of smaller countries, a general assembly, and an international court of justice. The forces of each nation, Roosevelt further proposed, should prevent deliberate preparation for war "through joint action when necessary."

A month after this general statement of policy, representatives of the United States, Great Britain, Soviet Russia, and China met in two conferences at Dumbarton Oaks, just outside Washington, for a series of exploratory conversations looking toward the adjustment and reconciliation of their respective plans for post-war co-operation. Without solving all problems, a tentative agreement was reached for the formation of a new world league, to be known simply as the United Nations. Its proposed charter followed the lines already forecast in Roosevelt's statement, with provision for a general assembly, a security council, an international court of justice, an economic and social council, and a secretariat. Far more important, the security council, controlled by the great powers, was to be authorized to check any threat to international peace through the use of armed forces placed at its disposal by member nations. These proposals were tentative, subject to further discussion by both governments and peoples before being presented to a full conference of the United Nations.

INVASION OF FRANCE

For all the progress made by both Allied arms and Allied diplomacy during the winter of 1943 and spring of 1944, these months were in reality a time of preparation. The bombing of Hitler's Europe became more and more effective; the Russian armies reconquered both the Ukraine and the Crimea; the Anglo-American forces in Italy finally broke through the German line anchored on Cassino, and, on the other side of the world, new amphibious operations in the Marshalls clearly opened the way for still further advance in the Pacific. Nevertheless, even these dramatic developments could not hide the fact that the global strategy of war was primarily directed toward the invasion of France and an assault upon Germany itself. The time was clearly approaching for the general offensive agreed upon at the Teheran Conference.

By May the nation was gripped by a feeling of great events impending which had been paralleled only by the tension of the months immediately following Pearl Harbor. But this time there was confidence that it was the United Nations and not the Axis

Powers that would take the initiative. The public waited nervously, feverishly, for the announcement that American and British troops had landed on the European coast. As the strategy of air raids changed from the bombing of industrial centers to greatly intensified attacks on airfields and transportation facilities in German-held territory, it became increasingly clear that D-day was close at hand. When would the Allied forces strike, and where? Twisting the dials on their radios every morning, the single thought in the minds of millions of Americans was the question: Is this the day?

The answer came on June 6. That morning the nation was electrified by the terse announcement that British, Canadian, and American troops had landed upon the coast of Normandy, and under the protection of mammoth air and naval forces were engaged in a crucial battle to secure a beachhead upon the shores of western Europe. Two days earlier, Rome had fallen, as Allied troops drove back the Germans in obstinate retreat up the Italian peninsula. It was the first Axis capital to fall. One down and two to go, President Roosevelt triumphantly told the American people. But this dearly won success in Italy paled before the momentous fact that the real second front had at last been opened, that the whole power of Hitler was directly challenged by the most gigantic landing operation in all the annals of modern history.

The war rose indeed to a frightening crescendo in June, 1944. As bombers and fighters made thousands of sorties overhead, the Allied forces clung to their toehold in Normandy, beat back savage German counter-attacks, and gradually extended their lines until the peninsula upon which they had landed was largely in their control, and the great port of Cherbourg successfully occupied. A heavy cost in casualties had to be paid for these gains in "the battle of the hedgerows," and at the same time the English home front was undergoing a new trial by fire. Germany launched an attack by robot bombs that took a deadly toll in lives, as well as causing widespread damage. It caused no slackening in support for the fighting in Normandy, however, and a miracle of supply was gradually building up the resources which were to enable the Allied troops to break through the ring of steel in which the Germans sought to enclose them.

What appeared to be a stalemate was shattered in early August. While the British and Canadians stubbornly held their pivotal position near Caen, the Americans crashed the German lines at Saint-Lo to swing out into Brittany and push ahead into the open country to the east. As this advance in northwest France gathered increasing power, moreover, new Allied landings were made on the Mediterranean coast. What had originally been a battle for a beachhead in Normandy became the battle of all France. French armies co-operated with the Anglo-American armies in both sectors of fighting, and underground forces rose against the oppressors who for four long years had held France in subjection. German resistance rapidly crumbled; city after city fell into Allied hands. Then, on August 23, as American armored columns closed in on the city, the citizens of Paris themselves rose to wrest control of the capital from the German invader. With our help, Paris was freed.

The break-through at Saint-Lo had proved to be a decisive turning-point in the war. The *New York Times* reported on September 3:

> The succession of triumphs made dazzling reading, a flashing roll-call of names carved on many battle-monuments. In a line reaching in from the Channel coast the Canadian First Army captured Rouen, drove straight on to Dieppe and Abbeville; the British Second Army raced through Beauvais, took Amiens, crossed the Somme, captured historic Vimy Ridge, struck for Arras, sealed off the robot coast; the American First Army roared through Belleau Wood, Chateau-Thierry, Soissons, Laon, Reims, to the fortress of Sead; the American Third Army hammered through Châlons, across the Marne and the Aisne, into the fortress of Verdun, on toward Metz, southward into Saint-Mihiel.

In Prime Minister Churchill's moving phrase, France was liberated "as if by enchantment."

For a time there were hopes that the German retreat might be turned into a rout, that the Allied armies surging across France and Belgium might crash through the vaunted Siegfried Line.

Paratroops were landed near the little Dutch town of Arnhem in a bold stroke to turn the German flank; the enemy's homeland was penetrated at Aachen. But whatever chance there might have been of decisive victory was tragically lost as determined German counter-attacks wiped out the bridgehead at Arnhem and firmly held the line at Aachen. Enemy resistance stiffened all along the front; the British and American troops had outrun their reserve support. While the momentum of the advance had carried to Germany's massive Westwall, any all-out offensive against this strongly held position had to wait until the Channel ports were cleared for bringing up additional supplies and the Allied armies had been regrouped.

Meanwhile, great events had also taken place in other sectors of what still remained a global war. Shortly after D-day, the long eastern front awakened to new activity. A Russian summer drive carried the Red armies deep within Poland, to threaten the capture of Warsaw. Then, as the German forces held along this central sector, the Russians launched another offensive in the north which was to liberate the Baltic countries, and struck out toward the south to break into the Balkans. Rumania collapsed on the very day that Paris was freed, and with his whole position in southeastern Europe endangered, Hitler began withdrawing his troops. As Bulgaria followed Rumania's lead in seeking peace, British troops landed in Greece and the Red army joined forces with the Jugoslavian partisans under Marshal Tito. An end was being written to the Balkan campaign. Still held up along the lower Vistula, the Russian forces then moved against Hungary, and as autumn came to a close they were advancing on Budapest.

CARRYING THE WAR TO JAPAN

The distant war in the Pacific also demonstrated the growing might of the United Nations, and particularly of the American Navy. Even as the eyes of the world had been fixed upon the grim fighting in Normandy, a tremendous naval task force, mounting greater offensive power than had ever been concentrated in the

Pacific or any other ocean, covered American landings in the heart of the Marianas, well within the inner circle of Japan's defenses. With a hold firmly established upon the island of Saipan, our ships and planes were then able to attack directly Japanese possessions and conquered territory throughout the western Pacific. And at the same time, new super-bombers — the B-29's — roared out from secret flying fields in western China to carry the war directly to Japan itself in bombing raids upon the homeland.

As both air and naval activity gathered increasing tempo in the Pacific war toward the end of summer, there was no question that the way was being prepared for the long-promised attack on the Philippines. The expected blow came in mid-October. Apparently taking the Japanese by surprise and scoring a great tactical success, troops under the command of General MacArthur landed on Leyte Island with the protection of both air and naval support by the American fleet. A flotilla of six hundred vessels — battleships, carriers, cruisers, minesweepers, transports, landing craft — made up the invasion forces. Clouds of carrier-based planes drove the Japanese out of the skies as the great guns of our warships demolished land fortifications and raked the beaches with screaming shells.

The Japanese were at first easily driven back. The initial landings were an immediate success. But the enemy had no intention of giving up the Philippines without a hard struggle. In a challenge to American sea power it had long avoided, the Japanese fleet made a desperate effort to break up our beachhead. Three separate naval forces were discovered steaming toward Leyte and an air-naval battle developed on a scale not seen since the battles of Midway and the Coral Sea. Once again the American Navy won a decisive victory, this time well within Japanese waters. It took such a heavy toll of the enemy fleet that only shattered remnants escaped the avenging arm of American air and sea power.

The way was open for further advance. While fanatical, last-ditch resistance reminiscent of Guadalcanal, Tarawa, and Saipan still continued on Leyte, General MacArthur made another daring landing on Mindoro Island and then, early in January, 1945, struck directly at the heart of the Philippines. Under cover of a huge air umbrella and with the support of even stronger naval units than those assembled at Leyte, some one hundred thousand troops were landed on Luzon. Again the Japanese were for a time unable to put up any effective opposition. Our troops drove steadily ahead toward Manila and entered the capital on February 3, some three years after it had been abandoned in the bitter aftermath of Pearl Harbor.

There was much bloody fighting before capture of the city was assured, and further operations both in northern Luzon and on other islands of the Philippines ran into stiff resistance. But the Japanese could not withstand the unrelenting pressure of our troops, and within three months our hold over the entire archipelago was virtually complete. The United States had made good its promise to free the Philippines from Japanese control.

Even as Manila was being invested, the navy carried the war still deeper into Japanese-controlled territory. While carrier-based planes from a task force venturing boldly within three hundred miles of the enemy coast blasted Tokyo with an unprecedented weight of bombs, two divisions of marines were landed on Iwo Jima. The conquest of this little island in the Volcano group, seven hundred and fifty miles from Japan proper, was to prove "the toughest battle" in the long history of the marines. Its Japanese defenders were not wholly overcome until after a month of almost hand-to-hand fighting over incredibly barren terrain covered with volcanic ash. It was a dearly won victory that cost some twenty thousand casualties.

The air war against Japan was in the meantime being stepped up spectacularly. Admiral Mitscher's great Task Force 58, roaming Japanese waters almost at will, launched hundreds of navy planes to wreak destruction upon the airfields, seaports, and naval stations of the enemy homeland. From their bases in the Marianas, fleets of superfortresses roared forth to rain thousands of tons of incendiary bombs on Tokyo, Nagoya, Osaka, Kobe, and other Japanese cities. Throughout March, the attacks continued on an unprecedented scale. In one series of raids alone, some seventeen Japanese warships were reported to have been damaged, over a thousand planes destroyed, and incalculable damage inflicted on shore installations and industrial plants.

Early in April, another island outpost within three hundred and sixty miles of Japan itself was invaded. In an operation again conforming to the now familiar pattern of heavy preliminary bombardment from the sea and from the air, American troops went ashore on Okinawa, principal island in the Ryukyus. This hard-won advance — for the Japanese forces fought back with fierce fanaticism — brought the United States to Japan's very doorstep, cut her life-line to what remained of her empire in southeastern Asia, and endangered her communications with China. The situation was indeed so critical for Japan that her depleted fleet made a desperate attack upon our supporting naval forces off Okinawa, only to suffer still another telling defeat.

The Pacific war had by the end of April entered upon a new phase. Our outposts threatened direct attack upon the Japanese homeland, new forces were gathering in China where the completion of the Stillwell Road had reopened the flow of supplies to Chinese troops, and bombing raids on the enemy's cities were daily growing in intensity. A blockade was being drawn about Japan; she was becoming hopelessly encircled.

ELECTION OF 1944

In the exciting autumn of 1944, with Germany threatened from the east, from the west, and from the south, with Japan reeling under the devastating shock of naval defeat in the second battle of the Philippines, the American people had gone to the polls to elect a President. Even more significant than the decision they then recorded, to entrust the country for a fourth successive time to the leadership of Franklin D. Roosevelt, was the very fact that an election was held. Nothing could have more forcefully demonstrated the vitality, the strength, and the faith of American democracy. In the midst of global war, at the very climax of the gathering attack upon Germany and Japan, close upon fifty million persons went quietly to the polls to decide whether or not it was to the best interest of the country to leave the existing administration in power. Once before the American people had held a presidential election during war. But to do so again under the circumstances of 1944 reaffirmed as could nothing else that there had been no betrayal or weakening of the ideals of freedom in whose defense the nation had taken up arms.

The campaign had not at first been able to make much headway against the background of war, but as November 7 drew near, it had developed into a hard-fought struggle whose outcome for a time appeared to be in some doubt. The Republicans had nominated Governor Thomas E. Dewey of New York, after Wendell Willkie, candidate in 1940, had withdrawn from the race following defeat in the Wisconsin primaries, and they adopted a platform pledging continued intensive prosecution of the war, American membership in a world organization for peace, and a post-war reconstruction policy to restore full employment through the encouragement of private enterprise.

Democratic renomination of President Roosevelt had long been assured. It met no opposition and the party platform stood squarely on the record. In its promise of continued support of the war effort, establishment of an international organization, and a domestic policy based upon faith in competitive private enterprise, the Democratic program, indeed, differed little in essentials from that of the Republicans. The issue in dispute was primarily which candidate, as a national leader, could most successfully steer the country through the critical days that lay ahead. The Republicans charged the Administration with incompetence, declaring it to be made up of tired old men. The Democrats countered with Dewey's youth and lack of experience. In the minds of many independent voters, party attitudes on foreign policy appeared to be more sharply defined than was the case in regard either to the war or domestic issues, again not through announced policies but on the basis of past records. For while Dewey tried to prevent American membership in a world peace organization from becoming a partisan issue, earlier Republican opposition to international co-operation raised the question of whether he would be able to pursue effectively the goal of full post-war collaboration.

The 1944 election was basically, however, a contest between two almost equally powerful forces in American life: the desire for a change in the national administration after twelve years, not only of Democratic rule, but of the presidency of one man, against the fear of making any change in the midst of a war which had not yet been won. Other factors naturally played their part in determining the people's final choice. Although subordinated to the larger issues of the conduct of war and future foreign policy, the old domestic quarrel over the New Deal itself was by no means dormant. But with millions of American troops poised for a direct attack upon Germany and fighting desperately in the Philippines, the war was decisive in making up the minds of the electorate.

Roosevelt was re-elected by a clear but relatively narrow majority. In the popular vote he obtained 25,603,000 ballots to Dewey's 22,006,000, or under 54 per cent of the total in comparison with 55 per cent four years earlier. This vote was so distributed, however, that his electoral college majority, 432 to 99, fell only seventeen votes short of that in 1940. The only states that Roosevelt failed to carry were Maine, Vermont, Ohio, Indiana, North Dakota, South Dakota, Wisconsin, Nebraska, Kansas, Colorado, and Wyoming — and even in these sections he generally trailed his opponent by a close margin. Moreover, the Democrats maintained their hold over the Senate and increased a precarious majority in the House.

The election was a close one because the Republicans narrowed the gap between their candidate's vote and that of Roosevelt to some 3,600,000 ballots in comparison with the latter's lead of 5,000,000 in 1940. The support of 22,000,000 persons for Governor Dewey was impressive. Nevertheless, the popular mandate could not be disputed. The American people had declared themselves in favor of Roosevelt's conduct of the war, and they expressed their confidence in his ability to lead them to final victory. Furthermore, the defeat in widely separated parts of the country of avowedly isolationist candidates for Congress, substantiated the interpretation of the President's re-election as endorsement of a foreign policy based upon American membership in the world peace organization outlined at Dumbarton Oaks. On these general grounds the public had taken its stand, and once the election was over the heated political controversy of the campaign quickly subsided. The country reaffirmed its united support of the war effort. There was to be no faltering in carrying through the job at hand.

An End and a Beginning

Almost as if awaiting the results of the election, the Allied armies on Europe's western front swung into vigorous action in the latter half of November. American hopes of an early victory over Germany soared as a great offensive ground slowly ahead on a three-hundred-mile front from the Netherlands to the Swiss border. Our forces threatened the Ruhr, invaded the Saar, and appeared to be closing in everywhere upon the barrier of the Rhine. But Germany still had a final powerful punch. Instead of triumph in 1944, the year closed with the furious battle of the Ardennes — "the battle of the bulge." Fiercely counter-attacking German forces — "the enemy is making his supreme effort," declared General Eisenhower — threatened to make what would have been a disastrous break-through greatly prolonging the war. It was prevented by heroic American resistance, and the situation was stabilized — but only after a month of the hardest fighting. Hitler had lost his last desperate gamble.

Not until late January, 1945, were the Anglo-American Allies able to re-form their badly bent lines, re-group their armies, and once again assume the initiative. The renewed offensive, however, developed under far more favorable conditions than had existed in December. For the Russians too were now under way and in a magnificent forward sweep along the entire eastern front, compelling the Germans to withdraw some divisions from the west, their armies advanced to the banks of the Oder. The stage was set for the long-planned, concerted assault upon Hitler's inner fortress. A three-front war — on the west, on the east, and in the air — opened in February with such massed strength, so overwhelming a force of arms that Germany's days were numbered.

The immediate plan of the Allied forces, as General Eisenhower stated on February 24, was the destruction of the German army west of the Rhine. There was no resisting this new drive. Within two weeks of its start, the vaunted Westwall was pierced and on the northern sector of the front, British and American divisions were drawing up to the banks of the great river which had for so long been their goal. Some of the enemy troops were able to make good their retreat, but our raging advance had broken the back of the Wehrmacht.

Even the Rhine could not stop the gathering momentum of Allied power. Through what appeared to be a lucky chance, a bridge at Remagen was seized before the Germans could destroy it. Compelled to divert troops in a vain attempt to break up this first Allied bridgehead, the German high command weakened its forces farther north. In the final week of March, a month after the start of the offensive, our troops were storming across the Rhine at several key points and the battle for Germany was fully under way. The stakes were final victory. Under the devastating blows of seven major Allied armies — one British, one Canadian, one French, and four American — the Germans reeled back in shattering defeat.

Armored columns swept ahead deep within the Reich. In a few areas the enemy kept up a fierce resistance, but there was no longer a cohesive front. Some of our tank units advanced so rapidly along Hitler's superb superhighways that they lost touch with Supreme Headquarters. One correspondent cabled the story that General Eisenhower, asked how far General Patton's Third Army spearheads had penetrated, replied that he did not know — he had not heard from them for three hours. Canadian troops pushed north to cut off Holland, the British advanced swiftly against Germany's northern ports, the Ruhr was encircled in one of the war's greatest single victories, the Ninth American Army raced ahead to the banks of the Elbe, and the First, Third, and Seventh Armies drove towards the borders of Czechoslovakia. The clear-cut objective of our strategy was to cut Germany in two and effect a juncture with the Russian forces, now advancing both from Austria, where Vienna had already fallen to the Red Armies, and from their expanding bridgeheads along the Oder.

The Allied bag of prisoners during these weeks was stupendous. A single day saw the surrender of almost 150,000 Germans. During the first two weeks of April alone, some 760,000 capitulated, bringing the total since D-day to more than two million. And at the same time that our ground forces were making such breathtaking advances, the air force was with devastating effect bombing German airfields (almost four thousand planes of the once-proud Luftwaffe were destroyed, largely on the ground, in two weeks), communication centers, railroads, and highways. Transportation within Germany was completely disrupted and her cities pulverized in final massive air raids. One day saw Berlin hit by a thousand Flying Fortresses, with some eight thousand planes in all operating over enemy-held territory.

The war was not being won without heavy sacrifice of American lives. From the first invasion of North Africa, through the Italian campaign, the battle of France, and the attack upon Germany, losses had steadily mounted. Even though the improved techniques of modern surgery, and especially the use of blood plasma, sulfa drugs, and penicillin, saved thousands of lives and greatly aided the wounded, the cost of victory was far heavier than during the first World War. Casualties in the fighting in Europe were over five hundred thousand, or more than half the total of nearly a million in all theaters during three and a half years of war. About twenty per cent of this over-all total were killed, something over half wounded, with prisoners or missing accounting for the remainder.

The closing days of April were climactic. As the Nazis appeared ready to drag down all Germany in the destruction which Hitler had foredoomed, the Allied armies in the West and the Soviet armies in the East pressed a tightening vise upon the heart of the nation. Elements of the two forces met dramatically on the banks of the Elbe in late April, and the war entered its last stage as a battle of still fiercely resisting pockets. The Russians overran Berlin in bloody house-to-house fighting; American armies swung south to storm what had been called Germany's national redoubt, and on the long dormant Italian front, Allied armies that had battled across the Po quickly shattered the German forces in northern Italy.

The first week in May brought a succession of further spectacular triumphs and the complete collapse of the Nazi régime. The German armies in Italy and western Austria surrendered and Mussolini was summarily executed by Italian partisans; Berlin fell to the Russians with Hitler reported dead amid its ruins, and the entire western front collapsed with the capitulation of all German forces in Holland, Denmark, and northern Germany. Finally, the Reich surrendered unconditionally to the United States, Great Britain, and Soviet Russia, and on May 8, 1945, there was formal proclamation of complete Allied victory. Germany was defeated; Hitler's dream of world conquest was forever dead. The grand coalition had held firm and the triumphant arms of the United Nations achieved the fateful triumph that had been in the making for so many long and bloody years.

Just two weeks before the juncture of Allied and Russian armies sealed Germany's doom, and as the decisive battle on Okinawa presaged the no less certain ultimate defeat of Japan, the great war President of the United States was suddenly stricken by death. Franklin Delano Roosevelt died of a cerebral hemorrhage on April 12, 1945. A shocked and benumbed people could not at first believe the news. When its tragic import was realized, the entire nation experienced a feeling of loss that was perhaps never before paralleled in all our history. Only the shock of Lincoln's death at the close of another great war could be compared with it. Nor was America the only country plunged into deep mourning. In all the Allied nations, in England and France, in Russia and China, the expressions of universal grief revealed as could nothing else the pre-eminent rôle that Roosevelt had assumed as a world leader of the forces of democracy.

The President had lived through only a little more than three months of his fourth term in office. In that brief period, however, he had achieved one more diplomatic triumph. Early in February a conference of the Big Three — Roosevelt, Churchill, and Stalin — had been held at Yalta, on the Crimean coast, and further strengthened the existing accord among the United States, Great Britain, and Soviet Russia. The three national leaders had not only reaffirmed their common determination to prosecute the war until Germany unconditionally surrendered, but in emphatic demonstration of their resolve to work together in peace as well as in war, they definitely fixed upon a date for a conference of the United Nations to draw up a charter for the international organization provisionally outlined at Dumbarton Oaks. It was to be held at San Francisco on April 25.

Roosevelt was succeeded in office by the Vice-President — Harry S. Truman. Even as the country still mourned its wartime leader, the new chief executive pledged himself, in a message to Congress and to the American people, to carry forward Roosevelt's policies. There would be no let-up in driving forward toward complete victory in both Europe and the Pacific, or in seeking a peace that would banish the age-old specter of war. "Let me assure the forward-looking people of America," President Truman also declared, "that there will be no relaxation in our efforts to improve the lot of the common people."

The international conference which Roosevelt had taken the lead in planning was not postponed by his death. It duly opened with the delegates of forty-six United Nations in attendance. Against the dramatic background of Germany's downfall and the mounting intensity of the sea and air blockade of beleaguered Japan, deliberations began upon a charter for world organization.

Could this impressive gathering provide a firm basis for that new international order of law and justice for which Roosevelt had given his life, for which so many young Americans had given — and were still giving — their lives? An era in American history — in world history — was drawing to a close as the conference began its momentous sessions. A new era was commencing.

"You members of this conference," President Truman told the delegates at San Francisco, "are to be the architects of the better world. In your hands rests our future. By your labors at this conference we shall know if suffering humanity is to achieve a just and lasting peace."

Bibliography

GENERAL AND BACKGROUND

Among books providing a general background of American history, dealing either in whole or in part with the twentieth century, may be cited S. E. Morison and H. S. Commager, *The Growth of the American Republic* (2 vols.); C. A. and M. R. Beard, *The Rise of American Civilization* (4 vols.), and, more particularly, *America in Midpassage*, vol. 3; A. M. Schlesinger and D. R. Fox, *A History of American Life* (12 vols.), with special reference to vols. 11 and 12:— H. U. Faulkner, *The Quest for Social Justice*; and P. W. Slosson, *The Great Crusade and After*; L. M. Hacker and B. B. Kendrick, *The United States Since 1865*; Mark Sullivan, *Our Times: 1900-1925* (6 vols.); and A. Nevins and L. M. Hacker, *The United States and Its Place in World Affairs.*

General studies in special fields include R. H. Gabriel, *The Course of American Democratic Thought*; Merle Curti, *The Growth of American Thought*; L. V. Parrington, *Main Currents of American Thought* (3 vols.); C. B. Swisher, *American Constitutional Government*; H. U. Faulkner, *American Economic History*; S. F. Bemis, *A Diplomatic History of the United States*; and T. A. Bailey, *A Diplomatic History of the American People.*

Two useful source collections are H. S. Commager, *Documents of American History*; and W. Thorp, M. Curti, and C. Baker, *American Issues: the Social Record.* See also C. L. and E. H. Lord, *Historical Atlas of the United States.*

BIOGRAPHY AND AUTOBIOGRAPHY

Among the more important political biographies are Henry Pringle, *Theodore Roosevelt* (1931), and *The Life and Times of William Howard Taft* (2 vols. 1939); C. G. Bowers, *Beveridge and the Progressive Era* (1932); Philip C. Jessup, *Elihu Root* (2 vols. 1938); N. W. Stephenson, *Nelson W. Aldrich* (1930); G. M. Stephenson, *John Lind of Minnesota* (1935); McAllister Coleman, *Eugene V. Debs* (1930); R. L. Neuberger and S. B. Kahn, *Integrity: The Life of George W. Norris* (1937); M. R. Werner, *Bryan* (1929); C. O. Johnson, *Borah* (1939); W. A. White, *A Puritan in Babylon* (1938); Harold B. Hinton, *Cordell Hull* (1942); and Gerald Johnson, *Roosevelt, Dictator or Democrat?* (1942). Also highly interesting is W. A. White, *Masks in a Pageant* (1929).

Revealing biographies of other figures include Joseph Dorfman, *Thorstein Veblen and His America* (1934); J. K. Winkler, *Hearst* (1928); J. A. Wechsler, *Labor Baron, A Portrait of John L. Lewis*

(1944); Allan Nevins, *Henry White* (1930); Harold Nicholson, *Dwight Morrow* (1935); Francis Biddle, *Mr. Justice Holmes* (1942); and R. H. Harvey, *Samuel Gompers* (1935).

Outstanding autobiographies that specially illuminate twentieth century history are Theodore Roosevelt, *An Autobiography* (1913); W. J. Bryan, *Memoirs* (1925); Robert La Follette, *Autobiography* (1913); Lincoln Steffens, *Autobiography* (2 vols. 1931); Samuel Gompers, *Seventy Years of Life and Labor* (2 vols. 1925); Henry Ford, *My Life and Work* (1922); O. G. Villard, *Fighting Years* (1939); Ray Stannard Baker, *American Chronicle* (1945); and George W. Norris, *Fighting Liberal* (1945).

SOCIAL CONDITIONS

BUSINESS

Business conditions prior to the depression are discussed in A. A. Berle, Jr., and G. C. Means, *The Modern Corporation and Private Property* (1932); H. R. Seager and C. A. Gulick, *Trust and Corporation Problems* (1929); R. G. Tugwell, *Industry's Coming of Age* (1927); H. W. Laidler, *Concentration of Control in American Industry* (1931); Stuart Chase, *Prosperity: Fact or Myth* (1929), and *Men and Machines* (1929); P. M. Mazur, *American Prosperity* (1928); W. Z. Ripley, *Main St. and Wall St.* (1927); Committee on Recent Economic Changes, *Recent Economic Changes in the United States* (2 vols. 1929); J. Klein, *Frontiers of Trade* (1929); P. M. Mazur, *America Looks Abroad* (1930); R. W. Dunn, *American Foreign Investments* (1926); and B. H. Williams, *Economic Foreign Policy of the United States* (1929). See also J. K. Winkler, *The Du Pont Dynasty* (1935); L. Corey, *The House of Morgan* (1930); Harvey O'Connor, *Mellon's Millions* (1933); and F. L. Lewis, *Lords of Creation* (1935).

AGRICULTURE

On the status of agriculture, with particular reference to conditions in the nineteen-twenties, reference may be made to J. D. Black, *Agricultural Reform in the United States* (1929); W. Gee, *The Place of Agriculture in American Life* (1930); E. R. A. Seligman, *The Economics of Farm Relief* (1929); J. E. Boyle, *Farm Relief* (1928); J. S. Davis, *The Farm Export Debenture Plan* (1929); Arthur Capper, *The Agricultural Bloc* (1922); E. G. Nourse, *American Agriculture and the European Market* (1924); and Edward Wiest, *Agricultural Organization in the United States* (1923).

LABOR

Labor studies include H. Harris, *American Labor* (1939); Mary R. Beard, *The American Labor Movement* (1931); R. H. Harvey, *Samuel Gompers* (1935); G. S. Mitchell, *Textile Unionism in the South* (1931); R. W. Dunn, *Company Unions* (1927); Edward Berman, *Labor and the Sherman Act* (1930); R. G. Fuller, *Child Labor and the Constitution* (1923); F. Frankfurter and N. Greene, *The Labor Injunction* (1930); L. L. Lorwin, *The American Federation of Labor* (1933); P. F. Brissenden, *The I.W.W.* (1919); J. S. Gambs, *The Decline of the I.W.W.* (1932); McAllister Coleman, *Eugene V. Debs* (1930); James Oneal, *American Communism* (1927); and Louis Adamic, *Dynamite* (1931). See also later section on The Rise of Labor.

OTHER PHASES OF SOCIAL LIFE

New inventions have their historians in E. D. Kennedy, *The Automobile Industry* (1941); D. L. Cohn, *Combustion on Wheels* (1944); M. Bardeche and R. Brasillach, *History of the Motion Pictures* (1938); Edgar Dale, *The Content of Motion Pictures* (1935); Margaret Thorp, *America at the Movies* (1939); Paul Schubert, *The Electric Word: the Rise of the Radio* (1928); A. N. Goldsmith and A. C. Lescarboura, *This Thing Called Broadcasting* (1930); F. C. Kelly, *The Wright Brothers* (1943); Victor Lougheed, *Vehicles of the Air* (1943); and H. L. Smith, *Airways* (1942).

On the experiment of prohibition, see E. H. Cherrington, *The Evolution of Prohibition* (1920); H. Feldman, *Prohibition, Its Economic and Industrial Aspects* (1927); G. W. Wickersham, *Report of the National Commission on Law Observance and Enforcement* (1931); Charles Merz, *The Dry Decade* (1931); and L. V. Harrison and E. Lane, *After Repeal* (1936).

Free speech and tolerance are treated in Z. Chafee, Jr., *Free Speech in the United States* (1941); E. S. Bates, *This Land of Liberty* (1930); M. L. Ernst and A. Lindley, *The Censor Marches On* (1940); G. Seldes, *Freedom of the Press* (1935); A. G. Hays, *Let Freedom Ring* (1937); and J. M. Mecklin, *The Ku Klux Klan* (1924).

Race relations are taken up in W. E. B. DuBois, *Black Reconstruction* (1925); E. R. Embree, *American Negroes* (1942); Roi Ottley, *New World A-Coming* (1942); R. W. Logan, *What the Negro Wants* (1944); Gunnar Myrdal, *An American Dilemma* (2 vols. 1944); and Oliver LaFarge, *The Changing Indian* (1942).

On immigration, see Louis Adamic, *From Many Lands* (1940); Carl Wittke, *We Who Built America* (1940); J. W. Jenks and W. J. Lauck, *The Immigration Problem* (1926); and R. L. Garis, *Immigration Restriction* (1927).

On other phases of social and cultural life, a highly selective list would include Dixon Wecter, *The Saga of American Society* (1937); A. M. Lee, *The Daily Newspaper in America* (1937); F. L. Mott, *American Journalism* (1941); A. E. Meyer, *The Development of Education in the Twentieth Century* (1939); E. H. Wilkins, *The Changing College* (1927); R. F. Butts, *The College Charts Its Course* (1939); W. A. Starett, *Skyscrapers and the Men Who Build Them* (1928); F. R. Dulles, *America Learns to Play: A History of Popular Recreation* (1940); Roger Burlingame, *Peace Veterans* (1932); R. L. Duffus and F. P. Keppel, *The Arts in American Life* (1933); A. D. Zanzig, *Music in American Life* (1932); J. W. Krutch, *The American Drama Since 1918* (1939); Alfred Kazin, *On Native Grounds* (1942); and Oscar Cargill, *Intellectual America* (1941).

THE PROGRESSIVE ERA

CHAPTER 5

The more general books include H. U. Faulkner, *The Quest for Social Justice* (1931); Mark Sullivan, *Our Times*, vols. 2-4 (1927-32); C. C. Regier, *The Era of the Muckrakers* (1932); John Chamberlain, *Farewell to Reform* (1932); Joseph Dorfman, *Thorstein Veblen and His America* (1934); Louis Filler, *Crusaders for American Liberalism* (1939); W. E. Garrison, *The March of Faith* (1933); F. L. Allen, *The Lords of Creation* (1935); and John Moody, *The Truth About the Trusts* (1919).

Contemporary discussions of special interest are Walter E. Weyl, *The New Democracy* (1912); Herbert Croly, *The Promise of American Life* (1909); F. C. Howe, *Wisconsin, An Experiment in Democracy* (1912); Charles McCarthy, *The Wisconsin Idea* (1912); Louis D. Brandeis, *Other People's Money* (1914); and R. S. Baker, *Following the Color Line* (1908).

Among the principal autobiographies of progressive reformers may be cited Lincoln Steffens, *Autobiography* (2 vols. 1931); F. C. Howe, *Confessions of a Reformer* (1925); C. E. Russell, *Bare Hands and Stone Walls* (1933); Jane Addams, *Forty Years at Hull House* (1935); Morris Hillquit, *Loose Leaves from a Busy Life* (1934); Brand Whitlock, *Forty Years of It* (1913); Tom Johnson, *My Story* (1911); and O. G. Villard, *Fighting Years* (1939).

For books on general conditions, including such topics as the growth of industry, status of agriculture, the labor movement, developments in transportation, and other phases of American social and cultural life, see the section on Social Conditions.

Chapters 6-8

In addition to the books cited, general studies of the politics of progressivism include J. F. Rhodes, *The McKinley and Roosevelt Administrations* (1922); F. A. Ogg, *National Progress, 1907-17* (1918); B. P. DeWitt, *The Progressive Movement* (1915); K. W. Hechler, *Insurgency* (1940); Dwight Dumond, *Roosevelt to Roosevelt* (1937); F. L. Paxson, *The Pre-War Years, 1914-1917* (1936); and M. Josephson, *The President Makers* (1940).

The biographies and autobiographies of Bryan, Roosevelt, Taft, La Follette, Root, Beveridge, Aldrich, and Debs (see section on Biography and Autobiography) are of obvious importance. Some other comparable, if somewhat less significant books, are J. B. Bishop, *Theodore Roosevelt and His Times Shown in His Own Letters* (2 vols. 1920); H. C. Lodge, *Selections from the Correspondence of Theodore Roosevelt and Henry Cabot Lodge* (2 vols. 1925); Paxton Hibben, *The Peerless Leader, William Jennings Bryan* (1929); Champ Clark, *My Quarter Century in Politics* (2 vols. 1920); L. W. Busbey, *Uncle Joe Cannon* (1927); A. W. Butt, *Taft and Roosevelt* (2 vols. 1930); H. H. Kohlsatt, *From McKinley to Harding* (1923); D. F. Houston, *Eight Years with Wilson's Cabinet* (2 vols. 1926); and Josephus Daniels, *The Wilson Era, Years of Peace, 1910-1917* (1944).

For Woodrow Wilson, see R. S. Baker, *Woodrow Wilson, Life and Letters* (8 vols. 1927-39); W. E. Dodd, *Woodrow Wilson and His Work* (1920); and William Diamond, *The Economic Thought of Woodrow Wilson* (1943).

Among contemporary political writings the most interesting are Theodore Roosevelt, *The New Nationalism* (1910), and Woodrow Wilson, *The New Freedom* (1913). See also Gifford Pinchot, *The Fight for Conservation* (1910); Carter Glass, *An Adventure in Constructive Finance* (1927). For constitutional developments during these years see C. B. Swisher, *American Constitutional Government* (1943); and Max Lerner, *The Mind and Faith of Mr. Justice Holmes* (1943).

Chapter 9

Among the more important books dealing with the consequences of the Spanish-American War are W. H. Haas, *The American Empire* (1940); A. T. Mahan, *Lessons of the War with Spain* (1899); M. Storey and M. P. Lichauco, *Conquest of the Philippines by the United States* (1926); J. R. Hayden, *The Philippines* (1942); A. C. Coolidge, *The United States as a World Power* (1908); J. H. Latane, *America as a World Power 1897-1907* (1907); C. R. Fish, *The Path of Empire* (1919); and L. M. Gelber, *The Rise of Anglo-American Friendship, 1898-1906* (1938).

Policy toward Latin America is discussed in Dexter Perkins, *Hands Off! A History of the Monroe Doctrine* (1941); G. H. Stuart, *Latin America and the United States* (1944); S. F. Bemis, *Latin American Policy of the United States* (1943); C. L. Jones, *The Caribbean Since 1900* (1936); W. H. Calcott, *The Caribbean Policy of the United States, 1890-1920* (1942); H. C. Hill, *Roosevelt and the Caribbean* (1927); and S. Nearing and J. Freeman, *Dollar Diplomacy* (1925).

On special countries, see J. Fred Rippy, *The United States and Mexico* (1931); C. W. Hackett, *The Mexican Revolution and the United States* (1926); J. M. Callahan, *American Policy in Mexican Relations* (1932); R. H. Fitzgibbon, *Cuba and the United States, 1900-1935* (1940); L. H. Jenks, *Our Cuban Colony* (1928); E. T. Parks, *Colombia and the United States, 1763-1934* (1935); D. C. Miner, *The Fight for the Panama Route* (1937); W. D. McCain, *The United States and the Republic of Panama* (1937); I. J. Cox, *Nicaragua and the United States, 1909-1927* (1927); C. Kelsey, *American Intervention in Haiti and the Dominican Republic* (1922); L. L. Montague, *Haiti and the United States, 1900-1935* (1940); M. M. Knight, *The Americans in Santo Domingo* (1922).

Sources for our policy in the Far East include A. W. Griswold, *The Far Eastern Policy of the United States* (1938); F. R. Dulles, *Forty Years of American-Japanese Relations* (1937); Tyler Dennett, *Americans in Eastern Asia* (1922); *John Hay* (1933), and *Roosevelt and the Russo-Japanese War* (1925); T. A. Bailey, *Theodore Roosevelt and the Japanese-American Crises* (1934); Herbert Croly, *Willard Straight* (1913); E. Tupper and G. E. McReynolds, *Japan in American Public Opinion* (1937); Paul S. Reinsch, *An American Diplomat in China* (1922); and F. V. Field, *American Participation in the Chinese Consortiums* (1931).

There is further interesting material on foreign policy during these years in Forrest Davis, *The Atlantic System* (1941); Merle Curti, *Bryan and World Peace* (1931); Harley Notter, *Origins of the Foreign Policy of Woodrow Wilson* (1937); H. and M. Sprout, *The Rise of American Naval Power* (1939); G. C. O'Gara, *Theodore Roosevelt and the Rise of the Modern Navy* (1943). See also S. F. Bemis, *A Diplomatic History of the United States*; and T. A. Bailey, *A Diplomatic History of the American People*, already cited.

THE STAKES OF WORLD POWER

CHAPTER 11

The most complete general account of American entry into the first World War is C. C. Tansill, *America Goes to War* (1938). Other studies are C. H. Grattan, *Why We Fought* (1929); Walter Millis, *The Road to War* (1935); N. D. Baker, *Why We Went to War* (1936); and three volumes by Charles Seymour: *American Diplomacy During the World War* (1933); *American Neutrality* (1935), and *Woodrow Wilson and the World War* (1921). See also F. L. Paxson, *Pre-War Years, 1913-1917* (1936); Alice Morrissey, *The American Defense of Neutral Rights, 1914-1917* (1939); Mark Sullivan, *Our Times* (vol. 5, 1933); and A. M. Arnett, *Claude Kitchin and the Wilson War Policies* (1937).

There is much interesting material in W. J. Bryan, *Memoirs* (1925); Robert Lansing, *War Memoirs* (1935); Charles Seymour, *Intimate Papers of Colonel House* (4 vols. 1926-28); B. J. Hendrick, *The Life and Letters of Walter Hines Page* (3 vols. 1922-25); J. H. von Bernstorff, *My Three Years in America* (1920); Constantin Dumba, *Memoirs of a Diplomat* (1932); D. F. Houston, *Eight Years with Wilson's Cabinet* (1926); J. W. Gerard, *My Four Years in Germany* (1920); and most importantly, R. S. Baker, *Woodrow Wilson: Life and Letters* (vols. 5 and 6, 1935-37).

Among many books on propaganda are H. D. Laswell, *Propaganda Technique in the World War* (1927); J. A. Wechsler, *War Propaganda in the United States* (1940); H. C. Peterson, *Propaganda for War* (1939); J. P. Jones and P. M. Hollister, *The German Secret Service in America* (1918); and G. S. Viereck, *Spreading Germs of Hate* (1920). Another relevant study is C. J. Child, *The German-Americans in Politics, 1914-17* (1939).

Chapter 12

Actual participation in the war is treated in F. L. Paxson, *America at War* (1939); P. W. Slosson, *The Great Crusade and After* (1930); L. P. Ayres, *The War with Germany* (1919); M. Sullivan, *Our Times* (vol. 5); and, with special reference to mobilizing national resources, B. Crowell and R. F. Wilson, *How America Went to War* (6 vols. 1921); H. S. Tobin and P. W. Bidwell, *Mobilizing America* (1940); Arthur Bullard, *Mobilizing America* (1917); G. V. Clarkson, *Industrial America in the World War* (1923); B. M. Baruch, *American Industry in the War* (1921).

Special related studies are E. L. Bogart, *War Costs and Their Financing* (1921); J. M. Clark, *The Costs of the War to the American People* (1931); A. D. Noyes, *The War Period in American Finance* (1926); W. D. Hines, *War History of the American Railroads* (1928); E. L. Hurley, *The Bridge to France* (1927); W. F. Willoughby, *Governmental Organization in War Time and After* (1919); and H. P. Davison, *The American Red Cross in the Great War* (1919).

On the army and military operations, see T. F. Frothingham, *The American Reinforcement in the World War* (1927); O. L. Spaulding, *The United States Army in War and Peace* (1937); Frederick Palmer, *Newton D. Baker: America at War* (2 vols. 1931); J. J. Pershing, *My Experiences in the World War* (2 vols. 1931); Shipley Thomas, *History of the A.E.F.* (1920); and J. G. Harbord, *The American Army in France* (1936).

Naval operations are treated in C. S. Alden and A. Westcott, *The United States Navy* (1943); W. S. Sims and B. J. Hendrick, *The Victory at Sea*; and Josephus Daniels, *Our Navy at War* (1922).

Other useful volumes on the war period include George Creel, *How We Advertised America* (1920); J. R. Mock and C. Larson, *Words that Won the War* (1939); Carl Wittke, *German-Americans and the World War* (1936); Norman Thomas, *The Conscientious Objector in America* (1923); Z. Chafee, Jr., *Free Speech in the United States* (1941); and W. G. McAdoo, *Crowded Years* (1931).

Chapter 13

On the problems of peace, in addition to many of the books already listed, important titles include R. S. Baker, *Woodrow Wilson and World Settlement* (3 vols. 1922); Robert Lansing, *The Peace Negotiations* (1921); Frederick Palmer, *Bliss, Peacemaker* (1934); D. H. Miller, *The Drafting of the Covenant* (2 vols. 1928); J. T. Shotwell, *At the Peace Conference* (1937); Allan Nevins, *Henry White* (1930); T. A. Bailey, *Woodrow Wilson and the Lost Peace* (1944), and *Woodrow Wilson and the Great Betrayal* (1945); and B. M. Baruch, *The Making of the Reparations and Economic Sections of the Treaty* (1920).

The rejection of the peace treaty is discussed in D. F. Fleming, *The United States and the League of Nations, 1918-1920* (1932); H. C. Lodge, *The Senate and the League of Nations* (1925); K. Colegrove, *The American Senate and World Peace* (1943); W. S. Holt, *Treaties Defeated by the Senate* (1933); and Karl Schriftgiesser, *The Gentleman from Massachusetts: Henry Cabot Lodge* (1944).

FROM PROSPERITY TO DEPRESSION

Chapter 14

Among important general treatments of social conditions in the nineteen-twenties and nineteen-thirties are C. A. and M. R. Beard, *America in Midpassage* (1939); P. W. Slosson, *The Great Crusade and After* (1930); Mark Sullivan, *Our Times* (vol. 6, 1935); F. L. Allen,

Only Yesterday (1931), and *Since Yesterday* (1940); H. M. Robinson, *Fantastic Interlude* (1943); R. S. and H. M. Lynd, *Middletown* (1929), and *Middletown in Transition* (1937); President's Research Committee on Social Trends, *Recent Social Trends in the United States* (2 vols. 1933).

Contemporary discussions include J. T. Adams, *Our Business Civilization* (1929); André Siegfried, *America Comes of Age* (1927); H. E. Stearns, *Civilization in the United States* (1922); Twelve Southerners, *I'll Take My Stand* (1930); J. W. Krutch, *The Modern Temper* (1930); Walter Lippmann, *A Preface to Morals* (1929); Waldo Frank, *Rediscovery of America* (1929); W. P. Webb, *Divided We Stand* (1937); T. Arnold, *The Folklore of Capitalism* (1937); and J. Daniels, *A Southerner Discovers the South* (1938).

See also books noted in the section on Social Conditions.

Chapter 15

In addition to such books as those by the Beards, Dumond, Slosson, and Sullivan already noted, political developments of the nineteen-twenties are taken up in J. C. Malin, *The United States After the World War* (1930); S. H. Adams, *The Incredible Era* (1939); Morris Werner, *Privileged Characters* (1935); L. M. Hacker, *American Problems of Today* (1938); M. E. Ravage, *The Story of Teapot Dome* (1924); W. S. Myers and W. H. Newton, *The Hoover Administration* (1936); and R. L. Wilbur and A. M. Hyde, *The Hoover Policies* (1937).

Biographies or autobiographies include Calvin Coolidge, *Autobiography* (1929); W. A. White, *A Puritan in Babylon* (1938); C. M. Fuess, *Calvin Coolidge* (1940); A. E. Smith, *Up to Now* (1929); H. F. Pringle, *Alfred E. Smith* (1927); Carleton Beals, *The Story of Huey Long* (1935); Herbert Corey, *The Truth About Hoover* (1932); Will Irwin, *Herbert Hoover* (1928); and George W. Norris, *Fighting Liberal* (1945).

Hoover's addresses are available in *American Individualism* (1934); *The Challenge to Liberty* (1934); *Addresses Upon the American Road* (1938); and *State Papers and Other Public Writings* (2 vols., edited by W. S. Myers, 1934).

Among studies of special topics are C. E. Russell, *Story of the Non-Partisan League* (1920); P. Odegard, *Pressure Politics* (1928); H. S. Raushenbush and H. W. Laidler, *Power Control* (1928); and T. C. Blaisdell, *The Federal Trade Commission* (1932).

Chapter 17

Among books describing the depression and its impact on American life (apart from the more general treatment in Beard, Hacker, Allen, Robinson, and other histories already noted) are L. Robbins, *The Great Depression* (1930); J. M. Blair, *Seeds of Destruction* (1938); J. N. Leonard, *Three Years Down* (1939); Gilbert Seldes, *The Years of the Locust* (1933); L. Corey, *The Decline of Capitalism* (1934), and *The Crisis of the Middle Class* (1935); A. R. Burns, *The Decline of Competition* (1936); W. B. Donham, *Business Adrift* (1931); M. Levens and Others, *America's Capacity to Consume* (1934); E. J. Nourse, *America's Capacity to Produce* (1934); F. C. Mills, *Economic Tendencies in the United States* (1933); H. G. Moulton, *Income and Economic Progress* (1935); Twentieth Century Fund, *Big Business: Its Growth and Place* (1937); Brookings Institution, *The Recovery Problem in the United States* (1936); and L. P. Ayres, *The Economics of Recovery* (1934).

THE NEW DEAL

CHAPTERS 19-21

Most of the literature dealing with the New Deal is of a rather ephemeral quality and no complete studies are available. The best treatment of the period as a whole is to be found in such books as C. A. and M. R. Beard, *America in Midpassage* (1939); Louis Hacker, *American Problems of Today* (1938); and Gerald Johnson, *Roosevelt, Dictator or Democrat?* (1942). The most important single source of information, however, is F. D. Roosevelt, *Public Papers and Addresses* (9 vols. 1938-41).

Among other discussions are C. A. Beard and G. H. E. Smith, *The Future Comes* (1934); E. K. Lindley, *The Roosevelt Revolution* (1933), and *Halfway with Roosevelt* (1936); H. A. Wallace, *America Must Choose* (1934), and *New Frontiers* (1934); George Soule, *The Coming American Revolution* (1934); Stuart Chase, *A New Deal* (1934); S. C. Wallace, *The New Deal in Action* (1934); Herbert Hoover, *The Challenge to Liberty* (1934); Norman Thomas, *After the New Deal, What?* (1936); Harry Laidler, *A Program for Modern America* (1936); W. C. MacDonald, *The Menace of Recovery* (1924); A. H. Hansen, *Full Recovery or Stagnation* (1938); A. M. Landon, *America at the Crossroads* (1936); E. Browder, *The People's Front* (1938) ; J. T. Flynn, *Country Squire in the White House* (1940); R. G. Tugwell, *The Battle for Democracy* (1935); W. F. Ogburn, *Social Change and the New Deal* (1934); and Basil Rauch, *History of the New Deal, 1933-38* (1944).

On the recovery program, see Brookings Institution, *The National Recovery Administration* (1935); A. A. Berle, Jr., *America's Re-*

covery Program (1934); G. B. Galloway, *Industrial Planning Under the Codes* (1935); H. S. Johnson, *The Blue Eagle from Egg to Earth* (1935); A. D. Gayer, *Public Works in Prosperity and Depression* (1935); and H. L. Ickes, *Back to Work* (1935).

Relief and the problem of social security are treated in J. C. Brown, *Public Relief, 1929-39* (1940); H. L. Hopkins, *Spending to Save: the Complete Story of Relief* (1936); M. D. Lane and S. Steegmuller, *America on Relief* (1938); D. S. Howard, *The WPA and Federal Relief Policy* (1943); W. Whitman, *Bread and Circuses* (1937); I. M. Rubino, *The Quest for Security* (1934); A. Epstein, *Insecurity: a Challenge to America* (1938); P. H. Douglas, *Social Security in the United States* (1939); M. Ezekiel, *Jobs for All* (1939); Nels Anderson, *The Right to Work* (1938); B. and E. K. Lindley, *A New Deal for Youth* (1938); and G. Adams, *Workers on Relief* (1938).

Books on agriculture relief and conservation include E. G. Nourse and Others, *Three Years of the Agricultural Adjustment Administration* (1937); H. H. Bennett, *Soil Conservation* (1939); Wilson Gee, *American Farm Policy* (1934); Cary McWilliams, *Ill Fares the Land* (1942); and C. T. Schmidt, *American Farmers in the World Crisis* (1941).

The T.V.A. is discussed in J. F. Carter, *The Future Is Ours* (1939); D. E. Lilienthal, *T.V.A.: Democracy on the March* (1944); C. H. Pritchett, *The Tennessee Valley Authority* (1943); the housing problem in L. W. Post, *The Challenge of Housing* (1938); M. W. Straus and T. Wegg, *Housing Comes of Age* (1938); Carol Aronovici, *Housing the Masses* (1939). Foreign trade is treated in H. J. Tasca, *Reciprocal Trade Policy of the United States* (1938); G. L. Beckett, *The Reciprocal Trade Agreements Program* (1941); financial reform in J. D. Paris, *Monetary Policies of the United States, 1932-38* (1938); R. L. Weissman, *The New Wall Street* (1939); and A. D. Gayer, *The Lessons of Monetary Experience* (1937).

Among available memoirs already published are James Farley, *Behind the Ballots* (1939); and Raymond Moley, *After Seven Years* (1939).

CHAPTER 22

Books on labor dealing with developments under the New Deal include H. Harris, *American Labor* (1939); M. R. Clark and S. F. Simon, *The Labor Movement in America* (1938); Edward Levinson, *Labor on the March* (1938); Samuel Yellen, *American Labor Struggles* (1936); K. White, *Labor and Democracy in the United States* (1939); H. Harris, *Labor's Civil War* (1940); R. R. Brooks, *When Labor Organizes* (1937); *Unions of Their Own Choosing* (1939), and *As Steel*

Goes (1940); C. R. Dougherty, *Labor under the N.R.A.* (1934), and *Labor Problems in American Industry* (1938); John B. Andrews, *Labor Laws in Action* (1938); E. Stein and Others, *Labor Problems in America* (1940); J. Rosenfarb, *The National Labor Policy* (1940); L. MacDonald, *Labor Problems and the American Scene* (1938); J. R. Walsh, *C.I.O., Industrial Unionism in Action* (1937); Benjamin Stolberg, *Story of the C.I.O.* (1938); Mary Vorse, *Labor's New Millions* (1938); and J. A. Wechsler, *Labor Baron, A Portrait of John L. Lewis* (1944).

Chapter 23

Constitutional developments leading to the Supreme Court struggle of 1937 may be most usefully studied in C. V. Swisher, *American Constitutional Government* (1943); Benjamin Wright, *The Course of American Constitutional Law* (1942); R. H. Jackson, *The Struggle for Judicial Supremacy* (1941); E. S. Corwin, *The Twilight of the Supreme Court* (1934); *Court Over Constitution* (1938); and *Constitutional Revolution, Ltd.* (1941); M. L. Ernst, *The Ultimate Power* (1937); I. Brant, *Storm Over Constitution* (1936); D. Alfange, *The Supreme Court and the National Will* (1937); R. K. Carr, *Democracy and the Supreme Court* (1936); and Charles Warren, *Congress, the Constitution and the Supreme Court* (1935).

PEACE AND WAR

Chapter 16

Among important general studies of American foreign policy in the nineteen-twenties and nineteen-thirties are D. V. Fleming, *The United States and World Organization: 1920-1933* (1938); Frank Simonds, *American Foreign Policy in the Post-war Years* (1935); Dexter Perkins, *America and Two Wars* (1944); C. A. Beard, *The Idea of National Interest* (1934), and *The Open Door at Home* (1934); W. S. Myers, *The Foreign Policies of Herbert Hoover* (1940); C. P. Howland, *Survey of American Foreign Relations, 1928-1931* (4 vols. 1928-31); and Council on Foreign Relations, *The United States in World Affairs, 1931-40* (10 vols. 1932-41).

See also H. and M. Sprout, *Toward a New Order of Sea Power* (1940); M. O. Hudson, *The Permanent Court of International Justice and the Question of American Participation* (1925); B. H. Williams, *The United States and Disarmament* (1931); P. C. Jessup, *International Security: the Rôle in Collective Action for Peace* (1935); R. M. Cooper, *American Consultation in World Affairs* (1934); W. E. Rappard, *The Quest for Peace* (1940); D. Bryn-Jones, *Frank B. Kellogg*

(1938); Harold B. Hinton, *Cordell Hull* (1942); D. F. Fleming, *The United States and the World Court* (1945).

Studies of the Kellogg-Briand anti-war treaty include D. H. Miller, *The Peace Pact of Paris* (1928); J. T. Shotwell, *War as an Instrument of National Policy* (1929); and J. E. Stoner, *S. O. Levinson and Pact of Paris* (1943). Our policy toward war debts is discussed in H. G. Moulton and L. Pasvolsky, *War Debts and World Prosperity* (1932).

Relations with Latin America are treated in G. R. Stuart, *Latin America and the United States* (1944); Dexter Perkins, *Hands Off! A History of the Monroe Doctrine* (1941); S. F. Bemis, *Latin American Policy of the United States* (1943); H. L. Stimson, *American Policy in Nicaragua* (1927); J. F. Rippy, *The Caribbean Danger Zone* (1940); and A. P. Whitaker, *Inter-American Affairs, 1941* (1942).

On the Far East, useful books include A. W. Griswold, *The Far Eastern Policy of the United States* (1938); F. R. Dulles, *Forty Years of Japanese-American Relations* (1937); R. L. Buell, *The Washington Conference* (1922); Y. Ichihashi, *The Washington Conference and After* (1928); R. W. Paul, *The Abrogation of the Gentlemen's Agreement* (1936); E. Tupper and G. E. McReynolds, *Japan in American Public Opinion* (1937); H. L. Stimson, *The Far Eastern Crisis* (1936); Frederick Moore, *With Japan's Leaders* (1942); T. A. Bisson, *America's Far Eastern Policy* (1945); G. L. Kirk, *Philippine Independence* (1936); J. R. Hayden, *The Philippines* (1942); G. E. Taylor, *America in the New Pacific* (1942).

Relations with Russia are taken up in W. S. Graves, *America's Siberian Adventure* (1931); F. S. Schuman, *American Policy Toward Russia Since 1917* (1928); and F. R. Dulles, *The Road to Teheran* (1944).

Chapters 25-28

On American involvement in the second World War, the more helpful books published so far are State Department, *Peace and War: United States Foreign Policy, 1931-41* (1942); J. W. Alsop and R. Kintner, *American White Paper: the Story of American Diplomacy and the Second World War* (1940); F. Davis and E. K. Lindley, *How War Came* (1942). See also F. D. Roosevelt, *Public Papers and Addresses;* J. E. Davies, *Mission to Moscow* (1941); and J. G. Grew, *Ten Years in Japan* (1944).

Among the controversial literature of pre-war days, there should be noted C. A. Beard, *A Foreign Policy for America* (1940); R. L. Buell, *Isolated America* (1936); A. W. Dulles and H. F. Armstrong, *Can America Stay Neutral?* (1939); E. Borchard and W. P. Lage, *Neutrality for the United States* (1937); H. F. Armstrong, *We or They*

(1936); E. M. Earle, *Against This Torrent* (1941); Jerome Frank, *Save America First* (1938); Hanson Baldwin, *United We Stand* (1941); Hubert Herring, *And So to War* (1938); and Max Lerner, *It's Later Than You Think* (1938). See also W. Johnson, *The Battle Against Isolation* (1944).

On the actual impact of war on America, the following highly selected books have already appeared: Pendleton Herring, *The Impact of War* (1941); Denys Smyth, *America and the Axis War* (1942); S. E. Harris, *Economics of America at War* (1943); Andre Maurois, *The Miracle of America* (1944); C. O. Hardy, *Wartime Control of Prices* (1941); W. F. Ogburn, *American Society in Wartime* (1943); D. W. Brogan, *The American Character* (1944); Selden Menefee, *Assignment: U.S.A.* (1943); John Dos Passos, *State of the Nation* (1944); H. A. Wallace, *Democracy Reborn* (1944); E. R. Stettinius, *Lend-Lease* (1944); L. W. Koenig, *The Presidency and the Crisis* (1944); Eric Johnston, *America Unlimited* (1944); and Carey McWilliams, *Prejudice* (1944).

The first accounts of military and naval operations include A. G. Clifford, *The Conquest of North Africa* (1943); Wes Gallegher, *Back Door to Berlin* (1943); *Target Germany, the Army Air Force's Official Story of the VIII Bomber Command's First Year Over Europe* (1943); Richard Tregaskis, *Invasion Diary* (1944); C. C. Wertenbaker, *Invasion!* (1944); Fletcher Pratt, *The Navy's War* (1944); Foster Hailey, *The Pacific Battle Line* (1944); Ernie Pyle, *Here Is Your War* (1943), and *Brave Men* (1944); Walter Karig and Welbourn Kelley, *Battle Report* (1945); *The Best from Yank* (1945).

Among many books dealing with the future peace and America's rôle in world affairs are N. J. Spykman, *America's Strategy in World Politics* (1942); Walter Lippmann, *U.S. Foreign Policy* (1943), and *U.S. War Aims* (1944); H. Hoover and H. Gibson, *Problems of Lasting Peace* (1942); Nathaniel Peffer, *Basis for Peace in the Far East* (1942); H. P. Howard, *America's Rôle in Asia* (1943); Hiram Motherwell, *The Peace We Fight For* (1943); J. M. Jones, *A Modern Foreign Policy for the United States* (1944); E. H. Carr, *Conditions of Peace* (1942); Wendell Willkie, *One World* (1943); H. A. Wallace, *The Century of the Common Man* (1943); Sumner Welles, *The Time for Decision* (1944); Owen Lattimore, *Solution in Asia* (1945).

Index